W9-BXT-887

# Explaining Buyer Behavior

# Explaining Buyer Behavior

*Central Concepts and Philosophy of Science Issues*

JOHN O'SHAUGHNESSY

New York          Oxford
OXFORD UNIVERSITY PRESS
1992

Oxford University Press

Oxford   New York   Toronto
Delhi   Bombay   Calcutta   Madras   Karachi
Kuala Lumpur   Singapore   Hong Kong   Tokyo
Nairobi   Dar es Salaam   Cape Town
Melbourne   Auckland

and associated companies in
Berlin   Ibadan

Library of Congress Cataloging-in-Publication Data
O'Shaughnessy, John.
Explaining buyer behavior : central concepts and philosophy
of science issues / John O'Shaughnessy.
p.  cm.   Includes bibliographical references and index.
ISBN 0-19-507108-5
1. Consumer behavior—Methodology.   I. Title.
HF5415.32.O74   1992   658.8'342—dc20
91-22140

1 3 5 7 9 8 6 4 2

Printed in the United States of America
on acid-free paper

# Preface

This book emerged from a series of notes I wrote for a seminar entitled "Explanation in Marketing." The aim of the seminar was to provide the fundamentals needed to feel comfortable in evaluating findings on buyer behavior and to feel confident in discussing the strengths/weaknesses and applicability to marketing of explanatory systems and methodologics employed in the behavioral sciences. This book is still directed toward this end and toward illuminating theories and findings on buyer behavior.

Most of the topics discussed in the book are controversial and complex, often made more complicated by an absence of agreement on terminology among philosophers and behavioral scientists. Hence I am grateful to the many colleagues and students who commented on the text as it developed. These include Stephen Bell, John Whitney, Lloyd Sandelands, Bernd Schmitt, Luis Araujo, Don Lehmann and Eric Gelb. Particular thanks go to Joel Steckel for pointing to omissions and loose thinking, to Morris Holbrook, whose unstinting help and encouragement kept me going, and to Roger Dickinson, who kept me informed about relevant references and provided detailed comments on an early draft.

I would like also to thank Maxine Freed and my secretary Liz Blair for being patient with me during the successive revisions of the book.

Finally, a special thanks is due to Herbert Addison of Oxford University Press, who in his gentle way nursed the book along and ensured the final draft took account of the wise comments of Oxford's reviewers.

*New York*  J. O'S.
*January 1992*

# Contents

# Explaining Buyer Behavior

# 1

# Marketing Management and the Behavioral Sciences

Art requires a long apprenticeship, being mechanical as well as intellectual.

John Constable (1776–1837)

No serious student of marketing ignores the behavioral sciences. Everything that is done in marketing must take account of human behavior: whether we seek to influence buyers, environmentalists, consumer groups, the government, competitors, or any other group whose decisions have an impact on market success or failure, we naturally turn for guidance to the behavioral sciences for sensitizing concepts, methods of inquiry, and relevant findings. Yet in turning to the behavioral sciences we encounter problems in evaluating claims when different scientists have different orientations giving rise to different conceptualizations of behavior, different methods of inquiry, and different possible weaknesses in findings.

Traditionally books for business students are concerned either with organizational or buyer behavior, focusing on behavioral science findings and models. Although such findings and models may have only a short life cycle before being displaced, the process is intended to create an awareness of behavioral problems in business so students remain mindful of behavioral issues throughout their careers. Every marketing manager, every student of marketing, should understand the behavioral sciences' contribution to marketing's theoretical base, but they also need to understand their philosophical underpinnings in order to know where each comes from, what each takes for granted about human behavior, and how each goes about the job of studying that behavior and checking on hypotheses. Knowledge of findings in buyer or consumer behavior is not sufficient to equip future marketing managers with what they need to get a feel for behavioral science, to evaluate approaches and interpret findings for validity and applicability to marketing problems. For these purposes managers need to be educated in the various modes of thinking in behavioral science and to be acquainted with the enduring philosophical conundrums that underlie all the behavioral sciences, so they can develop critical thinking in the area. The chapters that follow aim to provide such knowledge by focusing on the theme of explanation, since the ability to explain behavior is the major reason for studying the behavioral sciences and a firm understanding of each science's general orientation revolves around understanding the various explanatory modes and their limitations.

The behavioral sciences are often viewed as a set of antagonistic cults riven with disagreement, with the different protagonists demonstrating an unjustified dogmatism allied to a scorn for nonbelievers typically based on some caricature of their doctrines. In this book the different behavioral sciences are viewed as different windows onto a problem, with some windows offering better or sole viewing for certain types of problem. Consistent with this position, in the field of methodology, a pluralism of methods is recommended on the ground that different methodologies are likely to suit different types of questions; thus rejection of certain methodologies may mean ignoring whole classes of questions. When students of marketing in business schools are never exposed to more than one behavioral approach, it is highly unlikely other approaches will ever become a natural reference when working as a marketing manager. This is a loss both to them and to their companies.

The main aim of this chapter is to review the potential contribution of the behavioral sciences to marketing once we recognize management as a rule-governed technology and to discuss the relationship between that technology and science. This chapter, in discussing the job of management in terms of information acquisition and rule-governed action, allows us later to put the behavioral science contribution in perspective. Effectiveness in management depends on theories/information possessed and skill in application. Both are needed. Managers with good information are more likely to have correct beliefs about marketing and the market and so are *more likely* to act wisely, since managers do wrong things usually because they believe wrong things. But they are only "more likely," since skill in developing and implementing plans is not guaranteed by knowing all the right facts: there is a difference between "knowing that" and "knowing how." In making this distinction, Gilbert Ryle (1949) points out that a man who knows nothing about medical science could not be an effective surgeon. On the other hand, being an excellent surgeon is not the same thing as having a great deal of knowledge about medical science as it applies to surgery: skill at surgery is not simply a product of having the right knowledge base. While the surgeon must have learned a great number of "truths," he or she must also have practiced a great number of skills. Even where practice is simply the application of accepted rules, the intelligence and creativity involved in using the rules do not flow automatically from just comprehending the rules themselves.

One way the behavioral sciences enter into the marketing manager's job is by providing information. Such information acts like headlights to the night driver: it can illuminate the road ahead but does not dispense with the need for skill and good judgment in "driving." Thus practical marketing management, if it is to be successful, presupposes not only having the "right" information for decision-making but also having skill in application. Skill in application can be regarded as a technological skill. If technology is defined as consisting of rules or operational principles for the design and installation of systems that can succeed or fail (Polanyi, 1978), then skill in developing plans and implementing them is a rule-governed technology. Behind every decision are premises or rules, implicit or explicit, that govern action. For example, here are some rules, implicit in one debate among managers over whether to launch two new products or just one and, if so, which one.   . .

  • To be successful, we must choose just one of the products to market so as not to outstrip our resources.

- To be a success in the market, a product must have a distinct advantage.
- To be successful, it helps to concentrate where we have most know-how.
- To be successful, it helps to be in a big market with just one major competitor.
- To be successful in entering a market with a substitute product, it helps if customers currently are dissatisfied with existing offerings.
- To be a success in the market, it helps in penetrating the market if the firm already has a reputation in the field.

Some rules are just laid down for the manager to follow. Thus there are the "regulative rules," which represent company policies; the "authority-conferring rules," which are embodied in schedules of responsibilities; and, finally, the "constitutive rules," which define what constitutes, say, a creditworthy account, the market being served, a quality product, and so on, as well as laying down rules covering actual practices such as determining how quality standards are established and how markets to be served are actually to be found. But the rules or decision premises originating with the manager are not categorical directives, as are company policies; they are rules of action connecting rule to purpose, such as "In order to be a success in the market, all 'offerings' must have a competitive advantage." In information technology, so-called expert systems are modeled on humans to employ rules of action ("If the engine will not start, then check the battery") and some systems, called "expert systems shells," can even—like humans—combine rules and data to learn what can be learned from the data. Marketing managers operate "as if" guided by a stock of implicit rules. They are seldom absolute but in the nature of maxims, that is, rules with exceptions.

Even the most cherished principle of marketing, namely, the marketing concept, is simply a maxim. Hence there have been attempts to change this by redefining it so it becomes a truism ("We should know something about people's wants before trying to cater to them") or alternatively trying to define its exact domain of application ("The marketing concept is a rule of conduct appropriate to competitive markets composed of knowledgeable buyers who know pretty well what they want"). There will always be exceptions to any rule of business, but finding exceptions should not blind us to the fact that actions are rule-governed. Yet we do need to know the conditions under which a rule generally applies. Thus the maxim advising firms to "stick to their knitting" and resist entering other fields could, as Foster (1986) shows, be disastrous when new technologies are entering the market. We can take as another example the advice to decision-makers to take what they are currently doing as given and make only incremental adjustments so that the consequences of change can be better predicted and change more easily managed. But such advice, if universally followed, could spell disaster to any firm operating in rapidly changing markets or in need of a turnaround. A firm contemplating changes cannot just ignore the pace of change in the outside world but must change sufficiently to make the necessary adaptations to the changing environment.

Rules can be contradictory. This can on occasions be useful if opposing rules highlight the issues. For instance, opposing rules for pricing a new product, like skimming versus penetration pricing, make the manager think about the various options to determine which is more suited to prevailing market conditions. Antithetic rules may be reconciled by the understanding that each is a partial truth and that the whole truth involves both of them since each principle has a different domain of application. The truly skilled in any technology seem able to pluck one rule from here and another from there to produce some unique blend. This is true whether we are referring to the technology of cooking or the technology of doing research. As Polanyi (1978) points out, we can export the objective fruits of science throughout the world but we cannot export good research methodology. Just as research is a technology composed of rules of loose or vague texture learned by practice under the guidance of a master, the correct application of the rules in marketing is part of the art of marketing management.

Rules are said to be effective or ineffective, correct or incorrect—not true or false. However, rules do involve claims to truth in that they implicitly assume certain results are likely if the rules are followed. But the rules followed by a marketing manager will be less reliable than those followed by a cabinetmaker, who can be more sure of the presence of conditions under which the rules work. The marketing manager designs and carries out strategies that act as interventions in the market. Predicting the effects of such interventions means predicting the actions of people in circumstances never entirely identical to any situation in the past. There is thus more uncertainty in predicting outcomes.

Sometimes the word "principles" is used for rules that have demonstrated their effectiveness. Thus we have the so-called principles of advertising. Those propagated by David Ogilvy are very specific: include the brand name in the headline; don't try to be clever; avoid analogies and superlatives; write sentences of fewer than twelve words; make at least fourteen references to people per hundred words; avoid humorous copy; and use photographs instead of drawings (Fox, 1984). But as with any rules, principles are frequently violated to good effect (such as using humorous copy) and some rules (for instance, don't try to be clever) may be universally endorsed since everyone can read into them whatever they would endorse!

If successful marketing necessitates mastering certain technological skills, how do the behavioral sciences contribute? Before answering this question we need to discuss the relationship of any rule-governed technology to science.

## Technology Versus Science

The view of technology as consisting of rules or operational principles for achieving successful practical performances is that of Michael Polanyi (1978) and Stephen Toulmin (1977), who define technology as a population of techniques, recipes, processes, and procedures. However, a technology can be effective without being grounded in science. Thus the impressive technology reflected in medieval cathedrals owed nothing to chemistry or physics. This is germane to the argument of Charnes, Cooper, Learner, and Phillips (1985) that management/marketing science will continue to focus on developing new techniques rather than developing substantive theories because concern must be with solving problems and not with trying to make techniques fit theory.

Charnes et al. are claiming that management science is concerned with what Calder, Phillips, and Tybout (1981) call "effects application" research as opposed to "theory application" research. The goal of effects application research is to establish action effects in a research situation and gauge whether there is sufficient correspondence between the research situation and situations of interest in real life to expect the effects observed to be repeated in these real-life situations. In contrast, Calder et al. argue that theory application research seeks generalizable theoretical knowledge about events and relationships occurring in a variety of real-world situations and seeks to test such theory by trying to falsify it. Other writers in marketing talk about theory application research as basic research, contrasting it with decision-making research focusing on a specific problem or a class of problems (Myers, Greyser, and Massy, 1979).

The distinctions are those made in research generally. Traditionally scientists have spoken of *pure* research as advancing science regardless of potential application. This contrasts with *directed* research, which draws on all relevant disciplines to develop better solutions to certain *classes* of problem. Both differ from *applied* research, which is concerned only with solving a specific problem. What is being recognized in all these discussions is the distinction between technology and explanatory theory in science.

Both technology and science are involved in problem solving, but scientific solutions reflect explanatory theory whereas technological solutions need not do so. Technology is concerned with technique development and effects application research whereas science seeks to develop explanatory theory. Sometimes, of course, we speak of technological theory, but such theory is meant less to be explanatory than to specify what action to take to solve a problem.

The subject matter of technology cannot be fully specified in terms of science. Thus engineering cannot be specified in terms of physics since physics takes account neither of the purposes served by a machine nor (unlike engineering) with the way these purposes might be achieved. Yet science can explain technological failure. Thus, although engineering cannot be specified in terms of physics, physics may be able to show the necessary conditions for success and so be used to explain engineering failures. It is similarly true that market failure often can be explained by behavioral science theory. Yet, as already seen, some academics argue that research in marketing should focus on effects application research, problem orientation research, and the like, without being concerned with explanatory theory. But, as Merton (1968) points out, such naive empiricism is likely to lead to the chaotic accumulation of miscellaneous empirical generalizations. This is because empirical research is blind without some guiding theory, just as theory without empirical research can be empty. This is not to deny the contribution of technology to science since what may be possible by way of data collection and analysis depends vitally on technological advances. But explanatory scientific theory can give grounding to technology. Explanatory theory can also point to solutions to difficulties. In coming to grips with the problems of marketing, concepts and theories are what count and not just skills, since concepts and theories can help define a problem and the nature of its solution. Without theory, skills can be ill-directed and the advancement of marketing, beyond minor improvements, frustrated.

When we say that explanatory theory can give grounding to a technology, we mean that it can

1. justify the appropriateness of a technique;
2. provide some of the content of rules; and
3. sharpen judgment on behavioral issues.

We discuss each in turn.

## The Behavioral Science Contribution to Marketing Technology

### Technique Appropriateness

The techniques of any technology can be evaluated for appropriateness in the light of explanatory theory. For example, traditional techniques in personal selling are better evaluated for appropriateness when their theoretical underpinnings are exposed. The canned sales presentation or the ring-a-bell technique reflects the S-R (stimulus–

response) model of behaviorism. Hence the use of the approach presupposes the target audience has been conditioned to respond to the contents of the message so the technique is best suited to bargain offers and is not a technique that can be universally recommended. In barrier selling the salesperson guides the prospect into agreeing with a set of socially validated statements ("May I ask if you are interested in education?"). If at the end of the sequence of questions the prospect fails to buy, he or she is in the uncomfortable position of seeming to deny previous admissions. There are theories that explain why people would be uncomfortable and why people seek consistency between their beliefs and behavior. Still another technique is "AIDA" which aims to take the prospective customer through the supposed adoption process of getting attention, stimulating interest, arousing desire, and triggering action. The AIDA model is essentially the first of the hierarchy of effects models whose explanatory base lies in the information-processing approach of cognitive psychology. It follows from the preceding discussion that the behavioral sciences can contribute to rule formation by generating a knowledge base that might inform the specification of rules or give a grounding to existing rules of action.

## Providing Content

There are design rules and implementation rules. The design rules that find their way into marketing texts tend to focus on *how to go about* planning, how to segment a market, how to get out a competitive or advertising strategy or a distribution or pricing strategy. The focus is largely on procedure, not content or options, so that marketing planning typically describes the set of steps to be pursued in developing a plan. But systematic procedure represents procedural rationality and little more. Taken literally it suggests that rationality in planning is localized in the performance of a recommended fixed sequence of actions. But in developing an advertising strategy, for example, we want to know not just how to go about it but about the content of the message appeal, the format, and all other aspects. The role of the behavioral sciences lies in contributing to content and not only to procedure.

The claim that marketing, as a discipline, offers expertise is the basis of its use in helping marketing management to improve the content of its plans, or the options it selects. The claim that the behavioral sciences do and can contribute to the content of plans assumes that they can provide suggestions on courses or rules of action that seem behaviorally feasible. In general, the explanatory theory of interest is that which helps the marketing manager to understand the behavior of customers and to predict their actions under different suggested interventionist strategies. However, it is easy to exaggerate the potential contribution. As Lindblom and Cohen (1979) point out, the behavioral sciences can produce only a small portion of the total stock of propositions commonly employed in any type of social (e.g., marketing) problem solving. More typically, the behavioral sciences simply supplement, reshape, and refine the marketing manager's knowledge. Even when psychologists and sociologists focus exclusively on marketing phenomena, they produce only fragments of knowledge about behavior, which need to be pieced together with the fragments of management experience to form the needed informational base for action.

## Sharpening Judgment on Behavioral Issues

To focus exclusively on the contribution of behavioral science findings to marketing is to underrate the potential contribution of the behavioral sciences. It reflects a failure to appreciate the benefits of a broad social science training in both methods and philosophies. Such a training sensitizes the marketing student to behavioral phenomena, extending the range of alternative action plans considered while ruling out a host of suggestions based on erroneous ideas about behavior. Also, research in marketing long ago discovered the rich experience and store of methods developed by behavioral scientists for collecting information, operationalizing concepts, and testing ideas.

## What Is Science?

Up to now "science" and the "scientific" have been discussed but not defined. This has been postponed to now because the title "science" bestows such prestige that any definition of science or scientific will be controversial. Popper (1959) argues that science consists of propositions that have withstood attempts to falsify them. Nagel (1979) argues that science has three distinguishing features:

1. a set of problems;
2. a body of conclusions stated in propositional form and often general in content which are asserted as the warranted findings of special inquiries; and
3. most important of all—a certain method of inquiry.

No definition of science has been universally accepted. Kuhn (1970) points out the astrologers habitually test their predictions and acknowledge their failures, yet few academics would want to accept astrology as science. He also argues there is no unique scientific method for establishing "general, systematic and verifiable knowledge." The controversy has been carried into the debate over whether marketing is a science (Anderson, 1983; Peter and Olson, 1983). The concept of science is a fuzzy one that has varied in history. There is in fact an element of historical accident in what disciplines today are commonly accepted as sciences (O'Shaughnessy and Ryan, 1979). Some philosphers argue that there can be no definition of science that will be universally accepted until scientists and philosophers have developed and accepted a theory of what constitutes scientific rationality. This may be so. But the debate over the definition of science will not go away since it represents a way of ruling out of court, without further discussion, certain methods and explanations as nonscientific and therefore undeserving of consideration as advancing knowledge.

What is being argued in this book is that the goal of science is explanatory theory and that technologies with no grounding in explanatory theory will tend toward conservatism and be lacking in innovation. This is because the less understanding there is of what lies behind the technology, the more uncertainty there is over the consequences of change and the more reluctance there is to make changes. This tendency appears in marketing, where the lack of theoretical foundations leads to a fomulaic approach to all marketing, even though the rules of one game are seldom the rules of another.

## Plan of the Book

The book begins by considering in Chapter 2 the nature of explanation and the debates over what consitutes a "scientific" explanation and whether understanding rather than explanation should be the goal of the behavioral sciences. In Chapters 3, 4, 5, and 6, the traditional types of explanation are described and illustrated by examples from marketing. Chapters 7 and 8 classify the various branches of psychology and sociology in terms of their explanatory focus to discuss their limitations and application to marketing. Chapter 9 brings together behavioral findings and philosophical insights to come to grips with the subject of emotion to illustrate how a multidisciplinary approach is possible.

A subtheme throughout the book is whether all explanations of individual action are translatable into the reason-giving format which is the layman's way of explaining action and the one most understandable to the marketing manager. Chapter 10 pulls together the various sensitizing concepts in previous chapters into an overall reason-giving format.

Every discipline has a core of beliefs that generally remain unquestioned. In the behavioral sciences these beliefs typically relate to human nature and how human behavior consequently should be studied. Chapter 11 discusses the philosophical foundations of these largely unquestioned beliefs, and Chapter 12 describes and assesses the so-called scientific method as applied to behavioral research and its traditional biases. Finally, Chapter 13 considers recent developments in the philosophy of science and their implications for choices among methodologies and explanatory systems.

The last three chapters of the book raise perennial, fundamental problems in the philosophy of science. These problems need to be borne in mind to understand what social science can and cannot deliver. Typically, when examined abstractly, they are problems that defy solution; when raised in individual cases, though, they can often seem less intimidating. But it is not just in the last three chapters that controversies abound. Indeed the whole book can be regarded as focused on controversies. However the book generally does not choose sides in these controversies but sets out, as fairly as possible, the arguments on all sides so that the reader can consider the alternatives. Nonetheless, it could be said there is a hidden agenda to the book beyond wishing to promote a broader approach in courses on consumer behavior. This agenda consists first of a wish to promote methodological pluralism. All too often academics parody whatever fails to fit their methodological prescriptions for acquiring firm knowledge about behavior while presenting, by way of contrast, an idealized version of their own approach. There are limitations to all approaches and none discussed here is bankrupt in enlightenment. Another subtheme that runs without fanfare throughout the book is how explanation of all intentional action is rooted in the layman's explanation of action in terms of wants and beliefs. This is not always apparent given the many attempts to move away to something appearing more scientific or through the use of terms that only on close analysis turn out to be refinements or cognates of the terms "want" and "belief." This point is more important than appears. Students often feel obliged to memorize findings and theories about intentional behavior, as something discovered that has no commonsense rationale. In fact all such findings and theories about intentional action are making assumptions about people's wants and beliefs, and exposing such assumptions makes us see their common sense or the likelihood of the findings or theories being restricted to time and place. This is not to suggest that the social sciences are preoccupied with explaining intentional actions or that explanations of action should involve no refinements of concepts beyond laymen's language. This would be wrong since theoretical notions can sharpen everyday notions for research purposes, and the sensitizing concepts developed by behavioral scientists add a richness to understanding. On the other hand, it is easy to mystify rather than enlighten when vacuous abstractions claim scientific insight beyond commonsense understanding.

# References

Anderson, Paul F. (1983). "Marketing, Scientific Progress, and Scientific Method." *Journal of Marketing* 4, pp. 18–31.

Calder, B. J., L. W. Phillips, and A. M. Tybout (1981). "Designing Research for Application." *Journal of Consumer Research* 8 (September), pp. 197–207.

Charnes, A., W. W. Cooper, D. B. Learner, and F. Y. Phillips (1985). "Management Science and Marketing Management." *Journal of Marketing* (Spring), pp. 93–105.

Foster, Richard (1986). *Innovation.* New York: Summit Books.

Fox, Stephen (1984). *The Mirror Makers.* New York: Vintage Books.

Kuhn, Thomas S. (1970). *The Structure of Scientific Revolutions,* 2nd ed. Chicago: University of Chicago Press.

Lindblom, C. A., and D. K. Cohen (1979). *Usable Knowledge: Social Science and Social Problem Solving.* New Haven, CT: Yale University Press.

Merton, Robert K. (1968). *Social Theory and Social Structure.* New York: Free Press.

Myers, J. G., S. A. Greyser, and W. F. Massy (1979). "The Effectiveness of Marketing's 'R & D' for Marketing Management: An Assessment." *Journal of Marketing* 43 (January), pp. 17–29.

Nagel, Ernest (1979). *Teleology Revisited.* New York: Columbia University Press.

O'Shaughnessy, John, and Michael Ryan (1979). "Marketing, Science and Technology." In *Conceptual and Theoretical Developments in Marketing,* edited by O. C. Ferrell, S. W. Brown, and C. W. Lamb. Chicago: American Marketing Association, pp. 557–89.

Peter, J. Paul, and Jerry C. Olson (1983). "Is Science Marketing?" *Journal of Marketing* 47 (Fall), pp. 111–25.

Polanyi, Michael (1978). *Personal Knowledge.* Chicago: University of Chicago Press.

Popper, Karl R., (1959). *The Logic of Scientific Discovery.* New York: Harper Torch Books.

Ryle, Gilbert (1949). *The Concept of Mind.* New York: Barnes and Noble; London: Hutchinson.

Toulmin, Stephen (1977). *Human Understanding.* Princeton, NJ: Princeton University Press.

# 2

# Explanation

Men do not think they know a thing till they have
grasped the "why" of it.

Aristotle

In Chapter 1 it was claimed that the major reason for studying the behavioral sciences is to attain the ability to explain behavior; at the same time, it was argued that a firm understanding of any behavioral science revolves around understanding its mode of explanation. Yet up to now no attempt has been made to define "modes" of explanation or what constitutes an explanation. This chapter discusses the concept of explanation and the controversies that have arisen over the nature of a scientific explanation, explanatory adequacy, and the relationship between explanation and prediction.

An explanation is meant to enlighten: to make some event or action intelligible, or the thing to be expected given the explanation. Beyond this brief statement of purpose, there is no general agreement among philosophers as to what constitutes a *scientific* explanation. Most explanations that are commonly accepted as explanations are simply what Taylor (1970) calls "what explanations" in that they simply make clear what something is ("It's a premium offer"). Such explanations are important to a firm that is explaining what its new product does and how it can be used. But these would not be labeled scientific explanations. There are also the tautologies masquerading as explanations; for example,

1. Why does $X$ crave chocolate? Because she likes the taste.
2. Why does $X$ buy $Y$? Because she has an unopposed attitude toward doing so.

Pseudoexplanations frequently are accepted when the scientific explanation can be understood only after lengthy education. This is a reminder that explanations in buyer behavior may relate the unfamiliar to the familiar only to those already initiated into the behavioral science.

Given the dispute over what constitutes a scientific explanation it is not surprising that there are disputes over the distinct modes or classes of explanation. We like our classifications to consist of exhaustive and mutually exclusive categories, but the lack of agreement about the nature of explanation precludes this. For example, many philosophers divide explanations into causal explanations and reason-giving explanations. But some philosophers argue about the exhaustiveness of these two categories and others claim that all explanations that merit the title "scientific" are causal.

As we review different views about the nature of scientific explanation, the relationship between explanation and prediction, and so on, the controversies touched upon are important in that those seeking explanations have to make up their minds as to the type of explanation to seek.

## Explanation in Social Science

An explanation has two parts:

1. The *explicandum* is the thing to be explained.
2. The *explicans* is that which explains, that is, accounts for a certain state, conditions, or event.*

We speak of the explicans explaining a certain state or aspects of, say, an action. In other words, we explain a *described* condition or *described* action. As Danto (1965) says, it is only phenomena covered by description which are capable of explanation. We do not explain things per se but why such things are as they are, come into being, change their properties, or pass away. Although we do speak loosely of seeking to explain consumer behavior, we in fact explain specifically described consumer behavior. To explain behavior under one description is not necessarily to explain it under another: an explicans of the choice process under conditions of certainty or perfect knowledge will differ from an explicans of the choice process under conditions of uncertainty. Just because we give one name to phenomena does not imply the phenomena can be explained by a single explicans. There can be no single meaningful explicans for all buying behavior any more than there is a single meaningful explicans for all car breakdowns or holes in the road. This means there is always a problem in determining what dimension or aspect of a condition or an event is explainable and in need of explanation. Failure to recognize this leads researchers to think of finding some single explicans to explain, say, all brand choices. Such "overarching theory" can always be shown not to be all encompassing, but simply orienting the reader to what are considered to be the relevant variables.

## Explanation and Description

All explanations involve description but explanation is more than description. Even when the description consists of a well-confirmed generalization, it need not be explanatory. Thus in well-developed economies the capital–labor ratio is about 3:1, the rate of profit about 12%, and the share of gross national product (GNP) going to labor about 40%, but none of these generalizations is explanatory. There is a lingering controversy in the philosophy of science over whether explanation should be confined to purely descriptive *relationships* that never go beyond the observable. Many eminent scientists and philosophers in the nineteenth century claimed that science was interested merely in describing how things are connected. In the social sciences Handy and Harwood (1973) and others still argue that the objective of scientific inquiry is the description of what hap-

---

*Sometimes the explicandum is called the explanandum and the explicans is called the explanans.

pens under specified conditions. They claim that science should simply describe how things are connected, that the objective of science is to seek explanatory theories *only* if explanatory theory is confined to describing connections among things without assuming anything that is not observable. Since causal processes may not be observable, this has led to debates over the value of causal explanations.

Ernst Mach (1838–1916), the physicist and philosopher, rejected the very concept of cause and effect as being too theory loaded, arguing that scientific findings merely express functional (mathematical) relationships. He argued that such relationships must replace speculations about causal links since nature "merely goes on." While this viewpoint is by no means dead, the more general view is that scientific explanations will inevitably—if scientific knowledge is to advance—incorporate concepts (e.g., attitude, the electron) that are assumed to be operating yet are not observable. This is discussed in later chapters.

Perhaps the broadest and least controversial view of explanation is that put forward by Ryle (1949), Wisdom (1952), Toulmin (1960), Bambrough (1964), and Hanson (1965). Each of these philosophers proposed a *relational* view of explanation whereby explanation is simply a statement that relates the explicandum to other states or events to provide an illuminating network of interrelationships. But other philosophers have tried to define the nature of these relationships or connections more precisely. Thus Nagel (1961) sees explanation as a relationship between the explicandum and some law or principle accepted as true *or* as a relationship between the explicandum and some force with which it varies *or* as a relationship showing how the explicandum fits into some known system. We first discuss the relationship of the explicandum to a law or principle accepted as true and then discuss Nagel's other relationships later under model building and systems fit.

## Explanatory "Laws" or Principles

To identify the nature of scientific explanation, philosophers naturally turned to the mature sciences like physics, which rest on laws. Philosophers and social scientists who call themselves naturalists are committed to using the same methods in social science as those used in the natural sciences. Naturalists, like Nagel, believe that success in the social sciences depends on following the successful methods of the most mature sciences, which long ago rejected explanations that talked in terms of purposes. Nagel (1961), more than anyone else, is associated with that advocacy of applying the methods of the natural sciences to the social sciences. But Hempel's (1965) deductive—nomological model (the D-N model) is the one that held sway among philosophers as the exemplar of scientific explanation.

John Stuart Mill (1806–1873) first proposed the idea of there being just one type or pattern of scientific explanation. The single pattern that came to have wide acceptance was that the explicandum must follow as a logical consequence of the explicans. Some such deductive model of explanation was advocated by Hempel and Oppenheim (1948), Braithwaite (1960), Nagel (1961), and Popper (1965). Hempel's (1965) deductive–nomological model of explanation is the most well known.

Hempel aimed to set out the necessary and sufficient conditions for something to be accepted as a scientific explanation. To Hempel, scientific explanation consists of showing the explicandum to be an instance of some law (universal regularity). The explicans consists of a general law or set of laws plus a statement of the antecedent or initial conditions embraced by the laws. The law or set of laws is seen to account for the explicandum. In general terms, the deductive–nomological (D-N) model is composed of three elements:

1. A lawlike statement: "Whenever an event of type $x$ occurs, an event of type $y$ occurs."
2. A statement of initial/antecedent conditions: "$x$ happened."
3. The deductive conclusion: "$y$ happened."

That $y$ happened or will happen follows logically from the truth of the law acting as a premise. Such a law is meant to be universal in the sense of being true regardless of time and place. This means that generalizations like "all our customers are price conscious" will not suffice as they refer to some finite class. Hempel viewed a law as incorporating general terms referring to general kinds of things, not to individuals. In addition, the law must have withstood empirical testing. Expressed schematically, the D-N model consists of premises (which constitute the explicans) and the conclusion (constituting the explicandum), for example,

Explicans: $L_1, L_2, \ldots, L_r$    Laws               } Premises
              $C_1, C_2, \ldots, C_k$    Antecedent conditions

Explicandum: $E$                                  } Conclusion

*Example 1*

*Law:* All consumers who make a major purchase have postpurchase doubts about the wisdom of their buy.      } Explicans and Premises

*Antecedent or Initial Condition:* Consumer John Doe has made a major purchase.

*Explicandum:* John Doe has postpurchase doubts about the wisdom of his buy.      } Conclusion

*Example 2*

*Laws:* 1. High inflation always leads to the growth of discount houses in industrialized countries.      } Explicans and Premises

       2. Department store trading declines in countries where there is growth in discount stores.

*Antecedent Condition:* The United States is an industrialized country experiencing high inflation.

*Explicandum:* The United States will be experiencing the growth of discount houses and the decline in department story trading.      } Conclusion

The explicandum is subsumed under *premises* consisting of:

- a law or theory
- an antecedent or initial conditions that affirm membership of the class

The law or lawlike generalization "explains" a class of phenomena; the antecedent or initial conditions affirm that the explicandum is a member of the class. Hence the explicandum is a logical consequence of the explicans or premises.

The D-N model is also called the *covering law* model because it assumes some universal law. There are no non-trivial laws in social science or marketing regarding intentional action. At best we have statistical generalizations or probability statements. Hempel acknowledges this in his inductive–statistical (I-S) model of explanation. In the I-S model the lawlike statements in the D-N model become probabilistic. In other words, the explicans (premises) consists of some statistical law plus relevant antecedent/initial conditions. A statistical law takes the following form:

> The probability of an event of kind $E$ under conditions $C$ is $V$ where the statistical probability value $V$ is close to 1.

Such a statistical law can be used to explain why an event of kind $E$ occurred given conditions $C$. The probability statement must reflect all information relevant to the explicandum, that is, all the facts that affect the probability of the explicandum.

*Example*

*Probability Law:* The probability that a consumer from New York City will shop in New Jersey is proportional to the costs saved and inversely proportional to the distance to be traveled.

*Antecedent Conditions:*

1. John Doe lives in New York City where his shopping costs are $200 per week.
2. The same purchases in New Jersey would cost $120 per week.
3. The distance from John Doe's home in New York City to the shop in New Jersey is one mile.

} Explicans and Premises

*Explicandum:* John Doe will probably shop in New Jersey.

} Conclusion

The argument is deductive in structure but it is not a deductive argument since the truth of the premises (probability law plus antecedent conditions) does not imply the truth of the conclusion.

Hempel assumed that the probability law must be one of high probability but Salmon (1971) argues this need not be so. Salmon claims that an explanation is any set of statements that provides a basis for any inference about the explicandum. This inference need not claim the event definitely would, or even probably would occur; it merely must be a basis for inferring the probability (however small) of the event occurring. Salmon refers to this as the statistical relevance (SR) model of explanation. This statistical relevance model, as illustrated in certain brand-switching models, is more relevant to marketing than Hempel's I-S model since marketing is not just concerned with events of high probability.

Hempel regards the D-N model and the I-S model as the two basic patterns but accepts that not all explanations fall neatly into these two basic categories. He refers to three deviant patterns:

1. The "elliptical explanation" is one that does not make explicit all that it assumes. However, when its assumptions are drawn out, it falls into one of the two basic patterns.

2. The "partial explanation" is one that remains incomplete even when all that is understood by it is made explicit.

3. The "explanation sketch" remains incomplete but also vague about what might be the laws and initial conditions. The explanation sketch is regarded as common in history.

## CRITICISM OF THE D-N MODEL

There has been a good deal of criticism of Hempel's D-N model centering on its realism, utility, and universality. Scriven (1959) points out that Hempel was unable to produce a single perfect example of the D-N model. There are no laws that exact. Furthermore, it is assumed that the truth of the law has been established. Unfortunately, there is just no way of proving a universal law. Whatever the evidence, there always remains the possibility that the law will not hold up in the future. Scriven accepts the existence of "derivation explanations," which are derived from laws but in a generally more complex way than that suggested by the D-N model. But Scriven also talks of "selection explanations," whose focus lies in locating relevant causal antecedents since there are always rival hypotheses. Scriven's selection explanation highlights the fact that it is not the generation of hypotheses that often constitutes the problem but selecting the most likely hypothesis. It is only when the most likely hypothesis has been selected that it appears the obvious choice. As Scriven points out, explanations based on seeming truisms frequently represent selection explanations of the greatest value since the choice of the appropriate "truism" may be fundamental.

In social science there are *always* rival explanations. As Miller (1987) says the real problem lies in comparing and testing rival explanations to choose the best without necessarily referring to covering laws. There are no universal laws in psychology, economics, sociology, political science, anthropology, or history. Yet the social sciences do believe they offer explanations of scientific worth.

If the adequacy of an explanation relates to the purpose for which the explanation is sought, there are many explanations that do not fit the D-N model or even the I-S model. There are also statements that do fit the D-N model yet are not considered adequate in terms of explanation. Thus, on Hempel's view, Boyle's law relating temperature, pressure, and volume of a contained gas would be a law. But such a law lacks explanatory depth and needs the kinetic theory of gases to explain it. There is a difference between having grounds for expecting *y* to occur and explaining why it did or will occur.

Many philosophers like Toulmin (1960) claim that actual scientific explanation does not cohere to the D-N format of a deductive argument with laws as premises. An extreme example is evolutionary theory, which cannot be expressed within the D-N framework. When it comes to subjects like history, the D-N model is a world apart. As Kuhn (1977), a philosopher of the history of science, points out, historical explanation does not depend on the "power of a few scattered and doubtful laws but on the facts presented and their juxtaposition in argument."

For those who assert that all scientific explanations must be causal, the D-N model is unsatisfactory since causal explanations are just one subset of the model: the D-N model provides necessary but not sufficient conditions for a causal explanation since a universal regularity could embrace spurious relationships or reflect just correlations, not causation. Yet as Cummins (1983) argues, it is only in the case of causal subsumption that Hempel's D-N model provides any hint as to the nature of the explanation and that hint is limited by the failure to take causation explicitly into account. Hempel's laws can in fact be misleading in that, although *y* may always follow *x*, both may, for example, be the effects of a common cause *z*. Donagan (1966) claims Hempel confuses grounds for expecting an event to occur with *why it does* since the D-N model allows prediction but does not necessarily provide an explanation of the event after it occurs. This is because the laws in the D-N model are simply universal regularities that are not necessarily causal.

What also undermines the D-N model to those seeking causal explanation is the recognition that causal explanation does not necessitate any empirical law. In fact, as Miller (1987) says, reference to causal processes can do *all* the explanatory work that is needed without requiring or assuming any empirical *laws*. This is because causal processes can apply to nondeterministic systems, that is, to systems that do not make the assumption that if something causes an event, then it makes that event inevitable given the circumstances. As Miller says, this assumption that all causes are deterministic was never part of everyday causal analysis and is no longer part of physics. To quote Miller: "The basic reason for disbelief in determinism is the basic reason for disbelief in unicorns: the beast is unlike anything we have ever seen, and it was not found despite much looking" (p. 71).

Miller's own position is firmly on the side of causal explanation. For him, all explanations of observable phenomena (including human action) should be explained by reference to causal mechanisms even if such mechanisms are relatively unobservable (e.g., mental constructs like motives) and the testing of explanations should always be seen as choosing among rival explanations by testing and comparing them. This is a view that should have wide appeal to marketers.

Walker (1977), too, rejects the D-N model on the ground that all scientific explanations should be of the causal type. He stresses the word "type" because, like Miller, he acknowledges there may be doubts about what the actual causal mechanism is. His concept of "causal type" embraces both observable causal mechanisms and causal analogies:

1. Causal *mechanisms* can be observed to cause the phenomena in question; for example, bacteria eat cells.

2. *Analogies* or *metaphors* can connect certain phenomena by indicating that they behave "as if" some underlying causal mechanism or process is at work; for example, a person acts "as if" he or she has such and such an attitude, motive, or perception.

Analogies may later be found to be mechanisms (e.g., the initial pump analogy to represent the heart's function) but, more generally, analogies remain analogies and break down at some point; research seeks to establish their domain of application.

The philosopher Von Wright (1971) sees the primary test for the validity of the D-N model in whether it can capture reason-giving explanations. The only thing that comes near to a lawlike statement explaining action is the "principle of rationality," asserting that people rationally choose the best means to maximize their goals. But this principle is a rule and not a law of nature in that, like all rules, it can be broken without anyone believing that it is thereby falsified. In fact all rational choice theory based on the rationality principle (see Chapter 5) is essentially normative in pointing out what acting rationally would dictate even though some social scientists, like economists, assume people will actually act as the theory dictates. A commonly quoted rival to the rationality principle is that people adhere to the social norms or rules of society or at least to some subgroup of that society. Thus consumers are very much influenced by the expectations of the groups to whom they look for approval, and the behavior of purchasing agents is influenced by the rules or expectations of others emanating from the purchasing agents' role as buyers. But neither the rationality principle nor social norms are sufficiently compelling to form the basis for universal laws. In practice, which rules are dictated by the rationality principle and/or social norms is not always clear, since any action can be covered by a multitude of possible rules it could be said to follow; unless we know the wants and beliefs lying behind the action, the action could be in accord with any number of rules.

The ordinary language movement in philosophy, especially that branch of the movement that takes its inspiration from the later work of the philosopher Ludwig Wittgenstein (1889–1951), ridicules the idea that the explanation of human action involves subsumption under laws. Von Wright, a one-time colleague of Wittgenstein at Cambridge University, is typical in rejecting the notion that there is, or there must be, just one type of scientific explanation for both the physical and social sciences. But in deference to Hempel's D-N model of explanation and also to those who believe that scientific explanation is causal explanation, some social scientists prefer to talk of seeking *understanding,* not scientific explanation. They argue against making logical structure the major issue in defining scientific explanation as with the D-N model. More important for them is whether the explanation provides the questioner with understandable reasons. Whether the social sciences should focus on understanding, whether reasons operate as causes, and so on, are themes to which we return throughout the book.

LIMITATIONS OF I-S MODELS

No individual event can be predicted from a statistical law. Statistical laws *always* refer to classes of events, not to any single event. To say that seven out of ten new product launches, of which product XYZ is one, will fail says nothing specific about product XYZ. Product XYZ may fail or it may not fail, but saying that the probability of failure is 0.7 predicts neither one nor the other of these two possible outcomes. Statistical generalizations permit only inferences about the frequency of, say, new product failures in the class of cases of which product XYZ is a member. What we deduce from a statistical generalization is the relative frequency with which some event, belonging to the relevant class, will occur. As a consequence, it can be misleading to speak of deducing from some statistical law "with a probability of 0.7" that product XYZ will fail. Yet this is the shorthand we use instead of speaking more directly about relative frequency.

Much research consists of studies that make generalizations about such matters as product failure. Although these generalizations can be useful (e.g., in drawing attention to a problem), their value is often doubtful given that nothing can be said definitely about the individual case and managements are not dealing with a multitude of cases within a time span that would make sense. There is also the problem of class grouping in that the probability of failure may be high for all new product launches but less so for, say, new cereals and much higher for new perfumes; moreover, if all *company* new product launches are viewed as the relevant class, the probability may be different again.

The impossibility of forecasting the individual event means that the initial/antecedent conditions in the I-S model never refer to the individual event but to what happened in respect to some numbers of people or whatever. It might be added that if failure does not occur with the frequency predicted (after allowing for chance error), we regard the statistical generalization as falsified though in fact *no* statistical generalization can ever be conclusively falsified (see Chapter 12).

In marketing and the social sciences explanations do not in general mimic the D-N model though they do aspire to get out probability statements. Few, however, would claim that these are on a footing with the probability laws in the natural sciences, since these are based on frequency distributions not limited to time and place.

## System or Model-Building Explanations

When marketing academics talk about seeking explanations, they typically talk about building a model, though not one that aspires to the deductive–nomological framework. In marketing, "model" refers to just about any representation of some aspect of reality;

when used more precisely, it refers to structural similarity. When a study of the structure of system $X$ is useful for understanding the structure of system $Y$, then $X$ is a model of $Y$. Where the pattern of relationships among the elements in system $X$ (e.g., a diagram showing how the brain processes information) is identical to that of system $Y$ (the actual processes the brain follows), then the two systems are isomorphous. In practice, explanatory models in marketing consist of a set of variables and rules governing their interactions. Such variables and their interactions have a structure believed to be analogous to how real-world marketing phenomena behave. Where the relationships among the variables are causal, real-world events can be explained by manipulating the model to show how the results came about. (Such models relate to Miller's point about models of causal processes not presupposing universal causal laws, as in the D-N model.) If probabilistic relationships are assumed, the problem lies in judging the stability of the probabilities over time and situations.

Meehan (1968) and more recently Rescher (1986) speak of the model-building approach as the *systematization approach* to explanation to emphasize the contrast with the D-N model. With systematization or the model-building approach, the explanation might describe how the explicandum fits some system (like showing that what is bought fits the person's lifestyle) or contributes to the system's purposes (like the function of fear being its contribution to the organism's survival) or becomes the output of the system (e.g., buying intentions emanating from some mental information-processing system). The model-building or systematization approach is dominant among marketing academics.

Brody (1972) speaks of the "essential property" model of explanation, which could also fall under the systematization approach. Such a model does not explain how change comes about but shows the explicandum to be a property of some system. Brody's own example consists of the following argument:

*Explicandum:* This substance conducts electricity.

*Explicans:* This substance is copper: copper has the atomic number 29 and whatever has that atomic number conducts electricity.

This argument easily translates into the D-N format if we reword the explicans as a universal law. Brody would agree, but the idea that an explicandum can arise through being an essential property of a system provides extra explanatory depth. However, the application to marketing is not straightforward. We could, for example, say that an essential property of humans is to act in a rational way and use this to explain why consumers try to choose the most efficient means to meet their goals. We might even argue that the essential property of personality type $Y$ or psychographic profile $X$ is being self-assured and this explains why such people are innovators. But such explanations sound vacuous, tautological, or a restatement in behavioral terms of what is merely assumed to be an essential property. In other words, there is a problem in establishing any attribute or property as an essential one.

Cummins (1983), too, speaks of property theories but views them differently from Brody. Whereas Brody explains by showing the behavior of interest is to be expected given the system's properties or attributes, Cummins views property theories as seeking to explain the very properties themselves. Thus Cummins would explain dispositional states (or properties like a person's attitude toward a product) by analyzing the attitude itself or by analyzing the system (in this case the consumer) that has the property. Although the precise nature of such an analysis is not clear, Cummins is implying that analyzing a property into its interrelated components would on occasion constitute an appropriate explanation. This, of course, does occur when we explain attitude states in terms of the cognitive (belief) component, the affective (evaluative) component, and the conative (action) component. But is such analysis meaningful? We can talk of "attitudes" having these three components as a matter of definition, but what does it mean empirically? As Ryle (1949) pointed out, it has traditionally been supposed that the mind consisted of three ultimate classes of mental processes: thought (beliefs, cognition), feeling (emotions, evaluations), and the "will" (the conative or action component). Ryle argues that this traditional dogma (on which the concept of attitude is commonly based in the marketing literature) reflects "such a welter of confusions and false inferences that it is best to give up on any attempt to re-fashion it. It should be treated as one of the curios of theory" (p. 62).

Many of the models appearing in the marketing literature are focused more toward prediction than explanation and do not claim explanatory depth. This is the case with perhaps most marketing science models. But other models lack explanatory depth because they are too ambitious. This is the case with overarching theories of buyer behavior. In seeking to explain all, they end up explaining nothing in particular. It is not that they are useless but that at best they simply orient the reader to the types of variables that might be relevant. One orienting model is that of Webster and Wind (1972) covering organizational buying. Here the organizational buying decision is viewed as a function of (1) the individual characteristics of those participating in the decision, (2) social and group factors, (3) organizational factors, and (4) environmental factors. The criticism of such models is that it is not very helpful to be told that virtually everything could affect the buying decision, particularly when we have no idea how the variables can be measured or how their relative importance can be assessed in any particular situation. But Webster and Wind might legitimately reply that their model's purpose is merely to orient research to the nature and extent of the problem and not to offer any solution.

## Reason-Giving

We might stretch the concept of system fit to include the reason-giving explanation on the ground that actions can be explained by showing how they fit a person's system of wants and beliefs. Such an explanation makes the action intelligible and can expose the action's meaning and significance for the individual.

Many philosophers and social scientists claim that only involuntary behavior (like blinking) can be explained by mechanistic universal laws. Action, it is claimed, must be explained in terms of wants and beliefs or cognates of these terms (Rosenberg, 1988). Substitute terms for "belief" include cognition, convictions, and expectancies; substitutes for the term "want" embrace words like goals, utility, needs, desires, motives, and valences.

Those who see themselves as searching for laws tend to regard explanations in terms of wants and beliefs as nonscientific, as simply "folk psychology" that diverts attention from the search for laws, which distinguishes a true science. In fact, critics sought to substitute new categories like operant conditioning for mental constructs like wants and beliefs or to explain behavior in terms of social facts (e.g., poverty causing crime or culture and social pressure causing social conformity in buying). Although social facts are important, any statement linking external events to human action will always beg the question

"Why?" and demand an answer that speaks to motives and beliefs. An approach that focuses on understanding action, by showing it to be intelligible, typically seeks no laws since inquiry stops when intelligibility is reached. However, this does not mean that inquiry must stop at the individual level. The aim can be to move on to explaining the interactions among individuals that occur in a group setting and between groups. Such explanations would take account of group influences on beliefs and wants, but the explanation would still focus on interpreting actions in terms of wants and beliefs and not on formulating laws. In fact, those who seek simply to interpret actions believe that the search for *meaning* in actions and the search for laws represent incompatible points of view. Others disagree. While they do not dismiss the need for explanations that make action meaningful, they claim that the search for such meaning is not incompatible with the search for laws.

Many philosophers, however, contrast reason-giving and causal explanations. Taylor (1970) points out that whenever someone does something because it seems a good idea to do it, we speak of "reasons." In contrast, he argues that if a person does something that he or she cannot help doing, we speak of "causes." Von Wright (1971) argues that in the case of (intentional) action we attribute to others some degree of rationality in weighing certain considerations or reasons in determining what action to take. This contrasts with any concept of cause as compelling its effects. In making the distinction between causal and reason-giving explanations Howard (1982) argues that the distinction rests on the different methodologies from which they are derived. The causal explanation is based on controlled observation, experiment, and so on; in contrast, the reason-giving explanation is based on interpreting the meaning of actions. However, whereas identifying causes is primarily associated in science with experiment, this need not be so, and experimenting with consumers may involve interpreting the meaning of what is said. Similarly, establishing reason-giving explanations can involve laboratory-type experimentation.

Collin (1985) does not accept the sharp distinction made by Von Wright and Howard between causal and reason-giving explanations. He argues that causal ties are involved in *all* scientific explanations. However, for Collin this does not mean reason-giving explanations are causal explanations. The causal tie is implied whenever we say someone acted *because.* But a causal tie by itself is not an *explanation by causation* since the causal tie does not deliver the explanatory power and need not be the source of such power. This is a key distinction but, at this stage, we will leave open the question of whether all explanation could or should be reduced to a causal format, as Nagel (1961) suggests. For Nagel there is no special type of explanation peculiar to the social sciences since reasons can be regarded as causes.

## Explanation and Prediction

The capacity for prediction is commonly regarded as a major goal of science or at least the hallmark certifying certain types of knowledge as scientific. The weakness of the reason-giving explanation in terms of prediction was one basis for demanding something more scientific. It is not yet clear that we have developed any better tool.

Under the D-N model, to be able to explain is also to be able to predict. But it is possible to explain some event after it has occurred (e.g., the collapse of a bridge or the market failure of a product) without being in the position of being able to predict the event before it occurred (Scriven, 1962). This occurs because the conditions giving rise to the event cannot be foreseen.

There is also prediction without explanation (e.g., forecast from trends). As Scheffler says, "prediction may be made with or without rational grounds, and some rational grounds adequate for prediction fail to explain predicted occurrences" (1966, p. 280). When techniques like operations research (OR) yield reasonably accurate forecasts, firms may be content with just adapting to the forecasts. However, although explanations and forecasts both link the past to the future, explanation carries with it more potential for changing that future. This is because explanation presupposes understanding of the factors at work bringing about the action, whereas prediction is directed more toward control than changing background causes.

In principle we predict from theories or forecast from historical data. But theory in social science is not like theoretical physics when it comes to prediction: the predictions are limited to time and place and usually made contingent on other things remaining about equal. In particular, where competition is constantly introducing or making changes in market offerings and, as a consequence, changing beliefs and associated preferences, prediction becomes hazardous. Prediction is also complicated by any indeterminacy arising from the fact that consumers are subject to many cross-pressures and tradeoffs, making it difficult to say which particular wants and beliefs will dominate. Thus rather than discussing laws that suffer no exceptions Elster (1989) talks about "mechanisms" that make no claim to generality but simply add to our repertoire of ways in which various actions are prompted. Included in Elster's "toolbox" of mechanisms is acting on the rationality principle, which he contrasts (rightly or wrongly) with acting in accordance with social norms. In any case, it is easier to explain ex post facto than to predict accurately. Only in hindsight does what happened appear inevitable!

Rosenberg (1988) illustrates the problem of prediction based on using the rationality principle as some sort of law:

*Law: Principle of rationality:* For any consumer $X$, if $X$ has want $Y$ and $X$ believes that $Z$ is the best way to meet want $Y$, then $X$ will choose $Z$. (This is one assumption behind much advocacy of customer orientation in marketing.)
*Initial Conditions:*
1. Smith wants a toothpaste that will both clean teeth and prevent cavities.
2. Smith believes Crest toothpaste is best for both cleaning teeth and preventing cavities.
*Conclusion:* Smith buys Crest.

For Rosenberg, such prediction is beset with problems even if the rationality principle is accepted as valid. In the first place, the initial conditions concerning wants and beliefs are not easy to establish and the actual number of relevant beliefs that lead to action may be too numerous to identify, so the explanations may be incomplete. Moreover, whatever Smith might want and believe to date may change tomorrow since every new shopping trip can be a learning experience in which both wants and beliefs can change. What lightens this somewhat gloomy picture is that, as Gordon (1987) says, the argument assumes that people keep tabs on all the beliefs that might be relevant. Furthermore, it is not generally prediction at the individual level that is of concern but the prediction of the behavior of the masses.

Rosenberg correctly points out that unless we know two out of the three variables of interest—belief, want, and action—the third is not determinable. Thus to use beliefs to predict (buying) action we need to assume the relevant want (goals, needs, or whatever) is held constant. This is the assumption made when marketers predict buying intentions from consumer attitudes since attitudes reflect beliefs. Similarly, when we predict buying action from wants we assume beliefs remain constant. This is the assumption made when economists posit consumers who have perfect information and so just focus on maximizing the utility goal. The assumption of beliefs being held constant is also the assumption made by those in organizational behavior who seek to predict from motives (like Maslow's hierarchy of needs) that are assumed to lie behind manifest wants. What we cannot do is work back from buying itself to identifying the relevant wants and beliefs. Thus when the economist focuses on "revealed preference," he or she must abandon explanation at the individual level unless assumptions are made about either beliefs or wants since an action by itself "never identifies a single belief or desire" (Rosenberg, 1988).

Elster (1989) argues that explanatory theory may be predictively weak in that it is indeterminate and/or inadequate. A theory may provide indeterminate predictions because the theory is incomplete with the consequence that it does not yield unique predictions. Thus rational choice theory (see Chapter 5) does not yield unique predictions in that, for example, the consumer may find several alternative offerings equally acceptable. However, although the theory is not fully determinate, it may still be useful since it does exclude many possibilities that would otherwise be considered. A theory that does not predict wrongly but does predict weakly may also be inadequate. Thus a theory may help a manager predict how many will buy a product but not how many will buy a particular brand. Rational choice theory is also inadequate. Both the indeterminacy and inadequacy of rational choice theory emanate from its being first and foremost a normative theory saying what action should be taken and only second a predictive tool.

Many psychologists eschew talking explicitly about the rationality principle but instead talk about mental states and the probable action arising from those states:

If any consumer $X$ is in state $S_1$ in condition $C_2$, then the consumer will probably choose $Y$.

The state $S_1$ might refer to attitudinal states, expectancies, motives, perceptions, or states of confidence; conditions $C_2$ might refer to the time and place with its attendant social norms and pressures. Although such statements are couched in causal terms divorced from talk about reasons, there is no problem in translating them into a reason-giving format.

Gordon (1987) like many other philosophers claims that expressed intentions (e.g., I intend to buy $Y$) do not result from making deductive inferences along the lines of the D-N model but are the products of *practical* reasoning that is based on beliefs about the relevant facts and wants deriving from values and norms. Practical reasoning at its simplest has the following general pattern (Von Wright, 1983):

I want to attain $X$.

Unless $Y$ is done, $X$ will not be attained.

Therefore, $Y$ must be done.

The first premise expresses the want (not a law). The second premise expresses beliefs as to the conditions that must be fulfilled if $X$ is to be attained. The conclusion expresses a practical necessity that is both prescriptive and normative.

Gordon recommends what he calls "pretend-play" for predicting likely action. In pretend-play, we act out the decision based on knowledge of beliefs, wants, and the circumstances of those whose actions are to be predicted. The technique is concerned with the prediction of action that is not involuntary behavior. But much buying behavior is habitual or ritualistic—consumers responding in a somewhat mechanical way to replenishing their stocks, for instance—a response not unlike automatically carrying an umbrella when rain is predicted. Such habitual behavior does not involve the deliberation over means that characterizes true decision-making and would not be captured by "pretend-play."

Pretend-play is practical simulation to predict the action that best coheres with the wants and beliefs of the target group. But for those who talk primarily in terms of making behavior intelligible, prediction is not the main objective. We can understand a process (e.g., participation, a game of chess, a decision, or the plot of a novel) as it emerges or understand it after it happened, but this is different from predicting the outcome of a process or its evolution, since things could have gone otherwise in a way that might equally make sense.

Much of the prediciton that goes on in marketing owes little to explanatory theory but will nonetheless have some underlying rationale. As an example, we have the BCG (Boston Consulting Group) experience curve claiming that value-added costs decline 20 to 30% in real terms for each doubling of experience (operationally interpreted as doubling the volume of output). There is a rationale for the claim involving factors such as increased learning or greater specialization, but it is certainly not sufficient to justify such a precise claim. Although the experience curve was put forward initially by BCG as an established fact, the universality of any such claim has not been sustained. The BCG system was deterministic not only in its claims about the future of costs but also about a product's future based on its current relative market share and market growth rate. Whatever might be useful in the BCG system, the extent to which *its* dogmatic claims were accepted uncritically by many managers indicates the need for better thinking in the area of planning. What was most surprising, however, was the failure by some marketing professionals to see the implied claim, namely, that market success *always* relates to costs and the competitive advantage to be sought must *always* be lowest price.

## Adequacy of Explanation

Hempel argues that his D-N model of explanation constitutes an adequate scientific explanation providing

1. the explicandum was a logical consequence of the explicans, and
2. the law(s) in the explicans were *verified* general law(s).

But the D-N model may not provide the type of explanation that is sought. As Scriven (1959) says, what constitutes an adequate explanation is intimately related to purposes: an adequate explanation involves knowing all about something with respect to the question being asked. Achinstein (1983), too, argues that an explanation should relate to the interests of the questioner and so be of most value for the purposes in mind. Different types of explanation provide different windows through which to view a problem so that an adequate explanation, given the questioner's purposes, might involve several types of explanation. In line with this Kurtz (1965) recommends "coductionism," where different types of explanation make a contribution to overall understanding. Another view is that of Kuhn (1970), who argues that the adequacy of an explanation depends on the scientist's particular "paradigm" (theoretical and methodological orientation) as this indicates the type of problem solution considered satisfactory. What all this means is that what might be adequate to, say, a behavioral psychologist or ethnomethodologist might not be an adequate explanation from the viewpoint of the manager. In other words, there is a problem in choosing the right paradigm as not all social science paradigms will prove equally useful for all purposes.

As noted previously, explanations are always concerned with events or states under description (e.g., decision-making under uncertainty) and not with just explaining anything coming under some name. But what happens when no single existing explanatory system is adequate for the job? We might seek a multidisciplinary or multipronged approach (this is attempted in Chapter 9 on emotion) or we can treat the explicandum as provisional until the form of explanation has been decided on. In other words, the explicandum describing some aspect of reality may not be explainable under its current description. In practice, any explanation is likely to explain a little less or a little more than what was initially envisaged in stating the explicandum.

Meehan (1968) argues that scientific explanations should be judged beyond just adequacy for the purpose at hand if the development of a science is the aim. Explanations should seek accuracy, precision, reliability, power, and, last but not least, wide scope so that the explanation covers a wide range of states or events. This must be so if the purpose is to develop scientific theory.

An adequate explanation must also satisfy certain logical criteria. An explanation must, for instance, tell the questioner more than he or she must have known in order to ask the question. Homans (1967) illustrates this by what he calls explanation by concept, as occurs when someone "explains" why the Chinese do not like milk by saying it is because of their culture. This in effect says disliking milk is characteristic of the behavior of Chinese, which the questioner must have known to have asked the question in the first place. Sometimes it seems we believe that just naming a phenomenon explains it. Thus it is common in textbooks to find sentences such as "Consumers continue to buy the same brand, week in and week out, because they are brand loyal." Inventing names for unknown causes gives an illusion of explanation but may add nothing beyond giving a name to the phenomenon. We gain little by dubbing some effect "variety seeking," or whatever, unless we have independently established the concept of variety seeking as a causal or dispositional agent. The question is, of course, what evidence would we accept as being relevant to establishing the presence of such a disposition? Another common practice is to invent a synonym for some phenomenon to "explain" the phenomenon, as when we speak of "routinized response behavior" as a synonym for habit as if the term itself establishes an explanation. Economics is not immune from spurious explanation. As the economist Joan Robinson (1976) says, the word "utility" is of impregnable circularity. Thus to say the quantity of a commodity that an individual consumes will be cut back to the amount where marginal utility is equal to price is a tautology when price is the measure of marginal utility.

## Conclusion

What we might conclude from this chapter is that if the D-N format separates the true and adequate scientific explanation from the counterfeit, then *all* explanations in the social sciences are counterfeit. However, the evidence shows that the D-N model itself represents an unattainable goal and a dubious one at that. We will also be casting doubts on probabilitistic laws in the sense meant by Hempel in his I-S model. What must be said is that the type of explanation that is sought will relate to the investigator's purposes and such purposes may not encompass any hope of developing theory along the lines of physics. We can develop a very deep understanding of buyer behavior without being able to quote any explanatory laws along the lines discussed by Hempel.

In the four chapters that follow we discuss four types or modes of explanation as distinguished by Nagel (1961). These may not not be exhaustive, but they are probably the ones of most interest to marketing. These are

1. causal explanations where some precursor *X* results in or is invariably associated with some outcome *Y* under certain conditions;

2. causal temporal processes;

3. teleological or teleonomic explanations where the explicans makes reference to a person's *intentions* or the *goals, purposes,* or *wants* being sought, or, alternatively,

4. makes reference to the *function* which a component plays in some system.

# References

Achinstein, P. (1983). *The Nature of Explanation.* New York: Oxford University Press.

Bambrough, R. (1964). "Principia Metaphysica." *Philosophy* 39, pp. 97–109.

Braithwaite, R. B. (1960). *Scientific Explanation.* New York: Harper Torchbooks; Cambridge: Cambridge University Press, 1953.

Brody, B. A. (1972). "Towards an Aristotelian Theory of Scientific Explanation." *Philosophy of Science* 39, pp. 20–31.

Bromberger, S. (1966). "An Approach to Explanation." In *Studies in Analytical Philosophy,* edited by R. Butler. Oxford: Basil Blackwell.

Collin, Finn (1985). *Theory and Understanding.* Oxford: Basil Blackwell.

Cummins, Robert (1983). *The Nature of Psychological Explanation.* Cambridge, MA: The MIT Press.

Danto, Arthur C. (1965). *Analytical Philosophy of History.* Cambridge: Cambridge University Press.

Donagan, A. (1966). "The Popper-Hempel Model Reconsidered." In *Philosophical Analysis and History,* edited by W. H. Dray. New York: Harper and Row.

Elster, Jon (1989). *Solomonic Judgments: Limitations of Rationality.* Cambridge: Cambridge University Press.

Gordon, R. M. (1987). *The Structure of Emotions.* Cambridge: Cambridge University Press.

Handy, Rollo, and E. C. Harwood (1973). *A Current Appraisal of the Behavioral Sciences.* Great Barrington, MA: Behavioral Research Council.

Hanson, N. R. (1965). *Patterns of Discovery.* Cambridge: Cambridge University Press.

Hempel, C. G. (1965). *Aspects of Scientific Explanation.* New York: Free Press.

Hempel, C. G., and P. Oppenheim (1948). "Studies in the Logic of Explanation." *Philosophy of Science* 15, pp. 135–75.

Homans, George C. (1967). *The Nature of Social Science.* New York: Harcourt, Brace and World.

Howard, R. J. (1982). *Three Faces of Hermeneutics.* Los Angeles: University of California Press.

Kuhn, Thomas S. (1970). *The Structure of Scientific Revolutions,* 2nd ed. Chicago: University of Chicago Press.

Kuhn, Thomas S. (1977). *The Essential Tension.* Chicago: University of Chicago Press.

Kurtz, P. (1965). *Decision and the Condition of Man.* New York: Dell.

Meehan, Eugene J. (1968). *Explanation in Social Science: A System Paradigm,* Homewood, IL: Dorsey Press.

Miller, Richard W. (1987). *Fact and Method.* Princeton, NJ: Princeton University Press.

Nagel, E. (1961). *The Structure of Science: Problems in the Logic of Scientific Explanation.* New York: Harcourt, Brace and World.

Popper, K. R. (1965). *The Logic of Scientific Discovery.* New York: Harper Torchbooks; London: Hutchinson, 1959.

Rescher, Nicholas (1986). *The Limits of Science.* Berkeley: University of California Press.

Robinson, Joan (1976). *Economic Philosophy.* London: Pelican Books.

Rosenberg, Alexander (1988). *Philosophy of Social Science.* Boulder, CO: Westview Press.

Ryle, Gilbert (1949). *The Concept of Mind.* New York: Barnes and Noble; London: Hutchinson.

Salmon, W. C. (1971). *Statistical Explanation and Statistical Relevance,* Pittsburgh: University of Pittsburgh Press.

Scheffler, Israel (1966). "Explanation, Prediction and Abstraction." In *Philosophy of Science,* edited by Arthur Danto and Sidney Morgenbesser. New York: Meridian Books.

Scriven, M. (1959). "Truisms as the Grounds for Historical Explanations." In *Theories of History,* edited by P. Gardiner. Glencoe, IL: Free Press.

Scriven, M. (1962). "Explanations, Predictions and Laws." In *Minnesota Studies in the Philosophy of Science,* edited by H. Feigl, and G. Maxwell. Vol. III. Minneapolis: University of Minnesota Press.

Taylor, D. M. (1970). *Explanation and Meaning.* Cambridge: Cambridge University Press.

Toulmin, S. (1960). *The Philosophy of Science.* New York: Harper Torchbooks; London: Hutchinson, 1953.

Von Wright, G. H. (1971). *Explanation and Understanding.* Ithaca, NY: Cornell University Press.

Von Wright, G. H. (1983). *Practical Reason.* Oxford: Basil Blackwell.

Walker, N. (1977). *Behavior and Misbehavior: Explanations and Nonexplanations.* New York: Basic Books.

Webster, F. E., and Y. Wind (1972). "A General Model for Understanding Organizational Buying Behavior." *Journal of Marketing* 36 (April), pp. 12–19.

Wisdom, J. O. (1952). *Foundations of Inference in Natural Science.* London: Methuen.

# 3

# Causal Explanation

Happy is the man who knows the causes of things.
Ancient maxim

The type of explanation that is most popularly associated with the scientific enterprise is the causal explanation. In research on buyer behavior, causal relationships might be assumed to cover any of the following:

1. *External factors causing buying action.* The external factors viewed as causing buying response might be culture, reference group pressure, brand name, packaging, and so on.

2. *Mental state causing buying action.* The mental states viewed as causing buying response might be attitude, degree of involvement with the purchase, personality, and so on.

3. *External factors causing mental state.* The external factors viewed as causing the mental state (e.g., favorable attitude toward the brand) might be trial usage of the brand, advertising, medical recommendation, and so on.

4. *Mental state causing some subsequent mental state.* The mental state of involvement with the purchase might be viewed as causing subsequent complex mental processing.

There is no other mode of explanation that generates the same degree of interest for researchers as the causal explanation. In marketing we talk of identifying causes as a way of changing reality, or the way things are. Even when we talk to our customers about the function of a product we often describe that function in causal terms: "destroys bugs," "sweetens coffee," "fertilizes the soil," and so on. If we accept the premise that the firm's marketing endeavors can cause changes in buying behavior, then all our means of market control are causal means since all control involves changing behavior.

We all use the term "cause" to mean some sort of power bringing about some sort of effect. Yet the concept of cause is constantly being debated. No other form of explanation has been so elusive or given rise to so much conceptual confusion as the causal explanation. This chapter covers the major controversies: the nature of cause, the role of cause in marketing and the social sciences, whether reasons for action are the causes of action, the problems of identifying causes, and so on. If we believe that knowing causes can explain, that manipulating causes can change outcomes, that advertising can cause consumers to behave differently—then we need to be aware of the debates discussed here.

## The Nature of Cause

### Regulatory Theory

The natural scientist's view of the world is of how things are made to happen through cause and effect relationships. And social scientists implicitly subscribe to this view whenever they speak of the goals of their discipline being prediction and control since these goals are intimately associated with establishing causal relationships. It is not surprising then that Bagozzi regards the notion of cause and effect as key in marketing:

> Perhaps no single concept is more pervasive and important in marketing than the notion of cause and effect. Marketing practitioners depend on it in their planning and implementation of programs designed to obtain responses from consumers. Ideas of advertising affecting sales, opinion leaders influencing the adoption of new products, or promotion activities producing interest and preferences for one's wares all rely implicitly on mechanisms of cause and effect. Marketing scholars and researchers find causality at the heart of phenomena they attempt to understand and explain. Our propositions, theories, and methodologies are all fundamentally based on the concept of causality. (1980, p. 1)

Yet, as Bagozzi goes on to state, the nature of the causal relationship is full of controversy. The major controversy lies in whether we can ever show causes as necessitating their effects. This controversy goes back to David Hume (1711–1776), who claimed that observation tells us only that some things regularly follow other things; that is, observation does not reveal any special force or necessity that people intuitively feel must be involved in any causal situation. Hume argued that all that can be said is:

1. The cause $X$ and the effect $Y$ are contiguous in time and place.
2. $X$ precedes $Y$ or at least does not succeed it.
3. Causality is inferred from the constant conjunction between $X$ and $Y$.

Hume's concept of cause is consistent with his philosophy that the only entities of whose existence we can be certain are our perceptions. Given this, Hume argued that there was no necessary connection between perceived cause and perceived effect. The fact that people do see in some constant conjunction some necessity has to be explained by psychology since causal attributions stem simply from a person's experience and not from any external physical event. The assertion that $X$-type events cause $Y$-type events is not based on anything we actually see but arises as an inference from frequent repetitions of such conjunctions in our experience. Whenever we perceive constant conjunctions, we are likely to attribute a causal connection to the pairings. The belief that $X$-type events bring about $Y$-type events is just in the mind, nothing more. (This at least is the standard interpretation of Hume, but some philosophers point out that Hume consistently maintained that there are real powers and forces in nature. He was simply claiming they are not directly accessible to our senses. Because Hume maintains that all we know about causation is regular succession does not in itself imply he believed causation in the real world was nothing more than regular succession.)

Hume's thesis manifests itself in the *regularity theory of causation,* which claims that cause refers to any statistical regularity that obtains between some antecedent $X$-type events and some later $Y$-type events. As Robinson (1985) puts it, on this basis a causal law is just a shift in perspective from saying "$X$ has always been followed by $Y$" to "$X$-type events are followed by $Y$-type events," or "$X$" is the cause of $Y$."

Bagozzi upholds Hume for introducing a modern notion of causation. This is not because Bagozzi would rest content with defining cause as nothing more than the constant conjunction of events, for Bagozzi goes on to claim that "to say that *x* causes *y* is to say that *x* and *y* are related, and the relation involves some notion of mechanism, force, production, or the like between *x* as cause and *y* as effect" (1980, p. 2). Hume saw, as A. J. Ayer (1973) says, that the basis of ascribing causality in the first place cannot be anything more than a de facto correlation. Both the layman and the physicist depend on observed conjunctions or correlations to hypothesize about causes. Bagozzi might nonetheless be reading too much into Hume. Hume argued that it was merely "illusion" that lay behind seeing causal relationships as in some way being necessitated. Bagozzi interprets "illusion" as equivalent to "conceptual necessity." Since many statements in consumer behavior are accepted because of a seeming "conceptual necessity" (e.g., between customer satisfaction and the likelihood of repeat purchase), this interpretation of Hume has appeal. However, to substitute "conceptual necessity" for "illusion" is wrong. For example, there is a strong conceptual "necessity" to regard the following as sufficient conditions for consumer *C* to try to buy brand *B* because of the way we understand ourselves and other human beings:

- *C* wants such a product.
- *C* prefers brand *B* to rival brands.
- *C* believes there is no other way to obtain brand *B* than by buying it.
- *C* is in a position (e.g., financial, physical) to buy brand *B* and knows this.
- Brand *B* is readily available and its availability is known to *C*.
- *C* can think of no better use for the money than spending it on buying brand *B*.
- *C* can think of no reason why he should not buy *B*.

If we found that whenever such conditions arose, consumers sought to buy brand *B*, would we regard such conceptual necessity as equivalent to an illusion? Bagozzi is right about the role of conceptual necessity but he himself should take the credit. Although there are no constant conjunctions or non-trivial universal regularities in marketing, there is nonetheless considerable interest in establishing statistical regularities, whether explanatory or not, as long as they help in prediction. Elster (1983) classifies these regularity models into four groups:

1. *The deductive-statistical model.* This deduces some statistical regularity from the assumption that some stochastic process is at work. The base model is commonly a well-established model in statistics or mathematics. An example is the Markov chain or Markov process model, which has been used to predict brand-switching behavior. It is not clear that any explanation is involved beyond showing that the data fit the base model—perhaps with a little bit of juggling or curve-fitting!

2. *Hempel's inductive–statistical (I-S) model.* Here statistical laws are used to "explain" particular states or events, for example,
   If *X* is *Y*, then *C* is almost certainly *D*.
   *X* is *Y*.
   Therefore, *C* is almost certainly *D*.
   *Example:* If the firm is the lowest cost producer, then its market share will almost certainly be highest. The firm is the lowest cost producer. Therefore, the firm will almost certainly have the highest market share. Unless the probabilities can be given some empirical foundation or justified on theoretical grounds, there is always the possibility of the "explanation" (if any) being spurious.

3. *Probabilistic version of the causal model.* This is really a subset of Hempel's I-S model but its importance warrants separate treatment. It can be expressed as $X$ results in $Y$ in $T\%$ of cases, suggesting that some subset of $X$ causes $Y$ while the rest of the unknown set do not.

4. *Correlation analysis and associated techniques like path analysis.* Here the aim is to find systematic covariations among variables. In most cases the dependent variable $Y$ is only partially explained by the independent variable $X$, leaving a large unexplained residual. Typically such correlation analysis is used to eliminate a hypothesis as to cause when correlations are not significant.

## Criticism of Regulatory Theory

There have been many citicisms of Hume. After all, observing, say, bacteria-eating cells is more than just observing some things regularly following other things. Moreover, the fact that things do happen suggests that the constant antecedent event (or something coexisting with it) must be a factor in bringing about the effect. The fact that we can manipulate what we believe is the cause with the result that effects appear/disappear indicates cause is a mechanism. On the other hand, though we may be sure what causes what, it is generally true we never see the whole causal process. But unless the antecedent (or something coexistent with it) is instrumental in producing the effect, it would be pointless to manipulate the antecedent. Although there may be a perfect correlation between the number of storks born in Sweden and the human birth rate, no one believes that increasing the birth rate of storks will increase the Swedish human birth rate. Although every statistics text warns against assuming that a significantly high correlation implies some causal relationship, there is a tendency for people to act as Hume suggests. The PIMS [Profit Impact of Market Strategies] data base, for instance, consists purely of correlational data yet it is often assumed to be causal because it sounds as if it might be (conceptual necessity?). Thus the "sensitivity reports" and the "optimum strategy reports" of PIMS presuppose in their use that the data base does consist of causal relationships. There is a danger here of manipulating symptoms in the belief they are causes.

Because more than one single cause is usually at work, it is tempting to divide up the causal universe and present the resulting categories as an important discovery. It may be true that what we believe and what we do are results of our heredity and environment—but it is not that enlightening.

The first major criticism of Hume's position then is that it fails to distinguish spurious regularities from causal relationships. (Causal relationships, unlike spurious regularities, involve some power/mechanism within the cause itself to produce some effect through contact.) As a consequence, it offers dubious justification for drawing conclusions from what are believed to be causal laws over and above the justification for drawing conclusions from accidental regularities. Nagel (1961) calls causal laws "nomic generalizations" to distinguish them from mere accidental regularities for, to quote MacIntyre (1971), to any accidental generalization must be added, "do not be surprised if things turn out otherwise." This would not be so with a causal law. Harris (1970) similarly argues that causal laws in the natural sciences are not just Humean constant conjunctions; for him, they involve a principle of structure among the various objects and processes constituting the antecedent conditions, such that the entire system would be disrupted without the relation between the events in question.

Hume's regularity view allows anything to be the cause of anything providing there is constant conjunction. But causal laws are typically viewed as applying to what, as yet, are unknown cases just as the laws of physics are assumed to apply regardless of time and place in the universe. A causal law or nomic generalization should thus support

1. *A counterfactual statement:* if *X had* occurred, *Y* also *must* have occurred.
2. *A subjunctive conditional statement:* if *X were* to occur, *Y will* also occur.

There is however, a problem with counterfactuals in that they envision complete determinism. But as Miller (1987) says, what determines *Y* is not just the so-called cause *X* but *X* together with accompanying (often unknown) circumstances.

Hume's view presupposes frequent experience of the conjunction to allow inferences about causality. As Danto (1973) says, however, this means Hume's account of causation will not entertain the unique historical coupling of events as being causal. Yet singular sequences are recognized on occasions as causal just as some unique event in history can be regarded as causing subsequent events.

One final point: although most social scientists and marketers talk of causal relationships as being between states or events, Ayer (1973) argues that we should think not in terms of "events" but in terms of "facts" in that we can then talk of the cause of failure as the not doing of *X*.

## The Natural Necessity View

An alternative view to that of Hume is the "natural necessity" view. Those who regard cause as something more than constant conjunction claim there must be some *necessity* to the relationship (Bunge, 1963) and may argue (like the *realist*) that to identify *X* as the cause of *Y* necessitates showing how *X produces Y*. The "realist" takes it for granted that real causal mechanisms exist and need to be identified. Such mechanisms can refer to "powers," "capacities," "structures," and so on.

For the realist, citing the cause in itself is not enough since there is a need to specify the mechanism at work. Many realists happily accept reasons as the appropriate mechanism.

If there are no relationships in marketing that satisfy the condition of constant conjunction, then do we rest content with a relationship where *X* is frequently associated with *Y* or do we look for other justifications like trying to identify the mechanisms that might be at work? In social science it is doubtful whether we ever have explanations that contain a full understanding of the mechanisms at work. In practice, even the realist on occasion accepts grounds for believing *X* is the cause of *Y* other than direct observation of mechanisms at work. After all, we cannot directly observe how pressing numbers on a remote control unit changes television channels.

If cause is viewed as whatever is producing the effect, the concept of the likely cause of some effect assumes appropriate background knowledge since the idea that *X* is the cause of *Y* is tenable only against some background knowledge as to why this might be so. Thus if the manager accepts, without hard evidence, Porter's (1980) contention that the profit potential of an industry and the state of competition is determined by just the five factors of (1) threat of entry, (2) market rivalry, (3) pressure of substitutes from other industries, (4) bargaining power of suppliers, and (5) bargaining power of buyers, it is because it makes causal sense. Similarly, the selection of a marketing strategy is like the adoption of a causal hypothesis since it is assumed that the strategy will achieve certain effects. Again, the manager visualizes some causal process that makes sense as a way of producing the effects that are sought. This sort of thinking involves teasing out conceptual relationships since the marketing manager cannot draw on any behavioral laws.

For those realist philosophers who equate the search for scientific explanation with the search for causal mechanisms, a scientific explanation is a description of the causes that bring about the explicandum. But what antecedent or concomitant events are to count as causes? Miller (1987) focuses on the conditions necessary for triggering the effects. He rejects cause as embracing all the necessary and sufficient conditions since this would imply that all causes must be deterministic; that is, if $X$, then always $Y$. Except in classical physics (and relativity theory?) anything that is labeled cause $X$ brings about $Y$ only in certain circumstances "whose relevant features may be unknown even in broad outline." Miller argues that causal explanatory adequacy depends on the standards of the specific discipline but, in general, the causal factors singled out must actually exist and be causally sufficient in typical cases.

How do academics in marketing and the social sciences actually apply the term "cause"? On what grounds are they likely to speak of having established a causal relationship? Although social scientists and marketers do sometimes take high correlations to signify some sort of causal connection, it is usually only if there are reasons suggesting why it makes sense to think of the relationship in these terms. Consider the well-known finding of the positive relationship between market share and profitability. Although it is obvious that market share is not sufficient to ensure profitability (since, for example, high market share can come about from selling at unprofitable prices), acting "as if" the relationship was causal made sense to many people. But this did not mean that researchers in marketing did not see that substantial research was needed and one contribution was a study that cast doubt on the extent to which the relationship was actually causal (Jacobson and Aaker, 1985). More recently, Jacobson's (1988) research points to both market share and return on investment (ROI) as joint outcomes of successful strategies.

Relationships sometimes are accepted as causal when they have been validated in laboratory or field experiments. Even here we cannot just conclude that the factor being varied is the factor that should be labeled cause, any more than the cause of the increase in output in the famous Hawthorne experiment was viewed as varying the lighting rather than management interest and attention. Experiments that are well conducted, based on some theoretical position pointing to likely causes, and sufficiently varied and extensive in the way they are conducted to try to eliminate rival hypotheses can foster the acceptance of a causal relationship. If there is never any absolute certainty even in the case of an experiment (since all possible rival hypotheses are never tested), the problem is more difficult when the situation is nonexperimental. What we look for here first is a strong correlation that holds up wherever observed. Second, the high correlation must be considered theoretically interesting and make sense as causal on theoretical grounds. Finally, every attempt has been made (see Appendix: Tabular Analysis) to ensure the relationship is not spurious.

## Cause in the Physical Sciences

Causal laws are preeminently associated with the physical (natural) sciences. In what would appear to be an endorsement of Hume's position, as applied to the physical sciences, Von Wright (1983) views nomic (lawlike) causal relationships as adhering to two conditions:

1. The cause and the effect must be logically independent.
2. The cause and effect are connected such that whenever the cause in conditions $a$, $b$, $c$ occurs, the effect follows.

Even in the physical sciences the necessary and sufficient conditions for the effect to occur are never specified in full. Certain background constants are always assumed just as we say that striking a match will cause it to ignite, taking it for granted that oxygen will be present. This is the same point made earlier by Miller (1987). However, we are willing to extend a law of physics to unknown and imaginary instances regardless of time and place in the universe. This is not the case in marketing and the social sciences. The belief in the universal nature of physical laws is grounded in the fact that any particular law is backed by other laws into some form of theory, constituting for many philosophers a set of structural principles necessitating the predicted effects.

In the physical sciences there is a tendency to speak of functional dependence to describe what others might refer to as a causal relationship. This is the mathematical sense of a functional relationship. It has the advantage of being less controversial than the use of cause and offers a precise statement of the relationship. Thus quantity $Y$ is functionally dependent on $X$ if, for each value specified for $X$, there is a unique value of $Y$. Functional dependencies stated in this way sound purely descriptive and avoid any suggestion that mechanisms are at work. In marketing, however, it is common to exploit the functional notation for its association with a scientific image but not to deliver on what it promises. We often use the notation whenever it is believed one set of things varies with another set of things. Here there is the mathematical form but not the mathematical sense since there may be no way of measuring the variables; moreover, if the variables could be measured, whether there would be a unique value of $Y$ for each value of $X$ may be a matter of wild conjecture.

The adoption of the functional notation in science was supported by the debate over determinism in physics. Heisenberg's uncertainty principle of 1927 was generally interpreted as undermining determinism and the idea of absolute laws. In practice, the uncertainty principle was not that limiting since it was possible to attach probabilities to the behavior of particles and to predict with virtual certainty the behavior of particles en masse. Nonetheless, the principle raised the question of whether it makes sense to suppose that individual subatomic movements are caused when it is not possible in principle to discover their causes. One way to avoid answering this question was to argue that causation is irrelevant for physics. Bertrand Russell (1917) in particular ridiculed the concept of cause, arguing that the concept did more harm than good and should be replaced by discussion in terms of functional equations rather than the one-way relationship of cause and effect. But many would agree with Bagozzi that discussions of causality are very much part of all science and that the functional conception of causality where if $X$, then always $Y$ becomes $Y = f(X)$ can be "interpreted as a refinement and extension of the classical concept not a difference in kind." However, Kuhn (1977) claims there has been a decline of the causal mode of explanation in the natural sciences, which he attributes to the pragmatic success of other explanatory modes.

## Causes in the Social Sciences and Marketing

Whatever the problems involved with the concept of cause, the concept is basic to our thinking. Even to master a language is to master a causal picture of the world, as suggested by a word like "footprint," which implies a knowledge of the cause of what is observed. As has frequently been pointed out, managers—like plumbers and policemen—cannot resort to algebraic abstraction but must use a concept of cause near to the natural necessity theory by seeking the "mechanisms" at work. However, while marketing managers will draw on any findings regarding causal relationships, they are not in general producers of causal generalizations. Yet they are constantly being required to answer questions regarding the cause of individual events. Whether the singular causal statement ("Product failure was caused by sales force apathy") presupposes some universal is part of an ongoing debate over determinism.

In the social sciences the debate over the role and scope of causal explanation goes on. Walker (1975) denies there are any explanatory causal theories in psychology if causal theory demands knowledge of the mechanisms at work; explanations involving neurological mechanisms have so far proved of little value. He believes that emotions and reasons should be regarded as mechanisms on the ground that it is paradoxical to reject the only kind of causation directly experienced simply because the causes cannot be seen. He agrees, however, that the same emotions and reasons do not always produce the same effect so suggesting they are only part of the "mechanism" at work.

Cummins (1983) argues that causal laws would in any case be inadequate to fully explain psychological phenomena. For example, dispositional terms like attitude or personality traits, when used as causal variables, possess limited explanatory value. Cummins believes that causal "laws" operate best when they enter into "transition" theories. A transition theory explains some change of state in a system. It seeks to answer the question, Why does $S$ change state from $S_1$ to $S_2$? Subsumption under some causal "law," Cummins claims, would be the most natural way to answer the question. The method would be to fix on the set of variables describing the state of the system and show any change of state as being a function of some disturbing event $X$. Such a method might be used to explain "attitude change" or the transition from market growth to market maturity and from market maturity to market decline. But if attitudes rest on beliefs, it seems odd to many people to talk of *causing* someone to believe $Y$, since this implies some mechanical process at work. For many philosophers, a belief is not caused but endorsed on the basis of its conformity with other related beliefs, so that new beliefs "must win contests against conflicting claims in evidential showdowns" even though at times we do not have time (or whatever) to canvass all our beliefs.

Mohr (1982) refers to causal "explanatory" models as variance models viewing cause or "precursor $X$" as the necessary and sufficient condition for the outcome $Y$. He regards the "interaction problem" as the stumbling block to developing such causal models in social science. He defines interaction as occurring whenever the impact of some variable $X$ on $Y$ is dependent on some other factor $Z$. Being unable to take account of the mediating variable $Z$ gives rise to instability in results. Mohr is arguing, for example, that the effect of stimulus $X$ on response $Y$ fluctuates from study to study in large part because we do not know the mediating variable(s) $Z$. He suggests either that constructs such as attitudes are inadequate for the task or alternatively it has not been possible to measure their state with the degree of accuracy needed for predictive purposes.

Mohr leans toward a natural necessity theory in assuming that between the stimulus and the response is some causal chain consisting of a set of intervening or mediating variables. His position assumes some known antecedent condition is the initiating causal factor whose link to the effect can be vitiated or diluted by other mediating or intervening variables. But the assumed initiating causal factor may itself be an effect of some other factor that is the actual initiating cause.

Mohr's position calls into question whether we can ever get beyond establishing tendencies in social science and marketing. Bhaskar (1979), a realist, is skeptical. He argues that causal laws in social science will never amount to more than tendencies since causal laws manifest themselves only in empirical invariances under closed conditions. In other words, it may be possible on rare occasions to get "empirical invariances" in laboratory experiments when the causal structures of generative mechanisms can work without interference, but in the real world these generative mechanisms are normally *out of phase* with their effects. This is a position many of us would endorse.

## Are Beliefs and Wants Caused?
## Are Actions Caused?
## Is the Decision-Making Process a Causal One?

No one doubts that a good deal of behavior is caused in the sense of being involuntary. But many philosophers distinguish the "blink," which is an involuntary physical movement, from the "wink," which is voluntary and intentional and classified as action. Can we speak of the beliefs and wants lying behind actions such as winking as having been caused? Can we speak of the decision-making process as a causal one or that human actions are caused? These questions are major issues in the philosophy of social science. Perhaps the most key question here is whether the relationship between reasons and corresponding action is merely logical and conceptual or actually causal.

Robinson (1985), a psychologist, identifies three distinct positions relating to the foregoing questions:

1. *Hard determinism* claims that "for everything that ever happens at the level of observable human behavior, there are conditions such that, given them, nothing else could happen."

2. *Hard voluntarism* claims that when one's reasons are personal and not imposed, choices intentionally express wants and beliefs that authentically belong to the individual.

3. *Compatibilism* tries to reconcile determinism with voluntarism by claiming that actions can be caused and still appear to be freely chosen.

## Hard Determinism

The idea of reasons being causes is closely related to the question of determinism in human affairs. Nagel (1979) defines determinism as follows:

In the loosest relevant sense of this word, it is a label for the claim that all things, events, processes and traits come into existence, endure, or pass out of it, only under fixed and definite conditions.

Nagel goes on to comment on the relationship between determinism and human action:

The assumption or the discovery that our acts and choices are determined in some fashion does not mean that we are being coerced when we are engaged in deliberation and decision, nor does it mean that acts of deliberation and choice are irrelevant to what we may overtly do. But the mere absence of feelings of coercion does not itself warrant the conclusion that there are not determinants. (p. 268).

In sociology it is common to regard reasons as causes (Lazarsfeld, 1973), and motivational psychologists no longer consider beliefs and wants just "idle chatter in the mind" but posit them as causes (Brody, 1983). Bhaskar (1979) himself is concerned to bring the reason-giving or rule-following approach into a causal framework and argues that *real* reasons and rules must necessarily be causally efficacious.

Rosenblueth, Wiener, and Bigelow (1943) claim that all purposeful behavior is causal because goal-directed action is action directed by the goal-object through the mechanism of negative feedback. Mechanical systems incorporating negative feedback give the appearance of *purposefulness* and hence the appearance of teleology. They suggest this is the same with human systems. But intentional human action is not just purposeful action; it is also *purposive* action, which suggests consciousness and a mind at work with a *will* to achieve whatever purposes are chosen. Action is controlled or determined not just by the goal-object but by beliefs about the desirability and feasibility of attaining that goal-object (Collin, 1985).

In everyday conversation we do talk of reasons as causes if the reasons are particularly compelling, as when I say my father's death caused me to cancel my lecture. In marketing texts we also speak of market conditions *causing* a change of plans. Aristotle viewed basic desires as causal forces which reason merely directed.

Hard determinism regards all wants, beliefs, decisions, and actions as being caused, with the causes being drawn from natural, physical sources. Reasons on this basis are judged as effects of physical events *and* causes of action: reasons are contained in some neurobiological schemata in the brain and in this sense they are physical causes. Many determinists seek external causes of action because this lends itself to more quantitative techniques while offering the possibility of identifying observable causal mechanisms to displace the need for assuming invisible entities like motives, attitudes, and beliefs.

The problem for hard determinism is to show that "reasons" do in fact coincide with certain physiological conditions in the brain *and* that these conditions actually produce the action and at the same time the individual subject claims the action was freely performed. But can mental states be reduced to brain states? Can we reduce a person's attitude to physical matter such as saying the attitude $X$ reduces to the brain having $Y$ neurons in electrochemical state $B$? Those who accept that the mind is no more than the brain in action might argue that, when neurochemical explanations are that advanced, we would have no need of constructs like attitude.

## Hard Voluntarism

We should first distinguish between acting *with* a reason and acting *for* a reason. Both hard determinism and hard voluntarism are concerned with acting *for* a reason, which is *the* reason that leads to action, not just any reason that might be offered to explain action.

Hard voluntarism sees wants as being adopted, beliefs as being endorsed, decision-making as a reflective process of weighing up the pros and cons, and actions as being pursued in line with wants and beliefs. Voluntarism embraces several lines of interconnected argument: contrasting the causal with the reason-giving explanation; viewing rational processes as different in kind from causal processes; focusing on the absence of causal regularities; and finally advocating a *conceptual* as opposed to a causal relationship between reasons and action.

Causal explanations, as normally understood, are viewed as mechanical explanations showing why the event to be explained *had* to happen. They are appropriate, it is argued, only in explaining *involuntary* behavior since their aim is to find all the necessary and sufficient conditions that drove someone to do what he did. But buyers are not propelled by some stimulus to take action. They are usually conscious of the stimulus and can reflect on it and the buying situation before deciding what to do. Louch (1969) claims that mental events are causes only in the trivial sense that unless a person thought them, he would not have acted as he did. Although the temporal order of antecedent mental event and consequent action is present, the link between the two is a logical and not a physical one.

To the voluntarist, causal explanation points to the past: "*X* happened because *Y* had occurred." Reason-giving explanations point to the future: "This action *X* was taken in order to achieve *Y*." Purposive action looks to the final result to be achieved.

Voluntarism views people as free *agents,* not puppets on a string subject to the push and pull of uncontrollable stimuli. An agent, defined as an entity with authentic wants and beliefs, is someone able to frame plans based on considering various action–consequence sequences. This is not to regard all behavior as intended. Voluntarism accepts that there are reflexlike habits that may come under the causal framework. Voluntarism also accepts that agents do not have complete freedom in that they operate within constraints. But the acceptance of constraints (unless the constraints are imposed and coercive) results from a rational assessment of their significance. Rationally weighing the pros and cons may be a rule-following process but is not a causal one. Of course, people carrying out their plans will take account, where necessary, of the causal laws of nature while much of their behavior might be the automatic following of a set routine. This gives it high predictability but it cannot be said to be causally compelled.

Elster (1983) believes that causal explanations overlook the fact that human beings are "strategically rational actors" who are forever adjusting their plans to cope with a changing environment. He argues that causal explanations may account for the evolution of human *capacities* to behave strategically but do not explain intentional acts. Thomas Nagel (1970), in contrast to Ernest Nagel, argues in line with Kant that even basic desires are not causal forces but merely *input into the agent's reasoning process,* which influence both wants and beliefs.

Voluntarism sees wants, beliefs, and actions as logically connected through the principle of rationality. Actions, it is argued, cannot even be described (e.g., shopping) without implying a background of wants and beliefs, and the system of wants and beliefs relevant to some action can be described only in words that refer to each other ("I want *X* because I believe . . ." *or* "I believe I should do *Y* because I want . . ."). But the fact that wants, beliefs, and actions are logically related does not in itself exclude the relationship being causal. More difficult is the claim that beliefs and corresponding actions cannot be described independently of each other, that is, wants and beliefs cannot be described independently of their effects. This means that reasons (wants and beliefs) cannot be described independently of the action of which they are said to be the cause. It is this difficulty that has led naturalists to move away from reason-giving explanation to other types of explanation, since it makes the reason-giving explanatory system immune from testing.

The idea of there being actual causal *laws* lying behind action is commonly rejected. As Von Wright (1983) says, there are no fixed responses to the same stimuli over time since actions vary with the changing perceptions and judgments of the agent. In fact, we cannot even begin to see how intentional explanations relate to the causal framework. It is argued that only when we do not understand the point of some behavior should we search for physicalist, causal descriptions.

Even the idea of completely objective causal stimuli is challenged by those who see social reality as something the mind creates given that social reality is prestructured by the concepts the observer brings to the perception of events. Some of these philosophers urge social scientists to adopt the patterns of description, reasoning, and explanation people use in their everyday dealings with each other. In other words, explanations of human action should cohere with people's own ways of accounting for their actions. A good deal will be said in subsequent chapters about the validity of this viewpoint.

Winch (1958), who views action as rule-following, denies such rules can be viewed as causal. He regards the relationship between reasons/rules and actions as a conceptual, not a causal relationship. He argues that in the physical sciences the antecedent causal event is logically and conceptually independent of its effects. Thus, "If metals are heated, they expand"; the heating of metals is conceptually independent of their expansion. Winch claims that this logical and conceptual independence is the distinguishing feature of a causal science and is absent in the field of human action. But many philosophers (e.g., Bhaskar, 1979) have pointed out that Winch's argument rests on the discredited Humean concept of cause as constant conjunction, whereas Collin (1985) argues rightly that the *conceptual* connection between action descriptions and reason descriptions does not of itself rule out a causal interpretation of rule-following behavior. He argues that when a person acts *because* of this or that, it in fact implies a causal tie. Collin claims that *all* explanations must establish *causal* ties between explicans and explicandum but this does not *necessarily* make them causal explanations. The rule-following, reason-giving explanation involves causation but is not an explanation by causation *in that the causal tie neither delivers the explanatory power nor is the sole source of such power.* In the rule-following, reason-giving explanation, the explanatory power does not reside in the causal tie but in showing the rationality of the action given the person's wants and beliefs. Collin claims that in the field of human action, a purely causal explanation is meaningful in explaining only why action was initiated—in explaining things done *to* someone as opposed to things done *by* someone.

The problem for voluntarism is to demonstrate that wants and beliefs are authentic and not just "installed by conditioning and socialization." Establishing such authenticity would be difficult since self-reports would be rejected on the ground that they themselves have to be shown to be authentic.

## Compatibilism

To the compatibilist the reasons for taking action are not completely under a person's control but neither are they completely outside her or his control. Reasons, under this view, emanate from experience and so cannot be said to be entirely authentic: "They are his but not his own." Goldman (1970) argues that the very fact that the relationship between wants/beliefs and action is logical and conceptual ensures that the relationship is in fact causal. Here Goldman is viewing the rational imperative to do $X$ as causal.

Many philosophers, including Danto (1973), point out that there is no reason why, a conclusion having been reached, it cannot be regarded as a cause of subsequent action. MacIntyre (1971) similarly argues that although rational beliefs cannot be explained in causal terms, the actions based on these rational beliefs or wants and beliefs (reasons) can be explained causally. MacIntyre makes the point that treating the real reason for action as causal is necessary if we are to distinguish the reasons that are genuinely effective from mere rationalizations which are not. Harman (1973) also agrees that reasons can be treated as causes but, like Collin (1985), he argues that explanation by reasons is not causal explanation. His reasons, though, are different from Collin's. He simply claims that the sequence of considerations that make up the set of reasons for the action can be described without supposing that the sequence is causal. Like MacIntyre, he is rejecting the idea that the decision-making process is causal. This view—that rational beliefs and the decision-making process cannot be explained in causal terms, but the real reasons for action can be viewed as causes—is a claim many regard as the most defensible position to date.

## Conclusion

Reasoning and decision-making cannot yet be translated satisfactorily into causal terms. But can the beliefs and wants (reasons) that emanate from the decision-making process to form premises or rulelike reasons for action be regarded as causes? This is not the same as asking whether we can regard reason-giving explanations as causal explanations since we can accept that the explanatory force of the reason-giving explanation does not lie in its causal aspect. The relationship between reasons and actions is not, however, one that satisfies all three conditions laid down by Hume in that there may not be contiguity in time and place between the reasons and subsequent action and no one has yet been able to show any constant conjunctions between certain types of reasons and certain types of action. But if we view the causal relationship as essentially a set of conditions inducing some effect or consequence, it is reasonable to view the relationship as a causal one. But what about the point made earlier that reasons describe the proposed actions to be taken, which means cause and effect are not distinct entities? Such an objection does not stop us regarding the genetic code in a gene as part of the cause of what subsequently evolves in the womb, although the two are not independent. The major problem in practice lies in identifying the reasons for action in that expressed reasons may be merely rationalizations. We return to this question later in the book. In the next section we deal with the discovery of causes when the causal relationship does involve more or less distinct constant conjunctions.

## Discovering Causes

How are causes discovered? The answer to this question depends to a large extent on how cause itself is viewed. It is the Humean concept of cause that lies behind the so-called five canons of inductive inquiry popularized by John Stuart Mill in the nineteenth century. These methods embody a Humean concept of cause in that they assume cause $X$ and effect $Y$ are contiguous in time and place, that $X$ precedes $Y$, and that the relationship between $X$-type events and $Y$-type events is one of constant conjunction. For Mill the canons were methods for both discovering and proving causes. They were neither but are nonetheless useful. Mill's five canons are discussed next.

### The Method of Agreement

Mill's statement of this canon is as follows:

> If two or more instances of the phenomenon under investigation have only one circumstance in common, the circumstance in which alone all the instances agree is the cause or effect, or an indispensable part of the cause, of the given phenomenon.

Thus the canon argues that if

> $AB$ precedes $E$,
>
> $AC$ precedes $E$,
>
> $AD$ precedes $E$,
>
> and so on,

then $A$, being the factor common in all instances, is causally connected to $E$. The method of agreement depends on having a large number of instances that are different in all respects but one. It attempts to establish that $A$ is a *sufficient condition* for $E$. If $A$ is a sufficient condition for $E$, then if $A$ occurs, $E$ always follows. Thus if a sales manager employed a sales supervisor in a number of different regions and on each occasion labor turnover increased, the manager might conclude the supervisor was to blame.

The difficulty lies in ensuring the agreement is in one respect only since the method cannot distinguish between true cause and mere coexistance. We can never be sure, for example, that some additional factor is not at work in each region to which the supervisor was appointed. Never do all instances of phenomenon $E$ in marketing have only one other factor in common.

The method of agreement is commonly followed among business researchers. Thus Porter (1990) points to the four commonalities (agreement) among the 100 most successful export industries in various nations:

1. *Factor conditions*. The presence within the country of a technical infrastructure, needed human resources, and the other factors necessary in production.

2. *Demand conditions*. The presence of a sophisticated and demanding set of home customers whose needs anticipate those abroad.

3. *Supporting industries*. The presence of home-based suppliers and related industries that are internationally competitive.

4. *Firm strategy, structure and rivalry*. The innovativeness of the firm and its related strategies are important but most important of all is the stimulating effect of the presence of fiercely competing local rivals.

This method of agreement does not establish such conditions are necessary. In fact Japan, which has shown the largest increase in exports postwar, did it without having the four conditions.

The Peters and Waterman (1982) book *In Search of Excellence* also relied on the method of agreement, claiming that all its "excellent" firms had eight characteristics in common. No attempt was made, however, to show that, except for eight common characteristics, the firms were all different nor did the authors show that the eight characteristics were absent in the underachieving firms. In fact, there were no hard measures even demonstrating the presence of the eight characteristics in the "excellent" firms. The popularity of this book certainly owes little to its evidential base.

## The Joint Method of Agreement and Difference

> If two or more instances in which the phenomenon occurs have only one circumstance in common, while two or more instances in which it does not occur have nothing in common save the absence of that circumstance, the circumstance in which alone the two sets of instances differ is the cause or the effect or an indispensable part of the cause of the phenomenon.

The joint method of agreement and difference brings in negative instances together with the positive. It tries to establish both the necessary and sufficient conditions for event $E$. If $A$ is a necessary and sufficient condition for $E$, then if $A$ occurs, then *and only then* will $E$ occur.

Those who accept that the same cause always produces the same effect and the same effect is always produced by the same cause (providing the cause is analyzed as finely as the effect) believe, as a matter of faith, that it is the necessary and sufficient conditions that should be sought by science.

## The Method of Difference

If an instance in which the phenomenon under investigation occurs and an instance in which it does not occur have every circumstance in common save one, that one occurring in the former, the circumstance in which alone the two instances differ is the cause or an indispensable part of the cause of the phenomenon.

Thus the method of difference argues that if

$AB$ precedes $E$,

$\overline{A}B$ precedes $\overline{E}$

(where $\overline{A}$ or $\overline{E}$ indicates their absence), then there is a causal realtionship between $A$ and $E$. The method is reflected in the use of both experimental groups (to which stimulus $A$ is applied) and control groups (to which no stimulus is applied) in the design of experiments. As an example, the marketing manager notes some dramatic increase in sales. Nothing has changed except the salesman's incentive plan. The manager concludes that the incentive plan is the cause.

The method of difference requires instances that are alike in all respects except one. It attempts to establish a necessary condition for $E$ to occur. If $A$ is a necessary condition for $E$, then if $A$ does not occur, neither will $E$. $A$ must occur for $E$ to occur. This implies that the absence of $A$ is a sufficient reason for the nonoccurrence of $E$.

Thus the absence of the necessary conditions for market success is a sufficient condition for failure. This is the logic that lies behind the idea of identifying the "requirements for success," with the "critical success factors" being those that are not only necessary but also the ones most likely to present difficulties.

The method of difference is commonly employed in comparative research. In comparing Japan and the United States, it has been pointed out that the Japanese give lifetime employment, seek consensual decision-making, emphasize collective responsibility, promote on seniority of service, and so on—all in contrast to the United States. These differences have been presented by some management academics as explaining the relative success of the Japanese vis-à-vis the Americans in spite of the fact that many of these practices by the Japanese have traditionally been the factors quoted as explaining the general inefficiency of the U.S. civil service vis-à-vis American industry.

Both the method of difference and agreement assume the presence or absence of $E$ rather than changes in the degree to which $E$ can be present. Statistical analysis of variance takes into account that $E$ could vary by degrees, that several factors may affect $E$, and that the effect of each one on $E$ needs to be estimated. It also recognizes that all conditions cannot be controlled, so change plays a part in determining $E$.

With the results being analyzed by the analysis of variance, the most common application of the method occurs when identical groups are set up for an experiment, with one group constituting the control group and the other group the experimental group given the change treatment. The difficulties with the method lie in ensuring the situation remains the same except for the one change.

Bhaskar (1979), a realist, claims the essence of all science lies in the movement from knowledge of manifest phenomena to knowledge of the (causal) structures that generate them, but he argues that the sort of closed systems available to the physical scientist in experimentation are not available to the social scientist. As a consequence, tests of hypotheses even in experiments are always likely to yield mixed results. He argues for what he terms his RRRE model of explanation, consisting of a four-phase process:

1. *Resolution* of a complex event into its components (causal analysis);
2. *Redescription* of component causes;
3. *Retrodiction* to possible (antecedent) causes of the components;
4. *Elimination* of alternative possible causes of components. (p. 165)

What is neglected in this account of identifying causes is the recognition that what is to count as a causal connection depends somewhat on the theories held by the investigator. Thus two different theories might suggest quite different candidates for the status of cause and effect in any single event sequence (Hanson, 1971). Somewhat related to this theme is how professional expertise practically dictates where to look for cause. Thus in seeking the cause of the "black death" the bacteriologist names the microbe, the entomologist the microbe-carrying flea, and the epidemiologist the migrant rat. Similarly, the causes sought by the buying behavior researcher may have little significance for the marketing manager because he or she either does not see that cause as actionable (e.g., culture) or requires education as to why it is in fact significant.

## The Method of Concomitant Variations

Whatever phenomenon varies in any manner whenever another phenomenon varies in some particular manner, is either a cause or an effect of that phenomenon, or is connected with it through some fact of causation.

The method of concomitant variation assesses the variation between factors that may be causally related. The method of concomitant variations finds its contemporary expression in the techniques of regression and correlation in statistics. It suggests causation by establishing a high correlation between the independent variable (the "cause") and the dependent variable (the "effect").

In marketing we are frequently interested in establishing the relationship between some dependent variable $Y$ and some independent variable $X$. We might or might not have theoretical grounds for believing a causal relationship exists. In any case, we plot the relationship on a graph and use a method such as the method of least squares to fit a regression line through the scattering of points on the graph. We might then calculate the correlation coefficient $r$ to see how well the regression line fits the observed data. After that we may proceed to calculate the residual standard deviation to estimate the range of likely error in our predictions. The dependent variable, for example, might be the degree of commitment to intention to buy, and the independent variable might be some measure of attitude toward the buy.

When physicists do this type of exercise and use the regression line to predict, they assume the existence of a true regression line or line of best fit, so that the deviations from the straight line in the scatter diagram should represent just random scatter. The line of best fit will represent, say, the true causal law. It can also be legitimately assumed in calculating the residual standard deviation that the errors are normally distributed with the sample of points emanating from some normally distributed population to which the Gaussian theory of error can be applied.

Can such assumptions be made when undertaking regression and correlation in marketing? If we cannot define the future conditions under which the same regression line would be obtained, then our results are not repeatable and deviations of any individual score from the regression line cannot be said to be a deviation from any true value line. There is, of course, some stability in consumer behavior because so much behavior is routine, ritual, or habit (see Farley, Lehmann, Winer, and Katz, 1982). But the more basic question is whether there are any *natural* constants in the regression equation, as there are in physics, when in contrast to physics the subject is mental states where beliefs and wants change over time. Whereas the physicist uses regression and correlation already knowing a causal law is there, regression and correlation are too frequently viewed in marketing as if they in themselves were capable of establishing some probabilistic law. Also, in spite of warnings in every statistics text about extrapolating beyond the range covered by the observed data, such extrapolations are not uncommon.

Of course, any particular effect may be caused by many factors. This is sometimes forgotten, as when we rule out some explanation of an effect unless it completely explains the effect: it could in fact be just one of several factors. Multiple regression enables the statistician to take account of several causal factors. The techniques of multiple regression and multiple correlation are simple extensions of regression and correlation for one independent variable, so the comments made in this section apply equally here.

## The Method of Residues

> Subduct from any phenomenon such part as is known by previous inductions to be the effect of certain antecedents, and the residue of the phenomenon is the effect of the remaining antecedents.

The method of residues is not a distinct method but is supplemental to the others, and it depends on having explained some of the events already. The manager might explain a reduction in sales by pointing out that $X\%$ is accounted for as a result of discontinuing to sell a particular line and $Y\%$ as a result of losing certain accounts, so the remainder can be accounted for by the only other factor in the situation, namely, the weather.

We have dealt here with discovering causes but there is also concern with effects. Path analysis is a complex of techniques for estimating linear equation systems and decomposing total effects into direct effects, indirect effects, and joint effects.

## APPENDIX: TABULAR ANALYSIS

Tabular analysis is a useful technique initially developed by the sociologist Lazarsfeld to help test different relationships, causal or otherwise. The following discussion is based on Rosenberg's (1968) treatment of the subject.

In tabular analysis relationships are grouped into three broad categories: symmetrical relationships, reciprocal relationships, and asymmetrical relationships.

## Symmetrical Relationships

If $X$ and $Y$ have a symmetrical relationship, they are related without either influencing the other. This is because they may be expressions of the same thing. Thus if $X$ refers to buyers of well-known brands and $Y$ refers to being noninnovative, $X$ and $Y$ may be related simply because both express a similar disposition toward taking risks.

Alternatively, $X$ and $Y$ may be related in this way if they are effects of the same cause resulting from multiple-effect structures.

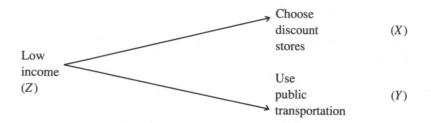

Any causal interpretation of the relationship between $X$ and $Y$ is spurious as both result from the antecedent event $Z$.

Finally, they may be part of the same system. Thus $X$, belonging to a country club, and $Y$, living in a wealthy part of suburbia, may both be part of a certain type of life style.

## Reciprocal Relationships

If $X$ and $Y$ form an interacting system, a reciprocal relationship exists in that both $X$ and $Y$ influence each other just as mental illness can cause physical illness and physical illness can cause mental illness. What in such circumstances is regarded as "cause" and what is regarded as "effect" depends on the problem addressed. In general, interest will focus on the factor or variable that is most actionable. Thus if beliefs influence brand choice and brand choice can change beliefs, it may be easier in certain circumstances to manipulate brand choice (for example, through favorable credit terms or discount pricing) to get a change in beliefs (as a result of sampling the product), rather than to try first to change beliefs to influence brand choice.

## Asymmetrical Relationships

If $X$ and $Y$ have an asymmetrical relationship, then $X$, the independent variable, influences $Y$, the dependent variable. Asymmetrical relationships take several forms in consumer behavior:

1. stimulus/response, for example, the stimulus of lower meat prices resulting in more meat being bought;
2. disposition/response, for example, cognitive dissonance leading the buyer to seek reassurance that he or she has made the best buy;
3. property/disposition, for example, age being related to the liking for "pop" music;

TABLE 3.1. Age and Radio Listening

| Dependent Variable | Independent Variable: Age | | Total |
| | Under 40 Years | 40 Years and Over | |
|---|---|---|---|
| Listen to radio program ABC | (78)   13% | (153)   26% | 231 |
| Do not listen to radio program ABC | (522)   87% | (447)   73% | 969 |
| | 100% | 100% | 1,200 |

4. property/response, for example, level of education influencing the type of magazine bought.

Asymmetrical relationships can be deceptive in that although $X$ and $Y$ are related, the association may be not what it appears to be but better explained by a third variable ($Z$). $Z$ can take a number of forms, the main ones being an extraneous variable, a component variable, an intervening variable, or an antecedent variable.

In seeking whether some relationship is better explained by $Z$, $Z$ is used as the test (or controlling) variable; that is, $Z$ is held constant to analyze the effect of $X$ (the independent variable) on $Y$ (the dependent variable). This division into subgroups on the basis of $Z$ can radically alter the interpretation of the original relationship and allow a more definite statement to be made about what influences $Y$.

## $Z$ = EXTRANEOUS VARIABLE

$X$ and $Y$ may not be inherently related but their relationship might be the result of $Z$ with which both $X$ and $Y$ are accidentally associated to different degrees. For example, Table 3.1 shows a relationship between the independent variable "age" ($X$) and the dependent variable "listening to radio program ABC" ($Y$).

The relationship between age and listening to radio program ABC may be better explained by different levels of education between the two groups. Table 3.2, as a consequence, is drawn up to stratify on education as the test variable. The relationship between age and listening to the radio has disappeared, suggesting the original relationship is explainable by the test factor education. If the relationship had persisted, further test factors might have been tried.

## $Z$ = COMPONENT VARIABLE

The relationship between $X$ and $Y$ might result from $Z$ being a component of $X$. Identifying which component of $X$ is the causal element can be important. For example, Table 3.3 shows the relationship between the independent variable $X$, "social class," and the dependent variable $Y$, "value placed on toothpaste with decay preventative."

TABLE 3.2. Education and Radio Listening

| Dependent Variable | Test Variable: Education | | | | Total |
| | High Education | | Low Education | | |
| | Under 40 Years | 40 Years and Over | Under 40 Years | 40 Years and Over | |
|---|---|---|---|---|---|
| Listen to radio program ABC | (27)   7% | (10)   11% | (51)   24% | (143)   28% | 231 |
| Do not listen to radio program ABC | (360)   93% | (77)   89% | (162)   76% | (370)   72% | 969 |
| | 100% | 100% | 100% | 100% | 1200 |

TABLE 3.3. Social Class and Toothpaste

|  | Independent Variable: Social Class | | |
| --- | --- | --- | --- |
| *Dependent Variable* | *Middle Class* | *Working Class* | *Total* |
| Value placed on toothpaste with decay preventive | (349)  53% | (146)  20% | 495 |
| No value place on toothpaste with decay preventive | (315)  47% | (590)  80% | 905 |
|  | 100% | 100% | 1,400 |

One element or component of social class is education. It is suspected that the component education might explain the relationship better. In Table 3.4 education is used as the test variable. Within each of the educational categories the difference between middle and working class is much smaller than the difference between the classes in the total group. Hence it might be concluded that the higher value placed on toothpaste with a decay preventive is due to educational level. If there were still a statistically significant difference in the percentages between middle and working class in each educational category, it would suggest that factors other than education are also at work. The implication for marketing is that members of the educated working class are a potential target audience which was not initially apparent.

## $Z$ = INTERVENING VARIABLE

$X$ may be related to $Y$ through $Z$ being a mediating or intervening variable giving rise to a causal chain: $X \rightarrow Z \rightarrow Y$. For example, suppose it had been established that heavy users of beer are men over thirty and under forty-five years of age. It might be suspected that $Z$, the nature of the work done, is a variable. Table 3.5 is computed using the nature of work as the test variable. The relationship between age and heavy beer use virtually disappears, with the table clearly showing that heavy beer use is tied to doing heavy manual work regardless of age.

Where there are a number of variables between $X$ and $Y$ there is a problem of which to choose as the cause of $Y$. The one selected is that which is the most actionable. Consider the following causal chain:

government tax on product with high elastic demand $\rightarrow$ higher prices $\rightarrow$ falloff in sales

TABLE 3.4. Education and Toothpaste

|  | Test Variable: Education | | | | |
| --- | --- | --- | --- | --- | --- |
|  | Under 12 Years | | 12 Years and Over | | |
| *Dependent Variable* | *Middle Class* | *Working Class* | *Middle Class* | *Working Class* | *Total* |
| Value placed on toothpaste with decay preventive | (78)  25% | (29)  7% | (271)  76% | (117)  38% | 495 |
| No value placed on toothpaste with decay preventive | (230)  75% | (400)  93% | (85)  24% | (190)  62% | 905 |
|  | 100% | 100% | 100% | 100% | 1,400 |

TABLE 3.5. Age and Beer Consumption

|  | Test Variable: Nature of Work | | | | | | | | | |
|---|---|---|---|---|---|---|---|---|---|---|
|  | Heavy Manual | | | Light Manual | | | Nonmanual | | | |
| Dependent Variable | Under 30 Years | 30–44 Years | 45 Years and Over | Under 30 Years | 30–44 Years | 45 Years and Over | Under 30 Years | 30–44 Years | 45 Years and Over | Total |
| Heavy user of beer | (160) 40% | (176) 44% | (164) 41% | (120) 30% | (132) 33% | (116) 29% | (60) 15% | (64) 16% | (68) 15% | 1,060 |
| Medium user of beer | (92) 23% | (88) 22% | (100) 25% | (60) 15% | (72) 18% | (48) 12% | (24) 6% | (32) 8% | (20) 4% | 536 |
| Light user of beer | (80) 20% | (68) 17% | (76) 19% | (48) 12% | (56) 14% | (40) 10% | (120) 30% | (100) 25% | (128) 29% | 716 |
| Nonuser of beer | (68) 17% | (68) 17% | (60) 15% | (172) 43% | (140) 35% | (196) 49% | (196) 49% | (204) 51% | (232) 52% | 1,336 |
|  | 100% | 100% | 100% | 100% | 100% | 100% | 100% | 100% | 100% | 3,648 |

TABLE 3.6. Advertising and Product Buying

| | Independent Variable: Exposure to Advertisement | | | | |
| | Seen Advertisement | | Not Seen Advertisement | | |
| Dependent Variable | Non–High Opinion of Product | High Opinion of Product | Non–High Opinion of Product | High Opinion of Product | Total |
|---|---|---|---|---|---|
| Subsequently bought product | (168) 63% | (1,007) 94% | (751) 63% | (297) 94% | 2,223 |
| Not-bought product | (100) 37% | (64) 6% | (436) 37% | (19) 6% | 619 |
| | 100% | 100% | 100% | 100% | 2,842 |

The falloff in sales could be explained as due to the government tax or to higher prices. If there is little than can be done about the government tax, the more immediate cause "higher prices" is the one to be addressed.

## $(z)$ = ANTECEDENT VARIABLE

Some antecedent variable $Z$ may influence the independent variable $X$, which, as a consequence, influences the dependent variable $Y$ to give the relationship

$$Z \rightarrow X \rightarrow Y$$

In such a case $X$, the independent variable, takes the role of an intervening variable between $Z$ and $Y$. If the antecedent variable $Z$ is controlled, the relationship between $X$ and $Y$ should be maintained since $X$, as the independent variable, will continue to influence $Y$. On the other hand, when $X$ is controlled and so tested as an intervening variable, the relationship between $Z$ and $Y$ should disappear since $Z$ goes through $X$ to effect $Y$.

In Table 3.6 there is a need to establish the relationship between what is suspected of being an antecedent influencing variable $Z$, exposure to the advertisement; the independent variable $X$, opinion of the product; and the dependent variable $Y$, subsequently buying or not buying the product.

To establish $Z$ as an antecedent variable there is a need to demonstrate the following relationships:

1. The independent variable $X$ (high vs. non–high opinion of the product) is related to the dependent variable $Y$ (subsequently bought vs. not-bought). Table 3.7 (deduced from Table 3.6) shows this to be so.

2. The antecedent variable $Z$ (exposure to advertisement) and the independent variable $X$ (high vs. non–high opinion of product) are also associated. This is shown in Table 3.8.

TABLE 3.7. Product Opinion and Buying

| | Independent Variable: Opinion of Product | | |
| Dependent Variable | Non–High Opinion of Product | High Opinion of Product | Total |
|---|---|---|---|
| Subsequently bought product | (919) 63% | (1,304) 94% | 2,223 |
| Not-bought product | (536) 37% | (83) 6% | 619 |
| | 100% | 100% | 2,842 |

TABLE 3.8. Advertising and Product Opinion

| | Antecedent Variable: Exposure to Advertisement | | | |
| Independent Variable | Seen Advertisement | Not-Seen Advertisement | | Total |
|---|---|---|---|---|
| Non–high opinion of product | (268) 20% | (1,187) | 79% | 1,455 |
| High opinion of product | (1,071) 80% | (316) | 21% | 1,387 |
| | 100% | | 100% | 2,842 |

3. The antecedent variable $Z$ (exposure to advertisement) is related to the dependent variable $Y$ (subsequently bought vs. not-bought). This is also true, as is demonstrated in Table 3.9.

4. The relationship between $X$ (opinion of the product) and $Y$ (subsequently bought vs. not-bought) should be maintained if the antecedent variable $Z$ (exposure to advertisement) is used as the test variable. Table 3.6 indicates this is so (94% vs. 63% in the first row).

5. The relationship between the antecedent variable $Z$ (exposure to advertisement) and the dependent variable $Y$ (subsequently bought vs. not-bought) should disappear if the independent variable is used as the test factor. Table 3.10 shows this is so.

All this assumes that $Z$ (exposure to advertisement) must operate via $X$ (opinion of product) to affect $Y$ (subsequently bought). It assumes that $Z$ (exposure to advertisement) is not a sufficient factor in itself to achieve a high product opinion. If $Z$ was a sufficient condition for $X$ and $X$ was a sufficient condition for $Y$, then $Z$ would be a sufficient condition for $Y$. In such cases $Z$ would be an extraneous variable and the postulating of $X$ would be irrelevant. In this view $Z$ (exposure to advertisement) has no effect on $Y$ (buying behavior) unless it first affects $X$ (opinion of the product). It assumes that $X$ can arise without $Z$ and so can affect $Y$ without antecedent $Z$.

There is the situation where $Y$ can be produced by one of several antecedent paths thus giving rise to multiple causal structures:

$$Z_1 \rightarrow X_1 \searrow$$
$$B \cup S \rightarrow Y$$
$$Z_2 \rightarrow X_2 \nearrow$$

where $B \cup S$ means $B$ or $S$ or both; for example,

falloff in motivation → fewer calls ↘

(fewer calls and/or consumers converted) → falloff in sales

invention of cheaper substitutes → consumers converted ↗

## Tabular Analysis and Segmentation

Tabular analysis is often useful, say, for explicating the relationship between segmentation variables and buyer behavior. Symmetrical relationships in segmentation analysis

TABLE 3.9. Advertising Exposure and Buying

| Dependent Variable | Antecedent Variable: Exposure to Advertisement | | | | |
| | Seen Advertisement | | Not-Seen Advertisement | | Total |
| --- | --- | --- | --- | --- | --- |
| Subsequently bought product | (1,175) | 88% | (1,048) | 70% | 2,223 |
| Not-bought product | (164) | 12% | (455) | 30% | 619 |
| | | 100% | | 100% | 2,842 |

are common. Thus it may be found that a certain type of lifestyle goes with using public transport. But both the lifestyle and the use of public transport may simply be an expression of low family income. The relationship between lifestyle and the use of public transport might in this case be regarded as a *nomic* (lawlike) *correlation,* or predictive rule, justifying the expectation that a certain lifestyle leads to using public transport. But nomic correlations in themselves are not explanatory.

VALS (Values and Life Styles) and other psychographic approaches to segmentation assume that each psychographic category constitutes a system that would embrace certain brand preferences. The claim is vacuous unless backed by empirical findings plus the logic relating category to preferences. The claim can take the form of a *nomic attribution* to the effect that buyers of product or brand *B* have the psychographic profile *P. Instantiation statements* can be derived from nomic attributions. These state how the property of interest is instantiated (exemplified) by some particular case. Thus it may be claimed that a certain personality or psychographic type is instantiated in, say, buyers of the Ford Escort car as reflected in their score on some questionnaire assessing personality or psychographic characteristics.

Asymmetrical relationships between segmentation variables and buyer behavior are frequently lacking in explanatory meanings. Thus some extraneous variable like fashion consciousness might account for the observed relationship between a woman's age and the buying of various types of pantyhose and stockings. Similarly, the relationship between social class and buying might be better explained by just one of the components of social class like income or occupation.

For explanatory purposes there is a need to specify the intervening variables between both demographic and psychographic data and brand choices. What is the causal chain? Unfortunately, tabular analysis is not a technique or a logic for discovering true intervening variables. But it does focus on the need to search for them when examining relationships.

TABLE 3.10. Opinions, Advertising, and Buying

| Dependent Variable | Independent Variable: Opinion of Product | | | | | | | | |
| | Non–High Opinion of Product | | | | High Opinion of Product | | | | |
| | Seen Advertisement | | Not-Seen Advertisement | | Seen Advertisement | | Not-Seen Advertisement | | Total |
| --- | --- | --- | --- | --- | --- | --- | --- | --- | --- |
| Subsequently bought product | (168) | 63% | (751) | 63% | (1,007) | 94% | (297) | 94% | 2,223 |
| Not-bought product | (100) | 37% | (436) | 37% | (64) | 6% | (19) | 6% | 619 |
| | | 100% | | 100% | | 100% | | 100% | 2,842 |

Many variables considered in consumer behavior—culture, social groups, situational factors, and so on—are generally antecedent variables in that they are not sufficient in themselves to produce $X$ and only contribute to bringing about effect $Y$ through acting on $X$. Although knowledge of antecedent variables or antecedent conditions furthers understanding and explanatory depth, their importance to marketing management depends on the extent to which they are actionable, that is, can be influenced by management. Mostly they are not actionable.

# References

Ayer, A. J. (1973). *The Central Questions of Philosophy.* London: Weidenfeld and Nicolson.

Bagozzi, Richard P. (1980). *Causal Models in Marketing.* New York: Wiley.

Bhaskar, Roy (1979). *The Possibility of Naturalism.* Atlantic Highlands, NJ: Humanities Press.

Brody, Nathan (1983). *Human Motivation: Commentary on Goal-Directed Action.* New York: Academic Press.

Bunge, M. (1963). *Causality: The Place of the Causal Principle in Modern Science.* New York: Meridian Books.

Collin, Finn (1985). *Theory and Understanding.* Oxford: Basil Blackwell.

Cummins, Robert (1983). *The Nature of Psychological Explanation.* Cambridge, MA: The MIT Press.

Danto, Arthur (1973). *Analytic Philosophy of Action.* Cambridge: Cambridge University Press.

Elster, Jon (1983). *Explaining Technical Change.* Cambridge: Cambridge University Press.

Farley, John U., Donald R. Lehmann, Russell S. Winer, and J. P. Katz (1982). "Parameter Stability and Carryover Effects in a Consumer Decision Process Model." *Journal of Consumer Research* 8 (March), pp. 465–70.

Goldman, A. I. (1970). *A Theory of Human Action.* Princeton, NJ: Princeton University Press.

Hanson, N. R. (1971). *Observation and Explanation: A Guide to Philosophy of Science.* New York: Harper and Row.

Harman, G. (1973). *Thought.* Princeton, NJ: Princeton University Press.

Harris, Errol (1970). *Hypothesis and Perception.* London: George Allen and Unwin.

Jacobson, Robert (1988). "Distinguishing Among Competing Theories of Market Share Effect." *Journal of Marketing* 52 (October), pp. 68–80.

Jacobson, Robert, and David A. Aaker (1985). "Is Market Share All That It's Cracked Up to Be?" *Journal of Marketing* 49 (Fall), pp. 11–22.

Kuhn, Thomas S. (1977). *The Essential Tension.* Chicago: University of Chicago Press.

Lazarsfeld, Paul F. (1973). *Main Trends in Sociology.* New York: Harper Torchbooks.

Louch, A. R. (1966). *Explanation and Human Action.* Los Angeles: University of California Press.

Louch, A. R. (1969). *Explanation and Human Action.* Los Angeles: University of California Press.

MacIntyre, Alasdair (1971). *Against the Self-Images of the Age.* New York: Schocken Books.

Miller, R. W. (1987). *Fact and Method.* Princeton, NJ: Princeton University Press.

Mohr, Lawrence B. (1982). *Explaining Organizational Behavior.* San Francisco: Jossey-Bass.

Nagel, Ernest (1961). *The Structure of Science.* New York: Harcourt, Brace and World.

Nagel, Ernest (1979). *Teleology Revisited.* New York: Columbia University Press.

Nagel, Thomas (1970). *The Possibility of Altruism.* Oxford: Oxford University Press.

Peters, Thomas J., and Robert H. Waterman (1982). *In Search of Excellence.* New York: Harper and Row.

Porter, Michael (1980). *Competitive Strategy.* New York: Free Press.

Porter, Michael (1990). *The Competitive Advantage of Nations.* New York: Free Press.

Robinson, D. N. (1985). *Philosophy of Psychology.* New York: Columbia University Press.

Rosenberg, Morris (1968). *The Logic of Survey Analysis.* New York: Basic Books.

Rosenblueth, A., N. Wiener, and J. Bigelow (1943). "Behavior, Purpose and Teleology." *Philosophy of Science* 10.

Russell, Bertrand (1917). "On the Notion of Cause." In *Mysticism and Logic and Other Essays.* London: Allen and Unwin. Quoted in H. Feigl and M. Brodbeck, eds., *Readings in the Philosophy of Science.* New York: Appleton-Century-Crofts, 1953, pp. 389–95.

Von Wright, G. H. (1983). *Practical Reason.* Oxford: Basil Blackwell.

Walker, Nigel (1975). *Behavior and Misbehavior: Explanations and Non-Explanations.* New York: Basic Books.

Winch, P. G. (1958). *The Idea of a Social Science.* Boston: Routledge and Kegal Paul.

# 4

# Causal Temporal Modes of Explanation

> Practically no sequence of (say) 3 or more causally connected con-
> crete events proceeds according to any single law. There are neither
> laws of succession nor laws of evolution.
>
> Sir Karl Popper (1957)

Most of the interesting causal models in marketing would come under the heading of causal temporal modes of explanation. These generally display more explanatory depth than do simple cause–effect conjunctions. Causal temporal modes of explanation are concerned with chains of *discrete* events, linked together through time in some causal way. The *temporal* linkage receives prominence because

- the time ordering of the events is crucial to the outcome; and
- the length of time taken for the consequences of one event to affect subsequent events allows time for unanticipated happenings to occur that might weaken or nullify the effect of earlier events.

There are different types of causal temporal modes of explanation. Ideally, all modes identify the mechanism, structure, or whatever it is that moves the process along from one stage to the next. But often no mechanism is specified and the relationship between stages is simply claimed to be probabilistic without theoretical justification as to why this should be so.

The following three temporal modes of explanation are discussed here:

1. *Evolutionary or developmental explanations.* These explain by presupposing that the explicandum or events of interest form some evolutionary pattern.

2. *Causal process explanations.* These explain by showing how the process is advanced from one stage to the next by delineating the causal factors involved at each stage. The focus is not on evolutionary pattern but on the causal process.

3. *Genetic explanations.* These explain in the manner of the historian, first defining the *specific* problematic situation then seeking its origin and how it evolved.

## Evolutionary Explanations

Evolutionary explanations explain a sequence of events by claiming it follows some pattern of *evolution.* For example, whenever it is claimed that sales follow the pattern of introduction (infancy), growth, maturity, and decline as represented by the product life cycle, the explanation is an evolutionary one.

Evolutionary explanations have a long history. Plato, for example, held that the history of society passed through stages, with society being ruled first by godlike men (kings), then by noblemen seeking honor and fame, then by rich families, then by the many (democracy), and finally by tyranny. The sociologist Auguste Comte (1798–1857) saw society as necessarily passing through three stages: (1) militarism, where society is bound together by force and fear; (2) legal society, where force and fear are replaced by law and constitutions; and (3) industrial society, where the ruler is science. In economics, we have Rostow's (1960) five stages of economic development: (1) traditional society, where the population is dispersed and close to the soil; (2) precondition stage for "takeoff" as the idea of economic progress develops; (3) sustained growth stage; (4) expansion stage; and (5) high mass consumption stage.

There have been attempts to establish life cycles in the growth of organizations. In both of the following models, the growth life cycle is not regarded as inevitable: moving from one stage to the next is viewed as contingent on solving the "crisis" that accompanies growth at each stage.

Greiner (1972) visualizes five stages conditional on solving the crisis that evolves at each stage:

| *Phase* | *Crisis* |
|---|---|
| 1. Creativity phase | Leadership crisis |
| 2. Direction phase under leadership (if the leadership crisis is resolved) | Demand for greater autonomy |
| 3. Delegation/decentralization phase (if the autonomy crisis is resolved) | Control crisis (need for control) |
| 4. Coordination phase (if the central control crisis is resolved) | Crisis of confidence between line and staff, headquarters and field—resentment of "red tape" |
| 5. Collaboration phase (if the red tape crisis is resolved) | Next phase? |

Greiner argues for knowing where a firm is along the "development sequence" so as to recognize the problems and the limited range of solutions and how, in turn, the solutions breed new problems.

Another organizational life cycle which builds on Greiner's is that of Kimberly and Miles (1980):

| *Stage* | *Crisis* |
|---|---|
| 1. Entrepreneurial stage | Leadership crisis |

At the entrepreneurial stage the focus is on creating a product and surviving in the market.

| | |
|---|---|
| 2. Collectivity stage (if the leadership crisis is resolved) | Need for delegation and control |

At this stage the organization develops clear goals and direction.

| Stage | Crisis |
|---|---|
| 3. Formalization stage (if the need for delegation and control is resolved) At this stage control and information systems developed. | Need to reduce red tape |
| 4. Elaboration stage (if the red tape crisis is resolved) | Need for renewal to avoid decline |

Interestingly, both these life cycles assume there are forces pressing for growth (the growth mechanism) and so look for factors that inhibit the release of these forces such as the absence of leadership.

Porter (1990) looks at stages in national growth as following a life cycle:

1. *Early development:* cheap labor as a basis.

2. *Growth:* resulting from huge investments in plant, equipment, infrastructure, and work force training.

3. *Maturity:* the innovation-driven period.

4. *Decline:* a wealth-protection stage wherein countries seek to protect what they have and firms tend to "harvest" their market positions by not continuing investment.

This national life cycle is unlikely to impress historians, who reject such work (even Toynbee, whose *A Study of History* sought to explain the growth, development, and decay of civilizations). The rejection comes not just from the arbitrariness and the forcing of generalizations but from the inadequacy of explanation. Thus in the case of Porter, the reader is left in the dark as to why a country stops increasing productivity and enters the wealth-driven stage.

In all evolutionary models there is the idea of movement through time conforming to a fixed pattern so that if we can identify the point reached, we can predict the general development (if any) from that point.

What Popper (1957) says on *historicism* is relevant to all such evolutionary explanations. Traditionally, a historicist is someone who claims that we cannot understand or predict the subsequent stages of some system without understanding the past states of the system. Karl Marx was a historicist in respect to society's development. But when the system of interest is society, historicism is specifically defined as the claim that each and every cultural tradition has its own laws and destiny: all cultural generalizations are historicorelative and can be comprehended only in terms of the particular culture's own development. It is associated with deterministic assumptions about inexorable historical laws—laws we are obliged to go along with—that are molding the evolution of cultures.

Popper (1957) defines historicism broadly as *any* approach to the social sciences which assumes that the principal aim is historical prediction, which is attainable through discovering evolutionary patterns. Those adopting a historicist perspective argue that plans must cohere with the main current of history if they are to be effective. In like manner, writers wedded to the product life cycle argue that marketing strategy cannot alter the evolutionary pattern of sales but must go along with it by adjusting the strategy to fit the impending changes. Like other historicists, these writers were not advocating inactivity or fatalism but teaching the futility of any attempt to alter the inevitable. Such a view contrasts with those who regard knowledge about the life cycle stage as simply inputs into a decision.

Popper claims that evidence for any *fixed* historical pattern is always weak, since the acquisition of new knowledge changes the pattern. What people cannot know is what they come to know only in the future. For instance, there is much that can happen in a market to revitalize a product. Beryl Markham's book *West with the Night* was recently on the *New York Times* best seller list for sixty-six weeks. This book, first published before World War II, was resurrected as a best-seller when the film *Out of Africa* and a television documentary of the life of Beryl Markham stimulated readers' interest. This example shows "laws and theories" can be overshadowed by unanticipated "events"—events that are resistant to prediction because they are contingent, resulting from the uncoordinated but convergent actions of people. But there are problems with all evolutionary explanations.

First, there is often disagreement on the overall evolutionary pattern or whether there is in fact just one pattern. As with the product life cycle, it can usually be shown that stages can be skipped, sequences can be truncated, or there can even be regression to earlier stages. So-called vital stages are often found to be less than vital, and the order of stages is seldom rigid. The resultant uncertainty as to what observations would test evolutionary models increases the difficulty of testing them.

The second problem with evolutionary explanations arises when time itself is regarded as a forcing variable. Time is not an independent event but one of the parameters to be estimated. Treating time as an explanatory variable can be justified but only if the process by which time is measured is known: time itself is not the cause of change. There are circumstances, however, where measures of time cannot be discovered, so resort is made to some arbitrary time scale; for example, in marketing a cyclical time scale containing the so-called *product life cycle* (PLC) stages may be used. Explanation here involves locating the life stage since, once located, it is assumed that the general pattern of preceding and future stages can be discerned.

If time cannot be the mechanism of change, the problem lies in identifying the actual mechanisms at work. It is easy here to confuse a logical with an evolutionary order. The two need to be distinguished. Thus sticks laid out according to size constitute a logical order but not an evolutionary one. The sequence of stages in the PLC may appear logical, but this does not make the sequence inevitable. It appears "logical" because the diffusion process takes time while new products typically come along to displace the old. It is this diffusion process that is quoted in support of the PLC curve. The diffusion process covers both the speed with which information about the innovation is dispersed and the spread of the innovation itself. But such a process varies with the many factors that influence the speed of diffusion and so cannot be decisive evidence for claims about the shape of the PLC curve. In any case, as Lambkin and Day (1989) point out, current diffusion theory simply reflects the demand factors at work in the market and not the supply position, the infrastructure, or other factors that also have an impact on diffusion.

But it is difficult to locate the life cycle stage when there is no definition of the stage in terms of the necessary and sufficient conditions characterizing the stage. All this is recognized by Midgley (1981), who accepts there are many product life cycles other than the classical bell-shaped PLC. He argues that if the PLC is to be useful, we must try not only to predict the specific PLC but to provide an explanation of why the particular sales pattern is to be expected. (Of course, no one would disagree that an explanatory base would be particularly useful but, contrary to Midgley, predicting the specific PLC would have many uses in product planning.) Midgley believes many of the different patterns of the PLC can be explained by the same underlying behavioral processes, but that "explanation" at present can only "take known or postulated outcomes of these behavioral processes, that is, the resulting distribution of first and interpurchase times, and compound them in some manner to predict various patterns of the PLC."

McNair (1958) coined the phrase "wheel of retailing" to describe a pattern of retail development, which Hollander (1960) defines as follows:

> This hypothesis holds that new types of retailers usually enter the market as low-status, low-margin, low-price operators. Gradually they acquire more elaborate establishments and facilities, with both increased investments and higher operating costs. Finally they mature as high-cost, high-price merchants, vulnerable to newer types who, in turn, go through the same pattern. Department-store merchants, who originally appeared as vigorous competitors to the smaller retailers and who have now become vulnerable to discount house and supermarket competition, are often cited as prime examples of the wheel pattern.

While pointing out that the wheel pattern does describe a common pattern in industrialized, expanding economies, Hollander concludes that the number of nonconforming examples means the wheel hypothesis is not universally valid. He lists various explanations offered in support of the wheel hypothesis but also shows the problem of trying to confirm such explanations.

Even where an evolutionary pattern has some empirical support there is the problem of explaining deviations. To explain why some observed sequence diverges from the assumed pattern while others do not presupposes the assumed pattern has some validity as the pattern to be expected. This, in turn, assumes the pattern has been established as being based on what amounts to a development law. A development law says in effect that if system $X$ has certain characteristics $A$ at time $T$, then it will at some later time go through the stages (or have the characteristics) $B, C, D, \ldots$, *providing* certain conditions $Y, Z, \ldots$, are present.

There are no development laws in marketing, although an *ideal type* may express a development generalization. An ideal type is an abstraction that may or may not correspond *exactly* to anything in the real world. Thus Max Weber's concept of "bureaucracy" and the economist's concept of "pure competition" are ideal types. Since an ideal type is an abstraction, based on what theoretically might be expected, exceptions do not disconfirm it. The product life cycle may be regarded as an ideal type. If so regarded, it becomes a basis for comparison with real situations. However, there are problems. Until we can order its logic so that it appears to be what would be expected to occur, we cannot make the most meaningful comparisons with actual life cycles.

## Causal Process Explanations

### Causal Processes

Hume spoke of cause $X$ preceding the effect $Y$, which suggests some time gap between cause $X$ and effect $Y$. Such a gap sounds mysterious unless it is assumed to be filled by a chain of causes. Of course, it is possible to be fairly certain that $X$ causes $Y$ without knowing the intervening steps by means of which $X$ causes $Y$. Yet scientists are concerned to discover and analyze more and more links in any causal chain to enhance explanatory depth. In marketing, seeking to fill a causal chain comes under the heading of "causal processing." But there are many such processes, including the following four.

SIMPLE CAUSAL CHAINS: $X \to Y \to Z$

There are intervening variables $Y$ between any marketing stimuli $X$ and effect $Z$, which we try to specify.

MULTIPLE CAUSAL STRUCTURES:

$$X \to Y \searrow$$
$$\qquad\qquad (Y \cup B) \to Z$$
$$A \to B \nearrow$$

(Note: Y ∪ B means Y or B or both)

Every effect can usually be attributed to several different causes.

MULTIPLE EFFECT STRUCTURES:

$$X \to Y \quad \begin{matrix} & & B \\ & A \nearrow \searrow & \\ \nearrow & & C \\ & & E \\ \searrow & & \nearrow \\ & D & \\ & \searrow & F \end{matrix}$$

There will *always* be multiple effects of any cause—some expected, some unexpected, some intended, some unintended. Path analysis is useful here since the technique helps decompose total effects into direct, indirect, and joint effects.

RECIPROCAL CAUSAL STRUCTURES: $X \leftrightarrow Y$

This is defined as $X$ causes $Y$ and $Y$ causes $X$. If reasons $X$ are regarded as the cause of buying $Y$, then $X$ causes $Y$, but the relationship between $X$ and $Y$ is still likely to be reciprocal. This is because buying $Y$ is a learning experience that might change buying reasons $X$ and hence brand purchase next time around. It is such learning that makes prediction at the individual level so difficult. The concept of reciprocal causal structures undermines, too, any belief that there must be a first term in any series. But this does not mean intervention cannot be guided. Thus if perceptions influence behavior and behavior influences perceptions, the question is to determine which "cause" is the more actionable by marketing strategy.

## Notion of a Process

The notion of a process is the key concept underlying all temporal causal modes of explanation. The word "process" is used loosely in ordinary language to refer to any sequence of steps that occur over time. However, a process that is intended to be explanatory should indicate how the events in the sequence are connected in a way that makes the flow of events seem compelling, that is, for the stages to possess sufficient conditions to bring about the next stage. A process defined along these lines is a nonunique, recurring sequence of discrete events that are interrelated in a causal way. This notion of a "sequence of discrete events" distinguishes a process from simply a movement of something through different positions, like a bullet fired from a gun. Also, a process explanation differs from an evolutionary explanation in that it does not focus on any overall pattern.

In marketing we commonly give the name "process" to any change in state leading researchers to talk of explaining the "process" when no process (only movement) is occurring. In any case, the process is not always the key issue. Although we have this interest in word-of-mouth communication with debates about the "trickle-down effect" or the "two-step flow hypothesis," product information is likely to spread among consumers without necessarily any hard-and-fast communications channels. Finding the source of information is less important than explaining why certain information spreads rapidly and finds fertile soil.

Ideally a process would be explained by a process law showing why, under certain conditions, each discrete link or stage in the process is the consequent of the preceding link (event, state, or stage) and, at the same time, a sufficient condition for the next link. A process law presupposes a specification of the system to which the process law applies. It assumes that, given the system at time $T$, it is possible to predict the future state at time $T_1$, $T_2$, and so on. No process laws exist in marketing since they assume a closed system for the law to operate without interference. A process law thus can be demonstrated only in experimental conditions (if at all, since it presupposes hard determinism).

## Dretske's General Model for Explaining Human Behavior

Dretske (1988) sets out to show what it means to explain human behavior in a naturalistic (natural science) way. He assumes a *causal process* normally involving

1. external conditions, events, or stimuli ($E$) that trigger the process and explain what causes the process to occur at that particular time;
2. internal conditions or states of mind ($C$) (including wants and beliefs) that shape, structure, and direct the process; and
3. effects or behavioral products ($M$) covering all movement and action.

Dretske rejects the identification of behavior with either the action effects $M$ that are caused or the internal conditions $C$ that caused the effects $M$. Dretske identifies behavior with the *process* that starts with the internal conditions and ends with the action, that is, the process of *causing* the resulting actions. In other words, behavior is the *producing* of the effects by some internal set of conditions. The process or behavior to be explained (the explicandum) is not some succession of events but the actual bringing about, the actual causing or producing of the terminal condition or behavioral products of the process (e.g., buying). A process does not cause its parts. Dretske illustrates this as in Figure 4.1 where a process is shown as beginning with internal conditions $C$ (states of mind) and proceeding through effects $M_1$, $M_2$, and $M_3$ with behavior $B_1$, $B_2$, and $B_3$. But $B_1$ does not cause $B_2$ since $B_1$ is in $B_2$ just as $B_2$ is in $B_3$. In other words, each is "nested, Chinese box fashion in its successor." Similarly, $B_2$ does not cause $M_2$, and so on, since $M_2$ is part of $B_2$ and not its effect.

The effects, behavioral products, or actions $M$ that are brought into being are an

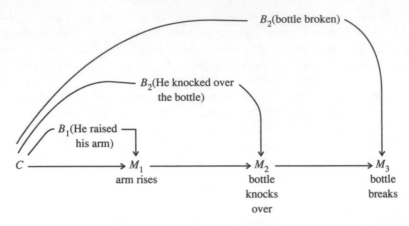

FIGURE 4.1. Behavior as a Process [*Source:* After Fred Dretske, *Explaining Behavior: Reasons in a World of Causes* (Cambridge, MA: The MIT Press, 1988).]

essential part of the total process but they are not of major interest when it comes to explanation. As Dretske says, the behavior of greatest interest is not the "printout" but the "printing" itself. To regard the behavior of interest as confined to the printout (e.g., some physical movement) would demand a neurological and not a psychological explanation. Reasons would have no role to play here. If psychological explanations are sought, the focus must be on the process producing the effect.

Dretske also rejects explaining by viewing external conditions $E$ like social facts as causes of actions. He argues that to view external conditions $E_1$, $E_2$, and so on (e.g., culture, reference groups), as causing $M_1$, $M_2$, and so on (e.g., buying a particular brand), and to ignore what happens internally (mentally) is both misleading and inadequate as a causal explanation. Thus if seeing a friend $E_1$ is regarded as the cause of my waving my hand to him $M_1$, it suggests that I myself had no role in producing $M_1$. As long as the effect (my waving) can be classified as the result of internal causes (reasons), the actual producing of this effect should be classified as the behavior to be explained. Nonmovements, like "just watching," if internally caused, would also be regarded as part of the total process to be explained by showing the causing (producing) of the watching.

Dretske, like many other followers of naturalism, aims at bringing the reason-giving explanation into a causal format but his book is essentially a rationale for cognitive psychologists who claim that they are not explaining actions but explaining the *capacity* (producing process) by which actions come into being. But not every cognitive psychologist would go along with the idea that this is a causal process, particularly as Dretske argues that there will be a different process operating from $C$ to $M$ for each form of $M$. Thus the process will differ somewhat between $M$ as "just talking" and $M$ as "talking loudly." But there is a problem here (as cognitive psychologists have discovered) in knowing which descriptions will involve different production systems.

Dretske is right in pointing out the fundamental nature of explanations that focus on the process by which movement and actions are produced. But this does not answer the question of what constitutes an *adequate* description of the process or whether for most marketing purposes we need to go beyond the reasons that lie behind action.

## Examples of Process Explanations in Marketing

Hierarchy Models

The adoption process propelled along by the diffusion process is a process model, often quoted in support of the bell-shaped curve of the PLC. This model consists of five mental stages, typically moving from product *awareness* to *interest/evaluation* and then onto *trial* and *adoption*. But as with the PLC such stages are by no means universal since stages can be skipped, the order can vary, and so on. Each stage is neither a necessary nor sufficient condition for inducing the next stage. In any case, adoption is likely to be a complex set of processes rather than a single unitary one as suggested; moreover, the adopting unit might be a committee rather than an individual.

The adoption process is a "hierarchy of effects model," where it is assumed that consumers pass through some set of stages on their way to buying intentions. The concept of some hierarchy of motives or hierarchy of stages in mental processing, common in psychology, recognizes that priorities must be established and that some mental stages must necessarily precede others. Thus we have Maslow's "hierarchy of needs" based on the assumption that people will seek to satisfy their most pressing needs first. However, the fact is that the strongest motives are not necessarily given priority. What people do also depends on their beliefs: thus death may be accepted before dishonor!

In consumer behavior, hierarchies are concerned with mental processing where the concept of "attitude" is basic since hierarchies of effects are assumed to occur in attitude formation, which is of central interest. Allport (1935) defined attitude as a "mental and neural state of readiness to respond, organized through experience, and exerting a directive influence upon the individual's response to all objects and situations with which it is related." Present-day social scientists have kept to this original view of attitudes, which is often interpreted as admitting three components: the cognitive, or knowledge, component; an affective, or evaluative, component (liking/disliking); and a conative, or behavior, component.

The current orthodoxy in consumer research (variously known as the cognitive orientation, the information-processing view, or the decision-making perspective) takes account of these three components in assuming some hierarchy of effects process going from cognition $C$ to affect $A$ to behavior $B$. This is so even though measures of attitude in practice tend to focus only on affect (the "feeling" or evaluative dimension). [Thus Fishbein and Ajzen (1975) view attitude as comprising solely an evaluative or affective response and ignore altogether the cognitive and behavioral dimension.] This $C \rightarrow A \rightarrow B$ model remains the dominant perspective in consumer research; this perspective takes for granted that buying is purposive, rational, reasoned, and deliberate (Holbrook, O'Shaughnessy, and Bell, 1990). The model views the consumer as first learning about the product or brand then developing a liking or disliking for it and finally acting in line with that knowledge and liking. The cognition $(C) \rightarrow$ affect $(A) \rightarrow$ behavior $(B)$ model or (as it is frequently known in advertising) the learn–feel–do hierarchy finds expression in many hierarchy models (see Figure 4.2) purporting to explicate what is involved in the cognitive, the affective, and the conative components of attitude. The formation of attitudes is thus considered key to understanding the persuasive process.

The hierarchy of effects models are views about the mental processing steps that comprise the cognitive and affective dimensions of attitude in which the conative dimen-

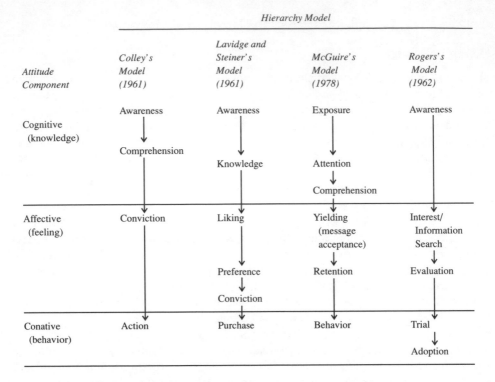

FIGURE 4.2.  Hierarchy Models Showing Mediating Processes Leading to Action and Their Link with the Alleged Components of Attitude

sion is identified with some action outcome. In Figure 4.2 Colley's (1961) model suggests the cognitive component necessitates awareness and comprehension, the affective component necessitates conviction, and the conative component necessitates action of some sort, though not necessarily actual purchase, as assumed in the Lavidge and Steiner (1961) model. McGuire's (1978) information-processing model chooses terms that stress the information processing that occurs; Rogers's (1962) model is that already mentioned as covering the alleged steps in the process leading to the adoption of an innovation.

It is claimed that the goals of advertising should be considered in terms of the various stages in the hierarchy on the assumption that this series of steps is typically undertaken by the target audience in becoming persuaded to buy the product. However, the universality of the sequence has been challenged by some researchers. Thus Ray (1982) posits three hierarchies, which in simple terms he describes as (1) learn–feel–do, (2) do–feel–learn, and (3) learn–do–feel. Ray regards the learn–feel–do hierarchy as applying only when consumer involvement with the product is high, product differentiation exists, and mass advertising is at work, with the product in the early part of its life cycle. The do–feel–learn sequence assumes consumer involvement with the product but low product differentiation, more reliance on personal sources than the mass media, and the product at the maturity stage in the life cycle. Finally, the learn–do–feel model posits low consumer involvement, low product differentiation, a mature market, and mass media is important.

Dröge (1989) argues that between cognition and any resulting conation there is always evaluation (or attitude if measured just to capture affect/evaluation). She thus regards the low-involvement hierarchy (learn–do–feel) as a "mirage." This makes sense since all awareness/comprehension of a product involves a form of acceptance or rejection where finding the "facts" is not a process separate from or prior to the evaluation of the product: there is a perceptual and procedural interdependence between the two. Even if we accept Ray's three processes, there is no problem in imagining the remaining combinations of feel–learn–do, feel–do–learn, and do–learn–feel. Lack of a theory to support the sequences does not rule out their regular occurrence.

Hierarchies can be said to explain in the sense that they point to the tasks to be accomplished by advertising. Although the hierarchies differ, each represents a defensible claim. However, even if the various information-processing steps suggested could be reconciled and shown to be descriptively correct, they would merely show what advertising had to do but not how to do it. Even if advertisers believe that creating awareness and comprehension is a technically solvable problem, they still want to know *how to* get conviction and buying action, and the hierarchy models do not tell them. Advertisers want to know about the mechanisms or appropriate appeals. Like the BCG matrix, hierarchy models tell you where you are and where you should go next but *they fail to tell you how to get there.*

As noted previously, the components of attitude are theorized as consisting of a cognitive, an affective, and a conative component. The cognitive component consists of beliefs, that is, dispositions to accept certain statements as more likely to be true than false (or vice versa) or that things should be done (or not done). It is claimed that attitudes may emanate from beliefs and attitude scores may be based on responses to questionnaires that tap beliefs (using, for example, a Likert scale, the semantic differential, or the multiattribute model), yet attitudes cannot be equated with beliefs since beliefs lack the affective (feeling/evaluative) and conative dimensions. However, it is not obvious that the evaluative beliefs involved in attitudes are neutral in affect, that is, do not incorporate affective dimensions. For example, I believe a certain advertisement to be grossly deceptive and whenever I see the ad the thought arises that "this is grossly deceptive" and I feel annoyed. The belief and the annoyance are simultaneous. The answer must lie in recognizing that a belief is not sufficient for producing the affect: values in some way must be involved. Thus we might take utilitarian beliefs about an ad and relate them to brand attitude but might find that measures of attitude toward the ad might relate still better to brand attitude. However, the position might change somewhat if we added more evaluative beliefs about the ad and related them to brand attitude. This is what in effect Mittal (1990) did. Mittal's study confirmed that including beliefs about image attributes of the ad (not just utilitarian beliefs) captured much of the relationship between measures of attitude toward the ad $A_{ad}$ and measures of attitude toward the brand $A_B$. But $A_{ad}$ was still found to be a better predictor of $A_B$. The question arises as to what was still missing in the belief set since conventional attitude measurement rests on answers to questionnaires that tap beliefs. It may be that the inclusion of more value-related beliefs might have done the trick.

Alternatively, we might look at a hint provided by Mackenzie and Lutz (1989). They claim that the focus when measuring $A_{ad}$ is more on affect than evaluation and that the causal antecedents of $A_{ad}$ are (1) ad credibility, (2) ad perceptions, (3) attitude toward the advertiser, (4) attitude toward advertising, and (5) mood. A mood is a generalized emotional state that has no object and it may be that this "mood" is not captured by the usual conventional listing of beliefs about the product. But neither might it be captured by the set of beliefs that make up the multiattribute model when used to measure attitudes.

Mackenzie and Lutz regard their factors as *causal* antecedents. This is misleading since the factors are a decomposition of $A_{ad}$ into components. Mackenzie and Lutz are engaging in what was termed "property analysis" in Chapter 2. Attitude measures toward the advertisement will be built up from beliefs about credibility, and so on, with answers reflecting mood.

Lutz (1985) speaks of four persuasive processes having been identified on the basis of whether involvement in the ad message was high or low and/or whether involvement in the ad execution was high or low.

The first process considered is the Elaboration Likelihood Model of Persuasion (ELM) of Petty and Cacioppo (1979), who claim there are two basic processes by which persuasion occurs. The "central route" to persuasion assumes the motivation, the opportunity, and the ability to evaluate the ad message but not the ad execution. As a result the force of the argument in the ad becomes important while the attitude toward the ad execution itself ($A_{ad}$) is unlikely to have much impact on attitude toward the brand ($A_B$). Under the "peripheral route" to persuasion, the ability, opportunity, and motivation to process the ad message are lacking, so that peripheral clues about the ad execution (humor in the ad, the celebrity endorsing the product) and not the quality of the argument becomes the key to persuasion. It is claimed that the relationship between $A_B$ and actual behavior is stronger for the central processing route.

Whether the two routes can be meaningfully separated like this (except in artificial laboratory conditions) is a matter of field research. On the surface, it would seem difficult to focus exclusively on the quality of the ad message and remain at the same time immune to how the message was presented: they interweave in producing an impact. Few would claim, for example, that students can or will assess the credibility of a lecture divorced from the way it is presented.

It is claimed that the central route to attitude change results in long-lasting, true, rational attitude change, and arises from processing cognitively the information contained in strong (valid) messages. The central route depends on the motivation and ability to elaborate cognitively the information presented. In the case of the peripheral route, there is short-term superficial acceptance of some message, not on the basis of its content but as a function of social and various affective cues such as the attractiveness of the source.

The Elaboration Likelihood model thus suggests that social comparison with reference group norms does not influence the perceived validity of messages being processed via the central route; that is, peripheral factors do not affect the perceived validity of the issues being processed. There is this suggestion in the model of persuasion being an objective property of arguments: just a matter of processing "good" information. Petty and Cacioppo argue that only the cognitive processing of strong arguments persuades. However, they acknowledge that they do not know what makes an argument persuasive, but simply define an argument as strong on the basis of its subjective effects: its rated persuasiveness and its capacity to stimulate favorable thoughts. Thus persuasion is identified with information processing of good, valid, and sound information, with good, valid, and sound information being defined as that which persuades! In ignoring the fact that what is considered good, valid, and sound is tied somewhat to social norms and conventions, the authors are regarding validity as somehow an inherent, objective property of the information being processed. But validity is not a property of information per se; it is a perception of the person doing the information processing, and such perceptions are not independent of social norms and conventions. This claim is essentially the basis of the criticism of the model by the social psychologist, John Turner (1991), but it would be supported by the work of Thomas Kuhn (1970), as discussed in Chapter 13.

The second of the four persuasive processes is the dual mode of persuasion, in which the individual is motivated to evaluate both the message and the execution. The third mode applies whenever the motivation to process both the message and execution is low, and the fourth mode applies whenever the motivation to process the message is low. Although each of these so-called persuasive processes is logically possible, it is not yet clear that they do form natural categories into which consumers watching an ad can be neatly categorized.

The concept of involvement here is crucial. As generally interpreted, consumers are said to have a high involvement with a product or brand or ad if it has high personal relevance for them in that it promises the benefits they seek or promotes the values they hold. Such a definition of "involvement" might be translated into the want/belief format by arguing that, say, my high involvement with an ad amounts to my believing that the ad has high significance for my wants. Thus Mitchell (1980), in line with those discussed earlier, argues that consumers who are highly involved with a product engage in a brand processing strategy with an in-depth processing of relevant information so that emerging attitudes reflect the persuasiveness of the presented information. On the other hand, when consumer involvement with the product is low, although consumers may still adopt a brand processing strategy, there will be an absence of critical attention so attitudes arise just from absorbing what is said rather than through assessing its persuasiveness. On the other hand, low involvement may lead the consumer to engage in a non–brand processing strategy away from the message content of the ad. "High involvement" can be replaced here by "believed in the high significance of the product (or whatever) from the point of view of their wants"; the term "low involvement" can be similarly translated.

But it is not at all clear that consumers who are highly involved with a product will in fact adopt a brand processing strategy. Much depends, for example, on how knowledgeable they are. The very knowledgeable might think they had no need; the ignorant might feel they are wiser to follow the advice of those considered "in the know." This is typically what occurs in the many protocols I have seen, recording before people buy, during buying, and after buying: there is often little in-depth processing of information but a resort to experts. What is troubling about all these generalizations is that they cannot be well-grounded since there is no validated theory from which they could be deduced and no surveys could draw on a true random sample covering all the different types of consumers and products; moreover, laboratory findings will always lack realism when it comes to generalizing the findings to the marketplace. Thus Dröge (1989) shows that non-comparative advertising generates a greater $A_{ad}$ but only an equal or less positive brand-related response $A_B$ than do comparative advertisements. She argues that research has not found the positive relationship between attitude toward the ad ($A_{ad}$) and attitude toward the brand ($A_B$) in the case of comparative ads.

Even if the findings such as those discussed in this section were highly probable, it is not clear how they can be used. They tell us next to nothing about how to persuade an audience, and they fail to identify who, under what conditions, falls into what categories. In any case it is doubtful that any target audience would fall into just one category that would allow one standard advertising appeal to be used.

In the consumer behavior literature, there is an assumed link between $A_{ad}$ and $A_B$. If attitudes both toward the ad and the brand are favorable, it is assumed they are likely to lead to purchase intention and purchase. But how good a predictor is attitude of behavior? After all, "attitude" is a dispositional term, meaning it will be activated only under certain conditions. Furthermore, attitudes will not predict behavior unless wants/goals are in line with the attitude; that is, we cannot predict how consumers with a highly favorable attitude toward product $X$ will behave unless we know the goals of such consumers in respect to buying. Yet attitudes, as generally measured, do not say anything about goals. Thus I cannot predict whether my friend's highly favorable attitude toward educational toys for children will lead to his buying them unless I know he is in the market for toys. If we were to rely on what was written in textbooks, confusion would reign since some writers are dismissive of any predictive power of attitude while others find a strong relationship between attitude and behavior.

Foxall (1984), in a review of the evidence, first quotes the classic study by Wicker (1969), who examined forty-six empirical studies of attitudinal–behavioral consistency only to conclude that it is more likely that attitudes will be unrelated or only slightly related to overt behavior than that attitudes will be closely related to actions. Foxall argues that more recent encouraging results have come about from researchers demanding "situational correspondence between the circumstances under which attitudinal and behavioral measurements occur."

With regard to the relationship between buying intentions and behavior, Jamieson and Bass (1989) claim that even knowledge of the relationship between purchase intentions and actual purchase is rudimentary at best. In particular, there is an absence of evidence on the predictive accuracy of intentions data for new products. In general, research finds substantial variation between stated intention to purchase and actual purchase behavior. They go on to suggest the need for adjusting intentions data to recognize likely contingencies.

Foxall discusses whether the concept of attitude has outlived its usefulness in consumer research. Certainly, as attitudes emanate from evaluative beliefs, would it not be better to focus on those beliefs and the bases of those beliefs rather than on attitude as "affect"? More specifically, should the focus be on beliefs and wants since beliefs lead to action only when combined to form reasons for action?

## The John Howard Model

Howard's (1989) most recent cognitive model of buyer behavior is along the lines of Dretske. Basic to the model is the view that consumers are in one of three different decision states corresponding to the first three stages of the product life cycle. At the introductory stage, the decision state is termed "extensive problem solving" (EPS), the growth stage is "limited problem solving" (LPS), and the maturity stage is "routine problem solving" (RPS).

EPS implies that the consumer has yet to form a concept of the product class or category. In the case of LPS, the consumer does have a concept of the product category but has yet to form a concept of the new brand falling into a familiar product category. In the case of RPS, the consumer has formed both a concept of the product category and a concept of each of the relevant brands.

Basic to all three decision categories is the concept of product category. Howard defines a "product category" as a group of brands that consumers view as close substitutes for each other. As Howard views product category it leads him to dismiss the utility of the PLC for brands, even though there are those who argue that the classic bell-shaped curve applies best to brands (Dhalla and Yuspeh, 1976). In this Howard is supported by Lambkin and Day (1989), who argue convincingly that the life cycles of brands and product forms (for example, sports cars) simply reflect competitive developments within life cycles rather than any overall life cycle pattern.

According to Howard, the movement from EPS to RPS is a movement toward a state of "total understanding" of a brand. Such total understanding does not mean that consumers become experts on brands but that they

1. know the brand's physical characteristics to allow *brand recognition* (*B*);
2. know the strengths of the brand on each of its relevant "benefits" as manifested in their *attitude* toward the brand (*A*); and
3. feel they have the *confidence* to judge quality (*C*).

This total understanding, what Howard calls the *ABC*'s of marketing (brand recognition, attitude, and confidence), constitutes for Howard the "brand image."

Howard's consumer decision model (CDM) is the process shown in Figure 4.3. It consists of six key, interrelated concepts:

1. *Information* (*F*). Howard defines information as the "precept" that is caused by the stimulus (e.g., advertisement), the precept being that which the buyer perceives from being exposed to the stimulus. But Howard measures the consumer's precept by recall, which makes information all that is recalled about the stimulus.
2. *Brand recognition* (*B*). Brand recognition involves categorization, which requires the consumer to have information on both the function of the product and its form. *B* is viewed as being causally linked with attitude (*A*) and with confidence (*C*).
3. *Attitude* (*A*). Howard defines attitude toward the brand as the measure of the extent to which the buyer expects the brand to satisfy certain requirements. Such a measure, he argues, should be multidimensional—weighting each benefit as to its relative importance for the consumer and multiplying each weighting by the corresponding expected performance of the brand, with the overall sum being the measure of attitude. Thus Howard supports the multiattribute model as reflected, say, in Fishbein's (1967) expectancy–value approach as the way to measure attitudes. Attitude (*A*) is viewed as being causally linked to intention to buy (*I*).
4. *Confidence* (*C*). Confidence is the degree of certainty felt by the consumer that his or her judgments about the brand and its benefits are correct. *C* is viewed as causally linked to *I*, particularly when *A* is high.
5. *Intention* (*I*). Intention to buy is the mental state reflecting the buyer's plan to buy some specified number of units of a particular brand in a specified time period. Intention (*I*) is a predictor of purchase (*P*).
6. *Purchase* (*P*). Purchase occurs when the buyer has either bought the brand or is financially committed to buying the brand.

Howard deals as follows with each decision state, describing the problems and the processes involved.

## EXTENSIVE PROBLEM SOLVING

In the case of EPS, the concept of product hierarchy is fundamental. The consumer classifies products into hierarchies. Thus vehicles are categorized into cars, buses, trucks, and so on, and cars themselves are categorized into standard, compact, subcompacts, and so

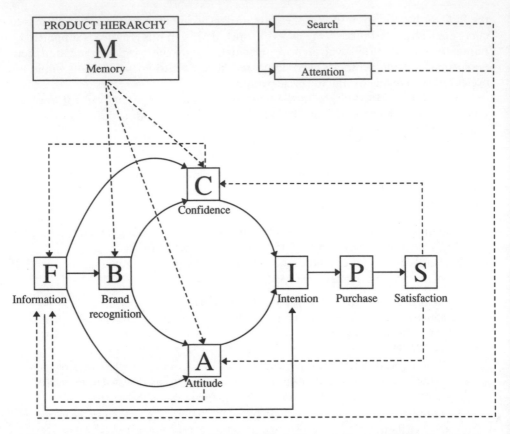

FIGURE 4.3. Information processing. [*Source*: John A. Howard, *Consumer Behavior in Marketing Strategy* (Englewood Cliffs, NJ: Prentice Hall, 1989). Reprinted by permission.]

on, with each subcategory subdivided into individual car brands. Within the product hierarchy is a basic level (here the car level). At the basic level the consumer has some standard/prototype, which represents what the consumer has in mind when speaking of brands of a product class. It is this prototype against which the consumer compares anything new falling within the basic level. For such comparisons, the consumer needs information regarding the product's functions (functional knowledge) and descriptive terms (lexical or word knowledge) to allow brand recognition (*B*) and the evaluation of benefits (*A*).

What activates this whole EPS process and the other two processes (LPS and RPS)? For Howard it is the consumer's objectives. He terms these personal objectives "motives." Motives/objectives manifest themselves in the importance weights attached to the various product/brand benefits. Long-term motives/objectives Howard views as "values." Short-term objectives/motives are viewed as simply the "physiological" satisfactions that are sought. Values (the long-term objectives/motives) are divided into (1) terminal values reflecting some preferred vision of the good life (e.g., an exciting life) and (2) instrumental values that relate to "modes of behavior" (e.g., ambitious behavior).

Terminal values give rise to the choice criteria (benefits sought) used in choosing product classes; instrumental values give rise to the choice criteria used to choose brands. Choice criteria, when used to evaluate a product class or a brand, result in beliefs about where a product or brand is located or ranked in respect to the criteria. These resulting beliefs determine the attitude toward the product or brand which influences intention ($I$) and purchase ($P$).

Short-term motives/objectives, Howard argues, motivate search, attention, memory, and choice because these physiological motives manifest themselves in arousal, feeling, and emotion. However, if short-term motives/objectives motivate in this way, the product hierarchy *guides* the search, attention, memory, and choice in EPS (and in LPS and RPS). But as the product hierarchy is less developed in EPS, short-term motives must play a more dominant role in stimulating the search for information. However, as Howard admits, with many low-priced products, there may be no exhaustive search; consumers may simply buy the new product and learn from using it (the do–feel–learn hierarchy).

Howard speaks of choice being at two levels in EPS since there is a choice of *both* a product category and a brand. He claims that under EPS consumers are responsive only to major price changes. Promotion is difficult given the need to get acceptance of both product and brand, and distribution often requires specialty stores to give initial advice.

## LIMITED PROBLEM SOLVING

Once a new brand is put into a product category, knowledge of the product category guides the process leading to intention ($I$) and purchase ($P$). Knowledge of the product category guides the search for information or for attention to whatever distinguishes the new brand from others and guides memory. Under LPS, price becomes more important while atmosphere and other conditions in the retail store become part of the consumer's image of the brand.

## ROUTINE PROBLEM SOLVING

Under RPS, a well-informed consumer may undertake little or no deliberation, so information (e.g., about household shortages) can lead directly to intention to buy ($I$). But many in RPS are not just creatures of habit but switch brands. In RPS, price is important since it is not part of brand image, and so it is considered separately by consumers. This contrasts with those in EPS and LPS who perceive price as part of the product, affecting attitude toward the brand itself. Product improvement is important in RPS, although the variables most likely to be manipulated are price, availability, and advertising focusing on benefits.

Howard focuses on how to use the whole or some modification of his model for dealing with the three decision states of EPS, LPS, and RPS while allowing for complexity. Thus he recognized feedback from consumer satisfaction to $A$ and $C$ while $A$ and $C$ feed back to information needs.

## GENERAL COMMENT

The Howard model (see Figure 4.3) offers an explanation of how $B$, $A$, and $C$ combine to convert $F$ into $I$. What might we say of this process model given the last two chapters? In essence the model is saying that beliefs about a brand ($B$) and its benefits in relation to wants ($A$) combined with confidence in those beliefs ($C$) lie behind whatever action is taken ($I$). This is the traditional rational model except that many would qualify the concept of confidence. Thus, as Harman (1986) says, people do not normally associate with their beliefs degrees of confidence of a sort they can use in reasoning. It is too complicated for them to do so: degrees of belief have to be implicit rather than explicit.

What Howard regards as a causal flow through $F$, $B$, $C$, $A$, $I$, and $P$ is debatable. If we believe that cause is something more than correlation, it is doubtful whether the whole flow could be considered causal. It could be argued that the consumer's reflections on a brand's function and distinctive form generates a distinct conceptualization of the brand ($B$) that finds *expression* in beliefs about a brand's costs and benefits in relation to what is sought ($A$) and beliefs about the strength of those beliefs ($C$). Where that *expression* is highly favorable in relation to competitive brands, it leads the consumer to the rational conclusion that the brand should be bought. Such a conclusion, regarded as sufficient reason for buying, might, however, be viewed as causal.

Discussion on the causal status of the model is important in considering its potential for prediction. Howard views the model as highly predictive once the regressions and correlations have been calculated for $F$ and the $ABC$'s. But a regression line will define a uniquely *true* value of $Y$ corresponding to particular values of $X$ only if the relationship is causal or in some other way can be shown to have stability. In any case, increasing advertising expenditure (as a surrogate of $F$ may have no *necessary* impact while such an expenditure might change the context (e.g., competitive activity) for which the regression is valid.

In line with current orthodoxy, Howard assumes a very rational consumer. But research findings can also be used to provide a different picture. Foxall (1990) points to the many studies that cast doubt on this progression from EPS through LPS to Routine Response Behavior (RRB) as the consumer acquires "total understanding" of a brand as alleged by Howard. Thus there are the studies that show consumers drastically limit their search for information even about durable products like furniture and cars while the "whole decision sequence assumed in comprehensive modelling appears to be absent from many instances of consumer buying." Foxall claims that the evidence taken as a whole suggests that consumers do not as a rule undertake comparative evaluations of brands on the basis of their attributes. Foxall, in line with his behaviorist stance (see Chapter 7), stresses situational variables, group pressure, and the physical arrangements of store displays in influencing consumer choice at the point of sale.

It is not surprising that these disputes exist since buyer behavior is unlikely to follow a standard set of rules everywhere and for everything bought. There will be occasions for heavy deliberation on carefully acquired information and there will be many occasions when habits or simple sense appeal or even random picking (see Chapter 10) dominates. We need to determine the relevant classes first if generalization is to be useful. What must be avoided are claims to *know* that *most* consumers will do this or that, as if we have statistical evidence covering all consumers, products, and circumstances.

## The Rossiter–Percy Model

If the more traditional causal process is the causal chain, the Rossiter and Percy (1987) model of advertising is an interesting example (see Table 4.1). The first four steps in Table 4.1 (exposure → mental processing → communication effects → target audience action) constitute the buyer response sequence. These four steps are regarded as necessary steps in the causal chain that results in any trial or use of a product brought about by promotion.

We discuss each of the four steps in turn.

TABLE 4.1. The Rossiter–Percy Model

| Exposure of target audience: selecting the target audience and exposure objectives | → | Mental processing: selection, rote learning *or* acceptance, and emotion | → | Communication effects: activating or intensifying category need, brand awareness, and brand attitude | → | Target audience action: trial or usage (repeat or switch) | → | Sales | → | Profit |
|---|---|---|---|---|---|---|---|---|---|---|

## EXPOSURE

Exposure, the first step, is the selection of both the target audience and the communication (exposure) objectives. Rossiter and Percy classify potential target audiences into four categories:

New (category) users (NCUs)

Brand loyals (BLs)

Other brand loyals (OBLs), those who are loyal to other brands

Brand switchers (BSs)

Which of these will be of interest depends on the stage in the product life cycle. At the decline stage, NCUs and OBLs are likely to have poor sales potentials, hence the focus would normally be on retaining the BLs and converting BSs to be loyal to our brand. [Rossiter and Percy measure brand loyalty in terms of both buying behavior (regularly buying the product) and favorableness of attitude toward the brand.] This classification into NCU, OBL, BL, and BS is the classification most useful for advertising segmentation. Other descriptions of the target audience in terms of demographics, psychographics, and the like, are regarded as useful (e.g., in selecting content and media vehicles) but secondary.

The authors segment target audiences for advertising purposes on the basis of new category users, brand loyals, brand switchers, or other brand loyals on the ground that such divisions reflect differences in awareness and attitude. They criticize defining segments in terms first of benefits. Thus they argue that "cavity prevention," "taste appeal," or any perceived benefits, do not represent segments of the toothpaste market as "brand loyals" and, say, "other brand loyals" would want the benefits to different degrees. We must first think in terms of target audience category, so Colgate, for example, might have two segments:

1. Colgate brand loyals whose category need is cavity prevention with the benefit of taste for children; and
2. Crest (P&G) brand loyals where Colgate is promoted vis-à-vis Crest as a brand of cavity prevention toothpaste that fights cavities as well as Crest.

*We think first of target audiences* and then of benefits they seek. Rossiter and Percy refer to any focus on benefits as a first step as a "student error," no doubt to show their contempt of any likely criticism. But the question is not this easy. The authors are right in the trivial sense that segmentation must involve both a customer target and a buying inducement. It is also true that for advertising purposes the customer target must come first since advertising must know to whom to communicate and the relevant mental state of that target audience. In fact, since, where profitable,

1. new (category) users are to be *attracted;*
2. brand loyals are to be *maintained* (or brand use *increased*);
3. brand switchers are to be *retained* (if favorable brand switchers) or *converted* (if other brand switchers); and
4. other brand loyals are to be *converted,*

the authors' approach is similar to that of those who focus on the goals of convert, increase, attract, or maintain. However, the authors are claiming that thinking in terms of segment benefits first would be an error. Their example points out that "brand loyals" and "other brand loyals" could both want cavity prevention and taste to different degrees. This example does not make it clear, however, which of the following the authors are saying:

1. Splits of the market into distinct sets of benefits may not coincide with divisions of the market into BLs, OBLs, NCUs, or BSs. This is correct if the various sets of benefits have not been shown to represent distinct wants. But benefit segmentation is segmenting a market on the basis of benefits *sought* (i.e., distinct wants sought), not on just what might appear to be distinct sets of benefits. Benefit segmentation should not simply be equated with divisions of the market into sets of what the segmenter *believes* are distinct wants.
2. Segments of the market representing different configurations of benefits *actually being sought* will not necessarily coincide with divisions of the target audience into BLs, OBLs, NCUs, or BSs. This could be true if benefits are confined to product attributes (properties), as in the authors' example. However, if benefits refer to *any* distinguishing characteristic of the *offering* (product attribute levels, price, promotion, and distribution) that constitutes a buying inducement for some part of the target customer group on some occasion, the distinct sets of benefits must distinguish target segments. If what they seek does not distinguish "brand loyals" from "other brand loyals," and so on, then we have no basis for differential advertising to them. In sum, it seems the authors are confusing benefit segmentation with various groupings of *product* attributes instead of thinking in terms of different *offerings* actually or potentially being sought.

Rossiter and Percy claim that while the objectives of advertising can be considered in terms of trial (attract), repeat (retain), switching (convert), or increased use, the effects to be generated to achieve these results are in terms of the more immediate communication (exposure) objectives of (1) *activating* category need; (2) *creating* brand awareness; and (3) *developing* a favorable brand attitude and/or triggering purchase intention and/or overcoming objections to components of the offering. These stages can be represented by the standard learning hierarchy of

- learn (awareness/comprehension)
- feel (conviction)
- do (action)

Other hierarchies such as the additional two mentioned by Ray are not considered.

*Activating category need* means for Rossiter and Percy appealing to the basic motives involved. The authors use Fennell's (1987) eight categories (see Table 4.2). This list does

TABLE 4.2. Eight Categories of Buying Motives

Negative or aversive origin

Problem removal (solve a problem)
Problem avoidance (prevent anticipated problem from arising)
Incomplete satisfaction (not satisfied with current brand)
Mixed approach avoidance (seeking new product to reduce disliked elements of current purchase)

Mildly negative origin

Normal depletion (seeks to maintain normal supply)

Positive or appetitive origin

Sensory gratification (seeks additional sensory enjoyment)
Intellectual stimulation (seeks extra psychological stimulation)
Social approval (seeks social rewards or personal recognition)

*Source:* Fennell (1978).

not repeat the psychological literature but categorizes goal-oriented reasons for buying. The list may not be operational (mutually exclusive) since the category of "mixed approach avoidance" suggests also "incomplete satisfaction," "normal depletion" relates to "problem avoidance," "social approval" could be sought as "problem removal" or "problem avoidance" or to "reduce an approach-avoidance conflict," and so on.

*Creating brand awareness* according to the authors can be in terms of ensuring *brand recognition* at the point of sale to activate category need or ensuring that whenever a category need arises there is *brand recall.* The assumption made is that the consumer *either* sets out with a shopping list (implicit or explicit) of brands to buy, in which case brand recall becomes important as he or she thinks about category need, or, alternatively, he or she goes shopping and chooses what to buy in the store, in which case brand recognition becomes important. (Most final brand choices for supermarket items appear to be made at the point of sale.) Inducing either brand recognition *or* brand recall makes for a more focused advertising strategy, though on occasion both may be of interest. (The empirical question is the extent to which target consumers fall into just one category.)

*Developing a favorable brand attitude* requires both influencing the cognitive (beliefs) and the affective (energizing, emotional) components of attitude to create, intensify, maintain, modify, or radically change attitudes. The authors recommend that strategies to influence attitudes take the following into account:

1. *The type of decision:* Is the decision low involvement or high involvement? As defined by the Rossiter and Percy, *involvement* refers to the degree of risk perceived by the buyer in purchasing the brand. Such perceived risk could be economic or psychosocial. With a high-involvement decision, consumers indulge in search behavior and conviction is required before purchase. In the case of low-involvement decisions, neither need occur. In the case of high-involvement decisions, it is claimed that the consumer's initial attitude limits the final attitude that can be obtained through promotion, as such decisions involve a limited latitude of acceptable choices. Hence the advertising strategy should make requests that fall within the limits of acceptance, that is, ask and expect only for a reasonable increase in favorable attitude change. On the other hand, in the case of low-involvement decisions, the strategy is to ask a lot to get a lot.

2.  *The type of motivation:* Is the motivation of negative or positive (appetitive) origin? *Negative* motives (problem removal, problem avoidance, incomplete satisfaction with the current product, approach-avoidance conflict, normal depletion) suggests *reason-why* advertising. On the other hand, *positive* (appetitive) motives suggest *image* advertising. The authors refer to negative motives as *informational* motivations and positive motives as *transformational* motivations. Both informational and transformational motivations may be involved on occasion.

Where motivations appear to be a true mixture of informational and transformational motivations the authors recommend the informational strategy.

The benefits promoted should be of importance ($I$) to the motivation and perceived as deliverable ($D$) and unique ($U$) to the brand. These $IDU$'s will differ for various target audiences such as brand loyals or brand switchers.

The authors deviate from Krugman's (1965) original definition of "involvement" as the "number of conscious bridging experiences, connections or personal references per minute that the viewer makes between his own life and the stimulus." Such a view cannot just be equated with degree of risk. If the term simply embraces risk, then why not simply use the term "risk" rather than add to the confusion over the meaning of "involvement"? In any case, a purchase that appears risky for one person may not appear so for another, hence a target audience for some product category may not fall neatly into the categories of high or low involvement, particularly given that the range "high" to "low" is a continuum. It is not clear that target audiences for some product category will fall neatly into the two categories of motivation or even whether those two categories are particularly meaningful. These doubts are a reminder that even the most thought about models in marketing are just groping their way.

## MENTAL PROCESSING

Rossiter and Percy claim two distinct processing sequences occur in reacting to an advertisement, depending on whether the decision or attitude reflects low or high involvement. This is illustrated as follows:

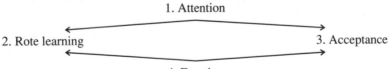

1. Attention

2. Rote learning                              3. Acceptance

4. Emotion

Regardless of whether involvement is high or low, the first stage in the mental processing sequence is *attention.* Advertising must gain target audience attention. However, in the case of low involvement, the aim is then to get *rote learning* of the message to create brand awareness in the form of brand recognition and/or brand recall. In the case of high involvement the aim is to get *acceptance* or agreement with the advertisement in respect of both category need and brand benefits. This is because attitudes in high-involvement situations must be confidently held—not passive rote learning but active, reflective deliberation—before the buyer will take action. Whereas a *soft sell* seems appropriate where low-involvement, rote learning occurs, a *hard sell* is needed where high-involvement, acceptance/agreement is required. With rote learning (low involvement) a paraphrase of the benefit claim is absorbed, whereas in the case of high involvement what is learned is the result of reflection and deliberation, so what is retained is a personal interpretation of the benefit claims.

But if high to low involvement measures *degree* of risk, then this is a continuum and not a dichotomy. How should a buyer be positioned along the continuum to indicate the extent of rote learning or personal interpretation that is likely to take place? More important, can it be asserted that low involvement always implies that rote learning is likely while high involvement leads to active deliberation? Rossiter and Percy refer the reader to cognitive response theory rather than actual evidence. If a person's existing beliefs, or just wishful thinking, predisposes him or her toward an advertisement's claims (and surely they will have some presuppositions), then rote learning might occur even in high-involvement situations. Does high involvement inevitably result in more reflection and thinking for oneself? Consumers may not have the confidence to depend on their own thinking but prefer to rely on the advice of others, brand reputation, and the like. Similarly, the mere condition of low involvement does not mean advertising claims will be just learned by rote. This assumes some sort of perception → absorption sequence without any evaluation. It could be argued that *evaluation* is inevitable in that experience is always a standard against which we will judge any incoming message. Unless the assertions are backed by field evidence covering a very wide range of circumstances, the assertions can be regarded only as sounding reasonable rather than established. In fact, if involvement is interpreted as degree of risk, then the involvement literature cannot necessarily be quoted in support.

The final element (in the preceding diagram) in mental processing of advertisements is *emotion*. It is claimed that emotions elicited by elements in the advertisement "feed" both the rote learning and the acceptance sequence.

COMMUNICATION EFFECTS

The third step, communication effects, might

1. activate or intensify category need;
2. create brand awareness (recognition and/or recall); or
3. create a favorable brand attitude.

Rossiter and Percy claim that in creating brand awareness we need to know whether the target audience chooses a brand by recognition or recall. It is important because advertising tactics differ for the two situations. The tactics for brand *recognition* are (1) to ensure sufficient exposure of the name and package, (2) a focus on category need, and (3) an initial high burst of advertising followed by reminder advertising. The tactics for brand *recall* are (1) to include both the category need and brand name in the main copy line, (2) keep the copy line short, (3) include a personal reference (e.g., you . . . ), and (4) use a bizarre execution and perhaps a jingle. It is not clear what the essential differences are here. Many would say that if you exchanged the tactics between the two, the exchanged tactics would still seem consistent with the goals.

The final set of recommendations are shown in Table 4.3 and summarized in Table 4.4.

If we were intent on explaining in terms of "wants" and "beliefs," we would work

TABLE 4.3.  Advertising Message Strategy Given the Decision and Motivation Strategies

| | Type of Motivation | |
| Type of Decision | Informational (Motives of a Negative/Aversive Origin) | Transformational (Motives of a Positive or Appetitive Origin) |
| --- | --- | --- |
| Low involvement | Give reasons<br>    Simple problem-solution format<br>    Easy to understand<br>    Likability of advertisement not necessary | Focus on image<br>    Emotional authenticity important<br>    Unique execution<br>    Advertisement liked<br>    Frequent exposure for liking |
| | Ask a lot<br>    Extreme claims | Ask a lot<br>    Benefits claimed linked to brand<br>    Dramatize use/possession/<br>    consumption of brand |
| High involvement | Give reasons<br>    Link to attitudes/beliefs<br>    Reasons given via comparative<br>    advertisements if competition is well<br>    entrenched<br>    Likability of advertisement not necessary | Focus on image<br>    Emotional authenticity important<br>    Appeal/format fits lifestyle<br>    Seek identification with brand<br>    Frequent exposure for liking |
| | Ask only what is reasonable<br>    Do not over- *or* underclaim | Ask only what is reasonable<br>    Some information may have to be put<br>    across<br>    Do not underclaim: *slightly* overclaim |

*Source:* After Rossiter and Percy (1987).


back from the behavior implied in Table 4.2 to how wants and beliefs appear to differ among the four categories.

For the low-involvement/informational category, consumers are assumed to want relief but at minimum cost in terms of effort since there is not much at stake. Further, because of the low risk, consumers are open to believing whatever is said, which, in turn, assumes the target audience harbors no inhibiting contrary beliefs or doubts.

For the high-involvement/informational category, consumers are assumed to want relief but, with the high risks attached to the purchase, consumers believe they need to equip themselves with more information to choose wisely and carefully.

For the low-involvement/transformational category, consumers want the good feeling associated with possessing, using, or consuming the product and, because of the low risks involved, are open to believing what they feel to be true.

For the high-involvement/transformational category, consumers want the good feelings associated with possessing, using, or consuming the product but, with the high risks involved, need more convincing that what they feel to be true is actually so.

We might sum up by saying that the Rossiter–Percy model assumes a fairly rational model for informational motivation whereas transformational motivation introduces some emotional bias. Rossiter and Percy do not enter into the current controversy over the relative difficulty of converting, retaining, attracting, and increasing sales by means of advertising. For example, Tellis (1988) and others argue that advertising seems to reinforce preference for the current brands being bought rather than stimulate brand switching. Also, advertising appears effective in increasing sales to current ("loyal") buyers but less effective in winning buyers.

TABLE 4.4. Recommendations for Various Target Segments

Low-involvement/informational product/brand

Target audience need not like the advertisement (it is the information to relieve their problem that counts)
Simple problem–solution format
Extreme claims for benefits
Easy to understand
Humor (if used) should be product-relevant

Low-involvement/transformational product/brand

Emotional authenticity important
Key benefits claimed linked to brand
Unique execution
Advertisement liked (to reinforce transformational theme)
Brand delivery made explicit in such a way that the target audience can put themselves emotionally in the role of using the advertised brand
Large number of exposures are needed, as liking increases with familiarity
Humor (if used) need not be product-relevant

High-involvement/informational product/brand

Emotional portrayal (if used) more relevant to the initial stage of the brand life cycle
Audience need not like the advertisement
Consumer's attitude should form the basis for directing advertising strategy
Should not overclaim
Should not underclaim
Consider refuting false beliefs, doubts, etc.
Consider comparative advertising if well-entrenched competition

High-involvement/transformational product/brand

Emotional authenticity paramount and in line with target audience's lifestyle
Get audience to identify with product/brand not just with advertisement itself
Some information may be required to be put across
Do not underclaim but slightly overclaim
Repetition of the advertisement both for building market share and for reinforcement

*Note:* Since members of the target audience categories NCU, OBL, BS, and BL may differ in precisely what they regard as emotional authenticity, further subsegmenting such audiences may be required.

*Source:* Rossiter and Percy (1987).

## The Weitz Model

Mohr regards process models as generally lacking a compelling flow of action: "One must also supply the external forces and probabilistic processes constituting the means by which the sequence of events is understood to unfold" (1982, p. 53). But what external force explanations would be compelling when the explicandum is voluntary behavior (action)? In other words, do we always need to know something about wants and beliefs (or cognates of these terms) for adequacy of explanation? We can take the Weitz (1981) model to examine this question since it seeks to explain effective salesperson interactions with buyers in terms of "facts" without resort to speculations about buyer beliefs or motivations. Weitz claims that the effectiveness of selling behaviors across customer interactions is *contingent* upon or moderated by (*a*) the salesperson's resources, (*b*) the nature of the customer buying task, (*c*) the customer–salesperson relationship, and interactions among *a, b,* and *c*.

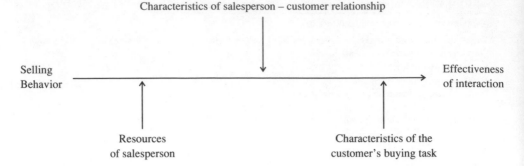

FIGURE 4.4. Contingency Model of Salesperson Effectiveness [*Source*: After Barton A. Weitz, "Effectiveness in Sales Interactions: A Contingency Framework," *Journal of Marketing* 45 (Winter 1981), pp. 85–103.]

The basic structure of the model is seen in Figure 4.4, where selling behaviors are depicted as determining the effectiveness of the interaction with the buyer, with the selling behaviors themselves being affected by (*a*) the resources of the salesperson, (*b*) the characteristics of the customer's buying task, and (*c*) the characteristics of the salesperson–customer relationship. We will discuss each of the elements of the model.

### SELLING BEHAVIORS

There are many ways of analyzing "selling behaviors," but Weitz's analysis reduces to just four components:

1. adapting to the buyer as opposed to being nonadaptive, as occurs in the canned presentation;
2. establishing an influence base resting on the various power sources of coercive power, reward power, legitimate power, referent power (identification with salesperson), or expert power;
3. influence techniques used; and
4. controlling the interaction.

These selling behaviors are the behaviors or external conditions that are viewed as causal in determining the effectiveness of the interaction. But Weitz's specification of selling behaviors is not clear-cut. In the first place, it is not clear that a canned presentation is always nonadaptive. On the contrary, where there is known customer homogeneity in susceptibility to a certain type of sales appeal (e.g., the bargain offer) the canned sales presentation could be regarded as *preplanned* adaptive. It is also not clear that the selling behaviors listed are in fact conceptually distinct. Is not "adapting to the buyer" equivalent to choosing the right "base of influence" and corresponding "influence techniques"? Is not "controlling the interaction" one of the purposes of the influence technique used?

In terms of our basic question, it is likely that we can ignore beliefs and wants when predicting effectiveness? It is doubtful. Thus whether control of the sales interview should even by attempted will depend on the expectations of the buyer. Buyers do have expectations about normative selling behaviors which, if frustrated, lead to passiveness or irritation.

## SALESPERSONS' RESOURCES

Salesperson's resources are a factor entering into the effectiveness of selling behaviors. Weitz defines these resources as the set of "skills or abilities, a level of knowledge about the product and customer, and a range of alternatives that can be offered to the customers." As it stands, this definition is much too embracing to be other than a truism in claiming such resources influence the effectiveness of the interaction. More difficult to determine is the extent to which such resources can be distinguished from selling behaviors since some of the selling behaviors as described presuppose certain salespersons' resources to be a fact, for example, to be able to adapt to the buyer.

The more basic question is what skills/abilities, what level of knowledge about product and customer, what range of alternatives will be needed to support the various selling behaviors? We cannot answer these questions without knowing *how* buyers make decisions.

## BUYING TASK

The buying task is a situational variable that mediates selling behaviors. The buying task might vary in terms of

1. newness of the buy;
2. risk associated with the buying decision outcomes; or
3. task structure defined by Weitz in terms of "the degree to which the product requirements are known by the customer, the degree to which a variety of products could satisfy the customer's needs, and the degree to which the customer is able to evaluate the performance of the product after the sale."

Weitz quotes research on the need for the salesperson to take account of these factors since they affect the *content* of the salesperson's appeals. But in precisely what way is the question to be answered? It is not obvious how selling behaviors such as "influence technique used" or "controlling the interaction" would be affected. In fact, we cannot know how variations in the buying task should guide selling behaviors without knowing how such variations influence the wants and beliefs of the buyer.

## CUSTOMER–SALESPERSON RELATIONSHIP

Customer–salesperson relationships are defined by Weitz in terms of the relative power between salesperson and customer, the level of conflict between them, and anticipations of future interactions. Selling behaviors need to consider the customer–salesperson relationship. (However, selling behaviors and customer–salesperson relationship form a reciprocal relationship: customer–salesperson relationships influence selling behaviors and selling behaviors influence the customer–salesperson relationship.) Weitz argues that a salesperson possessing unique information concerning a solution to a customer's problem would have power over that buyer. But again we cannot ignore beliefs and wants since whether power over the buyer does result in a sale depends on whether the buyer *perceives* the salesperson as possessing unique and useful information. It is a commonplace complaint of every consultant that managers do not recognize potential benefits from the adoption of some system.

Weitz claims that the level of conflict is reflected in the quality of the relationship, the amount of negotiating or bargaining associated with the sale, the level of competition the salesperson faces, and the degree to which the salesperson's offerings can satisfy the customer's needs. Again, these claims can be accepted only if we make certain assumptions about buyer perceptions and motivations. The fact is that none of these factors may affect the amount of *destructive* conflict between salesperson and customer. On the contrary, a high amount of negotiation or bargaining can lead to mutual respect, depending on how it is conducted, and the level of competition faced may or may not affect the relationship. Finally, if the salesperson's offerings do not meet the customer's wants, this need not generate conflict, yet if they meet the wants ideally conflict could still arise over, say, the tone of the salesperson's communications. Of course, expectations of future interactions may affect some aspect of selling behavior, although such expectations in themselves might be no more than the outcome of the interaction itself.

In sum, although Weitz sets out his model in a process format, there is no way anyone could use this model to predict outcomes in salesperson–customer interactions. The model is mainly an inventory of factors to consider, classified none too clearly, with the categories themselves defined only impressionistically while the nature of the relationships among the categories has to be inferred by the reader.

Weitz sets out a number of propositions for testing. It would certainly be a Herculean task to try to operationalize the variables in the propositions, and it is not surprising no one has attempted to do so. But, more relevantly, we might look at the propositions, like the following:

> Proposition 1: Engaging in adaptive sales behaviors across interactions is positively related to effectiveness in the following circumstances:
>
> (a) Salesperson resources—the salesperson has the resources, both personal abilities and product alternatives, to engage in adaptive sales behaviors.
>
> (b) Customer buying tasks—the salesperson's customers typically are engaged in complex buying tasks that could result in large orders.
>
> (c) Customer–salesperson relationship—the salesperson has a good relationship with the customer characterized by a low level of conflict and the salesperson anticipates future relationships with the customer.

We find the conditions under which this proposition is likely to hold are just those conditions that are either necessary conditions for success or necessarily contributing factors for helping along success. It is not certain that anything more could be learned from testing the hypotheses than could be inferred from the meaning of the words themselves. All this is not to deny that there is something of interest in Weitz's attempt to delineate the system and process involved in selling interactions, but it indicates we have a long way to go.

This criticism should not be interpreted as implying that focusing on how external events relate to the way people behave should be ignored. In fact, consideration of external events, conditions, and the like, is often needed to understand how people come to endorse the beliefs they hold or the wants they seek to satisfy. Also, for many purposes, establishing such relationships may be all that is required, particularly when it seems fairly obvious what the mental reactions will be. Thus we can generally take it for granted that employees will welcome an increase in salary or a promotion without checking on wants and beliefs.

## Organizational Buying

There have been attempts at applying the adoption process to organizational and industrial buying (Ozanne and Churchill, 1968) and also attempts at an overall modeling of the industrial buying process (Sheth, 1973). But perhaps most studies of industrial buying processes have focused on describing the sequence of stages in buying rather than seeking causal processes. Similarly, studies on the composition of the decision-making unit (DMU) have been mainly descriptive. More theoretically driven are the studies of the interactions and conflicts among members of the DMU given the buying situation and the differential self-interests of members. But the major studies in industrial buying have been concerned with developing a typology (a classification based on types) of buying situations in terms of the problems and uncertainties generated by the product buyer–supplier relationships, competitive conditions in the market and so on. A typical aim has been to discover categories that suggest what would be logically implied as to choice criteria. There are two problems here. The primary one lies in developing categories that imply *all* the likely factors and the relative weightings that will be brought to bear on the buying decision. The second problem is whether we can just assume that buyers will act rationally in line with the logic.

## Genetic Explanations

Some philosophers distinguish between "nomothetic" and "idiographic" disciplines. Nomothetic disciplines look for general laws connecting kinds of events so that inferences can be drawn from them. Idiographic disciplines do not seek laws or theories to cover whole classes of cases but focus on the "unique" event in all its individuality. But the idea of grasping connections among unique events, through some form of "intuitive understanding," rather than calling upon generalizations strikes many philosophers as nonsense. However, if we interpret idiographic studies as simply those that focus on explaining what happened on a particular occasion as opposed to explaining what generally happens in the circumstances, this is a common practice of both managers and historians. But neither the historian nor the manager is likely to rely solely on intuition, instead generalizing, where possible, about what would be a reasonable thing to do given the situation. Also, both historians and managers are likely to have hypotheses in searching out the facts, so their search is directed.

Marketing managers, then, insofar as they focus on particular market events, can be viewed as undertaking idiographic studies since their concern is often to explain the specific event. But idiographic studies in this sense need not rely solely on intuition. Even though the problem may be seemingly unique, it does not follow from this that treating the problem as belonging to a class of problems (and hence amenable to a certain type of treatment) is not useful. In fact, it is essential and the only way to interpret what is meant by experience.

The aim of the genetic explanation is to show how some specific problematic situation evolved. We start with the problematic situation and analyze retrospectively to tease out the chain of causal factors that brought about the situation. The genetic explanation is useful in explaining some particular event like a falloff in sales. It has never formally been adopted in the marketing literature (though not uncommon in case studies), perhaps because the focus in the genetic explanation is on explaining *unique* events rather than explaining *kinds* of events. In general, genetic explanations provide only weak, non-rigorous modes of causal, temporal explanation.

The first step in the genetic explanation is to define the problematic situation through a cross-sectional or *situational analysis*. The next step is a form of *historical review*. The factors that are believed to be at work in bringing about the problematic situation are identified and listed. This presupposes hypotheses as to what factors might be causally relevant. The next step is to show how the events involving these factors historically interrelate to bring about the problematic situation. In other words, we identify the events that seem to be significant in initiating the process leading to the current problematic situation. The criterion for choosing any event as part of the sequence of events is its appearance as a condition for subsequent events leading to the problematic situation.

The appendix to this chapter shows how a genetic explanation can be charted. Such charting helps to reduce the errors of omission in the causal chain and clarify sequences by picturing the interrelationships. (The appendix deals with the dropping of the Castle Stamping Company as supplier to the Scott Purchasing Group.)

# APPENDIX: LOMAX CASE

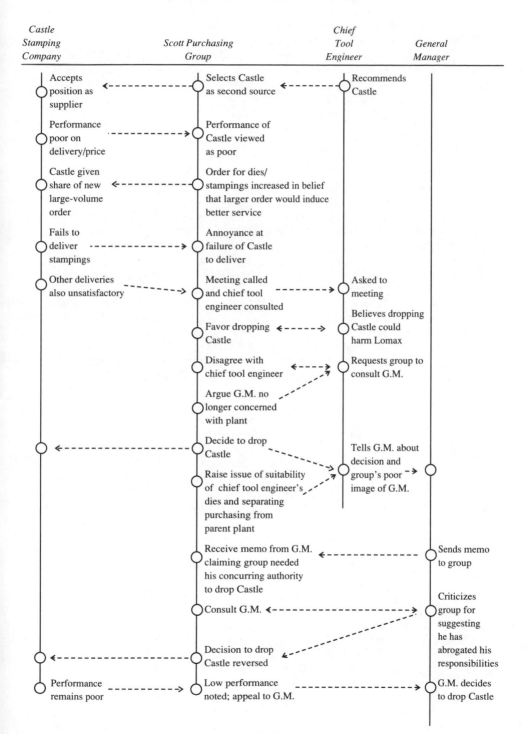

FIGURE 4.5.

# References

Allport, Gordon (1935). "Attitudes." In *Handbook of Social Psychology,* edited by C. Murchison. Worcester, MA: Clark University Press.

Colley, Russell H. (1961). *Defining Advertising Goals for Measured Advertising Results.* New York: Association of National Advertisers.

Dhalla, N. K., and S. Yuspeh (1976). "Forget the Product Life Cycle Concept." *Harvard Business Review* 54 (July–August), pp. 102–12.

Dretske, Fred (1988). *Explaining Behavior: Reasons in a World of Causes.* Cambridge, MA: The MIT Press.

Dröge, Cornelia (1989). "Shaping the Route to Attitude Change: Central Versus Peripheral Processing Through Comparative Versus Noncomparative Advertising." *Journal of Marketing Research* 26 (May), pp. 193–204.

Fennell, Geraldine (1978). "Consumers' Perceptions of the Product-Use Situation." *Journal of Marketing* 41 (April), pp. 38–47.

Fishbein, M., and I. Ajzen (1975). *Belief, Attitude, Intention and Behavior: An Introduction to Theory and Research.* Reading, MA: Addison-Wesley.

Fishbein, M. (1967). "Attitudes and the Prediction of Behavior." In M. Fishbein, *Readings in Attitude Theory and Measurement.* New York: John Wiley & Sons.

Foxall, Gordon (1984). "Evidence for Attitudinal-Behavioral Consistency: Implications for Consumer Research Paradigms." *Journal of Economic Psychology* 5, pp. 71–92.

Foxall, Gordon (1990). *Consumer Psychology in Behavioural Perspective.* London: Routledge.

Greiner, Larry E. (1972). "Evolution and Revolution as Organizations Grow." *Harvard Business Review* (July–August).

Harman, Gilbert (1986). *Change of View.* Cambridge, MA: The MIT Press.

Holbrook, Morris B., John O'Shaughnessy, and Stephen Bell (1990). "Actions and Reactions in the Consumption Experience: The Complemenatry Roles of Reasons and Emotions in Consumer Behavior." In *Research in Consumer Behavior,* edited by Elizabeth C. Hirschman. Greenwich, CT: JAI Press.

Hollander, Stanley C. (1960). "The Wheel of Retailing." *Journal of Marketing* (July), pp. 37–42.

Howard, John A. (1989). *Consumer Behavior in Marketing Strategy.* Englewood Cliffs, NJ: Prentice Hall.

Jamieson, Linda F., and Frank M. Bass (1989). "Adjusting Stated Intention Measures to Predict Trial Purchase of New Products: A Comparison of Models and Methods." *Journal of Marketing Research* 26 (August), pp. 336–45.

Kimberly, J. R., Robert H. Miles, and associates (1980). *The Organizational Life Cycle.* San Francisco: Jossey-Bass.

Krugman, Herbert E. (1965). "The Impact of Television Advertising: Learning Without Involvement." *Public Opinion Quarterly* 29 (Fall), pp. 249–356.

Lambkin, Mary, and George S. Day (1989). "Evolutionary Processes in Competitive Markets: Beyond the Product Life Cycle." *Journal of Marketing* 53 (July), pp. 4–20.

Lavidge, Robert J., and Gary A. Steiner (1961). "A Model for Predictive Measurements of Advertising Effectiveness." *Journal of Marketing* 25 (October), pp. 59–62.

Lutz, Richard (1985). "Affective and Cognitive Antecedents of Attitude Toward the Ad: A Conceptual Framework." In *Psychological Processes and Advertising Effects,* edited by L. F. Alwitt and A. A. Mitchell. Hillsdale, NJ: Lawrence Erlbaum Associates, pp. 45–64.

Mackenzie, Scott B., and Richard J. Lutz (1989). "An Empirical Examination of the Structural Antecedents of Attitude Toward the Ad in an Advertising Pretesting Context." *Journal of Marketing* 53 (April), pp. 48–65.

McGuire, William J. (1978). "An Information Processing Model of Advertising Effectiveness." In *Behavioral and Management Science in Marketing,* edited by Harry L. Davis and Alvin J. Silk. New York: Ronald/Wiley.

McNair, M. P. (1958). "Significant Trends and Developments in the Postwar Period." In *Competitive Distribution in a Free, High-Level Economy and Its Implications for the University,* edited by A. B. Smith. Pittsburgh: University of Pittsburgh Press, pp. 1–25 at pp. 17–18.

Midgley, David F. (1981). "Toward a Theory of the Product Life Cycle: Explaining Diversity." *Journal of Marketing* 45 (Fall), pp. 109–15.

Mitchell, Andrew A. (1980). "The Use of an Information Processing Approach to Understanding Effects." In *Advances in Consumer Research,* Vol. 7, edited by J. C. Olsen. Ann Arbor, MI: Association of Consumer Research.

Mittal, Banwari (1990). "The Relative Roles of Brand Beliefs and Attitude Toward the Ad as Mediators of Brand Attitude: A Second Look." *Journal of Marketing Research* 27 (May), pp. 209–14.

Mohr, Lawrence B. (1982). *Explaining Organizational Behavior.* San Francisco: Jossey-Bass.

Ozanne, Urban B., and Gilbert A. Churchill (1968). "Adoption Research: Information Sources in the Industrial Purchase Decision." *Proceedings,* Fall Conference (Chicago: American Marketing Association).

Petty, Richard E., and John T. Cacioppo (1979). "Issue Involvement Can Increase or Decrease Persuasion by Enhancing Message Relevant Cognitive Responses." *Journal of Personality and Social Psychology* 37 (October), pp. 1915–26.

Petty, Richard E., and John T. Cacioppo (1983). "Central and Peripheral Routes to Persuasion: Application to Advertising." In *Advertising and Consumer Psychology,* edited by Larry Percy and Arch Woodside. Lexington, MA: Lexington Books, pp. 3–23.

Petty, Richard E., John T. Cacioppo, and David Schumann (1983). "Central and Peripheral Routes to Advertising Effectiveness: The Moderating Role of Involvement." *Journal of Consumer Research* 10 (September), pp. 135–46.

Popper, Karl R. (1957). *The Poverty of Historicism.* New York: Harper Torchbooks: London: Routledge and Kegan Paul.

Porter, Michael E. (1990). *The Competitive Advantage of Nations.* New York: Free Press.

Ray, Michael L. (1982). *Advertising and Communication Management.* Englewood Cliffs, NJ: Prentice-Hall.

Rogers, Everett M. (1962). *Diffusion of Innovation.* New York: Free Press.

Rossiter, John R., and Larry Percy (1987). *Advertising and Promotion Management.* New York: McGraw-Hill.

Rostow, W. W. (1960). *The Stages of Economic Growth.* Cambridge: Cambridge University Press.

Sheth, Jagdish N. (1973). "A Model of Industrial Buyer Behavior." *Journal of Marketing* 37 (October), pp. 50–56.

Tellis, Gerard J. (1988). "Advertising Exposure, Loyalty and Brand Purchase: A Two-Stage Model of Choice." *Journal of Marketing Research* 30 (May), pp. 134–44.

Weitz, Barton A. (1981). "Effectiveness in Sales Interactions: A Contingency Framework." *Journal of Marketing* 45 (Winter), pp. 85–103.

Wicker, A. W. (1969). "Attitudes v. Actions: The Relationships of Verbal and Overt Responses to Attitude Objects." *Journal of Social Issues* 25, pp. 41–78.

# 5

# Teleological Explanation: Goal Ascription, Reasons, and the Rationality Principle

People are governed by the head; a kind heart is of
little value in chess.

Nicolas-Sebastien Chamfort (1741–1794)

Although the reasons that lead consumer *X* to buy brand *Y* can be viewed as causing the action (see Chapter 2), the explanatory power of the reason-giving explanation lies in the rationality of the action, interpreting rationality to be coextensive with the exercise of reason. The most basic assumption we typically make about human beings is that they can reason and in reasoning they aim at rationality. This is so even though attributing rationality to an action entails evaluating that action against some standard about which there can be disagreement. This chapter considers various views of rationality, whether there are defensible alternatives to the rational model, and whether explanations of large-scale phenomena are to be built from rational explanations of behavior at the individual level.

## Nature of the Goal Ascription Explanation

Ernest Nagel (1979) defines a teleological explanation as one that explains in terms of either goal ascription or function ascription. This chapter deals with goal ascription explanations; the next chapter deals with function ascription. The explanation of action in terms of its rationality falls under the goal ascription mode of explanation, even though all goal-seeking actions do not meet the full conditions for rationality.

Where goal ascription is used to explain action, it does so by specifying the goals of the action. Goal ascription explanations take the form of "he did it *in order to . . . , in order that . . . , for the sake of . . . , for the purpose of . . . ,*" and so on. Goal ascription is the way the nonspecialist explains action since to understand the goal or purpose of an action is to understand its meaning as action.

As a minimum, for an explanation to be rational it must be goal-directed. Goal ascription explanations are teleological in that they specify the action's purpose to account for it. Voluntary actions like buying are goal-directed in that they create conditions for bringing about some goal or remove the conditions impeding the realization of the goal.

Motivation is typically viewed teleologically in that we view people as being motivated to achieve some goal or want. But we need to distinguish between acting *for* a purpose (*purposeful* behavior) and acting *with* a purpose (*purposive* behavior). Intentional action is purposive, whereas psychoanalytic theory claims that unconscious motivation causes purposeful behavior that is not intentional (Robinson, 1985). If we accept that purposive behavior is causation by intentional states, we are likely to accept determinism, interpreted as asserting that every event owes its existence to some set of antecedents. In this chapter we focus exclusively on acting with a purpose.

Intentional action is generally considered conscious action, since having an intention suggests having a goal in mind; to act on an intention means believing that such action will lead to achieving the goal. Kagan (1989), a psychologist, denies the degree of consciousness that this implies. For him consciousness is analogous to life in a fire station: like firefighters who spring into action to fight fires only when the alarm goes off, we spring into conscious deliberation only when some problem arises. This may be true for much of what we term habitual buying.

Goal ascription explanations of intentional behavior, implicitly or explicitly, refer to wants and beliefs. In seeking goals, people try to coordinate their wants and beliefs into some coherent system. Such wants and beliefs are viewed by naturalists as reasons that operate, through intentions, to cause action. Nagel thus describes the goal ascription explanation along these lines:

> The "goal" G of an action or process is said to be some state of affairs intended by a human agent; the intention itself is an "internal mental state" which, coupled with the internal state of "wanting" G together with "believing" that an action A would contribute to the realization of G, is allegedly a causal determinant of the ensuing action A. "Goal-directed" behavior is then the action A undertaken by the agent for the sake of achieving the goal. (1979, p. 278)

But to make the connection between reasons and action conceptually watertight demands more than this. As Collin (1985) points out, a person who wants goal G to be the case, and who believes that performing the action A will bring about G, will perform A providing:

1. he believes G will not come about without his action;
2. he is able to do A and knows this;
3. the external conditions for doing A are present;
4. he knows of no better way of bringing about G than by doing A; and
5. he knows of no reason why he should not do A.

Providing reasons for an action makes that action meaningful. There is always a dissatisfaction with explanations that fail to show "how the actions of the people involved were the actions of conscious human beings, reacting to an environment, trying to make sense of it and pursuing various goals in their actions with more or less success. . . . Only explanations which take cognizance of the meaningful aspect of action will satisfy us as human observers" (Marsh, 1982).

Many social scientists agree with Nagel in viewing beliefs and wants as both *reasons for* action and *causes of* action, although they may use other terms for wants and beliefs: motive, need, or utility for want; cognition, expectancies, or subjective probability for beliefs. But if we accept that wants and beliefs are both reasons and causes of action, this does not mean that the reason-giving explanation is a causal one. If this seems like academic hair-splitting, Rosenberg (1988) regards the issue as fundamental. He argues that if the reason-giving explanation is causal, then naturalism is vindicated. If, on the other hand, the reasons for action explain, not because they are causes, but because they are reasons, then social science must focus on interpretation of action to demonstrate its intelligibility.

We will not reenter this debate but simply argue that we seem to expect people not to act against what reason suggests. If they do so, though there is nothing restraining them, philosophers use the Greek word "akrasia" for the weakness of "will" characterizing such situations. Reasoned action itself comes into its own when important choices have to be made, and there is uncertainty over the costs and benefits of various options. But most behavior is perhaps not based on any (highly conscious) deliberation to choose the best action–consequence sequence. As Dretske (1988) says, much behavior is like shivering, perspiring, coughing, weeping, salivating, dreaming, choking, or fumbling; or emotional reactions like blushing; or automatic reactions like withdrawing one's hand from a red-hot surface. Even behavior that is intentional may not be preplanned. Thus "impulse buying" does not evolve from any serious deliberation on action–consequence sequences but from a desire for instant gratification. Acting on impulse is, however, intentional in that consumers at the time of purchase had the intention of buying even if the intention was not preplanned and even if, after the purchase, there was regret.

## Rationality Principle

Lying behind the idea that people act for reasons is the rationality principle, which assumes people take the action that most promotes their goals. This principle is one criterion for rational behavior.

The most basic assumption in microeconomics, history, and anthropology (but not always in psychology or sociology) is that people act rationally. It is a basic assumption in marketing. Thus the adoption of benefit segmentation and the tenet of customer orientation assume that consumers are rational and informed and, as a consequence, will choose those offerings that come closest to what they seek. Other actors in the market are also considered rational. For example, in developing a competitive strategy, marketers take account of the inferred goals, beliefs, and situational constraints of major competitors and try to predict their behavior on the assumption they will act rationally. Game theory, or the theory of games, is the study of rational strategic action in competitive situations where the outcomes to each competitor depend on the decisions of others. The primary goal of the theory is to establish, *through formal reasoning alone,* what strategies competitors should adopt if they are to pursue their interests rationally. But rationality that confines itself to choosing the best means to achieve goals (the economist's view) is a narrow concept. Many social philosophers and social scientists would also demand some minimal degree of rationality in beliefs and wants. This is implicit in what Pettit lists as the postulates lying behind the notion of people being rational agents:

(i) Every human action springs from a desire or set of desires which, in view of the agent's beliefs, it promises to satisfy.

(ii) Every agent's desires, so far as they are properly human, are explicable by public standards of normality.

(iii) Every agent's beliefs, so far as they are properly human, are explicable by public standards of normality.

(iv) Beliefs and desires lead to action by familiar rational principles which it is the job of decision theory to spell out.

(v) Beliefs, desires and decision principles can sometimes be construed in advance of action from past behavior—assuming personal consistency—and from present circumstance—assuming commonness of response. Other factors, such as emotional expression, may also facilitate this sort of interpretation. (1978, p. 45)

Economists equate economic optimality with efficiency of *means* (the Pareto optimum) and ignore the content of goals. This may suit the economist's purposes but would elsewhere prove too restrictive. We can rationally criticize goals and even persuade consumers to change goal priorities. Thus, for example, consumers

1. may misconstrue their goals and wants: they may want what they do not think they want and may think they want what in fact they do not want because of erroneous beliefs;

2. may overlook goals they would pursue if made aware of what attaining the goal (what it *really* would be like) could do to enrich their lives; and

3. may lack the imagination to visualize what goals should be pursued since there is difficulty in knowing how much of the goal should be sought, how much of goal attainment is being provided by alternative offerings, and what different tradeoffs mean in terms of satisfaction.

These difficulties suggest that consumers may not have precise goals and may not know exactly what they want, simply setting out to see what is available, avoiding any attempt to tie up their precise wants in advance. Elsewhere in the social sciences, outside of economics, acting rationally typically takes into account the rationality of means *and* of ends. For example, few social scientists accept that wants that are injurious to health (e.g., use of heroin) are other than irrational unless there is a compensating reason (e.g., urgent need to overcome the pain of a dying man).

In economics, people are assumed to act rationally. Hence, in defining what is meant by "acting rationally," economists assume they are describing actual behavior (Sen, 1987). Economists have formalized the view that people act rationally and avoided some of the problems inherent to reason-giving explanations. This is not to say that economists do not speak of reasons. Hicks (1979) speaks of reasons for action and regards the reason-giving explanation, like all other explanations, as essentially causal. But economists generally speak of maximizing "utility," with the word itself being left uninterpreted or undefined so maximizing utility becomes the maximizing of any objectives or satisfactions you want to maximize. To the economist, rationality is the maximization of utility with utility itself simply reflecting the subjective valuation we put on the goods and services we buy. This allows the economist to talk of the ordering (ranking) of preferences or wants on the basis of their utility, which, conceptually at least, gets around the problem of having to say, for example, "that it is rational to choose brand $X$ *only* if there are no other overriding wants." Viewing consumers as ranking preferences on the basis of their relative subjective utility makes the rationality principle equivalent to the maximization of available utility.

Economists assume people *can* rank their preferences for various action–consequence sequences and convert the ordering into a utility function. In the simplest case, beliefs are held constant by the assumption of perfect knowledge of feasible options and corresponding outcomes (consequences), so that consumers can with certainty choose the higher ranking outcome to maximize utility. Where perfect knowledge cannot be taken for granted, beliefs cannot be held constant as beliefs about risks will vary. Where decisions are taken under conditions of risk, the option selected, economists suggest, will be that which maximizes *expected* utility. Expected utility is calculated by taking the value of the outcome and multiplying it by its probability of occurrence. Where such probabilities cannot be calculated from actual available data on long-run positive frequencies the decision-maker may rely on subjective probabilities (informed guesses or estimates). The rational expectations approach has the merit of being simple but has not had the predictive power that was intended.

Most economists focus purely on "revealed preferences." The economist in effect observes what the consumer buys and deduces preferences from these choices. This approach abandons any attempt to explain action at the individual level since beliefs and wants cannot be inferred from action alone. Sen (1987), an economist, argues that, as a consequence, the revealed preference approach leads to underestimating the influence on choice of other factors beyond self-interest.

Where complete uncertainty prevails the attitude of the decision-makers is said to determine the rule adopted. The "maximin" rule reflects a pessimistic attitude in assuming the worst outcomes for all options and so choice is the best of a bad lot, that is, the maximum of the minimum payoffs. On the other hand, the "maximax" rule reflects an optimistic attitude in assuming the best outcomes for all options and so choice is the best of the best, that is, the maximum of the maximum payoffs. The final strategy, the "minimax," assumes an attitude somewhere in between in choosing the minimum of the maximum payoffs.

## The Probability of Outcomes

We can never be entirely certain about the outcomes or the consequences of our actions. Because so many decisions involve estimating the probable consequences of actions, various methods have arisen for calculating probable outcomes. There are at least three methods with different justifications for applying the calculus of probability to real-world events: relative frequency, logical probability, and subjective probability.

### The Relative Frequency View

The relative frequency view identifies probability with the long-run relative frequency with which the event has occurred in the "same" circumstances in the past. As estimates of probability here will vary with sample size, the relative frequency view takes probability to be the *limit* of relative frequency, that is, the position where the estimates of probability change negligibly with further increases in sample size.

### Logical Probability

The decision-maker does not usually know the relative frequencies of the various consequences associated with various courses of action; moreover, historical data may no longer be representative. An alternative is "logical probability" (Keynes, 1921), where the probability adopted expresses the degree to which the evidence justifies a particular conclusion. Probability here is always relative to the evidence. But just as the probability of an event on the relative frequency view can differ according to the class to which it has been assigned, so logical probability can vary according to which evidence is called upon and how the evidence is interpreted and weighted. We can, of course, talk about logical probability being relative to the *total* evidence, but deciding what constitutes the total evidence is the problem.

"Expectation" is a term commonly used both in psychology and in economics for beliefs about the logical probability of an event. In economics, we speak of "rational expectations" when such expectations are based on the best information available. When used to predict the actions of others, however, danger lies in supposing that people living in society use the same models and the same information as the economist studying them (Elster, 1989b). Boland (1982) claims that the rational expectations approach assumes an inductivist theory of learning or the erroneous idea that *firm* knowledge about the future is available from inductive generalizations from historical data.

## Subjective Probability

Where evidence cannot be set out for evaluation, even the logical probability view is too demanding, hence a resort to subjective probability. The development of this view owes most to the work of Ramsey (1931/1950), Savage (1954), and de Finetti (1964). The subjective probability view is basic to Bayesian statistics and decision theory in general. We will illustrate its use and abuse in the "decision calculus" approach to estimating response functions such as the response of sales to advertising expenditure (Little, 1970) and the response of sales to increased selling effort (Little and Lodish, 1969).

Decision calculus rests on estimates of subjective probabilities being given by the decision-maker. Thus if the marketing manager is asked to estimate the likely sales resulting from a 50% increase in expenditure on advertising, he or she might produce something like Table 5.1 (Table 5.1 represents a more elaborate procedure than that adopted by Little and Lodish but is more suited to the purposes of exposition.) Column (1) shows the various sales ranges within any of which the resulting sales might fall. Column (2) gives the median of each of the ranges in column (1). Column (3) gives the subjective probability estimate of the sales falling within each of the ranges shown in column (1). Column (4) simply multiplies column (2) by column (3). The sum of column (4) is $10.4 million, which is the *expected value* of sales. The subjective probabilities in column (3) are viewed as representing degrees of belief, though, to ensure the probabilities conform to the probability calculus, the probabilities in column (3) are made to add up to unity.

When subjective probability estimates are equated with degrees of belief, degree of belief is commonly measured by the odds a person is prepared to accept in a bet. Popper

TABLE 5.1. Estimate of Likely Sales Given an Increase in Expenditure on Advertising of 50%

| *(1)* | *(2)* | *(3)* | *(4)* |
|---|---|---|---|
| | *Median of Range* | *Subjective Probability of* | |
| *Sales Range* | *in Column (1)* | *Achieving Sales Range* | *Expected Sales, Column* |
| *(million $)* | *(million $)* | *in Column (1)* | *(2) × Column (3) (million $)* |
| 2–6 | 4 | 0.20 | 0.8 |
| over 6–10 | 8 | 0.25 | 2.0 |
| over 10–14 | 12 | 0.30 | 3.6 |
| over 14–18 | 16 | 0.25 | 4.0 |
| | | 1.00 | $10.4 |

regards this as incredibly naive: "If I like to bet, and if the stakes are not high, I might accept any odds. If the stakes are very high, I might not accept a bet at all. If I cannot escape the bet, say because the life of my best friend is at stake, I may feel the need to reassure myself of the most trivial proposition" (1972, p. 79).

The strength of belief and the confidence we have in a belief can be distinguished in that additional evidence may increase the strength or intensity of a belief in the sense of making it harder to stop believing it true, yet this may not increase my confidence in the belief in the sense of my willingness to act on that belief. Although some distinction along these lines was made by Keynes, it is not always clear which is meant when we speak of degrees of belief. Yet it is important to know which is in fact meant.

The question arises as to whether subjective probabilities are part of some cognitive theory of psychology explaining how decisions are *actually* made or part of some *normative* theory of decision-making suggesting how decisions about response functions *ought* to be made by experienced managers in the absence of objective, empirical information on probabilities. These are the basic questions addressed by Kyburg (1983).

Those who claim that subjective probabilities capture what *actually* happens argue subjective probabilities represent degrees of belief in an outcome. Since it is impossible *not* to have a degree of belief in any outcome, it is always possible to provide a subjective probability. This argument offers support for the claim that Table 5.1 simply systematizes actual practice. But it is not clear that beliefs can be ranked in a *linear* array reflecting degrees of belief. A belief is a multidimensional construct embracing the intensity with which the belief is held, that is, the strength of belief and the degree of confidence with which it is held and its actual salience. Thus I could believe each of five sales ranges in Table 5.1 has the probability 0.2 yet hold each of these beliefs with different degrees of strength. On this basis it is not clear what is meant by degree of belief. If, as commonly supposed, it means the degree of confidence in the belief, it is not clear how different degrees of confidence can be equated with different degrees of subjective probability. In any case, as pointed out in Chapter 4, it is not clear that people in their reasoning or deliberating do normally associate their beliefs with explicit degrees of confidence since it would typically be too complicated for them to do so.

Another problem is that it is not clear that subjective probability estimates represent degrees of belief as opposed to being subjective estimates of relative frequencies. Moreover, in whatever way degree of belief is interpreted there is no evidence that the degrees of belief in an outcome will satisfy the probability calculus. The probability calculus, like arithmetic, is not innate. Hence on this basis alone Table 5.1 cannot be said to represent actual decision-making.

Finally, on reflection, managers may assign a probability, but this does not mean they had any such probabilities in mind until asked. Subjective probabilities can always be elicited. The question is whether such probabilities are reliable or possess any predictive validity. In fact, the actual subjective probabilities can vary with the method used to elicit them. Commenting on this, Elster (1989a) points out that if we were truly measuring something in the person's mind, the result should not depend on the method of measurement. Since it does, the probability is an artifact of the procedure.

If the subjective probabilities in decision calculus do not mirror any actual decision process, should they be part of some suggested normative process? The following are possible grounds:

1. Probabilities reflect the degree of evidence favoring the outcome. Can the subjective probabilities in Table 5.1 be regarded as proportionate to the degree of evidence? If

they were, they would no longer be subjective but logical probabilities. There is no guarantee that subjective probabilities do not just reflect hunch or fancy.

2. The procedure works. Does the decision calculus embodying subjective probability "work" in that predictions are correct? Subjective interpretations of probability vary from one individual to another. There is no way to resolve such differences except by changing to another type of probability (logical probability or the relative frequency view of probability). Therefore, the reliability of the technique cannot be asserted, so its predictive validity is automatically suspect. What we know about subjective probabilities does not increase our confidence in their validity. Thus Tversky and Kahneman (1983) found subjective probability estimates relate, for example, to the availability of items in memory with the result that people overestimate sensational cases like airplane crashes.

3. The procedure is rational. It could be argued (Little and Lodish, 1981) that the subjective probabilities in Table 5.1 would be based on knowledge of customers, market trends, competitive activity, and the like. But how can this assertion be verified unless such knowledge is set out? Of course, although managers will always have reasons for supporting the probabilities they offer, such reasons may or may not be reasons that would be accepted as supporting evidence. But could not subjective probability estimates arise from thought experiments? Kuhn (1977) points out that if thought experiments are to be successful, nothing about the imagined situation must be entirely unfamiliar or strange. Do expenditure levels and promotional campaigns *never before experienced* meet this requirement? Thought experiments embody no new information about the world, so the addition to knowledge is limited to deductions and corrections of conceptual errors.

4. The procedure is accepted by the relevant community of scholars. The procedure exemplified in Table 5.1 is in line with accepted procedure in decision theory. It is accepted because of the absence of rival approaches rather than satisfaction with the approach itself.

Subjective probabilities should reflect *relevant experience* in the same way that I might judge the probable conduct of a friend of long standing. Also, if subjective probabilities are just opinions, they are better captured by some interval (e.g., 0.3 to 0.6) than by some specific probability. On this basis Table 5.1 might be modified to Table 5.2.

A more fundamental approach is to try to specify the rules or factors used by managers to determine likely sales responses to different levels of expenditure or effort. A basis for such an approach is that given by Lilien and Little (1976) for determining industrial marketing budgets.

TABLE 5.2  Revised Expected Sales Calculation

| (1) Sales Range (million $) | (2) Median of Range (million $) | (3) Subjective Probability Range (million $) | (4) Expected Sales Range (million $) | |
|---|---|---|---|---|
| 0–6 | 4 | 0.20 ± 0.05 | 0.60 | 1.00 |
| over 6–10 | 8 | 0.25 ± 0.05 | 1.60 | 2.40 |
| over 10–14 | 12 | 0.30 ± 0.05 | 3.00 | 4.20 |
| over 14–18 | 16 | 0.25 ± 0.05 | 3.20 | 4.80 |
| | | | $8.40 | $12.40 |

We all have to deal with uncertainty as a fact of life, but many philosophers question whether probability theory will remain the dominant methodology by which to tackle uncertainty. Elster (1989b) makes the point that we simply hate to admit uncertainty and indeterminacy in decision-making. Rather than accept the limits to reason, we prefer "the rituals of reason" and, wanting to have reasons for what we do, we create reasons where none exist.

## Criticism of Rationality Models

Rational choice theory is first and foremost a normative theory and only secondarily an explanatory/predictive theory. As a normative theory it can be indeterminate in the sense that its prescriptions are often ambiguous. As an explanatory/predictive theory, it is inadequate in the sense that people frequently fail to follow its prescriptions (Elster, 1989b). Where rival offerings are undifferentiated, it is accepted that rational choice theory cannot be expected to predict as the consumer may just pick a brand on whim. But when rival offerings do have different strengths and weaknesses, it is commonly assumed that consumers can judge the relative utility of offerings, that is, order their preferences in line with the suppositions of the multiattribute model. But consumers may in fact be unable to rank and compare offerings, even when they fill in questionnaires as if they can. This is not because they are indifferent in choosing, say, which house to buy; that is, they may not know which house they prefer yet not believe the options were equally good. If they did believe that the options were equally good, a slight reduction in the price of one of the houses should—but may not—clinch the deal. It may just happen that the options are incommensurable, which means there can be only an incomplete ordering of preferences and no choice can be called the optimum choice. In any case, if, for example, industrial buyers do think in terms of the multiattribute model, they may be too uncertain to assign numbers and may have to fall back on rules of thumb like the maximin or maximax rules, in which case rational choice theory would be indeterminate. Rational choice theory may also be obliged to take account of the beliefs of others (e.g., in negotiation), and there may be no way of forming a rational belief about the future actions of others.

In economics, maximizing utility is interpreted as maximizing self-interest. On the surface, such a view would rule out public goods like roads and public libraries, in that everyone would seek to be a "free rider," enjoying the benefits and letting others pay. But economic self-interest need not be so narrowly interpreted. Thus there can be a "tit-for-tat" strategy. If firm X recognizes that everyone would benefit if competitors cooperated, firm X might start the ball rolling by acting cooperatively in the first round. In the next round firm X does what the competitor did the last time, which means further cooperative behavior or retaliation. In any case, the cooperative behavior and the imitative behavior continue until the competitor gets the message that tit-for-tat yields the largest payoff. Tit-for-tat is put forward to explain why the free rider phenomenon is not more widespread, but it does not adequately explain how cooperation comes about (Rosenberg, 1988).

Sen (1987) lists the major weaknesses of mainstream economic theory:

1. It takes goals as given so the object is to choose the best means to fulfill the goals.
2. It assumes actual behavior is rational behavior.
3. It assumes rational behavior can be identified with (a) the maximization of self-interest and/or (b) internal consistency of choice.

He acknowledges that identifying actual behavior with rational behavior leads to error but assuming, as an alternative, that irrationality governs behavior leads to even more error. Yet Sen questions the notion of maximizing self-interest since there is no evidence that the maximization of self-interest provides the best possible approximation to actual behavior or that maximizing individual self-interest leads to optimum conditions. He points out that even in a free market economy like Japan, a departure from self-interested behavior played a substantial part in economic success. Sen asks: "Why should it be considered uniquely rational to pursue self-interest to the exclusion of everything else?" He regards taking universal selfishness as a requirement for rationality to be patently absurd: the pursuit of self-interest is not the only motivation lying behind action. In particular, he makes a case for ethical motivation. As Sen says, a person's claim that he does not buy South African goods may well be relevant to determining the contents of his supermarket basket.

Sen argues that we need to see people as free *agents*. People as free agents form goals and values that lead them to consider more than their own well-being. Economics, with its roots in utilitarianism, ignores the agency aspect of people, an aspect where maximizing individual well-being is not likely to be the only thing valued.

Sen discusses the identification of rational behavior with consistency of choice. Consistency of choice is variously interpreted. One interpretation is that an individual must have consistent beliefs and wants so that if $A$ is preferred to $B$ and $B$ to $C$, then $A$ must be preferred to $C$. This transitivity rule is often broken. Take, for example, the so-called paradox of voting by which, in a majority vote for, say, the choice of the nation's capitol, Washington would be beaten by Boston. Boston, in turn, would be beaten by Chicago, yet in a vote between Washington and Chicago, Washington would win. Arrow's theorem shows such problems can arise with *any* conceivable method of aggregating individual preferences that meet certain conditions. In any case, when preferences are in a state of flux they are likely to violate any assumption about stable and consistent preference ordering; the cost of information and expectations about the market are additional unpredictable influences. Sen argues that consistency can in fact never be an adequate criterion of rationality in that rational choice must demand some correspondence between what people are trying to achieve and how they go about it.

Where tradeoffs are required in producing what Sen calls the "balanced complete ordering outcome," the ordering can mislead as people frequently have doubts about their orderings. Sen speaks of "partial ordering" since some options are left unordered because of the difficulty of finding a basis for ordering. This is similar to the point made earlier by Elster.

Many other economists have been equally critical. Frank (1988) regards as false the view of man as a rational, self-interested calculator. He focuses on the role of emotions in upholding ethical conduct in business and elsewhere (see Chapter 9). Gabor (1977) demonstrates that businesspeople are not just profit-driven when pricing but consider factors like social responsibility, reputation, and prestige.

The notion of maximizing is also questioned by Simon (1957), who uses the term "satisficing" to describe the more typical behavior of people searching until they find a workable (satisfactory) solution rather than an optimum one. There are difficulties in optimizing: knowing all the relevant alternatives and their consequences requires quantities of information; resources and time pressures are limited; and, finally, the "right" balance among multiple and conflicting goals must be found and sustained. Simon (1991) lists additional criticism of the rational model as reflected in the concept of subjective expected utility maximization (SEU). First, he argues that following the SEU rule would impose computational demands on decision-makers that could not be sustained. Second, he claims that the empirical evidence shows that people do not have comprehensive, consistent utility functions that would enable them to order any set of alternatives that is put before them; preferences are, in fact, highly contingent upon situational factors and upon the focus of attention of people to particular features of the environment. Third, the SEU theory fails to explain (1) how the utility function (if there is one) could obtain its content and shape, (2) how items are "placed on the agenda for decision making," (3) how problems are formulated, and (4) where the alternatives of choice come from.

Classical microeconomics assigns no role to generosity, social conscience, goodwill, or fairness, yet the evidence shows people resisting transactions they perceive as unfair and customers resisting price increases not seemingly justified by cost increases (Kahneman, Knetsch, and Thaler, 1986). Rawls (1980) regards acting purely from self-interest as "unreasonable" behavior on the ground that willingness to be guided by reasons from an impartial or intersubjective viewpoint defines what is called "reasonable" behavior. In line with this view Darwall (1983), a philosopher, claims that there are considerations other than self-centered ones that are reasons for action. Few social scientists have ever doubted this but Darwall's argument is pertinent to marketers.

Darwall distinguishes three sets of reasons, any of which might lie behind some action:

1. The *real* reasons why someone acted as she did.
2. The individual's *expressed* reasons for acting as she did. Reasons 2 may not be the real reasons or, alternatively, may not embrace all of the relevant reasons.
3. *Justificatory* reasons for the individual to so act, that is, the normative reasons that might justify action.

Darwall's argument focuses on the justificatory reasons. Darwall sides with Thomas Nagel in claiming an intimate relationship exists between something being a justificatory reason and its capacity to motivate even if only under ideal conditions. He argues there are *intersubjective* values, like justice, respect for privacy, or seeing meaning to life, that are basic to the idea of community. Such values translate into a set of shared, objective, justificatory reasons for action. They emotionally motivate in that there is a connection between upholding the values and having a sense of self-worth and self-respect; moreover, actively promoting such values expresses our identification with others and theirs with us. As Darwall says, if we were to always act on the strongest desire, then the very notion of settling tradeoffs by reasoning about the matter would probably make little sense: the strongest desire in practice may not be the desire to which we give greatest priority.

Darwall's fundamental point, however, is that practical reasons are at base *impartial* rather than entirely self-centered. This is because thinking about justificatory reasons can lead to new desires. For example, I may have no active desire to support "animal rights," yet seeing a film on cruelty to animals might activate a desire to do something about it. People (including people as consumers) can be moved by new considerations without there being any active antecedent want. As Quine (1987) points out, self-interest, however enlightened, affords no general rational basis for altruism. Yet there is altruism, stemming, partly at least, from the relationship between acting morally and maintaining self-respect: the capacity to care is tied to our emotional nature.

Campbell (1987), a sociologist, in line with Darwall, claims ethical ideas are central in our thinking about what to do since people feel the need to have "good reasons" for their conduct. Much "private talk" (deliberation about what to do) can take as much account of moral obligations as self-interest since morally idealized self-images can be just as much sources of pleasure as aesthetic ones. Etzioni (1989), also a sociologist, points out that human nature is a product of society, which means that behavior is social and so concerned not just with self-interest but with morality.

In terms of marketing, what Darwall would deny is a view of the consumer that is implicit in the customer orientation concept. This is the consumer as a bundle of wants that act as a filter, determing what products or considerations will motivate. As Darwall says, a person's motivational *capacities* are made up not just of a set of needs, wants, or desires but also of the capacity for imagination, sensitivity, and so on. People have a generalized need to show interest in things; to inquire about conditions that might bring about their realization; and, last but not least, to be moved by facts about things. Thus we cannot be absolutely sure what product benefits would lead someone to buy until we have made that person most vividly aware of the potential of those benefits for him.

If consumers considered rational self-interest only, it would be difficult to explain buying actions that reflect a concern for the environment, animals, fair dealings by companies, and so on. Consumers in fact have perceptions of themselves as moral agents and seek to bring their ideals into being. "True" brand loyalty also cannot be explained as purely self-interest. Loyalty, properly conceived (not as just anything that is habitually purchased and liked), implies devotion under conditions where rational calculation would suggest withdrawing support. It implies trust, that is, a partial relinquishment of the demand (at least in the short run) for equal reciprocity in the exchange relationship: loyalty is sticking to the subject through thick and thin, as the expression goes. Even in a market composed of objectively undifferentiated offerings there can be attachment to a brand, stemming usually from past associations, that can be compared to the devotion of a child to a nondescript security blanket.

Another question has to do with the extent to which people are in fact rational. If the proposition "all chosen action is rational" were put forward for testing, there would be no difficulty in finding supporting examples. But there would also be falsifying examples unless we make it just a matter of definition that all chosen action seeks to rationally maximize satisfaction *within the context of the person's own mental representation of the world.* However, it would, of course, be wrong to view someone as irrational simply because that person's knowledge was false since there exists no rational process to guarantee true knowledge (Boland, 1982).

We are all aware that rationality is limited by wishful thinking, emotional reaction, or lack of education generally. But some psychologists claim that most people are prone to certain fallacious intuitions that have nothing to do with emotional problems or intellectual deficiencies. Tversky and Kahneman (1986) show the type of heuristic (rules of thumb) that people use in everyday reasoning. It seems that a person's preference from among a set of options is not independent of the descriptions of those options. For example, variations in the framing of a choice problem can lead to very different preferences. Thus I may not use my credit card if the retailer imposes a 3% charge on credit cards yet continue to use it when there is a 3% discount for paying cash. Tversky and Kahneman, both cognitive psychologists, offer explanations of this and other violations of the accepted tenets of rationality. What has not so far been demonstrated to any degree is the significance for economics and marketing of these violations.

Rationality is a normative goal that, like the Christian ideals, is not disproved because it is never fully attained. Johnson-Laird (1982) shows that only those with training reason along the lines suggested by classical logic. Similarly, Cohen (1986) regards many violations of the tenets of rationality as something to be expected since the tenets presuppose a certain level and type of education. Thus when people infer from "If $p$ then $q$" the proposition "If $q$ then $p$" (the fallacy of affirming the consequent), it does not demonstrate much about how rationally people behave day-to-day. As Cohen says, the concept of a deductive problem in which only the information given should be considered is something inculcated by education. Thus in many real-life situations, people could safely conclude that "If $p$ then $q$, so if $q$ then $p$"; for example, "If you give him a tip, then he'll let you in." This is because in real life there can be situations where "If *and only if p* then $q$" may occur, in which case to infer "If $q$ then $p$" would commit no fallacy since the inference is valid. Experimenters, Cohen warns, should always be wary of supposing that a subject interprets a task in exactly the way the experimenter intends.

The economist's notion of rationality is unable to explain certain features of social living, like sharing of benefits and burdens of cooperation, because it fails to acknowledge that essential to what binds people together are social norms, like the social norm against being a free rider. Elster (1989a) maintains that norms can be internalized and can be emotionally based, and thus he denies that people obey norms only to seek certain self-serving outcomes like avoiding disapproval.

Herrnstein (1988) points to the limitations of the economist's view:

1. There are social motives at work, not just narrow egoistic ones. Neither evolutionary biology nor the evidence of everyday life would support reducing every generous act to self-interest.

2. People may not in fact hold any integral sense of their self-interest but have multiple and conflicting interests.

3. Social motivation cannot be accounted for by economic theory.

4. Every person will have some self-image that leads to the disapproval of certain types of behavior.

5. Indulging in certain types of stimulation produces opposite feelings (see opponent process theory of emotion in Chapter 9).

6. Interpersonal comparisons are a major source of motivation in that, for example, the fairness of a person's pay depends on what co-workers are receiving. Also, reciprocity—returning favors and the like—colors virtually all interpersonal relations.

## Alternatives to Rationality

Elster (1989b) regards rational choice theory as most applicable to medium-sized problems like buying a car, though even here the question of optimal search is largely indeterminate. He also sees the theory as more applicable to the individual buyer than some group of decision-makers. But he also argues, like Sen, that opposing theories are in worse shape.

Satisficing behavior, or Herbert Simon's claim that we stop searching once we have found something "good enough," is one of these opposing theories. Elster argues that this may well describe behavior on occasions but it does not explain, for example, why people have the aspiration levels they do. It also in practice has to make too many assumptions when applied to the theory of the firm, stipulating an aspiration level for each of the many subroutines of the firm.

Another opposing theory is prospect theory, developed by Kahneman and Tversky (1979). This description of how people make choices between probabilistic lotteries modifies subjective expected utility (SEU) theory to account for a series of experimental results which imply that the SEU model does not describe real behavior. Specifically, Kahneman and Tversky provide a number of significant interpretations of these results, all of which are inconsistent with SEU theory. First, people think of outcomes as additions to or deletions from current wealth and are more repelled by the idea of losing any of their wealth than they are attracted by gaining it. Second, people tend to give unlikely events more weight than they deserve in judging lotteries. Finally, people arbitrarily give some events more weight than they deserve. Prospect theory accounts for these by replacing utilities and probabilities with "value functions" and "decision weights." The value function allows people to be risk-averse in evaluating gains and risk-seeking in evaluating losses. The decision weights need not obey the usual probability calculus. These two components are then combined as in mathematical expectation.

Levi (1985) questions the work of Kahneman and Tversky at its roots, the interpretations of the experiments that supply the phenomena that prospect theory attempts to incorporate. He demonstrates that similar results could have been produced if subjects simply misinterpreted the instructions. Clearly, empirical investigation discriminating between the various interpretations would be a worthwhile task.

Biological explanations on the basis of animal studies offer another alternative. But they explain only the most naive forms of human behavior because people can use conscious thought processes to analyze the structure of a choice situation.

Finally, the theory of social norms, where action is either regarded as non–outcome-oriented or made contingent on past history or the behavior of others, is important but inadequate in scope. Yet social norms should not be underestimated, since shared social norms influence perception and behavior. Adhering to different norms from those within our social milieu induces instability and uncertainty in self-evaluation. This is the claim of social psychologists who argue that we conform because of group pressure or in order to be correct or to obtain better information about where we stand, and that conformity (for example, in buying) is likely to increase with the normative and informational dependence of the individual on the group.

## Methodological Holism and Methodological Individualism

This chapter has focused on the individual as a rational decision-maker. But do explanations of human behavior in markets, families, businesses, social classes, or decision-making units require anything more than aggregating the individual explanations of action? This question is answered differently by "methodological individualists" and "methodological holists," who represent two contrasting approaches to social science methodology.

### Methodological Individualism

The economists Schumpeter and Hayek and the philosopher Popper claim (as did John Stuart Mill in the nineteenth century) that social phenomena are wholly explainable in terms of facts about individuals. Schumpeter referred to this as *methodological individualism*. Watkins (1959) defines methodological individualism as claiming that

1. the ultimate constitutents of the social world are individual people who act more or less appropriately in light of their wants and beliefs about the situation, and

2. every event or institution is the result of a particular configuration of individuals, their dispositions, situations, beliefs, physical resources, and environment. All explanations of human actions, achievements, and the like, stem from the goals, wants, beliefs, resources, and interrelations of individuals. Social institutions and social change are explained by showing how they come into being as a result of the actions and interactions of individuals. Thus whenever we view diffusion theory, based as it is on the behavior of individuals, as explaining the product life cycle (PLC), we are assuming methodological individualism.

Watkins acknowledges that understanding group action presupposes understanding social facts like society's institutions or its bureaucratic structures but argues such understanding is also needed to interpret individual action. While agreeing that the behavior characterizing some group may not necessarily be just a simple summation of individual behavior and accepting therefore that group concepts and explanations may on occasions be useful, he argues that they are never "rock bottom" unless built up from explanations of individual behavior. However, Watkins does concede there are social regularities that are inexplicable in individualistic terms if they are the outcome of a large number of "accidents" or "automatic" type of behavior such as that following an earthquake.

Methodological individualism claims in general, though, that all social, political, economic, and marketing behavior is explainable in terms of the unintended/intended consequences of the actions of individuals. (An example here is Adam Smith's invisible hand.) Even large social processes like inflation and the trade cycle are viewed as explainable in terms of individual behavior. Methodological individualists consider concepts like "group mind," "national mood," "institutions," or "classes" as either reified nonsense or analyzable into the actions of individuals.

"Psychologism" underlies some forms of methodological individualism. Psychologism views the world as consisting of the physical contents of the universe and psychological states. Most philosophical problems as a result are viewed as questions of a factual kind to be answered by psychology. "Psychologistic individualism" relates to psychologism in identifying each individual with a given psychological state. Thus neoclassical economics is based on psychologistic individualism in that it identifies each individual with his or her utility function. But methodological individualism can be divorced from psychologistic individualism. For example, Popper subscribes to methodological individualism yet identifies individuals with their problem situation and not with their psychological state. Popper also believes institutions are never entirely explained in terms of individuals even though he regards all institutions as the creation of individual decision-making in the past.

## Methodological Holism

Methodological individualism is constrasted with methodological holism. If methodological individualists tend to discount the scientific status of social wholes, methodological holists discount the influence of individuals on social phenomena. Holists regard social groups as possessing a form of existence independent of their members as individuals. Methodological holism asserts that theories concerning social behavior are not reducible to the behavior of individuals and that collective entities like the "social group" are not specifiable in terms of individual behavior. Methodological holism postulates that social wholes like firms, competitors, and society have purposes or functions and can cause events to happen and the wants, beliefs, and actions of individuals to change. Emile Durkheim (1858–1917), the French sociologist, who saw holism as support for the distinctness of sociology as a social science, made the point that social forces work through individuals, whereas social facts influence and constrain individual behavior.

Holism itself gets its name from its advocates, who regard social phenomena as not reducible to individual psychology. Thus holists reject "reductionism," which is why Hempel regarded them as stifling scientific research. Reductionism seeks to reduce the macrosciences to the microsciences; thus psychology is explainable in terms of physics. Methodological holism is antireductionist in claiming there are autonomous levels in science that are not reducible to explanations or analysis at lower levels. (The tension between holism and reductionism finds expression in Hofstadter's [1979] book *Gödel, Escher, Bach: An Eternal Golden Braid*.) On the other hand, while methodological individualism is regarded as reductionist, it implicitly recognizes the problems of excessive reductionism by focusing at the level of the individual.

The debate between holism and individualism has a long history in sociology (e.g., the individualistic approach of Max Weber versus the holistic approach of Durkheim). However, in a way it is just the modern version of the older debate between realism and nominalism (see Chapter 11). Today the debate is less heated as few believe they must take sides. To many social scientists, the basic question is not whether group concepts or explanations are replaceable with concepts and explanations at the individual level but whether something is lost if explanations of social behavior are couched purely in terms of individual psychology.

# References

Boland, Lawrence A. (1982). *The Foundations of Economic Method*. London: George Allen and Unwin.

Brody, Nathan (1983). *Human Motivation*. New York: Academic Press.

Campbell, Colin (1987). *The Romantic Ethic and the Spirit of Modern Consumerism*. Oxford: Basil Blackwell.

Cohen, Jonathan L. (1986). *The Dialogue of Reason*. Oxford: Clarendon Press.

Collin, Finn (1985). *A Theory and Understanding*. Oxford: Basil Blackwell.

Darwall, Stephen L. (1983). *Impartial Reason*. Ithaca, NY: Cornell University Press.

De Finetti, Bruno (1964). "Foresight: Its Logical Laws, Its Subjective Sources," In *Readings in Subjective Probablility*, edited by H. E. Kyburg and H. Smokler. New York: Wiley. (Original work published 1937)

Dretske, Fred (1988). *Explaining Behavior: Reasons in a World of Causes*. Cambridge, MA: The MIT Press.

Elster, Jon (1989a). *Nuts and Bolts for the Social Sciences*. Cambridge: Cambridge University Press.

Elster, Jon (1989b), *Solomonic Judgements: Limitations of Rationality*. Cambridge: Cambridge University Press.

Etzioni, Amatai (1989). *The Moral Dimension: Toward a New Economics*. New York: Free Press.

Frank, Robert H. (1988). *Passions Within Reasons: The Strategic Role of the Emotions*. New York: W. W. Norton.

Gabor, Andre (1977). *Pricing: Principles and Practice*. London: Heinemann Educational Books.

Herrnstein, R. J. (1988). "A Behavioral Alternative to Utility Maximization." In *Applied Behavioral Economics*, edited by Shlomo Maital. New York: New York University Press.

Hicks, John (1979). *Causality in Economics.* Oxford: Basil Blackwell.

Hofstadter, Douglas R. (1979). *Gödel, Escher, Bach: An Eternal Golden Braid.* New York: Basic Books.

Johnson-Laird, P. N. (1982). "Propositional Representations, Procedural Semantics, and Mental Models." In *Perspectives on Mental Representation: Experimental and Theoretical Studies of Cognitive Processes and Capacities,* edited by J. Mehler, E. C. T. Walker, and M. Garrett. Hillsdale, NJ: Lawrence Erlbaum Associates.

Kagan, Jerome (1989). *Unstable Ideas: Temperament, Cognition and Self.* Cambridge, MA: Harvard University Press.

Kahneman, Daniel, Jack L. Knetsch, and R. H. Thaler (1986). "Fairness and the Assumptions of Economics." In *The Behavioral Foundations of Economic Theory,* edited by R. M. Hogarth and Melvin W. Reder, *The Journal of Business,* Vol. 59, No. 4, Part 2 (Oct.).

Kahneman, Daniel, and Amos Tversky (1979). "Prospect Theory: An Analysis of Decision Under Risk." *Econometrica* 47 (March), pp. 263–91.

Kahneman, Daniel, and Amos Tversky (1982). "The Psychology of Preferences." *Scientific American* 246, (January) pp. 166–73.

Keynes, John Maynard (1921). *A Treatise on Probability.* London: Macmillan.

Kuhn, T. S. (1977). *The Essential Tension.* Chicago: University of Chicago Press.

Kyburg, Henry E. (1983). *Epistemology and Inference.* Minneapolis: University of Minnesota Press.

Lazarsfeld, Paul F. (1973). *Main Trends in Sociology.* New York: Harper Torchbooks.

Levi, Isaac (1985). "Illusions About Uncertainty." *British Journal of Philosophy of Science* 36, pp. 331–40.

Lilien, G. L., and J.D.C. Little (1976). "The Advisor Project: A Study of Industrial Marketing Budgets." *Sloan Management Review* 17, pp. 17–31.

Little, J.D.C. (1970). "Models and Managers: The Concept of Decision Calculus." *Management Science* (April), pp. 466–85.

Little, J.D.C., and L. M. Lodish (1969). "A Media Planning Calculus." *Operations Research* 17 (January), pp. 1–35.

Little, J.D.C., and L. M. Lodish (1981). "Commentary on Judgment Based Marketing Decision Models." *Journal of Marketing* 45 (Fall), pp. 24–29.

MacIntyre, Alasdair (1971). "The Idea of Social Science." In *Rationality,* edited by Bryan R. Wilson. New York: Harper Torchbooks.

Marsh, Catherine (1982). *The Survey Method.* London: George Allen and Unwin.

Nagel, Ernest (1979). *Teleology Revisited.* New York: Columbia University Press.

Nagel, Thomas (1970). *The Possibility of Altruism.* Oxford: Oxford University Press.

Pettit, Philip (1978). "Rational Man Theory." In *Actions and Interpretation,* edited by C. Hookway and P. Pettit. Cambridge: Cambridge University Press.

Popper, Karl R. (1972). *Objective Knowledge.* Oxford: Clarendon Press.

Quine, W. V. (1987). *Quiddities.* Cambridge, MA: Belknap Press.

Ramsey, Frank P. (1950). *The Foundations of Mathematics and Other Essays.* New York: Humanities Press. (Original work published 1931)

Rawls, John (1980). "Kantian Constructivism in Ethics." The Dewey Lectures, 1980. *Journal of Philosophy* 77.

Robinson, Daniel N. (1985). *Philosophy of Psychology.* New York: Columbia University Press.

Rosenberg, Alexander (1988). *Philosophy of Social Science.* Boulder, CO: Westview Press.

Savage, Leonard J. (1954). *Foundations of Statistics.* New York: Wiley.

Sen, Amartya (1987). *On Ethics and Economics.* Oxford: Basil Blackwell.

Simon, H. A. (1957). *Administrative Behavior.* New York: Macmillan.

Simon, H. A. (1991). "Problem Formulation and Alternative Generation in the Decision Making Process." In *Progress in Decision, Utility and Risk Theory,* edited by Attila Chikan. Boston: Kluwer Academic Publishers.

Tversky, A., and D. Kahneman (1983). "Extensional Vs. Intuitive Reasoning: The Conjunction Fallacy in Probability Judgement." *Psychological Review* 90, pp. 293–315.

Tversky, Amos, and Daniel Kahneman (1986). "Rational Choice and the Framing of Decisions." In The Behavioral Foundations of Economic Theory, (eds.) R. M. Hogarth and Melvin W. Reder, *The Journal of Business,* Vol. 59, No. 4, Part 2 (Oct.).

Watkins, J.W.N. (1959). "Historical Explanation in the Social Sciences." In *Theories of History,* edited by Patrick Gardiner. New York: Free Press.

Winch, P. G. (1958). *The Idea of a Social Science.* London: Routledge and Kegan Paul.

# 6

# Teleological Explanation: Function Ascription

The question of commonsense is always "What is it good for?"—a question which would abolish the rose and be answered triumphantly by the cabbage.

James Russell Lowell (1819–1891)

This chapter discusses the functional explanation, a mode of explanation that is common in sociology and anthropology. This is not surprising since the functional explanation fits the holistic methodology. The chapter first defines the term "function," distinguishing it from words like "role" and "purpose" while showing its general indispensability in marketing. Next the functional explanation itself is defined and its grounding in the concept of system is discussed. Functional analysis, as a way of identifying functions, is then examined in general and specifically in cognitive psychology. Finally, after reviewing applications of functionalism (functional analysis and functional explanation) to marketing, we review the criticism of this approach.

## Nature of the Functional Explanation

### Definition of Function

All cultural and social phenomena serve some function, that is, contribute to the system of which they are a part. Thus consumer buying contributes to the maintenance of the economic system while individual purchases contribute to the lifestyle or consumption system of the consumer. Much of our thinking in marketing is driven by the belief that everything serves some function, as should everything about a product.

The word "function" and the word "purpose" are often used interchangeably, but there are differences. To speak of the function of $X$ is to speak about the intended and unintended contribution that $X$ makes to the system of which it is a part, whereas to speak of the purpose of $X$ is to speak of intended effects only, without invoking any explicit or implicit reference to the system of which $X$ is a part.

Just as we speak of $X$'s function in system $Y$, we speak of $X$'s *role* in system $Y$. The words "role" and "function" are also often used as synonyms. For example, we speak of the role *or* the function of distribution in the marketing mix. Yet there is a difference. The word "function" relates to a component's *contribution* to the system; the word "role" refers to a component's *pattern of expected behavior* or *activity* within the system. Thus the *function* of distribution in the marketing mix is the contribution distribution makes to achieving a satisfactory offering for the buyer; the *role* of distribution in the marketing mix covers the actual activities undertaken by distribution vis-à-vis the other elements in the mix.

When the concept of role is used to explain behavior, the explicans shows that actual behavior conforms to role expectations. For example, we might find that parents always choose the brand of baby food perceived as most nourishing and explain this as conforming to the rules or norms expected of men and women acting in the role of parent.

## Functional Explanation

Ernest Nagel defines a functional explanation as one that accounts for the presence of some item in a system by the contribution the item makes to the system of which it is a component; for example, "Fish have gills in order to obtain oxygen" (1979, p. 294). Thus cognitive psychology regards the function of consciousness to represent information about what is occurring outside and inside the human organism so the information can be evaluated and acted upon.

The functional explanation is a common form of explanation in sociology where it is usually assumed that all social phenomena must be beneficial to someone and the beneficial consequences explain the existence of the phenomena. The anthropologist Malinowski argued, too, that all social phenomena have beneficial consequences that explain the existence of the phenomena, regardless of whether the consequences were intended, unintended, recognized, or not recognized. Merton, in sociology, similarly claimed that whenever a social practice, custom, or the like, has functional consequences, these consequences explain its existence.

A functional explanation answers such questions as:

What does component *X* do in system *Y*?

Why is *X* part of system *Y*?

Why does *X* exist within system *Y*?

The first question asks about the function of *X* and is key to answering the other two questions. Thus I may claim that what accounts for the presence of humor in society is the function it serves in resisting or controlling the pressures arising from social living. But some particular activity can serve many functions, depending on its content. For example, communication is commonly regarded as serving eight functions (Condon, 1966):

1. *phatic communication,* or "small talk," facilitates general socializing;

2. *curb communication* indicates that further talk would not be welcome;

3. *transmitting communication* actually transmits information;

4. *instrumental communication* calls forth certain action from the target audience, as is typical in advertising;

5. *affective communication,* which flatters, praises, or compliments, conveys the feelings of the speaker toward the audience to, say, persuade by making them feel good about themselves;

6. *catharsis communication* simply "lets off steam" or allows one to get something "off one's chest";

7. *ritual communication* fosters a sense of sharing or community with others; and

8. *magic communication* suggests the possibility of magical intervention through exploiting people's belief in the power of words.

The concept of function is fundamental in marketing since a product's function identifies the market (system) in which it competes. A customer encountering a strange, novel product asks, "What does it do?" or "What is it for?"; that is, What is its function? This is because consumers type-identify an item within a product class on the basis of its function. Thus any object whose function is to be sat on is a seat and anything counts as a bed if its designated function is to be slept on. Whenever we talk in management of showing the point of some technique, we are talking about explaining that technique by showing how it functions in management. A failure to explain functions adequately is a failure to explain the full potential of the product or tool, which in turn can be a failure in persuasion. This is why we explain the need for each of the elements of the marketing mix (product, price, promotion, and distribution) by explicating the function of each within marketing.

## System Assumption

A functional explanation states the functions performed by the parts, thereby assuming some relevant system. In fact, the usefulness of the functional explanation lies in its focus on the interrelationships of the parts to the realization of the goals of the system.

A system is any set of interdependent or interacting parts which together form a unitary whole to perform some function. Unlike a mere heap (e.g., of stones), a system is held together from within through mutual dependencies. Every system is a subsystem of some larger system. Thus the marketing department is a system that is a subsystem of the firm, the firm is a system that is a subsystem of the economy, and so on. Any market segment is a system that is a subsystem of a market, a market is a system that is a subsystem of all markets, and so on. In practice, we draw the boundaries of any system to suit our purpose: to study too wide a system can be wasteful and cumbersome; to study too narrow a system can lead to suboptimal solutions. In any case, a functional explanation explains the presence of a part, element, or component of a system by showing its contribution toward maintaining or realizing the goals of the system. This means that the usefulness of the functional explanation rests on correctly specifying the system of interest. If the system is a lifestyle or consumption system, we need to be able to specify the distinct lifestyles or the distinct consumption systems as well as establishing that such systems are meaningful for our purposes.

Every system component serves some function, that is, makes some contribution to the functioning of the overall system, just as do the parts of any mechanical system like a watch. Thus the contribution of marketing planning to the business can be viewed as making the business more

1. homeostatic, that is, toward maintaining a constant operating environment in the face of random assaults from the external environment;

2. adaptive, that is, toward adjusting the state of the system to suit changing conditions; and

3. dynamic, that is, toward using feedback to keep the system changing through some sequence of unrepeated states along some desirable path.

## Holism and Functionalism

Methodological holism and functionalism are intimately related. Holism, in rejecting the claim that group phenomena can be explained by aggregating explanations of individual behavior, claims that social facts (e.g., poverty) can explain individual behavior (e.g., criminal activity). Like those who seek functional explanations, the holist asserts that the individual act takes its meaning and significance from its contribution to the social system of which it is part. Holistic and functional explanations of social phenomena are generally interchangeable in that both insist that explanations of social phenomena must either be in terms of the functions of the system itself within the wider system or in terms of the individual component's contribution to the immediate system. Thus I may explain the buying of a particular brand by some religious group by showing the function of the religious group within society and showing the contribution that buying the brand makes to that function or to some subfunction (e.g., increasing cohesiveness).

## Functional Analysis

Functional explanations explain the presence of a component by the function it performs, whereas functional analysis is concerned with first identifying the functions.

Of the functions that are functional or beneficial, not all are intended. Every manmade system—say, a product, an organization, or a market plan—will have *manifest* (intended) functions. Manifest functions can be contrasted with *latent* functions, which are beneficial effects that are neither recognized nor intended. Thus the manifest function of a penetration pricing policy might be to enhance market share, but the latent function might be to put pressure on the firm to achieve low-cost production. The *dysfunctional* consequences (those that undermine system goals) of the policy might be the lowering of the product's quality image. Similarly, the manifest functions of advertising are to persuade the target audience to think about the brand in the way advertising suggests. A latent function of advertising is the speeding up of the spread of knowledge about innovations; dysfunctional consequences might be the tarnishing of company image. Similarly, we can view the manifest function of a product as its design function; its latent or unintended functions might be to promote group cohesion or to subordinate the individual to the group (e. g., military uniforms); and it might have dysfunctional consequences like arousing envy.

In all cases functional analysis identifies a component $X$'s function(s) as whatever it does or whatever consequences it produces that contributes to the system's *formal* goals or (if latent functions are considered) whatever it does or whatever consequences it produces that confer benefits to the system. If it can be shown that the subtraction of component $X$ from system $Y$ (e.g., the removal of advertising from the marketing mix) leads to a failure of the system, this demonstrates that the existence of component $X$ is a necessary condition for system $Y$'s success.

Functional analysis need not be undertaken solely to explain. There are many reasons for inquiring about functions other than to explain a component's presence. For example, the technique of "value analysis" carries out a sort of functional analysis to assess the buyer benefits of a product's components to compare to related costs.

If we look at the functions of any product, there are design functions, use functions, and service functions. For instance, the *design function* of toothpaste is to clean the teeth and/or to freshen the breath and prevent cavities, tartar, or plaque. But *use functions* are the actual uses to which the product is put. These may not coincide with the design func-tion, as when toothpaste is used to remove white rings from furniture. The *service func-tion* describes what the product *actually* achieves. Thus the service function of toothpaste is the *actual* function performed. What should occur is for the design function to coincide with the user function and the service function to match the performance expectations incorporated into the design function.

## Functional Analysis in Cognitive Psychology

In cognitive psychology the term functional *analysis* is used to identify the brain's input, processing, and output functions leading to choices and actions. The brain is viewed as an information-processing unit that processes information in a way analogous to the computer. In the information-processing approach of cognitive psychology, the system of interest is the *program* describing how internal mental states combine with informa-tional inputs to yield other mental states and subsequent intention and action. To under-stand a certain type of mental state or mental process is to see what function such states or processes have in the overall program. A particular mental capacity is explained by detailing the program (processes) between the input of data and the output of action. Many cognitive psychologists argue that these programs must be viewed not as causal mechanisms but as *interpretation of the capacity to make a particular inference, take a particular action,* and so on (Cummins, 1983).

Mental states and processes are functionally defined in terms of the program or the overall processing system. Thus the function of "belief" is to represent "facts" about the world and offer prescriptions; the function of a "want" is to give direction; the function of perceptions is to yield new information about the world; and reasoning's function is to get truer representations of the way things are and ought to be.

Functionalism in cognitive psychology differs, though, from functionalism in soci-ology. Functionalism in cognitive psychology generally eschews teleology in the sense of showing the contribution of, say, attitudes to a person's goals but confines itself to show-ing the job performed by mental constructs like attitudes within some mental program or set of mental processes.

## Functionalism in Marketing

The functional concept has a long history in marketing, although interpretations of the word "function" have varied. Initial interest focused on describing the "functions of mar-keting" in the sense of the steps required to develop, produce, or move goods from pro-ducer to consumer. Marketing functions were described first by Shaw (1912), a Harvard economist, followed by the work of Ryan (1935) and Fullbrook (1940). Fullbrook defined the functions of marketing as the tasks required to get goods from producer to consumers, a definition that comes closer to defining the *role* of distribution. More recently, the focus has been on "function" as equivalent to "purpose." Thus Lewis and Erickson (1969) refer to two functions of marketing: to obtain demand (product planning, pricing, promotion) and to service demand (distribution including order processing, inventory management, warehousing, and transportation).

Wroe Alderson (1957, 1964) was the first to talk in functional terms about the work-ings of the marketing system. Alderson viewed the marketing system in terms of four elements: power, communication, operations, and internal elements/external adjustments. The marketing process he describes starts with the inputs into the firm of heterogeneous resources, which are then converted into meaningful assortments of goods for the consumer. Alderson's chief interest, however, lay more in systems thinking and analysis than in developing functional explanations.

In the area of consumer behavior, functional explanations are given to explain the functions served by attitudes, selective perception, emotion, and so on. Thus Katz (1960) argues that attitudes serve four functions: a utilitarian function, a value-expressive function, an ego-defensive function, and a knowledge function. The utilitarian function is to maximize reward and minimize costs. The value-expressive function is to give positive expression to core values relating to enhancing self-esteem. The ego-defensive function is to protect (rather than enhance) self-esteem from whatever would threaten it. The knowledge function is to help give order to events and make sense of the surrounding world. Few doubt that attitudes are often self-serving in this way. However, it is not obvious that *all* attitudes are so self-serving.

Leymore (1975), an anthropologist following the structuralist approach of Claude Lévi-Strauss, argues that the primary function of the human mind is classificatory, particularly into binary oppositions reflecting the human condition: rich–poor, loved–hated, and so on. Advertising at the deep level, she claims, influences consumer preferences through associating the product with the culturally preferred alternative—thus beauty, not ugliness. In this Leymore claims that advertising functions in the way myth functions in societies, namely, to (1) reinforce culturally accepted norms, values, and beliefs; and (2) reduce anxieties by offering the possibility of providing solutions to the "eternal polarities of the human condition."

Within precisely what system do these functions occur? Leymore states that the system of interest is that which affects the viewer. On this basis she identifies three possible systems:

1. The system composed of competitive brands. This system consists of all the brands to which the buyer is exposed in the same product class. These brands collectively constitute the system's structure. The advertising message depends intimately on this structure since it will vary according to what has been already conveyed by rival advertising.

2. The system composed of competing substitutes. This system might consist of different substitute product classes or a specific brand against the global market (e.g., Maxim coffee against all other beverages).

3. The system consisting of one brand constituting the whole product field. The advertising for the brand is obliged to do the whole job of getting the consumer to conceptualize the product and try it.

## Criticism of Functionalism

Functional analysis as an injunction to seek functions is very much alive. Much more controversial is functionalism as a form of scientific explanation.

In support of functional explanations in sociology, anthropology, and elsewhere, advocates quote the prevalence of such teleological explanations in the life sciences (e.g., the function of birds' song is to proclaim territorial ownership to avoid unnecessary fighting). But, as Rosenberg (1988) points out, functional explanations in biology are grounded in evolutionary theory, whereas there is no such underwriting in the social sciences. Nonetheless, Rosenberg believes that macro–social science requires functional explanations since discovering the social facts and the regularities that systematize these facts depends on assuming that these social facts and corresponding regularities serve functions.

Hempel (1965) and Rudner (1966) voice the major objections to functional explanations. The first objection is that functional explanations cannot be empirically tested. This criticism applies to functionalism in cognitive psychology, too, since mental entities like cognition are not observable, although they are treated "as if" they exist to perform some function. Miller (1987) shows how the functional explanation can be interpreted to get around this problem and also the criticism that functional explanations have no predictive value.

Miller argues that functional explanations succeed only if the specified function can be shown to be an underlying cause of the maintenance of the component of behavior in question: the fact that $Y$ serves function $X$ causes the causes that preserve $Y$. In other words, these preserving causes would not exist or would not come into being to preserve $Y$ unless $Y$ served function $X$. Functional explanations on this basis describe a cause of causes. To quote the simplest of examples, my action in buying an umbrella ($Y$) is to serve the function of keeping me dry in wet weather and the fact that it does this for me and others causes the preservation (manufacture, purchase, maintenance, and use) of umbrellas. Miller, however, sees functional explanations as more typically being employed to explain some enduring pattern of social behavior whose endurance is otherwise puzzling in that it seems to violate the individual self-interests of those involved. Consider those consumers who sacrifice self-interest by selling their shares in firms that invest in South Africa. This behavior ($Y$) serves the objective social function ($X$) of declaring where these consumers stand on the issue of apartheid and their hope to undermine that system. Such a declaration of public commitment causes group solidarity with those of like mind and a sense of sharing and loyalty to principle that leads to the preservation of $Y$, that is, more acts of sacrifice of material self-interest to further the cause. Miller's interpretation of the functional explanation can be represented by a set of causal events forming a circle: functional contributions causing events that in turn cause the functional contributions.

Hempel's and Rudner's further objection is that the functional explanation suggests the functional indispensability of the component. They argue such indispensability needs first to be demonstrated. If it cannot be demonstrated, then there is a need to explain why component $X$ rather than some other functionally equivalent $Z$ is performing the function. When there are many ways of fulfilling the same function, functional analysis in itself is inadequate for identifying with certainty what produces what. For example, it would not be easy to test Katz's functional explanation of attitudes because attitudes are not the only way of achieving the four functions. This means, it is argued, that the functional explanation is always problematical since there is a need to eliminate equally tenable ways of achieving the function. But this problem of eliminating rival hypotheses is a problem for all explanations, not just a problem for functional explanations.

Elster (1983) regards the functional explanation as too deficient to contribute much to the social sciences. Although he agrees that knowing something is there because of its beneficial consequences is useful, he claims we would understand it much better if we knew how it came to be there. This view is consistent with Miller, who (as discussed earlier) accepts the functional mode of explanation providing it is backed by an account of how the functional effects feed back on their cause and contribute to upholding that cause.

It has frequently been claimed that all functional explanations are in fact causal explanations. Thus Nagel (1979) argues that functional explanations say *B* is an effect of *A* instead of saying *A* is the cause or condition of *B*. However, Nagel admits that such a restatement is not an equivalence because it does not implicate the concept of system, which is basic to the functional explanation. For many sociologists and anthropologists, functions are the special consequences that arise from the way a system is constructed whereas causes are the factors that can lead the system to become active or inactive on any one occasion. Also, we cannot reinterpret a functional explanation as simply "*B* is an effect of *A*" since not every effect of *A* can be regarded as a function of *A* and not all functions relate to causes. Take the following functional type of explanation:

Warranties and guarantees arise to reduce buying risk.

The management hierarchy is instituted to coordinate and control all marketing activities.

The core function of a watch is to measure time.

None of these statements translates into a causal format, though each explains the existence of its subject by the function it performs.

Alan Ryan (1970) claims that in Merton's sociology the term "function" served no purpose except to make a nod to those who believe in the autonomy of sociology and to decorate the term "consequences" (particularly good consequences) with an impressive title. The distinction between "function" and "dysfunction" (which is derived from Durkheim's distinction between normal and pathological functioning), he argues, rests on moral not objective criteria. What is functional for one person may be dysfunctional for another. On the other hand, Merton's other distinction between manifest and latent functions (an extension of Durkheim's claim that functions are not always what they seem to be) is not a distinction that is clear-cut in practice.

Functional explanations are frequently claimed to justify the status quo and so to be unable to explain how change comes about. It is argued that the concept of function rests on a biological analogy that projects an image of cohesion. This is why functionalism seemed less relevant in the 1950s when applied to third world countries in the context of rapid change and upheavals. The distinction between functional and dysfunctional consequences is intended to rebut this charge by viewing change here as eliminating dysfunctional consequences. Although the distinction has not satisfied the critics, it is common to explain change by showing how some function has outlived its usefulness so it no longer makes a systemic contribution, or by showing there are more efficient ways of achieving the effects or consequences that are sought.

Functional explanations will continue to be sought in the social sciences because they can be enlightening. If the Miller viewpoint proves operationally feasible, functional explanation may become less controversial. But whatever happens in social science generally, the concept of a function is basic to marketing and particularly to buyer behavior since people buy products to perform some function within one of the subsystems that make up their total life system.

# References

Alderson, Wroe (1957). *Marketing Behavior and Executive Action*. Homewood, IL: Richard D. Irwin.

Alderson, Wroe (1964). "A Normative Theory of Marketing Systems." In *Theory in Marketing,*
    edited by R. Cox, W. Alderson, and S. J. Shapiro, Chicago: American Marketing Associa-
    tion, pp. 92–108.
Condon, John C. (1966). *Semantics and Communication.* New York: Macmillan.
Cummins, Robert (1983). *The Nature of Psychological Explanation.* Cambridge, MA: The MIT
    Press.
Elster, Jon (1983). *Explaining Technical Change.* Cambridge: Cambridge University Press.
Fullbrook, Earl S. (1940). "The Functional Concept in Marketing." *Journal of Marketing* 4 (Jan-
    uary), pp. 229–37.
Hempel, Carl G. (1965). *Aspects of Scientific Explanation.* New York: Free Press.
Katz, D. (1960). "The Functional Approach to the Study of Attitudes." *Pubic Opinion Quarterly*
    24, pp. 163–204.
Lewis, Richard J., and Leo G. Erickson (1969). "Marketing Functions and Marketing Systems: A
    Synthesis." *Journal of Marketing* 33 (July), pp. 10–14.
Leymore, Verda Langholz (1975). *The Hidden Myth.* New York: Basic Books.
Miller, R. W. (1987). *Fact and Method.* Princeton, NJ: Princeton University Press.
Nagel, Ernest (1979). *Teleology Revisited.* New York: Columbia University Press.
Rosenberg, Alexander (1988). *Philosophy of Social Science.* Boulder, CO: Westview Press.
Rudner, Richard S. (1966). *Philosophy of Social Science.* Englewood Cliffs, NJ: Prentice-Hall.
Ryan, Alan (1970), *Philosophy of Social Science.* London: Macmillan.
Ryan, Franklin W. (1935). "Functional Elements of Marketing Distribution." *Harvard Business
    Review* 13 (January), pp. 205–24.
Shaw, A. W. (1912). "Some Problems in Market Distribution." *Quarterly Journal of Economics*
    (August), pp. 703–65.
Simon, H. A. (1957). *Administrative Behavior.* New York: Macmillan.

# 7

# Explanatory Systems of Psychology

> Poor dear Psychology, of course, has never got far beyond the stage
> of medieval physics, except in its statistical developments, where the
> labors of the mathematicians have enabled it to spin out the corre-
> lation of trivialities into endless refinements. For the rest it is only
> too obvious that, up to the present, a great deal of Psychology con-
> sists mainly of muddle, twaddle, and quacksalving, trying to impose
> itself as science by elaborateness of its technical terminology and the
> confidence of its assertions.
>
> C. D. Broad (1949)

Previous chapters explored the four modes of explanation: causal (Chapter 3); temporal/
process causal models (Chapter 4); rational choice models (Chapter 5); and the functional
explanation (Chapter 6). Each of these four modes of explanation is present in the marketing literature on buyer behavior and we have illustrated some major applications.
However, we may explain marketing phenomena in any of these modes without claiming
the explanation is in any way grounded in the social sciences. Yet systems of psychology
and systems of sociology (see Chapter 8) both revolve around some preference for one of
the four modes. This is to be expected since, if science is concerned with explanation, such
explanations must necessarily reflect one of the given modes. This chapter describes the
various systems of psychology to reveal their assumptions, claims, and preferred explanatory mode.

Marketers, but particularly marketing academics, draw extensively on psychology
to direct their research and provide support for their models and assertions. But psychology itself is not monolithic: there are several explanatory systems of psychology, each
with its own basic conception of what needs to be explained and what factors to take into
account. We need to have a very clear idea of the strengths and weaknesses of the various
systems of psychology and to recognize that each system is just one viewpoint—albeit
sometimes a privileged viewpoint—with rival viewpoints acting as different windows to
provide additional perspectives.

How we study the consumer depends on what we take the consumer to be. Are consumers like machines responding to the push and pull of past impressed forces and immediate stimuli? Or is the consumer a free agent (as is popularly supposed) with goals, wants,
and beliefs, using past experience and immediate stimuli simply as input to a decision?
The more a system of psychology leans toward a strictly causal explanation, the more a

mechanistic model of man is assumed. The more a system of psychology leans toward the free agency concept, the more the tendency to assume the purposive, rational model of man. The systems of psychology or research traditions discussed here are behaviorist psychology or behaviorism, physiological psychology, psychoanalytic psychology, cognitive psychology, and interpretive psychology. Each of these is discussed in turn, with the criticism each makes of the other. These criticisms tend to be deeply rooted in different conceptions both of human behavior and the nature of explanation.

## Behaviorism

Behaviorism was the first system of psychology to influence marketing thinking, particularly in devising promotional strategies. Although now overshadowed by cognitive psychology, there is evidence of a revival of interest (Carey, Clicque, Leighton, and Milton, 1976; Foxall, 1987, 1990; Gorn, 1982; Rothschild and Gaidis, 1981).

Although there are several forms of behaviorism, all subscribe to the thesis that behavior is caused by external environmental factors that condition behavior to respond in certain ways. Behaviorism claims psychology should focus on relating environmental factors (the independent variables) to behavioral responses (the dependent variable) and not be concerned at all with mental processes. Although behaviorism has had an impact on sociology, political science, and economics, its main influence has been as a movement within psychology itself. This is because the behaviorist's concentration on laboratory research with animals has made generalization to humans somewhat problematic.

There are at least three forms of behaviorism:

1. Pavlovian conditioning, sometimes called classical conditioning or the contiguity model;
2. operant conditioning, preeminently associated with B. F. Skinner; and
3. Tolman's behaviorism, the particular form of behaviorism introduced by E. C. Tolman, consisting of relational and puposive behaviorism.

### Pavlovian Conditioning

Pavlovian, or classical, conditioning is also known as the contiguity model. It is the behaviorism of J. B. Watson, who, after an academic career, ensured the visibility of classical conditioning as a theory for advertising through his association with the advertising agency of J. Walter Thompson. Because classical conditioning is the earliest form of behaviorism, Watson is generally credited with being the founder of behaviorism in psychology, although it was Pavlov who pioneered the first experiments in "classical" conditioning. In classical conditioning there is a connection between some stimulus and a true reflex reaction, like that between the stimulus of food and the dog's reflex reaction of salivation. The dog reacts to the *unconditioned* stimulus of food by the *unconditioned* response of salivation. If a bell is sounded simultaneously with, prior to, or just subsequent to the introduction of the unconditioned stimulus of the food, this gives *contiguity* to the food stimulus and the bell stimulus. After repeated contiguity of the two sets of stimuli (food and bell sound), salivation will follow the bell sound alone. When salivation does follow the presentation of the bell sound alone, the sound of the bell becomes a *conditioned stimulus* and the salivation a *conditioned response*. Watson claimed that our physiological reflexes were the only behavior we inherit; all other behavior is the result of learning through Pavlovian conditioning. He saw Pavlovian conditioning as a way to construct a purely mechanistic theory of human behavior. Watson's methodological stance was "physicalism," which claims that all descriptive terms in science must designate only the observable properties of things. Psychological laws must therefore be translatable into observable, physical language to ensure the laws can be tested. Watson's views so dominated early on that criticisms of behaviorism today are often just criticism of his particular version.

Classical conditioning is a causal explanation in the form of stimulus $(S) \rightarrow$ response $(R)$, standing for cause $\rightarrow$ effect. There has been a revival of interest in classical conditioning with the development of the distinction between central and peripheral routes to persuasion in (say) viewing an ad on television (see Chapter 4). When identification with the product is low, the alleged influence of peripheral cues like humor or celebrity sponsorship is explained as the result of classical conditioning into normative conformity. Similarly, the relationship between $A_{ad}$ (attitude toward the ad) and its impact on $A_B$ (attitude toward the brand) is also typically explained as the result of classical conditioning. There is the assumption of some unconditioned stimulus being associated with the brand in the expectation that the brand itself will become the conditioned stimulus bringing forth a favorable attitude toward the brand advertised. However, classical conditioning is not just a matter of association, or the contiguity of events or images. In fact, classical conditioning was meant to replace the "associationist psychology" of the nineteenth century by providing a physiological basis for the behavior observed in terms of involuntary reflexes. Classical conditioning presupposes the existence of involuntary reflexes, which are said to make the associations compelling. In the absence of the relevant reflexes, the power of association must be justified in some other way, for example, by consistency theory—particularly the congruity model, which claims people seek congruence between their attitude toward a communication source and their attitude toward things linked to that source. Alternatively, it could be argued in a commonsense way that the efficacy of association rests simply on the proposition that whenever two things are intimately associated, the two things get recalled together so that the emotional aura of one rubs off onto the other.

All conditioning presupposes unconscious learning. At least this is the orthodox position. However, Allen and Janiszewski (1989) argue, on the basis of their experiments, that conditioning without awareness "need not follow from the Pavlovian position." They claim in fact that their work "does not corroborate the view that conditioned learning comes about through a noncognitive process and it is difficult to demonstrate conditioning in humans without subjects' awareness." Whereas the assumption of noncognitive conditioning means that one need merely expose the viewer to a series of pairings of unconditioned and conditioned stimuli for attitudes to be affected, the alternative assumption of a cognitive process being at work means that attempted conditioning must be done by promoting recognition both of the unconditioned stimulus (e.g., a beautiful woman in an ad directed at men) *and* of the conditioned stimulus (the brand being advertised) since the attention given to noninvolving products can be ephemeral.

## Operant Conditioning

True Pavlovian conditioning is dependent on the existence of a true reflex that can be stimulated (e.g., the salivary gland). This dependence limits the scope of any mechanistic psychology built on it since not much behavior is mediated by Pavlovian reflexes. Operant conditioning is a more embracing concept of conditioning. The central idea is that all living organisms are spontaneously "emitting" behavior and whenever this behavior is reinforced it increases the chances they will repeat the behavior. Although Skinner (1953) is most closely identified with operant conditioning, its basis is to be found in the work of Bechterev, a Russian physiologist, and the explanatory principle lying behind it is Thorndike's "law of effect." The law of effect states that acts that are followed by positive consequences are repeated whereas acts followed by negative consequences are not. More formally, the law states that any emitted behavior that continues to be reinforced will be repeated with greater frequency, intensity, and duration. This is the basic premise behind operant conditioning, which, unlike Pavlovian conditioning, assumes neither a true reflex nor some initial stimulus to start the process.

Foxall (1990) views operant conditioning as part of what is termed the "experimental analysis of behavior" (EAB). As a system of behaviorism, EAB consists of operant conditioning along with a philosophy that denies causal significance to mental events such as attitudes or motives but explains behavior purely by reference to the environmental consequences (i.e., whether the behavior is reinforced or not) of a person's behavior. For EAB, mental events are an epiphenomenon: they are caused and not causal in any way. The following analogy often is used to illustrate this: just as the body causes its shadow and that shadow has no causal effect upon the body or even upon other shadows, so the brain causes consciousness and mental events but these cannot affect the brain since the causal process is a one-way street. However, Skinner regards mental events (or, more in line with behaviorism, "within the skin events") not as causes but as important dependent variables in need of explanation. The third tenet of EAB is the belief that science proceeds through induction rather than the hypotheticodeductive method (see Chapter 12). EAB would deny goal ascription explanations and so deny that consumers act purposively with intentions, that is, with the aim of achieving certain goals (consequences), or act in line with attitudes or personality traits.

In operant conditioning, we wait for the behavior to be "emitted" by the subject. Thus Bechterev waited for his dog to lift its paw. If the dog is given food as a consequence of its lifting its paw, then the dog's lifting its paw is a response that acts on the environment to produce consequences (food provided) and hence is termed an "operant response." Responses are termed operant responses only if their rate of emission is affected by their consequences. The dog is *conditioned* to perform the act of lifting its paw and has *learned as a result of reinforcement.* All consequences that increase the rate of emission of a response (like the provision of food to a dog after it lifts its paw) in the same or similar circumstances are called "reinforcers." On this definition not everything considered to be a "reward" would necessarily qualify as a reinforcer. But since the dog's response is instrumental to producing the reinforcement, operant conditioning gives rise to "instrumental learning."

Responses with the same consequences are regarded as examples of the same "operant." Thus an operant is a class of responses defined in terms of their consequences. If these consequences increase the rate of response, then the consequences are "reinforcers"; if the rate of subsequent response drops off, the consequences are termed "punishers." In most texts, reinforcers are discussed under the heading of positive and negative reinforcement. Positive reinforcement is direct reward whereas negative reinforcement is the reward that occurs as a consequence of removing some adverse stimulus. Unless a response is reinforced, it faces extinction. In contrast to such reinforcers, there are also the punishments resulting either from the introduction of adverse stimuli or from the removal of some positive stimulus (e.g., a price discount).

Operant conditioning controls behavior by manipulating reinforcement so the "stimulus" is the whole set of conditions under which reinforcement takes place. Whatever it is about these conditions that communicates the likelihood of negative or positive reinforcement is termed the *discriminative stimuli;* more broadly, discriminative stimuli are those elements of the situation (e.g., brand name or package) that signal the opportunity for reinforcement (or punishment, though this is downplayed in behaviorism). Foxall (1990) represents the operant conditioning model as

$$S^D - R - S^R$$

where $S^D$ = a class of discriminative stimuli
$R$ = a class of responses
$S^R$ = a class of reinforcing stimuli

Although this model looks like a causal process, it is denied that the class of discriminative stimuli causes the response. The discriminative stimuli can control behavior in the sense of signaling an opportunity, but Skinner claims that any class of behavior is explained (caused) exclusively by its consequences. In the absence of reinforcement, the behavior may remain for a time under the control of the discriminative stimuli but it will eventually not be emitted because of the absence of reinforcement. Discriminative stimuli in marketing might take some form of promise about the beneficial consequences of buying. It is argued, however, that this will exert only partial control over behavior since the consequences (experiencing the benefits themselves) are key. Yet it is acknowledged that discriminative stimuli, if constantly paired with reinforcers, can become conditioned reinforcers themselves. This is the process known as "chaining." In any case, it is the specific reinforcement history of the consumer that determines what constitutes discriminative stimuli signaling what type of consequences.

The decision to try a product or brand is intimately related to past experience; repeat buying is, under the EAB system, tied to the past consequences of purchase. Because operant conditioning focuses on reinforcement in molding behavior, messages signaling untried benefits might have limited appeal. Hence those advocating operant conditioning are likely to downplay the role of advertising in product introductions. Under operant conditioning, complex new behaviors may be explained as emerging after a succession of preceding acts, each reinforced in turn, that together constitute successive approximations leading to the behavior observed. This process is referred to as "shaping."

Reinforcement may not occur every time the behavior is emitted; that is, there may not be continuous reinforcement. Reinforcement instead can be intermittent in the sense of occurring at fixed or variable intervals. All this influences the rate of learning and the rate at which extinction of the behavior takes place. Where every response is reinforced (the continuous reinforcement schedule), learning occurs rapidly but the behavior is also most likely to cease when reinforcement stops. Where responses are reinforced only periodically (the intermittent reinforcement schedule), learning is slower but drops off more slowly when reinforcement ceases. Both reinforcement schedules result in learning by what behaviorists call "shaping," which is the reinforcement of a succession of acts to guide behavior to making the desired response.

If the consumer receives reinforcement of one response (e.g., as a result of buying brand $X$ of company $Y$) and, as a result, is more likely to respond favorably to similar stimuli (e.g., buying other brands of company $Y$), then the behaviorist speaks of *response generalization*. If the reinforcement of the response in one situation leads to the same response in like situations, there is *stimuli generalization*. Foxall's (1990) example of response generalization is an individual purchasing one food product in a given store, which, if reinforced, may be followed by his buying a range of similar products there. His example of a stimulus generalization is a consumer buying a brand in a given store, which, if reinforced, may lead her to purchase the brand from similar outlets.

Skinner claims that operant conditioning replaces and incorporates classical conditioning. Unlike Watson, however, Skinner argues that unobservable thoughts and feelings can be scientifically studied if these thoughts and feelings are viewed as conditioned responses, not causes of behavior. He classifies thinking as covert behavior and verbal communication as overt behavior; both are conditioned since he regards all behavior (except certain innate reflexes) as explainable by conditioning.

Conditioning is assumed to act automatically irrespective of whether the subject is aware of what is happening. Conditioning occurs automatically or not at all. It is probably this view of conditioning that gives rise to so many charges of manipulation by advertising.

Skinner views operant conditioning as a scientific methodology for studying the precise effects of different schedules of reinforcement. But it is probably his explanation of superstitious behavior (e.g., wearing of a certain scarf) and reward (e.g., safe return from a bombing mission) that gave him most visibility outside academia. With every prospective purchase there are potentially reinforcing consequences (product benefits) and punishing consequences (cost and effort spent in obtaining the product). Hence the probability of purchase depends on the difference between the two sets of consequences.

## HULL'S DRIVE REDUCTION THEORY

Some behaviorists have sought explanatory mechanisms to account for conditioning. Hull's (1943) drive reduction theory is the most well known. This theory assumes a state of homeostasis: an organism is in a state of equilibrium until some internal metabolic deficiency or chemical imbalance becomes a (causal) "drive," driving the organism into a state of tension and trial-and-error learning until equilibrium is restored. Thus Hull sought to give a physiological foundation to behaviorism. Only a few biological drives (like hunger, thirst, and sex) were thought necessary to account for all behavior on the grounds that other "motives" were derivative and acquired through these basic drives. The "drive state" at any one time depends on the extent to which the organism is deprived. (Hull's drive reduction theory does not use the term "wants" though on this theory a person would want something only to the extent it had led in the past to drive reduction.)

The major attacks on Hull's drive reduction theory have come from several sources. Harlow (1953) showed that, for monkeys at least, problem solving could be self-rewarding, so monkeys continue on such tasks even without reinforcement. This curiosity motive is difficult to reconcile with the homeostatic assumption lying behind drive theory. Hebb (1955) also challenged the homeostasis assumption. In studies on sensory deprivation, it was shown that a certain level of arousal is necessary for the optimal functioning of the central nervous system. If deprived of such arousal, the organism seeks stimulation.

As Robinson (1985) says, if we take satiety as the equivalence of physiological equilibrium, many of life's goals (e.g., friendship, power) are not things with which we become satiated—unlike the biological examples Hull considers. According to Robinson, drive reduction theories do not say where in the system and in what manner equilibrium states reveal themselves. Any stimulation results in disequilibrium from a resting state, so that a resting state is not any more normal than a state of arousal.

Dretske (1988) makes the point that while a drive can be the cause of movement, unlike a desire, it is not *for* anything. This means we cannot explain behavior by an appeal to drives in the same way that we can explain actions by an appeal to wants and beliefs. The concept of drives lacks the intentional properties of reasons for action.

## CRITICISM OF OPERANT CONDITIONING

At the time of his defense of his doctoral dissertation, Skinner was asked what deficiencies there were in the theory. The story goes that Skinner could not think of any. Since then operant conditioning has become a favorite target for both philosophers and social scientists. No criticism has proved so damning as to push it into historical oblivion. This is partly because behaviorism explains some behavior in a more *useful* way than other approaches but also because it is doubtful if behaviorism can be empirically shown to be absolutely false. After all, the capacity to check predictions about an individual's behavior presupposes knowing the *total* reinforcement history. We will, however, review the major criticism which relates to behaviorism's explanatory emptiness, neglect of innate capacities and thinking, conflict with people's own experience, and simplistic assumptions, interpretations, and extrapolations.

*Explanatory Emptiness.* Operant conditioning is a technique (as Skinner says, a methodology) that is bereft of any theoretical underpinnings except for a simple hedonistic view of motivation in the law of effect. The trouble with the law of effect is that unless a reinforcer is defined independent of its effect on the probability of response, the law of effect seems devoid of empirical content, virtually saying that whatever it is that increases the probability of behavior tends to increase the probability of behavior (Dretske, 1988).

Skinner sees no need to explain what makes reinforcers reinforcing. Skinner does not deny that people talk of having motives. But for Skinner, a motive refers to some property of the stimulus by which the stimulus gains control over the resulting behavior (Robinson, 1979). Operant conditioning makes no distinction between behavioral responses in general and intentional action. Operant conditioning implicitly assumes that people behave not so much out of any conscious deliberation on anticipated consequences but because of the consequences that have followed similar behavior in the past.

*Neglect of Innate Capacities and Thinking.* Skinner's work has focused on showing how factors in the external environment (as opposed to internal wants and beliefs) can change animal behavior. But ethnologists have shown that much animal behavior outside the laboratory depends on an innately determined neural program. They argue that what is really distinctive about much of animal behavior is that it is fixed and cannot be eliminated or altered by the environment. To account for the existence of such instinctive behavior, ethnologists inquire about its survival value.

Garcia and Koelling (1966) challenged the Skinnerian thesis by showing that, although rats had no problem learning to associate a noise and light with an electric shock, they failed, for example, to learn the connection between a novel flavor and an electric shock. It seemed some types of association were just too implausible to consider or beyond what their survival programs were designed to accept.

Behaviorism claims that the direction taken by behavior is a function of stimulus–response connections that are either innate or have been built up through learning. The probability of a given type of response is deemed to be a function of previous conditioning and the state of deprivation. This answer can be shown to have some validity in many simple cases but applying it to all behavior becomes an act of faith. As Humphrey (1983) says, behaviorism is hopelessly inadequate to the task of modeling the subtleties of real behavior. He suggests that if a rat's knowledge of other rats were limited to what behaviorists have thus far discovered about rats, the rat would show so little understanding of its fellow rats that it would bungle disastrously every social interaction in which it engaged. (Humphrey, an experimental psychologist at Cambridge University, specializes in animal behavior.)

*Conflict with Experience.*    It is a common observation that people continue many activities (like betting) when there is no positive reinforcement (periodic wins) and cease the activity when they do receive positive reinforcement (e.g., a big win).

Behaviorist assumptions seem to be in conflict with what we know about ourselves. The inner debates, appraisals, and evaluations that go on in our mind to effect some decision can never be adequately accounted for in terms of the $S^D \rightarrow R \rightarrow S^R$ connections. *Intentional* actions appear to be mediated by meanings and considerations of consequences. Behaviorism does not see people (as we see ourselves) as strategically rational actors who are constantly adjusting their plans to cope with change.

Behaviorism belittles reason, yet reasoning is what distinguishes human beings from other forms of life. This does not mean going to the other extreme and assuming, like the existentialists, that all important human behavior is the result of human decision (so that even one's sadness is the result of choosing to be sad) but that people can and do reflect on past experiences and immediate stimuli. People do not learn from trial and error alone but can reason from general principles, imagined circumstances, and imitating others.

Malcolm (1977), a philosopher, points out that the statements people make about their intentions, wants, feelings, and so on, are the most important source of information about them. Yet such self-testimony cannot be checked by simply looking for relevant external influences; self-testimony is not replaceable even in principle by observations of functional relationships between physical variables. Malcolm also argues that the reasons that lie behind intentions and action cannot be shown to be functionally related to anything, that is, reasons cannot be shown to be some dependent variable resulting from independent variables operating in the environment. Elster (1989) agrees that reinforcing consequences may not be deliberately sought *through conscious intentions* but nonetheless argues that many social situations have little regularity and too much noise for reinforcement to really shape behavior in a fine-tuned way. He argues that the human capacity for conscious choice and the sheer complexity of human affairs reduce the importance of purely mechanical reinforcement in explaining behavior.

*Simplistic Assumptions, Interpretations, and Extrapolations.*    Behaviorism would seem appropriate to explaining involuntary behavior though probably not complex habits. Watson viewed habits as the result of a long chain of conditioned reflexes. However, Hilgard and Marquis (1961) show that simple chaining of conditioned responses will not account for the characteristics of complex habits.

Skinner assumes operant conditioning is conditioned behavior and as such is automatic learning. It can legitimately be argued that a person's response may be less automatically induced than designed knowingly to elicit a reward. Behaviorism proceeds from the assumption that the basic cause of behavior is sense experience to the erroneous view that, as a consequence, explanatory models must also be in terms of elements similar to the cause.

The behaviorist assumes that generalizations from experiments on animals are transferable to humans. But unlike a pigeon, whose reinforcement or conditioning history is easily tabulated to predict its behavior, the conditioning histories of people are just not available. Hence explanations of people's behavior in terms of their history must rest more on faith in the theory than on the evidence available. Also, although there may be something approaching a uniform rat or a uniform pigeon, humans in different cultures show a wide variation in behavior under similar circumstances.

However, a more fundamental criticism of generalizing from animal behavior is that animals have perceptions but do not think conceptually: they cannot use their nonverbal language to suggest abstractions that cannot be directly perceived through the senses. Signs for animals are meaningful only when they correspond to some physical object.

Even someone as sympathetic to behaviorism as Foxall (1987) regards it as naive to extrapolate from animal experiments to humans. Foxall (1990) acknowledges that generalization to human subjects cannot be taken for granted. Thus human subjects react differently from animals to different schedules of reinforcement (whether continuous or intermittent). He agrees with those researchers who attribute this to the human capacity to determine their own rules of conduct through reasoning about the likely consequences of their behavior. But, in any case, there are many operational problems in identifying what constitutes the operant responses and discriminative stimuli as well as over the extent to which responses must be similar to belong to the same operant.

Foxall believes it is only dogma that prevented Skinner from ascribing causal significance to discriminative stimuli. Such discriminative stimuli can be thoughts and feelings and not just factors in the environment. Foxall is thus arguing that the sequence $S^D \rightarrow R \rightarrow S^R$ could be a mental causal sequence, in which case we would have to reject Skinner's epiphenomenalism. Somewhat related to Foxall's point is the claim that humans, in their ability to reflect on what others are doing, can just imitate them in similar circumstances as well as anticipate to some extent the consequences of their behavior and take appropriate action.

Dennett (1986) argues that although behaviorists may claim their predictions are in terms of bodily responses to physical stimuli, such responses can be interpreted as appropriate rational action given the circumstances. Behaviorists are able to "sell" their interpretation by conducting highly artificial experiments designed to ensure that only one bodily response (e.g., eating) is available that is appropriate to the circumstances. Dennett points out that behaviorists also naively believe they are dealing only with the brute facts of behavior, failing to recognize that facts are not given but interpreted as facts. To designate something as a fact is to pass a judgment upon it.

Goldman (1970) claims Skinnerian events cause behavior only by first causing wants and beliefs, which in turn cause the behavior. In fact, what makes sense of the law of effect and concepts like response and stimulus and response generalization is that they make sense in terms of the reason-giving explanation. For many writers, the law of effect is just folk psychology dressed up in scientific jargon. Rosenberg (1988), while acknowledging that behaviorism has had success in animal experiments, claims that it has been no more successful in predicting human action than those approaches based on the reason-giving model. Behaviorists attribute this defect in prediction to there being no universals to go on, given that people have different reinforcement histories. This is also what leads them to downplay the influence of advertising, *except* for retaining current customers by reinforcing the customer's satisfaction with the brand.

## Tolman's Behaviorism

Tolman's behaviorism is the third category of behaviorism. It departs in major ways from the other forms of behaviorism in claiming that learning can arise from making stimulus–stimulus connections and not just from making stimulus–response connections. Tolman also incorporated into his behaviorism the idea of behavior being "purposive" with learning involving changes in people's expectations. These differences are so fundamental as to make it misleading to classify the Tolman system as behaviorism were it not for the fact that he used the term himself. Tolman's (1925) work anticipated later work in cognitive psychology.

Whereas with the contiguity (classical conditioning) and the reinforcement (operant conditioning) models, people learn and act through stimulus–response connections, in the case of *relational* behaviorism, learning and action arise through stimulus–stimulus connections, that is, the relation between the stimuli themselves. Tolman's *latent learning* is typical. Tolman showed rats learned a maze merely as a result of moving around in it, even though no response was reinforced directly. Tolman used the term "cognitive map"—the rat forms a map of the environment—to account for the animal's ability to improve by mere exposure.

Tolman saw no incompatibility between behaviorism and purposive explanations and regarded reference to purpose as necessary to understanding. He argued that what organisms learned was an "expectancy": a belief (cognition) that a particular response ($R$) in the presence of a particular situation ($S$) leads to the recurrence of some event ($E$). For Tolman, learning involves changes in expectations. Expectations always reflect probabilities about courses of action leading to desirable consequences. Tolman was willing to include the organism's expectancy as part of the explanation of behavior. Tolman named his system *purposive behaviorism*. He was *not* introducing teleology but simply saying that behavior pointed toward some goal, which was determined by antecedent causes.

In introducing the mental construct of expectations relating to the likelihood of achieving goals or purposes, Tolman was moving to a mental explanation based on intervening variables or hypothetical (assumed) constructs. The problem with all such variables lies in identifying their existence independently of their effects. This in turn depends somewhat on what evidence for their existence would be acceptable. For example, if consumers *say* they have certain expectancies and their subsequent actions are in line with those expectancies, most of us seem to be prepared to accept that consumers at least act "as if" they have expectancies.

The concept of expectations has found its way into economics, decision theory, and modern cognitive psychology. Expectations are commonly regarded as a cause or part of the cause of actions, although the traditional behaviorist would regard expectations simply as an epiphenomenon. It could be argued that the aim of marketing is not just to satisfy buyers (since competitors might go further to please them) but to match or exceed customer expectations, which, in turn, are based on what has been promised, what appears reasonable, what had to be given in exchange, and, most important of all, what competition is known to be offering.

What buyers seek, when they seek it, where they seek it, from whom they seek it, and how they go about buying—all are influenced by expectations. Action is much more a function of expectations than a function of the "objective" facts, although as a cognition or belief, expectations are just one determinant of action since they do not incorporate the want itself.

The concept of expectations is frequently cited in marketing to explain behavior. Thus Lattin and Bucklin (1989) argue that to use price discounting effectively, managers must understand the link between pricing and consumer expectations in that expectations are used as a reference point. The consumer reference price reflects consumer expectations based on past pricing of the brand. A response to an unexpected price decrease (below the consumer reference price) can signal a special opportunity with the result that the response is greater than the response to an expected price decrease. It follows that too much price discounting by increasing expectations can dampen consumer response to the decrease.

Tolman's behaviorism eschews the physiological or mechanistic explanations sought by other behaviorists, arguing that explanations of behavior should involve the use of psychological as opposed to physiological concepts. For Tolman, each person's stream of behavior was segmented into a variety of purposive acts and it was essential to include a reference to the goal toward which an action was directed if that action was to be understood. Tolman regarded the hallmark of purposiveness in behavior as characterized by "the persistence until . . ." aspect of behavior. However, not all human behavior is purposive (Brody, 1983). Unconscious causes and not the pursuit of goals, it is claimed, accounts for much behavior such as doodling, nail biting, and whistling, although such exceptions are unlikely to be relevant to those interested in intentional buying.

I have argued that behaviorism seeks a causal explanation. In the case of the contiguity model, the conditioned stimulus is regarded as the cause of the conditioned response. In the case of operant conditioning, the cause or stimulus of the conditioned response is the whole set of conditions associated with reinforcement. On the other hand, with Hull's drive theory (a favorite of writers in marketing) the cause is the deprived drive state leading to a conditioned response to seek drive reduction, that is, leading to actions which in the past led to drive reduction. In the case of Tolman's relational behaviorism, the stimulus is the pattern of connections emanating from stimulus–stimulus relations leading to a conditioned response based on indirect reinforcement. Finally, Tolman's purposive behaviorism views the stimulus as some pattern of connections which leads to a conditioned response, depending on the individual's expectancy that a certain response will in fact lead to whatever is sought.

## Conclusion

In spite of all the criticism, behaviorism does dramatize the importance of reinforcement so that we come to see that even the withdrawal of a reward can act like a punisher. In any case, operant conditioning has an impressive record of success in behavior therapy where deviant behavior is assumed to be the result of maladaptive learning. One way people learn is by positive or negative reinforcements. The whole process of socialization, for instance, is marked by behavior that is shaped this way.

If any support is needed, operant conditioning supports the case for customer orientation. Products that live up to expectations give positive reinforcement; products that do not give no reinforcement. But researchers like Skinner distinguished themselves not by demonstrating that behavior which is rewarding tends to be repeated but by devising techniques for ensuring that reinforcement takes place. There has been no corresponding creativity among marketing academics, although the success of the various "frequent flyer" programs can be interpreted as an application of operant conditioning imaginatively applied by management.

## Physiological Psychology

Physiological psychology correlates various physiological variables both among themselves and with environmental factors to identify the causes of mental states or behavior. Social science is often criticized for ignoring physiological factors like hormone balance and blood chemistry, which may affect how people behave and what they want and believe. For instance, the sex hormone testosterone at high levels acts as an aphrodisiac.

We typically use the word "craving" to indicate desire with a biochemical basis. For example, a craving for chocolate may arise because of a deficiency of the chemical serotonin in the brain. Physiological psychology and neuroscience can also explain certain types of habits like addiction and even aspects of perception without invoking any reference to consciousness (Kagan, 1989).

Neuroscientists and neurobiologists equate the mind with the brain in action and regard even wants and beliefs as simply complex categories of physical events. They avoid, though, terms like wants and beliefs, seeking explanations of behavior in terms of synapses, neurotransmitters, cortical excitation, or other brain states.

Developments in physiological psychology evoke interest because they hold out the possibility of reductionism, that is, the reduction of social science explanations to physiology or neurology and physics. Concepts like wants, beliefs, and intentions seem unconnected to the material world and so out of step with the natural sciences. But perhaps those materialists who dismiss "mind" may not be in tune with modern physics. As Paul Davies (1983), a physicist and writer on modern physics, points out, physics is now moving toward a more accommodating view of "mind" while the life sciences are trying to abolish mind altogether. Although biology draws heavily on physics (e.g., molecular biology), biology in recent years has become more mechanistic (treating organisms as machines) while physicists are seeing a less mechanistic universe. Davies claims that physicists are no longer hard materialists and have been moving away from strictly mechanical models of the universe. Davies rejects reductionism, asserting that we can no more understand the mind by reference to brain cells than we can understand brain cells by examining their atomic constituents. This does not mean that Davies rejects the idea of the brain being like a machine; rather, he contends that the mind is at a higher level of description (like the plot of a novel being more than the words themselves) so that to say the brain is a machine need not imply the mind is nothing but the product of mechanistic processes. To Davies, the essential ingredient of "mind" is information (not the ghost in the machine which the philosopher Ryle so ridiculed) and corresponds more to messages in circuitry, with the message itself transcending the means of its expression. Thus the relationship between brain and mind is more like the relation cognitive psychologists see between computer hardware and software, with the software being more integrated with the hardware.

Addictive habits seem more amenable to physical explanations than do actions. There is in fact a very important difference between explaining involuntary states or physical movements and explaining action. As Dretske (1988) says, in the social sciences we are not trying to explain why our limbs move but why we move them. It is because of this distinction that marketing has found few applications for physiological psychology.

In marketing, physiological psychology plays a peripheral role, commonly to supplement ways of pretesting advertisements. For example, because the pupil of the eye varies in size depending on subject interest, pupil diameters are sometimes used to gauge emotional reaction to proposed advertisements. Similarly, measures of brainwaves, pulse rate, and galvanic skin response are used to indicate reactions to advertisements. Physiological psychology has made a contribution to business but mainly through its human engineering applications (ergonomics). Such applications do have marketing implications, however, since ergonomics in design can suggest product differentiation and promotional appeal.

## Psychoanalytic Psychology

### Scope, Aims, Assumptions, and Methods

Psychoanalytic psychology is no longer considered a general psychology but a psychology that focuses on the unconscious inner conflicts to which we are subject as we strive toward wish-fulfillment (Edelson, 1989). Psychoanalysis, as the practical application of psychoanalytic psychology, seeks to identify the meaning of an individual's mental anguish so as to relieve that anguish through "unconcealment" of hidden wants, beliefs, and intentions (Leavy, 1988). It is difficult to explain neurotic behavior, dreams, and parapraxes (slips of the tongue) in rational terms and psychoanalytic psychology tries to fill that void. Yet psychoanalytic psychology is fundamentally teleological in that it assumes unconscious motivation serves some purpose for the individual. But since unconscious motivations are also viewed as causal "mechanisms," the resulting behavior, although purposeful, is not intentional (purposive) behavior.

The most basic thesis of psychoanalytic psychology is that we lead a life in which our conscious wants, beliefs, and intentions do not explain all that we say and do. Psychoanalytic psychology, as founded by Sigmund Freud, claims that the interplay of three structural systems in the mind cause behavior. These are:

*The id.* The id contains all our drives, reflecting the primitive urges of animal man. Behind the consciously expressed wants are those deeper unconscious drives. All drives are derived from just a few basic drives. Vintage Freud views the sexual drive, as expressed through our unconscious fantasies, the most important. Sexuality here embraces all pleasure obtained from parts of the body. But more recently, prominence has been given to the search for meaningful human relationships as a major motivational lever.

*The ego.* The ego deals with the real world and is the source of information about the world and about the means available to satisfy the id. The ego is the public and consciously known self. The ego has the job of reconciling the conflicting demands of the id, the superego, and the external reality.

*The superego.* The superego contains the social norms and rules of the social world and so acts as a conscience relating to the social obligations of civilized man.

The id, ego, and superego work together to produce behavior but individual well-being depends on how successfully the ego reconciles the demands of the id, the superego, and the external world. The social standards of behavior demanded by the superego may be too demanding for the id. One way to avoid any resulting conflict is through "repression," but repression is not elimination so that what is repressed continues to exist in the unconscious part of the mind sending into consciousness a disguised substitution for itself. This disguised substitute is a neurotic symptom giving rise to neurotic behavior, that is, behavior that the individual cannot help doing while not knowing why he does it. Whenever the repression of the id by the ego forces the id to seek alternative means to satisfaction, the result is some form of neurosis. What psychotherapy tries to do is restore the balance between the id and the ego. To do this the analyst must know what the patient really wants, bearing in mind that what the patient really wants is hidden in the unconscious. Psychoanalysis claims that the techniques of dream analysis and free association provide this necessary access to the unconscious. Once the hidden desires are discovered, the cure depends on getting the patient to recognize the unconscious desires and accompanying beliefs. With this deeper understanding, the patient may accept his behavior without continuing anxiety or may give up the unhealthy wants and beliefs or sublimate the desire by channeling attention elsewhere.

The interpretation of dreams was Freud's royal road to gaining access to the unconscious, but this is only one of the techniques used today when all sorts of free association techniques are available. In free association, patients recount whatever comes into their heads with the analyst occasionally asking questions and later offering interpretations. It is assumed that over time this process will lead to the uncovering of the unconscious repressed contents of the mind, which, when extracted and recognized by the patient, will have beneficial therapeutic effects. What helps in this identification of unconscious desires and beliefs is the assumption that drives are activated by specific happenings in the environment, so that there is an innate correlation between drives and external factors that is merely modified by maturation. Given this assumption, it is believed that knowledge of the goal to which behavior is directed will reveal the corresponding drive and hence the desire.

Freud claimed that infant traumas result in repressed emotions and memories being stored in the unconscious. These repressed emotions and memories are so painful that they cannot be brought into consciousness by any normal means, yet they remain sources of people's motives, feelings, and actions. The memory of absolute dependency is what affects all later relationships. What Freud meant by the Oedipus complex was that the family is the scene of the rivalry for the exclusive hold on one or both parents which influences the later developments of the individual. Under the rubric of "narcissism" Freud linked all matters of self-concern. Early damage to self-esteem can result in an everlasting desire for admiration, avoidance of criticism, and the urge for power and positions of dominance. Since death is the end of desire, conflict, pain, and disappointment, Freud posited a "death wish" to explain self-destructive urges.

What Freud in effect did was to extend the teleological model of explanation to behavior that was unintentional but served some unconscious motive (drive). Freud thus accepts behavior as meaningful but seeks deeper meaning in terms of unconscious motivation. Although Freud regarded unconscious motives as causes of behavior, he saw all such psychological accounts as simply a holding action until more mechanistic, biochemical explanations were found.

It would be wrong to give the impression that psychoanalytic psychology is limited to Freud. Alfred Adler's ego theory puts much more emphasis on the active self in contrast to Freud's focus on the unconscious urges of the id. Similarly, Carl Gustav Jung was much less concerned with repressed conflicts than with providing each patient with a faith or outlook by which to live. Other developments include object theory, theories of attachment, and the concept of the false self.

The attraction of psychoanalytic theory over behaviorism is its ability to come to grips with complexity of motivations. One has only to contrast the Freudian view of people—buffeted by conflicts, ambivalent in emotions, aiming to reduce the inner tensions in life with many defensive tactics—with the behaviorist view of people—acting simply in accordance with past conditioning. Whereas the behaviorist sees most human action as learned, psychoanalytic psychology regards instinctual drives as the basis of much human action.

Psychoanalytic explanations provide a causal *and* an interpretive explanation. As Davidson (1982) says, Freud wanted to extend the range of phenomena subject to reason explanations but to treat the phenomena as forces are treated in the natural sciences. However, the causal account of behavior is more apparent, with outside forces and inner drives determining critical decisions, lifestyles, and personal strategies.

## Psychoanalytic Psychology in Marketing

Psychoanalytic psychology is more likely to be applied in marketing to buying that is puzzling, seemingly not quite rational, involving sensual pleasure, fraught with risk, and so possibly involving unconscious anxiety and conflict between the id, ego, superego, and reality. But this need not be so (see Holbrook, 1988). Motivation research, whose heyday was in the 1950s, draws extensively on psychoanalytic psychology. Instead of a rational account of buying, motivation research seeks to reveal the "real" buying impulses, urges, drives, and feelings lying behind buying behavior. For example, the following explanation is given for the repeat purchase of the same model of automobile:

> A psychological survey revealed that the real reasons for the high percentage of repeat purchases were based on unconscious fear of automobiles as dangerous, powerful instruments, taking the form of fear of the unfamiliarity of a new make of car, fear of disloyalty to the old car which had demonstrated its safety, emotional attachment to the old car and similar factors.

With motivation research it is common to use free association to explore the symbolic meanings and hidden motives attached to buying a particular product. More often, interviewers use a structured approach in questioning followed by nondirective probes designed to elicit unconscious motives. Both focus groups and depth interviewing are techniques from psychoanalytic psychology. In depth interviewing individuals are asked to recall their thoughts and actions in buying. In the typical focus group three to ten participants or respondents assemble for an open-ended discussion of a product or brand (Calder, 1977).

Projective techniques are commonly used in both interviews and focus groups. Such techniques cover the inkblot (Rorschach) test, sentence completion tests, graphic techniques (Draw-a-Person), and finally construction tests (Thematic Apperception Test, TAT). Projective techniques assume that the more ambiguous the stimulus, the greater the scope offered for respondents to project into their answers their real motivations and beliefs. In the TAT technique, which is used most frequently, the respondent constructs a story around some sketch or picture. The aim is to get respondents to talk freely and revealingly by asking what is going on in the minds of those in the picture who are about to consider buying a car or whatever product the researcher is interested in.

Motivation research has fallen into disrepute among many academics (because of the difficulty in ensuring the reliability and validity of psychoanalytic interpretations of data), but the use of free association is common in marketing. Many marketers accept that buyers often act from unconscious motives.

Those who study nonverbal communication focus on nonconscious behavior. Thus they claim that liking another person reflects itself in sitting or standing close to that person, gazing at the person (up to a certain point), and so on. More broadly, it is claimed that *unconscious* nonverbal behavior is a guide to personality with, say, a sociable extrovert wearing brighter, more colorful clothes, the high-achiever speaking faster and sounding more confident, and the dominant personality exhibiting more loudness, smiling less, looking less at the audience, breaking gaze last, and so on. This gives no more than a flavor of the work on nonverbal communication, but such work has its critics. Thus Wiener, Devoe, Rubinow, and Geller (1972) deny that the study of nonverbal behavior is the study of a communication system, since the behavior is not intentional and they deny there is any socially shared code for understanding people's gestures and positions, particularly given the wide range of contextual factors to be considered when interpreting the behavior.

## Criticism of Psychoanalytic Psychology

Psychoanalytic terminology and thinking are common in the humanities and in social science generally. Many social scientists find Freudian concepts such as inner conflicts, repression, wish-fulfillment, and rationalization to be a matter of common experience and therefore demanding investigation. But in spite of this and the impact that psychoanalytic psychology has had on popular thinking, it has little support among academics other than its practitioners.

Gellner (1985) regards psychoanalysis as consisting of a self-maintaining, self-confirming set of ideas such that it "comes out right" whichever way clinical or experimental evidence happens to turn out. The various parts of psychoanalytic theory, he argues, defy testing because its vague and loose concepts make it difficult to know what observations are relevant to testing. Gellner regards only the concept of "transference" (whereby the patient comes to have positive feelings toward the analyst) as sufficiently operational to facilitate testing. If psychoanalysis does not come up to the claims made for it, how does Gellner explain its success in the market? This is the main question Gellner's book seeks to answer. Gellner offers seven reasons. These briefly are that psychoanalysis

1. offers a rationale to explain a disturbing experience;
2. makes sense according to the convictions of the age;
3. promises relief;

4. is convincingly asserted by professional figures;

5. suggests risk/tension in accepting the offer;

6. must be either accepted or rejected; and

7. offers no quick way of telling if it is true.

Biologists and neurophysiologists typically reject the Freudian view of dreams. To the neurophysiologist dreams are purely somatic, nonpsychical events; indeed, the very idea of subterranean mental forces seems arcane. For example, Hobson (1989) rejects the view that interpretation of the mainfest content of dreams is required to uncover their real meaning or latent content. To Hobson most dreams are not obscure but of transparent meaning. Although unconscious wishes may be expressed in dreams and may even shape the dream, this does not mean that unconscious wishes in any way cause a dream.

Grunbaum (1984) argues that the testability of psychoanalytic theory relates to showing the validity of the psychoanalytic interpretations allied to showing that the patient's acceptance of the interpretation is a necessary condition for a cure. Farrell (1981) claims that case studies, collected in psychoanalytic interviews, provide poor support to justify the interpretations made by analysts. Moreover, the patient's acceptance of the analyst's interpretation is not a necessary condition for a cure since patients do make spontaneous recovery. Even sympathetic accounts of psychoanalytic psychology (Fisher and Greenberg, 1977) find in it too much vagueness, too much appeal to authority, a lack of specificity in the concepts used, and unreliability in the application of techniques.

How do analysts respond to these criticisms? Many follow Freud in rejecting the utility of testing for establishing its value. Many regard psychoanalysis not as a search for causes and effects but a hermeneutical (interpretive) discipline, a search for a meaning in events to make the patient's problem intelligible to both analyst and patient. Robinson (1985), a psychologist of the more conventional variety, agrees that psychoanalytic explanations are not scientific; but, he argues, to maintain their validity is to mistake the purpose of psychoanalytic explanations. These explanations aim at getting the patient to accept fears and feelings as unjustified because they serve no purpose in the patient's present life. These explanations explain the "reason for" the patient's condition—a plausible rationale, which may or may not be completely true, but is a basis for getting the patient to reinterpret his or her problem. Gay (1985), a historian, who has been analyzed and sometimes propounds psychoanalytic explanations of history, defends psychoanalytic psychology by quoting the many insights that it offers. I think insights are provided. It is one of the reasons why projective techniques, focus groups, depth interviewing, and psychoanalytic interpretations are still so prevalent in marketing.

While psychoanalysis remains controversial, the idea of unconscious forces affecting behavior (including buyer behavior) has wide appeal. However, whether such techniques as free association offer access to the unconscious to identify these forces is still debatable. What can be said is that psychoanalytic explanations can "makes sense" and provide concepts we find useful. What has come generally to be accepted is the idea of childhood experience affecting adult behavior, sexuality as a pervasive drive, and the idea of behavior needing interpretation (Beloff, 1973). And many would accept that experience, as lived, is always a blend of fantasy, emotion, passion, and imagination as well as hard rational calculation. If psychology can tell us only what men and women respond to—not what they think or feel or about the emotional conflicts they endure—then we have a dull and impoverished psychology.

## Cognitive Psychology

Many psychologists saw behaviorism as lacking in explanatory depth and being unable to come to grips with the view of people as problem-solvers, decision-makers, and planners. Psychoanalytic psychology is viewed as too speculative to satisfy the commonly accepted tenets of a scientific psychology. Cognitive psychology is a response to the defects of these two systems. However, it can be misleading to view cognitive psychology as having no links with what has gone before. Cognitive psychology is not some discontinuous innovation but has its root in Tolman's purposive behaviorism and the subsequent cognitive behaviorism that accepted, contrary to Skinner, that mental events and processes can be causes of behavior. This led naturally to cognitive psychology's focus on decision-making involving how the mind processes information.

## Features of Cognitive Psychology

Gardner (1985), in the most sweeping historical review thus far of cognitive psychology, places it with artificial intelligence, linguistics, anthropology, neuroscience, and mental philosophy as collectively constituting the cognitive sciences. He identifies five features of cognitive psychology that distinguishes it from the other cognitive sciences. These five features are positing of mental representations as guiding behavior, the computer as the root metaphor of how the human mind processes information, the deemphasis of affect, an interdisciplinary approach, and a willingness to face philosophical issues.

### MENTAL REPRESENTATION

Cognitive psychology posits mental representations as guiding behavior. It is claimed that to explain conscious behavior psychology must relate the relevant internal processes or mental representations to mental processes like perception, attention, comprehension, and memory. Such processes suggest people learn by storing internal representations, which are then used to guide behavior.

Cognitive psychology postulates a level of explanation that relies neither on neurophysiology nor on reasons alone but lies somewhere between the two. Although all cognitive psychologists accept the need for mental representation, there are disputes over the form of that representation. There are different ways of characterizing the representational level as reflected in the use of terms like images, scripts, schemas, and mental models. The dispute stems from lack of knowledge about how the brain works. For example, in seeing, we know the eye throws a two-dimensional image of the world onto the retina and we know that particular points on the retina connect to corresponding points in the brain. But this is a far cry from knowing how all this translates into propositions such as "This is a detergent."

### COMPUTER ANALOGY

Cognitive psychology takes the computer as the root metaphor or model of how the human mind works. On this basis, the cognitive psychologist regards all thinking and reasoning as a form of information processing. Thus the study of mental representation is equated with how information is processed, that is, how information is stored and used in the mind: the study of mental representation takes the mind (as the brain in action) as an information-processing system. Does this mean then that those *mental* representations cause behavior or action? Cognitive psychologists do specify general causal relationships between mental states and behavior but take a physicalist stance in equating mental states with brain states. Cognitive psychologists, though, more typically claim their focus is on explaining mental capacities, not primarily looking for causes. This is because if we look at actions (as Ryle does) as a performance that exercises skills, we will then speak of the capacity to do something, whereas talk of such capacities being causes of action seems incoherent.

In cognitive psychology, human actions are viewed as manifestations of mental *capacities*; these capacities, *not* the actions themselves, are said to require explaining. The capacity to be identified is the *mediating processes* between input of stimuli and the output manifestations (actions). The other social sciences—sociology, economics, and so on—assume people have the capacity to, say, discriminate, perceive, and reason, but cognitive psychology is concerned with how these capacities come into being and operate. Thus instead of talking about the process of conditioning, the cognitive psychologist is concerned with explaining the capacity to be conditioned. Cognitive psychologists argue that the explanatory role of intervening variables like attitudes, motives, wants, and beliefs will inevitably remain mysterious until information-processing *capacities* are explained in terms of the programs at work.

The basic metaphor for understanding mental capacities is the computer. Describing mental capacities is like describing the computer's operations in terms of its programs (plus a physical level of description of the brain assumed to involve mechanisms corresponding to transistors, circuits, etc.). With no general agreement on terminology, various terms—like transformations, deletions, and conjunctions—currently are used to describe the processing operations acting on the mental events or representations of beliefs, goals, and so on. To some extent this reflects debate within the discipline. For example, there is debate over just how information is represented within memory; "icons" and "traces" are among the terms being used as tentative analogies to make up for current ignorance on the physiology involved.

The research strategy is first to identify the analogous computer programs and then to experiment to choose that which best describes the capacity of interest. When the capacity to perform some function such as perceiving is what is explained, cognitive psychologists typically speak of offering a functional explanation. This view has its antecedents in the psychology of William James in the nineteenth century. James viewed functionalism in psychology as being concerned with mental functions like perceiving, with the functionalist's task to discover how the process of perceiving operates, what it achieves, and under what conditions.

## DEEMPHASIS OF AFFECT

Cognitive psychology assumes highly rational thought processes and purposive behavior. The focus on rationality has meant that cognitive psychology neglects emotion or affect and motivation. It is agreed that emotions do have an impact on cognitive functioning but it is felt that at this time cognitive psychology cannot cope with this additional complexity (Gardner, 1985).

## INTERDISCIPLINARY APPROACH

Cognitive psychology has been open to ideas from all the other cognitive sciences, in particular artificial intelligence (AI). This is to be expected since the aim of AI is to develop computer programs (the chess example has been well publicized) that produce outputs that match the outputs of human intelligence.

## PHILOSOPHICAL ISSUES

Cognitive psychology, unlike other psychologies, has been prepared to confront many traditional philosophical issues. For example, is the mind simply the brain at work or something distinct? Are concepts and other ideas directly apprehended just as emotions are, or are ideas the means by which we apprehend and comprehend objects in the world outside? Although such questions are not directly discussed here, some of the criticisms of cognitive psychology emanate from these traditional philosophical controversies.

## Cognitive Psychology in Marketing

Cognitive psychology is generally considered the mainstream view in the study of consumer behavior. It has not been easy to transfer findings from the psychological literature, however, so that much of the marketing literature would not necessarily be endorsed as valid by cognitive psychologists. Hence the resort in the marketing literature to descriptions such as the "cognitive orientation approach" or the "decision-making approach" in addition to talking of an "information-processing approach"—all alternative terms for cognitive psychology. A number of interrelated streams of research draw on cognitive psychology:

1. Attitude formation on the assumption, say, that the consumers' decision process is captured by the multiattribute model.

2. Hierarchy of effects models concerned with the process leading to the formation of attitudes and purchase intention. Under this heading might also come research that identifies features of an ad that affect the processing of an ad's contents.

3. The concept of involvement and its influence on the consumer's mode of learning, attention to an advertisement, and sequencing of the mental stages in the hierarchy of effects model.

4. The relationship between attitude toward the ad and attitude toward the brand being advertised. Under this heading might also be placed research that relates *executional* aspects of an ad to the attitude toward the brand.

The Howard model discussed in Chapter 4 is one of the overarching cognitive models explaining how consumers make purchase decisions. The other two major models are those of Bettman (1979) and of Engel, Blackwell, and Miniard (1986). The general flow of such models is from motivating stimuli *to* cognition *to* attitude: the learn–feel–do sequence discussed in Chapter 4. Alternatively, it has been called the *C–A–B* paradigm with its hierarchical flow of effects from cognition (*C*) to affect (*A*) to behavior (*B*) (Holbrook, O'Shaughnessy, and Bell, 1990).

In all the models, motivation is just assumed without any enlightening discussion of how goals, wants, desires, values, or whatever, are acquired and changed. At best there may be discussion of problem recognition, occurring as a result of a perceived difference between the actual situation and the ideal. Alternatively, there may be talk about the ad appealing to either utilitarian or expressive motives or how the level of motivation (involvement) affects the process of attitude formation toward both the ad and the brand itself. Given a motivation, the consumer is assumed to embark on the acquisition of information. Consumers are viewed as highly selective in what communications they notice and absorb. As would be expected, consumers pay attention to what interests them, is useful to them, or excites their curiosity; they avoid communications that are at variance with their beliefs unless there is a need to think up counterarguments. The greater the perceived risk, the greater the tendency to seek information. It is accepted that consumers reflect on their reactions to things and such reflection is one basis for inferring their own attitudes toward the things to which they are reacting.

After information is received, it is organized in memory. How exactly it is represented within the data structures of human memory remains a mystery. The duplex theory of memory asserts the brain has two memories, an active short-term memory (STM) and a long-term memory (LTM), but there are also rival theories. STM is regarded as short on capacity for storing information so able to store information for a short time only. It is in LTM where knowledge of the meaning of things and the rules used for information processing are assumed to be stored. There are debates between those who regard information processing as a single process and those who adopt a multiple-process view. Allport (1980), for example, claims that there are no limitations to the amount of information that can come in through the various sensory channels; information inputs therefore should be regarded as parallel (multiple entries at multiple points) rather than serial (entering at a single point, one after another). There are even disputes over whether the particular forms of mental representation will vary with context, but these disputes will not be discussed here.

After information is absorbed and comprehended, consumers undertake the process of decision-making, which results in an attitude toward the brand. How the consumer processes information to arrive at an attitude is of particular interest. Does the consumer act as if he or she weights the individual attributes for relative importance and then combines the results in some simple additive way to arrive at an overall evaluation of one brand vis-à-vis another? This is the assumption of the compensatory (multiattribute) model and is the measure of *attitude* in the Howard model. It is termed a compensatory model because the consumer accepts that a product's weaknesses in one respect can be compensated by strength in another. Whereas a compensatory decision strategy assumes the consumer makes tradeoffs, a noncompensatory decision strategy makes no such assumption that a brand's weakness in one attribute can be compensated by strengths in another. Bettman (1979) defines these noncompensatory processing rules as follows:

1. *Conjunctive:* Consumers establish a minimum acceptable level for each choice criterion. They accept an alternative only if every criterion equals or exceeds the minimum cutoff level.

2. *Disjunctive:* Consumers establish acceptable standards for each criterion. A product is acceptable if it exceeds the minimum level on at least one criterion.

3. *Lexicographic:* Consumers rank choice criteria from most to least important. They choose the best alternative on the most important criterion. If a tie occurs, they select the best alternative on the second most important criterion, and so on.

4. *Elimination by aspects:* Consumers establish minimum cutoffs for each choice criterion. They select one criterion and eliminate all alternatives that do not exceed the cutoff level. They continue eliminating alternatives until one alternative remains.

Typically consumers, consciously or unconsciously, apply the appropriate rules when deciding to buy within a market segment and rule out other segments as a consequence. There is current interest in knowing how the compensatory model combines with noncompensatory rules and how the rules themselves combine. There is, for example, the claim that the compensatory model can be used to provide reasonably good predictions of choices made by using noncompensatory rules, but the universality of this has been called into question (Johnson, Meyer, and Ghose, 1989).

Ajzen and Fishbein (1980) regard a person's attitude toward taking some action (like buying) as determined by her beliefs that performing the action leads to certain outcomes and by her evaluation of these outcomes (consequences) in terms of her goals. This is the multiattribute model based on an expectancy theory conceptualization of attitudes. Attitude, as measured in this way or some other way, is typically used to predict intention on the assumption that intention is predictive of purchase, which is supported by some evidence (Kalwani and Silk, 1982). However, as noted in Chapter 4, the evidence supporting a positive relationship between attitudes and intention to buy and between intention to buy and actual purchase is not clear-cut.

What Ajzen and Fishbein refer to as a theory of reasoned action views intention to act as a function of

1. the individual's attitude toward taking the action;
2. the individual's perceptions of the social and group norms relevant to the behavior, given the situation; and
3. the individual's motivation to comply with these social and group norms.

The model assumes that attitude toward taking some action is independent of the individual's perceptions of social and group norms and independent of a motivation to comply with those norms. The fact that we can ask questions of respondents in a way that suggests independence does not mean actual independence exists. A person's attitude, traditionally defined as a predisposition to react in a particular way to some item, person, or thing, is the resultant of anything that affects related beliefs. Social and group norms clearly affect beliefs about socially appropriate behavior; the motivation to comply with such norms is likely to affect the intensity of attitudes. In any case, it is not clear that social and group norms also embrace personal standards of integrity, which surely affect behavior. Finally, it is not apparent that the three factors take account of any perceived risk that might affect buying intentions. If a customer is choosing between two brands, one believed to have the higher likelihood of achieving a lesser satisfaction but the other having a smaller likelihood of achieving a greater satisfaction, which will the consumer prefer? Howard's model (see Chapter 4) implicitly assumes that if the consumer has a high degree of confidence in her favorable judgment of the brand and its benefits, the perceived risk will be small. But I can be absolutely confident buying a house in Manhattan will be a good buy yet refrain from buying because of my attitude toward risk. Parents may have absolute confidence that their child will not take drugs but may still acknowledge there is high risk given the inner-city environment.

## Criticism of Cognitive Psychology

Robinson (1985) accuses cognitive psychology of passing off what are seldom more than metaphors as actual descriptions of what thought is like—usually accompanied by talk about processes without any explication of what a process is beyond saying it is like the processes occurring within a computer or a telephone switchboard. He regards much that occurs in cognitive psychology as retracing the "failed" program of "mentalism" that behaviorism replaced: even so-called pioneering work in cognitive psychology could have been done in Wundt's laboratory in the last century, so close is the orientation. Cognitive psychologists can claim that behaviorism's explanations are incomplete when the mind is ignored; behaviorists can reply that cognitive explanations must be incomplete when the causes of mental events and processes are ignored while the reliance on unobservable explanatory variables sets severe limits on testing (Foxall, 1990).

A common criticism of cognitive psychology is that the computer analogy is carried too far with functions attributed to the brain that belong solely to the computer. Do people think in a step-by-step procedural way as typified by the computer program, or does their thinking more typically involve rapid, intuitive, *creative* flashes of insight? Some writers (Roszak, 1987) argue that even mathematics at its highest levels has more to do with instruction and creativity than with programmed procedural thinking. On the other hand, people often behave in a "mindless" fashion in buying, as elsewhere.

Dreyfus (1979) criticizes the computer model as being unable to explain, on the basis of any formal calculus, even the most common everyday performance such as making our way around our home and picking up and manipulating objects. In fact, many eminent philosophers, including Fodor (1981), who take a specialized interest in cognitive psychology, express extreme skepticism over whether cognitive psychology will ever be able to explain any of the complex forms of reasoning.

Penrose (1989), a mathematician, argues that if the brain were just a digital computer, its power would be circumscribed by the limits on all computation, as demonstrated by Gödel's theorem. All computer programs are algorithms and Kurt Gödel, a mathematical logician, demonstrated that there are always statements about numbers that can never, even in principle, be proved either true or false on the basis of a fixed set of axioms. Gödel showed that a formal system of axioms and rules of procedure must contain some statements that can be neither proved nor disproved by means allowed within the system. It follows that minds cannot be equated with digital computers since humans can discover mathematical truths about numbers which a computer cannot prove for itself. The human mind seems able to apprehend the truth of some statements even though that truth cannot be formally established within the system. [This same point is mentioned by Davies (1983), who quotes Hofstadter in pointing out that the human capacity for discovering mathematical truths is itself limited.] Penrose also claims that ideas seem to be grasped as a whole, not as a series of logical steps, and speculates that the brain, if like a computer, would resemble a quantum computer and not a digital one. In any case, a computer might be programmed to answer questions in English that are asked in Chinese without being said to understand either Chinese or English. In other words, the way the brain produces conscious thought cannot be completely equated with implementing some formal computer program.

Rychlak (1979) regards cognitive psychology as just a variation of the $S \rightarrow O \rightarrow R$ (stimulus–organism–response) model with the additional concept of viewing responses as being derived from inputs through information processing. Malcolm (1977) argues that in respect to memory there is often no process involved at all in remembering or recognizing something. He claims that our understanding of human cognitive power is not advanced by replacing the $S \rightarrow R$ model with a *mythology* about inner guidance systems. Others have pointed out that the number of processing stages identified for some specific task or problem seems to depend more on the ingenuity of the experimenter than on any demonstrated fixed features of human information processing. Until more is known about the "hardware" of the mind, an infinite number of processing rules are possible for any given problem. As Dennett (1986) points out, there is no reason to believe that two people in the same logical state or functional condition will in fact use a similar program given the differences in their heredity and upbringing. Whether there are in fact any universal and precise processes to discover is a fundamental dispute. There are those who claim that mental processes are context- or task-specific (Allport, 1980). Thus Ray (1982), in positing the three decision process heirarchies (see Chapter 4), is refuting the universality of the learn–feel–do sequence that is implicit in the earlier discussion of cognitive psychology in marketing. As would be expected, with a little thought on viewing an ad, we can come up with many seemingly distinct tasks and hence with many categories of distinct mental processes. Thus MacInnis and Jaworski (1989) talk of there being at least six processing operations, each involving different levels of attention and utilizing different amounts of working memory. This is a central feature of their model concerned with the formation of brand attitudes. The model predicts that negative attitudes toward an ad generated by the presence of *affectively* disliked features of the ad need not carry over into a negative attitude toward the brand itself since "emotions have different impact on brand attitudes at different levels of processing." This is in line with the Rossiter and Percy model discussed in Chapter 4. When it comes to consumer decision processes, the computer (computational) model of step-by-step symbolic processing may correspond only to what consumers can be directed into doing in a laboratory experiment but seems far removed from the messy process that actually occurs.

Searle (1980), a philosopher, denies the need for mental representation models, arguing there is a need simply for neurophysiological explanations of what the brain does in realizing intentional states and the reason-giving explanation that explains at the level of intentionality. Searle in fact argues that a programmed computer could never have real intentional states and that only things having the "causal power" of real brains can genuinely think.

Harré and Secord (1973) object to the very conception of people as information-processing machines rather than as information-seeking and information-generating agents. In the typical experiment, where subjects play the part of information-processing machines, the authors argue that the judgmental aspect of behavior is emphasized and those other aspects of the perceptual process that operate in nonlaboratory situations, such as exploration, are excluded. In fact the information provided to subjects in an experiment in information processing is such that there is virtually only one way that the person can process it—the way that fits the hypothesis!

Taylor (1983), also a philosopher, claims that what cognitive psychologists say about the cognitive processes is not how people themselves experience action. People have an understanding of themselves as agents and so act to realize their goals in terms of what they want to be and do. It is this self-understanding that gives significance to mental states and events. Taylor argues that the crucial difference between people and machines is not consciousness but this significance feature: things have significance for people which cannot be captured by any computer program analogy. This question of significance relates to whether the aspects of mental life concerned with knowing are independent of those concerned with feeling or willing. Others have claimed that human functioning typically involves a direct relation with the world without the mediation of mental representations.

The representational theory of the mind, implicit in cognitive psychology, raises many old philosophical controversies. Thus there is the claim that the mind is like a computer, or a "syntactic engine," which acts upon symbolic representations like a computer operates on some symbolic language. Thinking on this basis that "I want $X$" or "I believe $Y$" is to have stored in the brain mental sentences with the same meaning as "I want $X$" or "I believe $Y$." Such a hypothesis, if true, would help us explain why mental states can act as causes, given that there is a corresponding physical structure in the head which acts in the causal chain that leads to action. But many objections can be raised to refute this representational theory. Thus what gives meaning to these representations if not other representation in another language? A representation is a representation for someone but the brain cannot be said to know what it represents without some further assumption about, say, internal observers doing the job of interpreting. This, of course, can lead to infinite regress since the same argument can be applied again to the observers. The fact is that no one has actually seen a mental sentence and, even if one could be identified in the neurology or chemistry of the brain, there would still be the problem of intepreting its meaning. Cognitive psychologists reply to this infinite regress objection by pointing to artifical intelligence programs, which do not contain observers. But humans interpret the AI simulation of natural intelligence—humans who, unlike AI, possess intentionality so that behavior is not merely purposeful but purposive.

Gardner (1985) points out that experimental psychology has had a disastrous history when it comes to producing useful findings, and the most impressive models in cognitive psychology are based on experiments that have little or no relevance to human action. In fact, cognitive psychology has not yet succeeded in developing a psychology that makes a substantial contribution to understanding how the mind works.

In spite of the foregoing criticism, cognitive psychology, in seeking to understand underlying capacities for knowing, learning, and thinking, represents a search for a fundamental form of explanation. As Dretske (1988) says, to be able to explain how the system works to produce the light in the bulb is more fundamental than knowing that the light comes on when the switch is pushed down or knowing that electricians put in the system of wiring that works to produce the light. On the other hand, at its present stage in development, it would be wrong for marketing academics to put all their eggs in this one basket by focusing exclusively on cognitive psychology.

## Hermeneutics: Interpretive Psychology

### Definition and Scope

Interpretive social sciences include symbolic interactionism, ethnomethodology, cultural anthropology, phenomenological psychology, and ethogeny (and perhaps psychoanalysis?). Phenomenological psychology and ethogeny are discussed in this chapter; the others, in the next.

"Hermeneutics" has become an umbrella term for all interpretive approaches in social science. Hermeneutics was traditionally defined as the methodology of interpretation for recovering the true meaning of ancient texts like the Bible. Gadamer (1975) and Ricoeur (1981) have expanded the term to embrace the interpretation of all behavior (including records of behavior like interview narratives). Messer, Sass, and Woolfolk's (1988) review of hermeneutics deals with applications and issues, and there have also been review articles for marketers (O'Shaughnessy and Holbrook, 1988).

All the interpretive social sciences reject the doctrine of "methodological monism," which asserts that all disciplines that aspire to be science must follow the methods of the natural sciences. The term used by critics to categorize such a claim is "scientism," which is rejected by the hermeneutic disciplines on the ground that the goal of the social sciences should be understanding, not the establishment of predictive laws in the manner of physics. Indeed, there are many who claim that the very idea of psychological "laws" is misplaced: human actions occur within a certain historical context and within certain cultural institutional constraints, so that behavior is always being formed anew as circumstances change.

The hermeneutic or interpretive social sciences seek the meaning of action for the individual. This concept of meaning includes significance and symbolic meaning, not to be equated with the narrower concept of meaning in cognitive psychology, which is restricted to intentional mental state. On a hermeneutical basis, buying is not viewed simply as a matter of rational calculation with buyers deliberating on the objective facts; rather, the buyer has *felt expectations* as to how the buying and consumption episodes will be *personally experienced.*

The hermeneutic social sciences do not include all those opposing methodological monism. Thus humanistic psychology opposes methodological monism but is generally not grouped within hermeneutics. Humanistic psychology developed as the so-called third force in psychotherapy, in opposition to the narrow, deterministic vision of human nature seen in behaviorism and psychoanalysis. Thus Abraham Maslow, one of the originators of humanistic psychology, returned to a more humanistic, Aristotelian view of the human being through the hierarchy of needs. Humanistic psychology points to people's self-actualizing tendencies and somewhat downplays the role of understanding; as such it is outside the mainstream of hermeneutics.

Although hermeneutics as a methodology is usually given the spotlight, Gadamer (1975) regards hermeneutic understanding as just something that is necessary for social living in that without the intersubjective understanding that emanates from interpreting others, coordinating one's actions with those of others would be impossible. This intersubjective understanding results from an ability to see the sense, the rationality, of the action from the agent's point of view. The hermeneutic approaches seek the meaning to action, or the pattern to action, or the rule governing actions. They are rooted in the rational (goal ascription) explanation, providing "rational" is interpreted as making sense within the context of the person's situation, perceptions, beliefs, wants, and feelings.

The basic idea is to observe, listen, and interpret what is being said and done and make sense of it. Interpretive explanations show the purpose of action, the semantic meaning of the action, the patterns to action, or the rules being followed in the action.

People interpret the behavior of others all the time. Even the significance of physical movement depends on interpretation. Thus interpreting a facial muscular response as a smile or just a nervous twitch determines its meaning and hence its significance for the observer. Intentional action like shopping is not just physical movement. To say someone is shopping is an interpretation of behavior that presupposes that those undertaking such action are guided by the concepts and purposes implied by the word "shopping." Shopping is a social activity, and how it is carried on is greatly influenced by the social institutions, conventions, and internalized social norms that suggest what is socially appropriate. A correct interpretation of people's behavior does not come from viewing actions as discrete events to be rendered intelligible by subsuming them under general laws but by understanding what an agent is likely to do in the circumstances, given the culture and conventions of that person's social milieu.

Hermeneutics commonly claims that an individual psychology is not possible without the intersubjective understanding people have of each other; to understand action means interpreting the *meaning* or *significance* of the action for the person taking it. When it comes to beliefs about, say, products, these beliefs constitute a socially constructed reality rather than an entirely objective one. In hermeneutics the focus in general is on how consumers come to construct and share these meanings and how such shared meanings guide behavior.

Interpretive psychology does not deny that things can happen *to* people that cause them to behave in a certain way (e.g., the involuntary closing of the eyes in a sandstorm). However, when actions are intentional, people act as *agents* directing their own lives while trying to make things happen their way. Of course, intentional action is influenced by stimuli, but such stimuli are just input to thought, sometimes compelling physical movement but never completely determining action.

The methodology of hermeneutics makes a number of assumptions:

1. The data of the social sciences are meanings: beliefs, wants, plans, goals, and purposes. (See Chapter 8 for an explication of the concept of "meaning" as used here.)

2. Each person's actions or descriptions of those actions can be read *as if a text*. The metaphor of the text replaces the metaphor in cognitive psychology of the mind as a computer.

3. People's actions are never isolated events but are embedded in some context that needs to be identified to understand the action.

4. There are no noninterpreted givens that can serve as a foundation for knowledge: facts are not neutral, objective, or value-free but are interpreted as "facts" only against some conceptual scheme or theory. People see what they have been taught to see and all methods of inquiry direct and constrain interpretion (e.g., statistical methods).

## PHENOMENOLOGICAL PSYCHOLOGY

The basic phenomenological assumption is that the reality of interest to social scientists is what people perceive it to be. Hence phenomenological psychology seeks to understand the meanings of social phenomena from the perspective of the individual. Phenomenological psychology is frequently combined with the philosophy of "existentialism" (Thompson, Locander, and Pollio, 1989). This is not surprising since existentialism emphasizes the uniqueness of the individual, *subjective* experience and the belief that we must accept responsibility for everything about ourselves, not just our actions but our attitudes, character, and even our emotions. Such a philosophy rejects the idea of any compelling external causes of *action* but instead seeks its meaning for the individual, that is, belief about its significance for the individual's wants. As every single person is a coherent whole and not just a bundle of unrelated wants and habits, the fundamental choices people make are key to understanding all their behavior.

Thompson et al. claim existential phenomenology (EP) blends the philosophy of existentialism with the methods of phenomenology as influenced by the Gestalt ("the whole is more than the sum of the parts") perspective. In EP, people are not studied in isolation or as individual units interacting with each other but as part of a whole comprising the individual with his environment. Thus individual experience is described *as it is lived.*

The interview is the basic source of data. The aim of the phenomenological interview is to elicit a first-person description of the experience (e.g., of buying). Only descriptive questions are asked: "*What* was *X* like?" The answers are recorded in the respondent's own words, and transcribed recordings of the interview constitute the "text" to be interpreted. The interpretation keeps to the respondent's own language, avoiding any abstract theorizing or resort to external verification of what is said; thus the interpretation remains at the level of the "lived experience." All theoretical hunches are held in abeyance and bracketed for later consideration. This process is helped if several people do the interpreting, acting as a check on each other.

Interpreting a text means operating within the "hermeneutic circle" (Gadamer, 1975) by moving back and forth between parts of the text and a general conception of the text as a whole. The hermeneutic circle means that the parts are always interpreted within some understanding of the whole, which in turn is understood by coming to understand the constituent parts. This highlights the hermeneutic belief in the contextual nature of knowledge. A "fact" is judged to be so not in isolation but by taking account of context and whoever is doing the interpretation. Thompson et al. acknowledge that hermeneutics in general accepts that there can be equally defensible interpretation but that in EP there is a search for *the* interpretation describing the respondent's experience.

After the process of interpretation, a search is made for common patterns. These common patterns, if found, are termed "global themes." These global themes are not extracted and then expressed in abstract terms or theoretical explanations but stay rooted at the level of experience. For instance, part of a global theme quoted by Thompson et al. was that when shoppers felt knowledgeable about what they were shopping for and enjoyed the shopping, they viewed salespeople as intrusive and coercive. There has to be support for global themes in all transcripts of the same experience.

Most social scientists seek interpretations that get away from observational langauge, adapting abstractions like the concept of "displaced meaning" in anthropology (see Chapter 8), but EP keeps to the level of respondent experience. The price of this is a lack of richly exploitable global themes. The philosopher Rorty (1979) is supportive of this; Gadamer (1975) is not. For Gadamer it is not enough to recover meanings, but what is said must be illuminated by a "fusion of horizons"; that is, the researcher's own perspective and thinking must be fused with the meanings emerging from interpretation. This, it is claimed, is the way to achieve depth of understanding. A fusion of horizons allows the interpreter to bring to bear on a text the whole range of sensitizing concepts developed in the social sciences.

ETHOGENY

Existential phenomenology seeks global themes or recurring experiential patterns. An alternative approach is to view action *as if* rule-following and seek to identify the rules.

We all accept "manners" as reflecting the habitual rules followed in someone's culture and "etiquette" as reflecting the formal rules of behavior. We may also define "skills" as following rules in different combinations and we might well use a checklist (a set of formal rules) for choosing a used car. But in what sense is all action said to be rule-following?

One argument is that identifying the meaning of action is like deciphering a text and to understand that text is to understand the language or the rules it follows (Rosenberg, 1988). Another approach is to say that intentional action is planned action and, since plans are guideline rules, (intentional) action is rule-following (Baker and Hacker, 1984; Winch, 1958). The buyer is viewed as a collection of practices or rules which, though constantly under review and revision in the light of experience, nevertheless guide buying actions. It is claimed that as long as consumers believe there is the possibility of making a mistake, buying actions will be guided and constrained by rules designed to avoid making mistakes. This does not imply that buyers are conscious of the rules they follow but simply that their behavior is rule-governed. Still another view of rule-following is the original one put forward by Wittgenstein, who spoke of rule-governed behavior in the sense that a rule could describe the behavior; it is the behavior that determines the rule not vice versa. [Winch, who was a student of Wittgenstein, is accused by Schatzki (1983) of incorrectly interpreting Wittgenstein on this issue.] Under the the Wittgenstein view, rules cannot be the cause of action but simply describe customs or the regularities of what are generally unreflective acts.

Harré and Secord (1973) regard all action (as opposed to involuntary behavior) as rule-following and advocate "ethogeny," a new social science discipline modeled on ethology. Just as ethologists seek patterns of instinctive behavior in animals, ethogeny seeks the implicit or explicit rules that underlie everyday social action. The basic tool is the protocol statement, which is a record of what the subject—here the consumer—has to say as he or she thinks aloud

1. before buying (the anticipatory account),
2. during buying (the contemporaneous account), and
3. after buying (the retrospective account).

The protocol statement constitutes the "text" to be interpreted to reveal the goals, wants, beliefs, or rules being followed. In the most general terms, the process of rule identification consists first of showing buying actions to be the outcome of reasons. Explicating the key concepts employed in these reasons reveals the rules being employed. Thus if the consumer said she bought the brand because it was the most familiar, it is in the concept of "familiarity" that the rule can be found—"other things remaining equal, I buy the brand that is most familiar." We can explicate the key concepts used in self-reports to describe a respondent's behavior to identify the rules while at the same time operating within the hermeneutic circle. There is no conflict between traditional hermeneutics and the idea of action as rule-governed.

Harré and Secord (1973) neatly summarize ethogeny's assumptions:

- Human beings must be treated as agents acting according to rules, and it must be realized that it is unscientific to treat them as anything else.
- Social behavior must be conceived of as actions mediated by meanings, not responses caused by stimuli.
- The theory of movements, physiology, must be clearly separated from psychology, the theory of actions.
- It must be clearly appreciated that most human social behavior cannot be made intelligible under the mechanistic, causal paradigm.
- Reasons can be used to explain actions, and not all reasons can be treated as causes in the mechanistic sense, though in some special cases causes may be cited as reasons.
- Lay explanations of behavior provide the best model for psychological theory, and properly considered they can be seen to be more in accordance with the actual methodology of real natural science than is the positivist methodology, which provided the old models of science that psychologists have copied.

Interpretation involves operating within the hermeneutic circle with attention to intelligibility, internal consistency, coherence, and comprehensiveness.

There are limits, of course, to what consumers can reveal about their thinking or reasoning processes, and there is sharp debate over this issue (Nisbett and Wilson, 1977, versus Miller and Smith, 1978). Ericsson and Simon (1980) claim that people asked to think their thoughts aloud are likely to supply reliable data given no intent to deceive.

However, there is more likelihood of bias if people are asked to recall from long-term memory. But a problem remains in identifying the reasons (those that were *truly* motivational), but this is no more disturbing than the "impossibility in the physical sciences of knowing for certain whether one's theoretical explanations are correct" (Harré and Secord, 1973). Biehal and Chakravarti (1989) point to two problems that potentially threaten the validity of verbal protocols:

1. task "impact" effects caused by the need to talk out loud while making a choice, and

2. subjects' conscious attempts to manage the impression given to the experimenter.

Their experiment used a no-protocol group of subjects and a protocol group. Although differences in information processing occurred (the no-protocol subjects did more brand processing and fewer holistic comparisons, initially focusing on the chosen brand's features), the verbalization of protocol subjects did not affect either first or second choice outcomes.

Ericsson and Simon stress the importance of interpreting protocol statements in the light of the circumstances (i.e., the buying situation) under which they were obtained. This means that those recording the anticipatory, contemporaneous, and retrospective accounts should note possible unconscious influences on the respondent's behavior. Agents or consumers are not always aware of everything that influences them at the time.

No investigative technique is free from potential bias. Just as we can misinterpret what we observe or bias behavior by our presence during an experiment, so too can testimony be biased. There is always a need for vigilance and a willingness to discard protocols that may be biased. But ethogeny is criticized on other grounds. Typically those committed to phenomenological psychology find ethogeny too "mechanistic" for their liking in spite of denials of this by Harré and Secord and other practitioners. For some critics, hermeneutics is a matter not of discovering rules but of showing meaning. But much depends on how specific we expect the rules to be and how we interpret "meaning." For many philosophers advocating the concept of rule-following, the rules are not like the clear-cut, specific rules of chess but the "diffuse notion of 'knowing how' rather than following specific instructions." In any case, ethogeny, in identifying the rules of action, shows the meaning of that action. Rules are deduced from knowing the meaning of the situation to the agent (see Chapter 11).

## Interpretive Psychology in Marketing

The application of an interpretive psychology is inevitable in marketing since marketers are obliged to interpret the verbal reports of customers. However, few would say that such interpretation was grounded in any principles drawn from interpretive psychology. But applications are growing. For example, the rule-following approach has been applied to individual brand choice (O'Shaughnessy, 1987); to use patterns in clothing and food consumption (Kehret-Ward, Johnson, and Louie, 1985); to gift giving (Caplow, 1984); and to competition among firms (Thomas and Soldow, 1988).

## General Criticism of Hermeneutics

One criticism lies in the difficulty of ensuring that the contents of verbal reports are representative since what people say about their actions does not exhaust all their inner thoughts. Also, people cannot always put into words the things they feel. When respondents make a statement, the statement itself can be viewed as an interpretive expression of thoughts. If this is so, then the view of communication as a coding and decoding activity is a little misleading. In any case, people are not always infallible commentators about their own wants and beliefs. Self-understanding cannot in all circumstances be accepted as the final authority; the understanding offered by "experts" may override its verdict.

As Humphrey (1983) says, people have privileged access to themselves as a model for studying others. As humans ourselves we can *look in* on our thoughts and the passions that accompany our behavior. Without introspection, deciphering the behavior of other people would be impossible. However, Humphrey would probably claim that for any interpretation to have real depth, there must be a shared cognitive environment and shared assumptions about the world. Understanding is always constrained by what we ourselves have experienced and having the relevant experience makes us better judges of how people are likely to react. Thus ex-alcoholics are in a better position to understand alcoholics, and so on.

Those viewing actions as rule-following (e.g., Winch, 1958) incurred a good deal of criticism (Bhaskar, 1979; Gellner, 1971; MacIntyre, 1971; Rudner, 1966; Thompson, 1981) in suggesting the approach constituted an overall methodology for social science. For example, Churchland (1981) points out that such a psychology could never explain mental illness, creative imagination, or the *capacity* to perform action. Doubts are raised as to whether an interpretive social science can generate scientific theory as generally conceived by philosophers of science (Collin, 1985; Mandler, 1975). Thus Collin argues that the richness of human action will never reduce to orderly systematic theory as long as explanations of actions are couched in terms of meaning, rules, goals, and the like. He maintains that all interpretive explanations of human action are necessarily confined to intervening variables operating between the environmental stimuli and the action taken but that theory-building requires knowledge of the causes or generative mechanism that shape action from behind. However, Collin acknowledges that to do this would require a causal vocabulary as rich as the varied reasons given for action.

The answer to the foregoing charges is not to deny their truth but to claim such criticism assumes hermeneutics has the same goals as natural science. Interpretive social science seeks intelligibility or the meaning of action, not laws for subsuming into theory. To accept the natural science goal would be to accept the goal as realizable and to underwrite methodolgical monism, which is what is being rejected.

The oldest criticism is the claim that interpretive approaches generate only hypotheses that need to be tested in the same way that natural science hypotheses are tested. This criticism is generally considered unfair. As Thompson et al. say, their conclusions are empirically based; their research seeks to be free of personal prejudices; an "outsider" would agree that the conclusions are justified by the data; and attempts are made to rule out rival interpretations. Others point out that interpretivism does entail falsificationist procedures (Hirsch, 1967; Ricoeur, 1976). This is a key controversy to which we return later.

The criticism that is taken most seriously relates to the fact that there is no unique interpretation of a text or set of protocol statements (Derrida, 1981). The philosopher Quine (1970) speaks of the "indeterminacy of translation," which applies to all psychological theories that rely on the interpretation of verbal behavior as data. Hence his argument encompasses much of marketing research. He demonstrates that researchers can never be absolutely sure their interpretations reflect the structure and meaning of the thought which the speaker intended to communicate. Those in hermeneutics generally accept that no one can prove a translation is absolutely true (Ricoeur, 1976, 1981) but argue that no one can ever be sure in the natural sciences that their explanations are absolutely true.

## Conclusion

The various systems of psychology discussed here provide alternative perspectives or additional windows through which to view behavior. None has a monopoly on the truth and each is but a partial viewpoint engendering its own insights leading to both successes and failures. But this is a difficult message to get across to adherents of one system or another. Those who have gradually and painfully mastered a discipline are loath to admit its weakness and the claims of others, particularly when those others caricature the methods and attainments of other fields. Each of the systems of psychology discussed here slices the mind in different ways, with some ignoring the mind altogether. In any case, each is likely to have some advantages for certain types of problems. The final justification of any system must be the extent to which it enables us to understand the problems with which we are dealing and to come to grips with a solution. But whatever the system, let us not use it to produce the banal "findings" so common in textbooks on buyer behavior.

What must be rejected is any presumption by practitioners that their own particular system of psychology has all the answers or at least is the only road to enlightenment. No system of psychology has much of a track record in marketing, which in itself should suggest modesty and an openness to other approaches. While the individual researcher may be obliged to bet on just one system, he or she should nonetheless recognize that at present this is an act of faith, not dictated by any irrefutable logic pointing to the inevitable winner. We return to this theme in Chapter 13.

## References

Ajzen, Icek, and Martin Fishbein (1980). *Understanding Attitudes and Predicting Social Behavior.* Englewood Cliffs, NJ: Prentice-Hall.

Allen, Chris T., and Chris A. Janiszewski (1989). "Assessing the Role of Contingency Awareness in Attitudinal Conditioning with Implications for Advertising Research." *Journal of Marketing Research* 26 (February), pp. 30–43.

Allport, D. A. (1980). "Patterns and Actions: Cognitive Mechanisms Are Context Specific." In *Cognitive Psychology: New Directions,* edited by G. Claxton. London: Routledge and Kegan Paul.

Baker, G. P. and Hacker, P.M.S. (1984). *Scepticism: Rules and Language.* Oxford: Basil Blackwell.

Beloff, John (1973). *Psychological Sciences.* London: Crosby, Lockwood, Staples.

Bettman, James R. (1979). *An Information Processing Theory of Consumer Choice.* Reading, MA: Addison-Wesley.

Bhaskar, Roy (1979). *The Possibility of Naturalism.* Altantic Highlands, NJ: Humanities Press.

Biehal, Gabriel, and Dipankar Chakravarti (1989). "The Effects of Concurrent Verbalization on Choice Processing." *Journal of Marketing Research* 26 (February), pp. 84–96.

Broad, C. D. (1949). "The Nature of a Continuant." In *Readings in Philosophical Analysis,* edited by H. Feigl and W. Sellars. New York: Appleton-Century-Crofts, pp. 472–81.

Brody, Nathan (1983). *Human Motivation: Commentary on Goal-Directed Action.* New York: Academic Press.

Calder, Bobby J. (1977). "Focus Groups and the Nature of Qualitative Marketing Research." *Journal of Marketing Research* 14 (August), pp. 353–64.

Caplow, Theodore (1984). "Rule Enforcement Without Visible Means." *American Journal of Sociology* 89, pp. 1306–23.

Carey, J. R., S. H. Clicque, B. A. Leighton, and F. Milton (1976). "A Test of Positive Reinforcement of Customers." *Journal of Marketing* (October), pp. 98–100.

Churchland, Paul (1981). "Eliminate Materialism and the Propositional Attitudes." *Journal of Philosophy* 78, pp. 67–96.

Collin, Finn (1985). *Theory and Understanding.* Oxford: Basil Blackwell.

Davidson, Donald (1982). "Paradoxes of Irrationality." In Richard Wolheim and James Hopkins (eds.), *Philosophical Essays on Freud.* Cambridge: Cambridge University Press, pp. 289–305.

Davies, Paul (1983). *God and the New Physics.* New York: Simon and Schuster.

Dennett, Daniel C. (1986). *Brainstorms: Philosophical Essays on Mind and Psychology.* Cambridge, MA: The MIT Press.

Derrida, J. (1981). *Positions,* translated by A. Bass. Chicago: University of Chicago Press.

Dretske, Fred (1988). *Explaining Behavior: Reason in a World of Causes.* Cambridge, MA: The MIT Press.

Dreyfus, H. (1979). *What Computers Can't Do.* New York: Harper and Row.

Edelson, Marshall (1989). *Psychoanalysis.* Chicago: University of Chicago Press.

Elster, Jon (1989). *Nuts and Bolts for the Social Sciences.* Cambridge: Cambridge University Press.

Engel, J., R. D. Blackwell, and P. W. Miniard (1986). *Consumer Behavior,* 5th ed. Chicago: Dryden Press.

Ericsson, K. A., and Herbert A. Simon (1980). "Verbal Reports as Data." *Psychological Review* 87, pp. 215–51.

Farrell, B. A. (1981). *The Standing of Psychoanalysis.* Oxford: Oxford University Press.

Fishbein, M., and Ajzen, I. (1975). *Belief, Attitude, Intention and Behavior: An Introduction to Theory and Research.* Reading, MA: Addison-Wesley.

Fisher, Seymour, and Roger P. Greenberg (1977). *The Scientific Credibility of Freud's Theories.* New York: Hassocks.

Fodor, J. A. (1981). *Representations: Philosophical Essays on the Foundations of Cognitive Science.* Cambridge, MA: The MIT Press.

Foxall, Gordon R. (1987). "Radical Behaviorism and Consumer Research: Theoretical Promise and Empirical Problems." *International Journal of Research in Marketing* 4, pp. 111–29.

Foxall, Gordon R. (1990). *Consumer Psychology in Behavioral Perspective.* London: Routledge.

Gadamer, H. G. (1975). *Truth and Method,* translated by W. Glyn-Doepel: edited by G. Barden and J. Cumming. New York: Crossroad.

Garcia, John, and Robert Koelling (1966). "Relation of Cue to Consequences in Avoidance Learning." *Psychonomic Science* 4, pp. 123–24.

Gardner, Howard (1985). *The Mind's New Science.* New York: Basic Books.

Gay, Peter (1985). *Freud for Historians.* New York: Oxford University Press.

Gellner, Ernest (1971). "Concepts and Society." In *Rationality,* edited by Bryan R. Wilson. New York: Harper Torchbooks.

Gellner, Ernest (1985). *The Psychoanalytic Movement.* London: Paladin Books.

Goldman, A. I. (1970). *A Theory of Human Action.* Princeton, NJ: Princeton University Press.

Gorn, Gerald J. (1982). "The Effects of Music in Advertising on Choice Behavior: A Classical Conditioning Approach." *Journal of Marketing* (Winter), pp. 94–101.

Grunbaum, Adolf (1984). *The Foundations of Psychoanalysis.* Berkeley: University of California Press.

Harlow, H. F. (1953). "Mice, Monkeys, Men and Motives." *Psychological Review* 60, pp. 23–32.

Harré, R., and P. F. Secord (1973). *The Explanation of Social Behavior.* Totowa, NJ: Littlefield, Adams.

Hebb, D. O. (1955). "Drives and the C.N.S. (Conceptual Nervous System)." *Psychological Review* 62, pp. 243–54.

Hilgard, E., and D. Marquis (1961). *Conditioning and Learning.* New York: Appleton-Century-Crofts.

Hirsch, E. D., Jr. (1967). *Validity in Interpretation.* New Haven, CT: Yale University Press.

Hobson, Allan J. (1989). *The Dreaming Brain.* New York: Basic Books.

Hofstadter, Douglas R. (1979). *Gödel, Escher, Bach: An Eternal Golden Braid.* New York: Basic Books.

Holbrook, Morris B. (1988). "Steps Toward a Psychoanalytic Interpretation of Consumption: A Meta-meta-meta-analysis of Some Issues Raised by the Consumer Behavior Odyssey." In *Advances in Consumer Research,* Vol. 15, edited by M. J. Houston. Provo, UT: Association for Consumer Research.

Holbrook, Morris B., John O'Shaughnessy, and Stephen Bell (1990). "Actions and Reactions in the Consumption Experience: The Complementary Roles of Reason and Emotion in Consumer Behavior." In *Research in Consumer Behavior,* edited by Elizabeth C. Hirschman. Greenwich, CT: JAI Press.

Howard, John A. (1989). *Consumer Behavior in Marketing Strategy.* Englewood Cliffs, NJ: Prentice Hall.

Hull, C. (1943). *Principles of Behavior.* New York: Appleton-Century-Crofts.

Humphrey, N. (1983). *Consciousness Regained.* New York: Oxford University Press.

Johnson, Eric J., Robert J. Meyer, and Sanjoy Ghose (1989). "When Choice Models Fail: Compensating Models in Negatively Correlated Environments." *Journal of Marketing Research* 26 (August), pp. 255–70.

Kagan, Jerome (1989). *Unstable Ideas: Temperament, Cognition, and Self.* Cambridge, MA: Harvard University Press.

Kalwani, M. U., and A. J. Silk (1982). "On the Reliability and Predictive Validity of Purchase Intention Measures." *Marketing Science* 1 (Summer), pp. 243–86.

Kehret-Ward, Trudy, Marcia Johnson, and Therese Louie (1985). "Improving Recall by Manipulating the Syntax of Consumption Rituals." In *Advances in Consumer Research,* Vol. 12, edited by Morris Holbrook and Elizabeth Hirschman. Ann Arbor, MI: Association for Consumer Research, pp. 319–24.

Lattin, James M., and Randolph E. Bucklin (1989). "Reference Effects of Price and Promotion on Brand Choice Behavior." *Journal of Marketing Research* 26 (August), pp. 299–310.

Leavy, S. A. (1988). *In the Image of God.* New Haven, CT: Yale University Press.

MacInnis, Deborah J., and Bernard J. Jaworski (1989). "Information Processing from Advertisements: Towards an Integrative Framework." *Journal of Marketing* 53 (October), pp. 1–23.

MacIntyre, Alasdair (1971). "The Idea of Social Science." In *Rationality,* edited by Bryan R. Wilson. New York: Harper Torchbooks.

Malcolm, Norman (1977). *Thought and Knowledge.* Ithaca, NY: Cornell University Press.

Maloney, Christopher J. (1991). *The Mundane Matter of Mental Language.* Cambridge: Cambridge University Press.

Mandler, G. (1975). *Mind and Emotion.* New York: Wiley.

Marsh, Catherine (1982). *The Survey Method.* London: George Allen and Unwin.

Messer, S. B., L. A. Sass, and R. L. Woolfolk (1988). *Hermeneutics and Psychological Theory.* New Brunswick, NJ: Rutgers University Press.

Miller, F. D., and E. R. Smith (1978). "Limits on Perception of Cognitive Process: A Reply to Nisbett and Wilson." *Psychological Review* 85.

Nisbett, R. E., and T. D. Wilson (1977). "Telling More Than We Know: Verbal Reports on Mental Processes." *Psychological Review* 84, pp. 231–59.

O'Shaughnessy, John (1987). *Why People Buy.* New York: Oxford University Press.

O'Shaughnessy, John, and Morris Holbrook (1988). "Understanding Consumer Behavior: The Linguistic Turn in Marketing Reseach." *Journal of the Market Research Society (U.K.)* 30, pp. 197–223.

Penrose, Roger (1989). *The Emperor's New Mind.* Oxford: Oxford University Press.

Quine, W.V.O. (1970). "On the Reasons for the Indeterminacy of Translation." *Journal of Philosophy* 62 (March).

Ray, Michael L. (1982). *Advertising and Communication Management.* Englewood Cliffs, NJ: Prentice-Hall.

Ricoeur, P. (1976). *Interpretation Theory: Discourse and the Surplus of Meaning.* Fort Worth: Texas Christian University Press.

Ricoeur, P. (1981). *Hermeneutics and the Human Sciences,* translated by J. B. Thompson. Cambridge: Cambridge University Press.

Robinson, Daniel N. (1979). *Systems of Modern Psychology.* New York: Columbia University Press.

Robinson, Daniel N. (1985). *Philosophy of Psychology.* New York: Columbia University Press.

Rorty, R. (1979). *Philosophy and the Mirror of Nature.* Princeton, NJ: Princeton University Press.

Rosenberg, Alexander (1988). *Philosophy of Social Science.* Boulder, CO: Westview Press.

Roszak, Theodore (1987). *The Cult of Information: The Folklore of Computers and the True Art of Thinking.* New York: Pantheon.

Rothschild, Michael, and William C. Gaidis (1981). "Behavioral Learning Theory: Its Relevance to Marketing and Promotions." *Journal of Marketing* 45 (Spring), pp. 70–78.

Rudner, Richard S. (1966). *Philosophy of Social Science.* Englewood Cliffs, NJ: Prentice-Hall.

Rychlak, Joseph F. (1979). *Discovering Free Will.* New York: Oxford University Press.

Schatzki, Theodore (1983). "The Prescription Is Description: Wittgenstein's View of the Social Sciences." In *The Need for Interpretation,* edited by Sollace Mitchell and Michael Rosen. Atlantic Highlands, NJ: Humanities Press.

Searle, J. (1980). "Minds, Brains and Programs." *Behavioral and Brain Sciences* 3, pp. 417–57.

Skinner, B. F. (1953). *Science and Human Behavior.* New York: Free Press.

Skinner, B. F. (1957). *Verbal Behavior.* New York: Appleton-Century-Crofts.

Taylor, Charles (1983). "The Significance of Significance: The Case of Cognitive Psychology." In *The Need for Interpretation,* edited by Sollace Mitchell and Michael Rosen. Atlantic Highlands, NJ: Humanities Press.

Thomas, Gloria, and Gary Soldow (1988). "A Rules Based Competitive Interaction." *Journal of Marketing* 52, pp. 63–74.

Thompson, C. J., W. B. Locander, and W. R. Pollio (1989). "Putting Consumer Experience Back into Consumer Research: The Philosophy and Method of Existential-Phenomenology." *Journal of Consumer Research* 16 (September), pp. 133–46.

Thompson, John B. (1981). *Critical Hermeneutics.* Cambridge: Cambridge University Press.

Tolman, E. C. (1925). "Purpose and Cognition: The Determiners of Animal Learning." *Psychology Review* 32, pp. 285–97.

Tolman, E. C. (1948). "Cognitive Maps in Rats and Man." *Psychological Review* 55, pp. 189–208.

Tolman, E. C. (1951). *Collected Papers in Psychology.* Berkeley: University of California Press.

Tolman, E. C. (1967). *Purposive Behavior in Animals and Men.* New York: Appleton-Century-Crofts.

Watson, J. B. (1924). *Behaviorism.* New York: People's Institute Publishing Co.

Wiener, M., S. Devoe, S. Rubinow, and J. Geller (1972). "Nonverbal Behavior and Nonverbal Communication." *Psychological Review* 79, pp. 185–214.

Winch, P. G. (1958). *The Idea of a Social Science.* London: Routledge and Kegan Paul.

# 8

# Explanatory Systems of Sociology

> Society is a masked ball, where everyone hides his real character, and
> reveals it in hiding.
>
> Ralph Waldo Emerson (1803–1882)

We come now to the explanatory modes in the various systems of sociology. Sociology is the study of society and societal relations. Auguste Comte (1798–1857), in advocating a scientific study of society, was the first to use the term sociology. But there are many aspects of society that can be studied. Hence, not surprisingly, the focus of sociology has varied depending on the sociologist and the particular period in history. For Emile Durkheim (1858–1917) the focus was social cohesion. For Max Weber (1864–1920) it was types of social action; for example, the legal system represented rational action and religion nonrational. After World War II, the writings of Talcott Parsons (1902–1979) dominated sociology—so much so that, as Alexander (1987) shows, subsequent sociologists defined themselves vis-à-vis the Parsonian position.

Marketers are interested in sociology, in particular sociological studies of subjects like class structures, class mobility, and population patterns. But the theories and findings of sociology are of relevance to all studies of buying behavior since buying is a social activity.

Psychologists—especially practitioners of social psychology—are also interested in social behavior. The individual in a social setting is their main interest, but social psychology focuses more on laboratory experiments and how individuals are influenced by others than does sociology. More specifically, social psychology studies how the behavior, thoughts, and feelings of individuals are influenced by the actual, imagined, or implied presence of others. Sociology is also distinguished from anthropology, which studies the whole culture. However, sociology, social psychology, and anthropology overlap in interests, so the following discussion draws on studies in all three disciplines.

Within sociology there are the usual debates over whether human beings are best viewed as rationally calculating, self-serving agents or as organisms propelled by past events and immediate stimuli or as social animals guided by wants, social norms, or unconscious motivations. But the most intense debate is between methodological individualism and methodological holism. Individualistic theories in sociology reduce it to psychology, claiming that social organizations and other structures result from a myriad of individual choices. On the other hand, methodological holists as "collectivists" view individual actions as caused by collective forces like culture, social pressure, and other environmental factors.

Probably most social scientists seek a "causal" (collectivist) explanation of people's dispositional state (e.g., attitudes, motives) and an intentional (individualistic) explanation of a person's actions, given the dispositional state. Sociology today is probably no exception. In any case, the following systems of sociology reflect a diversity of viewpoints: structural functionalism, conflict theory, exchange theory, symbolic interactionism, ethnomethodology, and cultural sociology/anthropology.

## Structural Functionalism

Functionalism focuses on how a system attains its ends through the contributions made by its components (see Chapter 6). Functionalism in sociology asserts that the job of sociology is to study the subsystems of society (e.g., social classes, institutions) to explain their persistence or immutability and examine whether their existence and persistence are explainable by the contribution the subsystem makes to the maintenance of society.

Structural functionalism in sociology developed from functionalism in social anthropology. It conceptualizes society or small units such as communities or organizations as systems and seeks to explain particular features of their social *structure* by means of a functional explanation, that is, in terms of their contribution to maintaining the system as a viable entity. Structural functionalism, as developed by Talcott Parsons (1951a), explains the existence and maintenance of *social order* in society by our internalization of the norms (accepted standards of behavior) of society. Parsons views structural functional analysis as involving several steps. These briefly are

1. identifying the functional requirements for system survival and effective operation;
2. describing how these requirements are typically met; and
3. identifying compensating mechanisms that compensate for the malfunctioning of the usual mechanisms involved in meeting functional requirements.

In building marketing systems, we typically think in terms of the functional requirements of success and how these requirements should be met but typically fail to think of contingency plans to compensate for component failure (e.g., of the advertising strategy), as would be recommended by Parsons.

Parsons viewed human beings as goal-seeking agents, constrained by personality and external conditions, but otherwise guided by social norms in deciding what to do. Social/cultural norms have commonly been perceived as determining what is done and how it is done. One is reminded here of Lenin's remark that Germans always buy platform tickets before they storm a railway station! Social norms are the socially approved means for achieving goals. Adherence to social norms facilitates social acceptance and, through that acceptance, a greater sense of personal worth. This focus by Parsons on the social appropriateness of action contrasts with the view of action as individualistic and narrowly self-serving. The social norms that guide action (including buying action) Parsons regarded as having been internalized through both the socialization process and the process of social control (e.g., social sanctions).

The Fishbein model of reasoned action (see Chapter 7) specifically takes account of social norms. But there is a major difference in that Fishbein takes into account the agent's *motivation to comply* with situational norms, whereas Parsons took this motivation for granted. For Parsons social action was preeminently normative (norm-driven) action exercised within constraints. Reason is much more to the forefront in the Fishbein model. However, while social norms do not compel a specific action, they can, on occasion, be the most important consideration.

There has been a neglect of the role of social norms in deciding *who* has a say in organizational buying. The current focus is on power-bargaining. But group norms are likely to develop in any well-established decision-making units (DMUs) in respect to (1) territorial rights (beyond scheduled responsibilities) through respect for what has been the case in the past, and (2) avoiding undermining the power base of other members of the DMU. Thus if members of a DMU recognize they will have to continue to act jointly, members will not wish to undermine other members by, say, appeal to their bosses.

Several Parsonian insights are of interest in marketing. One is the claim that people's deepest needs are not for tangible objects but for *symbolic rewards* that suggest love, respect, and prestige. Marketers who manage to symbolize these values in their offerings tap deep motives.

Parsons claimed that infants identify with external things and such identifications are generalized to analogous objects later in life. If this is true, it may account for the effectiveness of nostalgic advertising appeals and the latent goodwill attaching to old brands when rejuvenated.

Parsons conceptualized society as a series of *social roles* with each role having attached to it certain obligations or expected patterns of behavior for each person playing that role. But there can be "role conflict," "role strain," and "role anomie." Thus a professional purchasing department's role of "adviser" conflicts with its role of "policeman" in ensuring that commercial aspects of the purchase are given due weight. There is role strain whenever purchasing is pulled in different directions and role anomie when purchasing is unclear about its exact role.

Of interest to selling is Parsons's concept of equilibrium in a dyad. When two people are interacting, the expectations of the two participants must be complementary; otherwise, frustration or withdrawal occurs. Thus, for example, if the buyer expects consultative selling, a unilateral selling spiel may lead to buyer frustration.

Parsons advocated the priority of developing systems of concepts over trying to establish systems of hypotheses. But Merton (1949) argued that Parsons's attempt at developing an all-encompassing system of concepts would prove both futile and sterile. Instead of initially developing a system of highly abstract concepts, Merton suggested the need for theories of the middle range with concepts that could be operationalized. Early models of buyer behavior ignored this advice and got nowhere.

The most common criticism of Parsons is the emphasis he gives to the role of social norms in guiding behavior. Bleicher (1982), an advocate of a hermeneutic social science, claims that under Parsons the spontaneity of individuals is all but obliterated with the intentionality of action merely reflecting norms, that is, society-approved values. Other criticism is the usual criticism of any functional approach applied to society as being ahistorical, too insensitive to the place of symbolic structures in society, and too concerned with how society maintains equilibrium rather than with how society changes. In any case, it can be debated as to whether social norms today in Western societies are exercising as much influence on directing action. This is because, in conditions of high social and geographical mobility, people mix less with close friends and associates but are obliged to spend their time with casual acquaintances who are much less likely to frown on the violation of social norms.

## Conflict Theory

Conflict theory arose in opposition to "Parsonianism," caricatured as "order theory." But early attacks were somewhat muted, with Dahrendorf (1959) simply portraying functionalism as a consensual, static view of society. Coser (1956) in fact critiques functionalism within a functionalist framework, pointing to the positive aspects of conflict for maintaining social systems: all conflict, he argues, need not be destructive.

The most bitter attack on Parsonian functionalism was made by Rex (1961), who argued that the root metaphor or model for functionalism is human physiology, which does not undergo fundamental changes after maturity but maintains equilibrium or breaks down altogether. Parsons, it was argued, assumes that conformity to social norms leads to social stability, disregarding the fact that such conformity depends completely on individual internalization of social values and norms.

Rex views actions as self-serving and plays down the role of social norms in bringing about social stability. Instead Rex sees conflict bringing about change, not social norms bringing about stability. The basic question for Rex is to explain how order does come about when everyone is pursuing individual self-interest. (This is a problem for all individualistic theories.) The answer for Rex is that order is imposed by those with the coercive power to enforce their will, although Rex on occasion does speak of the possibility of a "truce" whereby selfish motives are curbed in the interest of society as a whole.

In the organizational buying literature there is an echo of Rex. There is, for example, the idea of the dominant decision-maker who can enforce his "will" or the claim that power bargaining is *the* mode of resolving conflicts in group buying. A truce corresponds to the position where an "analytic" mode of resolving conflict predominates in that reasoned argument is used to select the supplier.

A basic problem in conflict theory is the definition of "conflict." Obviously, participants in a DMU will have differences arising from differential self-interest, differential perceptions of reality, differential information possessed, and differential views about the consequences of proposed purchases. If these differences lead to *violent* confrontation, there is obviously conflict. But if all disagreement involving heated discussion is defined as conflict, then some conflict is constructive and educational.

Conflict theory comes under the goal ascription mode of explanation providing rationality is defined broadly. There is further scope for marketing applications of conflict theory to the resolution of conflicts among rival firms and to conflict with resellers over loss leader practices, full line stocking, servicing, display support, and so on.

## Exchange Theory

Exchange theory is another challenge to the view that internalized social norms govern action. Its most influential form, exchange behaviorism, favors methodological individualism in claiming individual negotiation with others determines social exchange phenomena. The explanatory mode is essentially that of goal ascription.

### Exchange Behaviorism

Exchange behaviorism, associated with George C. Homans (1961), combines operant conditioning and economic rationality. The two are connected through exchange behaviorism, which is a variant of the view that people act to maximize utility (rewards) and/ or minimize costs (punishments). Exchange theories borrow from behaviorism the notion of "reward" and substitute "cost" for the notion of "punishment."

Like Rex, Homans claims functionalism focuses on social norms as a basis for understanding society. Homans argues social norms change all the time and are never detailed enough to predict behavior. He wants the focus to be on actual behavior.

For Homans, social interactions are a matter of offering rewards and applying sanctions (costs); thus responses in interactions depend on the calculation of net profit. The net profit from an exchange is reward minus cost. In interaction with $B$, $A$ tries to persuade $B$ to give up something that is less costly to $B$ than it is valuable to $A$ in exchange for something more valuable to $B$ than it is costly to $A$. For an exchange to proceed it must be profitable to both parties.

Homans's "rationality principle" involves the concept of *expectancy:* people choose the highest expected value. Thus if $X$ is highly valued (say 10) but the probability of getting it is low (say 0.2), whereas $Y$ is less highly valued (say 5) but the probability of getting it is higher (say 0.5), then $Y$ is chosen since $10 \times 0.2 = 2$, whereas $5 \times 0.5 = 2.5$.

Houston and Gasseheimer (1987) sum up the prerequisites for marketing exchange as implied by exchange behaviorism as follows:

1. Behavior is directed toward goals that have the preferred anticipated consequences.

2. For exchange to take place, at least two parties must be involved.

3. Each party must have something that might be of value to the other party.

4. Each party must be capable of communication and delivery.

5. Each party must be free to accept or reject the offer of the other party.

6. Each party believes it is appropriate or desirable to deal with the other party.

If Parsons underplays self-interest and overplays the normative, moral dimension, Homans redresses the balance with his emphasis on "calculable motives": feelings and value inclinations are simply the result of profit anticipations. As a methodological individualist, Homans (1950) claims sociological concepts are reducible to concepts describing individual behavior, although he does not deny the utility of group concepts.

Houston and Gasseheimer take marketing critics of exchange behaviorism, like Ferrell and Perrachione (1980), to task. They claim that the all-rational, utility-maximizing entity is clearly alive and well if there is to be a theory of exchange. But the real issue lies not in whether consumers occasionally behave like economic man (they clearly do) but in how much buying behavior can be adequately explained by such a narrow view of human motivation. The economist's view of rationality opens Homans to criticism leveled against all who draw on economic rationality, namely, as to whether (except in a laboratory setting) people calculate only individual costs and rewards (see Chapter 5). Douglas (1986) predicts that any rational choice theory based purely on individual self-interest will fail to explain the behavior of individuals in groups (e.g., in industrial buying). Douglas is struck by the universality of "self-sacrifice" despite the fact that opting out—being a free rider—is more enticing. In ignoring feelings and sentiment, sense of obligation, and the like, exchange behaviorism represents the "egoistic hedonism of a reward-maximizing, cost-avoiding image of man."

There is, for example, the question of the "trust" that can emerge between parties to an exchange. Trust implies a willingness to accept vulnerability in the belief that the other party would have acted likewise in the circumstances. If loyalty means sticking to someone through "thick and thin," then lying behind loyalty is always trust, which implies a willingness to act without calculating immediate costs and benefits. Whenever the parties to an exchange trust each other, there is a sense that reciprocity will operate to even things out in the long term. On the other hand, when each transaction is conducted with self-interest only in mind, then distrust colors the whole process.

There is danger in assuming a one-dimensional view of man, motivated solely by self-interest, and in assuming universal man where people are motivated similarly at all times and places. Buying, when a search for status, prestige, and personal integrity, cannot be accommodated in exchange behaviorism. In any case, social norms always enter into buying since (as Homans was later to acknowledge) valuation reflects such norms.

## Exchange Structuralism

Exchange structuralism is the exchange theory of Peter M. Blau (1964). This version broadens the concept of rewards to embrace intangibles like social approval, esteem/respect, and power over others. In fact, Blau defines social exchange as embracing *all* behavior that is motivated by the *expectation* of some return or response from another. But this is still a limited view of human motivation in that it still excludes behavior motivated by duty or integrity.

In rejecting the concept of economic man (basic to exchange behaviorism) Blau points to a view that is all too easily forgotten in marketing, where people rarely pursue just one goal to the exclusion of all others, are frequently inconsistent in their preferences, rarely have complete information on alternatives, and are never free from social commitments that constrain their choices.

## Emerson's Power Exchange Theory

The exchange theories of Homans and Blau are vulnerable to the charge of being tautologous. The tautology arises from the difficulty of defining and measuring the "values" of participants *independently of their behavior.* With Homans and Blau it is easy to say, when predictions prove false, that the measurement of "values" was wrong, so it becomes impossible to try to falsify their theories. Emerson (1976) sought to bypass this issue by viewing the exchange relationship itself as the *unit* of analysis. The individual actor's values are less central when the focus is on the relationship itself, though this is at the expense of explanation at the individual level.

Emerson distinguishes exchange theory in microeconomics from exchange theory in sociology. Exchange theory in microeconomics assumes transactions (i.e., the individual paired exchanges where something concrete passes) are *independent* single transactions. In contrast, Emerson regards sociological exchange theory as concerned with the *ongoing relationship,* the social relationships that continue over time. People, according to Emerson, generally act to produce consequences that are beneficial to them, though such actions are subject to satiation and diminishing marginal utility. However, an *ongoing* relationship results in a sense of interdependence, which leads to less than rational (self-interested) motives coming into play; these include the norm of sharing, continuation of the group, and altruism. In other words, from repetitive exchanges emerge normative (rule/norm-governed) constraints on the use of power. Thus the longer the relationship between salespeople and their customers, the harder it is likely to be for either the buyer or the salesperson to be purely "hard-nosed." The other person becomes a beneficiary of allegiance through supportive interactions and resulting identification with the other's fortunes.

Like Homans, Emerson employs the principles of operant conditioning. What he wants to know is how established relationships are affected by the use of *power* and the lack of balance in power among participants. If the exchange relation reveals a higher dependency of $B$ on $A$ for reinforcement, then $A$ has a "power advantage" over $B$. Hence $A$ can elicit increasing costs on $B$ within that exchange. But every power advantage creates an imbalanced exchange, which in turn gives rise to pressure for balance, such as

1. pressure for decreasing the value for $B$ of $A$'s rewards,
2. pressure to increase the number of alternative sources for $B$, or
3. pressure to increase the value of the reinforcers provided by $B$ to $A$.

Whenever a supplier is a monopolist, the supplier has a power advantage over the buyer. The foregoing strategies are those likely to be adopted by customers to redress the power balance.

Under the marketing concept producers take instructions from the market as to what offerings to produce. It is too easily forgotten, however, that manufacturers would prefer the market to take instructions from them. Customer orientation brings with it problems, like the need for flexible production and the uncertainty concerning whether people will still want the same thing at the end of the conversion period. Hence the attraction of any insights that promise the power to manipulate demand through changing consumer values, perceptions, or attitudes.

## Heath's Exchange Decision Theory

Of particular interest to marketers is the addition of decision theory to exchange theory (Heath, 1976). The focus here is on choosing from among alternatives, whereas the other exchange theories, linked as they are to conditioning, suggest the process of conditioning removes alternatives over time, bringing about habitual behavior.

Heath claims that exchange theorists typically adopt a rational choice model that assumes consumers choose in conditions of certainty, which means people are able to rank alternatives in order of preference and select the one that comes top of the list. He argues rightly that such riskless choices are rare in practice. On these grounds Heath criticizes the compensatory (multiattribute) model because of its failure to take account of risk. Thus although the perceived outcomes or consequences of purchasing one or the other of two products may suggest identical utility, in practice the probability of actually achieving these outcomes may differ. This means there is a need to consider the probability of success.

Of particular importance to Heath is *consumer expectations,* which are based not just on what is offered but on past experience or the experiences of one's social group. This is why it is argued that customer orientation should be viewed as matching or exceeding customer expectations with the recognition that customer expectations will be based on what can be reasonably expected, what competition is offering, what has been promised, and what costs (money and effort) are involved. Heath believes that any theory of rational choice should take account of

1. the lack of complete information that would be needed to distinguish between the truth of the consumer's actual beliefs and knowledge and the rationality of what she does given her beliefs and knowledge;

2. the likelihood of information being collected to the extent needed only to determine a brand preference, not to become an expert on the product class;

3. time pressures; and

4. goals other than self-interest.

Rational choice theory as applied to buyer behavior does not at present take adequate account of these factors.

## Exchange Theory in Marketing

Exchange theory is of interest to marketing academics since it offers the possibility of both explaining and predicting the amount of $X$ exchanged for $Y$. The following common-sensical behaviorist propositions are suggested by exchange theory:

Consumers buy whatever brands yield most reward for least cost.

Consumers repeat buy whatever has proved rewarding in the past, other things remaining equal.

Present stimuli (e.g., shopping at a particular store), associated with past rewards, will evoke buying similar to that in the past.

Repeat buying occurs only as long as the practice continues to yield a net reward.

Consumers display emotion if their actions (e.g., looking for a favorite brand) previously rewarded in a similar situation suddenly go unrewarded (e.g., store being out of stock).

The more the same reward follows the same effort (e.g., buying a particular brand), the less rewarding the behavior and the more extensive the search for other types of reward.

The greater the number of rival brands, the less dependent is consumer $A$ on any one brand.

The more brand $B$ provides more sources of reward for $A$, the more dependent is $A$ on brand $B$.

The less satisfied consumer $A$ is with brand $B$, the less the likelihood of $A$ continuing to buy brand $B$ as more brands become available.

The greater the relative advantages of brand $B$ over its rivals, the more consumer $A$ will try to get it.

It is claimed that the basic focus of marketing should be on the exchange relationship (Bagozzi, 1975; Hunt, 1983; Kotler and Levy, 1969) or the transaction (Kotler, 1972). This suggests a marketing exchange theory different from exchange theories in microeconomics and sociology. This has not yet been developed. Bagozzi's (1979) attempt to develop a theory of *marketing* exchange has been rightly criticized as relying too much on the economic model and so accepting the "obsolete" concept of the consumer as "totally rational, maximizing, utilitarian economic man" (Ferrell and Perrachione, 1980).

Whether or not there is or can be a specific marketing exchange theory, Dwyer, Schur, and Oh (1987) claim that marketing theory has persistently focused on exchange. If this is so, it is more in lip service than in research. In the case of buyer behavior the tradition has been cognitive psychology. The authors go on to claim that research on the exchange relationship in buying has treated buyer–seller exchanges as discrete events (as the economist tends to do), not as ongoing relationships. In making a case for the ongoing relationship, they are recommending (in line with Emerson) a move away from a microeconomic viewpoint toward a sociological one. One ongoing relationship in marketing is franchising, where franchisees invest in the franchiser's supplies and promotions while franchisors undertake training and provide specialized know-how on running the business. To back up their claim about marketing's focus on exchange Dwyer et al. quote several authors (Frazier, 1983; Weitz, 1981) whose writings in marketing deal with the exchange relationship. The question is, however, whether day-to-day consumer shopping (choosing from a display and paying for it at a sales desk) captures the core meaning of exchange. In any case, exchange theory, as thus far developed, simply shows the rationality of the overall act of exchange and is inadequate for the job of explaining individual actions.

## Symbolic Interactionism

The study of social interaction is of major interest to sociologists. The focus is on how people interact with others and the world. George Herbert Mead (1934) pioneered the study of interaction. Basic to Mead's view of our interaction with others is his concept of the "generalized other." The generalized other manifests itself in our awareness of ourselves from the perspective of others in social settings. It is only in this way that we are able to realize what is expected of us. Mead accepted the behaviorist position that reinforcement guides behavior. However, while people choose whatever promises to provide the most gratification, Mead regarded *social adjustment* as being the most important gratification sought: people choose whatever best facilitates such adjustment. It was argued earlier that we need to interact with others for material, emotional, and intellectual sustenance but do not want to lose our individuality, "to be lost in the crowd" or at the mercy of its dictates. Hence the problem of social adjustment is largely a matter of getting the right balance between going along with the group and maintaining individuality. This theme is exploited constantly in advertising promising group acceptance or freedom to be oneself.

Symbolic interactionism is the study of the process by which people in interaction come to interpret the situation. There are at least four versions of symbolic interactionism.

### Symbolic Meaning

The first version is associated with Herbert Blumer (1969), who was Mead's student. Blumer focuses on the importance of symbolic meaning for sociology. Symbolic meaning is concerned with what a thing symbolizes: signifies, or connotes for the individual. For Blumer, *the meaning of things directs action*. Symbolic meaning is not, of course, the only type of meaning in the social sciences. Peter and Olson (1987) list sensory meaning, episodic meaning (interpretation of past personal events), cognitive meaning (factual beliefs), and evaluative meaning (attitudes) as well as symbolic meaning. In any case, symbolism is a key concept in marketing as symbols can activate the emotions so that, for example, viewers of a commercial can come to believe they have a special relationship with the characters in the advertisement and respond as strongly as if the relationship were genuine. As Humphrey (1983) says, there is the symbolism of characters performing under the viewer's own banner or there is sympathy with the character's situation emanating from actual experience or imagination. But there is much more to be learned about the conditions that give rise to such sympathetic identifications.

The claim that it is the "meaning" of things that defines, directs, governs, and delimits action is a position maintained by many interpretive social scientists. "Meaning" is viewed as mediating between incoming communications and responses to determine the nature of the action. Whereas "perception" is the apprehension of ordinary sense-objects such as houses, horses, and chairs and "sensation" is the apprehension of isolated sense qualities like the smell of something, "meaning" is of a higher order than either sensation or perception since it involves interpreting the significance of things for the individual.

How does this view of "meaning" as directing action relate to talk about "motives" and reasons? Motivation refers to the process of motivating, that is, of providing others with a motive for doing something. A motive, as commonly conceived, is a disposition to seek certain goals and/or to relieve certain inner tensions. The psychological study of motivation presupposes generalities about the motives of people in the sense that people are generally disposed to be stimulated by certain specific needs or to seek a certain common set of goals or at least to avoid punishment and seek reward. In terms of the reason-giving explanation, a motive is simply a psychological term for a general category of "want." On this basis, a motive, as a want, cannot predict action since there is a need to know relevant beliefs. If we accept that this is so, then "meaning" is more than a motive since it implies a set of beliefs. When we say meaning directs behavior, we are saying in effect that it is *beliefs about what something signifies for a person's wants* that determine his or her actions. On this basis, meaning is not something distinct from wants and beliefs but a convenient way of capturing in one construct the idea of wants and beliefs directing action while linking beliefs and wants together in a way that narrows the search for the appropriate beliefs.

Blumer's methodology is interpretive. Interpretive social scientists typically regard themselves as seeking not explanations but understanding. They view the search for explanations as the search for laws as in physics and they reject the idea of any such laws being found in the social sciences. However, on any broader view of explanation, we would speak of interpretive explanations which fall under the goal ascription mode of explanation (see Chapter 5).

For Blumer, interpretation is a process into which the symbolic meanings of things enter to be molded by people's needs, particularly the need to act in a confident manner with others. Interpretations change with experience, so that what things mean in social interaction depends on how these things relate to our current presuppositions, concepts, and ideas. On this view, what things conjure up or symbolize for people is key:

> The idea of going out to eat at a restaurant interacts with the meanings of the various types of establishments to fit the sex and age grading, and family status dimensions. . . . Lower class cafes and fancy restaurants are adult in meaning, placed for adults at work away from home (truck stops, executive business lunches). At the heights, haute cuisine with its subtle sauces and other exotic efforts symbolizes an elite use of leisure, an extreme degree of refinement of the palate, and attendant sybaritic sensibilities. People eat dishes they never have at home and go beyond ordinary meats to expensive cuts and seafoods. (Levy, 1981, p. 58)

Human beings do not so much respond to the so-called objective facts of the social world as interpret that world to make sense of it for their purpose. Although Blumer acknowledges that social forces can initiate action, they are for him simply a framework within which actions are carried out and are not determining of individual action. Blumer thus downplays the causal role of social forces. People instead interpret (give meaning to) a situation which becomes the basis for action.

If conflict theory and exchange theory ignore how individuals interpret the meaning of a situation, Blumer makes the process central to all interaction. People construct their own social world and knowledge of that "reality" emanates from understanding the process by which that reality is constructed.

To say that each individual constructs his or her own social world points to Blumer's individualistic stance; interpretations for Blumer are always personal. But more controversial than the view that interpretations are idiosyncratic is Blumer's view of symbolic meanings being completely created by the process of interaction. For example, Blumer would argue there is no way to understand the decisions of a decision-making unit (DMU) except as the decision unfolds or the outcome emerges in the process of interaction with others; it is as if participants do not bring to the process any accumulated beliefs or norms but meanings arise through interpretations occurring during the process of interaction. Are interpretations so idiosyncratic and specific to a situation? As Alexander (1987) points out, Blumer is obliged on occasion to acknowledge that people bring with them certain standard meanings, which correspond to what Parsons called social norms or values.

## The Collective Behavior Approach

The second version of interaction theory is the collective behavior approach. This holistic approach takes account of the influence of collective social factors. The approach seeks to develop case histories showing how change comes about as the processes of opinion formation and consensus building get under way. Such an approach has application not only to research on strategy implementation issues but also to research on organizational buying, as is suggested by a study by Pettigrew (1973).

## Self-Theory

The third approach is Manfred Kuhn's (1964) self-theory. In sharp contrast to Blumer, who regards people as active in creating the world to which they respond, Kuhn focuses on social systems as causal in molding an individual into the type of actions taken. This approach is holistic (collectivist), seeking causal explanation.

## The Dramaturgical Model

Erving Goffman's (1959) dramaturgical model of interaction, whereby life is viewed as a stage where each individual is an actor/player with an audience looking on, is the fourth approach. It is the expectations of others that guide behavior and Goffman speaks of three types of expectations as influencing an actor's behavior in a role:

1. expectations from the "script," that is, the norms attached to the position;
2. expectations from *other* players (demands of other people in the situation); and
3. expectations from some audience (real or imagined "reference" groups).

The extent to which the actor's behavior is guided by his or her role depends on the extent to which expectations are internalized, sanctions/rewards are attached to conforming, and the fulfillment of expectations acts as a yardstick for self-evaluation.

People act to influence the impressions others have of them. This means that whatever people say or do in interaction with others, they do not admit of any one, conclusive, interpretation since people deliberately conceal beliefs and feelings for the purpose of manipulating perceptions. All of us, as actors, are concerned with "impression management." Goffman's key distinction is between expressions given and expressions given off: people "give off" as well as give information about themselves. What is perceived by others includes what is "given off" (for example, in facial expressions and gestures) by an individual in ways which he or she does not intend. In order to claim to be a certain type of person, the messages given off need to be consistent with what is said. The problem is to make our behavior consistent since any appearance of inconsistency generates doubts about the "performance." As in selling, consistency is important for upholding credibility. Furthermore, we must not appear to be trying too hard or not hard enough in conveying that impression.

Goffman to many people presents a depressing view of social life, made up of Machiavellian individuals using stealth and falsity to manipulate others. All "fronts," or appearances, are invented and assumed for impression management. Goffman uses the term "role distance" to cover the ways people can manipulate some role they are playing to fashion some preferred image of themselves that contrasts with the (lower status?) role they are playing—for instance, the man who plays the ignorant fool when doing the cooking. But Goffman does acknowledge there are "standard fronts" attached to *established* social roles. These influence an actor's behavior, stemming out of a desire to socially conform.

Goffman's dramaturgical model brings together role playing and exchange theory: the role can provide the script and exchange theory the rationale for following the script. It thus comes under the goal ascription mode of explanation. The concept of role (particularly what is known as the scripted role) relates also to the idea of rule-governed action in that the norms attached to a position act as rules in directing action. However, role theory and the concept of rule-governed action emanate from different traditions. In any case, actors practice impression management to improve the social terms of trade and reconcile cross-pressures (stemming from social demands and the demands of the private self) by trying to convey the front most likely to engender the cooperation of others. Given this is so, tactical rules change with time and occasion.

Although the applicability of Goffman's work to salesmanship is recognized, the Goffman approach has yet to be fully exploited in selling. Advertising, though, has long recognized the consumers' desire for image management in what they buy to support the "look" they seek.

As in Goffman, the broader interactionist tradition tends to combine symbolic interactionism and role theory (Park, 1955). This is because a person's role in a group or organization influences behavior while role expectations are influenced by the norms attached to the position and by real or imagined reference groups. A *reference group* is any group that is used as a point of reference to influence one's behavior. It is a concept well established in the buyer behavior literature. Buyers, like others, are likely to be influenced by some reference groups (e.g., the family) when

1. contact with the reference group is common, though there can be groups to which a consumer aspires that may not be a group to which the consumer currently belongs (e.g., a higher status group);
2. there is dissatisfaction with alternative group membership;
3. there are perceptions of rewards from group membership; and
4. there is an understanding of the reference group's norms.

Implicit, if not explicit in much of the interactionist literature is also the concept of self. The concept has at least three meanings (Kagan, 1989):

1. *Self-concept/self-image,* or the properties a person believes apply to him or her. These properties can be intrinsic ("I am blond") or comparative ("I am taller than most people").

2. *Self-esteem* (self-worth, self-respect, self-regard), or the private valuations we put on the properties constituting our self-concept or self-image. These valuations, and thus the view we have of ourselves, are tied to the cultural, subcultural, or societal values acquired through interacting with others.

3. *Self-confidence,* or feelings of competence and potential for having an impact on others.

Feelings of self-esteem, relative status, and sense of confidence emanate from social living and changes in motives can occur rapidly when self-esteem, status, and feelings of competence are threatened. Emotional appeals in advertising commonly promise enhancement of self-esteem/status and confidence since our concern with these things makes us prone to accept self-serving delusions. We might add a fourth concept of self to Kagan's list:

4. *Symbolic self* (ideal self-image), or the self we wish others to take us to be. This symbolic self, though tied to self-image, can be remote from the true self. Nonetheless, it provides the model self that can act as a screen for choosing products and brands that are supportive of the image we wish to project, for example, of having good taste. The concept of ideal self-image is exploited in so-called aspirational advertising, which relates to what the consumers would like to be rather than what they are.

Solomon (1983) argues that the symbolism that is culturally associated with a product can be sought by consumers to help them establish a self-image that facilitates their performance in certain social roles. In the absence of such products their behavior in the role would be more inhibited, typically because he or she has not mastered the repertoire of behaviors associated with successful role performance. In this sense such products can be said to orient behavior, analogous to the way the symbolic interaction with other people influences our behavior.

## Ethnomethodology

Ethnomethodology has its roots in phenomenology. Phenomenology literally means the study of appearances, although Edmund Husserl (1859–1938), the most influential writer on phenomenology, defined it as the science of the subjective. (Phenomenology must be distinguished from "phenomenalism," with which it is easily confused. Phenomenalism is the philosophical claim that *only sense data* can be known and that we cannot know the ultimate nature of reality itself: it denies the existence of material bodies, reducing them to ideas or mere sense data.) In Chapter 7 we argued that phenomenological psychology seeks to understand the meanings of social phenomena from the perspective of the individual since the reality of interest is what people perceive it to be. To give a phenomenological account of *y* is to say how *y* is experienced by some person or group. Phenomenology is always concerned with "reality" as experienced: as part of social science, it is concerned with understanding people's own subjective interpretations of their actions and incorporating them into a picture of the social world. Phenomenology is regarded as the subjective viewpoint focusing, as it does, on how people view the world as opposed to what objective facts suggest.

Today, the term phenomenology is commonly used to cover any method that explains action by interpreting the meaning of that action for the person taking it. In viewing reality as a social creation, the phenomenological perspective challenges the idea that there is objective knowledge of the *social* world. There is thus a phenomenological dimension to symbolic interactionists like Blumer, and in consumer research that focuses exclusively on consumer perceptions as being the reality of interest.

Phenomenology is one aspect of Gestalt psychology with its focus on how wholes are perceived from different viewpoints (e.g., the picture of the woman who from one view is old and ugly and from another young and beautiful). Gestalt psychologists show how objects that are close together tend to be grouped together in perception (the principle of proximity); the more symmetrical some closed area, the more it tends to be seen as a figure (the principle of symmetry); and so on. Gestalt psychology claims that the way parts are seen depends on the configuration of the whole rather than vice versa. The foregoing principles do suggest how information might be organized in the mind, but the Gestalt concept of organization has not become part of cognitive psychology, which relies on more "mechanistic" models to explain the same facts (Gardner, 1985). Although it is common to regard Gestalt psychology as a spent force (Beloff, 1973), Gestalt notions are to be found in diverse places, including the psychology of feeling and chaos theory.

Alfred Schutz (1967), who built on Husserl's work, argues that all human action makes sense, that is, appears rational within the context of each person's mental representation of the world, and, in order to understand a person's mental representations of the world, there is a *need to explore the concepts* people use to describe and structure their environment. Basic for Schutz is the distinction between the constructs of common sense and those of science. Commonsense constructs (concepts, idea, notions) combine to form commonsense knowledge, which Schutz views (following Husserl) as intersubjective, or common knowledge, in the sense that "I know it, you know it, I know you know it, and you know I know it" (Howarth-Williams, 1977). Schutz claims we assume a reciprocity of perspectives because most of any person's knowledge is socially mediated. Thus, according to Schutz, people carry in their minds, as part of commonsense knowledge, conceptions of appropriate social conduct, allowing them to function effectively in society.

Schutz believes all explanations of a person's actions must be understandable to the subject and not just to the researcher. This is in line with his claim that social science theory should be based on people's own interpretations of their actions. Ethnomethodology draws on Schutz's phenomenology but does not subscribe to the view that the agent's own interpretation must be taken at face value; instead it accepts, like Goffman, that social action may be staged to deceive the audience. Ethnomethodology started as a critique of mainstream sociology, which tends to accept social facts as indeed facts instead of recognizing that social facts emerge from social processes. Ethnomethodology is the study of the "folk" (ethno–) methods people employ to create a sense of social order. Interest centers, as in existential phenomenological psychology, on people's own words, not the abstractions of social scientists. Hence ethnomethodologists ignore traditional sociological constructs like *social* norms, structure, and values to study how people construct, reinforce, or change their perceptions of reality. Ethnomethodologists thus are interested not in knowing specifically how social norms emerge but in how people come to agree upon an impression that there are social norms to follow. Ethnomethodologists are concerned with *how people create a sense of a common reality* and *how this sense of reality is constructed, reinforced, or changed* (Leiter, 1980). In line with phenomenology, the reality of interest is that contained in people's accounts of reality (what's out there).

"Indexicality" is the key concept in ethnomethodology. It relates to the meaning of words and rests on the distinction between the agreed-upon meaning of a word as found in a dictionary and the specific contextual meaning. The indexicality of a word, phrase, or sentence is that part of its meaning that is specific to the context in which it occurs; the indexicality of a word is unknowable without knowledge of that context. Ethnomethodology claims that all interactions are highly indexical, yet such indexicality is lost when social science attempts generalization.

Garfinkel (1967), the originator of ethnomethodology, claims orthodox sociology (read Parsons) portrays action as completely determined by social norms. Like Blumer, ethnomethodologists accept that it is the *meaning* of things that directs action, yet such meaning rests completely on people's own interpretations and is not fixed by social norms. Alexander (1987), in rebuttal, points out that Parsons simply claims interpretation is impossible without standards and such standards he is calling "norms." Parsons did not conceive norms as outside causal forces but as conceptual tools used by the mind to create a sense of social structure—as do ethnomethodologists. If Alexander is right, then the Parsonian "norms" are rules that govern (rather than completely determine) action. Garfinkel is not far different in seeing rules as procedures to be followed in going about everyday activities and showing how violating such rules can upset others by failing to meet their expectations.

Ethnomethodologists view people as interpreting cues, gestures, words, and data to sustain their particular vision of reality: people's behavior is in general "reflexive" in that it is undertaken and carried out to support their beliefs even in the face of contrary evidence. This is not to suggest that people will believe that black is white just because they want to do so but that evidence will be weighed and evaluated to support any system of beliefs found to be comfortable. This is a major reason why "wise" marketers are more likely to change perceptions to make the message fit beliefs rather than seek to undermine a well-established, comforting set of beliefs.

The importance of using a respondent's own words finds support in the problem of trying to substitute synonymous descriptions for any belief or want statement without distorting the intentions of the respondent. This is a subject discussed later under the heading of the "intension" and "extension" of words and phrases because of its implications for marketing research.

Ethnographic studies in marketing can be related to the work of Belk (1987), Hirschman (1986), Holbrook (1987), and Belk, Sherry, and Wallendorf (1988). One criticism of ethnomethodology is its dismissal of social and cultural norms as if the meaning of action can be understood without reference to the broader cultural framework in which action takes place. There is also objection to the view of indexicality as implying that social scientists can never generalize from context-bound meanings because meanings are specific to situation. Also, as Collin (1985) says, one gets the impression in ethnomethodology that social action is never what it pretends to be but, following Goffman, is always something of an illusion. A criticism that is pertinent to marketing is that because perceptions of reality may not always coincide with the objective facts, under some conditions changing the facts may not be relevant to changing interpretations, perceptions, and attitudes.

## Cultural (Hermeneutic) Sociology/Anthropology

Cultural sociology, like Blumer's interactionism, ethnomethodology, and phenomenology, stresses the need for an interpretive understanding of action. Cultural sociology/anthropology is frequently called hermeneutic to emphasize this interpretive aspect. Hermeneutical social science manifests itself in interpretive psychology, cultural sociology, and cultural anthropology. In anthropology the well-known writers in English are Clifford Geertz (1964), Mary Douglas (1966), Douglas and Isherwood (1979), and Victor Turner (1969), all major influences in cultural sociology.

Interpretation leads to understanding to the extent it enables us to "see" how things happen in the social world. Although such understanding can be regarded as a form of explanation, those who advocate an interpretive social science frequently reject this contention on the ground that no laws are sought and understanding does not carry the same logical force as do the laws of natural science. But to insist that there can only be an interpretive social science, while at the same time insisting there can be no explanations in the social sciences, is to claim that explanation is impossible in the social sciences. This runs against common usage and is likely to confuse. Hence the decision here is to regard certain interpretive accounts to be a form of explanation.

All hermeneutic traditions accept the need for subjective input into social sciences. Although hermeneutics is used today as a rubric to cover any interpretive approach to understanding, cultural sociology typically makes the following claims:

1. Understanding action is made possible by a common culture or, at least, cultural overlap. This contrasts with conventional phenomenology, which claims the ability to understand derives from the ability to generalize from the individual experiences themselves, not the culture. Cultural sociology also contrasts with those versions of hermeneutics that confine themselves to the subjective meanings, paying little or no attention to identifying general, underlying (cultural) systems of meaning.

2. Action is less a matter of rational calculation than felt expectations as to how the action will be experienced since people are motivated by meaning.

3. The meaning of an action (like the buying of a product or brand) mirrors somewhat the patterns of interconnected meanings constituting the individual's cultural or social milieu. This view contrasts with Blumer's relativist position, which stresses the uniqueness of each individual's own world of meaning.

Blumer's relativist position rules out any generalization of findings. Instead of understanding emanating from a common culture, he suggests the need for empathy in order to interpret another's actions. Geertz (1964), an interpretive anthropologist, rejects the idea of interpretation being dependent on empathy. For him the task is not to put oneself in the other's shoes but to find out "what they think they are up to."

Ricoeur (1981) points out that all action can be treated as text simply because actions are a cultural product and, as such, are guided by a "supraindividual" cultural order. Cultural sociology rests on there being intersubjective meanings of actions based on cultural affinities, which in turn implies that interpretive social science can have some objective basis.

The concept of culture is basic. Whereas society itself is typically identified with the people themselves, culture embraces all the people's shared beliefs, values, knowledge, meanings, and ideas. There are some, however, who would prefer a definition of culture that focuses purely on what is observable, that is, what can be seen, heard, smelled, or touched. But, as would be expected, Geertz does not take the view that culture must be defined in terms of observables.

For Geertz, culture is above all a system of symbols, not symbols in the abstract but *the* symbols (e.g., language) used to convey meaning in social situations. For him, the task of the anthropologist is to identify the symbol systems of a culture that give rise to the rules governing behavior. If undirected by rules reflecting the culture, human behavior would be chaotic since, unlike animals, human beings do not have any broad, comprehensive set of fixed, instinctive response patterns. What has characterized evolution has been the increasing reliance on symbols (language, art, myth, and ritual) for understanding the world, communication, and self-control.

Geertz views the mind as consisting of symbolic models that are used to interpret the real world. These symbolic models are the source of conceptions of how things are to be understood and how things should be done. All conscious perception to Geertz involves identifying an object by pairing it with something that is already part of the mind's symbolic models so that culture, as a symbolic model, acts as a road map, transforming "mere physical locations into places."

This claim that people interpret or understand the world only through symbolic models of experience contrasts with the view that people simply make sense of experience (Blumer's view) or weigh the objective material facts to choose the most rewarding action (Homans's view) and many consumer decision models like the multiattribute model.

In studying a culture, Geertz aims to grasp the subject's point of view to determine what members of this group or that take to be the point of what they are doing. It is this focus on purposes that makes interpretive social science an explanation in the goal ascription mode (Chapter 5). Explanations in social science for Geertz issue not in "laws" but in an "unpacking of the conceptual world" in which the person lives. He recommends that anthropologists seek explanations of culture "connecting action to its sense rather than behavior to its determinants." This is done not by using empathy (as Malinowski, an earlier anthropologist, had recommended) but through hermeneutics. To understand a culture we need to determine what the people take to be the point of what they are doing, search out and analyze their symbol systems, and not proceed as if the native point of view can be ignored if understanding is the goal. The cornerstone of Geertz's interpretive anthropology is the concept of "thick" description. This is a phrase coined by the philosopher Gilbert Ryle and used by Geertz to mean drawing large conclusions from small but very densely textured facts.

Geertz, as an anthropologist, does not accept that the world's peoples are growing more and more alike; there is dissensus rather than convergence of cultures. This is one expert opinion that might be borne in mind when considering global marketing. As Montaigne said: "If we were not alike, we could not be distinguished from the beasts but, if we were not different, we could not be distinguished from each other." And while cultures overlap, they do differ nonetheless and subcultures—based, say, on racial and ethnic groups, social classes, and geographic location—flourish. In fact it could be claimed that marketing is wise to look for subcultures and not be content with identifying cultural commonalities. Western cultures at least are rife with competing subcultures seeking, as Collins (1990) says, self-legitimation of their cultural products, striving to persuade those who consume them that the subculture and it alone speaks the language of truth about life and how it should be lived. Collins argues that high culture has not been dominant since the eighteenth century and low culture is better viewed as a rich plurality of beliefs/behavior systems. This is a view that advertising has long accepted.

As pointed out in Chapter 7, if reliance is placed on what people say, then individual statements need to be considered in the context of the whole to see the contribution to the broader theme. However, protocols cannot be studied as *indivisible* wholes but only in terms of their relationships between individual statements. This implies the wholes are conceptualized from the individual parts, yet the parts can be understood only as parts, providing a whole is assumed. This is the "hermeneutical circle" touched upon in Chapter 7. Gadamer (1975) claims that understanding a way of life means operating within this hermeneutic circle, moving back and forth between parts of the text and a general conception of the text as a whole. Thus the interpretation of protocols involves moving back and forth between interpreting the individual statements and repeated readings of the whole protocol to get a feel for central themes.

But any set of protocol statements is simply a sample from a population of protocols. When allied to the possibility of the sample being drawn from a less than familiar subculture, this means there is always some conjecture involved. Derrida (1981) makes the point that no single interpretation can claim to be the final one. He demonstrates this not by showing how the text meaning is reconstructed, but instead by *deconstructing* a text in the sense of showing its failure to be interpreted unambiguously. The text at its literal level is shown to be intensely metaphorical, so that intentions are never fully transparent even to the subject. The practice of deconstruction gives rise to alternative readings that are equally defensible. Foucault (1982) argues, however, that some interpretations are more fundamental than others, so a choice can be made. Ricoeur (1981) agrees, arguing that though a text may allow for several interpretations, the better ones emerge from a process of argumentation and debate.

The hermeneutic tradition is more European than American. The dominant figure in Europe is Gadamer (1975), who, like many hermeneutic philosophers, speaks of understanding actions rather than explaining them as a way of emphasizing the difference between the natural and social sciences. What is distinctive about Gadamer, however, is his rejection of the idea of objectivity and open-mindedness in the interpretation of action. He argues that it is only our preconceptions that make our understanding of others possible. It is, in fact, not possible to interpret in a completely objective way since the mind is not a tabula rasa upon which experience records impressions without distortion. Understanding others arises not from abandoning our own sets of meanings or trying to put ourselves in others' shoes. On the contrary, any depth of understanding arises from fusing, or integrating our meanings with those meanings we want to understand. Gadamer claims it is inadequate simply to recover meanings of, say, an alien culture, since the need is to illuminate that culture by fusing its concepts with one's own way of thinking. It is the interplay of the social scientist's own beliefs and practices and those being studied that gives rise to depth of understanding.

## Criticism of Cultural Sociology/Anthropology

Those who reject interpretive approaches to social science argue about the validity of its methodology for developing scientific theory. Others, who support alternative positions, claim, for example, that there are often unconscious causes at work, or that objective external causes should be sought, or that functional analysis should be used to understand capacities for action, and so on.

## Anthropology and Marketing

Perhaps the most well-known contribution of anthropology to marketing is that of Mary Douglas (see Douglas and Isherwood, 1979). Douglas claims that buying typically tracks the social goals and values of promoting community with others and making sense of what is happening in the world around: consumer goods are bought to transmit and receive information about the social scene to help build bridges or erect social fences. Goods on this basis are sought to signal to others the user's self-image, rank, and values; to mark social events like marriages and births; to reduce chores and so provide more time for social involvement; and, finally, to give order to events through newspapers, television, books, and so on, to make sense of the world around.

A recent book by McCracken (1988), *Culture and Consumption,* seeks to apply anthropology more broadly to understanding consumer behavior. McCracken argues that goods express *and* create a whole range of cultural meaning, that without consumer goods certain acts of self-definition and collective definition (i.e., defining who and what we are) would be impossible. Thus goods help the consumer lay claim to status, compete for status, or legitimize status.

A major theme in the book is what McCracken terms the movement of meaning from culture to goods and on to the consumer. He claims that whatever *meaning* is imputed to goods ultimately derives from the culture itself. One reason is that culture determines the subdivisions of the world into categories like male and female. Thus clothing projects the supposed delicacy of women and the supposed strength of men. (It is not entirely clear that this would be the interpretation of someone outside Western culture, since it is the women who are less protected from the cold with their skirts and stockings as contrasted with the men in their trousers and heavy sweaters.)

McCracken focuses on the role of promotion in the transfer of meaning to products. What advertisers try to do is to get the consumer to see the advertised brand in accordance with the cultural categories, norms, and values most favorable to a sale. McCracken, however, recognizes there are other means of transferring meaning from a culture to its goods and services (products). Thus fashion makes associations with the relevant persuasive cultural categories and principles and can, on occasion, create new cultural meanings.

The final step is the transfer of meaning from products to the individual consumer. McCracken sees four rituals involved: exchange, possession, grooming, and divestment. Under *exchange* rituals, McCracken focuses on the exchange of gifts, seeing the giver as being able, through gift-giving, to insinuate certain symbolic messages into the lives of recipients. We may agree with McCracken that gifts do say something about the giver's perceptions of the recipient, but it is surely not obvious that givers in general seek to pass along their own values. Many of us in giving think about what others would like, not about what symbolic meaning we wish to convey. Thus if someone is known to like smoking we are still more likely to give him or her duty-free cigarettes from abroad than a medical kit to reduce the addiction.

The second ritual is the *possession* ritual, in which owners establish access to the meaning or meaningful properties of goods through time spent discussing, comparing, showing off, cleaning, and even photographing their new possessions. What McCracken does not discuss is how advertisers try to capture what access to those meaningful properties might do to enrich the target audience's lives. On the other hand, it is because advertising can never substitute for the possession ritual that the personal experience is so important.

The third ritual is the *grooming* ritual, whereby there is a continual transfer and renewal of a product's meaning by repeating the act of consumption (the "going out to dinner" ritual) or repeating some activity (cleaning the car). Finally, there is the so-called *divestment* ritual, which seeks to empty goods of their existing meaning so that contagion cannot take place. For example, McCracken claims that the (latent?) function of cleaning a newly purchased, previously owned house is to erase the meaning associated with the previous owner. Similarly, when a person sells or gives away items of clothing he or she will clean them or otherwise feel strange, thinking of someone else wearing them. But this can be questioned. My thoughts in cleaning the house might be to have it to my taste, and I might wash my divested clothing to avoid the shame of being known to give someone dirty clothes; each is simply a matter of adhering to social norms.

McCracken discusses the "trickle-down" hypothesis in relation to the diffusion of fashion in clothing. In Simmel's (1904) original version of trickle down, influence is seen as flowing down from higher to lower status levels as subordinates imitate the fashion of those considered their immediate social superiors. McCracken rightly points out that the name "trickle down" is a misnomer in that the move comes from below as the subordinate social group "hunts" the status of the next higher level group while the higher level group seeks hasty flight by further fashion differentiation. McCracken acknowledges this trickle-down hypothesis has lost favor, being replaced by a "trickle-across" model or by a "multiflow" viewpoint suggesting all flows can occur. But McCracken says the trickle-down view helps us predict fashion change, whereas the other views involve a major problem of identifying the influence source. He proposes a revised version of trickle down that would be truer than the old yet preserve this feature of prediction. In his revised version, superordinate (superior) status need not reflect social position but such things as gender, age, and ethnicity, while imitation need not be "wholesale appropriation" but selective borrowing to an extent that still signals the type of status being sought but preserves those individual qualities the borrower group seeks to preserve.

It is not clear how this revision differs from a multiflow viewpoint in that any type of borrowing from any group seeks to enhance "status" as defined by McCracken. It could be argued that selective borrowing has always been the case since complete copying is usually beyond the subordinate's means. It is also not even clear how the revised version would improve prediction of a fashion change since the relevant reference ("status") groups would still be unknown, as would be the prediction of what will be selectively borrowed. McCracken does offer some guide by saying we should concentrate on the "end to which imitation is devoted." Thus he argues that women adopt the clothing of male colleagues in the workplace to get accepted as competent and equal partners in the world of work. But unless we are to assume just this one objective, this hint is not very helpful. On this basis, however, McCracken predicts men will react to the imitation by women by seeking differentiation to create once again an exclusive male clothing style. He quotes an article in *Esquire* talking about the development of the "heroic" look, which breaks with the conservative, understated symbolism of men's clothing. In fact, he argues that the emergence of this new style could have been foreseen from the moment women began to appropriate the "authority" look.

Is McCracken really serious in saying we could have predicted the exact style? If so, there are fortunes to be made! The fact is, of course, that one swallow does not make a spring. If men's styles are changing in the direction of the heroic look, it is not obvious in New York or London, where dress codes remain surprisingly uniform and conservative. In the City of London, only the bowler hat—which did differentiate men from women—is being abandoned. Also, if we look around, with men adopting earrings and necklaces and using cosmetics, it is not at all apparent that men are seeking to distance themselves from competing women. There is a *cultural determinism* about McCracken's writings that results in exaggerated claims for cultural influences.

Another major theme for McCracken is the concept of *displaced meaning*. Campbell's (1987) "dream longings" (see Chapter 9) would fall under "displaced meaning" in that McCracken claims that people's hopes and ideals remain alive through the strategy of displaced meaning. This strategy reconciles ideals with harsh reality by what amounts to wishful thinking that the ideal is to be a reality in the future (e.g., "after we have socialism," "after marriage," "in heaven") or that the ideal is already a reality elsewhere (e.g., in another country). McCracken offers a functional explanation of displaced meaning in claiming that it helps us cope with life and sustain hope in the face of impressive grounds for pessimism. Consumer goods, according to McCracken, can act as bridges to the hopes and ideals constituting the displaced meaning. Such goods allow people to have a link with the lifestyle of their dreams (e.g., people in the third world buying American products). However, when goods are chosen as a bridge they are goods that typically stretch the individual's purse, so they are exceptional buys, bought in anticipation of eventually obtaining the whole dream package. For McCracken, the concept of displaced meaning offers a functional explanation for the willingness of consumers to make costly purchases.

One subtheme in the book lies in showing how cultural meanings can change. Thus "newness" in earlier centuries was associated with "commonness" while "patina" (an indicator of age that accumulates on the surface of valued objects) was a guarantee of standing—proof of a family's longevity and the duration of its genteel status. But the advent of fashion changed all that since fashion required frequent replacement, investment in learning, and more emphasis on individualism. Although no doubt the possession of ancient riches did and does add to status, McCracken gives it too much weight, as if more direct knowledge about who constitutes the true gentry was not at hand. If it were not, it would surely have been easy for the newly rich to buy heirlooms and other goods to signal title to ancient status.

Another topic discussed is the coordinated nature of purchases. In speaking of lifestyle and consumption systems, marketers draw attention to the nonrandom nature of goods assembled in ownership. Goods purchased in ownership exhibit a coherence to a lifestyle or fit together to achieve some overall function. Douglas and Isherwood (1979) claim individual purchases are always coordinated with other purchases on the basis of what the purchaser wants to signal to the world. This belief that consumers maintain a certain consistency in their complement of goods McCracken calls the Diderot effect (Diderot in the eighteenth century recorded an incident illustrating it).

After pointing out that the concept of lifestyle has no explanatory base to allow its exploitation, McCracken claims that the "unities," or coordination themes, found in the same set of purchases reflect

1. the nature of meaning contained in the goods themselves: the Rolex watch and the BMW car go together because they have a structural similarity in that they occupy the same relative position in their product categories;

2. the way in which meaning enters into things: the associations between Rolex and the BMW car could be the result of advertising; and

3. the manner in which the meaning of goods is already built into the culture: goods that go together tend to have the same symbolic properties. This is one reason why firms like Burberry and Ralph Lauren can sell across so many product categories. McCracken focuses on this, asserting that products travel in complements because they project the same symbolic properties. Like Douglas, McCracken argues that the things we buy affirm who we are and what we aspire to be while acknowledging that the pattern of purchases can change as people seek new ideas, react to changed circumstances like marriage, or experiment with new concepts of self.

What McCracken has to say about the principles underlying coordinated purchases has intuitive appeal yet is disappointing since he assumes there are no problems in the identification of symbolic properties. Take the matter of sports. Why do those who prefer running also prefer canoeing and cross-country skiing? What symbolic properties unite them? If the commonality of preference reflects a general preference for "moving through nature in an autonomous and self-propelled way," can such a reason be categorized on the basis that all these sports have common symbolic properties?

McCracken takes to task those like Alison Lurie (1983) who apply the metaphor of language to clothing without seeing that the differences overwhelm the similarities. He argues that the message we read into what a person is wearing is much too stereotyped. On the other hand, when people dress in an unconventional manner, observers seem unable to read the message; moreover, clothing cannot convey emotion or affect. While all analogies and metaphors break down at some point, none of the points raised by McCracken would seem to destroy the utility of the metaphor. After all, much language interpretation is fairly standardized, too; an inability to read clothing mixtures is analogous to not knowing that particular language. Lurie does show in fact how clothing mixtures can be and are interpreted. Finally, although it is not clear that clothing does not convey emotion, it surely can arouse a great deal of it.

## Conclusion

In reviewing these various research traditions, it is tempting to agree with T. H. Huxley's reminder that history warns us that it is the customary fate of new "truths" to begin as heresies and to end as superstitions. It is a temptation to be resisted, for it would suggest nothing substantive has been achieved beyond the pursuit of fashion. In fact, each of these systems offers useful sensitizing concepts and additional windows onto social life.

We might, however, agree with the observations of Perry (1984) in *Intellectual Life in America: A History,* where he claims that the social sciences today are not a coherent movement but a set of alternative approaches to knowledge—with diminishing likelihood that any one approach could be used to disprove another. Perry goes on to say that although the individual scholar might feel his choice was the best one, in actual fact, choice is often simply a matter of chance like admiration for a great teacher or social rewards for one style of research. He also notes the willingness of most social scientists to concentrate on some small patch of human experience and cultivate it without ever asking fundamental questions about either approaches or methodology.

But need there be this fragmentation? Jerome Bruner (1990), an eminent psychologist, claims that the boundaries that separate psychology, anthropology, sociology, and philosophy are matters of administrative convenience rather than intellectual substance. His own vision for psychology is that it join forces with "its sister interpretive disciplines in the humanities and the social sciences." He seeks a cultural psychology that is organized around human "meaning-making" and "meaning-using" processes since these are what connect people to their culture. For Bruner it is culture and the quest for meaning within a cultural setting that are the proper "causes" of human action. Culture and the search for meaning constitute the "shaping hand" with a person's biological makeup acting as a constraint to some extent. We find much here that is an echo of Geertz and Alexander, mentioned earlier.

Bruner, one of the pioneers of cognitive psychology, points out that the cognitive revolution in psychology started as an all-out effort to establish "meaning" as the central concept of psychology but that early on it became seduced by the metaphor of the mind as a computer. With the concept of "mind" being equated to a computer program, there was no place for any concept of mind in the sense of intentional states like believing, desiring, and seeking meaning. Even the concept of humans as "agents" was attacked. Although cognitive psychologists accept the idea that behavior is goal-directed, the concept of agency has been typically eschewed as implying that people act for reasons, that is, act under the sway of intentional states. Although cognitive psychologists have no objection to speaking of humans acting "as if" acting on the basis of intentional states, typically they reject the idea that this is a factual state of affairs.

Bruner argues that psychology must link up with culture because human actions are tied to culturally shared meanings and concepts; to shared "modes of discourse" by which differences in meaning and interpretation are negotiated among people; and, most important of all, tied to a culture's account of what makes human beings tick. The culture's account of what makes humans tick is what we have been calling "folk psychology," though Bruner prefers the term ethnopsychology. Bruner argues that it is through folk psychology that people "anticipate and judge one another, draw conclusions about the worthwhileness of their lives and so on." Human beings react to one another in terms of their own psychology (folk psychology) rather than the psychologists' psychology, so we need to study it to give meaning to human experience. Folk psychology must be the base of any cultural psychology together with its basic premise that people have beliefs and wants that activate behavior. A culturally oriented psychology would not dismiss what people have to say about their mental states or just accept such statements are predictive of behavior. What would be central to psychology would be the recognition that the relationship between expressed feelings or mental states and actions is, in the ordinary conduct of life, interpretable. For Bruner, then, cultural psychology should be the major thrust of psychology. It should be an interpretive psychology in much the same way that history, anthropology, and linguistics are interpretive disciplines. Such a psychology, he argues, need not be unprincipled or without methods, even hard-nosed ones. What it would seek, however, are the rules that people bring to bear in creating meaning in cultural contexts.

This focus by Bruner on "meaning" as the key property of action is a focus shared by the interpretive social sciences (hermeneutics). Ethogeny, for example, focuses on how action is made meaningful by those who carry out the action and those who observe the action being carried out. Ethnomethodology studies the "folk methods" used by people in everyday life to give meaning to the roles they and others play in life and to the nature of the institutions that surround them. Symbolic interactionism views interaction between people as symbolic exchanges and aims at discovering the ways by which such exchanges are rendered meaningful. Finally, in cultural anthropology there is Geertz, who focuses on symbols and how they function to mediate meanings. Although all these approaches may differ somewhat in what they look for, they would seem to share some notion that the meaning of action involves understanding the point of the action, its significance, and the beliefs and wants that guide and shape it.

# References

Ajzen, Icek, and Martin Fishbein (1980). *Understanding Attitudes and Predicting Social Behavior.* Englewood Cliffs, NJ: Prentice-Hall.

Alexander, Jeffrey C. (1987). *Twenty Lectures: Sociological Theory Since World War II.* New York: Columbia University Press.

Bagozzi, Richard (1975). "Marketing as Exchange." *Journal of Marketing* 39 (October), pp. 32–39.

Bagozzi, Richard (1979). "Toward a Formal Theory of Marketing Exchanges." In *Conceptual and Theoretical Developments in Marketing,* edited by O. C. Ferrell, S. W. Brown, and W. Lamb. Chicago: American Marketing Association.

Belk, Russell (1987). "The Role of Odyssey in Consumer Behavior and in Consumer Research." In *Advances in Consumer Research,* Vol. 14, edited by Melanie Wallendorf and Paul Anderson. Provo, UT: Association for Consumer Research, pp. 357–61.

Belk, Russell, John F. Sherry, and Melanie Wallendorf (1988). "A Naturalistic Inquiry into Buyer and Seller Behavior at a Swap Meet." *Journal of Consumer Research* Vol. 14 (March), pp. 449–70.

Beloff, John (1973). *Psychological Sciences.* London: Crosby, Lockwood, Staples.

Blau, Peter M. (1964). *Exchange and Power in Social Life.* New York: Wiley.

Bleicher, Josef (1982). *The Hermeneutic Imagination.* London: Routledge and Kegan Paul.

Blumer, Herbert (1969). *Symbolic Interactionism: Perspective and Method.* Englewood Cliffs, NJ: Prentice-Hall.

Bruner, Jerome (1990). *Acts of Meaning.* Cambridge, MA: Harvard University Press.

Campbell, Colin (1987). *The Romantic Ethic and the Spirit of Modern Consumerism.* Oxford: Basil Blackwell.

Collin, Finn (1985). *Theory and Understanding.* Oxford: Basil Blackwell.

Collins, Jim (1990). *Uncommon Cultures: Popular Culture and Post-Modernism.* London: Routledge.

Coser, Lewis (1956). *The Functions of Social Conflict.* New York: Free Press.

Dahrendorf, Ralf (1959). *Class and Class Conflict in Industrial Society.* Stanford: Stanford University Press.

Dahrendorf, Ralf (1967). *Essays in the Theory of Society.* Stanford: Stanford University Press.

Derrida, J. (1981). *Positions,* translated by A. Bass. Chicago: University of Chicago Press.

Douglas, Mary (1966). *Purity and Danger.* London: Penguin.

Douglas, Mary (1986). *How Institutions Think.* Syracuse, NY: Syracuse University Press.

Douglas, Mary, and B. Isherwood (1979). *The World of Goods.* New York: Basic Books.

Dwyer, Robert, Paul H. Schur, and Sejo Oh (1987). "Developing Buyer–Seller Relationships." *Journal of Marketing* 51 (April), pp. 11–27.

Emerson, R. M. (1972). "Exchange Theory," Parts I and II. In *Sociological Theories in Progress,* edited by J. Berger, M. Zelditch, and B. Anderson. Boston: Houghton Mifflin.

Emerson, Richard (1976). "Social Exchange Theory." In *Annual Review of Sociology,* Vol. 2, edited by Alex Inkeles and Neil J. Smelser. Palo Alto, CA: Annual Reviews.

Ferrell, O. C., and J. R. Perrachione (1980). "An Inquiry into Bagozzi's Formal Theory of Marketing Exchanges." In *Theoretical Developments in Marketing,* edited by C. W. Lamb and P. M. Dunne. Chicago: American Marketing Association.

Foucault, M. (1982). *Social Theory and Transgression.* New York: Columbia University Press.

Frazier, Gary L. (1983). "Interorganizational Exchange Behavior: A Broadened Perspective." *Journal of Marketing* 46 (Fall), pp. 68–78.

Gadamer, H. G. (1975). *Truth and Method,* translated by W. Glyn-Doepel: edited by G. Barden and J. Cumming. New York: Crossroad.

Gardner, Howard (1985). *The Mind's New Science.* New York: Basic Books.

Garfinkel, Harold (1967). *Studies in Ethnomethodology.* Englewood Cliffs, NJ: Prentice-Hall.

Geertz, Clifford (1964). "Ideology as a Cultural System." In *Ideology and Discontent,* edited by David E. Apter. New York: Free Press.

Geertz, Clifford (1965). "The Impact of the Concept of Culture on the Concept of Man." In *New Views of the Nature of Man,* edited by John R. Platt. Chicago: University of Chicago Press.

Geertz, Clifford (1984). *Local Knowledge: Further Essays in Interpretive Anthropology.* New York: Basic Books.

Goffman, Erving (1959). *The Presentation of Self in Everyday Life.* Garden City, NY: Doubleday.

Habermas, J. (1974). *Theory and Practice,* translated by John Viertel. Boston: Beacon Press.

Heath, Anthony (1976). *Rational Choice and Social Exchange.* Cambridge: Cambridge University Press.

Hirschman, Elizabeth C. (1986). "Humanistic Inquiry in Marketing Research: Philosophy, Method, and Criteria." *Journal of Marketing Research* 13 (August), pp. 237–49.

Holbrook, Morris B. (1987). "From the Log of a Consumer Researcher: Reflections on the Odyssey." In *Advances in Consumer Research,* Vol. 14, edited by Melanie Wallendorf and Paul Anderson. Provo, UT: Association for Consumer Research, pp. 357–61.

Homans, George C. (1950). *The Human Group.* New York: Harcourt Brace Jovanovich.

Homans, George C. (1961). *Social Behavior: Its Elementary Forms.* New York: Harcourt Brace Jovanovich.

Houston, Franklin, and Jude B. Gasseheimer (1987). "Marketing and Exchange." *Journal of Marketing* 51 (October), pp. 3–18.

Howarth-Williams, Martin (1977). *R. D. Laing: His Work and Its Relevance for Sociology.* London: Routledge and Kegan Paul.

Humphrey, N. (1983). *Consciousness Regained.* Oxford: Oxford University Press.

Hunt, Shelby D. (1983). "General Theories and the Fundamental Explanada of Marketing." *Journal of Marketing* 47 (Fall), pp. 9–17.

Kagan, Jerome (1989). *Unstable Ideas: Temperament, Cognition, and Self.* Cambridge, MA: Harvard University Press.

Kotler, Philip (1972). "A Generic Concept of Marketing." *Journal of Marketing* 36 (April), pp. 46–54.

Kotler, Philip, and Sydney J. Levy (1969). "Broadening the Concept of Marketing." *Journal of Marketing* 33 (January).

Kuhn, M. (1964). "Major Trends in Symbolic Interaction Theory in the Past Twenty Five Years." *Sociological Quarterly* 5 (Winter), pp. 61–84.

Leiter, Kenneth (1980). *A Primer on Ethnomethodology.* New York: Oxford University Press.

Levy, Sidney J. (1981). "Interpreting Consumer Mythology: A Structural Approach to Consumer Behavior." *Journal of Marketing* 45 (Summer) pp. 49–61.

Lurie, Alison (1983). *The Language of Clothes.* New York: Vintage Books.

McCracken, Grant (1988). *Culture and Consumption.* Bloomington: Indiana University Press.

Mead, George Herbert (1934). *Mind, Self and Society,* edited by Charles W. Morris. Chicago: University of Chicago Press.

Merton, Robert K. (1949). *Social Theory and Social Structure.* Glencoe, IL: Free Press.

Park, Robert E. (1955). *Society.* New York: Free Press.

Parsons, Talcott (1937). *The Structure of Social Action.* New York: McGraw-Hill; reprint New York: Free Press, 1968.

Parsons, Talcott (1951a). *The Social System.* New York: Free Press.

Parsons, Talcott (1951b). *Towards a General Theory of Action.* New York: Harper and Row.

Parsons, Talcott (1967). *Sociological Theory and Modern Society.* New York: Free Press.

Perry, Lewis (1984). *Intellectual Life in America: A History.* Chicago: University of Chicago Press.

Peter, Paul, J. and Jerry C. Olson (1987). *Consumer Behavior: Marketing Strategy Perspectives.* Homewood, IL: Richard D. Irwin.

Pettigrew, A. M. (1973). *The Politics of Organizational Decision-Making.* London: Tavistock.

Rex, John (1961). *Key Problems in Sociological Theory.* London: Routledge and Kegan Paul.

Ricoeur, P. (1981). *Hermeneutics and Human Sciences,* edited and translated by J. B. Thompson. Cambridge: Cambridge University Press.

Schutz, Alfred (1967). *The Phenomenology of the Social World.* Evanston, IL: Northwestern University Press.

Simmel, G. (1904). "Fashion." *International Quarterly* 10, pp. 130–55.

Solomon, Michael R. (1983). "The Role of Products as Social Stimuli: A Symbolic Interactionism Perspective." *Journal of Consumer Research* 10 (December), pp. 319–29.

Turner, Victor (1969). *The Ritual Process.* Ithaca, NY: Cornell University Press.

Weitz, Barton A. (1981). "Effectiveness in Sales Interactions: A Contingency Framework." *Journal of Marketing* 45 (Winter), pp. 85–103.

# 9

# Emotion: A Multidisciplinary Approach

What matters most is the underlying emotion, the music, to which
ideas are a mere libretto, often of a very inferior quality.

                                        Sir Lewis Namier (1955)

## Emotion and the Behavioral Sciences

Chapters 7 and 8 reviewed psychology and sociology, showing how their explanatory
modes fit the four categories of explanation discussed in Chapters 2 to 5. What was missing in these two chapters was any discussion of emotion and its relationship to buying.
Yet, as Elster (1989a) says, emotions are the "stuff of life"—so much so that an affectively
neutral experience (if we can even envisage such an experience) would be wooden and
pointless. Buying is certainly not an affectively neutral experience but can at times be
highly emotional. Because this is so, the distorting effects of emotion are commonly cited
to explain deviations from what rational choice theory would predict. But this is to under-
estimate the influence and pervasiveness of emotion. This chapter draws together the
fragments of theory drawn from the systems of psychology, sociology, and philosophy to
seek a coherent overview.

De Sousa (1990) regards emotion, as have many others before him (see MacMurray,
1935), as entering into all motivation. As de Sousa points out, no logic determines the
salience of things—what to notice, what to attend to, what to inquire about, and, it might
be added, how to do the tradeoffs that are involved in buying. When we say that such
activities depend on our interests, values, gut feel, or whatever, we are indirectly bringing
emotions into play. When Elster (1989b) speaks of the motivational basis of motivation,
of how some unconscious motivational mechanisms shape desires "behind our backs,"
he is making reference to the emotional base of motivation. Thus he quotes, as an example, Festinger's (1957) model of cognitive dissonance, which would assert that every
choice made by a buyer is a potential source of dissonance as the perceived loss of the
alternatives that might have been chosen is dissonant with the knowledge that another
product has been chosen. As a result the buyer will tend to strengthen his or her decision
through, say, the selective interpretation of information, so that the decision will come to
seem more justified than when it was first made. The aim is to reduce emotional tension
as expressed in sayings such as "I paid a lot for it so it must be good."

Where emotions more or less determine motivation, this affects actions just as those
who fear a weight gain may avoid going on the bathroom scales or avoid buying their

favorite dessert. Such emotionally dominated motivation can distort cognition. Elster speaks of belief-oriented dissonance reduction as a form of wishful thinking.

In the buyer behavior literature it is accepted that emotion can be generated by both the executional elements of an advertisement and the brand's relevance to self. While it is also accepted that $A_{ad}$ (attitude toward the ad) has both a cognitive and affective dimension, Holbrook and Batra's (1986) work points specifically to the influence of emotion on $A_{ad}$. More recently, Burke and Edell's (1989) work suggests that expressed feelings (as indicators of emotional state) generated by an ad not only influence the consumer's evaluations of the ad, but also influence judgments of the ad's characteristics, brand attribute evaluations, and attitude toward the brand.

In spite of regarding emotions as being of central importance in all human actions, Elster (1989b) argues that the nature, causes, and consequences of the emotions are among "the least understood aspects of human behavior, matched only by our poor understanding of the social norms to which they are closely linked."

In social science generally the role of emotion receives too little prominence. As Goldman (1970) points out, social scientists have "scientific" counterparts for "wants" and "beliefs," but the emotions of "fear," "anger," "delight," "pride," "embarrassment," and the like, do not have "scientific" counterparts. This is because many psychologists have tried to get by, as far as possible, without involving concepts of various emotions, which are difficult to define and deal with operationally. This is not to suggest that the various systems of psychology and sociology have ignored emotion but simply that none of them offers anything like a comprehensive view. Since the emotions are so central to buying, this chapter tries to make sense out of what philosophy and the various branches of psychology and sociology have to say about emotion.

De Sousa (1990) reviews the theories of emotion as found in psychology and sociology:

1. *Behaviorism.* Skinner regards the emotions as "dispositional dispositions," as illustrated by "If I like the salesperson I may excuse the incompetent service but if I do not like the salesperson I will find the service intolerable." On this basis emotions are second-order dispositions, modifying the conditions of first-order learning. While de Sousa argues the behaviorist uses emotions as an ad hoc rescue hypothesis to protect behaviorist hypothesis against counterevidence (e.g., any failure to corroborate hypotheses about learning rates or the "probability of emission" of different groups of operants can be explained away by positing an emotional state), he argues the behaviorist does capture an important feature of emotions, namely, that emotions have an effect on the way mental states, events, and dispositions are organized.

2. *Physiological psychology.* Here attention is drawn to the physiological changes accompanying an emotion. Emotion, however, cannot be equated with any definite feeling or sensation. Thus fear may induce in one person a shaking of the knees; in another person fear may be accompanied by a dryness of the mouth; and so on. As Carroll (1990) says, the feelings that accompany emotions can vary from person to person and may also vary within a single subject on different occasions.

3. *Cognitive psychology.* Cognitive psychology focuses on the informational content of emotions. One view argues that emotion arises from the receipt of information that conflicts with existing intentions or distracts from the carrying out of our intentions. In any case, there is the acceptance that strong evaluative judgments are involved in generating emotions. De Sousa regards these insights about the role of information and the presence of strong evaluative judgments as important, providing we keep in mind there is a physiological dimension to emotion.

4. *Feeling theories.* A traditional view in the behavioral sciences has been to treat emotion simply as a certain felt experience. But de Sousa argues that the very identification of an emotion involves an object (the object of the emotion) while emotions in any case need to be distinguished from other types of feelings.

5. *Freudian views.* The Freudian tradition is not discussed by de Sousa yet it is important. In the Freudian tradition, the reasons given for action are commonly regarded as rationalizations (reasons but not *the* reasons for behavior) that hide the real unconscious motives and beliefs. In other words, unconscious reasons determine behavior. On this basis, it is not conscious reasons but only hidden drives that operate in producing behavior. Some such view lay behind the claim of motivation research in the 1950s that buying was not the rational activity generally assumed. A common theme was of behavior being driven by emotions such as guilt; thus an airline advertisement directed at men stressed safety, stirring feelings of guilt over the possibility of leaving families bereft.

There have, of course, been many other views of emotion. Sartre (1948) views emotions as intentional strategies adopted to bring about change in the world, though not in a realistic or rational way. But as de Sousa says, though the emotions can on occasion serve some purpose for the individual, there is also something in the view that the emotions are generally passive and not freely chosen. It is this view of the emotions that led Descartes to speak of them as passions. The pretense of having complete control over one's emotions, according to de Sousa, is one indicator of phoney emotions. The extent to which we do have control depends on the extent to which attention itself is within our control. We may not always find it possible in the short term to redirect our attention. As Elster (1989a) says, in the short run our emotional patterns are given but in the long run they can be at least partially under our control.

De Sousa views emotions as a kind of perception where the objects of the emotion have axiological properties. In other words, whatever it is that arouses the kind of perception called emotion, it is something closely tied to our values. The properties of objects of emotion are axiological (related to values) through being tied to certain past experiences or what de Sousa calls "paradigm scenarios," which are "little dramas in which our natural capacities for emotional response were first enlisted." On this basis emotional reactions are very dependent on experience and social context. This chapter first discusses the nature of emotion: the various definitions and functions of emotion; its supposed contrast with reasoned action; the problem of identifying emotions and their importance for marketing. We next set out a model of the process generating emotions, viewing the process as rooted in values, triggered by evaluations related to these values, with the processing itself involving wishes and beliefs. The third section deals with emotional effects: cognitive effects, physiological effects, behavioral expressions, and actions. The final section discusses how emotional responses are predicted and how emotions can be influenced.

## Nature of Emotion

Emotion is a layman's term, an umbrella category to cover such mental states as joy, love, fear, and anger. Psychologists sometimes use the word "affect" as a synonym although this term is more commonly interpreted to embrace not only emotions but all feelings, moods, and temperament. With the demise of behaviorism and the acceptance of mental entities, psychologists conceptualized emotion along the lines of the layman's intuitions supplemented by the psychologists' own conceptions. In general terms, emotion is defined as a mental state, periodic or dispositional, associated with certain physiological conditions, and brought about by thoughts and happenings perceived as highly desirable or highly undesirable. An example of a periodic emotional state is the academic's joy at solving a tricky intellectual conundrum; an example of an emotional dispositional state is the sympathy that disposes people to help others. All emotional states are characterized by bodily effects on pulse rate, blood pressure, adrenal secretion, blushing, trembling, crying, fainting, and so on.

Lyons (1980), a philosopher of mind, argues that someone is in an emotional state if, and only if, an evaluation of an event is accompanied by an "abnormal" physiological state. Neither the evaluation nor the physiological state is sufficient: only jointly are they sufficient to produce an emotional state. Emotions imply very positive or very negative evaluations, whereas autonomic physiological effects (the term "autonomic" is better than the dubious word "abnormal") are a necessary condition for any emotional experience. This is demonstrated by findings that show loss of bodily sensation is accompanied by loss of emotion. Carroll (1990) adopts a similar view of emotion. He too claims that to be in an emotional state, a person must undergo some concomitant physical agitation, registered as a sensation, and also have evaluative beliefs and thoughts about the properties of the object of the emotion. However, Carroll acknowledges that there can be counterexamples in that a condition like neurasthenia (a nervous debility with several emotional symptoms) does not seem to have an object. Others argue that dancing can be emotional even though based purely on rhythm and physiology rather than on cognition and evaluation. This example, however, can be questioned. What will be argued later is that emotion can relate purely to the evaluative judgments made about one's thoughts and these thoughts may not mirror any fact or truth in the world "out there." This is important for advertising.

Lyons claims that the physiological effects associated with an emotion need not be actually felt (e.g., an increase in blood pressure), which suggests a strong evaluation can lead to an emotional state without feeling anything physiologically. Although we can accept on this basis that people can be in an emotional state without being conscious of it, the question arises as to whether people can *believe* they are in an emotional state without feeling any physiological effects.

In the Lyons's model (what he calls his "causal–evaluative" theory of emotion) the focus is on the process of evaluation. It has much in common with the PAD (pleasure–arousal–dominance) model in psychology (Merabian and Russell, 1974), which claims that every emotional state is positioned somewhere on a continuum of three dimensions:

pleasure/displeasure————arousal/nonarousal————dominance/submissiveness

We can relate this to Lyons's focus on evaluation in that every *evaluation* of an emotion-arousing situation must reflect a pleasure/displeasure dimension and a consequent sense of increased/decreased standing (dominance or submissiveness) vis-à-vis the world at large, whereas physiological effects are always arousing.

The concept of evaluation in emotion links emotion to "attitude" in that attitude measures reflect an evaluation. Recognition of the connection between emotion and evaluation leads some writers to use "evaluation" and "affect" interchangeably. But attitude measures include not just measures that reflect strong evaluations, that is, those that incorporate affect, but the whole range of measures that are actually found. If a researcher is concerned with affect only, then less confusion would arise if measures were said to simply measure affect. Attitudes are not emotions. We can look at emotions as presupposing both values and attitudes in that a person must already be disposed to something to be, say, sad or fearful. Thus citizens of a country must share certain values and attitudes to be emotionally moved by their national anthem and flag.

Adjectives that describe emotional states—embarrassed, delighted, fearful, and so on—suggest an involuntary state brought about by an external cause since all these adjectives are past participles implying being acted upon. This suggests that the emotions are "passions" for which we are not responsible. It is in reaction to such a viewpoint that R. C. Solomon (1984) (following Sartre) states the case for viewing emotions as voluntary choices. To Solomon, emotions are rational and purposive; we choose our emotions much as we choose a course of action. Emotions to Solomon are rational in the sense that they serve a purpose and change as beliefs change. Emotions are judgments (usually rather rash judgments) which, like other judgments, can be "defused" or changed by other judgments (e.g., fear of a snake may disappear on learning that it is a stuffed version). On this basis we are all responsible for our own emotions since they are our own choice. Although this view is designed to free us from the belief that we are at the mercy of our emotions, it imposes a formidable burden of responsibility.

Calhoun (1984) challenges the Solomon thesis. Although she agrees that emotions are often tied to cognition (that emotional life is influenced by beliefs), she argues that emotions (paradigmatically) are things that happen to us, are involuntary, and are a- or ir-rational. Thus emotions can be in conflict with beliefs in that, given our emotions, we ought to believe something other than we do. There can be emotions too that lack any roots in belief. For example, people with an obsession realize their thoughts are both unwanted and silly, yet they are unable to stop them; or people with compulsions say they do not want to perform the activity but find anxiety builds up until they do. Calhoun concludes by noting that ordinarily emotions do go hand in hand with supportive beliefs, not because emotions are beliefs but because we believe things are as they seem.

Gordon (1987), another philosopher, takes the middle ground, claiming that both the preceding positions are wrong. He argues it is fallacious to regard emotional states as entirely involuntary just because emotions are triggered by external causes. On the other hand, it is an error to assume that just because emotions are not entirely involuntary, they must therefore be entirely voluntary. While uncontrollable events or situations trigger emotion, emotional responses are generally neither entirely uncontrollable nor entirely within control. As Frijda (1988), a psychologist, says, we are subject to our emotions and cannot just engender them at will. An emotional *response* is controllable only in its outward expression. Thus I cannot control the depth of my grief but I can hide the extent of my grief. I may also try to take my mind off my grief by doing other things. However, this is a far cry from being able to switch emotional states on and off, since repressed emotions may resurface later. An emotional state can, however, be changed by helping the subject to reinterpret the triggering event or situation. Moreover, reason might lead us to think of ways of avoiding situations that generate unpleasant emotions.

## Function of Emotion

The most fundamental explanation of emotion would be a demonstration of how emotional states are produced. This is the approach adopted here. But a satisfactory explanation for many purposes is the "functional" explanation: the contribution made by the emotions to the system to which it belongs, in this case the system of strategies used consciously or unconsciously to cope with the world. Plutchik (1980) claims that emotions help people survive. On this view emotions are adaptive. But emotions can be adaptive only if they influence behavior, that is, affect motivation. Plutchik lists these adaptive functions as relating to exploration, orientation, reintegration, reproduction, protection, rejection, incorporation, and destruction. In line with this Frijda (1988) claims that the negative emotions exist to signal situations demanding a response, whereas positive emotions signal situations needing no response. He argues this is why positive emotions (e.g., joy) are of such relatively short duration compared to negative emotions. Thus for Frijda anger helps gain docility in others, fear saves on efforts to overcome risks, guilt serves community morality, grief confers the right to be treated with consideration, and so on.

Unger (1984) focuses on the emotions that arise in social living, arguing these are aroused whenever the situation threatens the uneasy balance between the need for others and the need to be ourselves. This to him is the major source of human anxiety. Even the function of humor, for example, may be to fend off social pressure. In any case, Unger views emotional behavior as a gamble to discover the kind and degree of freedom to act individually while associating with others. Emotions are one way of living out *the* problem posed by the conflict between the need for others (for material, intellectual, and emotional sustenance) and the need to avoid subjugation. The deepest demand for acceptance is that which says "accept me for what I am regardless of my position and what I'm able to offer." All this is consistent with the humanistic philosophy of Maslow, who suggested that people cannot be fully adjusted if they are still prisoners of society.

Advertisers are very conscious of the human need for social acceptance, and the promotion of certain products like deodorants exploit this. Advertisers are also aware of the desire to avoid being just one of the crowd and/or accepting traditional subservient social roles, as witness the Charlie fragrance advertisement. Unger views the search for novelty as originating from a sense of isolation and a need to relieve boredom. On the other hand, a desire for luxury signals a wish to deny dependence on others. Unger defines a luxury product as something that is above minimal needs, is relatively scarce, and whose possession asserts social rank while providing an intrinsic pleasure over and above any utilitarian function the product might have. Consumers find refuge in luxurious possessions which make them feel less vulnerable to the need for others. This may be why the newly rich are more likely to seek luxury: they have the money but not necessarily the social acceptance of "old money."

The most fundamental and the most relevant view of the function of emotion is that put forward by de Sousa, who argues that the function of emotion is to make up for the insufficiency of reason. Emotions deal with the insufficiencies of reason by controlling salience. Emotion fills the gaps left by pure reason in the determination of action and beliefs. Emotions, related as they are to values, determine the "patterns of salience among objects of attention, lines of inquiry and inferential strategies." Emotion limits the range of information a person will take into account, the inferences actually drawn "from a potential infinity," and the set of live options from which he or she will choose. When faced with two competing choices, arguments, or claims, between which reason cannot decide, then emotion can endow one set of supporting arguments, considerations, and the like, with more salience than the other. In other words, emotion supplies the weightings that "break the tie when reason is stuck." Emotions, de Sousa argues, "provide a framework for our beliefs, bringing some into the spotlight and relegating others to the shade." *This is because emotions are a kind of perception—a perception of what values are to govern behavior.* These can differ among individuals because values have their origins in the relevant paradigm scenarios in the individual's background, although no doubt there are certain cultural or subcultural values. And as Solomon (1976) says, many values are linked to self-esteem.

## Emotion and Rationality

The emotions have traditionally been associated with acting in an irrational manner. De Sousa attributes this to the recognition of the power of the emotions to reinterpret the world and the view that the emotions are passions to which we are subject. But, as we have seen, de Sousa himself regards emotions as a kind of perception (rooted in the paradigm scenarios in which they were first learned) which play an essential role in decision-making by filling the gaps left by pure reason through providing salience to the various considerations that enter into decision-making. Without the emotional ingredient, decision-making can be stymied.

De Sousa claims that the faculty of emotion is required for the more conventional mechanisms of rationality to work. He points to three considerations that link emotions to rationality. First, emotions can be assessed for rationality in that they can be judged to be reasonable. In other words, not only can reasons for action be ascribed to someone's emotional state, but we can on occasion show such emotions to be reasonable given the circumstances (e.g., getting angry at some insult). Second, emotions can even be cited to justify the action (e.g., buying a sports car). Finally, most emotions are thought-dependent in that they are responsive to beliefs. Thus a change in beliefs can radically alter an emotion, as is the case with embarrassment, shame, grief, and anger. For example, my anger at being shortchanged in a store will evaporate when I find this hasn't happened. But de Sousa argues that there are some emotions like worry and hope that seem impervious to beliefs. But surely beliefs are in fact involved in that people believe they have something to hope or worry about. The problem lies in changing such beliefs. De Sousa agrees that we think of emotions as being grounded in beliefs but argues that it is better to regard emotions as operating by evoking a whole paradigm scenario "at a metalevel in relation to beliefs." This is because belief touches only the cognitive aspects and not the axiological level, which constitutes the core of the emotions viewed as a kind of perception.

Somewhat of a contrast to the view that emotions generate irrationality was the recognition in the eighteenth century that some emotions (e.g., compassion) are "moral sentiments," forming the basis for social and moral life. An extension of this idea is that emotions enforce adherence to social norms. Thus shame and guilt in particular support social norms in that they typically arise from violating the norms of society. As de Sousa says, emotions move and disturb us and through their links with social norms help to stabilize social life.

In buying, the emotions act, too, to fill the gaps left by reason. However, emotions are multiple and often conflicting since value systems do not necessarily have an overall coherence. We see this conflict in the indecisiveness, for example, over whether to go for instant gratification or exercise forbearance in the interest of long-term gain. Thus the concept of the "impulse buy" carries the notion of being emotionally based so that some considerations do not receive the weight we would normally attach to them if given time to reflect. Of particular interest is how emotion provides singular reference in the sense that the child will insist on clinging to its security blanket and reject other blankets that are objectively the same. In other words, emotions can lead to attachments to singular objects which are (presumably) linked through past associations to paradigm scenarios. This emotional attachment is what we call "devotion." We can thus have "devotion" to a brand. This idea of devotion to a singular brand that is undifferentiated from its rivals may seem to run counter to the claim that the consumer always seeks a configuration or bundle of benefits. If this were always so, devotion to a brand would not occur if rival brands possessed the same objective benefits. But devotion to a brand may be such that even when the brand is at a disadvantage (e.g., in respect to price) it is still bought. This is true loyalty. If we are to explain such loyalty, we must explain how emotions come to surround a singular object. Of course, we can rescue the concept of the consumer always seeking some bundle of benefits by arguing that there are psychological benefits that are unique to the brand to which one is devoted, but this is to move away from the conventional meaning of "seeking a specific bundle of benefits" toward stating a truism of little operational significance. We might round off this section by returning to the topic of emotional response and our ability to control such responses.

The term "emotional response" can refer to an emotional inner state or the manifest (observable) behavior triggered by an emotional state, or it can refer to a combination of both. If we interpret emotional responses to mean only the emotional inner state, then emotional responses are involuntary and not reasoned action. However, the actual manifest behavior may or may not be involuntary. Although we cannot stop emotions from arising, we may be able to exercise control over their expression and even take reasoned *action*. Emotional behavior need not be against long-term interests or defy social norms; on the contrary, it can be on the side of doing "good."

## Identification and Classification of Emotions

If presented with a list of emotions, we can usually categorize them into positive–negative or pleasant–unpleasant experiences. We say "usually" because a few emotions like "suspense" can be either pleasant or unpleasant, depending on the situation. However, beyond this simple dichotomy, we run into the problem of knowing whether we are classifying emotional events or classifying different bodily states. In other words, does the multiplicity of types of emotion in the language reflect a multiplicity of bodily states or only a multiplicity of situations giving rise to just one or two distinct bodily states? Is there, for example, any difference in *felt bodily state* between "fear" and "anxiety," or is it simply that being in a bodily state of fear is called anxiety when the cause is diffuse or unknown? In psychology, the early view was that emotional labels did represent distinct physiological states. Lange, a nineteenth-century Danish physician, accounted for the distinctive quality attributed to different emotions as arising from perceptions of different bodily changes caused by different emotion-arousing situations. On this basis we are afraid because we are trembling rather than trembling because we are afraid: it is the bodily expression that causes the perception of an emotion. For Lange, emotions are identified through *and* with feelings. This is an *epiphenomenalist* position—that mental events are the effects of physical happenings but exert no causal influence on the body.

William James (1890) in the so-called James–Lange theory of emotion reaffirmed the view that it is the autonomic arousal that causes the emotion: experiencing different emotions corresponds to different types of physiological happenings, and it is the perception of these physiological changes that gives our consciousness a particular emotional quality. Thus we have the well-quoted example by James: "We do not weep because we are sad but rather we are sad because we weep." This claim conflicts with the common-sense view that we are angry with $A$ because $A$ slighted us, which then brings about the physiological reaction. As Cannon (1927) pointed out, *bodily* changes do not seemingly differ from one emotional state to another even though people are sure about what emotions they are experiencing. While *artificially* induced bodily changes said to define the emotion do not produce the experience of true emotion, Cannon himself believed that the bodily changes and the corresponding experience of emotion occur simultaneously. This, however, has proved difficult to demonstrate.

A more recent view in psychology is Schachter's (1971) *cognitive-arousal theory of emotion,* a cognitivized version of the James–Lange theory. Schachter argues that people, as rational social animals, explain their emotional state not just in terms of their feelings but also in terms of the emotion-arousing event or situation. On this basis, anger results from a *belief* we are in a certain physiological state brought about by a perceived slight. This is an application of *attribution theory* in that the *causal* attribution we give for the bodily happenings determines the attribution or label given to the particular emotion. Schachter agrees with James that to experience emotion a person must feel some bodily arousal, but Schachter also argues that *beliefs* about the situation must be consistent with the attribution of the emotion. The conscious experience of being in an emotional state involves first having information about some emotion-arousing situation then making some evaluation of that situation in conjunction with information about one's physiological state. While James accepts that different emotions represent different bodily states, Schachter claims it is mainly the subject's beliefs that determine the emotional label given to the bodily state. Schachter's theory implies that feedback to the brain about the subject's bodily state simply gives rise to a state of arousal that is not in itself differentiating. The emotion itself is determined by the *label* the person assigns to the aroused state. This *labeling process* is a cognitive process in that people use past experience and current perceptions to interpret their feelings. Hence the title of Schachter's theory: the cognitive-arousal theory of emotion.

The Schachter thesis is supported by the well-known Schachter and Singer (1962) experiment. However, Gordon (1987) argues that this experiment does not demonstrate that *actual* emotional states depend on beliefs as to the cause of the physiological (bodily) arousal but only that the *labeling* of emotion depends on beliefs as to the cause of the physiological arousal. Gordon does not deny that beliefs about the cause of an emotional state determine the label we give to the emotional state. But we cannot infer from this that the particular bodily state or physiological arousal may not represent a distinct emotional state. Gordon points out that if Schachter is right, and anger (or any emotion) is not a particular bodily state caused by some insult but simply an emotional state caused by a belief that I am in a state caused by some insult, then we are in a position to manipulate people into different emotional states by manipulating their attributions. If, on the other hand, the physiological states reflect real, distinct emotional states, then emotional states are not malleable by manipulating beliefs. Gordon uses the analogy of being hungry, thirsty, or sleepy. Just as people can be misled about being hungry or thirsty or sleepy, people can be misled about their emotional state. However, in neither case does it mean that people's own labeling always represents the true position.

Countering Gordon is the fact that research has thus far failed to discover any physiological states that are unique to different emotions. However, this may simply reflect the crudeness of our measuring instruments since, for example, different specific facial expressions do relate to different emotions. Thus the facial expressions of happiness, disgust, fear, and anger appear to have universal meaning regardless of culture. Tomkins (1981) in fact argues that different emotional stimuli activate innate structures of the brain representing primary emotions like fear and anger, with each of these innate structures being linked to a specific facial display. The question thus remains open as to whether each emotion corresponds to a distinct physiological state. In dismissing the notion of distinct physiological states for different emotions, we may be like the fisherman using a net with four-inch holes who declares there are no smaller fish because he never catches any!

Early writers on emotion, including Descartes (1596–1650), sought to compile lists of basic emotions. Like attempts to compile lists of motives, there have been many different lists but no general agreement. One recent attempt was made by Plutchik (1980), who identified eight primary emotions and regarded all other emotions as combinations of these eight. These eight are fear, surprise, sadness, disgust, anger, anticipation, acceptance, and joy. Plutchik claims these primary emotions can be expressed at different degrees of arousal as follows:

| Primary Emotion | At Low Intensity | At High Intensity |
| --- | --- | --- |
| Acceptance | Tolerance | Adoration |
| Fear | Timidity | Terror |
| Surprise | Uncertainty | Amazement |
| Sadness | Pensiveness | Grief |
| Disgust | Boredom | Loathing |
| Anger | Annoyance | Rage |
| Anticipation | Mindfulness | Vigilance |
| Joy | Serenity | Ecstasy |

If Plutchik, in line with Schachter, is talking about how we apply emotional labels, then it is not always easy to make sense of his categorization without doing violence to the English language. Although sadness at low intensity is said to be "pensiveness," "pensiveness" need not involve any sadness but may even have a hedonic tone. Or however minor one's "disgust," it need not involve "boredom" since disgust is always active toward whatever is inspiring the disgust whereas boredom is always a passive turning away. Hardly any of the emotions said to reflect the primary emotions at a low or high level could not be similarly contested. In fact, it is not even clear that the so-called emotion of acceptance is in fact a recognizable emotion at all. But Plutchik is saying there are just eight basic physiological states or feeling states, with other states being combinations of these basic eight. In saying this, Plutchik is going beyond what current knowledge can deliver.

The most theory-driven classification of the emotions is that put forward by Gordon (1987). He classifies emotions into factive and epistemic. *Factive* emotions necessitate the subject *believing as a fact* that the emotion-arousing event or situation has happened. If a customer is upset at, annoyed with, ashamed of, embarrassed by, amused by, pleased with, and so on, she must believe *as a fact* that the state, event, or situation which triggered her emotional state did in fact occur or does in fact exist. In contrast, *epistemic* emotions stem from uncertainty as the relevant facts are not yet known to the subject. For example, a person hopeful of winning the next state lottery is acting *as if she believed* she could be a winner; she does not yet know whether she has won.

Gordon claims that the distinction between factive and epistemic emotions is preferable to that between "forward"- and "backward"-looking emotions. This is because it is possible to speak of someone desperately *hoping the train arrived safely,* since the facts about the train's arrival are already known but not to the subject. The key distinction is knowledge possessed. A consumer can have fears about a product's safety only when she does not know *as a fact* that the product is safe or unsafe. To be in a state of fear about some possibility, like the safety of some product, it is not necessary to even think the possibility likely. On the contrary, it is possible to be in a state of fear when the possibility feared is believed by the subject to be very unlikely or considered by others to be a delusion, as happens in hypochondria. Epistemic emotions may be without evidential support. Yet when an emotion is epistemic, we *act as if we believe* that our fears or hopes could be true.

If we regard "moods" as emotional states, it is not clear whether they are factive or epistemic since moods cannot usually be tied to specific facts or specific uncertainties or even to any specific object. A mood is a diffused emotional state or persistent feeling tied to personality or perceived quality of life rather than to any one event or situation. But moods can be brought about by events generating specific emotions whose aftereffects linger on as moods. If national moods exist, it is important to marketers since a mood constitutes a tendency to make certain types of evaluation and to selectively perceive facts that can be evaluated that way (Nozick, 1989). Thus Carroll (1990) explains the cyclical popularity of horror films in terms of public mood in arguing that horror films dramatize the prevailing malaise in times of stress. He demonstrates a correlation between horror film themes, their popularity, and prevailing social stresses. Thus in the 1950s the popularity of horror films featuring extraterrestrial invaders reflected public concern with the international communist menace.

## Importance of Studying Emotions

This brief review of the nature of emotion suggests emotions influence decisions. The extent of this influence is a matter of debate ranging from economists, who equate actual decision-making with the normative rational model where emotions play no role, to sociologists like Etzioni (1989), who in the preface to his recent book writes:

> The notion that people rationally seek the most efficient means to their goals is replaced with a new-decision making model that assumes that people typically choose means largely on the basis of emotions and value judgments, and only secondarily on the basis of logical-empirical considerations. Even when they are making decisions within the rather limited zone in which they wish to draw only on logical-empirical considerations, their decisions are still sub-rational due to their rather limited intellectual capacities.

If emotions enter into decision-making, it means that explanations of actions lack explanatory depth when emotional motivation is ignored. Emotions can activate behavior, provide salience, direct choices, and strengthen other motives; thus the social motive to be fashionable is reinforced by pride in exhibiting one's possessions. Even arousing a mild affective state in buyers can induce a more sociable, cooperative relationship with the seller (Isen, 1987). But while emotions, as motives, can be used to explain choices, emotional arousal and emotion avoidance can be ends in themselves, just as I might decide to shop for the excitement of shopping or act to avoid embarrassment or fear. In other words, the consumption experience in itself matters. This is part of the joy of living, though, as Elster (1989b) says, you may not be able to have the highs without exposing yourself to the lows. There are couplings between the emotions just as you cannot feel hope at the thought of $X$ if you don't feel joy at the reality of $X$. Emotional experiences

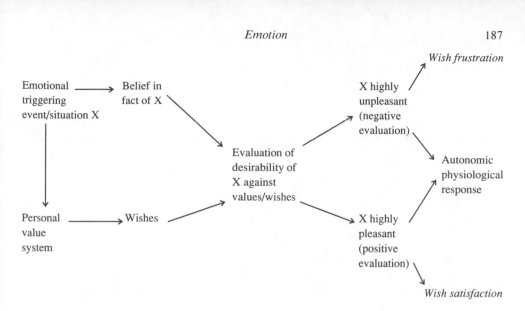

FIGURE 9.1.  Belief-Wish Condition: Factive Emotions

also influence future choices; thus a bad experience with a product turns the consumer off it. But perhaps the philosopher Nozick (1989) provides the best reason for studying the emotions when he argues that it is the emotions that link us to our values. Emotional responses link us closely to the values we perceive in the emotionally charged situation. Emotional responses signal what we value.

## A Model of the Emotional Process

This section brings together a number of viewpoints from psychology and philosophy to explain how emotional states are produced. As seen in Figures 9.1 and 9.2, the model has four components: (1) the subject's personal value system; (2) the events/situations con-

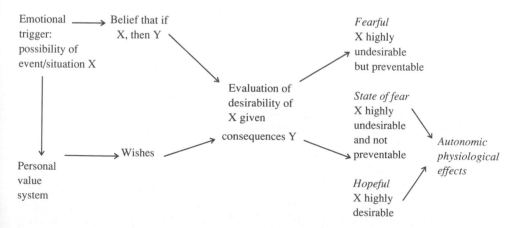

FIGURE 9.2.  Belief-Wish Condition: Epistemic Emotions

stituting the emotional triggers; (3) the production process itself; and (4) the emotional responses and their effects. Each of these four components is discussed in turn.

## The Subject's Value System

As Frijda (1988) says, emotions arise in response to events and situations that are important to the individual's concerns. These events and situations need not be real but may simply be thought. On the other hand, they must be matters of concern that develop from paradigm scenarios rooted in life's experiences (if we are to go along with de Sousa) and that are related to the individual's *system of values.* Something will always become our concern if we can be persuaded that it threatens what we hold dear, that is, what we value. When we refer to a person's system of values we refer to that person's intrinsic preferences for rules to live by or the principles lying behind where a person stands on an issue.

A person's values tell us what will be significant for him. The consumer values that are likely to enter into buying may relate to

1. projecting a certain self-image tied to self-esteem (e.g., being practical and efficient);
2. protecting one's sense of integrity (e.g., helping others, buying "green");
3. enhancing interpersonal relations (e.g., buying what conforms to group norms);
4. avoiding risk (e.g., buying well-known brands); and
5. a concern with achievement (e.g., on the job).

This list is not unlike the four basic dimensions of emotion suggested by Davitz (1969):

1. *Activation:* association with being alive and full of vitality as a move away from sluggishness.
2. *Relatedness:* association with warm, close, loving relationships as a move away from loneliness and isolation.
3. *Hedonic tone:* association with inner harmony as a move away from tension.
4. *Competence:* association with self-fulfillment/accomplishment/being in control of one's life as a move away from being dependent on others or being unable to cope with life.

MacDonald (1968) says: "To assert that 'Freedom is better than slavery' or 'All men are of equal worth' is not to state a fact but to choose a side. It announces This is where I stand." It is because values are so fundamental to choice criteria that Meehan (1969) regards values as a necessary condition enabling us to choose among alternative possibilities. As Meehan says: "Values are the tools needed to make choices or to express preferences, to order or scale potential outcomes on some reasoned basis," (p. 27). And: "Without sets of values, all human actions are equally significant or equally meaningless" (p. 25). The role that Meehan attributes to values is the role de Sousa attributes to emotion, namely, to determining salience or how various considerations are to be weighted. What de Sousa would claim is that it is not the values themselves but their tie to the emotions that determines the importance given to various considerations. But it is because values are so pervasive that the whole teleological process of striving, choosing, and selecting is value-driven. Values are expressed as value judgments. Such judgments are not provable but can be defended. As MacDonald says: "We do not refer to Mill's proof but to his 'magnificent defence' of civil liberty. For a successful defence involves much more than statement of facts. The facts of the case are known to both prosecuting and defending counsel." Because values reflect ultimate concerns, commitment to them can be emotionally arousing and direct appeals to values can be much more motivating than appeals to immediate technical and economic benefits. To quote MacDonald again:

> I mentioned earlier that in the late war, propaganda appeals to defend our comforts and privileges would have been rejected as uninspiring but that appeals to defend the rights of all men to freedom and equality obtained the required response, at least in all but the depraved and cynical. I now suggest that they did so because they accorded with our decision about these ultimate social values.

It might also be added that such superordinate values promise emotional unity and friendship from sharing in the achievement of common goals.

We have spoken of appealing to values rather than trying to change values. Because values are not open to factual proof, they are difficult to change, though they can be changed by a dramatic defense of some alternative value system, as shown by Mill's defense of liberty. It is also possible to change value judgments without changing underlying values. This is because value judgments are contingent upon descriptions of the situation and the anticipated consequences of choices. Thus it may be possible to redescribe situations and consequences to fit values. This is what is meant by changing perceptions. Thus the anti-abortion movement does not seek to change the values of the pro-choice group but, by describing abortion as murder, it hopes to link its case to more deep-seated human values.

Another way to view values is through the concept of a preferred life vision (O'Shaughnessy, 1987). We are all sensitive to contrasts in the human condition (being rich versus being poor, being healthy versus being ill) and seek a life that captures the more preferred polar extreme. However, all aspects of the good life cannot be pursued with equal vigor, so that a person's *value system reflects through emotional commitment the weightings given to the components of the life vision.* Indifference to situations and events is equivalent to giving equal weighting to each of the polar extremes, a possibility that can generally be dismissed for all practical purposes.

Nozick (1989), like de Sousa, views emotions as a response to events and situations involving our values, particularly things having intrinsic value, that is, being valuable in themselves. He sees the emotions as a map—a psychophysical replica or analogue of value—where the psychophysical configuration of an emotion actually models the structure of the particular value to which the emotion is a response. Thus whatever is emotionally arousing is a guide to values. Nozick uses the term "value" to denote some overarching category for everything good, acknowledging there are many different kinds of value because there are many different ways something can be good. Nozick's concept of intrinsic value is something that brings unity into diversity to provide an internal unified coherence. But while all things possessing intrinsic value will possess such coherence, it does not follow that everything having such coherence will be regarded as having intrinsic value: because all $X$ are $Y$, it follows only that some $Y$ are $X$. For Nozick "good" music, "good" paintings have value because the diverse elements within each of them form an integrated and united whole. The greater the diversity that gets unified within an item and the tighter that unity, the greater the organic unity and the greater the relative intrinsic value of the item within its class.

## Emotional Triggers

Emotions are activated by evaluations of events, situations, or thoughts that relate to values. But the individual values are not all of equal concern to all people. People will differ in their attachments, for example, to hedonic, utilitarian, social, or ethical values (Holbrook, 1986). The more important the value, the greater the potential intensity of the emotion aroused. Value systems are fairly stable, so that the same things can retain their power to elicit emotions almost indefinitely (Frijda, 1988).

Frijda claims that whenever a situation can be viewed in alternative ways, there is a tendency to interpret it so as to minimize the negative emotional load and maximize the emotional gain. Of course, we are dealing here in generalities. Thus there are people who force themselves to face up to reality and others who seem constitutionally unable to look on the bright side.

The question of whether we can imagine situations that are *known to be false but felt to be true* to generate *genuine* emotions is a controversial one. Campbell (1987) claims that we do this all the time. Advertisers certainly try to stimulate emotions via the appeal to the imagination, often asking us to imagine what it would be like (what it **really** would be like) to be in a particular situation, thus to conjure up an emotional state at least in small doses. Gordon would deny that the imagination would generate the same autonomic physiological effects as emotions, since emotions, like those generated at the theater, are different in kind from genuine emotions. But if emotions cannot just be turned on by the imagination, this still leaves open the question of whether emotions can be generated by imitating the physical signs. Is it, for example, true that making ourselves smile in adversity will help us feel happy? There is evidence for such a relationship (Laird, 1974).

Carroll's (1990) study of horror films perceptively analyzes the relation between fictional events and the emotions. People can be frightened when watching horror films, Carroll claims, but he asks (1) how we can be frightened by what we know does not exist and (2) why anyone would be interested in horror films, since being horrified is unpleasant. (His answer to the second question is given later in the chapter.)

As Carroll says, the first question is all of a piece with answers to such questions as "How does the plight of Oedipus move us to pity and fear?" He might also have said it is all of a piece with such questions as "How does the plight, the joy, the fear—whatever— of the actors in a commercial move the target audience?" Carroll claims that when we are moved by real situations (e.g., being indignant in the face of injustice), our emotions change if we find the situation is not as we believed it to be. In other words, emotions typically rest on beliefs, so that emotions change as beliefs change. If this is so, how can we have emotional responses to what we know to be fiction? He rejects the "illusion theory of fiction," which claims we actually do believe or, alternatively, there is a willing "suspension of belief" on the ground that people accept the monsters as fiction and cannot just believe at will that something exists. Similarly, Carroll rejects the "pretend theory of fictional response," which denies that we are genuinely responding with emotion, that the fear is make-belief or "pretend-fear." This, he argues, would presuppose that the emotions can be engaged at will.

Carroll supports the "thought theory of emotional response" to fiction. He argues that emotion can be generated by entertaining just the thought of something terrible, something beautiful, something disgusting, and so on. With thoughts, the content is merely entertained without necessarily any commitment to its being the case. We can reflect on a collection of properties (e.g., the attributes evoked by a name or a brand image), and such reflection can generate affect. The belief that this is so is presumably why politicians might call an opponent a "sick, pathetic, permissive, tax-spending, bureaucratic liberal" and themselves a "humane, visionary, candid, hard-working reformer." Carroll speaks of entertaining thoughts rather than imagining certain things on the ground that to imagine implies we ourselves are the primary source of the contents of our thought, when the fictional story or film itself provides all that is needed. In linking his views to those of Lyons, Carroll claims we are only "art" horrified if and only if

1. in a state of abnormal, physically felt agitation such as shuddering,

2. which has been caused by some thought that the monster is a possibility and is evaluated as both threatening and impure. (If only threatening, the emotion is fear; if only impure, the emotion is disgust.) And

3. thoughts are usually accompanied by some desire such as not to touch the monster.

## The Production System

Events, thoughts, or situations (typically novel or unexpected) that enhance or undermine a subject's value system trigger the process of emotion generation. But not all emotions are generated in the same way (compare Figures 9.1 and 9.2): there is a difference in the generation of factive as opposed to epistemic emotions, although both depend on what Gordon (1987) calls the *belief-wish condition (BWC)*. Gordon's model of the generation process involves the two concepts of "wish" and "belief," hence he calls it the "belief-wish condition model of emotion."

In the case of factive emotions, the BWC consists of a belief that relevant events occurred or exist and the subject wishes to experience or avoid them. Whether the wish is for or against something depends on beliefs about the positive or negative impact of the event on the subject's system of values or preferred life vision.

The BWC formulation suggests one belief and one wish when several wishes and beliefs might be involved in explanation. Thus, as Gordon points out, the emotion of "indignation" presupposes not only the belief relevant to anger (about some insulting action having occurred) but the belief that what occurred was unjust. Also, a person may at the same time be emotional (e.g., annoyed) about a number of things, so it is possible to frustrate several wishes and not just one wish at one time.

Is all emotion based on some form of belief? Lyons claims all emotion need not be based on belief in that we can be conditioned to react to some situation with, say, fear yet believe there is nothing really to fear. In other words, the evaluation need not be a conscious current evaluation but may be one formed some time before. Similarly, de Sousa argues that some emotions like worry and hope seem impervious to changes in belief. Gordon gets round this problem by saying that people sometimes emotionally react "as if" they believe something was the case rather than actually believing it is so. In other words, people act "as if" they believe there is something to fear, worry about, and so on. This may be a satisfactory way of explaining the vast majority of such emotions. However, when explaining emotional responses to fictional characters, can we claim we are acting "as if" we believe, say, the monster is a real threat to ourselves or to others? An affirmative answer leaves us open to the objections to the illusion theory or the pretend theory of emotional response criticized by Carroll. When Carroll argues that genuine emotions can be generated by just entertaining the thought of the monster, he is rejecting the need for any corresponding beliefs such as a belief in the existence of the monster. He claims that to have a belief is to entertain a proposition assertively (I believe $X$ as a fact or I believe I should do $Y$), whereas a thought is merely entertained without any commitment to its being the case that $X$ is true or one should do $Y$. In other words, one can entertain some thought (e.g., of jumping off a cliff) and be emotional as a result without having any corresponding belief (that we are about to jump off the cliff). This can be questioned since thoughts that generate emotion (as Carroll admits) involve a strong evaluation about something being highly pleasant or unpleasant, and this evaluation implies a belief that something is so. However, this is not to imply that such judgmental beliefs are necessarily articulated.

Carroll denies that every emotion links up with a desire (want or wish). Thus he argues that a person may feel sad by the sudden realization that he or she will die someday without that leading to any desire, such as wanting to live forever. This example is not very convincing since it is very likely the person would have some desire or wish—perhaps to be able to choose how and when to die.

Drawing on the work of Lyons and Gordon, the process of generating *factive* emotions consists of the following:

1. a belief that something is so;
2. a strongly positive or negative evaluation that what is so is either in line with value system wishes or out of line with value system wishes;
3. an autonomic physiological response following the evaluation;
4. a sense of wish frustration if there is a very negative evaluation allied to the physiological response and a sense of wish satisfaction if there is a very positive evaluation allied to the physiological response; and
5. positive or negative emotional state caused by wish satisfaction or wish frustration (see Figure 9.1).

Gordon uses the term "wish" rather than want or desire on the ground that the term wish suggests more of a yearning with less concern about feasibility in that a wish may happily be entertained even when incompatible with other wishes.

*Wish frustration* is a state in which someone simultaneously wishes something were not true yet believes that it is. *Wish satisfaction* is a state in which someone simultaneously wishes something were the case and believes as a fact that it is the case. *Wish satisfactions and wish frustrations cause factive emotions.*

Gordon accepts as a limitation that emotions like surprise involve frustration of expectation rather than wish frustration, whereas the emotion of disappointment involves both expectation frustration and wish frustration. But this limitation may be less real than appears. Although words like surprise or disappointment do not in themselves signal whether they are negative or positive, situationally they must do so in that to arouse emotion there must be a negative or positive evaluation of the emotion-arousing event.

Epistemic emotions typically involve fear and hope. If we fear $X$ happening, we wish $X$ not to occur because $X$ brings with it undesired consequences $Y$. Similarly, if we hope $X$ will happen, we anticipate consequences $Y$ to be pleasant.

The generation of *epistemic* emotions (see Figure 9.2) depends on three of the conditions listed for factive emotions:

1. a belief that something is so, or at least reacting "as if" something is the case;
2. a strong positive or negative evaluation that what is so is either in line with value wishes or out of line with value wishes; and
3. an autonomic physiological response following the evaluation.

The actual type and intensity of the emotional state generated by epistemic emotions will depend on attitudinal and epistemic reasons. We have *attitudinal reasons* (ARs) for *wishing* $X$ to occur or not to occur. These attitudinal reasons relate to why the consequences $Y$ of $X$ are viewed as desirable or undesirable. Thus I may fear $X$, a heart attack, because the consequences $Y$ might be death and I value life. We also have *epistemic reasons* (ERs) for *believing X* can or cannot be prevented when we wish to avoid the consequences $Y$ of $X$, the same heart attack, *or* our epistemic reasons for expecting $X$ to occur when we wish to experience the consequences $Y$ of $X$, winning the lottery. "Epistemic" means pertaining to knowledge, so epistemic reasons are concerned with the knowledge base of beliefs. Epistemic reasons refer to the reasons for thinking the occurrence or non-occurrence of $X$ to be uncertain.

The epistemic reasons might be *objectively* more supportive of *not* believing in, say, a heart attack than in believing even though the person may act *as if* he believed otherwise. This is a key point made by Gordon about epistemic emotion: the evidential base of $X$ occurring may be very small indeed. In fact, the intensity of epistemic emotions may have little relation with either the possibility of $X$ occurring or the expected value (probability $X$ weighted by consequences $Y$) since people can get extremely emotional over what, even they admit, is the small possibility of a negative or positive happening—thus we refer to getting emotional though we are just entertaining some thought. When the thought of something is highly pleasant or unpleasant, we still have attitudinal reasons for wishing or not wishing for something to occur but no epistemic reasons, yet we may still get emotional.

If we wish to avoid consequences $Y$ of $X$ and believe the $X$ cannot be prevented, then the emotional state will be one of *fear*. If, on the other hand, $X$ can be prevented, we may be *fearful* though not in a full state of fear. In either case, the subject's focus will be on reducing vulnerability. On the other hand, if we wish $X$ to occur and also expect it to occur to produce desired consequences $Y$, then the emotional state will be one of *hope*.

## Mood

Can the BWC model accommodate "mood" as an emotion? As noted previously, moods can be the lingering effects of a series of events that are emotionally charged. Moods are regarded as ranging from positive to negative and capable of influencing product evaluations. Hence there is interest in the buyer behavior literature in how moods can be engendered or manipulated (see Hill and Ward, 1989). Moods are diffused in that they are attached to no specific object but are a class of dispositions toward many objects. At the simplest level, marketers cater to moods by playing music appropriate to the mood desired to facilitate buying.

Cantril's (1942) classic study of deviant social movements like the Nazi party shows how national moods can develop. Cantril argues that cultural norms are reflected in society's customs, conventions, laws, institutions, way of life, and expectations about life. Such norms become the social values of society, which, in turn, provide the standards lying behind general attitudinal judgments. People within a nation tend to identify with such values, which are closely tied to perceptions of national and personal self-esteem and status in the world at large.

Whenever social values are under attack or changing so that expectations are not being realized, people face uncertainty. Because social values act as anchors that make life meaningful, when they are threatened it creates instability and a floating anxiety about status and actions become less certain. When things become unstable, people lose the informational anchors that help them understand what is happening. The result is a sense of lost competence and a mood suggesting life is unmanageable. An antidote in advertisements is to exploit nostalgia, which advertisers do by using symbols typifying the earlier period: celebrities, songs, old brand names, original brand slogans ("Timex takes a licking but keeps on ticking"), and the like. On the other hand, appeals to the optimistic young might be deliberately antinostalgia, condemning the past (e.g., for its lack of equality for women) and pointing to the advantages of the present ("You've come a long way baby"). Where social values have become too rigid and too predictable, the result may be a national mood of lethargy/boredom; an antidote in advertising is to project brands as adding excitement to life.

This analysis by Cantril can be tailored to the BWC model. When people in society wish to maintain social values which they believe are being undermined, there is persistent wish frustration and a corresponding negative mood. People, too, may be fearful or be in an actual state of fear about the future for the attitudinal reason that changing social values threaten their status and self-esteem and for the epistemic reasons of believing the erosion of social values will continue. The net result is vulnerability-avoidance action either to stop the tide of change or to protect oneself from its consequences.

## Illustrations of BWC Model

The discussion has focused on the emotions as a class. Thus we have talked about wishes and beliefs without saying much about what might be wished and what might be believed, although the content of the BWC model would vary with different emotions. We next consider content for specific emotions that are commonly exploited in advertising, drawing initially on Taylor's (1985) work on the self-assessment emotions (pride, envy, shame, guilt, integrity, etc.), which are directed toward self, personal status, and the need to believe in one's own self-worth. The self-assessment emotions are factive in that such emotions presuppose as a fact (1) that the subject has risen above or fallen below some personal expectation or standard, *and* (2) that in so doing there is a change in his or her status or standing in the world. If, as one of our values, we wish our status in the world to be increased or at least maintained, then an increase in status leads to *wish satisfaction,* whereas a decrease in status leads to *wish frustration.*

Taylor sets out the belief conditions behind each of the self-assessment emotions. In doing so she distinguishes between *explanatory* beliefs and *identificatory* beliefs. Explanatory beliefs are beliefs about the event that emanate from evaluating the event. These beliefs are explanatory in that they make the emotional state understandable or rationally intelligible. Identificatory beliefs are those that identify the particular emotions. Inferences from explanatory beliefs entail the identificatory beliefs (assuming, of course, that the subject understands the language sufficiently to know the reference of terms like guilt and pride).

We will not follow Taylor to discuss each of the self-assessment emotions at length. Instead the appendix to this chapter sets out the BWC of each of the emotions. Following the Taylor format we have added the epistemic emotions of fear and hope. In each case a brief note is given of advertisements linked with these emotions. The link need not actually arouse emotion but it must be an oblique promise of fulfilling some positive emotion or avoiding a negative emotion. Advertisements can put an audience into an emotional state (think of the anger that can be aroused through ads showing the killing of baby seals) but more typically "emotional" advertisements arouse something less than full-blown emotions with accompanying physiological changes.

## Enjoyment-Seeking

Campbell (1987), a sociologist of mass culture and religion, distinguishes enjoyment-seeking from satisfaction-seeking. (Campbell actually uses the term pleasure-seeking rather than enjoyment-seeking but the ambiguity of the word "pleasure" makes the term "enjoyment-seeking" clearer.) Satisfaction-seeking is to fulfill biological needs to relieve discomfort arising from deprivation (e.g., hunger). In contrast, enjoyment-seeking seeks a quality of experience arising from certain patterns of sensation.

Satisfaction-seeking is the *push* of needs demanding satisfaction; enjoyment-seeking is the *pull* of hope about experiencing fresh stimulation. Marketers who cater to satisfaction-seeking stress the relationship between the inner discomfort (e.g., acid indigestion) and their brand's ability to relieve the situation better than rival brands. But those catering to enjoyment-seeking appeal to the senses. Whereas satisfaction-seeking means trying out real products to see which are effective in relieving the discomfort, enjoyment-seeking always aims at stimulating the senses. Campbell argues that whereas satisfaction depends on *what a product is,* a product's pleasurable significance depends on *what it can be taken to be,* since in this case illusion and delusion operate to provide pleasure. But Campbell claims that the opportunity to experience enjoyment is limited when confined to the human contact senses. Thus the taste buds and sense of smell are confined to just the four categories of salty, sweet, bitter, and sour, and although sight and hearing offer wider possibilities, they too are limited, even when aesthetic appreciation enhances enjoyment.

Campbell sees two traditional strategies for the pleasure-seeker. The first is to indulge as much as possible in each of life's pleasures (e.g., more eating or listening to music). The second is to squeeze as much pleasure as possible from individual experiences. However, for Campbell, the key to understanding today's *hedonistic buyers* lies in understanding how people use (and came to use) "daydreaming" to generate feelings. Although no great pleasure can be derived from imagined *sensations,* it is comparatively easy to imagine *situations* and *events* that have the capacity to stimulate an emotional experience. This emotional enjoyment is derived from imagined situations or through the manipulation of meaning given by emotional events. For Campbell, modern hedonism is characterized by daydreams giving rise to illusions *known* to be false but *felt* to be true. The crucial premise is that we can suspend belief or manipulate our beliefs to give enjoyment because beliefs are seldom such firm convictions as to prevent this from happening. The claims about suspension of beliefs can be criticized on the grounds used by Carroll (1990): we cannot just will what to believe. Carroll in fact would see no need to make such assumptions since just entertaining the thought itself can generate emotion. In any case, Campbell claims that gratification from the use of a product cannot be divorced from the image and other associations (e.g., between champagne and the luxurious lifestyle) attached to the product. From the consumer's point of view images and other symbolic meanings are as much a real part of the product as are the raw materials of which it is made.

The ability to indulge in such enjoyable daydreaming was and is facilitated by products such as novels, films, compact discs, television, and radio. It is in daydreams that the idealized self-image takes shape to influence buying in line with that image. The modern hedonist looks to novel products as offering the hope of realizing some of the idealized pleasures imagined in daydreams. However, since reality will fall short of the dream, disappointment is inevitable. The result is a return to the longings. The whole cycle then starts afresh. "Hope dwells eternal in the human breast / man never was but always to be blessed." To Campbell modern consumerism is self-illusory hedonism that reflects itself in a longing to experience in reality the pleasure enjoyed in imaginative daydreaming. The net result is a longing for novelty because novelty allows the consumer to attribute to the product imagined meanings and images. However, the pleasure of longing can rival actual gratification since consumption is unlikely to live up to the dream. Hence the never-ending search to match the dream. As the poet says, "not for us quiet, content nor peace of mind / for we go seeking a city that we shall never find."

Campbell does not suggest that modern hedonism be equated with self-indulgence. In fact the self-illusory pleasure-seeker may be led in the direction of idealistic commitment. Campbell argues that motivation involves not only self-interest but perceptions of moral obligations, since our thinking about what to do has to be justified to ourselves. As a consequence, the distinction between motivation and justification (legitimization) is not as sustainable as first appears since legitimizations "may simply be the actor's articulations of his or her motives." He argues that morally idealized self-images can be just as much sources of pleasure as aesthetic sources of pleasure.

In terms of the BWC model, Campbell is highlighting wishful thinking and assuming wishes can be entertained while beliefs about the facts can be submerged. Campbell's concept of daydreaming can be related to the strategy of displaced meaning discussed in Chapter 8 (McCracken, 1988). This strategy consists of reconciling our hopes and ideals with harsh reality by what amounts to wishful thinking to the effect that the ideal will either be a reality in the future ("after we have socialism," "after marriage," "in heaven") or the ideal is already a reality elsewhere (e.g., in another country).

No marketing professional is likely to doubt the seeming insatiability and inexhaustibility of wants or that people have diffuse longings. Social historian Loren Baritz (1989) sums up the frenzy to accumulate with the bumper sticker slogan: "Whoever dies with the most toys wins." He goes on to show how the middle classes act as if looking for some intangible element missing from their lives while they follow any orgy of spending with an "is-this-all-there-is?" malaise. What is much less credible is Campbell's claim that the ability to indulge in imaginative daydreaming is of recent origin. He seems to regard the ability (as opposed to the capacity) to daydream as analogous to the ability to read, that is, as something that requires a particular type of exposure and learning. Csikszentmihalyi (1990) seems to agree, quoting Jerome Singer (1973) in claiming that daydreaming is a skill that some children never learn to use. He points out that daydreaming can help bring emotional order to the mind by allowing both children and adults to rehearse imaginary situations so that the best strategy for confronting some situation can be adopted. He claims that when used with skill, daydreaming can be enjoyable, for it can "help increase the complexity of consciousness." Strangely, Campbell sees little opportunity for learning to daydream before the eighteenth century, when a certain ethic developed to encourage pleasure-seeking for its own sake. But it is easy to imagine that children have always day-dreamed and are better at this than adults. As the poet says: "What can a tired heart say/ which the wise of the world hath made dumb/ save to the lonely dreams of a child,/ return again come!" In fact, if children are those most likely to develop this ability, it would seem to run counter to the idea of the need for much learning. It seems more likely that most of us have daydreams about our future, our children, some future holiday, changing our image by facelift, or even how much easier life would be with a dishwasher. But is such daydreaming relevant to the bulk of novel new products? And are people really able to get emotional pleasure by imaginative daydreaming about something other than romance? If visualization is a credible technique for doing this, it should be formally taught and practiced as a way of making this life more pleasant. It seems as likely that people are constantly made miserable by emotional states they are unable to control, for people would love to be able to substitute pleasurable emotions but find this beyond them.

Carroll (1990) explains both the enjoyment of horror films and the relationship between the audience and the characters in a film or book in a way that provides insight for advertising. Carroll shows that the source of our enjoyment in horror films is our curiosity as the horror story engages its audience. We are involved in the processes of disclosure, discovery, proof, explanation, hypothesizing, and confirmation. He shows how the way the narrative is constructed stimulates a desire to learn more about the monsters and a desire to know about the outcome. Curiosity is aroused by the plot and the objects of horror. Disgust is more or less mandated for the pleasure involved in engaging our curiosity in the unknown and drawing it into the revelations and other processes. Compensating for whatever negative emotions are stimulated, whatever distress is evoked, is the fascination with impossible beings, since we know the monsters do not actually exist.

Carroll asks whether a positive response to fictional characters is based on some identification with them. Do audiences watching a "slice of life" commercial identify with the characters? To Carroll the word "identification" suggests some sort of sharing with the characters, for example, of interests, feelings, values, circumstances. But such identification is rejected by Carroll as a necessary or sufficient basis for evoking positive (emotional) responses. He points out that an audience does not always identify with fictional characters in any meaningful sense. While the responses of characters often do cue the emotional responses of the audience, this may not happen. Thus the audience may feel suspense when the characters in a mystery film do not. What Carroll claims is that we do not so much identify with the fictional characters as *assimilate the situation* in that we come to see the situation both from the point of view of the characters in the film (commercial) and from the outside as well. In neither case is it necessary to identify with the characters. This may be so, but it then leaves open the mechanism at work since to talk of assimilating the situation seems somewhat inadequate. There are, of course, alternatives to identification to act as mechanisms. Thus a positive response or evaluation could arise through conditioning (e.g., a loving child) or contagion in that the behavior of others (e.g., laughter) can be infectious.

## Emotional Effects

Emotional effects can be considered under the headings of cognitive effects, feelings and physiological effects, behavioral expressions, and inputs to action.

### Cognitive Effects

There is a strong tradition dating back to Plato that views emotion as the enemy of reason. Thus fear inhibits learning, perception, and concentration, as we tend to forget newly acquired information after some emotional experience. Frijda notes the tendency of emotion to be closed to judgments about effects and to the requirements of goals other than the goal of the particular emotion (e.g., revenge). With intense emotions there is a self-righteous absoluteness of feeling, with the emotion so occupying center stage that other

concerns tend to be ignored. On the other hand, Frijda cites the tendency for every emotional impulse to elicit a secondary impulse that tends toward dampening the potential
consequences of the initial emotion.

As we have seen, de Sousa, while agreeing that emotion limits the range of information and options taken into account, argues that the emotions fill the gaps left by pure
reason in the determination of wants, beliefs, and action. Emotions determine the
salience of things noticed and considered and so control the parameters of rationality,
although the emotions themselves may be subject to rational appraisal. Emotions act as
arbitrators among reasons, dealing with the insufficiencies of reason by influencing the
selection and controlling the salience of the factors reason takes into account.

## Feeling and Physiological Effects

Frijda points to findings showing pleasure is contingent on change. Also, pleasure tends
to wear off with continuous satisfaction, whereas pain is likely to persist, though perhaps
not with its initial poignancy. This relates to the so-called opponent process theory of
emotion (Solomon, 1980; Solomon and Corbit, 1974), whose central tenet is that the
brain is set up to oppose or suppress emotional responses regardless of their nature. Every
emotional reaction is followed by an opposing emotion, just as the pleasure high of drugs
is said to diminish in intensity while the opposing low emotion intensifies. This would
seem to have implications for marketing, perhaps partially explaining variety-seeking
behavior. Yet this opponent process theory must be set against Frijda's additional claim
that a loss of satisfaction leads not to a neutral condition but to positive misery while a
loss of misery yields a sense not of normality but of positive happiness.

## Behavioral Expressions

Behavioral expressions include body posture, gesture, and facial expression. There is evidence suggesting that different specific facial expressions relate to different emotions.
Moreover, facial expressions of happiness, disgust, fear, and anger appear to have universal meaning regardless of culture (Ekman and Friesen, 1975; Tomkins, 1981).

## Inputs to Action

R. C. Solomon (1984), while claiming that emotions are purposive choices, agrees that
emotions can prompt intentional actions at variance with long-term interests. Acting on
the strongest desire due to a strong emotion may not be acting in ways which in more
sober moments would be given priority. But people are not generally wanton in simply
acting on inclinations; they tend to exercise some control. Without some control over the
ordering of inclinations, integrity would be meaningless in guiding action. As Darwall
(1983) says, in line with Campbell, there is a close connection between judging that there
are good and sound reasons for taking some action and, as a consequence, being motivated to take such action. Emotions can be multiple and conflicting, with some emotions
pressing for instant gratification and other emotions pushing for the long term. There is
nothing contradictory in saying someone has an emotional commitment to trying to be
rational, a person of integrity, or a good citizen.

An emotional reaction can alter future wants and actions. In Chapter 5 we mentioned Darwall's point that someone seeing animals cruelly treated may evaluate the situation negatively and wish it had never occurred, which in turn can activate a strong desire to prevent such things from happening again. What Darwall brings out is how we can never tell whether some fact or whatever should be a reason to act (or buy) until we have made someone *vividly aware* of that fact and its significance for him or her. Thus consumers typically cannot say finally whether they would want product $X$ until the seller has made them fully aware of what the product could really do for them and they have considered the costs.

A belief throughout the ages has been of the "energizing" effects of the emotions: the emotions do not just act as motives but provide that extra push and sustained effort (persistence) to achieve relevant goals. If having intentions to do something is like going into gear with the "will" being needed to press the accelerator (McGinn, 1983), then the emotions may provide the will. Psychologists who agree with MacIntyre (1971) that acts of so-called will simply refer to resolving, deciding, and intending, and not to mysterious volitions, may yet see the will's distinctive role as a hypothetical construct in considering the emotional motor behind actions.

Hume in the eighteenth century insisted on the emotional basis of doing the right thing, that is, that emotion lies behind ethical conduct. Ascribing an instrumental role to the emotions was typical of eighteenth-century philosophy, in line with the view of emotions as moral sentiments on which social and moral life was built. Comte went further in arguing that the intellect had no energy of its own, so altruistic emotions were needed for people to be motivated to serve humanity. Frank (1988), an economist, returns to this theme of emotions and altruistic behavior. Frank's title *Passions Within Reason* is an apt one in that he argues that there are good reasons for being passionate. He rejects the economist's model that equates rational behavior with narrow self-interest. In what he calls his "commitment model of emotion," Frank sets out to show how unselfishness can have a material payoff for the individual as well as society.

Frank explains deviations from the economist's rational model of behavior as arising through emotional commitments. He claims that the rational model takes one of two forms reflecting two different concepts of rationality:

1. The "present aim theory" of rationality, where rationality is defined as the use of efficient means in the pursuit of goals that are of immediate interest.
2. The "self-interest theory" of rationality, where a person's actions are considered rational providing they promote self-interest.

Frank argues these two views differ in that pursuing the goals of the moment may not be consistent with self-interest more soberly considered. It is the self-interest theory of rationality that dominates and it is this theory that Frank seeks to modify. Thus people do not behave as predicted by the self-interest model. For example, the evidence does not support a major implication of the theory that people will always seek to be "free riders" for public goods. Also, people often ignore narrow self-interest in giving anonymously to charity, enduring pain and high expense to ensure justice, walking away from profitable transactions when the terms appear inequitable, and so on. Frank endorses the philosopher Parfit (1984), who argues that people have *and* profit by having much broader concerns than would be indicated by the self-interest models of rational behavior. Frank points out that the self-interest model ignores the role played by the emotions, yet emotion can bias action away from the solutions suggested by pure self-interest. Frank never really sorts out the self-interest concept: although he claims material self-interest is exaggerated as an incentive, much of what he says about emotional commitments rests clearly on material benefits acting as the carrot.

Frank interprets being rationally self-interested as implying a short-term, opportunistic stance. In contrast he regards his so-called commitment model as a step toward a theory of nonopportunistic behavior. This commitment model claims that behavior which deviates from rational self-interest may sometimes be explained by emotional predispositions that generate commitments to solve certain dilemmas in a particular way. Thus people who feel guilty when they break the law will be disposed not to break the law (e.g. cheating on income taxes), even when rational calculation as to self-interest suggests otherwise. Although the outputs of rational calculation based on self-interest do enter as inputs to decisions, Frank argues that feelings and the stronger feelings of emotion are the proximate causes of most behavior. Thus when a person buys something, the anticipated consequences of possessing, using, or consuming the product come to mind to trigger certain feelings. Some good feelings (contemplating eating the chocolate bar) may compete with unpleasant feelings (about weight gain) in determining what action is taken with such tradeoffs intimately depending on existing commitments that are emotionally based (like the value of being slim).

Frank sees an "impulse control" problem in many decisions. This problem arises because of the desire for instant gratification. He quotes with approval one of the properties of Herrnstein's matching law to the effect that the attractiveness of a reward is inversely proportional to the delay, with delay defined as the amount of time that elapses before the reward is received. Addiction is regarded as a direct consequence of the law. Although the rational model *could be* interpreted as suggesting that choices should reflect long-term self-interests, Frank argues that the motivation is usually lacking when there is no emotional commitment. What emotions do is shift the relevant future payoffs into the current moment of choice. Thus the person's emotional commitment to slimness dramatizes and so weights negatively the unpleasant consequences of overeating. Similarly, a person's aversion to feelings of guilt can radically alter the payoffs that the person faces when given a golden opportunity for material advantage in breaking the law: the anticipated guilt feelings act as a deterrent to cheating. As far as Frank is concerned emotions develop commitments in the same way that feelings of hunger commit a person to seek food: such commitments act as strong incentives, but like incentives generally they are neither binding nor irrevocable.

Frank argues in effect that, over the long term, people are better off being honest than being dishonest. This may not be true, he argues, for any one individual transaction but over many transactions it would tend to be true. To pick and choose the occasions on which to be honest is to weaken the commitment; this is likely to be noticed by others, undermining one's reputation. Similarly, a bargainer can add to his reputation as a tough bargainer by being committed to rejecting unfair deals (even if favorable), which in turn can lead to better terms being offered in the future. It is easier to refuse such terms if accepting them makes the bargainer feel bad. The emotional support provides the backbone to reject the offer: the impulse to accept is effectively blocked by the imagined emotional consequences arising from accepting. Frank is not arguing that the material advantages always accrue to those with principles. He acknowledges that the person who risks his life to save others may actually lose his life. On the other hand, people are seldom called upon to undertake such risks, and the empathetic person is generally favored by those with whom she has dealings.

Frank argues that people who seek only self-interest typically fail to feel morally committed. Even though they might actually believe honesty pays in the long term, each situation will be viewed opportunistically. On the other hand, those committed to honesty will have few such doubts, with each temptation and rejection reinforcing the will to avoid cheating.

If adherence to certain emotional commitments (particularly the moral commitments to avoid feelings of guilt and shame) are in harmony with a wider, more coherent theory of rational behavior, the question to be answered is how such commitments lead to enhanced material reward. If commitments anchored in emotion are to be rewarding, then others must be able to discern such predispositions. Frank claims that others attribute these predispositions to us on the basis of our reputations and/or our manner. People do acquire a reputation over time and the reputation does influence how others treat and trust them. Much more difficult is judging character or emotional dispositions from observation of manner, although Frank believes that reasonable inferences can be made about the character traits of others. He argues that the signals of character traits that would be costly to fake (e.g., long years helping in "meals on wheels") and difficult to feign (e.g., blushing) are the most credible. He discusses the research on what can be inferred (and is unconsciously inferred) from body language, voice, facial expression, and so on. Thus with regard to facial expression, the focus should be (and presumably unconsciously is) on those muscles that are least subject to conscious control. Only 10% of people can deliberately pull the corners of their lips downward without moving their chin muscles, yet we do it automatically when we experience sadness or grief. In fear, eyebrows are raised and pulled together, yet again only about 10% of people can produce this expression voluntarily.

Although Frank agrees that there is a strong connection between self-reports and objective reality, he argues that people's fantasies often provide a deeper insight into how people actually feel. He accepts the TAT (Thematic Apperception Test) as probably the best way of assessing a person's motivational state.

## Predicting and Influencing Emotional Responses and Corresponding Actions

### Predicting Emotional Responses

Gordon claims that predicting emotional responses is just the same as predicting people's actions. The best approach to predicting someone's *actions* is *not* by trying to invoke "laws," as suggested by the deductive–nomological model (Hempel, 1965), as no such laws exist. The best approach lies in simulating the *practical* reasoning of those whose actions are to be predicted. Gordon refers to this method as the "play-pretend" method of prediction and recommends the same method for predicting *emotional* responses. Play-pretend is not simply acting out another's situation. Unless both actor and subject are tokens of each other, much more is needed: we need to understand the beliefs and the wishes/wants of the person or persons whose emotional responses or actions are to be predicted. Gordon's argument here is in line with Taylor's insistence on knowing explanatory beliefs. The aim would be to select the hypothesis about emotional responses that would seem to give the best fit to the wishes and beliefs of the subject in the situation. Gordon speaks of "hypotheticopractical" reasoning for predicting action and "hypotheticoemotional" reasoning for predicting emotional responses as counterparts to the hypotheticodeductive method of the natural sciences.

When action is intentional, the role of beliefs is to identify appropriate means to achieve goals. However, in the case of emotions, beliefs are mobilized to establish explanatory beliefs from which are inferred identificatory beliefs. In other words, the focus is not on goal attainment but on understanding the cause and nature of our feelings.

Emotions, though, like motives generally, can activate behavior, but typically the direction of that behavior cannot be taken for granted without knowing beliefs. Thus the success of one firm of cereal makers in spreading fear of colon cancer among a body of consumers does not guarantee that consumers will flock to buy their cereals. There are other alternatives that may be adopted by the consumer even if the consumer accepts the cancer link that is suggested by advertising.

## Influencing Emotions

If we wish to change a person's rational action, the focus will be on getting the subject to think about the merit of the proposed action in relation to goals or the desirability of the goals themselves. If we wish to make counterarguments to a rational argument we question assumptions and inferences. With regard to changing a subject's emotions, however, the focus is on getting the subject to interpret the actual or potential emotion-arousing situation in a different way and/or to reassess its significance. Thus a buyer who is angry at not receiving an order to time and specification is not likely to be pacified by being told that getting angry is not the best way to behave. Instead the salesperson will sympathize, pointing out that the last thing his firm would want to do would be to antagonize such a valued customer—the unfortunate mistake will be remedied at once. However, whereas changing emotions and emotional states is a matter of reinterpreting the situation and its significance (i.e., changing evaluations), making emotional changes to stimulate action favoring the seller may involve changing beliefs that are not in line with the suggested action. Because emotions can be influenced by normative beliefs as to what is or is not socially appropriate behavior, they are responsive to persuasion. This means that people can be talked into an emotional state, talked out of an emotional state, or even talked into a more intense emotional state.

In the case of *epistemic emotions* like "fear" the focus will be more on getting the subject to reinterpret the epistemic reason (ER) rather than the attitudinal reason (AR). It is the epistemic reason that is more likely to be open to persuasion. For example, if the aim is to enhance fear, the strategy would be to stress the extreme likelihood of $X$ and how the occurrence of $X$ is outside the control of the target audience. Such a strategy is likely to be more effective than stressing the negative consequences $Y$ about which attitudes are already formed. Thus to reduce the fear of hair loss the strategy would be to stress

1. the nonlikelihood of $X$ (hair loss), as is frequently done by medical practitioners who have patients who think they are going bald because they notice a lot of hair in their hairbrush after brushing; and
2. that the occurrence of $X$ (hair loss) can be prevented if certain medical treatments are followed.

In the case of the *factive emotions,* the focus lies in getting the subject to reinterpret the facts. For example, if we wish to stimulate feelings of pride or the anticipation of pride in possessing our product, we will represent the product as (1) highly esteemed by the relevant reference groups, (2) no longer beyond the target audience's aspirations, (3) socially visible, and (4) enhancing of self-esteem and status. On the other hand, we may want to stop the pride people have in some possession. This is not uncommon in the fashion world when designers or decorators wish to promote their own creations at the expense of what is currently in vogue. Promotion here focuses on getting the target audience to reinterpret the facts leading them to perceive what is currently fashionable as no longer esteemed by those "in the know" and as no longer a boost to self-esteem and status.

Nozick (1989) speaks of "fit" among the components of an emotion whenever beliefs are true, evaluations correct, and feelings proportionate to the evaluations. When such a fit is lacking (false beliefs, wrong evaluations, and disproportionate feelings) the emotion is defective.

We have focused on changing emotion but not directly on changing actions through emotional appeals. As de Sousa says, the point of reasons in an emotional argument is not to lead to an inference but to have the audience share a particular perspective or conjure up a certain experience. Although to get people to see something from a different perspective is to get them to reinterpret that something, to speak of getting someone to reinterpret the facts does not sufficiently capture the idea of emotional arguments, which, if successful, aim at generating a new experience. Emotion in advertising tries to show the product in a certain light, to induce certain experiences involving the product. Thus "transformational" advertising associates the possessing, using, or consuming of the product with certain values and experiences that are highly desirable. The aim of transformational advertising is to create brand associations that transform the consumer's use-experience with the brand, so the user feels, for example, more confident, beautiful, or socially adjusted. Of course, for this to be done, the ad must tie into the values of the audience and evoke the type of experiences (the paradigm scenarios) that led to the values in the first place. There are difficulties here. Whatever scenario is evoked may not be adequate to impress others either because the scenario itself is not that meaningful to the target audience or because it evokes a set of associations or images entirely different from those intended.

The key problem is to find the set of values and paradigm scenarios that appeal to a wide target audience. One way is to look to the culture or subculture. There are myths in every culture which, though questionably accurate, suggest the origins of the culture's preference for certain beliefs and values and in the process reaffirm that set of preferences. Every culture or subculture, too, has its heroes in its myths who act as role models personifying the values of the culture or subculture. Emotional advertising may exploit this set of culturally shared beliefs and values by linking the product to these values and supporting paradigm scenarios. We might take as an illustrative example the cowboy in the ad for Marlboro cigarettes. This ad links the cigarette to the cultural values exemplified by the Western lifestyle as portrayed in countless movies, rugged independence and a simple life without bureaucracy where the bad and the good can be easily distinguished and "real" men exhibit an independence and strength in manly pursuits. The theme projected of the cowboy, usually on his faithful horse, is not of aloneness but of independence, a declaration of individuality that is welcome to those feeling the dependence on others for emotional, intellectual, and material sustenance. The same advertisement has been used throughout the world with only minor changes (e.g., a black cowboy in Nigeria). This suggests that the values are fairly universal while the illustration using the cowboy was symbolic for many a target audience all over the world. One reason for this, beyond the theme itself, is that America for many throughout the world, exemplified by the Western movie, is still a land where dreams can be fulfilled. There was always a risk, though, that the ad might bring forth an interpretation that highlighted the cowboy's isolation. Thus an ad for a British cigarette called a Strand showed a lone man, cigarette in hand, on an isolated dockside. The caption: "You are never alone with a Strand." The suggestion that a cigarette was a substitute for human companionship proved not to be believable; a man in isolation on a deserted dockside conveyed not independence but isolation or rejection by others. Needless to say the ad was not a success.

With respect to emotional advertising with links to subcultural or group values, we have the campaign slogan for Schlitz beer: "You only go around once in life, so go for the gusto." This slogan stemmed from a psychographic profile of the heavy drinker *as* more of a risk taker, more self-indulgent, more interested in sports, less concerned about responsibilities, and more strongly preferring physical, male-oriented action than the non–heavy drinker. The slogan coheres with the value system of the heavy drinker and offers comfort by endorsing those values since values are made more meaningful when endorsed by others. The aim is to get the target audience to see Schlitz as part of that value system, assuming the association of welcome message with the particular brand will enhance its attractiveness by a carryover from attitudes toward the ad to attitudes toward the brand.

What we have in both the cigarette and beer cases is the importance of symbolism. Symbols, as signs with meaning and significance, are particularly important when there is ambiguity surrounding which brand to buy in a market where brands, within a segment, seem tokens of each other. With ambiguity within the market segment, symbols or slogans that capture cultural or subcultural values can evoke appropriate scenarios to enlist emotion in persuasion.

## Conclusion

A philosopher of history once argued that psychology should focus not on the rationality of man but on man's emotional nature because rationality varies with the times and the culture, whereas the same basic emotions have persisted at all times in all places. It is doubtful whether any psychologist would agree with focusing exclusively on the emotions, but there is no doubt an awareness of its neglect. Even if we were to reject the idea that emotion lies behind all action and that without emotion reason is impotent, it is nonetheless true that we cannot claim to have an adequate view of the consumer until we have come to grips with the emotional elements in buying behavior.

## APPENDIX: BELIEF-WISH CONDITIONS

PRIDE

1. Wishes. Whatever has occurred by way of achievements, possessions, or personal qualities, they are states that would have been wished.
2. Explanatory beliefs that:
    - what has occurred would be perceived as worth having by relevant reference groups.
    - that which occurred is connected in some way with self through ownership, kinship, or whatever.
3. Beliefs linking explanatory beliefs to entail identificatory beliefs:
    - that what occurred would be normally beyond his expectations *and capabilities* as

based on past experience, own sense of limitations and the expectations that others have of him.

- that what occurred is something the person cares about, values highly, and will increase his standing.
- belief that something of which he is proud did in fact occur.

*Example.*  Aston Martin Lagonda ad: "Every Aston Martin motorcar is hand built for its owner. Every chassis is identified by its owner's initials."

## SHAME

1. Wish to uphold certain internalized cultural or social norms.
2. Explanatory beliefs that:
   - others would condemn him (or those with whom he identifies) for what has been done.
   - he is in fact connected and accepts that connection with what occurred.
3. Linking explanatory beliefs to entail identificatory beliefs:
   - that his standing or status is reduced in his own and other people's eyes.
   - reduced sense of self-respect, self-esteem, and self-worth.

*Example.*  Antidrug campaign: "Anyong taking drugs is fostering crime and destroying society."

## ANGER AND INDIGNATION

1. Wish to uphold self-esteem and other interests of self or quasiselves.
2. Explanatory beliefs:
   - action $X$ carried out by $Y$ threatened interests of self or quasiselves.
   - action $X$ perceived as a slight or insult.
3. Beliefs linking explanatory beliefs to entail identificatory beliefs:
   - that standing or status had been reduced.
     *or*
   - in the case of indignation, a belief that action $X$ created an injustice.
   - sense of a need to hit back.

*Example.*  Greenpeace ad against the killing of baby seals in Canada.

## FEAR

1. Wish that either $X$ could be prevented or could be protected from consequences $Y$ of $X$.
2. Explanatory beliefs:
   - situation or event $X$ has unpleasant consequences $Y$.
   - either $X$ may occur unless preventive action is taken or $X$ cannot be prevented so protection against $Y$ is needed.
3. Beliefs linking explanatory beliefs to entail identificatory beliefs:
   - self-threatened.
   - uncertainty about occurrence of $X$.

*Example.*  Ad for hair restorer: "If you're concerned about hair loss. . . ."

## EMBARRASSMENT

1. Wish own behavior and that of others to be socially appropriate.
2. Explanatory beliefs that:
   - he or others being observed have done something that is being viewed by the audience as gauche or in some other way socially maladroit.
   - the audience is perceived as in fact viewing the behavior that way.
3. Link explanatory beliefs to entail the identificatory beliefs:
   - he or others being observed seem unable to respond in some socially appropriate way to remove embarrassment.

*Example.*    Ad for Close-Up toothpaste: "When he's this close, you'll be glad you used the new improved Close-Up."

## GUILT

1. Wish he or she had not violated the taboo or rule or law.
2. Explanatory beliefs that:
   - he has broken the rule of some authority.
   - authority is perceived as a voice of conscience. (Even if rationally he rejects that authority. Emotional reactions are not always in step with current reasoning.)
3. Beliefs linking explanatory beliefs to identificatory beliefs:
   - that his standing or status is reduced in his own eyes.

*Example.*    Ad by Columbia University Community Service on behalf of the homeless: "Isn't it time you stopped looking away?"

## INTEGRITY

1. Wish to uphold his values.
2. Explanatory beliefs that:
   - a threat or appeal has been made to his sense of integrity.
   - unless his values are upheld by him he will lose self-respect and sense of standing in his social milieu.
3. Beliefs linking explanatory beliefs to identificatory beliefs that:
   - action $X$ does or would lower his own sense of standing in his social milieu.
   - there is a need to defend personal values (integrity) against $X$.

*Example.*    Wartime recruitment poster: "Your country needs you."

## HOPE

1. Wish for consequences $Y$ of $X$.
2. Explanatory beliefs:
   - that if $X$ occurs, then consequences $Y$ will occur.
   - uncertainty about the possibility of $X$ happening.
3. Beliefs linking explanatory beliefs to entail identificatory beliefs that:
   - consequences $Y$ are highly valued.
   - $X$ can yet happen.

*Example.*    Cosmetics advertising generally.

# References

Baritz, Loren (1989). *The Good Life: The Meaning of Success for the American Middle Class.* New York: Knopf.

Burke, Marian Chapman, and Julie A. Edell (1989). "The Impact of Feelings on Ad-Based Affect and Cognition." *Journal of Marketing Research* 26 (February), pp. 69–83.

Calhoun, Cheshire (1984). "Cognitive Emotions." In *What Is an Emotion?,* edited by Cheshire Calhoun and Robert C. Solomon. New York: Oxford University Press.

Campbell, Colin (1987). *The Romantic Ethic and the Spirit of Modern Consumerism.* Oxford: Basil Blackwell.

Cannon, W. B. (1927). "The James-Lange Theory of Emotions: A Critical Examination and an Alternative Theory." *American Journal of Psychology* 39, pp. 106–24.

Cantril, Hadley (1942). *The Psychology of Social Movements.* New York: Wiley.

Carroll, Noel (1990). *The Philosophy of Horror.* New York: Routledge.

Csikszentmihalyi, Mihaly (1990). *Flow: The Psychology of Optimal Experience.* New York: Harper and Row.

Darwall, S. L. (1983). *Impartial Reason.* Ithaca, NY: Cornell University Press.

Davitz, Joel R. (1969). *The Language of Emotion.* New York: Academic Press.

De Sousa, Ronald (1990). *The Rationality of Emotion.* Cambridge, MA: The MIT Press.

Ekman, Paul, and W. V. Friesen (1975). *Unmasking the Face: A Guide to Recognizing Emotions from Facial Expression.* Englewood Cliffs, NJ: Prentice-Hall.

Elster, Jon (1989a). *Nuts and Bolts for the Social Sciences.* Cambridge: Cambridge University Press.

Elster, Jon (1989b). *Solomonic Judgements: Limitations of Rationality.* Cambridge: Cambridge University Press.

Etzioni, Amitai (1989). *The Moral Dimension.* New York: Free Press.

Festinger, Leon (1957). *A Theory of Cognitive Dissonance.* Stanford: Stanford University Press.

Frank, Robert H. (1988). *Passions Within Reasons.* New York: W. W. Norton.

Frijda, Nico H. (1988). "The Laws of Emotion." *American Psychologist* 43 (May) pp. 348–58.

Goldman, A. I. (1970). *A Theory of Human Action.* Princeton, NJ: Princeton University Press.

Gordon, R. M. (1987). *The Structure of Emotions.* Cambridge: Cambridge University Press.

Hempel, C. G. (1965). *Aspects of Scientific Explanation.* New York: Free Press.

Hill, Ronald Paul, and James C. Ward (1989). "Mood Manipulation in Marketing Research: An Examination of Potential Confounding Effects." *Journal of Marketing Research* 26 (February), pp. 97–104.

Holbrook, Morris B. (1986). "Emotion in the Consumption Experience: Toward a New Model of the Human Consumer." In *The Role of Affect in Consumer Behavior,* edited by R. A. Peterson, W. D. Hoyer, and W. R. Wilson. Lexington, MA: Lexington Books.

Holbrook, Morris B., and Rajeev Batra (1986). "Assessing the Role of Emotion as Mediators of Consumer Responses to Advertising." Research Working Paper No. 86-AV-10, Columbia University.

Isen, Alice M. (1987). "Positive Affect, Cognitive Processes and Social Behavior." In *Advances in Experimental Social Psychology,* edited by Leonard Berkowitz. Vol. 20. New York: Academic Press.

James, William (1890). *The Principles of Psychology.* New York: Holt.

Laird, J. D. (1974). "Self-Attribution and Emotion: The Effects of Expressive Behavior or the Quality of Emotional Experience." *Journal of Personality and Social Psychology* 29, pp. 475–86.

Lyons, W. (1980). *Emotion.* London: Cambridge University Press.

MacDonald, Margaret (1968). "Natural Law and Natural Rights." In *Readings in the Philosophy of the Social Sciences,* edited by May Brodbeck. New York: Macmillan.

MacIntyre, Alasdair (1971). *Against the Self-Images of the Age.* New York: Schocken Books.

MacMurray, John (1935). *Reason and Emotion.* London: Faber and Faber.

McCracken, Grant (1988). *Culture and Consumption.* Bloomington: Indiana University Press.

McGinn, C. (1983). *The Character of Mind.* New York: Oxford University Press.

Meehan, Eugene J. (1969). *Value Judgment and Social Science.* Homewood, IL: Dorsey Press.

Merabian, A., and J. A. Russell (1974). *An Approach to Environmental Psychology.* Cambridge, MA: The MIT Press.

Namier, Lewis (1955). *Personalities and Powers.* London: H. Hamilton, p. 2.

Nozick, Robert (1989). *The Examined Life.* New York: Simon and Schuster.

O'Shaughnessy, John (1987). *Why People Buy.* New York: Oxford University Press.

Parfit, Derek (1984). *Reasons and Passions.* Oxford: Clarendon Press.

Plutchik, Robert (1980). *Emotion: Psychoevolutionary Synthesis.* New York: Harper and Row.

Sartre, Jean-Paul (1948). *The Emotions: Outline of a Theory.* New York: Philosophical Library.

Schachter, S. (1971). *Emotion, Obesity and Crime.* New York: Academic Press.

Schachter, S., and J. E. Singer (1962). "Cognitive, Social and Physiological Determinants of Emotional State." *Psychological Review* 69, pp. 379–99.

Singer, J. L. (1973). *The Child's World of Make-Belief.* New York: Academic Press.

Solomon, R. C. (1973). "Emotion and Choice." *Review of Metaphysics* 27, pp. 20–40.

Solomon, R. C. (1976). *The Passions: The Myth and Nature of Human Emotions.* New York: Doubleday.

Solomon, R. C. (1984). "Emotion and Choice." In *What Is an Emotion?,* edited by Cheshire Calhoun and Robert C. Solomon. New York: Oxford University Press.

Solomon, R. L. (1980). "The Opponent-Process Theory of Acquired Motivation." *American Psychologist* 35, pp. 691–712.

Solomon, R. L., and J. D. Corbit (1974). "An Opponent-Process Theory of Motivation: I. Temporal Dynamics of Affect." *Psychological Review* 81, pp. 119–45.

Taylor, Gabriele (1985). *Pride, Shame and Guilt: Emotions of Self-Adjustment.* Oxford: Clarendon Press.

Tomkins, S. (1981). "The Quest for Primary Motives." *Journal of Personality and Social Psychology* 41, pp. 306–29.

Unger, R. M. (1984). *Passion.* New York: Free Press.

# 10

# Understanding Consumer Actions Using Social Science Sensitizing Concepts

> If one does not understand a person, one tends to
> regard him as a fool.
>
> Carl Jung (1875–1961)

## Sensitizing Concepts as Diagnostic Criteria

In discussing the explanatory systems of psychology and sociology in Chapters 7 and 8, the focus was on how these systems go about investigating and explaining human behavior. In these and previous chapters explanations and findings useful in marketing were also presented. But to date the record here is more one of promise than of substantive achievement, though the potential is there. Of considerable importance, however, are the concepts developed to describe different facets of behavior. We refer to these concepts as *sensitizing* concepts since they direct our observation in what to look for if we are to interpret buyer behavior with some degree of subtlety and sophistication.

In studying consumers we are drawn to what we have been sensitized to observe and describe what we observe in terms of the concepts we have learned. Thus the more refined the concepts, the more narrowly can behaviors be labeled and more widely can categories of behavior be noticed. An analogy can be drawn with the garage mechanic looking at a car engine. Because he can label the parts, he notices more than the mechanically ignorant driver who has a label only for the engine itself. The various behavioral concepts developed by social scientists constitute a stock of labels that sensitize the observer to various buying phenomena for diagnostic purposes. These different sensitizing concepts often suggest rival hypotheses to explain action. In interpreting behavior to explain it, we compare and choose from among these rival hypotheses the hypothesis that best fits the evidence.

This chapter brings together, within a reason-giving framework, *some* of the sensitizing concepts discussed in earlier chapters and elsewhere. The basic framework (O'Shaughnessy, 1987) is based on a categorization of want states depending on the type and extent of the deliberation involved in buying (see Figure 10.1). The aim is to provide a coherent, recognizable picture of the buyer by describing behavior and behavior patterns in terms of concepts that make sense in that they can be affirmed by everyone's buying experience. In other words, we are concerned with people's own likely interpretation of buying episodes, reflecting as it does a "folk" psychology but introducing more

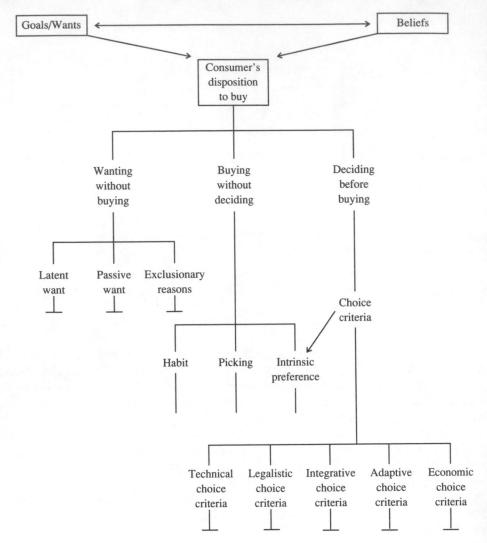

FIGURE 10.1. Basic View of the Consumer

refinements in line with social science. As the Oxford psychologists Clarke and Crossland (1985) argue, the first requirement of a more mature psychology is that at least some branches should be built upon the foundations of ordinary commonsense experience, as folk psychology is far too important, not to mention interesting and credible, to be abandoned.

## Goals in Buying

Purchase behavior, like all human action, is purposive. Whether through daydreams about idealized lifestyles, past experience, or the strategy of displaced meaning, consum-

TABLE 10.1. Consumer Purchases Track a Preferred Life Vision

| Track the Good Life | Seek to Avoid the Poor Life |
|---|---|
| To be healthy | Being unhealthy |
| To be secure | Being physically at risk |
| To be loved/admired | Being hated/disliked |
| To be full of life | Being miserable/sluggish |
| To be an insider | Being an outsider |
| To be confident | Being socially insecure |
| To be serene/relaxed | Being tense/anxious |
| To be beautiful/handsome | Being ugly |
| To be knowledgeable | Being ignorant |
| To be in control of one's life | Being at the mercy of events/others |
| To be entertained | Being bored |
| To be free of guilt | Being guilt ridden |
| To be consistent | Being inconsistent |

ers in their purchases seek "the good life." This vision of the good life reflects sensitivity to contrasts in the human condition with the more agreeable polar extreme representing the preferred life vision. Consumer purchases track that vision (see Table 10.1).

The good life is the preferred life vision, but not all components of that vision can be pursued with equal vigor. How people assign priorities to the various components depends on their system of values, which reflects their emotional nature as manifested in what people envy in others, fear about the future, and so on. We weave our lives out of memory, imagination, and hope and the consumer's pattern of purchases emanates from that same weave. Of course, the pursuit of the good life is not the only human goal: we generally have some vision of what we would like to achieve in life, and this may be something over and above the "good" life itself.

All advertising should be linked, however obliquely, to the consumer's diffuse longings for the good life. Although advertising may affect values by dramatizing what a change in values can mean in terms of enriching life, advertising more typically presents the case for claiming the advertised brand "gives more bang for the buck" in achieving the existing preferred life vision. It is because persuasion can influence values or show why some goal can be more efficiently pursued by some alternative means that we come to want something not sought previously. Consumers can overlook, misconstrue, or be unable to visualize what the pursuit and attainment of certain goals would be like. What advertising can do is give new meaning to the product in terms of its significance for the good life. People can even be persuaded on occasion to change their lifestyle. Such a conversion may not come about by any comparisons of lifestyles (since they may be so different as to be incommensurable) but by dramatizing what adopting the alternative lifestyle would be like.

## Reasons (Wants and Beliefs)

### Wants

The consumer's preferred life vision, as reflected in his or her system of values, gives rise to "notional" product wants, that is, for products in line with the preferred life vision. A

TABLE 10.2. Propositions Regarding Wants

---

Each consumer has a multitude of wants.

Different consumers have different wants or want priorities.

Every consumer would prefer to satisfy more rather than less of a want.

There is a strict limit to the number of wants that can be met by any one product.

There are always costs attached to the satisfaction of any want and such costs are best reflected in the alternatives displaced.

The way the consumer satisfies his or her wants is constrained by perceptions of what is an efficient and socially appropriate way of meeting the want.

The same lifestyle can find expression in many equally acceptable ways, so many different products are substitutable without any corresponding sense of loss.

The consumer is *not* always conscious of his or her wants.

*Active* wants take account of the feasibility of satisfying the want, so that expressed wants do not necessarily take account of all "secret" wishes. Hence asking people what they want in a product or offering is unlikely to generate truly innovative ideas. Perhaps asking them about their secret wishes would stimulate more novel suggestions.

A want for a product can be thought of as a *cluster of attributes* being sought to generate certain satisfactions, not all of which must be possessed by the firm's offering for the consumer to feel the want is being met satisfactorily. Every indivdual want will have unique aspects that the standard mass-produced product will have had to ignore.

Consumers may actually want something they do not consciously believe they want or may think they want what in fact they do not want.

An active want is not just a want for anything that would meet the core want. Thus water may quench the consumer's thirst but the active want is for a cold beer.

A consumer's *total* want is not necessarily captured by any product not just because some of the benefits sought are absent but because of the presence of things not wanted (e.g., carcinogens in cigarettes).

Some wants seek immediate satisfaction; others are intended to be realized in the future.

---

"notional want" is a cluster of dispositional states pointing to the satisfactions that are sought, whereas a "specific want" is a disposition to possess, use, and/or consume some specific product. Notional wants combine with beliefs to provide reasons for buying. A want is typically represented in the mind as benefits sought; a "belief" is a disposition to accept that certain things are true (or false) or that certain things should be done (or not done). Wants are always comparative in that whatever is wanted, it is wanted through comparison with alternatives displaced. Whereas wants point to the satisfactions that are sought, beliefs take account of achieving the satisfactions given the circumstances, application, or occasion for use.

Several propositions can be put forward regarding wants (see Table 10.2). The following terms in popular usage are refinements of the term want or specific species of wants:

- *Desire.* A desire is a want that the consumer is acutely aware of not having realized,. One aim of advertising is to elevate wants to desires so that the consumer thinks often about the product, inquires about it, and is moved by facts about it.

- *Need.* A need is a basic requirement. On this basis we may need things we do not actively want (car safety belts) and want things we do not really need (cigarettes).

- *Impulse.* An impulse is a strong notional want that finds expression in a response to some stimuli without the consumer being acutely conscious of what is being sought. Product attractiveness when allied to seemingly effortless, low-cost buying can activate impulse buying.

- *Wish.* A wish, unlike the typical want, is a yearning for some state of affairs regardless of the feasibility of attainment. Emotional stimulation is often tied to appeals to wishes.
- *Craving.* A craving is a desire that is biologically compelling.
- *Lust.* Lust is a biologically driven desire that has the potential to lead to actions that defy social norms and morality.
- *Obsession.* An obsession is any cycle of repetitive behavior from which a person finds it difficult to break free.
- *Addiction.* Addiction is the paradigm case of obsession when the object of the obsession is some consumable product.

We can never cater to everyone's full want in all its detail but seek to meet or exceed *expectations* which depend on what the product costs in terms of money and effort, what competition is offering, what the consumer has been promised, and what appears reasonable to expect from past experience. Whenever expectations are seriously violated, the emotions generated inhibit repeat purchase.

## Beliefs

The want for a specific product or brand is a derived want, generated by beliefs (tacit or otherwise) about how to track the preferred life vision. Thus wanting product XYZ depends on beliefs about what consequences, outcomes, or effects flow from possession, use, or consumption of XYZ. The wants we seek to meet are not necessarily the strongest but preferably those that cohere with beliefs about what is wise, or the sensible thing to do in the circumstances. Thus if the consumer believes (as many do in Portugal) that too frequent consumption of ice cream can give rise to throat problems, this inevitably affects the amount of ice cream that is bought, however strong the desire. As this example shows, although changes in beliefs can lead to not-wanting some specific product, there may still remain the more general want awaiting satisfaction. This is why a product may fail yet be successfully reintroduced by eliminating or adding some ingredient, component, or feature that is considered necessary before the consumer will buy it.

Beliefs lie behind attitudes and control and inform action all the way from shaping wants into specific product preferences to guiding postpurchase actions such as returning an unsatisfactory product. It is beliefs that convert a notional want for a certain type of satisfaction into a specific want for a certain product and brand.

### BELIEFS AND INFORMATION

Dretske (1988) conceptualizes beliefs as internal structures that steer and control actions in line with the informational content of the beliefs. As more information is acquired about a product, beliefs become more refined and specific in steering action. Initial beliefs at the start of the buying process may thus be few and general but, whenever shopping is a learning experience, beliefs become more detailed and firm.

Beliefs are tied to information in that new information affects beliefs. Beliefs are thus parasitic on the interpretation of the information that beliefs encode. Of particular significance in changing belief structures is information that adds to the consumer's repertoire of concepts. The learning of new words to describe brand *B* or the meaning of product features can lead to the consumer endorsing a new set of beliefs. Thus in learning about the mouse as a feature of the Macintosh computer, I may come to endorse that feature, that is, come to believe in its benefits. Where consumers have failed to grasp the concept of the product and its differences from rivals, they cannot develop a genuine preference for it.

Typically beliefs about products are issue-bound in that the consumer believes one thing as opposed to another. All consumers wish their beliefs to be based on the best information available, but time pressures and cost factors usually rule this out. Consumers therefore are likely to collect enough information to determine a brand preference but not to become experts on the product class.

### BELIEFS AND EMOTIONS

Beliefs are not just based on objective facts or personal experience but are linked to loyalties, hopes, fears, self-interest, and social conditioning so that beliefs only imperfectly relate to supporting evidence. Self-deception occurs when false beliefs are accepted for the sake of some noncognitive goal. Wanting something to be true can influence the selection of facts, so that the consumer selectively perceives, remembers, and interprets to filter out disconfirmations of emotionally held beliefs. Also, consumers do not generally have the time or the desire to canvass or discover all their beliefs, so that, when disposed to believe $X$, the result can be an automatic endorsement and choices in line with that endorsement. This is one reason why appeals to emotion can, on occasion, be so effective.

### BELIEF NETWORKS

Beliefs seldom are isolated but typically are part of a system of beliefs and wants. This is why some beliefs are more fixed and less easily given up or imagined to be false than others. It is also a reason why attacking a single belief (e.g., smoking is not all that bad for the health) may be ineffective when it is part of a supporting network of beliefs. New beliefs are more easily endorsed when not in competition with other sets of beliefs.

### TACIT BELIEFS

Most beliefs involved in buying are tacit beliefs. Memory stores the resources out of which beliefs come into being, so that most beliefs are probably "manufactured" from information possessed, just as the consumer arrives at her belief about the overall cost of shopping by calling on the rules of addition. This is another reason for claiming that product evaluations are likely to be much less thorough than is suggested by consumer experiments in the laboratory.

### STRENGTH OF BELIEF

It is common in statistics to speak of the strength of belief but others (e.g., Levi, 1967) argue that belief is not a probabilistic notion but an all-or-nothing concept, since the notion of dogmatic belief is necessary if we are to understand the role of belief in decision-making. What we can say is that some beliefs are more easily surrendered than others.

## Wanting Without Buying

Wanting a product may be a necessary but is not a sufficient condition for buying it. Wants are not in themselves reasons for action; the relevant beliefs need to be present. When the want for a product is latent, consumers have yet to acquire the relevant beliefs about the product's potential for them. When a want is passive, consumers are aware to some extent of the product's potential for them but are held back from buying by beliefs about the wisdom of buying. Finally, when a want is excluded, there are exclusionary reasons precluding buying, that is, reasons that have nothing to do with the relative merits of the offering itself.

## Latent Wants

Consumers may not be actively aware of wanting a particular product or brand but would come to want it if made aware of what it could do to enrich their lives. This is because *conceiving* the potential of a product comes before actively wanting it. Thus we may be aware of a product (e.g., antilock brakes) and the functions of the product (allowing the driver to retain control of a vehicle while stopping on a slippery road) yet still not know enough to buy it. If we are current consumers of the product, we may still be activated to increase our consumption when made aware of other benefits. Thus my consumption of potatoes may increase dramatically after being told by some nutritionist that the potato has "almost no fat with a laundry list of vitamins and minerals that makes it come close to being the perfect source of nourishment." Consumers do not want a product per se but the effects/functions/benefits that stem from possessing, using, and consuming it. Consumer knowledge of products can be superficial, so there is a need to teach consumers about benefits to activate their want for it. Consumers, like everyone else, can be moved by new facts to actively want something. They can come to want something never previously considered as a result of appeals to their imagination and rationality.

It is sometimes assumed that buyers know what they want and this knowledge acts as a screen determining what products are bought. This ignores the fact that consumers can be stimulated to imagine what something really would be like to possess, consume, or use and in the process come to want it. But consumers are not motivationally empty until injected with the new want. Wants are not created but activated, since the underlying motivational disposition toward the preferred life vision is already there. As Nozick (1989) says, people in Chaucer's time did not know of Shakespeare yet were not conscious of missing anything. He asks "What comparable voids exist now waiting to be filled?"

Reasoning can lead to wanting something since rational deliberation involves making oneself aware of the relevant facts and assessing what they mean in terms of one's system of values. The process of deliberation in consumer decision-making can be viewed as a process of *coming to prefer* something. In sum, the appeal to the imagination aims to change perceptions, whereas the appeal to rationality is to provide justification (in terms of values or preferred life vision) for new beliefs to emerge to activate latent wants. The problem lies in grabbing the consumer's attention since, when wants are latent, emotions may not direct attention to the relevant communications.

We can never be certain whether consumers would want product XYZ sufficiently to buy it (if able to do so) until we know what they would do after being made most completely and vividly aware of what the product can do for them. Consumers are seldom aware of a product's full potential or the potential of some single feature. Moreover, consumers are often in doubt about the lifestyle that most suits them and are open to persuasion. Thus repositioning a product in the market can give new life to the product.

## Passive Wants

A latent want, when activated, may become a passive want in the sense that the prospective customer may know about the potential benefits yet still be inhibited from buying. The consumer is in effect saying, "Though I want product XYZ, I do not intend to buy it." The move from a latent want to a passive want corresponds to "unfreezing" the consumer; removing inhibitions to buying corresponds to "moving" the prospect into buying. To complete the Kurt Lewin (1968) trinity, there is "refreezing" in ensuring the purchase lives up to expectations.

Inhibitors to buying include the following:

1. *Price* may be more than the consumer is willing to pay; that is, the relative weight given to price is higher than the perceived benefits.
2. *False beliefs* in that the evaluation of benefits may be based on erroneous information. False beliefs often resist being changed because they are usually part of a system of beliefs. Hence an attack on one belief may stimulate robust counterargument based on these other beliefs.
3. *True beliefs.*
4. *Doubts* about the claims made for a product. Doubts abound about
   - "revolutionary" advances in a product's functions
   - multiuse products (unless versatility is sought)
   - product advances (not being at the expense of losses elsewhere)
   - the firm's competence across several product areas
5. *Social norms* in that consumers often act as if big (social) brother is watching their purchases; even when the product is not visible socially.

Firms seek to overcome such inhibitors by choosing the appropriate *promotional focus:*

*Price:* Minimize the impact (e.g., offer of credit) or perceptions of importance (e.g., suggesting the price is an investment).

*False beliefs:* Challenge the *set* of beliefs of which the false belief is a part.

*True beliefs:* Depreciate the importance or compensate.

*Doubts:* Show untenability or nonapplicability.

*Contrary to social norms:* Show social approval and/or depreciate the importance.

## Exclusionary Reasons

Consumers may want a product but various incapacities may take them out of the market. The set of known product alternatives is not the same as the set of feasible options when the consumer considers personal constraints on buying. Exclusionary reasons for not buying are those reasons that have nothing to do with the objective merits of the offering but everything to do with not having the money to pay for the product, being unable to obtain the product, promises to parents not to buy the product (e.g., a motorcycle), and the like.

Activating latent and passive wants is part of the cost of entry to a new market and the difficulties involved in doing this can affect the diffusion process. Estimates of what can or will be done to overcome latent and passive wants are often key to determining the sales forecast. It might also be argued that activating latent and passive wants is what development selling is all about.

## Choosing Without Deciding

Although "deciding" and "choosing" are often treated as synonymous, they should be distinguished. Whereas deciding always involves choosing, not all choosing involves deciding. The core meaning of deciding presupposes deliberation over uncertainties regarding feasible options and the costs and benefits attached to them. Choosing, on the other hand, involves making choices that are regarded as unproblematic, that is, no practical uncertainties need to be resolved.

Choosing without decision-making follows three distinct rules:

1. *Habit:* buy the same brand as before.
2. *Picking:* buy any brand within a cluster of brands as any will do.
3. *Intrinsic preference:* buy the brand that most appeals to the senses—that sounds best, feels best, smells best, or tastes best.

## Habit

With habit, current choices are the same as past choices, that is, repeat buying is the rule. Habitual buying suggests a one-to-one correspondence between a recurrent want and a certain purchase. Although habitual buying is associated with day-to-day buying, it can also extend to infrequently bought products like annual vacations. With habitual buying, choice is automatic in that although consumers know what they are about, habitual choices occur without monitoring or deliberating on the alternatives available. In other words, learning is no longer active in that current actions follow rather than improve upon past practices. There is a tendency toward habitual buying as confidence increases with each repeat purchase since habits save time, effort, and expense; mitigate risk; and reaffirm the wisdom of past practices. Acting on habit can be a rational strategy in that the consumer, instead of weighing the options, falls back on the generalization that there is no better way to meet a particular want than to act as in the past. Without much buying being habitual, shopping would be impossibly time consuming.

Once a brand becomes the habitual buy, there is less attention to seeking and evaluating information. Indeed, having invested heavily in the current habitual purchase, consumers are loath to seek and accept evidence raising uncertainties; thus the anticipated psychological costs of changing and making an error can be weighted disproportionately to anticipated likely gains.

In other words consumers are unlikely to seek disconfirming evidence of their beliefs about their habitual buys but are more attuned to accepting their brand's advertising copy. A brand habitually bought need offer no objective advantage over rival brands since the habitual buy always has an advantage over a rival that is objectively equivalent in all relevant respects. This is because the consumer has more familiarity with the habitual buy and so has more confidence in it and liking for it. There is a disposition to hold on to good things associated with the past so that any change (as in the Coca-Cola formula), even for the better, is in danger of being resented. We may in fact come to be devoted to a particular brand because of past association when objectively the same bundle of benefits is available in rival brands. We may even continue to buy the brand when it is at a disadvantage (e.g., on price) so that loyalty alone explains the habit. However, there are always counterpressures toward change, including social norms on appearing progressive ("don't be an old stick in the mud"), toward enjoying variety, and toward making sure today's choices are still the wisest. Hence buying habits can be broken when consumers are persuaded the rival brand offers enough additional benefits to compensate and there is appeal to social norms about being progressive and wise.

Consumers have more experience with the habitual buy and wish to believe they are already buying the best available, which makes it easier to retain customers than to convert from rivals. Habits receive support through their integration into a particular way of life just as someone may feel lost without a wristwatch. To retain customers we must reassure customers they are already buying the best while upgrading the offering to match or preempt competition. What helps in restraining customers from trying nonequivalent brands is the potential ambiguity over the value of different attributes or the particular combination of attributes.

## Picking

Puzzled consumers tend to have no set allegiance and consumers are often puzzled about differences among brands. One strategy for choosing among brands is to choose at random or on whim. This is "picking" just as cigarettes are picked from the pack.

Picking occurs for several reasons. First, there may be a belief that all offerings are alike, that is, whatever differences there are, these differences are not discernible from inspection or from the package information. Second, there may be the belief that the rival offerings, even if not undifferentiated, are not sufficiently different to undertake inquiry. Third, the consumer's want for a class of product may be "holistic," that is, there is no want for any refinement. The holistic want is the counterpart to the concept of "cluster brands," groups of brands any of which the consumer finds equally acceptable. When wants are holistic, price is usually key.

When writers sometimes hold that much buying is mindless, they may be referring to the large amount of picking behavior that occurs. But where differences among brands, within some segment of a market, are not regarded as significant, picking is as rational a solution as any. Picking can be regarded as a way of avoiding the anxiety arising from there being too many options from which to choose or the rational thing to do when circumstances suggest that further investigation of differences is likely to be a waste of time or result in lost opportunities. But consumers hate to just pick: this resort to seemingly nonrational processes makes us generally uncomfortable.

Although what the consumer actually "picks" can be said to represent the picker's preference, the picker cannot genuinely be said to have a preference, since no preference is implied when several offerings are equally attractive. And with the absence of preference comes a lack of resolve in the choices that are made, which, in turn, means that the choice itself is devalued.

Consumers who initially pick a brand on whim might go on to rationalize the choice and so continue to buy it on a habitual basis. There is pressure to rationalize since one social norm is to justify choices and avoid making errors. Consumers therefore seek to avoid picking, which risks later discovering that a difference between brands is significant. Some implications follow from this discussion of picking:

1. When picking is extensive, the firm that provides a relevant difference and *proclaims* it will catch the pickers.

2. When a firm cannot distinguish its product, price, or distribution, it may still catch the pickers by increasing brand familiarity and/or associating it with an attractive image or giving it visibility in the store.

3. When a brand makes no claim to possessing a significant advantage over rivals, it will lose out to the brand that does make such a claim.

## Intrinsic Preference

Some brand preferences reflect nothing more than an intrinsic preference, that is, a preference based on nothing more than anticipated pleasure or enjoyment. Products bought on this basis are bought to provide enjoyment or pleasure to the senses and nothing else. The reasons for buying are purely subjective. There are no objective reasons for choosing since pleasure is an end in itself, so reasons can do nothing more than describe the enjoyment expected or the form of pleasure experienced:

> The *taste* is refreshing.
>
> The *smell* is fresh.
>
> It *looks* appetizing.
>
> The name *sounds* soothing.
>
> It *feels* pleasant.

Some writers distinguish pleasure from enjoyment. Thus Csikszentmihalyi (1990) defines "pleasure" as that feeling of contentment that arises whenever expectations set by biological programs or social conditioning are met. "Enjoyment," on the other hand, is more complex than pleasure, involving both pleasure and a sense of having achieved something unexpected, adding to one's sense of psychological growth. Enjoyment of activities goes beyond mere pleasure because of the investment of time, energy, concentration, and skill involved in controlling the activity. Although we generally speak of pleasure as being sought for its own sake, Csikszentmihalyi reminds us that pleasure does have a function in being a reflex response that is built into the genes for the preservation of the species. Thus eating is an efficient way of ensuring the body gets the nourishment it needs while even listening to music for pleasure helps bring order into consciousness to ward off boredom and the tendency of the bored mind to dwell on unpleasant images. Intrinsic choices can also be made to appear instrumental by making reference to the (vacuous) superordinate goal of utility maximization. However, this said, the fact remains that pleasure is not consciously sought for anything beyond itself.

Pleasures do vary. Csikszentmihalyi draws on the work of the French anthropologist Roger Caillois in analyzing the type of pleasure provided by games. Thus with competitive games, pleasure arises from meeting the challenge of an opponent; games of chance give pleasure by creating an illusion of controlling the future; games like riding the merry-go-round provide pleasure by transforming the way we perceive reality; and games involving pretense and fantasy create the feeling of our being more than we actually are. Films, novels, and similar diversions provide pleasure by conjuring up an emotional curiosity about answers to the questions implicitly raised by the narrative as well as by the fascination evoked by the characters themselves. Curiosity and the desire for novelty are intrinsic in that satisfaction is sought as an end in itself. But curiosity and novelty are not activated by all that is new but by those products that are neither too similar nor too dissimilar from what is currently being bought. If too similar, there is an absence of novelty and curiosity is not aroused. If too dissimilar, there is the problem of understanding and accepting the utterly strange.

Intrinsic preferences are likely to enter into all aspects of buying, not just brand choice. Thus consumers may avoid shops and shopping districts that make them feel uncomfortable—those in run-down areas of town or those considered boring, for example.

Although many products are bought purely on the basis of intrinsic preference, as a percentage of all consumer purchases, they are likely to be only a small proportion. Even with food items, anticipated relative enjoyment tends not be the sole criterion: consumers typically take account of calories, convenience in use, nourishment, health, and, last but not least, price. Yet anticipated pleasure is typically one criterion. Thus a major reason for choosing a "luxury" brand is not just belief in extra quality or snob appeal but the fact that luxury gives intrinsic pleasure beyond any utilitarian function.

Yet the pleasure generated by a certain type of activity or food or whatever diminishes over time unless addiction is involved. In other words, variety is needed to put off the point of satiety.

When it comes to products bought solely for pleasure, it is difficult to generate single-minded loyalty to a single brand. Consumers seek pleasurable novel experiences as a way of warding off boredom. The more frequently the same reward follows purchase, the less rewarding is the purchase and the broader the search for other types of reward. The search for variety is one component of pleasure, and equivalent pleasure can be found in a wide range of offerings which are interchangeable from the consumer's point of view. As D. H. Lawrence said, "I love trying things and discovering how I hate them." There is, to some degree, cultural homogeneity of likings, particularly in respect to aversions. Thus in Western societies there is an aversion to eating insects, dogs, lizards, and anything that is alive (except plants and some invertebrates). But associations count. Thus teenagers seeking to act like adults will suddenly find children's movies and stories no longer pleasurable; moreover, many a taste has been changed (e.g., in music) by education or new associations.

Intrinsic preferences often present a problem in marketing. In the first place, consumers have difficulty in verbalizing their likes and dislikes in a way that can be concretely tied down. Second, expressed likings can reflect socially prudent or socially appropriate replies rather than true intrinsic preferences. Also, firms find it difficult to educate consumers into changing their likings but find it easier to change choices from being purely intrinsic by associating their brand with people, symbols, events, and so on, with which the consumer can identify or to add features appealing to other criteria (e.g., fewer calories).

## Aspects of Consumer Decision-Making

Deliberation in buying consists of canvassing reasons and assessing them with a view to reaching a decision. In the process of deliberation, reasons that were initially given little consideration may come to be weighted heavily so that views about product attributes and combinations of attributes can change. This is not only because deliberation can involve rational calculation but because deliberation puts us in touch with our gut feelings (emotions) about the salience for us of various tradeoffs.

We commonly assume that consumer decision-making, as practical reasoning, is means–end reasoning. But this is an oversimplification, for it suggests that wants are already in place and fixed. In fact, rationality involves reflecting on the wants themselves and modifying them if there are good reasons to do so. Thus as I think about my real wants in the future, I may change my mind about a second car or station wagon. This is not to suggest that through reasoning alone the consumer will reach a decision. Rationality proscribes rather than prescribes; pointing to inconsistencies between immediate desires and long-term goals and distinguishing real differences from distinctions without a difference (de Sousa, 1990). But the actual tradeoffs themselves are value-laden. This means that where the consumer's values, as sensed by the consumer, form a coherent set for the purpose of buying, the weighing of options and tradeoffs is made easier. When value systems are vague, however, and outcomes sought are vague, decision criteria are correspondingly vague and, unless such vagueness is recognized and corrected, deliberation will inevitably be perfunctory and open to manipulation by persuasive communications. But even when such vagueness is absent there may still be the problem of determining how much of any particular product attribute (e.g., size of car engine) is wanted and how much of it will be provided by each of the options considered. Certainly the process of deliberation is often a learning process that moves from some initial (antecedent) set of wants and beliefs to a new or modified set. Thus beliefs about what is practically feasible can affect wants (the "sour grapes" phenomenon) in that consumers may end up desiring what they know is possible for them. On the other hand, it is possible for the consumer to feel emotionally bound to look further for feasible options or to reduce the number of options by exaggerating the uncertainties or risks attached to certain options.

Although the compensatory model does implicitly acknowledge the value-laden judgments involved in the weighting of attributes, it may still distort the actual process. Thus it may be that consumers simply choose on the basis of *felt expectations* as to how each brand will be experienced after purchase. This does not mean that anticipated benefits do not receive acute attention but simply that the compensatory decision strategy demands more than consumers will or know how to give. We would suspect that experiments using the model yield results that give undue weight to choosing efficient means for performing functions while neglecting the importance of social norms in buying. Yet choices in practice take account of both efficiency and social appropriateness. In general, there often remains enough doubt about the consequences of buying that the likelihood that deliberation will yield an absolute sense of certainty about having chosen the best remains doubtful. This is particularly so when product options possess very different strengths and weaknesses so that they cannot readily be compared but essentially remain incommensurable. Here there is not indifference as to what choice is made (as in the case of true picking behavior) since a slight change (e.g., reduction in price) in one of the options would not overcome the problem of which to choose. This is where gut feel (emotion) most clearly comes into play.

The conjunctive and disjunctive choice strategies can be regarded as descriptive of efforts to reduce the total set of options considered. Where the purchase is important too many options can create anxiety as a wide range of choices is intimidating. For example, more than 350 different car models are sold in the United States, 50% more than in 1984. Even where rationality comes into its own in proscribing options, it may not be exercised as would be expected. Deficiencies can arise in *receiving information* through functional illiteracy, expectations, wishful thinking, or time pressure. Deficiencies can also arise in *processing information* through lack of competence, faulty reasoning habits, wishful thinking, erroneous beliefs, emotions like fear and anxiety, overweighting more recent events, or fatigue.

But none of these limitations undermines the fundamental truth of the following:

- The greater the number of rival brands, the less dependent is the consumer on any one brand.

- The more brand $B$ provides more sources of perceived reward for consumer $A$, the more dependent is $A$ on brand $B$.

- The less satisfied consumer $A$ is with brand $B$, the less the likelihood of $A$ continuing to buy brand $B$ as more brands become available.

- The more the perceived advantages of brand $B$ over its rivals, the more consumer $A$ will try to get it.

Even if consumers are not as systematically rational as suggested by decision theory, they may not act on the strongest want (desire) since such wants may conflict with an emotional commitment to beliefs about what considerations should be given priority. Choices are not necessarily in line with the relative strength of wants. Wants are not so much compelling forces as key imformation to be taken into account. Consumers, like people in general, internalize social norms about the need to act rationally and such norms can dictate forbearance and the need to think more about the long-term consequences. However, the strongest desires do start with an advantage in that their pursuit seems to promise instant gratification.

## Choice Criteria in Buying

Deliberation involves canvassing and assessing reasons. Such reasons in buying constitute *choice criteria*. There are just six categories of choice criteria that in some combination enter into every buying decision: technical, legalistic, integrative, economic, adaptive, and intrinsic (enjoyment and pleasure).

We have already discussed intrinsic preference. The other five categories are not pursued for their own sake, as is enjoyment and pleasure. They describe the considerations that might be addressed to reach a satisfactory decision.

## Technical Criteria

Ignoring the case where a product is bought simply for enjoyment, products serve some function or functions. The *core* technical function is the primary function for which the product was designed. The name of the product typically suggests the core function. Thus a seat is to be sat upon and toothpaste is to clean teeth.

*Ancillary-use* functions are permanent or optional technical functions associated with the performance of the core function: the core function of a clock is to measure time, whereas an ancillary-use function would be an alarm. *Convenience-in-use* functions are additions, modifications, packaging, and so on, designed to make the performance of core and/or ancillary-use functions easier, such as the toothpaste pump.

Marketers always need to consider

1. the core function for which the product was designed versus the function for which the product is used, so that the two coincide;

2. the level of performance sought by consumers versus the level technologically possible: technological performance must not become an end in itself; and

3. the way consumers infer performance/quality of a product versus the way the firm signals its quality or level of performance: the two ways should cohere even though the seller might recognize the need to supply what it considers quality.

Many a market leader has taken the lead by discovering the true core functions sought or by adding ancillary-use and/or convenience-in-use functions. The importance of technical attributes of products does change when such attributes can no longer be used to discriminate among brands. Thus with the introduction of quartz (liquid crystal) technology, watch accuracy ceased to be a discriminator since a watch with an accuracy of plus or minus fifteen seconds per month could be purchased for less than ten dollars. Also, as new indicators of the good life evolve, new products arise whose function is to provide the new indicator. For example, when a sun tan began to symbolize a rich, leisured existence rather than a laboring life in the fields, products arose to provide the tan to symbolize the lifestyle.

## Legalistic Criteria

Buyers take account of legalistic choice criteria whenever their buying is determined by the law (e.g., in respect to safety belts) or the desires of those *directly* affected by the purchase. Thus if I am buying on behalf of someone else, I need to keep that person's instructions or wants in mind. On the other hand, my purchase might be for the family (e.g., an apartment) where I give priority to what others seek since I believe it means more to them, or they will use it more, or others are perceived as just being more knowledgeable about such purchases. Although I might have been happy just to pick, I will be more happy if, instead of just picking, I choose in a way that pleases my family. Advertisers recognize this whenever advertising reminds its audience of what others (for whom the purchase is being made) really want.

## Integrative Criteria

Some brands have more appeal to the consumer because

1. they promise more social integration and/or standing in the community as a result of their purchase and possession, or
2. they promise better integration with a person's ethical values or personal integrity.

There is constant tension between these two purposes. We need other people for emotional, intellectual, and material sustenance yet also seek privacy, individuality, and independence. The problem is to achieve the appropriate balance to avoid despair. Advertising, in appealing to integrative criteria, tends to stress one or the other, that is, either the joy of a supportive network of friends or the satisfaction of being independent of others.

### SOCIAL INTEGRATION

Under this heading comes adherence to the conventions of the consumer's own social milieu, fashion, fads, and the desire for status and prestige. Community or group support mitigates against life stresses. But dependence on others makes us sensitive to group norms, whose violation can jeopardize such support. The belief that certain purchases might foster or destroy the needed support of those who share our values is commonly exploited in advertising. The fewer the number of people with whom we have a sense of sharing of values and background, the more important they are to us. Hence meeting a countryman in some foreign land can be an emotional experience.

*Convention and Social Norms.* Consumers, like everyone else, have a conception of appropriate social conduct. Indeed, they must have if they are to function effectively in society. An outstanding peculiarity of human beings is the influence that social conventions have on their behavior, and they will typically trade off the satisfaction of making a completely independent decision for social acceptance. Conventions act as social norms so that even when people appear not to be conforming to society at large their behavior may still be conformative to some social group (e.g., some punk group). Following conventions, unlike habits, is not the result of any initial deliberation but emanates from the socialization process. Conventions influence the type of house chosen, its location, its furnishings, and whatever we eat and how we eat it. What makes a convention a convention is that violations of convention are viewed by others as wrong behavior. As one woman said about using a diaper service: "I would get a lot of flack from friends for using a diaper service: 'Why do you want those dirty diapers lying around' they would ask." Thus columnist William Safire (*New York Times,* October 25, 1990) finds wearing a tie "a pain around the neck," but nonetheless finds himself compelled to wear one "when going tieless would make a fashion statement discomforting other guests, and cause them to think me a too-secure slob." Thus adherence to conventions relates to what the consumer views as expectations of various reference groups. Convention can dictate a good deal of buying at the product level and rule out a host of brand alternatives and buying locations. Consumers are seldom free from social commitments that constrain their choices. Following the conventions and social norms of society and/or the groups with whom we mix contributes to social adjustment and the acceptability that is so keenly sought,.

Sometimes a distinction is made between conventions and social norms. Conventions are viewed as instrumental to coordinated action (e.g., driving on the right-hand side of the road) and being backed by sanctions in the event of violation. On the other hand, social norms need not necessarily aid coordination or be enforced by external sanctions so much as by internalized rules whose violation causes embarrassment or guilt. But social and geographical mobility weakens the hold of society's norms in favor of specific group norms, and what may be socially appropriate for one group (buying an expensive car) may not be socially appropriate behavior for those in another group where such buying is viewed as distancing rather than sharing behavior.

*Fashion.* There are conventions in fashion, but basic motivations differ. Whereas we adhere to conventions to avoid conflict and coordinate our actions with others, we adopt certain fashions as part of image management to signal social aspirations and identifications. The role of fashion designers is to anticipate trends in tastes and accelerate the movement to that trend by showing its social appropriateness through promotion by credible fashion experts. Fashion in clothing helps us camouflage our deficiencies and savor the fantasy of being like some famous figure or part of some lifestyle. This fantasy induces people to buy flying jackets but never fly, to buy ski clothes and never ski—and it even penetrates the bedroom! Simulating a new identity may be an expression of McCracken's displaced meaning (Chapter 8) in that fantasy helps people cope with life and sustain hope "in the face of impressive grounds for pessimism." Fashion frequently allows us to possess the symbols of success when whatever the symbols represent may be beyond our attainment.

*Fads.* Faddish products, unlike fashion, are noncyclical. They are adopted with intense zeal when, as is typically the case, they generate some in-group feeling and sharing of status emanating from mastering skills associated with the product (e.g., the hula hoop).

*Status.*    A concern for status is a concern for social recognition and prestige. People keep diaries or take family pictures to suggest a certain lifestyle, certain values, and a certain status: self-image is never far from the center of one's interest. The desire for status is directly linked with the desire for power, fame, and wealth.

All these things facilitate our acting in a more confident manner with others by reducing our dependence on others. Status helps shift the power balance in our favor when we deal with others, which, in turn, increases the likelihood of getting our way. The subjective manifestation of the ego is in self-esteem (self-respect, self-regard). Although self-esteem is not entirely dependent on status, it is an important determinant of it. People wish to signal their status; possessions lessen the danger of that status going unrecognized. When being deprived of status symbols is viewed as a threat to self-esteem, there is the likelihood that consumers will overstretch their budgets to possess the symbols. A good deal of advertising is concerned with associating the product with status, social recognition, and a certain lifestyle. A key to service is the symbolization of status through customized execution involving personal recognition. To gain social recognition, consumers may buy products with more technical features than they will ever need.

What firms would like to do is create a prestige brand image "on the cheap" to draw a corresponding premium price. But brand images are not easy to manipulate. A brand's image, as a collection of properties, characteristics, and attributes associated with the brand, encapsulates a brand's connotations as shared by the public at large or by some particular target group of buyers. A favorable brand image signals a set of benefits without involving the consumer in exhaustive information processing. However, at the level of the individual consumer, brand image will always vary somewhat since the experiences that determine that image are never quite the same for any two people. Brand image is the consumer profile of beliefs about the brand as captured by consumer predictions about the performance of the brand on all choice criteria. Where those predictions embrace what the consumer seeks, the brand is perceived as a "good product." Goodness (as Artistotle points out) rests on a "conditional wanting rule"; that is, to call a product good is to say that it will do for us whatever we want from that type of product.

Typically brand image focuses on the social meaning of the brand. In any case, whether the whole brand image or the social image is of interest, firms try to manage that image (see Park, Jaworski, and MacInnis, 1986). But attempts to establish, say, a prestige brand image can be defeated by the consumer refusing to go along. Consumers recognize projected images can be deceptive and many factors contribute to brand image that are beyond the control of the seller. Consumers generally are more impressed with information they believe cannot be manipulated for purposes of deception (e.g., the materials out of which the product is made). Manipulating brand image is easier when objective contrary evidence is not available and others seem to accept the image projected, while packaging, distribution and pricing are supportive.

## INTEGRITY

We now turn to the second component of integrative criteria, the desire for products that fit ethical values. Consumers have a sense of themselves as moral agents with their buying behavior expressing their ethical values. Buying, like all social conduct, includes not only self-interest but some promotion of ideals. The particular balance that is adopted is intimately tied to an individual's self-image and emotional nature. Support for firms believed to act in a social and morally responsible manner makes consumers feel good about contributing to a better life while at the same time getting a glow of pleasure arising from living up to an idealized self-image. There is a connection between adherence to some set of community values and respect for oneself. The emotions of pride, shame, and envy are intimately related to self-image/self-esteem/self-worth. In pursuing intersubjective community social values in buying, consumers not only perceive themselves as fostering such values but are expressing an identification with others in a way that gives deeper meaning to their lives.

In summary, we can say about integrative criteria that one way of enhancing a brand's value to the consumer is by building into the offering (product, price, promotion, and distribution) whatever signals

- social acceptance,
- social esteem,
- fashion,
- status, and
- consumer values.

Integrative criteria can be key in buying socially visible products.

## Adaptive Criteria

Uncertainty is inherent in buying: consumers are not always sure what they want and cannot be experts on every product they buy. Consumers have to adapt or come to terms with their lack of knowledge or the information overload that occurs when they try to master all the information available. Yet choosing wisely to avoid error is a social norm, and violating this norm can lead to a sense of guilt and a loss of self-esteem. Although consumers inspect the product where possible, inspection is seldom all-revealing. It affords some certainties (presence of some feature) while typically just providing probable truths (e.g., on quality) or telling us nothing at all (e.g., on the effectiveness of some non-prescription drug).

In adapting to uncertainty consumers adopt a number of strategies. One is to *imitate* those "in the know." Following social convention is "social conformity"; imitating those in the know is "informational conformity." Informational conformity is common in certain product categories like stocks and bonds. A second strategy is to seek *advice*. We may believe others know better than we do what, for example, suits us; thus we implicitly accept the advice of service station attendants when we leave the selection of the motor oil to them. Consumers are typically uncertain about tradeoffs and generally will seek advice on major purchases to avoid unpleasant surprises. But the advice of salespeople frequently presents a problem. Interactions with strangers who may or may not be impartial advisers is always fraught with uncertainties revolving around the risk of losing control of the situation. Where the salesperson is much more knowledgeable, the power balance can be perceived by the prospective buyer as on the side of the seller with a consequent sense of powerlessness and fear of embarrassment, humiliation, and subjection to pressure tactics.

A third strategy is to look for *guarantees* beyond the legal ones like the Chrysler Corporation's money-back guarantee that buyers who change their mind within thirty days or one thousand miles can get their money back. Guarantees are important when information is lacking. The fourth strategy is to *sample,* which offers an opportunity for direct experience: the product is used at minimum cost by a consumer whose behavior is considered socially approved (wise). Finally, when ambiguity prevails, we tend to fall back on preconceived images about different company/brand reputations, so that a firm that is known and respected (as was IBM when it entered the PC market) has a distinct edge over firms that are not.

All the foregoing strategies substitute to some extent for *comparison shopping* and extensive homework, which are costly not only in effort but in the postponement of gratification. Yet keeping one's options open until one knows more about the options and the risks involved can on occasion be a sensible strategy.

## Economic Criteria

Every buying situation is an approach/avoidance situation. The approach is the anticipated benefits; the avoidance is the sacrifice in terms of the price to be paid and the effort to be expended in obtaining the product. We can refer to this anticipated sacrifice as manifesting itself in applying economic criteria. Consumers instinctively rank brands on the basis of the sacrifices to be made in exchange. Each sacrifice is usually measurable, so that indecision is more associated with uncertainty about benefits. Even so, consumers are constantly trying to balance benefits against corresponding sacrifice.

The maximum sacrifice or price obtainable (if the rest of the sacrifice is of no consequence) depends not just on the importance of the product but on the consumer's dependence on the brand:

1. Its centrality for the consumer's purposes.
2. Its uniqueness to the seller's firm.
3. Social perceptions of the wisdom of the purchase at that price: spending too much may be viewed as foolish by peer groups.
4. Where the brand is purchased, since location and outlet make a difference in willingness to pay a premium price: paying a high price in a low-class outlet is regarded as "getting stung" and is a blow to self-image.

A high price, given the right product, supportive promotion, and appropriate distribution, can help project a desirable social image, signaling exclusivity and status for a socially visible product. With a standard product and standard application, where performance is regarded as the same in all respects, price becomes key. However, when consumers are unable to judge quality, they tend to avoid the lowest priced brand as a risk-aversion tactic. The problem with all bargain offers is making the offer credible, for bargains often create suspicion, that is, the feeling that the price is just too good to be true. On occasions, there is (contrary to the Boston Consulting Group) no way to dominate a market by low price. Purchases relating to fashion, to mark occasions, to signal status, and so on, are seldom if ever dominated by the lowest priced brand. This suggests that perception about price can be key and this can depend on the framing of the choice situation. Thus a 3% charge by the retailer for payment by credit card is perceived differently from an offer of a 3% discount for cash.

The cost or price of the product is not the only sacrifice. There is also the effort involved. Although shopping can be a highly pleasurable activity, most day-to-day shopping lacks the novelty aspect and can be a chore. Hence the consumer may demand a brand be readily obtainable in the local store where shopping is not a hassle. For products bought infrequently or for the first time, there is also the effort involved in learning about rival offerings. Consumers will tend to seek only enough information about the product to determine a preference. At some point consumers come to believe that major mistakes are unlikely, so that refining search and learning still further is not worth the effort.

## General Comments

Brands that perform the same core use functions are substitutes for each other but brands are close segment rivals only when they cater to the same intrinsic preference and coincide in terms of technical, economic, integrative, legalistic, and adaptive appeal. If brand offerings within a segment are perceived as undifferentiated, then habit, picking, or just liking (say of the brand name) will direct choices. Since these processes favor the pioneers, market shares can still be uneven, making little sense in terms of the objective differences among brands. Whatever criteria are stressed, the target audience is being invited to believe these are the important ones. Thus if only economic and technical criteria are emphasized, the focus is on value for money. Hence it should not be surprising if customer patronage is merely rented.

### Surrogate Indicators

Even when consumers apply the same choice criteria, the process may not lead to the same preference since applying the criteria is a skill and not a straightforward process of measurement. Visualizing the outcomes of choosing one brand rather than another typically necessitates the use of surrogate indicators. We can usually accurately gauge the sacrifice but estimating potential benefits is something else. Thus consumers may seek to enhance social recognition and prestige from a car purchase but will differ somewhat in deciding which of the makes is most likely to provide this. The consumer has to estimate such benefits from viewing the product, promotional material, advice, and other information sources. Those surrogate indicators that consumers generally use to make inferences about the presence of attributes at the level sought need to be identified. Thus consumers are likely to associate plastic parts with cheapness and have all sorts of indicators to suggest low quality in foods. As several respondents said in one focus group, transparancy and homogeneity in honey suggests artificiality of manufacture, which would inhibit purchasing such brands. A firm's indicators should be in line with the symbolization consumers take to be indicative of what they seek.

What can be said is that the consumers in general are open to persuasion right to the point of sale because

1. consumers collect only enough product/brand information to state a preference;
2. where determining a preference involves deliberation, consumers are always uneasy about tradeoffs made;
3. even when satisfied with past choices, consumers recognize that things could have changed;
4. until the full potential of a product/brand is revealed to them in the most persuasive way, consumers cannot be said to definitely not want the product/brand; and
5. until people have tried all brands, they cannot be absolutely convinced about their preferences.

## Preference

The output of the buying decision is a preference in the sense that consumers can state which brand is their choice. In this sense, listing preferences results in a ranking where we would expect preferences to be transitive; that is, if I prefer $A$ to $B$ and $B$ to $C$, I would prefer $A$ to $C$. But an intransitive preference (preferring $C$ to $A$) is irrational only if it can be shown that $A$ is better in all respects and at all times and on all occasions. Intransitive preferences involve inconsistency only when it can be shown that the judgments cannot be simultaneously maintained without contradiction. The fact is, of course, that preferences are not absolute but vary over time and occasion. Also, the weighting of attributes or choice criteria can vary through time just as the "accuracy" of watches became no longer a problem with the development of the quartz watch: accuracy, being taken for granted is no longer a differentiating criteria for choosing.

## Intention

All voluntary buying is preceded by an intention to buy though not necessarily with a *planned intention* to buy. But consumers can have a brand preference without any intention to buy, and the intention to buy a particular type of product can occur before a brand preference has occurred.

An intention to buy is not an unconditional promise to buy. It is not equivalent to saying "I will" or "I promise to buy brand $B$ tomorrow." However, an expressed intention to buy $B$ does contain some resolve to buy $B$ since buying intentions and actual purchase are linked much more closely than wants and buys. Nonetheless, expressed intentions are contingent, like saying "If the buying situation envisaged is the same next week, I will buy brand $B$." We can compare forming an intention to going into gear, but the will is needed to take the final step of pressing the accelerator. Many expressed buying intentions are like New Year's resolutions: they are made in good faith and given up when difficult to implement. Modern psychology makes no distinction between "motivated" and "willed" behavior. The term "will" is eschewed because of its association with "volition," used in the sense of something in the mind putting muscles into action, which, in turn, assumes the mind is a "secondary field of special causes," to use the expression of Gilbert Ryle. But the concept of the will as a self-promise ("I will") to indicate firmness of resolve seems a useful concept for marketing as an improvement on using only "buying intention" in forecasting future sales.

## Postpurchase Behavior

It is a truism to say that consumers come to know better what they want after buying, possessing, using, and consuming the product. Experience with a product typically presents additional benefits and deficiencies. A product can be found to have worthwhile features not sought at the time of purchase but sought thereafter (e.g., wash-and-wear trousers) or a product can live up to expectations in terms of technical performance but still prove to have major flaws (e.g., a luxury soap that does not dry one's skin—the reason for purchasing—but lasts only two weeks).

A purchase in fact can perform outstandingly on all the criteria that entered into the decision to buy it—yet the customer may still be dissatisfied. This is not uncommon in buying a house, where many things that should have been considered at the time of purchase were not considered. It may even be that certain things were taken for granted; consider the dissatisfied European customer of satellite television who assumed that he would be able to see all European TV channels, reception would always be excellent, and foreign programming was going to be superior to that in his own country! By and large, though, consumers try to show their choice was clearly superior to alternatives in order to avoid the discomfort arising from the thought of not having chosen wisely. Even when consumers have been unable to buy what is commonly regarded as the best, they are likely to rationalize that they would have bought what they did regardless of whatever wealth they possessed. But with increases in wealth such rationalizations disappear as consumers are less prepared to make do with second best.

The above view of the consumer captures much that is discussed by Olshavsky & Granbois (1979). As these writers point out, for many purchases a decision process never occurs, not even on the first purchase.

> Purchases can occur out of necessity: they can be derived from culturally mandated life-styles or from interlocked purchases: they can reflect preferences acquired in early childhood: they can result from simply conformity to group norms or from imitation of others: purchases can be made exclusively on recommendations from personal or non-personal sources: they can be made on the basis of surrogates of various types: or they can even occur on a random or superficial basis (p. 89).

# References

Clarke, David D., and Jill Crossland (1985). *Action Systems: An Introduction to the Analysis of Complex Behavior.* London: Methuen.

Csikszentmihalyi, Mihaly (1990). *Flow: The Psychology of Optimal Experience.* New York: Harper and Row.

De Sousa, Ronald (1990). *The Rationality of Emotion.* Cambridge, MA: The MIT Press.

Dretske, Fred (1988). *Explaining Behavior: Reasons in a World of Causes.* Cambridge, MA: The MIT Press.

Foxall, Gordon (1990). *Consumer Psychology in Behavioral Perspective.* London: Routledge.

Levi, Isaac (1967). *Gambling with Truth.* New York: Borzoi Books.

Lewin, Kurt (1968). "Group Decision and Social Change." In *Readings in Social Psychology,* edited by Eleanor E. Maccoby, T. M. Newcomb, and E. E. Hartley. New York: Holt, Rinehart and Winston.

Nozick, Robert (1989). *The Examined Life.* New York: Simon and Schuster.

Olshavsky, Richard W., and Donald H. Granbois (1979). "Consumer Decision Making—Fact or Fiction?" *Journal of Consumer Research* 6 (September), pp. 93–100.

O'Shaughnessy, John (1987). *Why People Buy.* New York: Oxford University Press.

Park, C. W., B. J. Jaworski, and D. J. MacInnis (1986). "Strategic Brand Concept-Image Management." *Journal of Marketing* 50 (October), pp. 135–45.

Ryle, Gilbert (1949). *The Concept of Mind.* New York: Barnes and Noble; London: Hutchinson.

# 11

# Philosophical Controversies Underlying Explanatory Systems and Methodologies

> It is a great advantage for a system of philosophy to
> be substantially true.
>
> George Santayana (1863–1952)

The different explanatory modes discussed in Chapters 3 to 6 give rise to different methodologies as to what data to collect and how the data are to be collected, manipulated, and interpreted. As shown in Chapters 7 and 8, each of the various systems of psychology and sociology adopts a methodology that fits the pursuit of one of the four modes of explanation. Thus the methodology of existential phenomenology pursues a goal ascription type of explanation and adopts a methodology for interpreting behavior. But there is no exact one-to-one correspondence between methodology and the type of explanation sought. Thus if I believe reasons are causes, I can still adopt a methodology that relies on interpreting verbal protocols and need not, like the behaviorist, resort to experimentation. However, regardless of the explanatory mode and corresponding methodology adopted, there is no avoiding philosophical controversies as researchers implicitly or explicitly take a position on issues like rationalism versus empiricism or realism versus idealism. The purpose of this chapter is to discuss both the philosophical underpinnings and the controversies involved in the various explanatory modes and the presuppositions inherent in any methodology.

Given the successes achieved in the natural sciences, it was inevitable that some attempt would be made to describe the methodological and philosophical prescriptions of these sciences and argue that every discipline making a claim to be a science should adopt these prescriptions. The movements known as "positivism," "logical empiricism," and their various subbranches like "naturalism" aim to different degrees to set out such prescriptions to guide all scientific inquiry. This chapter discusses these movements and the movements that oppose them, like hermeneutics, and philosophies that largely opt out of the debate, like pragmaticism, instrumentalism, and conventionalism.

## Positivism

Positivism was the name given by Auguste Comte, the founder of sociology, to the application of the methods of the natural sciences to the study of society. Comte believed that nineteenth-century society had reached a "positive" stage, that is, an era that was ready to use "positive" (observable, physical, empirical) data about the social world to create a better society.

Positivism today is more associated with the logical positivist movement. The movement developed in the late 1920s around Moritz Schlick (1882–1936), a professor of inductive science at the University of Vienna who formed the so-called Vienna Circle, members of which came to be called "logical positivists." Among the members of the Vienna Circle later to emigrate to the United States were Rudolf Carnap, Herbert Feigl, and Kurt Gödel. The term "logical" was added to positivism to suggest the antispeculative stance and the use of logical analysis and symbolic logic in making knowledge statements clear and unambiguous. The major goal of the logical positivists was to provide criteria for distinguishing between those problems and assertions that deserve to be considered science and those that do not. A later generation, which included A. J. Ayer, Richard Braithwaite, Carl Hempel, Ernest Nagel, and May Brodbeck as well as some of the original members of the Vienna Circle, like Carnap and Feigl, developed logical positivism into "logical empiricism," which had a major impact on the social sciences following World War II. The logical empiricists are less united in doctrine than were the logical positivists but still share with the positivists the central tenet of methodological monism (discussed later).

Positivism seeks to reduce all scientific knowledge to an empirical basis with reductionism as the ultimate aim. Positivism thus has its roots in early British empiricism associated with George Berkeley (1685–1753), David Hume (1711–1776), and John Locke (1632–1704). *Empiricism* claims that all factual knowledge is based on experience, and that *sense experience* is the building block for all knowledge. Also, because claims to knowledge must be justified by experience, science must be tied to direct observation. Empiricism has traditionally been closely related to the doctrine known as "phenomenalism," which asserts that all material things amount to nothing but a series of sensations and so can be reduced to statements about sense data, the irreducible givens of all knowledge. (Phenomenalism should be distinguished from phenomenology discussed in earlier chapters.) This traditional tie of empiricism to phenomenalism is no longer tenable. Phenomenalism is fundamentally wrong in asserting that statements about material things can be reduced to statements about sense data since there is no sensation vocabulary. As Ryle says, we can observe only a conceptualized reality not because our vocabulary is deficient but because the very notion of an unconceptualized reality is absurd. Thus observations cannot be reduced to sensations (elements of an unconceptualized reality) that can be verified.

An empiricist position contrasts with *rationalism* (associated with Plato and Descartes), which claims that the world is knowable only through reason, since sense data need to be connected in the light of reason. For the rationalist the criterion of truth is intellectual, not sensory. In the most general terms, a rationalist is someone who stresses reasoning or thought as the basic factor in knowledge in contrast to the empiricist, who stresses the role of observation and sense data. Successes in experimental science have invested the empiricist with great prestige, yet the laws of logic seem to precede any data to which they might be applied and mathematical knowledge seems more certain than any amount of observation. The typical social science researcher is empirical by inclination, but many mathematical model builders find rationalism more to their taste. Cognitive psychologists lean more toward rationalism than empiricism and hence receive support from rationalist philosophers like Fodor, who regard mental events as having causal power (Gardner, 1985). On the other hand, behaviorists are clearly empiricists.

## Tenets of Positivism

We now consider some of the specific tenets of logical positivism as represented by the Vienna Circle. These tenets were not necessarily held by every member of the circle. More important, all of these tenets are not necessarily those that are implied today when a social scientist speaks about positivism or a positivist orientation. Although the term "positivism," as used today, still shows ties to its roots in the Vienna Circle by implying that the study of human behavior must proceed by using the methods believed to be employed in the natural sciences, the term also connotes a host of other images depending on how particular social scientists characterize the methods of natural science.

A logical positivist *suggests* someone disposed toward the following:

1. *Methodological monism,* which asserts that all sciences, if they are to be sciences, must follow the same scientific method regardless of subject matter. If a discipline is to be called a science, it must follow the same methods as the physical sciences. The word "monism" asserts this oneness and contrasts with *methodological pluralism,* which asserts there is more than one acceptable method. Positivists see no reason why human action should be treated differently from the way events are treated in natural science.

   Methodological monism is the tenet most associated with positivism, so that logical empiricists and others who adhere to this tenet tend to be (in spite of their protests of denial) classified as positivists. If methodological monism is a necessary condition for being a positivist, then few academics in marketing can be pure positivists in practice.

2. *Empiricism,* which claims that what we know we know only because the empirical evidence so far happens to point that way. Positivists confine reality to that revealed by sensory experience. This is the most basic tenet of positivism, from which many of the other tenets follow. On this basis, explanation is descriptive and amounts to no more than showing that the explicandum is an instance of some *descriptive* regularity. Phenomenalism (as discussed earlier) accompanied the logical positivist's empiricism to emphasize the priority given to observational sense data. *Physicalism,* too, as embraced by Carnap, goes with logical positivism. Physicalism asserts that any science should be translatable into terms that refer to observable events. In other words, mental events should be translatable into observable behavior. This stress on observation assumes there is an observation language that is independent of theory. In other words, it assumes observation can be a check on theories without such observation being "contaminated" by the theory itself. In this way conflicts among scientists (and the various systems of psychology and sociology) can be settled empirically so that the development of science can proceed in a linear and cumulative way. (We return to this claim in later chapters.)

3. "Laws of nature" that simply *describe what happens* so that if the term "cause" is adopted at all it is the Humean concept of cause. (As stated in Chapter 3, Hume dismissed as an illusion the idea of cause as compelling an effect and simply viewed it in terms of constant conjunctions of events or the set of conditions always present during the occurrence to be explained.) Like Comte, the Vienna Circle repudiated the search for causes that was associated with the prepositivist, metaphysical stage in the development of science. The acceptance of physicalism meant that science was to be built on empirically established universal regularities as exemplified by Hempel's deductive–nomological (D-N) model (see Chapter 2), since talk about "causes" was talk about the unobservable. Whereas many in marketing might have to be content with "explanations" resting purely on correlations or conjunctions of events, not many would subscribe to the Humean concept of cause and never seek to go beyond descriptive regularities, eschewing all unobservables like "attitude."

4. *Nominalism,* which recognizes only individual particulars, denying that general abstract concepts offer additional insight onto the world. Nominalists claim that only individual things are real, that universal categories like man, society, and market are mere names applied to classes of things. Nominalism, implicit in empiricism, was initially a reaction against the realism that makes realities of general concepts. The belief that one's abstract categories represent real divisions in nature is regarded as fallacious. A moderate nominalist position, however, would accept the idea of members of a category having a special relationship of similarity with each other. Methodological individualists tend to be nominalists in claiming that only individuals are "real," but collective entities like society are not. Nominalism in marketing finds expression in the rejection of any talk about group mind in favor of talk about how individuals behave in groups. The decision-making unit (DMU) would be regarded less as a decision-making entity than as an arena in which individual members exchange views, bargain, and so on, to reach some consensus or majority view to proceed in a coordinated way.

5. *Avoidance of explanations involving nonobservable (theoretical) entities,* since reality consists only of that which can be observed. If theoretical entities like the electron, attitudes, motives, and expectancies, are adopted, they are to be regarded only as useful fictions to help resolve temporary puzzles. As the puzzles get resolved, the fictions can be dropped. However, as with nominalism, there was no unanimity here among logical positivists. Whereas some claimed that only assertions about observable phenomena could be given the status of being knowledge, Carnap was prepared to accept theoretical terms as having partial meaningfulness to the extent they could be partly interpreted in observational terms—"partly interpreted in observational terms" because, if theoretical terms were fully definable in terms of observational data, then no problem would arise. But such terms would then have no "surplus meaning," being purely descriptive. Yet it is because some theoretical entity such as "self-esteem" is more than the specific local observations that the term can be generalized and potentially made rich in explanatory power and in possibilities for generating hypotheses. If to be a positivist a researcher must confine herself to just the observable and forsake all nonobservable theoretical entities like attitudes and motives, then few (if any) marketers are positivists. In psychology, only behaviorists subscribe to this tenet.

6. The *nonvalidity of teleological explanations,* that is, explanations in terms of functions, intentions, goals, purposes, and so on, *unless* they are transformed into non-teleological form. Adherence to this particular tenet would confine psychology to behaviorism. If this tenet is necessary to be a positivist, then again there are few positivists in marketing.

7. *"Reality" consisting only of what is observable,* leaving to science the job of identifying the (as yet) unknown but nonetheless observable states and events. As consistent with nominalism, all science is regarded as starting with direct observation of *single* facts. The idea of the world consisting of unambiguous facts waiting to be observed and generalized about is a central tenet of positivism.

8. *The role of theory as systematizing observations* and not guiding research if this involves embracing theoretical entities not definable in observational terms. The process of theory formation proceeds, therefore, from observation. In general, logical positivists share with instrumentalists (discussed later) the view of theories as merely instruments, not true or false but merely useful or not useful since theories (in line with nominalism) are regarded as lacking in empirical content.

If the prescriptions of the Vienna Circle positivists were adopted in the study of buyer behavior, methodology would be confined by the constraints of methodological individualism and behaviorism. Collective terms such as culture, reference group, and social norms, or mental terms/representations could not be treated as causal factors on the ground that such entities are not observable. This suggests that there are few such positivists in marketing. Hunt (1991a) argues that the antipositivists typically claim that positivists sought causal, mechanistic explanations, reified abstract concepts, and endorsed realism. As the preceding discussion makes clear and as Hunt makes clear, the positivism of the Vienna Circle embraced none of these doctrines. But such criticism ignores the modern usage of the term "positivism." In the first place, as Von Wright points out (1971, p. 4), positivism can be said to seek causal explanation "in a broad sense" of the Humean concept of cause or the idea of subsuming individual cases under hypothetically assumed laws of nature. More relevantly, because the central tenet of positivism came to be identified with methodological monism as exemplified by the exact natural sciences, the views of all philosophers subscribing to this doctrine came to be regarded as positivist. On this basis, any methodology for studying human behavior that cannot be used in the natural sciences (e.g., attitude measurement) is nonpositivist while any methodology that seems to follow the methods of natural science (e.g., behaviorist laboratory experiment) are labeled positivist. Thus a positivist frequently is defined as a social scientist who follows the methods of the natural sciences and damn everything else. This can be irritating to those who see some advantage of terms keeping their original, historical meaning. There is less confusion when words have the same reference for all, but whether Hunt's article or any other will change current practice is doubtful.

Hunt in the same article points out that there is an emerging consensus for methodological pluralism or at least critical pluralism which modifies the former by recognizing the need to subject theories to critical scrutiny. This implies that someone can be an antipositivist in rejecting methodological monism and still accept as legitimate the use of a positivist methodology in the study of behavior. This needs to be said because antipositivists are typically viewed as necessarily rejecting every methodology associated with the natural sciences. Some may do so but many do not.

## Criterion of Meaningfulness

Logical positivists argue that statements are either "meaningful" or "nonsensical" (nonsensical). A meaningful statement is either synthetic *or* analytic. A *synthetic* statement is always an empirical statement, which means there are observable facts that are relevant to its truth. On the other hand, an *analytic* statement is true as a matter of definition or because it just follows from the meaning of the words used in the statement; for example, if buying is voluntary, consumers must think they want $x$ to buy it. Analytic statements explain why we cannot imagine certain statements not being true. The truth or falsity of an analytic statement is decidable with the help of logic alone. Whereas a proposition $P$ is synthetic *if and only if* its negation (not-$P$) entails no inconsistencies, this is not so of analytic statements. Many of the so-called findings of PIMS are analytic though paraded as synthetic.

If all meaningful statements are either synthetic or analytic, this means references to entities not accessible to observation are meaningless. Value judgments, ethical declarations, or religious pronouncements are regarded as simply emotive or nonsensical, matters of assertion or preference. In particular, the logical positivists sought to dismiss all metaphysics as nonsense. [The word *metaphysics* was originally the collective noun for the fourteen books of Aristotle that had been placed after (meta) Aristotle's treatises on physics, the latter being the study of nature in general.] Metaphysics deals with the most general questions about the universe. A major interest, for example, lies in *ontology*, which is concerned with what kinds of things exist—material objects, persons, minds, numbers—or the existential standing of some entity. Any particular theory about what exists can be called an ontology. The major ontological question in psychology is whether there are bona fide mental entities. But how we view the ontological status of something will in turn depend on our *epistemology* (theory of knowledge), that is, what modes of knowing (knowledge justification) we accept. (Epistemology is the study not so much of what we know but rather what it is to know something.) Thus, as Robinson (1985) says, to ask whether mental entities exist is to ask for a certain type of evidence, which in turn presupposes the validity of a certain mode of inquiry.

Metaphysics was anathema to the positivist because it gives the illusion of knowledge without actually giving any "real" knowledge. For positivists, the success of Newtonian physics demonstrated what could be achieved by the rejection of all metaphysical systems in favor of controlled and disciplined observation combined with the precision of symbolic logic.

But categorizing nonanalytic, nonsynthetic statements as meaningless cast doubt on the status of those laws in science that involve hypothetical entities like the electron since such laws were neither purely definitional nor strictly empirical. Yet the claim that there is a sharp distinction between truths of fact, justified by observation, and conceptual truths, justified by logic alone, goes back at least to Leibniz (1646–1716) and Hume. Quine (1953) attacked the distinction on the ground that we cannot define analytical propositions unambiguously: there are no universally valid criteria of "sameness of meaning," so the concept of analyticity itself cannot be satisfactorily defined. We cannot classify "man is a rational animal" as an analytic proposition when we cannot give an independent definition of what constitutes a synonym. To Quine there are no so-called analytic statements that in principle could not be rejected in the light of future knowledge.

Analytic propositions in fact are never immune from revision on empirical grounds, so that none are beyond dispute. Thus the logical and mathematical components of a scientific theory, that is, the so-called analytic components, cannot in practice be sufficiently disentangled from the empirical components for the two to be regarded as subject to different criteria of truth. Quine in fact argued that the analytic truths of logic and mathematics are just part of the overall system of science and differ from the rest of science only in our reluctance to abandon them when some contrary experience dictates a revision of our system of beliefs. All philosophies of science embody certain metaphysical assumptions that can be said to be neither analytic nor synthetic. Consider the proposition (any sentence involving a judgment) "Every event has a cause." Its negation is not self-contradictory, so it is not analytic. Yet advocates accept no single piece of evidence as refuting the proposition.

However, Ayer (1982) still regards the distinction between analytic and synthetic propositions as useful since many statements propounded as hypotheses for testing are simply definitionally true. However, there can be problems. Take, for example, the statement "A source of high credibility enhances message impact." Although this does not mean that a noncredible source will always eclipse the message, it does state that a credible source adds something by way of persuasive impact. It could be argued that this is true by definition since persuasive impact is part of the concept of being a credible source. In other words, if the message's impact were not enhanced, other things remaining equal, it would imply that the source was not in fact highly credible. However, it might be claimed that the hypotheses being tested are concerned with establishing the *operational meaning* of high credibility. Possible hypotheses are:

1. If societal rules suggest a certain source is highly credible on an issue (e.g., a famous cancer researcher talking about smoking and lung cancer), the audience will be more inclined to believe that source than someone who, on the basis of societal rules, is considered less credible even though saying the same things.

2. A person who displays highly relevant technical expertise will be perceived as a highly credible source and hence exert more influence with the audience.

Analyticity implies a priori. An *a priori* proposition is one whose truth is not contingent on experience. A priori propositions contrast with *a posteriori* propositions, whose truth is contingent on experience. A posteriori implies syntheticity. Rationalists claim there is a priori knowledge of general principles. Empiricists deny this possibility unless such knowledge consists of analytic statements. But the Austrian school of economics insists there are fundamental axioms of human action that are a priori. Others claim there can be synthetic a priori statements arguing, for example, that causality is a matter of synthetic, a priori judgment. In other words, the claim is made that a proposition can be known to be true a priori, although its content can be known only through experience. This in turn implies that there are statements which describe states of affairs that can be known with certainty.

The synthetic a priori concept emerged from Kant's (1724–1804) attempt to synthesize or reconcile rationalism and empiricism. Rationalists accept the existence of a priori synthetic propositions. In denying that there could be synthetic a priori knowledge of the world, positivists sought to undermine rationalism, in which the criterion of truth is not sensory but intellectual and deductive.

## Verifiability Principle

To the Vienna Circle the "meaning" of any statement in the sense of significance or meaningfulness was its method of verification, the so-called principle of verifiability. To the logical positivist there was no difficulty in distinguishing analytic statements since they follow from definitions. The question was how to test synthetic propositions. This was to be the role of the verifiability principle. Any assertion that did not conform to the verifiability principle was either analytic (hence needing no confirmation) or "nonsensical" (just emotive). The verifiability principle has not, however, withstood criticism. In the first place, the principle itself is neither an analytic proposition nor an empirical one, although the logical positivists did not regard it as nonsensical. Schlick regarded the principle as a truism. Carnap regarded the principle simply as a rule demanding that theoretical concepts be expressible in observational language. But the question remained as to whether "to verify" meant "to prove" absolutely or just to test. Because of the problem of verifying in an absolute sense, Carnap (1945) abandoned the word verifiable in favor of *confirmable* or *testable* on the ground that insistence on absolute verifiability rules out as nonsensical all universal laws, that is, all propositions of unrestricted generality. In recognizing that universal scientific laws cannot be absolutely verified, Carnap sought to develop a system for measuring the degree of confirmability of a hypothesis. He focused on ways to assess the probability of a hypothesis relative to the evidence or empirical support. But measuring the degree of confirmability provided by supportive evidence has proved much too elusive.

A. J. Ayer (1936) suggested a weaker version of the verifiability principle. Ayer claimed that a sentence is factually significant to someone if and only if that person knows what observations would lead him or her, under certain conditions, to accept it as being true or reject it as being false. Ayer's principle supplies a criterion for determining only whether a sentence is meaningful; it does not take the further step (like Schlick's Vienna Circle version of the principle) of giving a procedure for determining what meaning a statement has. Ayer (1973) claims the distinction has substance in that his weaker principle avoids condemning as nonsense those scientific laws not reducible to descriptive experience.

A belief in the verifiability principle tended to go hand in hand with a *correspondence theory of truth*, which asserts that something is true if it can be correlated with the facts. However, not every logical positivist agreed with the correspondence theory. Neurath favored a *coherence theory of truth*, which asserts that something is true if it coheres with other systems of knowledge. We take for granted, if systems of knowledge cohere, that this is something more than saying the systems are "consistent," since any two statements are consistent providing they do not contradict each other. Coherence implies the systems are connected by some common principle or that they logically entail each other. The coherence theory may have some applicability to buyer behavior. When evaluating a product in advance of any experience of possessing, using, or consuming a product, the consumer is in effect obliged to judge on the basis of a coherence theory of truth, that is, coherence with the consumer's current beliefs assumed to be true. But a coherence theory of truth may apply more broadly in that consumers in their decision-making seek coherence with existing beliefs more than they seek disconfirmation of their beliefs by seeking out and reflecting on new evidence.

Neither the coherence theory nor the correspondence theory has proved generally acceptable to philosophers. Coherence of hypotheses or systems of knowledge with systems already accepted does not make any of them true. Similarly, the correspondence theory of truth has limitations. Under the correspondence theory, something is true by virtue of its correspondence with the world. The problem arises in asserting we can check a hypothesis against neutral "facts" reflecting some unconceptualized reality. What are considered the facts depends on the theories we hold. The reality "out there" is not transparent and there is no way we can be absolutely sure we have grasped the independent structures of the world as they really are. On this basis, there is no way of establishing the *extent* of the fit between science theory and the world. This means, it is claimed, that only a softened version of the correspondence theory is defensible.

But in spite of the fallibility of correspondence and coherence as truth criteria, their use is inevitable in the absence of infallible guides to establishing truth. In marketing there are no universal laws from which predictions can be deduced to provide guidance in the selection of strategies and tactics. We do have, however, a store of knowledge built up from company experience, research findings, and social science theory. We want our strategies and tactics to cohere with such knowledge as it represents our best guide. Along the same lines, whenever we argue, in support of interpretations of findings, that the interpretations are consistent with or cohere with behaviorism, statistical theory, or whatever, we are assuming a coherence theory of truth. On the other hand, the knowledge bank itself to which our actions or interpretations are said to cohere may have been accepted on the basis of the correspondence theory of truth in claiming that the "facts" (established by surveys, experiment, etc.) support the assertions. In this way both the correspondence and coherence theories are drawn upon in practice.

## Logical Empiricism

Carnap preferred the term *logical empiricism* to logical positivism because, unlike early positivists, he saw the focus of the Vienna Circle to be on logical analysis as a tool for clarifying concepts. Logical empiricism today is typically regarded as a more sophisticated version of logical positivism. For example, between 1935 and 1955 logical empiricists sought a better criterion of cognitive significance or meaningfulness than that provided by the verifiability principle. Carnap suggested confirmability or testability. Scientific hypotheses were to be distinguished by being testable, which meant collecting evidence to confirm or disconfirm the hypotheses. Hypotheses, it was suggested, might be ranked on the basis of the degree to which there is confirming evidence. However, as pointed out, measuring the degree of confirmability has proved an elusive pursuit. There are even logical problems in deciding what evidence counts as supportive. In any case, it is not just a matter of establishing the probability of hypothesis *A* but the probability of *A* in relation to the probability of alternative explanations. The early view of the logical positivists was that theories only describe; the logical empiricists, however, typically assert that the goal of science is explanation through the unification of the maximum number of facts and regularities in terms of the minimum number of theoretical concepts and assumptions.

## Falsificationism

Popper (1959), who does not consider himself a positivist, suggested *falsifiability* be substituted for verifiability. However, Popper's *falsifiability principle* was to be the method for demarcating scientific from nonscientific statements, not (as in the case of the verifiability principle) to act as a criterion of meaningfulness or significance. What observations would falsify, say, Freud's concept of the unconscious? As we saw in Chapter 7, Popper's falsifiability principle has commonly been used to attack psychoanalytic psychology and any other unpopular theories.

The aim of the falsifiability principle is to distinguish statements that can be tested from those that cannot be tested (like "Many forms of buyer behavior are caused by the unconscious projection of infantile desires"). In other words, to apply the falsifiability principle we must be in a position to describe the state of affairs if a statement is true and the state of affairs if the statement (hypothesis) is false. Popper argued that universal lawlike statements cannot be proved (verified) absolutely but can only be absolutely falsified by asking what predictions would follow if the hypothesis were true and demonstrating the falsity of such prediction. The original statement of Popper's falsification principle has come to be known as "dogmatic falsificationism." There are later versions culminating in "sophisticated falsificationism," wherein Popper accepts that refuting facts can be problematic and theory-dependent. This topic is discussed further in Chapter 13.

Falsificationism has not proved easy to implement. In recent years attention has shifted from the search for criteria to distinguish scientific propositions to the problem of evaluating competing theories or research traditions. Yet the concept of falsification is important since it directs attention to the search for counter or refuting instances. This is important in marketing, given the tendency to seek confirming rather than counter instances of some proposition (e.g., of successful firms practicing the marketing concept).

Popper does not regard himself as a positivist even though he believes in methodological monism or the unity of the scientific method. Popper claims that theoretical orientation always gives direction to observation in scientific activity and, contrary to positivism, scientific knowledge does not start from the particulars of experience. On the contrary, he argues that scientists use what he calls the *method of conjecture and refutation* in that scientists start with a hypothesis and try to falsify it. This is what in Chapter 12 we refer to as the "hypotheticodeductive method," which is commonly associated with empiricism in that it goes along with the testability principle and falsificationism.

## Naturalism

Although Ernest Nagel, a philosopher of science, held many positivist viewpoints such as methodological monism, he does not subscribe to one of the most central tenets of positivism, namely that science must be built on direct sensory experience and not go beyond what is observable. Nagel (1961) argues that if this were accepted, it would severely restrict scientific progress since not every theoretical term in a theory can be defined operationally, that is, captured or measured in some observational language. He argues that theoretical terms or entities not directly linked to something observable should still be accorded "cognitive significance" if there is successful confirmation of the theory in which they are embedded.

Nagel is classed as a logical empiricist though his own particular philosophy of science was *naturalism,* which asserts that whatever occurs, including mental events, is contingent upon the occurrence of physical-chemical-physiological events and structures. The doctrine, which is closely associated with philosophers Nagel, Randall, and Buchler at Columbia University (see Krikorian, 1944), goes back to David Hume. As an approach to the social sciences, it asserts that people can be studied in exactly the same way as the rest of the physical world: human behavior can be explained *in terms of causes* without resort to supernatural explanation. In philosophy, Hempel and Nagel were the major advocates of naturalism; in sociology, it was Emile Durkheim. (Naturalism should not be confused with the term "naturalistic observation," which is the "observation and description of events as they occur in nature or naturally"; see Agnew and Pyke, 1969. The term naturalism also should be distinguished from "naturalistic inquiry" as a type of ethnographic research—see the study by Belk, Sherry and Wallendorf, 1988.)

Nagel's (1961) defense of the natural sciences as a model for the social sciences is the classic one. Nagel would not have thought it profitable to discuss whether marketing is a science. He argued that it was more important to achieve clarity on issues of methodology than to award or withhold honorific titles. Nagel demonstrated that it was *not logically* impossible for the social sciences to adhere to the methods of the physical sciences. But, as Bernstein (1976) shows, Nagel, in the process, indicated the immense practical obstacles to doing so. Interestingly, while recommending that the social sciences focus on *overt* behavior, Nagel accepts the need to understand people's subjective states if we are to understand their actions, even claiming that the logical canons used to address the evidence for imputing such subjective states are not essentially different from those used in science generally. On the question of *value judgments* entering into all social science research, Nagel distinguishes appraising judgments from characterizing judgments. In *appraising* value judgments, one simply expresses approval or disapproval on the basis of a commitment to some ideal. On the other hand, in *characterizing* value judgments, one can at least discuss them objectively since they involve methods for estimating the degree to which some quality is embodied in the example under discussion.

Carnap, too, was to move away from the view that only propositions about observable phenomena be granted the status of knowledge. Just as the concept of, say, attitude as "a predisposition to react in a certain way to some item, person or thing" is never fully captured by measures of attitude, Carnap came to recognize that theoretical terms can be captured only partially in observation language. Both Nagel and Hempel criticized the movement known as *operationalism* for its demand that all theoretical terms be fully operationalized. Operationalism (Rapoport, 1953) treats concepts as logical positivists treat statements: it demands that all concepts be defined in terms of the synthetic operations employed in applying the concepts.

Suppe (1977) in the "Afterword—1977" argues that logical positivism itself has gone into near total collapse because of its failure to

1. demonstrate the validity of the analytic–synthetic distinction;
2. discover a procedure for verifying hypotheses;
3. deal with the process of discovery; and, finally,
4. stem the retreat of philosophers from the notion of a neutral observation language.

What has come to be recognized is the tenuous connection between high-level theoretical terms and their corresponding counterparts in observation, that is, their operational definition. The notion too of a theory-neutral observational language has had to go. We see what we are trained to see and interpretations of sensory perception are "contaminated" by theory: a nonspecialist looking through a microscope lens does not perceive what the biologist perceives. This means that the dichotomy between "fact" and "theory" (basic to the correspondence theory of truth) is no longer tenable. If observation is theory impregnated and therefore not entirely neutral, how should observational evidence count in the verification/confirmation of hypotheses and how can it be said that scientists are simply detached, unbiased observers of an independent external reality? The undermining of the privileged position of observation as neutral and unbiased has been most damaging to the logical positivist position. We return to this theme in Chapters 12 and 13.

## Scientific Realism

Miller (1987), a realist, describes the various kinds of positivism as the worship of generality in the philosophy of science. He argues that positivism is still the most frequently espoused philosophical position and is still concerned to resolve methodological questions through a priori rules that are claimed to be valid for all time and in all fields. In contrast, Suppe (1977) claims positivism—with all of its assumptions now undermined—truly belongs to history. This seeming conflict of viewpoint reflects the confusion over how the term positivism is used today.

Realism is often associated with positivism because certain positivists deviated from Vienna Circle positivism to embrace realism and certain realists were (wrongly) called positivists. But *scientific realism* does not subscribe to many of the tenets of positivism, in particular, to the logical positivists' view of theoretical entities and theories. However, there is some overlap between the two in that both logical positivism and realism are empiricist, and realists commonly support methodological monism, providing it is liberally interpreted.

There are several forms of realism, all involving claims about the actual existence of certain entities. "Naive" realism or "commonsense" realism concedes to observation direct acquaintance with the physical world, that is, that we perceive reality not through sense impressions but directly (Ayer, 1973). But *scientific* realism is something different. Hacking (1983) argues that there are two kinds of scientific realism:

1. Realism about theories: Realism asserts that theories are either true or false since truth is how the world is.
2. Realism about unobservable theoretical entities: Realism accepts the existence of many theoretical entities even if they are unobservable. (This is the usual interpretation of realism and is a position that would not be supported by positivists.)

There are those who are realists about theories but not about entities and vice versa. Thus Bertrand Russell was antirealist when it came to theoretical entities but was a realist about theories. Also, some people may be realists about *some* theories and *some* theoretical entities and antirealist about others. (Most of us probably fall into this category.) In general, controversies about realism have centered on realism about theoretical entities. Hacking's own realism is a robust belief in the independent existence of certain theoretical entities ("If you can spray them, then they are real") but does not believe in the objective truth of models or theories. His position might or might not be what Putnam (1981), an instrumentalist, refers to as "metaphysical realism." He contrasts this with *relativism* (discussed later) but argues both positions are "incoherent in the end." Putnam defines metaphysical realism as the view that the world consists of some fixed totality of mind-independent objects and that there is exactly one true and complete description of that world. He criticizes such realism on the ground it assumes a "God's Eye point of view" of the relation between words and the world. Putnam, on the other hand, rejects relativism, which he defines as claiming there are no standards of truth or rationality that transcend *particular cultural or linguistic communities.* He rejects relativism on the ground that it undermines the distinction between a belief's being right and merely seeming to be right.

To the scientific realist, the scientist's job is to find the mechanisms, structures, or powers that cause the effects of interest. Realists do not in general reject the existence of theoretical entities like the "ego" or the "electron" just because they are unobservable. Such a view rejects the logical positivist assertion that the meaning of any statement resides in the way the statement is verified. Realists generally argue that a statement is true or false independently of whether we can verify or falsify it. Whereas the positivist focus is on the observable events themselves, the focus in scientific realism is on the causal powers of entities and their interrelationship in bringing about effects. The realist does not take a simple view of single causes being linked to single effects but argues that any particular effect results from complex interrelations among mechanisms, structures, and background conditions. Thus realists (e.g., Bhaskar, 1979) are not concerned with individual cause-and-effect relationships but look for distinct structures that causally mesh.

The real causes of events are often complex, unobservable structures and processes; the job of science is to identify and define such causes. Realist explanations always refer to structures and processes. These causal structures and processes may be out of phase with the events they cause, with the result that the relationships are often hidden. This occurs because the world is an "open system," that is, a system open to intervening and countervailing causes, giving an instability to cause-and-effect relationships. This is particularly so given the fact that structures/processes combine in different ways to produce what is happening. Thus to the realist, prediction is always somewhat problematic: we can never be sure which set of generative mechanisms will be at work. This means that even scientific laws typically describe a tendency (probability law), not a universal law as in the D-N model.

If prediction is always somewhat problematic, then the acid test of a theory is not necessarily its predictive power. Hence realists regard science as primarily interested in what kind of causal mechanisms there are and what they tend to do, with predictive success being expected and sought only in the "closed system" of the experimental laboratory. If the positivist sees explanation as a deductive argument, exemplified by the D-N model where cause (if admitted at all) is simply constant conjunction, the scientific realist seeks explanation in terms of causal necessity.

Given that scientific realists deny that what exists must be restricted to what is observable, they reject positivism's *methodology,* which precedes from the particulars of experience, on the ground that such a method would never approve the postulation of unobservable theoretical entities.

Any view that asserts the actual existence of some particular kind of thing can be called realist. To the argument that objects do not exist in the world independently of how we conceptualize them, Hacking (1983), as a realist, asserts that the fact that we do partition the world into what are possibly incommensurate categories does not itself prove that all such categories are mind-dependent. For the realist, whenever the consumer sees, feels, smells, and touches a product, these experiences are not created by the mind but are abstractions from an independent reality.

Realists typically assume the reality of general terms so that, for example, *social realism* denotes a belief in the reality of social entities like "society" over and above the individuals who compose it. This view of reality is important when general terms like society, social norms, and attitude are used to signify real mechanisms or structural causal agents. The reality of general terms contrasts with the nominalist position of logical positivism. The nominalist argues that whatever is "out there" does not come to us already categorized. How we categorize the world into sheep, dogs, fields, mountains, whatever, results from our language and way of thinking. A more sophisticated nominalism acknowledges that any conceptual scheme would take into account that there are, say, trees and animals in the world but argues that categories do change and there are no uniquely fixed or right set of categories for each aspect of nature.

Bhaskar regards social relationships as the structures and processes causing social life. These social structures—the product of individual decisions and action (in line with methodological individualism)—influence people collectively and individually (in line with methodological holism). The realist does not emphasize methodological individualism over methodological holism or vice versa. Bhaskar accepts intentional behavior (action) as caused by reasons but argues that these reasons have their origin in social happenings (e.g., social norms and relationships), psychology (e.g., personality), and physiology (e.g., hunger). The search for structures and processes typically requires *retroduction* (also called retrodiction), that is, working back from manifest effects to hidden causal structures and processes. The manifest effects would take account of the individual's or the group's own account of its purposes, intentions, wants, and beliefs and proceed from there. This realist view has great appeal for many social scientists.

For realists like Miller (1987), the view of the atom as no more than an abstract construct of the imagination considered useful for making sense of reality is not a reasonable option. Yet quantum physics is held by many to be antirealist. If the atom really exists as a distinct entity, it would have location and a definite motion. But the Heisenberg uncertainty principle says you can have one or the other but not both: you cannot at one time know where an atom or an electron is and how it is moving. As Davies (1983), a physicist, says, the atom is a ghost which only materializes when you look at it. The experimental evidence in physics suggests some reality can be triggered into being by observation and some events can happen without causes.

Most so-called antirealist philosophers are not so much disbelievers as doubters (agnostic) but nonetheless claim that disbelief (and not just doubt) is a reasonable option when the entity or theory is not observable. Ernest Nagel was such an agnostic, although he was the most passionate advocate of the need for theoretical entities if science was to progress.

## Idealism

Realism contrasts with *idealism,* which asserts that reality is in some way mental. Idealism is the doctrine that the only things that exist are ideas or mental entities—the contents of the mind are all that there is in experience. In a more commonsense way, idealism can be viewed as asserting that whatever reality there is "out there" is unknowable: all we have consists of ideas about what the world is like. Those in sociology who equate the nature of any object with its meaning for the individual and talk about a socially constructed reality are assuming an idealist position for their purposes.

We have said realism contrasts with idealism, but there are degrees of idealism. A full-blooded idealism asserts that what we call reality is simply what is in the mind. *Critical idealism* acknowledges that there is a reality "out there" but argues that we know how this reality is, not in itself but only as a result of what is revealed through the senses. This was the position of Kant, who accepted the existence of an independent reality but argued that how that reality appeared to us was determined by the structure of the human mind: objective empirical knowledge was possible but only of appearances, so that all attempts to know the world "as it is in itself" are doomed to failure.

The term "idealism" has a specialized use in psychology. *Psychological idealism* is the doctrine that ideas or judgments are causes of thought and behavior and not mere effects. In contrast, *epiphenomenalism* claims that mental phenomena are entirely caused by physical phenomena in the brain or central nervous system and they themselves have no effects, mental or physical—just idle chatter in the mind. Few today believe that bodily phenomena cannot be caused by mental phenomena, which are relevant to action. Moreover, many believe that bodily illness can cause mental illness, and mental illness can cause bodily illness.

We may recall that Geertz claims (see Chapter 8) that social reality is interpreted, understood, and created through the symbolic systems (e.g., language) used to convey meaning in social situations. An antirealist position that fits this view is that of the philosopher Nelson Goodman (1987). Goodman argues that it is pointless to try to find out what the facts "really are" independent of how we conceptualize them. Goodman's *constructivism* holds that the mind adds to incoming stimuli in the course of producing a precept. This, of course, is what cognitive psychologists also claim. However, his constructivism also claims that, contrary to common sense and what most cognitive psychologists believe, there is no unique "real world" that preexists and is completely independent of mind. For Goodman, there is no pure given, no innocent eye—no perception without conception. Even the astronomer's observations are dependent on the concepts he or she uses: "sun," "star," "orbit," and so on. Goodman suggests we are never in contact with some sort of aboriginal reality independent of our own minds and the minds of others around us and from the past. The activity of "world-making" is a process of construction through language and other symbolic systems.

If there is no true, unique reality "out there," independent of the conceptual lens through which we interpret the world, then the correspondence theory of truth loses some of its appeal. Goodman, though, also rejects as an alternative the coherence theory on the ground that it degenerates into *relativism* (discussed later). A version of the world can hold together but still not hold true. Right or true versions are true in some world: there are many right or true versions, each true for some world. Thus the physicist's view is true for his world even if it makes little sense for the layman. Goodman is essentially a *conventionalist* (discussed later) advocating a revised correspondence theory of truth in that every right version has a world corresponding to it.

Goodman argues that one of the attractive features of nonrealism of the sort he advocates is that it allows the possibility of alternative right versions of the world without advocating relativism. Under the Goodman thesis we will have good reasons for justifying our particular version of reality. However, under the Goodman view ontology seems pointless since worlds in a sense are neither real nor ideal.

## Realism Versus Idealism, Pragmatism, Instrumentalism, and Conventionalism

Scientific realism accepts that many unobservable entities, states, and processes exist when a theory is correct. Unless such entities, states, or processes do exist, there would seem little point in using them in explanations. Antirealists, on the other hand, deny there are such things as "protons," "electrons," "fields of force," or "attitudes," regarding them as simply useful fictions or tools for thinking or prediction. There are several movements, idealist by inclination, that take such a view. These are pragmatism, instrumentalism, and conventionalism, all of which manifest themselves in management and marketing science.

### Pragmatism

Pragmatism is a response to the failure to certify what constitutes true knowledge. Pragmatism regards the practical success of a theory as the criterion for judging its truth. Pragmatism is the philosophy developed by Charles Sanders Peirce (1839–1914) and William James (1842–1910). Peirce sought a more intellectually satisfying substitute for the correspondence theory of truth. What he did was to substitute method as the signifier of truth. Pragmatism views the meaningfulness or justification of a statement, belief, or idea with the practical consequences ("cash value") emanating from holding such a statement, belief, or idea as true. But what practical consequences are of interest? For Peirce it meant consequences that were subject to experimental investigation; for James practical consequences were those related to influencing human beings.

The "cash value" of any statement is measured by the difference it would make to a decision if it were true or false. In science, the focus of pragmatism is purely on the utility of concepts, laws, theories, and the like. For the pragmatist, knowledge consists of assertions that have practical value in solving practical problems. This implies that a description of the problem must accompany any claims to knowledge. It follows there is no absolute truth since knowledge itself depends on its value in problem solving. A view *of*

*man* as a pragmatist is implicit in interactionist sociology. A prominent modern pragmatist philosopher is Rorty (1987), who regards both language and scientific knowledge
as *tools for coping with the world.* On this basis, evaluative criteria are always relative to
purpose and interests. As he says:

> The culture of positivism thus produced endless swings of the pendulum between the
> view that "values are merely 'relative' (or 'emotive,' or 'subjective')" and the view that
> bringing the "scientific method" to bear on questions of political and moral choice was
> the solution to all our problems. Pragmatism, by contrast, does not erect Science as an
> idol to fill the place once held by God. It views science as one genre of literature—or, put
> the other way around, literature and the arts as inquiries, on the same footing as scientific
> inquiries. Thus it sees ethics as neither more "relative" or "subjective" than scientific
> theory, nor as needing to be made "scientific." Physics is a way of trying to cope with
> various bits of the universe; ethics is a matter of trying to cope with other bits. Mathe-
> matics helps physics do its job; literature and the arts help ethics do its. Some of these
> inquiries come up with propositions, some with narratives, some with paintings. The
> question of what propositions to assert, which pictures to look at, what narratives to lis-
> ten to and comment on and retell, are all questions about what will help us get what we
> want (or about what we *should* want). (p. 61)

## Instrumentalism

John Dewey (1859–1952) referred to his own version of pragmatism as instrumentalism.
Instrumentalists like Putnam claim that theories, concepts, and so on, are simply tools or
instruments for organizing descriptions of phenomena and for drawing predictive inferences. This is in line with the logical positivism of the Vienna Circle. Whereas realists
generally regard theoretical entities as real so that the theories or hypotheses that incorporate them can be tested as true or false, instrumentalists regard theories and theoretical
terms as simply heuristic (rules of thumb) instruments that are effective or ineffective.
Like pragmatism, instrumentalism justifies science in terms of its ability to predict and
control.

   If scientific theories are merely instruments for prediction and control, this leaves no
independent explanatory function for theories. Whether or not they capture hidden
aspects of reality is subservient to their predictive ability; theories in fact are not true or
false but merely useful or not so useful. Economist Milton Friedman (1953) represents
this view. As an instrumentalist he downplays explanation to focus on choosing the best
predictive instrument. Friedman's instrumentalism leads him to support simple, rational
principles to explain buying and selling on the grounds of their simplicity and common
sense. Instrumentalists like Friedman are, of course, right in claiming that theories do not
have to be true to be successful in prediction. Yet good instruments do not generally come
about by chance and true theories obviously help, although demonstrating the truth of
theories is a problem.

## Conventionalism

Like pragmatism, conventionalism has its origins in the failure to solve the problem of
*proving* scientific propositions. Conventionalism regards the truth of any statement as
determined not by empirical fact but by social agreement or usage. For a conventionalist,
scientific laws and theories are not true or false descriptions of some external reality but
are *mental constructions* of the scientist. What theories are constructed or what theories

are accepted or rejected will simply depend on the scientist's practical interest in light of current convention. The objectivity assumed by the positivist is rejected by the conventionalist. For the conventionalist, once a law or method is found useful for analysis or prediction, its acceptance becomes a matter of convention. It is no longer subject to scrutiny or criticism, though on occasions the scientist may have to make choices among conventions.

Kuhn and Feyerabend are among the prominent critics of the claim that traditional philosophy of science captures the actual methodology of the natural sciences (see Chapter 13); both have a conventionalist orientation. Paul Samuelson (1965) is the most prominent conventionalist in the field of economics (see Boland, 1982).

Although theoretical research in marketing is commonly regarded as positivist or logical empiricist in orientation (Deshpande, 1983), this is misleading if the terms refer to Vienna Circle philosophy and the philosophy of Carnap. What is probably meant is that theoretical research in marketing favors empirical research and the empirical testing of hypotheses. If there is positivism in marketing, it has been far from pure but has been interwoven with strands of realism, pragmatism, instrumentalism, and conventionalism. This is not surprising since some philosophers, too, like C. I. Lewis (1946), mixed their logical empiricism in with pragmatism. Thus Hunt, one marketing academic who has been willing to declare his colors, calls his own position "modern empiricism," describing it as a blend of scientific realism, logical empiricism, falsificationism, and pragmatism. If logical positivism prevailed, there would be no references to the social level of reality as such a level is not observable. It would be illicit to talk like McCracken (see Chapter 8) does about cultural influences in buying or about personality influences. It would also be illicit to assign terms like attitudes and intentions as causal factors in buying. But few (if any) marketing academics eschew all references to mental constructs and do talk of attitudes, needs, wants, intentions, and the like, as causally related to buying. Also, particularly if they are cognitive psychologists, they are disposed to believe that some of the mental entities they discuss are real even if prudence requires them to speak of such entities "as if" they exist. Without the assumption of mental entities, social scientists proscribe many rich hypotheses regarding how behavior comes about even though the problem remains of showing how such entities are causally linked to behavior when they cannot be directly observed. The difficulty (as behaviorists like Skinner constantly emphasized) lies in establishing that the unobservable mental states are conceptually distinct from the behavior itself.

In the natural sciences there are also realists, pragmatists, instrumentalists, and conventionalists. Many physicists deny that physics is about truth but claim it is simply about building models that can relate observations in a systematic way. Quantum theory led many even to deny there is an objective reality "out there" and to argue that theories are not right or wrong but useful or not useful for connecting a wide range of phenomena. In any case, as Davies points out, many physicists are no longer hard *materialists* (those who deny the existence of mind altogether) but are moving toward a more accommodating view of the mind.

## Alternatives to the Methodological Monism Thesis of Positivism

The most general objection to both logical positivism and logical empiricism is that they endorse methodological monism. The most violent objection to methodological monism comes from those behavioral researchers who claim that the methods of the natural sciences are ill-suited to the goal of understanding human actions. Others (e.g., Elster, 1989) argue that behavioral scientists have even been wrong to seek as analogies the models from physics and biology, which have tended to be more misleading than helpful (e.g., society or an organization as an organism). But many who object to methodological monism recognize there are many areas of behavior that can be studied by the methods used in the natural sciences. What is denied is that these methods constitute the only scientific way to proceed. What pervades much of this criticism is a general dissatisfaction with the methods associated with the name positivism. Thus it is claimed that the focus on verification has given rise to methodological rather than conceptual innovation, driving social science toward false precision, and trivial, misleading correlation studies (Alexander, 1987). To the extent that positivistic philosophies assume that what explains and what confirms must be the same for every field, they are seen as wrong.

In this chapter we limit the term antipositivism to those who not only reject methodological monism but who also believe that the study of human action demands different methods from those used in the natural sciences. Antipositivism in this sense has a long and intellectually respectable lineage, with philosophers as eminent as Immanuel Kant in the vanguard. In general it is claimed that the major job of the social sciences is not to study behavior per se but to study human *actions,* which have meanings for those who perform them. These meanings cannot be grasped by the methods used in the natural sciences: we can never adequately explain why a consumer responds to some offering unless we understand the meaning of the offering within the social context. Whereas natural scientists are not concerned with the attitudes, motives, and intentions of atoms, antipositivists believe such concepts as meaning, motivation, and intention are at the core of understanding people. Human behavior, it is claimed, must be understood in terms of its intentionality and such understanding cannot be treated as a stopgap explanation waiting to be replaced by more fundamental physicalist accounts. This means that action is to be explained by interpreting it—giving it meaning and significance. In practice, this signals that social science must build on language more, rather than merely focus on observable behavior (Rosenberg, 1988).

Wilhelm Dilthey (1833–1911) attacked the idea that there was just one scientific method. He made a sharp distinction between causal explanation *(Erklären)* as applied in the physical sciences and understanding *(Verstehen)* as applied in the humanities. This relates to the further distinction between *Naturwissenschaft* (science) and *Geisteswissenschaft* (hermeneutics). Dilthey argued; "Nature we explain: psyche life we understand." To make his distinction more dramatic, Dilthey equated explanation with causal explanation. He argued that actions are meaningful only in terms of purposes and intentions. People are agents because they have purposes. Unless actions are recognized as expressions of purposes, emotions, and intentions, knowledge of human behavior will never amount to anything more than knowledge of statistical regularities. We can understand others only if their actions are subsumed under categories like purpose, wants, and feelings. For Dilthey hermeneutic understanding provides the foundation for the human sciences.

Benedetto Croce (1866–1952), along the same lines as Dilthey, argued that the problem in history and elsewhere is not to grasp the facts ("to designate something a fact is already to pass judgment on it") but to understand how people describe the world to make it intelligible for them. Croce recommended *empathetic* understanding, claiming that historians should resort to theories and models only when such understanding is lacking.

*Verstehen* as empathetic understanding was to be achieved through imaginatively reenacting the thoughts and likely mental states of those studied. This view of *Verstehen* as empathetic understanding is associated primarily with Max Weber. Today *Verstehen* need not be so interpreted. Charles Taylor (1964) takes *Verstehen* to be the set of intersubjective meanings that constitute social life, to be grasped not by empathy but through some hermeneutical (interpretive) approach. (This is in line with the view of Peter Winch discussed later.)

R. G. Collingwood (1889–1943), drawing on Dilthey, denies the idea that universal regularities can be applied to human nature (Martin, 1977). In particular, Collingwood (1946) argues that there is a total dissimilarity in the long term between men at one time and men at a later time since beliefs as well as social settings change. He saw actions both as the output of rational, reflective thought and as resulting more directly from feelings (impulse, emotion, and sensation). It was rational man who changed through time: basic emotions were unchanging.

The attacks on particular forms of positivism have intensified since the 1960s with much more subtlety and sophistication of argument. Suppe (1977) as a result regards positivism as near total eclipse. If this is so, there is the danger of "throwing out the baby with the bathwater" in that there is much in positivism to be commended. However, as Hegel (1770–1831) pointed out, great liberating ideas can become rigid orthodoxies and turn into suffocating straitjackets (Bernstein, 1976).

Explanation in the natural sciences is assumed to take the form of subsumption under predictive laws along the lines of the deductive–nomological model described in Chapter 2. This is contrasted with understanding. But positivist critics argue "understanding" is merely the first stage in groping around for something more lawlike. This debate continues with the claim that the methods of "verification" applying to each are fundamentally different, *testing in the one case and interpreting in the other.* Louch (1969) even sets out to show the impossibility of *any* social science going beyond mapping the conventions of a particular society. He views the search for hidden laws as a pipe dream. To Louch, we already have a rich store of knowledge about human nature, which so-called social science simply rehashes in jargon while invoking artificial and ungainly hypotheses to suggest science. However, more specifically the major challenges to positivism have come from

1. linguistic or ordinary language philosophy inspired by the work of Ludwig Wittgenstein;

2. interpretive social science, as discussed earlier; and

3. recent developments in the philosophy of science. (This is dealt with more extensively in Chapter 13.)

Each of these challenges is discussed in turn.

## Linguistic Philosophy

Analytic philosophy includes logical positivism, logical empiricism, certain aspects of instrumentalism and pragmatism, and linguistic philosophy. What brings these very divergent philosophies together as analytic philosophy is the view that philosophy is a form of logicolinguistic analysis and that philosophical problems are best approached as problems about the linguistic expression of thought. However, Cohen (1986) argues convincingly that the problems investigated by analytic philosophy are not so much about language per se as they are all, in one way or another, problems about reasons and reasoning.

Although Wittgenstein's early writings were generally credited with giving a stimulus to logical positivism, his later writings provide the major intellectual base for attacks on positivism (1958, 1969). This later work spawned the *linguistic* school of analytic philosophy, which rejected positivism on grounds stemming from arguments about the nature and language of action. Linguistic philosophy is concerned with examining the use of words as a basis for problem solving. Linguistic philosophy is a method for undertaking conceptual analysis like examining the use of the term "loyalty" in social life and in marketing. On the other hand, the philosophy of language is a subject area that tries to philosophically illuminate certain general features of language, whereas linguistics seeks to describe the actual structures of human languages. Here we are concerned only with linguistic philosophy. Initially there was a positivist stage in linguistic philosophy when the following was claimed:

1. All thought consisted in the mental processing of linguistic forms. This claim was undermined by psychological studies such as those showing the possibility of nonlinguistic thought as occurs with infants.

2. The meaning or meaningfulness (significance) of a sentence depends on the method used to verify it (the verification principle). But meaning could come about in other ways such as through analogies like the concept of the life cycle.

Wittgenstein believed it instructive to think of language as a set of games in which different interactions with others are seen as different games, each having its own rules. Wittgenstein (1958) argued that the rules followed in social life are analogous to the grammatical rules of speech in that just as grammatical rules facilitate the creation of sentences, so social rules help people create appropriate actions in new situations. Instead of thinking in terms of mental processing like today's cognitive psychologist, the focus on rules suggests studying language games as a way of understanding social life.

Contrary to logical positivism, Wittgenstein claims that the meaning of any word, statement, or utterance is a matter of its use within the "language game," or social context. Words and statements differ in meaning depending on context, just as the word "sanction" in one context can mean "approve" and in another context imply to "punish." Meaning cannot be divorced from usage and the same applies to intentional action. What a buyer is doing when carrying out certain bodily movements can be understood only in terms of the meaning the buyer attaches to the movements within that social context and not by subsuming the movements under some general law. The only way to grasp such meaning is to learn the rules and conventions that operate in that particular social context.

Wittgenstein posed the question, "What is left over if I subtract the fact that my arm goes up from the fact that I raise my arm?" What distinguishes the action of raising my arm from mere bodily movement is the "meaning" of the movement: *action is behavior described not just in terms of bodily movement but in terms of intentions, reasons, or rules.* An action cannot be treated as a category of bodily movement since the same bodily movement can be involved in carrying out many different actions.

To infer an action presupposes an understanding of the act of which the action is part. If someone lacks the concept of "shopping," it is conceptually impossible to shop or describe an act as shopping since what counts as "shopping" is determined by the rules governing the use of the concept and not by the properties or attributes of the movements themselves. As Hartnack says:

> It is from the behavior a person displays that I am able to infer what kind of act he is performing. I observe that he is walking and I infer that he is taking a walk (and not just going to the grocer's). I observe that he is looking at an open book and that his eyes are moving in a special way, and I infer that he is reading a book (and not just heeding the kinaesthetic sensations caused by the movements of the eyes). . . . It is only because I already understand the language of acts that I am able to infer an act from a particular instance of behavior. Behavior is a necessary but not a sufficient condition for inferring another person's acts. (1972, p. 111)

The distinction between involuntary bodily movement and meaningful action is accepted by philosophers of science. But many would argue that the two differ in the nature of their causes, not in the fact that action is uncaused whereas involuntary movement is caused (see Chapter 5). Thus May Brodbeck (1968, p. 671), a logical empiricist, argues that action is determined by the choices made, that what someone does causally depends upon what he wants. Brodbeck accepts determinism, which she claims is often confused with fatalism, or the view that because everything is predetermined whatever happens is never affected by what we do. Scientific determinism, she argues, in the field of human conduct, is simply the view that there are circumstances—in our makeup, background, or environment—that are jointly sufficient conditions for our behavior, including the choices we make. She rejects historical determinism (the view that there are laws covering the social process that are independent of the actions of individuals) as a form of fatalism: historical or social determinism is not only different from scientific determinism; it is inconsistent with it.

In rejecting positivistic philosophies (including logical empiricism), interpretive social scientists typically hold that such philosophies view causes as compelling their effects. This is so even though the Vienna Circle positivists and many logical empiricists accept the Humean concept of cause and dismiss as an illusion the idea of cause as compelling an effect. But positivism in practice is equated with methodological monism and the belief that the natural sciences seek, like realism, causal explanation. Antipositivists typically reject the concept of cause when it comes to explaining action. However, Brodbeck argues that cause compels *only* if it is of a certain kind in a certain context. If the cause is my own choice, she argues, then I am not compelled but instead act freely, although my choice causes my actions. Therefore, I act freely and am responsible for my actions. [Brodbeck (1968) uses the term "cause," but she believes that although it is useful where "knowledge is only partial, as in the social sciences," it tends to be eliminated in mature sciences. This is in line with the opinion of other philosophers who view sophistication in science as finding its expression in mathematical relationships, not in talk about causes.]

But antipositivists like Meldon (1961) and Anscombe (1972) reject *any* conception of motivation as necessitating a process leading to action. They are opposed to construing motivation as antecedent mental processes causing action. They claim motivational explanations should simply bring out the intentions, reasons, or rules a man had for acting as he did, recognizing that reasons are essentially evaluative: they are views about what makes some course of action of value.

Antipositivists contrast teleological explanations with causal explanations and deny that teleological explanations can be translated into causal form. One form of teleological explanation is that which explains *action as rule-following.* As Baker and Hacker (1984) argue, "We are, above all, rule-making and rule-following creatures." They point out that the understanding of a rule emanates from knowledge of *how to apply it and how it is applied, not from looking at the rule itself.* This is as true in understanding social life as it is in understanding the legal system. To speak of a person's action as being rule-governed is to say that the person thinks there are good reasons for doing what the rule requires. Rules are constitutive here of the action so it cannot be claimed a person is doing something independent of the rules. Only intentional action is rule-governed, since "the intention to take the action will contain the rule just in the way that the rules of chess are related to the intention to play a game of chess." To understand a rule is to know what acts would count as compliance with it. Such a view of rules as a guide for action is distinguished from other senses of the word rule that vary all the way from a rule as a statistical regularity to the rule of a monarch.

Harré, a realist philosopher, and Secord, a psychologist, give the general form of a rule as: "In order to achieve $A$ (the act), do $a_1, \ldots, a_n$ (the actions) when $S$ (the occasion or situation) occurs" (Harré and Secord, 1973). They argue (unlike Wittgenstein) that rules are tied to ends, that the goal-directedness of action is implicit in the very notion of action being rule-following. The focus is not, as in cognitive psychology, on the information-processing rules (the software programs) of the mind but on the rules to which the individual actions can be said to conform. They can be described at different levels of generality. Thus in the highest level, particular lifestyles (e.g., active rather than passive, ostentatious rather than private, cosmopolitan rather than local, career-oriented rather than family-oriented) can be described in terms of the general rules being followed. On the other hand, through the use of protocols there can be detailed description of the rules being followed on, say, a buying episode.

Traditionally rule-following behavior is regarded as the *conscious* application of a rule with everything else being regarded as habit or automatic response. This view is no longer tenable. Rule-following behavior is not necessarily conscious. In fact people can be following rules that no one has even formulated before researchers made their observations. Goffman (1963) and others have shown that even though a person is *not* consciously following any set of rules, his or her departure from expected behavior elicits the same response from others as that brought forth through breaking some formal set of rules. There is a good deal of agreement among philosophers and the behavioral researchers who promote the concept of action as rule-governed, that rules not only can be unconsciously followed but are (1) something groups and societies share, and (2) not absolute but conditional and guide rather than determine action. The idea that rules are not absolute but conditional and guide action rather than determine action is also a reminder that even though certain rules may be internalized (e.g., to buy the cheapest brand of coffee), they may have little influence on action unless the individual is directly exposed to and recognizes the relevant contingent circumstances.

Both positivists and logical empiricists have been more prepared to accept the notion of action being rule-governed providing the rules emanate from some known role being played (see Chapter 8). Thus a researcher might seek to discover the relationship among role expectations, social situation, and actions. But the rules here will also be inevitably loose since "actors" interpret roles somewhat differently, as do the researchers themselves. Researcher interpretations will differ even more if only observable behavior is used to infer the rules. This is because an action can be in accord with very different rules unless we know about a person's intentions. To infer the relevant rules of action is equivalent to inferring the relevant wants and beliefs. Yet, as stated earlier in the book, in looking at wants (or cognates like desire or goal), beliefs, and action, we need to know two of them to predict the third. In observing behavior, we know only about the action taken. In any case, rules are not like laws in science: they can be modified or broken or there can be errors in application.

Using the game of chess as a model of rule-governed action, Ryle argues that rules can explain the overall game but not the exact moves. The rules are the same for all games of chess, yet chess games are not uniform and there is plenty of scope for displays of cleverness, stupidity, and deliberation. The rules restrict what is done, though what is done might still be bad tactics. The tactical rules or principles conform to but are not reducible to the rules of chess. If we regard consumers as chess players writ large (Peters, 1958), we might follow Ryle in regarding the overall pattern of their actions as being explained by the rules of the game of shopping. On the other hand, while specific tactics can still be expressed in the form of rules and conform to the rules of the shopping game, they are not reducible to those rules. On this basis, although all action might be regarded as rule-governed or rule-following behavior, we can give an overall explanation only in terms of rules: the individual moves, though following some tactical rule, are too rooted in individual circumstances and experience to be predictable.

What should be said at this stage is that this discussion of what constitutes rule-following behavior is not grounded in actual research. Harré and Secord (1973) point out that philosophers like Ryle in philosophical psychology, mental philosophy, theory of action, or whatever name is used to discuss the philosophy of action, are not engaged in empirical inquiries. They are undertaking an examination of the criteria used by behavioral scientists and doing conceptual analysis, that is, examining the logical properties of the various words (want, choice, decision, intention, preference, etc.) used to describe decision and action and distinguishing them conceptually. The only experiments they undertake are the thought experiments necessary to judge borderline uses of a word.

Probably the most influential post–World War II philosopher to attack methodological monism and promote the concept of action as rule-following is Peter Winch, a student of Wittgenstein. We discuss at length the work of Winch (1958), since many writers define their own position in terms of his seminal work. The social sciences, according to Winch, should be concerned with meaningful behavior. For action to be meaningful it must "count as something." To "count as something" means to be governed by a rule determining what actions are to count as choosing, buying, using, and so on.

Winch, though a philosopher, writes within the phenomenological tradition so that his views echo the sociology of Schutz and are supportive of the anthropology of Geertz (see Chapter 8). Borrowing from Wittgenstein, Winch argues that action must always be understood in the context of the language game or form of life in which it occurs. In other words, we must understand the rules of the game if we are to understand the plays. Until we understand the meaning of the action, we cannot understand what is going on; thus the language game being played must be clear to us.

Winch's major contribution lies in his elucidation of the relationship between the concepts people use to think about social life and the actions (e.g., shopping actions) they take. He argues that any reflective understanding of an individual's action should reflect that individual's own *unreflective* understanding of his or her actions. Actions, in other words, must be conceptualized in the person's own terms. The social scientist can extend from this but the base must be the person's own account. Thus Winch sees social science developing on the conceptual possibilities of commonsense knowledge. He claims that if we deny the actor's own "theories" of his or her actions, we change the criteria for identifying the actions being studied and, as a consequence, cease to study what we set out to study. Winch is adamant in insisting explanation of individual action in social settings must be intelligible in terms of the individual's own concepts. Winch argues that social scientists must be concerned with the concepts used in social life and employ the same concepts and conceptual frameworks as employed by those whose actions they aim to explain. In other words, any marketing manager intent on explaining buyer behavior must first understand the vocabulary, the way of looking at things, the perceptions, and so on, of his target segment. What is to count as a "bargain," a "quality" product, a "contract," a "high-class" store, a "complex buy"—this can be settled only *within* the relevant form of social life. As with ethnomethodology, the mode of understanding sought must be that of those being studied. Buying action is social behavior partly because it is *meaningful* to others engaged in that same activity. Just as knowing the meaning of a word or sentence in a language game equals knowing the social rules governing its use, so social behavior (like buying behavior) is rule-governed behavior in the same way.

To Winch all behavior is rule-governed or rule-following whenever it makes sense to distinguish between a right and a wrong way of doing things; the notion of following a rule is inseparably bound to that of making a mistake. To ask for an explanation of human action simply reflects our ignorance of the rules being used. To discover such rules is to explain the action. Action is a performance and like every other performance it can be good or bad according to the rules being used (Peters, 1958). Thus a poor performance in buying is to violate the rules, that is, to make a mistake. Hence to ask what might go wrong is a guide to the rules being used.

For Winch, understanding human action is a matter of grasping the point or meaning of what is being said or done, which, in turn, necessitates understanding the concepts being used. For Winch, people's actions are a reflection of the concepts they use and types of action presuppose types of concepts. Concepts used by people to describe their actions reflect the rules being followed. The development of concepts goes hand in hand with the development of rules. As concepts change so do perceptions of the world, and actions change as a result. Hence if we wish to change perceptions, we should focus on changing underlying concepts: *changing concepts is basic to changing intentional action as the concepts mirror the rules being followed.*

Winch regards regularities in social behavior not as indicating scientific laws that relate stimuli to responses, but as evidence for the existence of rules. Discovering these rules is a matter of explicating the concepts being used, which mirror the rules being followed. Thus a woman, choosing a product for the first time, says she chose that brand because it was advertised, and therefore "familiar." Winch would add that the rule being followed is embodied in the concept of "familiarity."

Winch does not regard actions as caused. In the physical sciences, he argues, an antecedent causal event is logically and conceptually *independent* of its effects. Thus in saying "if metals are heated, they expand," we find the heating of metals to be conceptually independent of their expansion. Winch claims that this logical and conceptual independence is the distinguishing feature of a causal science but is absent in the field of human action. This leads Winch to reject the type of empirical research concerned with testing hypotheses by checking whether predictions correspond with reality. He argues that what is needed are better and better interpretations. In brief, Winch argues for conceptual analysis rather than a search for scientific laws: "To give an account of the meaning of a word is to describe how it is used; and to describe how it is used is to describe the social intercourse into which it enters" (1958, p. 123).

Thus people's actions are a reflection of the concepts they use and types of action presuppose types of concepts: "If N does not grasp the concept of industrial peace it must be senseless to say that his reason for doing anything is a desire to see industrial peace promoted" (Winch, 1958, p. 47). Winch's *Verstehen* is very different from Weber's. Winch argues that Weber never gives a clear account of the logical character of empathetic understanding *("Verstehen")*. Winch rejects the view of *Verstehen* as some sort of psychological technique for achieving empathy ("a matter of putting oneself in the other fellow's position") as this is not in line with the conceptual type of analysis advocated by Winch. In spite of this, Winch is often misrepresented as advocating mere empathy, so strong is the identification of this with *Verstehen*. Winch agrees, for example, that many a taboo would not be "directly intelligible to anyone brought up in a different tradition"; empathy as a technique for understanding would simply be inadequate.

Winch believes knowledge of rules can lead to good prediction of behavior. Thus Winch writes:

> If O wants to predict how N is going to act, he must familiarize himself with the concepts in terms of which N is viewing the situation; having done this, he may, from his knowledge of N's character, be able to predict with great confidence what decision N is going to take. (1958, p. 91)

However, he warns against believing in perfect prediction:

> But notions which O uses to make his predictions are nonetheless compatible with N's taking a different decision from that predicted for him. If this happens, it does not necessarily follow that O has made a mistake in his calculations; for the whole point about a decision is that a given set of "calculations" may lead to any one of a set of different outcomes. (p. 92)

In the natural sciences predicting from event *A* the occurrence of event *B* requires agreement among scientists as to *what is to count* as an event *A* and an event *B*. However, in the behavioral sciences everything depends on what the subjects themselves *perceive* as an event *A* or *perceive* as an event *B*. Following a rule depends on recognizing similarities in situations. But what counts as similar under one rule might not count as similar under another. It is *not* what the observer thinks but what the subject thinks that counts as "doing the same thing." Hence as a first step the researcher must become familiar with the concepts through which the agent views the situation.

Winch's work gave and continues to give considerable philosophical support to interpretive social sciences. Inevitably his position has stimulated a good deal of criticism. One of the most commonly quoted criticisms is that made by the philosopher Rudner (1966), who accuses Winch of the "reproductive fallacy" by denying the possibility of developing and employing generalized categories other than those of the participant. This distorts Winch's position. Winch does not reject the idea of developing and employing sociological concepts and categories other than those of the actors being studied. He simply insists such categories must be mediated through the participant's own world of meaning. Nonetheless, Winch's insistence on the uniqueness of individual life forms and social contexts left him open to the charge of relativism (Hunt, 1991). Other writers, including Habermas, argue for the intersubjectability of different forms of life while Gadamer speaks of the need to fuse horizons.

MacIntyre (1971) dismisses criticism of Winch that views his work as a revival of discredited ideas and agrees with Winch that establishing reasons, motives, and intentions must be a first step to understanding human action. Nonetheless, he criticizes Winch's framework as inadequate, incomplete, and limited in scope.

1. It is inadequate because Winch dwells on what people do and not what they are or suffer; social science cannot be concerned *just* with intentional action but must also seek the background environmental causes and effects (e.g., of being unemployed). There is a need on occasion for collectivist explanations. Also, to accept Winch means we cannot go beyond society's own self-description, which severely limits "developing standards of intelligibility through criticism." It is necessary on occasion to go beyond the rules governing the use of an expression to the purpose these rules once had if we are to understand the concept.

2. It is incomplete because Winch does not indicate what would constitute sufficient conditions for action: a person may have reasons for action but the question remains whether he was moved to action by those specific reasons.

3. It is limited in scope. It is not always possible to distinguish between a right and wrong way to do something. If this is the criterion of rule-following behavior, it is necessary for the behavior to be part of a coherent mode of behavior (e.g., buying) where the individual has a role to play. This relates to a criticism made by Schatzki (1983), who accuses Winch of moving away from Wittgenstein's concept of rule-governed behavior. Schatzki claims that Wittgenstein, in suggesting all behavior can be described as rule-governed, is using the term "rule" in the sense of describing some regularities in behavior, that it is the behavior that determines the rule and not vice versa, as seems to be assumed by Winch.

Gellner (1971) agrees that to understand the workings of the concepts of a society is to understand its institutions, but he argues that this does not mean that to understand the concepts of that society in the ways its members do (as Winch advocates) is to understand that society. Concepts can on occasion mask reality. Thus the concept of "gentlemen" may be applied to military officers for image management, though this can mask the true reality.

Bhaskar (1979), a realist philosopher, takes Winch to task for claiming that the analysis of concepts exhausts the range of social science. He agrees that social science is *concept*-dependent and concepts are the distinctive feature of social reality, but he argues this is something different from saying concepts exhaust the subject matter of social science. What can be said is that social causation is conceptually *and linguistically mediated* and that *Verstehen* is necessary because of the concept-dependent nature of social causation. Bhaskar makes a number of other criticisms. Winch does not deal with the origin of rules: Why is one rule rather than another selected? How do people cope with conceptual conflict? Bhaskar, as a realist concerned with bringing the concept of rule-following into a real causal framework, argues that *real reasons* (or rules) are those that are causally efficacious. Like Harré and Secord, Bhaskar also points out that Winch's rejection of the natural science model is based on acceptance of a positivist conception of science (e.g., cause as constant conjunction), which is erroneous.

Von Wright (1971) criticizes Winch for his focus purely on rules on the ground that it fails to highlight sufficiently the intentionality of human action.

Thompson (1981) adds further criticism:

1. Winch (unlike Wittgenstein) argues that the process of following a rule involves a *reflective decision* in determining how rules are to be applied to a particular case. But Winch gives an inadequate account of this reflective decision. Thus carrying over what is important in past experience to a new (buying?) situation ignores the creative element in such decision-making. In line with Thompson, Schatzki (1983) points out that Wittgenstein claimed people may achieve their goals without much conscious

thinking but simply react in an *unreflective* manner to the meaningfulness of the situation facing them. Hence rules may describe the regularities in people's unreflective actions rather than be something consciously applied.

2. Winch ignores the "how come" or genesis of the conditions within which individuals make their reasoned decisions.

3. Winch's concept of meaningful action is deficient. To say that action is meaningful only if it is performed in accordance with a rule simply shifts the weight of the analysis onto the concept of rule, which Winch does not adequately discuss; he merely says it is inseparable from the notion of making a mistake. But are all mistakes violations of rules? Thompson quotes MacIntyre in saying it is not clear what would be meant in violating a rule in, say, the way we walk.

4. Winch seems to use Wittgenstein's claim that the meaning of an expression is specified by the intersubjective rules that govern the use of the expression to illicitly deduce the view that *all* social relations presuppose concepts or that *all* social relations between men exist only in and through concepts. Thus, following Gellner (1971), Thompson points out that the concepts of domination–subordination may enter into a relationship but be actually concealed by other concepts articulated by the participants.

5. Winch views social science as concerned with understanding rather than explanations per se. Such understanding relates to the extent one comprehends the rules that govern the action. Thompson argues that the elucidation of rules is not always necessary or even sufficient for the understanding of action. Thus the action of "smiling" is understood by description alone and action may have meaning/significance beyond the meaning endowed by the rules (e.g., the buying's effect on the firm from which the product was bought).

Thompson would supplement the hermeneutical approach to obtain *both understanding and explanation* by considering the circumstances surrounding the action such as institutional factors and the origins of the action. He argues that the distinction between the reasons for action and causes is artificial, based on the erroneous Humean concept of cause. There are always forces acting on an "agent" of which the agent is unaware, and knowledge of these help in achieving a deeper explanation. A social science cannot remain at the level of lay actors' accounts of their own actions, as ethnomethodologists suggest. We should try to identify the (collective) factors that help generate the action of which the agent may be only dimly aware. (This is a return to Weber's claim that an explanation should be adequate both at the level of meaning and at the level of cause.) Thompson comes to grips with the problem of validating interpretations. He supports the *principle of self-reflection,* which insists interpretations be endorsed by the actors themselves.

Harré and Secord (a realist philosopher and a psychologist) have been in the forefront in developing the rule-following approach into a fully fledged model as an alternative to positivism. They reject Hempel's D-N model of explanation and the view of causal laws as simply expressing constant conjunctions. To Harré and Secord human behavior is typically the *conscious* following of rules and the intentional carrying out of plans. Their nonpositivist approach to explaining behavior is a two-stage process:

1. Determine the "episode" to be explained. An episode is any organized activity in which human beings engage which has some unity. Thus any act of buying can be regarded as an episode. A shopping episode would cover the set of actions that comprise buying.

2. Identify the generative "mechanism," structures, or powers giving rise to the behavior associated with the episode. Because this process of discovery and identification is termed *ethogeny,* the Harré and Secord approach is called the *ethogenic model of action.*

Harré and Secord acknowledge some episodes are enigmatic in that there is uncertainty over whether the behavior is best explained by rule-following or by *external* causes. They thus speak of *formal* (rule-following) *episodes* and *causal episodes.*

Assuming a formal episode where behavior is clearly intentional (done *by* the agent, not *to* the agent), ethogeny consists of discovering the *meaning* of the situation for the agents (buyers) and from this deducing the rules being used. This is because similarities in behavior do not necessarily derive from similarities in stimuli but from shared meanings and acceptance of the same rules.

Ethogeny involves collecting accounts (anticipatory plans, ongoing commentaries, and retrospective comments) from the agents (buyers). The meanings of the situation emerge from the reasons given in the accounts justifying the action in the episode. Human action acquires its meaning through being recognized as the *performance* of an act with reasons for that performance. Performances are good to bad and so governed by rules that are not true or false like scientific laws but effective or ineffective to differing degrees.

The description of the actions performed and the acts achieved is called a description of the act–action structure. Different accounts of this act–action structure may have to be negotiated with the respondent (agent). In any case, the sequence is from a description of the act–action structure to reasons, meanings, and rules being followed. The key lies in identifying meanings. A greater precision in specifying meanings corresponds to achieving greater accuracy in the physical sciences.

The preceding discussion is consistent with Winch, although Winch rejects Harré and Secord's realism. Thus for actions done *by* an agent, both would claim that past buying action is first made intelligible by being shown to be the outcome of reasons. Past buying actions are made even more intelligible by explicating the concepts employed in these reasons and, step by step, moving back to the rules governing the action itself. However, Harré and Secord spell out their methodology in much more detail than Winch. Thus they deal with the concept of role, recognizing that rules associated with roles are essentially normative rather than actually followed to the letter and they impose (additionally) stylistic elements onto a performance. In respect of enigmatic episodes they recommend imagining a set of rules that might account for them and then seeking the limitations of whatever is imagined as an explanation before regarding the behavior as involuntary.

Harré and Secord argue that the verifying of self-reports is no more disturbing than the impossibility in the physical sciences of knowing for certain whether one's theoretical explanations are correct. They point out that so-called controlled experiments are far from immune to criticism. The participants in an experiment are not passive, so their interpretations of what is going on can affect results, even helping the experimenters achieve the results sought. They claim that work on information processing in cognitive psychology involving experiments is frequently useless because the information provided is so restricted that the only way to process it is by "confirming" the hypothesis being tested.

Returning to the question of rules, Black (1970) suggests a continuum rather than just using the one category of rule-governed to cover all types:

1. *Rule-invoking rules* are formally set out and invoked, thus constituting an explanatory "mechanism" (e.g., bidding or negotiation rules in industrial buying).

2. *Rule-governed rules* are consciously remembered and followed (e.g., when the consumer always looks for the same things in evaluating a used car).

3. *Rule-accepting rules* are followed without active attempt to remember them (e.g., the thirteen rules of differential calculus).

4. *Rule-guided rules* are followed loosely, with less of a sense of following rules than in the case of rule-accepting rules (language is rule-guided with wide individual variations).

5. *Rule-covered rules* are followed when the agent is completely unconscious of following any rule (e.g., in riding a bike, where once a particular skill is mastered, the body seems to take over and do the required thinking). The less conscious the rule, the more difficult is the problem of identifying *the* reasons and working back to the relevant rules regulating the action.

Bhaskar (1979), among others, believes both positivists and antipositivists base their case on outdated concepts of science. As a realist he criticizes positivism on the ground that experimental science is interested less in showing a constant conjunction of events than in identifying generative *mechanisms* that explain events. In fact, unless experiments are controlled, he argues, there is likely to be no constant conjunction of events because other events intervene. Hence causal laws in the real world only express tendencies (no blanket determinism).

Bhaskar agrees that intentional action is caused by reasons and it is only because action is caused by reasons that it is properly characterized as intentional behavior. He nonetheless claims that the behavioral sciences, like the natural sciences, are concerned with moving from knowledge of manifest phenomena to knowledge of the structures or mechanisms that generate them. However, in the case of behavioral sciences as opposed to the mature sciences, (1) manifest phenomena are the phenomena of social life and so must be conceptualized in the way they are conceptualized by those whose behavior we seek to explain, and (2) the generative structures of "mechanisms" consist of social relationships. On this basis, the study of buyer behavior should move from acquiring knowledge first of the manifest phenomena of buying actions (as described in terms of the concepts used by the buyer) to knowledge of the situations, roles, lifestyle, and other social relationships relevant to buying. In more general terms social science must (on the Bhaskar thesis) follow a three-step process:

1. Identify the behavior as some specific action rather than simply being movement or involuntary behavior. This presupposes some intersubjectivity of social meaning. As stated earlier, if someone lacks the concept of "shopping," it is conceptually impossible to describe behavior as shopping.

2. Establish the meaning of the action for the actor (its significance, what it symbolizes, how it is experienced) and the resulting reasons (goals, wants, and beliefs) leading to the action.

3. Identify the influences, factors, and considerations that were taken into account by the actor and can be said to have initiated, pressed, induced, or caused the action.

## Interpretive Social Science

While philosophers debate the nature and meaning of action, antipositivist social science has continued to grow along lines suggested by the philosophical criticism of positivistic social science. Antipositivists speak of understanding behavior *(Verstehen)* or, more commonly, interpreting behavior (hermeneutics). The importance of interpretation for understanding action is now generally recognized. It is also accepted that such interpretation cannot be bypassed or eliminated by studies of regularities.

Antipositivist social science includes interpretive sociology and interpretive psychology, cultural anthropology, and a host of other movements loosely grouped under the heading of the *hermeneutical* approach to social science. In broad terms these movements receive their intellectual inspiration from philosophy and the hermeneutic phenomenological movement on the continent. This movement is associated on the continent with Heidegger (1962), Gadamer (1976), Habermas (1974), and Ricoeur (1974) (see Chapter 8).

The hermeneutic approach necessarily assumes some rationality in action. Hence side by side with the interest in hermeneutic social science has been the study of rationality (Elster, 1983; Pears, 1984).

Those who argue that positivist-type approaches are inadequate rather than wrong claim they merely need to be supplemented by a hermeneutic approach to uncover and interpret the meaning of the actions from the perspective of the agents themselves. Like Max Weber, such social scientists argue for adequacy of explanation at the level of cause *and* the level of meaning. They accept the distinction between the *reason* for an action and the *cause* of an action. The *reason* for an action is an appeal to some accepted rule that *justifies* the performance of the action; the *cause* of an action is an appeal to statistical regularities, some mechanism, structure, or process depending on whether the Humean concept of cause or realism is accepted.

## INTENTIONAL STATES

In ethnomethodology and elsewhere, there is an emphasis on keeping to the respondent's own words. There are good reasons for this when it comes to "wants" and "beliefs," since wants and beliefs represent *intentional states.* Understanding intentions means understanding what happens when you make seemingly minor changes in the sentence expressing the intention (Rosenberg, 1988).

We can speak of the *sense* and the *reference* of a word or sentence. The sense of a word or phrase is its meaning (connotation, or intension) and its reference is what it denotes (denotation, or extension). To illustrate the distinction, consider the "morning star" and the "evening star." Both have the same reference (denotation, extension) but may not have the same sense meaning. I may believe Venus is the morning star without believing that Venus is the evening star. Thus the sense meaning of a word or phrase can be something different from the object to which the word or phrase applies. This implies that the words used in an intention statement expressing wants and/or beliefs have a significance that is absent in statements expressing nonintentional *facts,* which is why we cannot freely substitute alternative words and phrases for statements expressing wants and/or beliefs (intentions) without the risk of turning a truth into a falsity. In other words, we cannot guarantee that the substitution will occur without changing the sense meaning for the respondents. Thus a respondent might agree with the statement that "abortion should be allowed" but disagree with the statement that "killing unborn babies should be allowed." As Rosenberg says, when two people have the same want (e.g., within some segment) or belief, then that "sameness" is due to an identity of some statement they both believe or want to be true. Any change in the words or phrases in which the wants or beliefs are expressed and the result might not be what the respondent would have endorsed. Respondents are not necessarily as knowledgeable about what are essentially equivalent statements as is the investigator. Although some market researchers have yet to learn this lesson, political pollsters have long known how to exploit it in the interests of their candidate.

## RELATIVISM

Several writers in marketing (e.g., Anderson, 1983; Peter and Olson, 1983) have talked about supporting a relativist orientation in marketing science; others (e.g., Hunt, 1991) have damned much antipositivism as relativism. We need first to know what the term means. To say something is "relative" is to say it varies from time to time and/or with circumstances. "Relative" contrasts with "absolute"—that which does not vary with time or circumstances. As Muncy and Fisk (1987) state, the core of relativism is the notion of something being relative to something else, for example, moral relativism claims morals are relative to an individual, circumstances, or society. They distinguish relativism from "relativity" in that relativity in the sense of cultural relativity would simply claim that cultural entities must be understood in their cultural setting. The relativist would go further and claim the culture provides the standards of evaluation. Muncy and Fisk also point out that relativism is not rejecting something being true but replacing the idea of absolute truth with the idea of relative truth.

*Relativism* is the doctrine that beliefs and principles are not universally valid across time and across cultures but are valid only for some historical period, some social group, or the individuals holding them. Relativism is commonly associated with historicism (see Chapter 4), which, when applied to society, claims that all cultural generalizations are historicorelative and can be understood only in terms of a culture's own development. Cultures are, of course, relative in some ways in that what may be the right thing to do socially in one culture may not be the right thing to do in another. But cultural relativism, as first expounded by Melville Herskovits (1895–1963), makes a greater claim, namely, that the values and institutions of any culture must be taken to be self-validating. Cultural relativism, by extending the debate over the unity of man and leading naturally to the further question of whether rationality itself is relative (cognitive rationality), is a major area of controversy in anthropology. A *strong* relativist position is one that denies there are any universal standards. This position reflects an extreme skepticism. Thus a strong moral relativism claims all moral beliefs are relative to the culture or the group or the individual: they are right for them. The most common objection to strong relativism is that in denying universal standards, it denies its own universal that everything is relative! Although we may not be able to verify moral standards by the methods of natural science, we are typically in a position to show the dysfunctional consequences for society of following no moral standards. Also, some moral standards can be better defended than others in terms of, say, our basic need for survival, the need to belong, and the need for order and security. As Rapoport (1953) says, there is no point in trying to justify our pursuit of these four invariant needs. Similarly, with regard to *cultural cognitive relativism,* we can point to the consequences: beliefs all become equally acceptable, so that evidence becomes meaningless.

There are positions other than that of strong relativism. A "modest" relativist simply claims that principles and beliefs *may* be relative to time and place. But such relativism lacks a cutting edge. Although this position is popularly adopted to signal open-mindedness and toleration of opposing views, when challenged, it elicits a tendency to move to strong relativism or to "weak" relativism. Weak relativism claims that *some* particular beliefs and principles can be shown to be justifiably different for different groups or individuals depending on the circumstances. Weak relativism is, of course, a defensible position since some principles and some beliefs are indeed linked with certain historical periods or places.

Muncy and Fisk argue that it is cognitive relativism that is most germane to marketing. They distinguish between *aletheic* relativism, which asserts that truth itself is relative to circumstances, and *epistemic* relativism, which asserts that it is the criterion of truth only that is relative to circumstances. But what might truth or the criteria of truth be relative to? The authors suggest the following:

1. An individual's beliefs and values. If truth itself is relative to individual beliefs and values, it is termed *subjective aletheic* relativism; if the criteria used to evaluate truth are relative to individual beliefs and values, it is termed *subjective epistemic* relativism.

2. A particular position or purpose. If truth itself is relative to a particular position or purpose, it is termed *objective aletheic* relativism; if the criteria of truth are relative to a particular position or purpose, it is termed *objective epistemic* relativism.

3. The conceptual scheme involved. If truth itself is relative to the conceptual scheme in which the theory or whatever was developed, it is termed *objective aletheic* relativism; if the criteria of truth are relative to the conceptual scheme in which it was developed, we have *conceptual epistemic* relativism.

Muncy and Fisk dismiss subjective relativism and aletheic relativism and focus on conceptual epistemic relativism and objective epistemic relativism. Conceptual epistemic relativism claims that the criteria used to evaluate any theory must be based on the conceptual framework in which the theory was developed, whereas objective epistemic relativism claims that the criteria used to evaluate a theory are relative to purpose or position. Hunt (1991), who, perhaps more than anyone else, has brought to the marketing literature a needed debate over the philosophies of research, is a passionate advocate of freeing marketing from all forms of what he defines as relativism. What Hunt finds most objectionable is the implication in relativism that there are no objective appraisal criteria for evaluating beliefs and principles. He points out that the mere fact that no evaluative criteria guarantee certain knowledge does not mean that everything is relative to the culture, group, or individual. This is in line with what A. J. Ayer once said, to the effect that it is in demanding impossible standards of perfection that the skeptic feels secure. Just because we cannot *absolutely* prove scientific laws does not mean we have no good reasons for believing them. This has been a standard argument against those advocating instrumentalism and conventionalism, but Hunt casts his net wider.

With respect to cultural relativism, Hunt points out that the evidence suggests that the basic elements of morality and rational thinking are the same in all cultures. But Hunt does not confine himself to cultural differences in morality and ways of thinking. He focuses on what he calls the three major subcategories of cognitive relativism: rationality relativism, reality relativism, and conceptual framework relativism as represented by historical relativism. Rationality relativism would seem to fall under Muncy and Fisk's subjective relativism, reality relativism would seem to embrace conceptual aletheic relativism, and conceptual framework relativism seems equivalent to conceptual epistemic relativism. With respect to "rationality relativism," Hunt attacks the "strong program" (see Chapter 13) in the sociology of knowledge (Bloor, 1983) which views the adoption of scientific and other theories as determined by social factors/group interests rather than rational reasons supporting the validity of the knowledge claims. He supports the view that we should look for such causes only when it is evident there are no rational reasons underpinning the scientific claims. As a pragmatic rule, I would support this position; nevertheless, it could be argued that whatever led to the adoption of the knowledge claims is always a matter of empirical inquiry and never one for dogmatism. If the strong program is wrong to assume the universality of (collective) causal social factors in adoption, it may also be wrong to assume that, because a knowledge claim can be rationally defended against all criticism, such reasons were the basis or the sole basis for adoption. Group interest may in fact be determinate in the adoption of some knowledge claim even though the claim is rationally and objectively defensible. Hunt is asking for a privileged position for science which no sociologist would be prepared to accept. In any case, it is not clear that "relativism" is involved or merely "relativity" in that the claim being made is that to understand how a scientist comes to hold such views we need to take account of social factors and group interests.

Of more interest is Hunt's attack on what he calls "reality relativism," which he identifies with any "constructivist" thesis such as Goodman's (discussed earlier). Hunt makes clear he is not attacking the idea that people may view the same phenomenon differently or the idea that theory directs observations. What he is attacking is the view that we cannot rationally and objectively compare or evaluate the truth of different conceptualizations of reality, which would deny that we can choose the reality most likely to be true. In the vocabulary of Muncy and Fisk, reality relativism would appear to be conceptual aletheic relativism, which they dismiss as a straw man.

Are there *always* rational evaluative criteria available for rational choice? To claim this so is to assume the following:

1. This is always so in practice if not in theory. This assumption would have to be established empirically, if possible.

2. All right-minded people agree on what constitutes evidence and what evidence is relevant to establishing the knowledge claim. Of course, social scientists do *not* agree and there is a danger in arguing that those who do not agree are not just not right minded but simply irrational.

3. There will always be a balance in the evidence favoring one knowledge claim over another. This again cannot be dogmatically asserted since the weighting of various types of evidence varies among scientists. As Cohen (1986) says, it is in the nature of fundamental issues that they do not admit of universally acceptable solutions. If we look at the different explanatory systems of psychology and sociology, we find the various advocates of these different systems do not agree even on the nature of man or how action is to be explained. As a consequence, they do not agree on evaluative criteria. Thus the logical empiricist or positivist traditions in psychology claim that the psychoanalytic view does not square with the evidence, yet its practitioners continue to practice. Is it that the strong program is right and knowledge-based claims are adopted for self-serving reasons or could it be that psychoanalysts do not accept what the positivist would call the objective evidence?

Hunt puts Winch in the category of reality relativism on the ground that Winch is saying our concepts construct reality and is tolerant of different cultural realities. Hunt seems to misunderstand Winch's purpose and by implication the purpose of sociologists like Blumer, Schutz, and Garfinkel and anthropologists like Geertz. Their aim is to *understand how other groups view their actions, not to inquire about the truth of their constructions.* It is a fact that there is no perception without conception and this claim is entirely neutral in respect to whether particular perceptions of reality are more rationally defensible than others. Understanding others means seeing it their way: it does not mean we accept their versions of reality as equally correct as our own views. There seems to be a confusion here between relativism and relativity. Winch is surely right in arguing that to understand others, particularly other cultures, we must understand the thought models with which others comprehend the world.

To demonstrate the absurdity of strong relativism when applied to all beliefs, Hunt points out that relativism would consider the views of those who deny the holocaust occurred as equally acceptable. Although it is true that strong cognitive relativism, if extended beyond the domain of cultural beliefs to all beliefs, does have this implication, it is simply a debating ploy to treat such an extension as some position being actually advocated by any body of social scientists. If relativists were to argue that all beliefs and not just cultural beliefs or just some beliefs are equally defensible or equally true, they would not survive long to cause much trouble. When not concerned with moral principles, relativists have typically been concerned with different cultural beliefs. If Feyerabend (1987) refuses to condemn fascism because of relativism, he could more easily have got that attitude from the positivists, who ruled out from the realm of meaningful discourse all ethical, aesthetic, religious, and value statements as being just emotive discourse.

Hunt claims that the same arguments that undermine cultural relativism can be used to undermine the reality relativism of Goodman's constructivism. This is to trivialize the arguments of one of America's most distinguished philosophers. Does the denial of some 'aboriginal' reality imply an anything-goes relativism? Goodman in fact denies his position supports relativism. Hunt is quick to point out how the term "received view" is slightingly applied to those of a positivist or logical empiricist orientation (and I agree), but he has returned the compliment by branding opposing viewpoints relativist.

The final category of cognitive relativism considered by Hunt is what he terms conceptual framework relativism. He claims this holds for philosophers Kuhn and Feyerabend. This is the conceptual epistemic relativism of Muncy and Fisk, who point out that supporters of this view claim (1) that all theories are underdetermined in that no theory is uniquely demonstrated by the evidence available, so that resort must be made to the conceptual scheme of the researcher to establish coherence with what is accepted as true and (2) that theories may not be comparable but may be incommensurable. They argue that the first claim does not justify relativism and that the other claim about incommensurability can be disputed. We return to this discussion in Chapter 13. We will also be further considering Hunt's criticism along with others in Chapter 13.

## Philosophy of Science

Critics of positivism and logical empiricism have generally restricted their criticism to disputing the idea of a social science based on the natural sciences. It was generally taken for granted that some version of positivism faithfully described the methods and prescriptions accounting for the success of the natural sciences. But doubts began to grow as to whether the positivist picture describes actual practices in the natural sciences and whether positivism and modified versions of it were not in themselves highly flawed as a model of rationality for the pursuit of scientific knowledge. Attacks came from critical realists like Wilfrid Sellars (1963), critical rationalists like Imre Lakatos (1971) and Paul Feyerabend (1977), and historians of science like Thomas Kuhn (1970). But first there is a need to describe in more detail the recommended methodology of science associated (often wrongly) with positivism and logical empiricism, what has come to be known as the "received view" (Suppe, 1977).

## Conclusion

The debate between positivists/logical empiricists and interpretationists has been going on for a long time. Plato in the *Phaedo* in fact is credited with advocating that human action be explained by interpreting it in the sense of giving it meaning and significance. The debate will continue not only because both sides can quote successes but because purposes differ. Positivists/logical empiricists seek explanatory models for prediction and control; interpretationists seek intelligibility, that is, the meaning of action. But is the major focus of science to understand/explain things as they "really are" (if that is a feasible goal) or is it rather to predict and control? The pragmatist/instrumentalist/conventionalist despairs at finding truth and opts for control and prediction or regards whatever we accept as simply dependent on what convention suggests is defensible. There has been no attempt in this chapter to resolve these issues, which have vexed philosophers for generations and centuries. The aim has been to stimulate theoretical curiosity to conceive philosophical positions and visualize perspectives other than one's own.

## References

Agnew, Neil McK., and Sandra W. Pyke (1969). *The Science Game.* Englewood Cliffs, NJ: Prentice-Hall.

Alexander, Jeffrey C. (1987). *Twenty Lectures: Sociological Theory Since World War II.* New York: Columbia University Press.

Anderson, Paul F. (1983). "Marketing, Scientific Progress and Scientific Method." *Journal of Marketing* 47 (Fall), pp. 18–31.

Anscombe, G.E.M. (1972). *Intention.* Oxford: Basil Blackwell.

Ayer, A. J. (1936). *Language, Truth and Logic.* London: Gollancz.

Ayer, A. J. (1973). *The Central Questions of Philosophy.* London: Weidenfeld and Nicolson.

Ayer, A. J. (1982). *Philosophy in the Twentieth Century.* London: Weidenfeld and Nicolson.

Baker, G. P., and P.M.S. Hacker (1984). *Skepticism, Rules and Language.* Oxford: Basil Blackwell.

Belk, Russell W., John F. Sherry, and Melanie Wallendorf (1988). "A Naturalistic Inquiry into Buyer and Seller Behavior at a Swap Meet." *Journal of Consumer Research* 14, pp. 449–470.

Bernstein, Richard J. (1976). *The Restructuring of Social and Political Theory.* Philadelphia: University of Pennsylvania Press.

Bhaskar, Roy (1979). *The Possibility of Naturalism.* Atlantic Highlands, NJ: Humanities Press.

Black, Max (1970). *Margins of Precision.* Ithaca, NY: Cornell University Press.

Bloor, David (1983). *Wittgenstein: A Social Theory of Knowledge.* New York: Columbia University Press.

Boland, Lawrence A. (1982). *The Foundations of Economic Method.* London: George Allen and Unwin.

Brodbeck, May (1968). *Readings in the Philosophy of the Social Sciences.* New York: Macmillan, Introduction, Section 8, on Freedom, Determinism and Morality.

Carnap, R. (1945). "On Inductive Logic." *Philosophy of Science* 12, pp. 72–97.

Cohen, Jonathan L. (1986). *The Dialogue of Reason.* Oxford: Clarendon Press.

Collingwood, R. G. (1946). *The Idea of History.* Oxford: Oxford University Press.

Davidson, Donald (1984). *Inquiries into Truth and Interpretation.* Oxford: Oxford University Press.

Davies, Paul (1983). *God and the New Physics.* New York: Simon and Schuster.

Deshpande, R. (1983). "Paradigms Lost: On Theory and Method in Research in Marketing." *Journal of Marketing* 47 (Fall), pp. 101–10.

Elster, Jon (1983). *Sour Grapes: Studies in the Subversion of Rationality.* Cambridge: Cambridge University Press.

Elster, Jon (1989). *Nuts and Bolts for the Social Sciences.* Cambridge: Cambridge University Press.

Feyerabend, Paul (1977). *Against Method.* London: New Left Books.

Feyerabend, Paul (1979). *Science in a Free Society.* London: New Left Books.

Feyerabend, Paul (1981). "How to Defend Society Against Science." In *Scientific Revolutions,* edited by Ian Hacking. Oxford: Oxford University Press.

Feyerabend, Paul (1987). *Farewell to Reason.* London: New Left Books.

Friedman, Milton (1953). "The Methodology of Positive Economics." In *Essays in Positive Economics.* Chicago: University of Chicago Press.

Gadamer, H. G. (1976). *Philosophical Humanities.* Berkeley: University of California Press.

Gardner, Howard (1985). *The Mind's New Science.* New York: Basic Books.

Gellner, Ernest (1971). "Concepts and Society." In *Rationality,* edited by Bryan R. Wilson. New York: Harper Torchbooks.

Gibbon, Guy (1989). *Explanation in Archaeology.* Oxford: Basil Blackwell.

Goffman, E. (1963). *Stigma: Notes on the Management of Spoiled Identity.* Englewood Cliffs, NJ: Prentice-Hall.

Goodman, Nelson (1987). *Of Mind and Other Matters.* Cambridge, MA: Harvard University Press.

Habermas, J. (1974). *Theory and Practice,* translated by John Viertel. Boston: Beacon Press.

Hacking, Ian (1983). *Representing and Intervening.* Cambridge: Cambridge University Press.

Harré, Rom, and P. F. Secord (1973). *The Explanation of Social Behavior.* Totowa, NJ: Littlefield, Adams.

Hartnack, Justus (1972). *Language and Philosophy.* Paris: Mouton.

Heidegger, M. (1962). *Being and Time.* Oxford: Oxford University Press.

Hogarth, R. M., and M. W. Reder (eds). (1986). "The Behavioral Foundations of Economic Theory." *Journal of Business* 59 (October), pp. 185–209.

Hunt, Shelby (1991a). "Positivism and Paradigm Dominance in Consumer Research: Toward Critical Pluralism and Rapproachment." *Journal of Consumer Research* 18, I, pp. 32–44.

Hunt, Shelby (1991). *Modern Marketing Theory: Critical Issues in the Philosophy of Marketing Science.* Cincinnati: Southwestern Publishing Co.

Krikorian, Tervant H., ed. (1944). *Naturalism and the Human Spirit.* New York: Columbia University Press.

Kuhn, Thomas S. (1970). *The Structure of Scientific Revolutions,* 2nd ed. Chicago: University of Chicago Press.

Lakatos, Imre (1971). "History of Science and Its Rational Reconstructions." In *PSA 1970: In Memory of Rudolf Carnap. Boston Studies in the Philosophy of Science,* Vol. III. Dordrecht, Holland: D. Reidel, pp. 91–139.

Lakatos, Imre, and Alan Musgrave, eds. (1970). *Criticism and the Growth of Knowledge.* Cambridge: Cambridge University Press.

Lewis, C. I. (1946). *Analysis of Knowledge and Valuation.* Lasalle, IL: Open Court.

Louch, A. R. (1969). *Explanation and Human Action.* Los Angeles: University of California Press.

MacIntyre, Alasdair (1971). "The Idea of a Social Science." In *Rationality,* edited by Bryan R. Wilson. New York: Harper Torchbooks.

Martin, Rex (1977). *Historical Explanation.* Ithaca, NY: Cornell University Press.

Meldon, A. I. (1961). *Free Action.* London: Routledge and Kegan Paul.

Miller, R. W. (1987). *Fact and Method.* Princeton, NJ: Princeton University Press, Chapter 6.

Muncy, James A., and Raymond P. Fisk (1987). "Cognitive Relativism and the Practice of Marketing Science." *Journal of Marketing* 51 (January), pp. 20–33.

Nagel, Ernest (1961). *The Structure of Science.* New York: Harcourt, Brace and World.

Nagel, Ernest (1979). *Teleology Revisited.* New York: Columbia University Press.

Pears, David (1984). *Motivated Irrationality.* Oxford: Clarendon Press.

Peter, J. Paul, and Jerry C. Olson (1983). "Is Science Marketing?" *Journal of Marketing* 47 (Fall), pp. 111–25.

Peters, R. S. (1958). *The Concept of Motivation.* London: Routledge and Kegan Paul.

Popper, K. R. (1959). *The Logic of Scientific Discovery.* London: Hutchinson.

Putnam, Hilary (1981). *Reason, Truth and History.* Cambridge: Cambridge University Press.

Quine, W. V. (1951). "Two Dogmas of Empiricism." *Philosophical Review* 60, pp. 20–43.

Quine, W. V. (1953). "Two Dogmas of Empiricism." In *From a Logical Point of View.* New York: Harper and Row.

Rapoport, A. (1953). *Operational Philosophy.* New York: Wiley.

Ricoeur, Paul (1974). *The Conflict of Interpretations: Essays in Hermeneutics,* translated by Willis Domingo et al.; edited by Don Ihde. Evanston, IL: Northwestern University Press.

Robinson, Daniel N. (1985). *Philosophy of Psychology.* New York: Columbia University Press.

Rorty, Richard (1987). "Pragmatism and Philosophy." In *After Philosophy: End or Transformation?* Cambridge, MA: The MIT Press.

Rosenberg, Alexander (1988). *Philosophy of Social Science.* Boulder, CO: Westview Press.

Rudner, Richard S. (1966). *Philosophy of Social Science.* Englewood Cliffs, NJ: Prentice-Hall.

Ryle, Gilbert (1949). *The Concept of Mind.* New York: Barnes and Noble; London: Hutchinson.

Samuelson, Paul (1965). "Professor Samuelson on Theory and Realism: A Reply." *American Economic Review* 55, pp. 1164–72.

Schatzki, Theodore (1983). "The Prescription Is Description: Wittgenstein's View of the Social Sciences." In *The Need for Interpretation,* edited by Sollace Mitchell and Michael Rosen. Atlantic Highlands, NJ: Humanities Press.

Sellars, Wilfrid (1963). *Science, Perception and Reality.* London: Routledge and Kegan Paul.

Suppe, Frederick (1977). *The Structure of Scientific Theories.* Champaign/Urbana: University of Illinois Press.

Taylor, Charles (1964). *The Explanation of Behavior.* New York: Humanities Press.

Thompson, John B. (1981). *Critical Hermeneutics.* Cambridge: Cambridge University Press.

Von Wright, G. H. (1971). *Explanation and Understanding.* Ithaca, NY: Cornell University Press.

Winch, P. G. (1958). *The Idea of a Social Science.* Boston: Routledge and Kegan Paul.

Wittgenstein, Ludwig (1958). *Philosophical Investigations,* translated by G.E.M. Anscome. London: Oxford University Press.

Wittgenstein, Ludwig (1969). *Preliminary Studies for the "Philosophical Investigations", generally known as the Blue and Brown Books.* Oxford: Basil Blackwell.

# 12

# Research Methodology

Where it is impossible to obtain good tools, it is all the more important to know the defects of those you have.

John Stuart Mill (1806–1873)

In Chapter 11 we reviewed the objections to methodological monism's assertion that any discipline aspiring to be a science must follow the scientific method employed in the mature sciences. Opponents, though, encompass a wide spectrum. In the broadest terms there are those who do not deny the applicability of the methods of science to the study of human action but claim such methods do not exhaust the realm of useful methods and techniques. This is the position of those who proclaim the virtues of methodological pluralism. But there is a second category of critics: those who do not deny that the methods of the natural sciences apply to the study of human physiology and involuntary behavior but deny their appropriateness for understanding human action. This chapter considers the methodology to which this group of antipositivists typically object. This is the methodology that is commonly regarded as positivist in orientation. But it is positivist only in terms of today's common usage of the term positivism. It is not the pure logical positivism of the Vienna Circle. It is perhaps in recognition of this that many writers prefer to use the term the "received view," although this alternative label may be considered pejorative.

Methodology describes the procedures used to attain knowledge in a discipline. In a more specific sense, methodology is synonymous with the "scientific method," a procedure intended to generate scientific knowledge by considering (1) the aims of science; (2) its major concepts (like explanation and causality) and the methods (e.g., experimentation) used to attain its aims; and (3) the form in which the knowledge claims are expressed in laws and theories. Much of this methodology focuses on justifying claims to knowledge and theory building. When this methodology proves inadequate researchers typically resort to conventionalism, as reflected in statistical approaches to hypothesis testing. A critical review of this so-called positivist methodology should help us decide among methodological monism, methodological pluralism, and the antipositivism that denies a role to the methods of science in the study of action. My own position favors methodological pluralism. This needs to be said in case my critique of much that passes as sound methodology is interpreted as a rejection of the application of such methods to the study of buyer behavior. But what every researcher must bear in mind is the absence of any perfect tools for studying human subjects. In any study of buyer behavior many so-called facts are unreliable, concepts fuzzy and malleable, and findings somewhat tentative whenever they go beyond (as science must) the common experiences that accompany social living.

## Goal of Science

The major aim of science is the development of theory. Since for the logical positivist, theory consists of descriptive regularities, positivist theory seeks true descriptions of that reality. The ultimate goal is the *substantive unity* of the sciences to be achieved by reductionism.

It is debatable whether psychological theories involving mental constructs will ever be expressible in the vocabulary of the physical sciences, for example, that $X$ having attitude $Y$ is equivalent to $X$ number of $F$ neutrons in electrochemical state $G$ (Dennett, 1986). For the logical positivist this would constitute another reason for rejecting any theory involving mental constructs. Not that every philosopher advocating reductionism (also called reductivism) regards it as necessitating concept reduction. Nagel (1961), in fact, rejects the view of reductionism as reducing all the *concepts* of one science to those of another. Reductionism for him involves the idea of a hierarchy of sciences whereby explanatory theories of any science higher in the hierarchy could be explained by the preceding science, with all being ultimately explained in terms of physics. But reductionism even in the natural sciences remains more an act of faith than accomplishment. Davies (1983) claims physicists, especially those in quantum physics, long since abandoned a purely reductionist approach to the physical world and he doubts whether collective behavior is ever comprehensible in terms of its constituent parts.

Perhaps the most frequently quoted goal of science is the attainment of truth. Since accuracy in prediction and success in solving technical problems suggest the truth of the theories from which the predictions are derived, truth is declared (particularly by the realist) the major goal of science. Where truth is advocated as the goal of science, a simple correspondence theory of truth is adopted: to say a statement is true is to say that it corresponds with the way things really are.

It is not clear that truth can be the goal of science as we do not know the conditions that unequivocally signal its attainment. There are particular problems in the social sciences whenever hypotheses are tested by considering the replies to questionnaires or verbal reports of respondents. There is first the problem of ensuring that the questions themselves do not change the way respondents perceive the issue; further, there is no method of interpreting verbal reports that is certain to reflect the meaning of the thought lying behind what is said. A good interpretation is not the same as a true one (Gibbon, 1989). It could, of course, be argued that truth in science is like holiness in religion in that it is simply a normative goal, an ideal for which we strive rather than actually achieve. But this presupposes that we can measure progress toward truth. Scientists seek better and better prediction because it appears to signal continuing progress along the path to truth. But such prediction can be misleading. Barrow (1988), a writer on physics, shows how we may use a scientific law to accurately predict for years, improve upon it, and build around it an entire view of nature's mechanical workings, yet find in the end that the law is in fact part of something very dissimilar from what we had believed. Although there has been progress in improving our theories over the years, this does not prove such theories are nearer the truth.

## Induction Versus the Hypotheticodeductive Method

### Induction

Traditionally, philosophy of science has sought to establish *the* scientific method by which science proceeds to establish truth and to predict and explain. Two contrasting methods have emerged. One is known as "induction"; the other, the "hypotheticodeductive method." Hacking (1983) contrasts the two methods by comparing Carnap's verification and Popper's falsification. Carnap's is a bottom-up approach, whereas Popper's is a top-down approach. Hacking points out that Carnap wrote in a tradition that referred to the natural sciences as the "inductive sciences" in that the scientist was viewed as making precise observations, conducting experiments, then making generalizations, and finally drawing on analogies to work up to hypotheses and theories. Carnap in the positivist tradition regarded the scientist's observations as the foundation of knowledge, seeing how they added up to confirm some general proposition even if only in a probabilistic sense. As Hacking says, he spent the later part of his life in an attempt to develop an inductive logic to explain "how observational evidence could support hypotheses of wide application." Popper, on the other hand, believes there is only one logic—deductive logic— and that rationality in science is the method of conjecture and refutation.

For those who subscribe to the scientific method known as induction (see Figure 12.1), science always begins with the direct observation of single facts on the ground that nothing else is observable, certainly not regularities. (Methodological individualism goes with such a program.) The observed facts are then defined and classified on the basis of similarities and differences. Once the facts are so ordered, *inductive* generalizations are made. Only when numerous observations are compared is it possible to generalize. The supposed passage from the observed facts to generalization is known as *induction*. Such generalizations are then tested and evolve into laws if they withstand testing. Laws in turn can be related to other laws to form some theory. Science, on this view, is concerned primarily with the collection of data, forming generalizations from these data, with laws and theories later emerging through the testing process. Induction would seem to go with the tenets of logical positivism and certainly early positivists like Auguste Comte (1798– 1857) and Herbert Spencer (1820–1903) argued that the scientific method was induction. But Ernst Mach (1838–1916), whose views about science had such a strong impact on the logical positivists, was not concerned with laying down any specific method as long as the method used was empirical and had predictive power. Today, those of a positivist orientation, mainly logical empiricists, are more likely to support the hypotheticodeductive method.

In its broadest sense, induction is any process that proceeds from statements made about some things of a certain kind (e.g., a sample of customers in a market segment) to a conclusion or generalization about some or all the remaining things of that kind (all of the customers in that segment). In brief, any rationale of induction would need to *justify* such statements as "All observed $X$'s are $Y$'s, so all $X$'s are $Y$'s."

*Justificationism* is the doctrine which asserts that claims to knowledge must be based on demonstration that the knowledge is true. Induction and justificationism are related

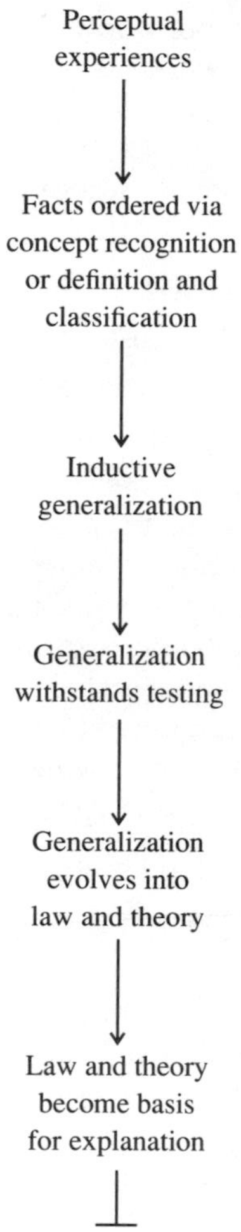

Perceptual
experiences

↓

Facts ordered via
concept recognition
or definition and
classification

↓

Inductive
generalization

↓

Generalization
withstands testing

↓

Generalization
evolves into
law and theory

↓

Law and theory
become basis
for explanation

⊥

FIGURE 12.1. The Induction Process

through the positivist doctrine of *inductivism,* which asserts that justifying knowledge claims rests ultimately on verifiable singular observations.

Those who accept induction as a procedure that can be rationally justified are called *inductivists.* The problem for the inductivist is to find a method that provides inductive proof, that is, to show how observational evidence can be used to validate laws of wide generality or at least to provide criteria that would certify "good" inductive inferences. With David Hume (1711–1776), it was the constant conjunctions signaling "causality," but inductivists now defend the validity of their inductive inferences on several shaky grounds.

Since universal laws cannot be absolutely verified or confirmed by any form of inductive logic, one rationale used to justify induction is simply the claim that it works. However, its having worked in one set of circumstances in the past is no guarantee of future success. A second rationale to justify induction cites the uniformity of nature. But even if nature is uniform, this does not imply that the particular uniformities being observed (e.g., in a market segment) will hold in the future. A final rationale relates to probability sampling theory, but sampling theory, which depends on induction, cannot justify induction.

Many sociologists, including Homans, recommend an inductive strategy for building sociological theory:

1. Observe how people behave in different groups.
2. Develop concepts and generalizations to describe such behavior.
3. Move on to other groups to confirm, modify, and augment earlier concepts and generalizations.

This procedure is misleading if it suggests that equally intelligent people will be "good" inductivists; it ignores the probability that those with a social science background will be guided in their observations by the sensitizing concepts they have learned. Thus a physicist and a sociologist, with differing theories and categories, are unlikely to perceive experience the same way. All observation is selective, and the more fruitful observations are likely to be made by those already knowledgeable in the area.

Zaltman and Bonoma (1979) recommend induction as a basis for theory building in marketing. They suggest moving from observing successful marketing practices to the building of sound theory by adopting a two-stage approach:

1. Observe the rules of thumb used by good marketing managers.
2. Deduce from these rules of thumb the model or set of propositions lying behind the rules.

Although a study of what managers do might reveal hypotheses and creative tactics, the procedure suggested is misleading if it gives the impression that identifying such rules is a simple matter of observation since all scientific observation is inevitably selective *and* theory-driven.

Foxall (1990) points out that behaviorism seeks inductive generalizations from "the intensive analysis of the behavior of single subjects" and argues that this is common also in qualitative marketing research (e.g., focus groups). While acknowledging that the hypotheticodeductive method may be inevitable in the physical sciences, he claims that in the study of human behavior it is usually trivial and unnecessary.

## Hypotheticodeductive Method

Critics of induction argue that science does not proceed from first assembling individual facts and then assuming these facts will in themselves suggest some theory. The only fact is that there are no pure facts since the assembled facts are *described* facts. Moreover, the facts that are considered relevant depend on the theories we hold. As Popper (1959) says, the simple command to observe cannot be followed since an indefinite number of things might be observed: observation is necessarily selective and science is a combination of inspiration and deduction called the *hypotheticodeductive method* (see Figure 12.2). Inspiration is needed to postulate some hypothesis or model, which in turn directs perception. Explanations do not emerge from vast collections of facts but from ideas incorporating concepts that provide a criterion of what to look for. Major advances in science

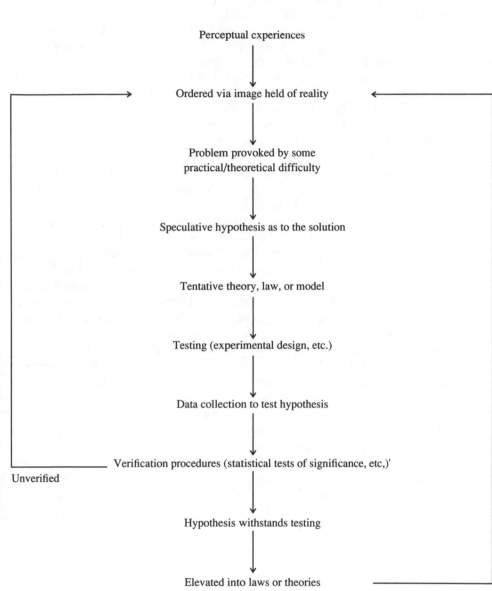

Perceptual experiences

↓

Ordered via image held of reality

↓

Problem provoked by some
practical/theoretical difficulty

↓

Speculative hypothesis as to the solution

↓

Tentative theory, law, or model

↓

Testing (experimental design, etc.)

↓

Data collection to test hypothesis

↓

Verification procedures (statistical tests of significance, etc,)'

Unverified

↓

Hypothesis withstands testing

↓

Elevated into laws or theories

Confirmation

↓

Become basis for explanation

FIGURE 12.2.  The Hypotheticodeductive Model

are occasioned by major changes in concepts. Indeed, a faulty conceptual baggage can hopelessly bias the selection and description of the facts.

Popper argues that all observation in scientific inquiry rests on theoretical assumptions so that scientific knowledge, contrary to logical positivism, does not start with sensory experience. Scientists follow the hypotheticodeductive method, whereby bold hypotheses are suggested, tested, accepted, rejected, or modified. Popper (1959) refers to the hypotheticodeductive philosophy as *deductivism* to distinguish it from inductivism.

Popper would claim that induction, as recommended by Zaltman and Bonoma for marketing, takes little or no account of how conceptual and theoretical presuppositions determine what "facts" are seen and how they are ordered. Theories are not just outcomes emanating from the laborious collection of facts. Thus Kuhn (1970) argues that scientists come to their research with a theory-loaded conceptual lens, without which certain phenomena would be overlooked so that scientists from different disciplines with different conceptual lenses are likely to see things differently. Theoretical presuppositions affect observation by blocking out perceptions that depend on concepts not embraced by the theoretical presuppositions.

The hypotheticodeductive method is associated with Popper's falsifiability principle in that scientists are said first to formulate a hypothesis and then seek to falsify it. The hypotheticodeductive method came to enjoy wide acceptance among social scientists because it legitimized the postulation of unobservable theoretical entities. In contrast, the inductive approach to theory building (Figure 12.1) seeks purely observational sciences made up of descriptive regularities. This is strange since even in the eighteenth century some of the most successful theories in physics and chemistry assumed unobservable entities. As Nagel (1961) argues, no interesting scientific hypothesis restricts itself to what can be directly observed but includes nonobservable constructs like the electron. Such transcendent hypotheses cannot be inferred from direct induction.

Whereas the inductivist views scientific progress as occurring through the steady accumulation of facts leading to theories becoming increasingly general in scope, this is not necessarily so with the hypotheticodeductive account. The hypotheticodeductive approach views science as progressing through successive formulations, modifications, and rejections of theories without any absolute assurance that scientific knowledge will necessarily be steady and cumulative.

The hypotheticodeductive method, which has wide acceptance among logical empiricists, is not strictly deductive, as the name suggests. The method does not lead to certainty since its success rests upon induction, a fact obscured by Popper's use of the word "deductivism" to describe the method. Thus critics argue that the hypotheticodeductive method does not circumvent the problem of induction and its justification. The basis for expecting unfalsified theories or hypotheses to remain unfalsified and falsified theories or hypotheses to be continually falsified regardless of their domain of application remains questionable. There is an inductive element in weighing the significance of each falsification or nonfalsification and we need some way of rationally defending why so many nonfalsifications in such circumstances lead us to accept the hypothesis. Usually, the criterion is conventionalist: we select what conventionally is acceptable.

## Retroduction/Abduction

Mowen (1979) argues that researchers can develop marketing theory through a process of *retroduction*. Charles Sanders Peirce (1839–1914) uses the term retroduction or abduction to refer to the observation of facts and the construction of theory to explain these facts. Peirce viewed retroduction (or abduction) as the process of moving from consequent to antecedent. It is a mode of reasoning that proceeds from the observation of an unexpected fact to a hypothesis that would explain the fact. Thus the marketer might be faced with the unexpected failure of a product launch and seek to explain that failure. Abduction or retroduction contrasts with induction in that induction merely generalizes from what is already known and does not provide us with any new explanatory hypothesis. For Peirce, abduction is the mode of reasoning underlying hypothesis formation, whereas induction merely classifies. Abduction—typified by medical diagnosis and detective novels like the Sherlock Holmes series—is illustrated in science by Kepler reaching his hypothesis about the elliptical path of Mars from the observed irregularities in the movement of Mars.

Hanson (1958), building on Peirce, argues that contrary to the inductivist position, a theory is not pieced together from observed facts; instead, the observed phenomena are fitted into systems. If the retroductive process seeks an explanation in terms of the historical events that gave rise to the facts observed, then the result is a genetic type of explanation. However, this need not be so since other types of explanation may be sought. Of more concern is whether retroduction uses the hypotheticodeductive method. This seems to be implicitly admitted by Mowen, who says that Peirce today would have probably followed Popper in labeling retroduction the process of theorizing by conjecture. However, retroduction is assumed to arise from observation of some surprising fact, whereas the origin of Popper's conjectural hypotheses remains unexplained.

Both induction and the hypotheticodeductive method assume knowledge must be empirically based. However, not all social scientists agree. There are still those of a rationalist orientation, including members of the Austrian school of economics, like Hayek (1952) and Von Mises (1949), who claim that reason alone can be used to judge the validity of economic theories since such theories are rooted in self-evident axioms. Since these axioms refer to individual behavior, Hayek and Von Mises subscribe to methodological individualism.

## Theory Development

When writers in social science speak of "theory," they often mean classifications, broad ideas, or hypotheses. In this sense we all have theories since we have no other choice, for theories in this sense provide the decision guidelines without which we would have mental overload in considering options. But this use of the term "theory" and the everyday use of the term to suggest some speculative hypothesis differ from its use in the philosophy of science. In traditional philosophy of science, a theory is a system of mutually supporting laws. Each law in the theory is supported by the evidence collected to test it and by its coherence with the theory's laws that have withstood testing. Under the coherence theory of truth, a hypothesis may be accepted if it fits into a theory and not just because it fits the facts. It can be argued that a scientist must be guided by a theory on the ground that we can interpret a "fact" only if we have a theory to guide us: facts rest on theory and not the other way round. On the other hand, the insistence that novel hypotheses be consistent with existing theory can be dysfunctional. An established theory is never one that is absolutely certain (proved) but one seemingly more probable than its rivals.

"Theorizing" is used to cover several distinct levels of explanation:

1. Factual description:
   Q. Why did Jane buy brand X?
   A. Jane always buys the cheapest brand.

2. Lawlike generalization:
   Q. Why did Jane, after purchasing brand X, start to compare her purchase with other brands?
   A. All consumers behave that way when the price is high.

3. Theory: Whereas a law (as above) simply subsumes the event to be explained under a general regularity, it is the theory as a whole that offers an explanation of why a particular law holds to the extent it does. Thus cognitive dissonance might at one time have been quoted to explain Jane's behavior in (2). Theory is viewed as achieving its explanatory power through interrelating some set of lawlike generalizations.

There are several received views of how best to go about theory building. As would be expected, one dispute relates to whether the basic procedure must be based on induction or the hypotheticodeductive method. In recent years some version of the hypotheticodeductive method has held sway. This is because few in social science would want to restrict theory to descriptive regularities eschewing all references to unobservables. Figure 12.2 shows the hypotheticodeductive approach to theory building as consisting of the following major stages:

1. The researcher's initial *image* or conceptualization of the domain of interest.
2. The identification of problems for research.
3. Speculation as to a solution.
4. Tentative model or formal representation of the scientist's image of the relevant reality. From such a model some set of hypotheses or *tentative* theory may be derived.
5. Preparations for testing the hypotheses or tentative theory. This involves defining terms, classifying, and operationalizing the model.
6. Testing hypotheses.

This list of stages cannot be considered sacrosanct. Research can be an iterative process, and stages can be skipped or collapsed in practice. However, the stages can be made conceptually distinct for the purpose of exposition.

## Domain Image

The first stage in the hypotheticodeductive method is to have some image or conceptualization of the domain of interest. Every researcher in marketing as elsewhere has a set of mental images about how the consumer "ticks." These mental representations may be based on theories already held, readings of the consumer behavior literature, or prior experience. In any case, such mental images embody presuppositions. Thus when Homans argued that adequate explanations of social phenomena could be given only by learning theory, this inevitably influenced how he viewed social phenomena and conducted research. Similarly, all researchers in buyer behavior will bring to the job some body of knowledge, some system of psychology, and some beliefs about preferable explanatory modes. These are their biases, which color everything they do and every decision they make. This is not to suggest, however, that these biases cannot be rationally defended—and some biases better than others.

The researcher's image is basic, for unless it is changed through further learning, all else flows from that overarching conceptualization of the domain. A major element of the domain image is how consumers or buyers are to be viewed, whether as simply responding to the push and pull of past impressed experiences and immediate stimuli or as agents who can act from habit alone but can also deliberate on the pros and cons of alternative actions.

## Problem Identification

All research has some practical or theoretical goals. The achievement of the goal constitutes the task at hand. Thus the behavioral researcher may have the task of explaining why people on the beach, when asked about the maximum price they would pay for a certain brand of beer, agreed that the maximum they would pay depended on whether the beer was to be purchased at the fancy hotel restaurant or at the equally nearby deli. Why would people be prepared to pay more at the fancy restaurant? The researcher has an image of the buyer as a free agent acting in accordance with his or her beliefs and wants. The researcher might say the problem lies with how consumers evaluate the two different outlets. Identifying the problem thus means choosing the correct category of solution. Naturally, problems tend to get categorized within the researcher's field of competence. For example, one can imagine a firm having difficulty in delivering to time and specification and consulting the "experts." The OR specialist would be biased toward defining the problem as one of inventory control; the systems and procedures specialist as the order-handling system; the personnel specialist as a recruitment and training problem; the organizational behavior expert as a problem of motivational climate; finally, the ergonomist might speak of the problem as being a man–machine compatibility problem.

## Speculative Hypothesis as to a Solution

Based on the researcher's domain image and the identification of the problem, speculation arises as to how to solve the problem. What hypothesis does the researcher have about how evaluations come about? The researcher might hypothesize about consumer expectations and what might be considered a reasonable, just, equitable price given the different overheads and pretensions of the different outlets. What can be said is that the process by which fruitful speculations (hypotheses) are generated has been neglected by philosophers, although there are exceptions (e.g., Hanson, 1958). As Putnam (1981) says, philosophers talked as if hypotheses just came from the sky while methods for testing them were highly developed, rigid, and predetermined. He argues that there are in fact maxims for discovery, like having extensive experience in the domain of interest, which allows "thought experiments" based on the experience. More generally, hypotheses are often suggested by analogies between something understood and whatever it is that seems puzzling.

## Tentative Model

### MODELS

Initial speculations are likely to be somewhat vague, so an attempt is made to model what the speculations suggest. When a study of the *structure* of system $X$ is useful for the understanding of system $Y$, then $X$ is a model of $Y$. Where the pattern of relationships among the elements $A$, $B$, $C$ in system $X$ is identical (has an exact correspondence) to elements $R$, $T$, $U$ in system $Y$, then systems $X$ and $Y$ are isomorphs of each other. However, in marketing the term "model" is used much more loosely. It is used to mean *any* representation of the properties of the larger system (Montgomery and Urban, 1969). This loose use of the word model has some justification as a reminder that every person has a set of beliefs about how the world works that acts as a filter in dealing with problems.

Models describe patterns into which events, items, or situations can be fitted. They are not necessarily constructed from induction but postulated. This relates to the question of whether science is discovered or invented. Is science like finding the bits and pieces of a jigsaw puzzle or do scientists impose some order on what they take to be out there? The answer is that science is not simply discovery. Yet neither is it pure speculation. It is more like invention: inspired and constrained by our concepts and our perceptions of the relevant events and actions.

In Chapter 4 we examined a number of process models that sought to model the process of attitude change and also to provide an understanding of the "mechanisms" that move along the process. *Stochastic* models involve processes whose outcomes are assumed to be governed by probabilistic mechanisms in contrast to deterministic models. In mathematical models such processes are typically expressed using differential, or difference, equations. *Structural* models, on the other hand, represent the structure of, say, social relations using techniques like graph theory, matrix algebra, and topology theory; they are typically deterministic in format if not in practice.

The key to any model building is identifying appropriate concepts (e.g., expectations). A concept is defined by abstracting common features of objects or situations and so can be as mundane as "whiteness" or as contrived as "product life cycle," "attitude," "involvement," "variety seeking," and so on. The word "construct" is often substituted for the term "concept" when the concept is part of a scientific vocabulary. The concepts themselves, like the model they compose, may be idealizations. However, the explanatory usefulness of such ideal types (e.g., pure competition) may depend not on their being true to reality but on suggesting what would be if certain conditions prevailed.

In model building we try to explicate the concepts involved in a way that removes ambiguity and vagueness. Typically, concepts are measured to become variables and formed into propositions with the final model showing how the propositions or hypotheses themselves are interrelated; examples include

Concepts like brand loyalty

Variables like degree of brand loyalty

Variables into propositions; for instance, brand loyalty is a function of . . .

Propositions interrelated to form a model of brand loyalty

Pragmatists and instrumentalists typically draw on models already developed, like mathematical models such as the Markov chain and the random walk. They may seek *robust* models—models that predict consequences in a wide range of conditions—but such robustness may be at the expense of precision in prediction. Many models in marketing are simply "boxology," defined as "the construction and ostentatious display of meaningless flow charts as a substitute for thought."

Textbooks (see Ackoff, 1968) typically advise checking a model to ensure

1.  all the concepts or variables are relevant to the problem;
2.  no relevant concepts or variables have been omitted;

3. the proposed measures of the concepts are adequate;
4. the type of relationships among the variables makes sense; and
5. the model's assumptions are reasonable.

These guidelines are more suited to microlevel models than to those at the macrolevel such as ASSESSOR (Silk and Urban, 1978), designed to forecast sales prior to test marketing, and TRACKER (Blattberg and Golanty, 1978) and NEWS (Pringle, Wilson, and Brody, 1982), which were developed to forecast sales from test market data. These models have an instrumentalist rather than an explanatory orientation. Such models are commonly devised by statisticians and operations research staff in industry without enlightenment from courses in marketing. When evaluated on criteria such as Ackoff's they can be shown to be highly deficient (Narasimhan and Sen, 1983). Perhaps, however, they should be judged solely on their success in prediction, as with all other instrumentalist models.

A constant problem in model building lies in determining the right degree of complexity: models that are very simple may be too remote from reality, whereas complex models are difficult to work with and comprehend. In any case, no model perfectly reflects the structure of the problem, so solutions derived from models will only approximate the optimal solution. However, mathematical models can simplify multitudes of relationships that would otherwise be too complex to handle. Nonetheless, demonstrating the formal possibility of mathematical modeling does not in itself demonstrate its practical feasibility in the individual case. Like all rules, models provide guidance but are also like blinders on a horse—focusing in one direction but sometimes promoting tunnel vision. The concepts create awareness of what is being conceptualized but they also ensure we see only what the concepts alert us to see.

Because rationality is best exhibited by a preparedness to identify and react to novel situations with an open mind, many marketing managers tend to be uncomfortable with formal models reflecting a fixed viewpoint. This is why formal marketing models are best promoted as decision support systems (DSSs) rather than solutions and judged on the basis of their relevance, consistency, and simplicity. Most practical problems have unique aspects, and it is easy for those who have all the facts on that uniqueness to carry the day (if they have a mind to do so) against whatever is suggested by the model. There are other problems in managerial acceptance in that (1) many mathematical models have overly naive assumptions; (2) pseudoconstants that cannot be checked by independent and impersonal operations may be introduced in the equations, and (3) arbitrary coefficients may be plugged into equations to fit a formula to some series of numbers with no warrant for assuming such coefficients will apply to the next stage in the series.

Although model building is accepted by positivists, it is subject to scrutiny in case it degenerates into pure rationalism. Handy and Harwood (1973) argue that rationalism is still the dominant orientation among formal model builders, giving rise to models like "game theory" and "utility theory," which confuse warranted assertions about the particular model with warranted assertions about some aspect of human behavior. They take model builders to task for not investigating the presumed connections between the model and observed behavior with any degree of thoroughness: typically it is the *internal* aspects of the model that are examined rather than matching the model to actual behavior. Handy and Harwood claim that *internal tests* are seldom adequate since assumptions often seem unchallengeable, reasoning absolutely sound, and conclusions inescapable, when in instance after instance the assumptions are later shown to be unfounded, the facts proved wrong, and errors in reasoning detected. They take econometricians to task for often "obtaining plausible numbers to provide ceremonial adequacy for a theory." A little cleverness "will get you almost any result you want," and that is why "few econometricians have ever been forced by the facts to abandon any firmly held belief." The Handy and Harwood claims receive support from many studies. Thus Lockhart (1979) demonstrates and explains the inadequacy or inappropriateness of formal, rational, economic, and psychological models for the study of severe international conflicts.

## THEORY

Even at this early stage a model might be elaborated into a tentative theory. Although the word "theory," as suggested earlier, is often used as a synonym for any speculative hypothesis, in the philosophy of science a theory has always been regarded as something more substantial.

The logical empiricist presents a systematic view of theory, laws/hypotheses, and models. Hypotheses and laws are always synthetic statements whereas the statements that relate them, being merely deductive inferences, are analytic. Theories are tested by testing the implied models, thus always embrace models. A model's focus is on the structural relationships among the variables; the theory's focus is on the theorems themselves. The laws or hypotheses in the theory are interrelated, so evidence for the truth of one law provides evidence for the support of the other. Whereas a law simply subsumes the event to be explained under a general regularity, it is the theory as a whole that offers an explanation of why a particular law holds to the extent it does. A hypothesis may be concerned with some unique event, but theories and laws always seek to explain kinds of events. The aim of science is to find laws and theories that are unrestricted in application over space and time. But no such laws or theories have been discovered in social science or in marketing.

Nagel (1961) views a theory as having three components:

1. An abstract calculus or logical skeleton of the system.

2. A set of rules of correspondence that assigns an empirical content to the abstract calculus by relating it to the concrete materials of observation and experiment.

3. A model or interpretation for the abstract calculus which supplies flesh for the skeleton structure in terms of visualizable materials.

Campbell (1920) has a more elaborate breakdown of what constitutes a theory:

1. A vocabulary of terms:
   a. Logical terms like "and" and "or."
   b. Extralogical terms consisting of
      - primitive terms, which are those terms or basic concepts that remain undefined in the theory.
      - defined terms, which may or may not be formed from the primitive terms.

2. Hypotheses embodying the vocabulary of logical and extralogical terms:
   a. Primitive sentences which are the axioms of the theory. *These are generalizations that do the explaining.*
   b. Derivative sentences formed from the axioms or primitive sentences. These derivative sentences are termed *theorems.*
   c. A logical syntax or set of formation rules to be used to derive the theorems from the axioms.
   *The primitive terms, axioms and formation rules make up what is termed the calculus of the theory.*

3. Models, in which the various hypotheses are brought together and the structural implications of these hypotheses are expressed.

4. A dictionary setting out the correspondence rules or operational definitions relating the abstractions of the theory or model to events or items in the real world.

Campbell's "axiomatic theory," as this system is called, received a great deal of support, although even theories in the natural sciences are not generally formulated axiomatically. Perhaps much of microeconomic theory is put forward as essentially axiomatic, and there appears to be a scattering of axiomatic theories in physics, chemistry, and biology. In social science there have been attempts at axiomatic theory (e.g., exchange theory) but in marketing there is no reported case of any researcher spelling out a theory in the form and detail recommended by Campbell. There is a great gap in all the social sciences between what is said to constitute a theory and what is actually produced. But the absence of theory is less of a loss for the logical positivist than it is for some other empiricists. This is because, for the Vienna Circle positivist, theory has no role beyond systematizing the findings of observation. However, for those empiricists who pin their faith in the hypotheticodeductive method the loss is greater. Under the hypotheticodeductive method, theory generates additional hypotheses for testing by further exploiting the theory's basic concepts, which are never fully captured in operational definitions.

In marketing the focus is on model building and not on explicating any abstract background theory, although this does not mean such a background is not being assumed. The term "theory" in marketing covers any set of factors that orients the reader to what might be relevant to a problem. Some writers even argue that buying behavior is created anew with changing circumstances so that orienting or sensitizing models are all that can be demanded. As Humphrey (1983) says, there is doubt whether "the mountain of human complexity can be turned into a molehill of scientific laws."

## Preparations for Testing

MEANING

Until the terms (concepts, etc.) of a theory, model, or hypothesis are defined, the hypothesis or theory cannot be tested. But terms cannot be satisfactorily defined until their meaning in the language is explored. It is this recognition that meaning needs to precede verification that leads many researchers to reject the logical positivists' verification principle that the meaning (significance or meaningfulness) of a statement is its method of verification.

In scientific research we cannot explicate the meaning of terms merely by looking up synonyms in a dictionary. Such an approach to meaning does not provide the understanding and precision needed. We start by thinking about the "sense meaning" (intension, connotation) of the word and its "referent" (denotation, extension).

The sense meaning of a word is the sense (connoted) inside one's head, that is, the thought it evokes. Every word evokes some sense meaning, which is likely to be forgotten when brand managers choose computer-devised brand names in the hope of avoiding all associations. The sense meaning of some words seems very personal, so referents differ from one person to another. We wish words to have the same shared referents. The "referent" of a word is that to which it refers. The same referent may have several sense meanings. Thus "Ivory soap" and "the only soap that floats on water" have the same referent but somewhat different sense meanings. Advertisers are interested in promoting the more persuasive of the sense meanings. When terms, however, have sense meaning but no referent (e.g., angel), debate lacks concrete examples, thus dispute about meaning can go on indefinitely. This is why the theoretical meaning of terms and propositions should combine both sense meaning and referent.

Concepts in marketing tend *not* to have fixed meanings (consider words like "loyalty," "habit," "motive") since meanings can differ with theoretical orientation (e.g., a "motive" to a behaviorist versus "motive" to a psychoanalytic psychologist) and tend to evolve with experience. Nonetheless, for any piece of research, meanings of terms need to be explicated with justification given for any change from those meanings already established. Without some intuitive understanding of the terms in a hypothesis, there would have been no hypothesis in the first place. But intuitive understanding is not enough. There is a need to explicate the meaning of the terms to serve the objectives of the research.

When it comes to the meaning of words, concepts, and statements, logical positivists are "semantic empiricists" in claiming that meaning in the sense of significance or meaningfulness is, like knowledge generally, dependent on experience. For the logical positivist the meaning of a term is its concrete referent, that is, what it stands for in observational terms. This is an approach to meaning known as the *referential viewpoint*. But two terms can have the same reference yet have differences in sense meaning. Consider the referents of the terms "brand-loyal buyer" and "habitual buyer." Both terms could be said to refer to purchasing the same brand. However, most explications of the term "brand loyalty" would distinguish it from mere habitual buying; without this distinction it would be less misleading to consistently use the term "habitual buying."

The referential viewpoint can be equated with the logical positivist's claim that the meaning or meaningfulness of a word or statement is its method of verification. It finds expression in operational philosophy ("IQ is whatever IQ tests measure"). To the question, for example, "What is emotion?," the operational philosopher would seek to identify the shared experiences to which people refer when they use the word "emotion." Sense meaning here, if it comes at all, follows as a byproduct. Yet the referential viewpoint captures several truths. The first is that scholars come to agree on the meaning of theoretical terms only when the theory in which the terms are embedded is linked to methods that tie the abstract terms to empirical referents, as the concept of learning in operant conditioning is tied to the deprivation of food. As Kagan (1989) makes clear, the meaning of terms, statements, and concepts in social science is *in part always dependent* on the procedures by which they are operationally defined. He takes to task Thomas (1979), who claims that the meaning of a theoretical term is determined *only* by the theoretical network of which it is a part.

In marketing it is often difficult to contest many statements because of uncertainty over referential meaning; consider "Brand image makes the difference between market success and market failure" or "The more successful firms long ago adopted customer orientation." Without concrete referents to act as standards, words, too, like light/heavy, comfortable/uncomfortable make sense but depend completely on the audience's frame of reference to interpret concretely.

We might take specifically a PIMS statement that "relative market share and quality are partial substitutes for each other as far as determining return on investment is concerned." The "quality" incorporates the sense meaning that the product is positively evaluated, but the descriptive referents that lie behind the positive evaluation are crucial to testing the proposition. Experts and buyers can differ widely among themselves as to what constitutes quality. As Zeithaml (1988) demonstrates, although there is a shared sense meaning of the term product quality as connoting a product's overall excellence or superiority, referential properties signal that quality may be not only product-specific but individual-specific. In any case, she points out that because the concept of quality has never been adequately explicated, it tends not to be distinguished from concepts like "value," "goodness," "luxury," and overall attitude.

Many philosophers claim that questions about sense meaning are different from questions about which thing is meant (referent) in that questions about sense meaning boil down to questions about the use of a word in general. The meaning of a word on this basis is a function of the way in which the word is used by speakers of the language. Words have the meaning they do only because of what people do when they use the words. Thus departure from that usage can lead to failures in communication.

Ordinary language philosophy sees a close connection between meaning and use. The use of a word or expression within a particular context or language "game" is governed by rule or convention. As Wittgenstein argues, to explain the meaning of a word is to elucidate the rules for its use. To Wittgenstein the slogan "the meaning of a word or expression is its use" meant simply that the meaning of a word or expression is the role it plays in the corresponding action. Thus to grasp the meaning of the word "slab" in building is to see how it is used in a certain *language game* of receiving and giving orders on a building site. This view of meaning is in line with that of the instrumentalist John Dewey, who similarly claimed that there was no more to the meaning of a word or expression than the overt use made of the expression.

This *usage theory of meaning* is essentially an attack on the view that meanings are already there before we choose words to designate them. It contrasts, too, with viewing words as pictures of some aspect of reality. Instead it views words as merely tools. "Meaning in use" is a functional approach to the interpretation of concepts. On this basis, a word would have meaning only if it did indeed have a use and its use could be taught.

Many empiricists particularly object to this view of *meaning as use* since it suggests the same term or expression in a theory need not have one stable meaning. This has implications for falsifying and replicating studies. Whereas the logical positivist's "meaning is the method of verification" suggests a unitary account of meaning, "meaning as use" rejects the very possibility of a uniform account. The belief in a stable meaning leads to a reluctance to face up to new evidence that challenges existing meanings. On the other hand, many philosophers argue that theoretical terms need only retain some core meaning, being allowed a specific interpretation for each application providing it coheres with that core meaning. For example, the concept of "involvement" would have to be reinterpreted but not redefined to apply to organizational buying as opposed to its consumer application. Sameness of "meaning as use" in different contexts or applications suggests not a constancy of reference but a family resemblance in the pattern of its references. Such a dispersion of references, it is argued, can still be consistent with a stable core meaning. More difficult is when the various referents cannot be made to cohere with one core meaning. This might be so in the case of the expression "*A* prefers brand *B*." This expression could mean:

*A* likes *B* best.

*A* gets more satisfaction out of *B*.

*A* believes *B* is the most efficient and socially appropriate way of meeting the goals he has in mind.

*A* believes it would be more correct to choose *B*.

*A* actually chooses *B*.

It is "meaning as use" that has come to dominate Winch's (1958) view of interpretive social science. Thus Winch states: "To give an account of the meaning of a word is to describe how it is used; and to describe how it is used is to describe the social intercourse into which it enters" (p. 123).

When Wittgenstein argued "Don't look for the meaning, look for the use," it signaled the decline of older philosophical views. Wittgenstein viewed the "meaning" of a word or expression with its use, function, or purpose in the language. Words/concepts are adopted to serve some function and when our forms of life change so do concepts change in meaning *or* become extinct. Hence to understand meaning as "meaning in use" requires that we investigate the situation and occasion in which the word or expression occurs, that is, investigate how the word or expression is being used in the particular context or language game. Wittgenstein spoke of language games as consisting of the language itself and the action into which it is woven.

The most serious criticism of "meaning as use" is the claim that it may not be possible to discover the use to which a word is being put without first knowing its meaning. As Gellner says, meaning cannot always be easily inferred from use in some context; we often need to know what a word connotes before we can fully understand its use: "The meaning of the term 'of one's own free will' is not defined in terms of smiling bridegrooms, but on the contrary the behavior of smiling bridegrooms is interpreted in such a way as to make those terms applicable. The interpretation may be mistaken" (1968, p. 37).

The final view of meaning is *response meaning,* which defines meaning in terms of effects on behavior (Morris, 1964). We do not understand the meaning of a nation's flag by identifying it but by noticing how people act and react to it in different circumstances. Effects on the individual can be in terms of beliefs, emotions, or overt behavior.

A common objection to this view is the practical problem of gauging the variety of possible effects. Osgood's "semantic differential" is meant to get around the problem in that the semantic differential is designed to capture the responses evoked by the word or expression (see Osgood, Suci, and Tannenbaum, 1957). But the debate lies in determining the extent to which response meanings are likely to be idiosyncratic. Yet if meanings were not to some extent universal, there would be little point in advertisers carefully choosing their words and symbols. There are general gut reactions to the word "cheap" versus "inexpensive," "payment" versus "investment," "senior citizen" versus "old-age pensioner," "homely" versus "plain," and so on. Gut reactions to words as symbols were termed by the semanticist Alfred Korzybski (1879–1950) "identification reactions," since reaction occurs on identification without making what may be necessary distinctions. Such identification reactions are regarded by semanticists as confusing the symbol with reality, which in turn can lead to racial stereotyping, prejudice, or other unanticipated results. For semanticists meaning is whatever something symbolizes, with human behavior as a consequence being "conditioned, shaped and mediated by symbols" (Hayakawa, 1950).

Under the response view of meaning, meanings would differ with context while differences in meaning would correspond to differences in the effects on the hearer. A corollary is that all concepts that evoke the same effects are equivalent and that concepts not related to any known effects have no meaning!

In explicating the meaning of terms and phrases, the researcher generally needs to provide both sense meaning and referent. In other words, in explicating the meaning of X, we list those things the word X stands for and its qualities, functions, and characteristics, thus developing a criterion of what it is to be an $X$. The next step is to convert that meaning into a definition precise enough for research purposes, since looseness of terms leads to vagueness in the hypotheses that incorporates them.

## DEFINITION

To define a word is to follow some procedure for specifying meaning to facilitate understanding, data collection, classification, and hypothesis testing. As Quine (1987) says, to define is in effect to explain how to get along without the term being defined. But many definitions are really theoretical assertions since acceptance of the definition can be fundamental to accepting an argument. Thus if I accept alcoholism as a disease, I will go along with those who believe the Veterans Administration or insurance companies should support alcoholics as they would support those incapacitated by lung cancer. Similarly, there are different implications arising from viewing a "motive" as something that activates behavior and gives it direction as distinct from viewing a motive as simply the reasons a person has to justify his actions. Because different definitions suit different purposes, it is inevitable that writers will adopt slightly different definitions of the same term. What marketing writers need to do is demonstrate which definition(s) would suit marketing's purpose best. Thus in defining the term "market," there is at least a choice between viewing a market as a network of dealings (the market in . . . ) or market as function(s) sought by those composing the market (the market for . . . ). The "market for" is generally chosen as best for identifying competition and breaking down a market into segments. Throughout this book we have seen the lack of agreement on definitions on even basic concepts like "cause" and "scientific explanation" because various definitions have theoretical implications.

There are a number of different types of definition not all of which enter into research. Among those considered here are the analytic, operational, ostensive, contextual, and synonymous definition.

*Analytic Definition.* The traditional definition is the analytic definition, which states the class or category to which the term belongs and differentiates the term from other members of the class, for example, "man is a rational animal." Within any theory analytic definitions are common. Analytic definitions should be reversible. Thus the analytic definition of learning as "behavior modification resulting from experience" is weak since it would include madness as a species of learning.

By assuming things have essences, analytic definitions elevate definition to being a doctrine of essences. But most things do not have essences or, at least, there is controversy over wherein the essence lies. Thus there are no differentiae for distinguishing qualities like "red" within the class "color." Moreover, the salient features of words like "attitude" often change as theoretical conceptions change. The analytic definition by assuming essential qualities are known and agreed does not admit of provisional definition. This brings with it the danger of premature closure on what is the essence of the thing to be defined. There is generally no once-and-for-all answer to the question of whether there is an essential essence that defines the nature of whatever it is that is being defined. Essential features, or essences, are often matters of dispute as different consequences follow from accepting different analytic definitions. Thus not everyone follows Osgood in defining an attitude as simply an expression of taste. Analytic definitions are often a means for changing perceptions, valuations, and orientations while masquerading as factual and objective. As pointed out earlier, definitions—particularly analytic definitions—may in reality be merely asserting a theoretical position or a recommendation or making an exhortation (e.g., "marketing is the art of creating and maintaining customers").

In spite of these limitations, analytic definitions are the most frequently quoted in textbooks. But even well-known writers can err in their use. For example, take the following definition of strategy: "Strategy is a pattern in a stream of decisions" (Mintzberg, 1978). The definition distinguishes strategy from other components in a stream of decisions by saying strategy follows a pattern. The fact is, of course, everything has a pattern, even if it is not one we recognize. This definition also implies that *any* pattern in a stream of decisions is a strategy. Since any decision can be broken down into a stream of decisions that contains patterns, this definition does not distinguish strategy from decision-making generally.

The definition would not be particularly helpful to anyone who believes there is a distinction between strategy and tactics. It also fails to capture the traditional use of the word "strategy" in terms of its being a broad conception of how resources are deployed to overcome resistance to the attainment of objectives. Traditional uses are important, for whenever we define a word or expression that departs from a traditional use within that particular language game, we are likely to sooner or later fall back on the more traditional meaning and so confuse the meaning of the term. Any move away from the traditional use of a word (as opposed to just tightening the definition to focus on core meaning) needs justifying, perhaps on the ground that the stipulated definition provides new insight that changes our conceptualization of the term.

*Operational Definition.*    Unless a theory or hypothesis is given some interpretation in observational terms, its usefulness is questionable. But how can we tell what items in the real world are represented by the terms $X$ and $Y$ in the theorems or abstract model? The primitives of the theory are linked to the real world by a set of interpretive sentences. This job of anchoring the empirical meaning of abstract terms was the purpose of Campbell's dictionary. But a host of terms have come to be used for the interpretive sentences. Perhaps the most favored term is "operational definition."

The physicist Bridgman (1927) showed how the development of physics had been stymied by the practice of defining concepts in terms of their properties (essences) and that it was only after Einstein abandoned property (analytic) definitions that he made his crucial discoveries. Under the operational definition, all concepts are defined in terms of observations and procedures. An *operational definition* lists the operations to be carried out and the observations to be made, the performance of which will define the term. The idea was to get agreement by using criteria based on observation. When Bridgman argued that a scientific concept can be defined only in terms of the operations that are necessary to measure it, he was claiming that definitions of concepts should be *measured* operational definitions.

The operational definition implies that for every theoretical term there corresponds some set of operations involved in using the term. Further, to know these operations is to grasp the concept, that is, not to know the operations is equivalent to not knowing the scientific meaning of the term. But the question arises, Can someone really grasp a concept this way without some sense meaning? This definition presents a problem in identifying the operations whenever performance of the operations is in some way different. After all, the operational definition covers all those operations not specifically excluded by the definition. Yet it is the operational definitions or operational measures that are important when it comes to testing hypotheses, that is, it is the referential meaning captured in some measurement rather than sense meaning that is tested. Sense meaning is being tested only to the extent that the operational definition reflects it. Thus when Ajzen and Fishbein (1980) define "intention to act" in terms of attitude toward taking the action, perceptions of relevant group norms, and motivation to comply with these norms, it is the measures of "attitude," "perceptions," and "motivation to comply" that are key since poor measures ensure poor testing. Ensuring that a particular measure does reflect the sense meaning intended is what we mean by "construct validity," but tests designed to check this are never any substitute for good judgment.

Kagan (1989) argues that the sense meaning of theoretical terms in practice is always partly derived from the operational definition/measure. MacCorquodale and Meehl (1948) distinguished between the two in their distinction between "intervening variables," which are the referents, operationally defined and measured, and the "hypothetical constructs," which are the abstractions representing sense meaning. Although the authors promoted the use of intervening variables, they acknowledged that on occasion the hypothetical constructs alone may have to assume the burden of explaining findings. This has frequently been necessary in cognitive psychology where it has not proved possible to develop intervening variables or operational measures for the various mental representations (hypothetical constructs) assumed. The following terms are used as rough synonyms for "hypothetical construct":

1. Concept of postulation. Northrop (1959) distinguishes between a "concept of postulation" and a "concept of intuition." The concept of intuition is the immediately apprehended fact. Thus blue as a color is the concept of intuition, whereas blue as a number on a wavelength is the concept of postulation.

2. Genotypic level of description. Coombs (1966) distinguishes between the "genotypic level of description" and the "phenotypic level of description." The phenotypic level is the behavior that is actually observed, whereas the genotypic level is what is inferred to exist lying behind the behavior observed.

There can be many operational measures of the same construct and these measures may not just reflect different aspects of the underlying theoretical construct but may represent different conceptualizations of the construct. Thus the Fishbein operational measure of attitude represents a different conceptualization of attitude than that reflected in the Likert scale or the semantic differential. Any change in an operational measure can change the researcher's conceptualization (sense meaning) of the theoretical term. This is important since research in marketing may not be sufficiently alert to this possibility when changes are made in operational measures. Unless sense meaning is clearly understood, there is a danger of the various operational measures not capturing the key defining features of the hypothetical construct; that is, construct validity can be questioned. The concept of involvement is a case in point. Krugman (1965) never fully explicated the concept. In fact, the concept would seem to be equivalent to the sociological concept of "meaning" discussed in Chapter 8. Thus when we say $X$ has a good deal of meaning for $Y$, we are saying that $Y$ believes that $X$ has high significance for her wants. This seems the same as saying that $Y$ has high involvement with $X$. We might also point out that the confusion of attitude measures with measures of affect stems from a poor conceptualization of "affect."

In marketing it is more typical to measure first than to initially reflect on sense meaning. Thus we may be quite happy with operationally measuring "loyalty" as "buying the same liked brand five times in succession," which certainly does not capture the most key feature of loyalty, namely, sticking to someone or something through "thick and thin." Not surprisingly, Jacoby and Chestnut (1978) found 53 different operational measures in over 200 studies of the concept of brand loyalty—involving many different conceptualizations of the term. Of course, different operational measures may reflect different views about sense meaning. When different subbranches of social science use different operational measures, this frequently reflects different hypothetical constructs. Thus the Thematic Apperception Test (TAT) for measuring motivation may not be highly correlated to measures of motivation based on speed and persistence of response. Similarly, measures of a respondent's fear using self-reports do not seem to coincide with biological measures. Also, operational measures of hypothetical constructs like attitude change through time as new views of its defining features arise. This means that historical and interdisciplinary comparisons of studies involving the "same" theoretical terms can be hazardous at best. In any case, new procedures for obtaining operational measures can provide fresh insight leading to revised meanings.

Some measures are only possible indicators of what we are trying to measure. Thus audience measurement simply measures exposure to the vehicle, not exposure to the advertising itself within the vehicle. Different operational measures in marketing can serve different purposes, although sometimes it is not too clear what purpose is being served beyond adding to confusion and a lack of interstudy comparability. This seems to be the position of studies involving the concept of quality. The PIMS measure of quality is simply management's own view of customer perceptions. When such a measure is used it is difficult to take seriously conclusions about, say, the positive impact of quality on price—even though some researchers expect us to do so (see Jacobson and Aaker, 1987). A number of recent studies (Curry and Reisz, 1988; Lichtenstein and Burton, 1989) have taken the quality ranking of *Consumer Reports* as quality measures. The attributes forming the basis of such a ranking, however, may not capture all of what the consumer would include in defining a quality product within the product class. Rao and Monroe (1989), using the consumer's perceptions of quality as a measure, showed that for the consumer products in their sample the relationship between price and perceived quality was positive. Zeithaml (1988), on the other hand, claims a general price–perceived quality relationship does not exist. More correctly, she regards the proposition as untestable (given the problem of collecting a random sample of all products and buyers) while more usefully pointing out that price as an indicator of quality depends on individual factors, information available, and product category. The factors to consider include

1. availability of other clues to quality,
2. price variation within a class of products,
3. product quality variation within a category of products,
4. level of price awareness among consumers, and
5. consumers' ability to detect quality variation in a group of products.

Self-reports (questionnaires or interviews) are typically used in marketing to get operational measures of attitudes, moods, motivation, beliefs, and wants and personality factors like self-esteem. They are used because states like "mood" cannot be unambiguously recognized and assessed by direct observation. There is, though, a need for many measures. It is unsound to use just one measure and in the physical sciences multidimensional measures predominate. Thus measuring "arousal" by the single measure of galvanic skin response and "attention-processing effort" by pupil dilation should be supplemented by other methods, just as there should be several measures of attitude.

Self-reports are important in marketing when we are concerned with the subjective (phenomenological) point of view, though such self-reports cannot always be expected to coincide with observational measures (e.g., expressed fear and biological measures of fear). In designing the questionnaires, marketers typically take variables to be continuous, so that responses can be assigned along some continuum. This ignores the fact that extreme values (e.g., on an attitude scale) may generate states involving emotions not captured by the measure. There is the additional problem in structured questionnaires of forcing respondents into ticking some category when it may amount to no more than mindless choice. In such cases the tabulated results may reflect nothing more than the method of elicitation.

Other terms used as synonyms for operational definitions are operational measures, correspondence rules, bridge rules, coordinating definitions, text/dictionary, epistemic correlations, semantical rules, and rules of interpretation. These definitions never capture the full meaning of a hypothetical construct in all possible applications. If they did, the theoretical terms could be dispensed with altogether as the terms would no longer function in explanations.

The development of operational definitions turns theoretical hypotheses into *experimental* ones. Such experimental hypotheses are immediately intelligible independently of the theory itself. But theoretical terms strictly speaking are never linked directly with reality itself but to empirically meaningful words, which in turn are connected to reality. Furthermore, where a concept has several dimensions each dimension may have to be given meaning by a separate operational definition. Thus the different individual measures may be predictively weak, and all the various measures may not necessarily pull in the same direction.

Because theoretical concepts can be articulated with a high degree of precision beyond that which can be captured in observational terms, concepts can be defined operationally in many different ways without capturing the whole meaning of the theoretical concept. Hence theoretical terms have "surplus meaning." If theoretical terms could be reduced to observation, they would be dispensable and their potential explanatory scope and power would be reduced to mere description. Except to the positivist, operational definitions are regarded as only *partial* interpretations of the theoretical terms.

A hypothesis that is not operationalized is like a map with no key. All terms in a proposed theory, model, or hypothesis, though, need not be operationalized (not all theoretical terms can be), but enough must be so that a variety of consequences of the hypotheses can be tested. For social scientists, the theory as a whole must stand up to testing—not every single constituent of the theory (several terms in Keynes's General Theory still remain without operational definition). This is because not all the terms, concepts, or constructs in a theory are abstractions of sense experience. Some concepts cannot be instantiated in observations. Yet such concepts may be legitimately posited on the ground that any adequate explanation of observed phenomena would need to assume their existence. As Nagel says:

> [In] disciplines like psychology . . . a proposed explanation of phenomena is to be rejected as meaningless if it contains terms for which operational definitions are not provided. These are, however, unduly severe requirements for scientific constructions. . . . Indeed, the explanatory power of theories is in general directly proportional to the remoteness of their key concepts from things capable of direct observation. What is essential, however, is that at some point in the deductive elaboration of a theory, suitable links be established between some of its concepts and experimentally identifiable properties of macroscopic objects. (1979, p. 17)

One approach to defining a theoretical (hypothetical) construct operationally is to think of the empirical consequences or implications of that construct and deduce from these consequences operational definitions. Thus if customer loyalty exists as described earlier in this book, it would suggest loyal customers would typically personify in affectionate terms the brand to which they are loyal and would be less inclined to switch brands in response to a lower price offer by a competitor.

Bagozzi (1984) in marketing uses the term "correspondence rules" as the overall label for ways of giving empirical meaning to theoretical terms. He distinguishes three models of correspondence rules. The first is the operational definition, which is synonymous with some set of operations. He argues that different operational definitions imply different theories. This was certainly what Bridgman believed. But as Kagan (1989) says, if different methods of operational measurement refer to the same defining features of a term (because, say, they are linked to the same mediating processes), the meaning of the theoretical terms and hence the corresponding theories remain unchanged. Bagozzi's claim though echoes Kuhn (1977), who argues that when operational definitions or correspondence rules differ as between different investigations such differences may constitute reconstructions of slightly different theories. Although it is true that the various operational measures of a construct can be so different as to suggest different theoretical meanings, different measures can be consistent. (Kuhn himself sees no role for correspondence rules in the physical sciences. He argues that correspondence rules are not explicated in science texts but their role is taken over by the *exemplars,* or standard examples of concrete problems, together with their solutions. These exemplars inform the student of what is empirically meant by such theoretical terms as force or electron. He argues that correspondence rules in fact can represent premature closure of concepts.)

Bagozzi's second model is the "partial interpretation model." It is called a partial interpretation on the ground that the meaning of the theoretical entity is specified only under specific test conditions. This leads to a measure that only partially captures the full meaning of a hypothetical construct. In terms of our earlier discussion, this is still an operational definition. As we have said, operational definitions can rarely capture a construct's full meaning. In fact, it is the surplus meaning of constructs that lies behind their fruitfulness in supplying hypotheses. Bagozzi's third model of correspondence rules is what he calls the "causal indicator model." Here a causal link is specified between the hypothetical construct and observations in an experimental setting. Earlier it was pointed out that one way of defining a term operationally is to think of the empirical consequences of the construct assuming its presence. Again this model is not distinct from the operational definition but is one way of going about operationalizing a construct.

Churchill (1979) deals with the problems of developing better operational measures in marketing when questionnaires are used. Since such operational measures can be contaminated by the respondent's state (e.g., mood, willingness to express feelings), situational factors (e.g., room heating), interviewer differences, questionnaire design, and errors in coding, Churchill lists eight steps in developing better operational measures. His first step emphasizes the need to explicate the sense meaning of the concepts or terms themselves. He points out (as I have) that different conceptualizations of terms give rise to different operational measures. (On this basis it would be of interest to compare the extent to which different measures of attitude converge since the Likert, Guttman, and Thurstone scales, Osgood's semantic differential, and the Fishbein multiattribute model do reflect differences in the conceptualization of attitude.) Poor initial conceptualization of the concept of "consumer involvement" has led to all manner of confusion (Laurent and Kapferer, 1985).

Although the focus here has been on operational definitions of theoretical terms, operationalization is, of course, of vital interest to marketing generally. Thus when consumers speak of wanting a "dry" alcoholic beverage, managers seek to identify what this means in terms of the drink's constituents, which in turn implies knowing what "dry" means subjectively.

*Other Definitions.* There are other types of definitions in addition to operational and analytic definitions. An *ostensive* definition simply defines by pointing to an example ("That's what I mean by a point-of-sale aid"). A *denotative* definition simply lists all the items to which the term applies, as when a firm defines its competition by listing the brands or firms with which it does battle. A *contextual* definition is one that has to be deduced from the context in which the word or expression is used. Most people learn the meanings of words this way in spite of the problems associated with gauging meaning from usage. A *recursive* definition defines a thing in terms of a simpler rendering of the thing itself. Thus $n!$ ($n$ factorial) is defined by $n(n - 1)!$. The concept of a recursive definition is a key one for mathematics. Finally, there are definitons that are merely *synonyms*. However, words that are regarded as synonymous are usually synonyms only for the purposes at hand, and there are nice distinctions between them. Thus, in this chapter, construct and concept, property and attribute, set and class, are regarded as synonyms and therefore interchangeable, though distinctions could be made between them.

## CLASSIFICATION

In testing hypotheses definition is often a prelude to classification, which consists of grouping items (objects, subjects, or events) on the basis of their shared attributes (properties or characteristics). This means that all items being grouped have to be defined and labeled in terms of the shared attributes of interest.

We classify to order observations and enable generalizations to be made. Thus if we classify respondents on the basis of social class, it is because we believe that social class implies something about behavior and so can be related to other variables. But classification in research is not a matter of identifying "essences," for the basis of classification simply reflects our purposes. Thus Bartos (1982) classified women into (1) stay-at-home housewives, (2) plan-to-work housewives, (3) just-a-job working women, and (4) career-oriented working women, because she was interested in determining whether the different groups had different attitudes to the way women were portrayed in commercials (they did).

What we call each class or where we draw the line between classes depends on purpose. Thus an advertisement may classify a cereal as a health product so that the target audience will feel or act in the way suggested by the classification. Sometimes advertisers, in asking us to classify ourselves with some character in the advertisement, are trying to elicit empathy to generate identification with the character and thus with the brand.

Since all perception involves classification, we classify all the time. The extent to which consumers' classification of products is crude and general reflects the extent to which they are sensitive to differences. One of the aims of advertising is to teach consumers to make fine subdivisions within some product class (e.g., coffee) on the basis of differences that help sell the advertised brand. But classifying a brand consistently in one way leads to difficulty in classifying it in another way. This is one of the reasons why repositioning a brand in the market can prove difficult if its original positioning is well established in the target audience's mind. Interestingly, it appears that human beings build categories around a prototype or representative example of the class. This is suggested by the work of Rosch (1973) and adopted by Howard in the model discussed in Chapter 4. On this basis, a sparrow is more likely to be a prototype of a bird than is a kiwi. A move away from the prototype representing some class of product suggests newness and innovativeness but can also generate uncertainty about additional learning. People tend not to form categories with firm boundaries, so that researchers cannot expect perceptions of product class, segment boundaries, and so on, of consumers to be as tightly drawn as research categories.

The items within a class often have more in common than is revealed by the basis used to classify. Darwin, for example, found in the classification system of Linnaeus evidence for the theory of common descent. This is why experimenting with classifications may lead to the discovery of more profound similarities. Hence we may classify buyers as heavy users, medium users, or light users of a brand to discover the additional characteristics such consumers have in common as an aid in developing market strategy.

Classifications are often theory-loaded and constitute a model. Thus classifying buyers into situations characterized as "extensive problem solving," "limited problem solving" and "routine problem solving," when taken in conjunction with the belief that these situations occur at different stages of the life cycle, allows Howard (see Chapter 4) to deduce a number of implications for marketing strategy. Similarly, the categories of new category user (NCU), other brand loyals (OLB), brand loyals (BL), and brand switchers (BS) of Rossiter and Percy are theory-loaded with implications for likely consumer behavior and corresponding competitive strategies.

The system of names given to each class is its "nomenclature." A good nomenclature suggests relations between classes. Thus in biology, the higher classes have distinct names and the subclasses are distinguished by adding a distinctive attribute to the genus. In chemistry, names indicate relationships by modification of their form.

*Taxonomy* is often used as a synonym for a formal classification scheme, although it more properly refers to the theory of classificatory systems. Strictly speaking *classification* is grouping individuals or "species" into classes; breaking down a class into subclasses is known as *logical division*. Grouping (classification) is generally superior to logical division as logical division can end up with classes containing no members. Logical division can proceed as in a decision tree with branches that form dichotomous subclasses. A "hierarchical definition" of a market is illustrated in Figure 12.3. This approach to breaking down a market into segments amounts, in the absence of theory about consumer behavior, to stating an a priori model, which can be misleading. With every classification relating to purpose, substantial knowledge of subject matter is needed to decide the basis that best suits each purpose. Thus the purpose of segmentation relates to having a more homogeneous "want" on which to focus marketing strategy, but choosing the right basis for segmentation depends on having substantial knowledge about buyers and competition.

Every classification in research is theory-loaded since it is theory that determines what properties are considered significant for the purposes at hand. When several classifications are equally acceptable, the relative efficiency in data storage, retrieval, and naming classes and constituents become additional criteria. However, once having said this, it must be acknowledged that the marketing literature has a penchant for producing completely useless classificatory schemes. Useful classification presupposes knowing what properties or attributes are important for the purposes at hand. This in itself suggests the theory-loaded basis of useful classifications.

A classification scheme meets the requirements of logic if it contains exhaustive and

Women's stockings

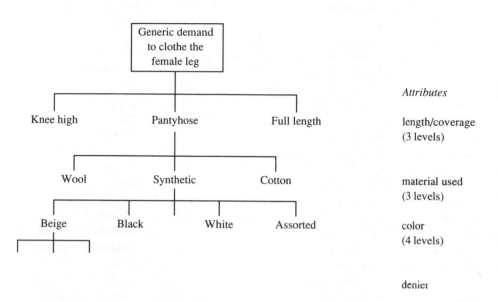

FIGURE 12.3. Hypothetical Hierarchical Definition of the Women's Stocking Market (Partial Representation)

mutually exclusive categories at each step in the classification. Categories are exhaustive when there is a place for every item, and categories are exclusive when there is one and only one place to put an item. This means that each subclass must be defined in terms of the necessary and sufficient conditions for membership, even if boundaries are somewhat arbitrary. Of course, data do not always fall into distinct groupings since there can be variations in degree to which an attribute or property is possessed.

*Monothetic* classification occurs when membership of a class is based on the presence or absence of just one attribute. Monothetic classification is typically associated with logical division since successive logical divisions define monothetic classifications. In segmentation, a hierarchical market definition is a monothetic classification. Where such segments (see Figure 12.3) are based on real knowledge about the consumer, the representation has a distinct advantage over a one-level classification (segmentation) into broad groupings of individuals, where many important distinctions are lost. On the other hand, a classification that preserves all distinctions will contain too many groupings. The stepwise disaggregation illustrated in Figure 12.3 can be helpful in suggesting when to stop.

Classification, strictly speaking, is reserved for situations where the individual items can be neatly pigeonholed into homogeneous classes because variations that occur are variations *of kind.* The term "ordination" is used when continuums are involved, that is, when the variations are variations *of degree,* not of kind. Scaling is ordination that assigns numerical values to order subjects or items along a continuum. The "latent" continuum basis is called the scale and subjects or items are represented by points on the scale. When we deal with continuous variables, we are forced to specify class limits along the continuum before we start grouping into classes.

A *polythetic* classification usually involves ordination and occurs when membership in a class (type or taxon) is based on more than one attribute being shared. When items are to be grouped on the basis of the number of dimensions ($N$), this means measurements on $N$ variables. Each item is specifiable when values have been assigned to all $N$ variables in respect to each item. Polythetic classification implies the need for criteria for weighting characteristics or properties of the items. This depends on theory and theories can change. For example, taxonomists no longer give high importance to wings as a condition for classifying something as a bird since the kiwi, which has no wings, is classified as a bird. *Typological* systems provide for the arrangement of items along several axes and thus replace strict classification by references to spaces of several dimensions. Such ordering (ordination) has the advantage over strict classification in that it allows for subtler distinctions.

In a polythetic classification, the members of a class will share several attributes (features, properties, characteristics), but no single member in the class need possess *all* the features used to identify the class. Still there remains the problem of assigning subjects or items to classes when grouping depends on measuring degrees of affinity. This is where the techniques of *multidimensional scaling* prove useful in measuring and representing, as points in space, the various attributes and their dimensions.

Where there is a good deal of uncertainty, using logical division to arrive at, say, market segments by the hierarchical classification may not yield meaningful categories; the grouping of wants into classes (segments) may be much more realistic. This will involve polythetic classification involving multidimensional scaling to allow perceptual mapping. Psychographic segmentation is a polythetic classification. The VALS (Values and Life Styles) system is the most well known. Its various categories are viewed as segments of consumers with dispositions toward different configurations of product benefits and susceptibility to different promotional appeals. The most recent VALS is VALS2, which classifies consumers into eight segments along two dimensions:

1. *Self-orientation.* This refers to the need to define a social self-image and a hospitable environment for personal growth. There are three subcategories of self-orientation:
   a. *Principle orientation.* Consumers in this subcategory are inclined to base their decisions on strongly held principles, following the established codes of family, church, or nation.
   b. *Status orientation.* Consumers in this subcategory are concerned with social position and so take account of the anticipated reaction of reference groups.
   c. *Action orientation.* Consumers in this subcategory are concerned with action that will affect the world around them in tangible ways.
2. *Resources.* This refers to the range of resources (psychological and material) the consumer can draw on to sustain the self-orientation or social self-image. These resources embrace education, income, health, energy level, self-confidence, interpersonal skills, inventiveness, intelligence, and so on.

Based on self-orientation and resources available, consumers are said to fall into eight segments: fulfilleds, believers, actualizers, achievers, strivers, strugglers, experiencers, and makers. Both fulfilleds and believers are principle-oriented; achievers and strivers are status-oriented; experiencers and makers are action-oriented; actualizers are guided both by principle and by a desire that their actions have an impact on the world; strugglers have no strong self-orientation since their life is focused on the needs of the moment.

Why should we expect the eight categories to be predictive of different patterns of buyer behavior? From an advertising point of view, they could be regarded as segments of consumers holding different values to which to appeal. But VALS2 holds a simplistic view of buyer motivation. Although VALS interprets "self-orientation" very broadly to embrace what in Chapter 10 was described as "integrative criteria," it is still not broad enough to embrace all the other motives at work. But more important, in setting out the eight categories it assumes consumers have one dominant motive (or at most two) in buying. This is a simplistic view of buying. In any case, what consumers buy also depends on their beliefs about how to satisfy the motive. Until such beliefs are known, prediction is hazardous. Thus the actions of status-oriented consumers will depend on what they consider in buying to be status enhancing. VALS2 is presumably assuming that there will be some cultural agreement on what constitutes status symbols. In the case of the principle-oriented, they are assumed to already hold beliefs about what rules ought to be followed in many areas of life, although there will inevitably be differences among the principle-oriented as to the principles they hold dear. In the case of action orientation, it is difficult to see how this category can be given any beliefs predictive of behavior beyond concern with actions that have an impact on the consumers' environment; this is not all that helpful in predicting either product or brand choice.

Are the segments mutually exclusive? Logic would suggest they are not in that there is no logical inconsistency between being a fulfilled and an achiever, yet the segments may be empirically distinct. But are consumers likely to fall consistently into just one segment? In buying books and newspapers I might behave as if I am an actualizer but in buying clothes I might behave as an achiever. Also, it is not clear that being principle-oriented and being action-oriented can be easily separated in that being principle-oriented has led many people to be concerned that their actions have an impact on the world. Looking at the categories in still more detail, we find fulfilleds and believers are both principle-oriented. The fulfilleds are described as moderately active in local community affairs and politics with their leisure centering on the home; education and travel are valued; and this group is also health-conscious and politically moderate and tolerant. The believers, on the other hand, respect rules and authority figures; enjoy a comfortable, predictable existence; socialize with family and established groups; are reasonably well-informed and politically conservative. Unless we are to assume that these differences between the two segments of principle-oriented consumers stem from the two groups having different sets of resources at their command, then it must be the content of the principles that gives rise to the difference. Has such content been identified, examined, and categorized? Finally, there is a richness of the segment description that cannot be deduced from the two relevant basic dimensions and their subcategories. Thus regardless of the range and quantity of resources available, there is no way we could deduce from the concept of being principle-oriented the lifestyles described under the headings of fulfilleds and believers. As with the first VALS, academics will continue to be skeptical of the claims for VALS2. In respect to some of this criticism, the response may be that more is being asked or expected of VALS2 than those promoting VALS2 are attempting. It may be that promoters and users would be satisfied if VALS2 simply helped advertising link the product or brand to the values of different target groups of consumers. But, even given this modest aim, it is not clear that such a system does distinguish categories of consumers with distinct value orientations.

Statistical techniques used to identify classes include principal components analysis, factor analysis, cluster analysis, linkage analysis, profile analysis, and discriminant analysis. Each makes different assumptions about the items and their attributes, but the basic principle in all of them is to establish comparative similarities so as to be able to assert that $X$ is more similar to $Y$ than it is to $Z$, and so on, to allow classification to proceed. Collectively these techniques have made polythetic classification a realistic goal.

Perhaps the most popular of the techniques is factor analysis. Where a large number of factors determine attitude, researchers may use factor analysis to reduce the set of factors to a more manageable number and to assess the contribution of each factor (assess loadings) to bringing about the results of interest. But factor analysis, like the other techniques, cannot anticipate which class of similarities will prove useful. There is also a danger in undertaking classification without necessarily thinking first of purposes. Again, factors have to be given names with scope for misleading labels in that the labels may not capture the key features of the factor; moreover, the evaluation of the loadings admits of no unique solution. Finally, factor analysis cannot certify causal links since it is based simply on tables of intercorrelations. In spite of all this and the fact that factor analysis cannot demonstrate a unique pattern of factors, it can reveal possible regularities and provide a more helpful taxonomy.

The problem of operationally defining *and* describing categories is important. Take, for example, the following categories recommended by Drucker (1964) for classifying a firm's products:

|                              |                               |
|------------------------------|-------------------------------|
| Today's breadwinners         | Repair jobs                   |
| Tomorrow's breadwinners      | Unnecessary specialties       |
| Productive specialties       | Unjustified specialties       |
| Development products         | Investment in managerial ego  |
| Failures                     | Cinderellas                   |
| Yesterday's breadwinners     |                               |

These categories are not operational and using them would more likely reflect one's prejudices than objective classification. This is particularly so given the emotive category labels. In any case, the categories are not mutually exclusive in that, say an unjustified specialty could also be an investment in managerial ego.

Another well-known classification is the five-category classifcation of roles in industrial buying (Webster and Wind, 1972):

*Users:* those who will use the product.

*Influencers:* those who can influence choice by, say, defining choice criteria or providing information on other offerings.

*Buyers:* those who have the formal authority for choosing suppliers.

*Deciders:* those who determine the ultimate supplier.

*Gatekeepers:* those who control the flow of information to participants.

This classification would cause problems in practice. In the first place a "user" does not define a role in the buying decision process but defines a consumption role. In the second place every participant to a buying decision is an "influencer."

Sometimes a classification is put forward and found useful and later expanded giving fresh thought to its theoretical base. This has been the case with the classifcation of products into convenience, shopping, and specialty on the basis of the consumer's alleged typical buying relationship with the product (Copeland, 1923). This classification was expanded by Holbrook and Howard (1977) to include "preference" goods, which has stimulated other writers (Enis and Roering, 1980; Murphy and Enis, 1986) to suggest a more meaningful theoretical base for the classification based on the dimensions of the risk and effort attached to buying.

Some classifications, like the assumed segments of a market, are meant to be predictive of behavior. There is a need to demonstrate this. Thus why should lifestyle or demographics be predictive of product demand? We might argue that

1. buying product XYZ goes with such and such a lifestyle,

2. each product category fits different lifestyles, and

3. a certain type of lifestyle is a quasi-necessary condition for using a certain product. (e.g., a car).

All such arguments establish the reasonableness of the relationship but only empirical evidence can decide.

There are different ways of classifying phenomena and these give rise to different descriptions of the same thing, each of which may be valid for its purpose. Thus one can claim to "disprove" a particular description of behavior by describing that behavior in other terms. Consider Humphrey's (1983) two descriptions of the same scene in the British House of Commons:

> Between 16:00 and 18:00 hours on Friday afternoon, men and women on each side of the chamber shouted at each other, threw bits of paper, clapped their hands, stamped their feet, and talked about cod; then, at a signal from an old fellow in a curly wig, everyone got to their feet, and those who had previously been sitting on the right side of the chamber all made their way out through a door marked A Y E, while those who had previously been sitting on the left side all made their way out through a door marked N O E. (p. 11)

and the second description:

> Following Prime Minister's Question Time, there ensued a lively debate on the White-Fish Fisheries Bill; the Speaker called for a vote, whereupon the House divided, and, under the influence of a three-line whip, the motion to give the Bill a second reading was carried for the Government. (p. 12)

As Humphrey says, both these descriptions are perfectly valid descriptions of what occurred but from different points of view. Neither view disproves the other. Yet we have Mintzberg's (1973) rejection of the claim that managers plan, organize, coordinate, and control, on the ground that the actions of managers as described by observers suggest otherwise. But planning, organizing, coordinating, and controlling are categories based on the purpose served by each managerial activity. Just observing activities would not reveal such categories.

## Testing Hypotheses

The last feature of the scientific method—testing—is critical: there is always a need to check hypotheses. Novel hypotheses can appear absurd without empirical support. Thus William Harvey was ridiculed when he introduced the idea that the blood did not ebb and flow but circulated in the body. The traditional view is to check the correspondence between the hypothesis and reality; the approach in hermeneutics is to check the interpretation against the "text" (e.g., self-reports).

Traditionally, once hypotheses are stated in operational terms, the testing of the hypotheses proceeds by deducing the empirical consequences of the hypotheses. This is not always straightforward, and debates may occur over whether the consequences assumed are legitimate derivatives from the hypothesis. The hypothesis is set out as an antecedent proposition with the deduced consequences shown as the consequent proposition. If the consequent is confirmed, this raises the likelihood of the antecedent hypothesis being true. The deduced consequences themselves need to be defined, which may also require careful operational definition and measurement.

The conditions for the formulations of a hypothesis are that it should explain and be formulated so that verifiable consequences can be deduced. Ideally these consequences should be "surprising," as there is always a danger of creating a hypothesis to explain events and then "confirming" the hypothesis by showing that these events are actual consequences. There is never any difficulty in devising some hypothesis to explain what is already known. The problem is to devise a hypothesis that explains the present facts but also leads to the prediction and confirmation of what is currently thought unlikely to be true. But such predictions are not always easily tested. Thus Einstein in the general theory of relativity predicted that the violent birth and death of stars would produce gravitational waves, blanketing the earth in a unique kind of radiation. Scientists are still trying to confirm this unlikely prediction.

Many problems are formulated in ways that disguise the fact that they consist of a hypothesis to be tested. For example, a company executive might ask, "Will a price cut lead to retaliatory action on the part of competitors?" The question is better posed as "To what extent do we have evidence to support the hypothesis that a price cut will lead to retaliatory action by competitors?" The first question merely elicits opinion; the second question demands consideration of evidence.

The problem of what constitutes an adequate test of a hypothesis is not straightforward. Thus Churchman (1966) points out: "Hypothesis- and theory-testing are delicate operations, and, as yet, in the history of science we have no very clear ideas how they should be performed."

If we could confirm every possible consequence, we could verify the hypothesis. This cannot be done with a *scientific* hypothesis, which extends to an infinite population of occasions. (It can be done for a *descriptive* hypothesis, e.g., "this country is in a state of depression," providing we get agreement on the operational measures.) In any case, the mere confirmation of just any consequence or repeated confirmation of the same consequence will not do. The interest lies in identifying consequences that, if confirmed, rule out rival hypotheses.

It was argued that the degree of confirmation of a hypothesis is the degree of evidential support for the hypothesis. The higher the degree of confirmation, the higher the probability of the hypothesis being true. What is meant by "degree of evidential support"? Some philosophers argued that the confirming instances must differ from each other so each instance tests a different consequence of the hypothesis. Others claimed that a hypothesis is confirmed only by these instances of attempted confirmation that disconfirm rival hypotheses. Still others claimed that the ability to predict unexpected new phenomena was the best sort of confirmation.

All three approaches (tests of different consequences, disconfirming rival hypotheses, and predicting surprising consequences) can be applied but the truth value of the hypothesis, somewhere between a probability of zero and one, still must be established. Marketers, like social scientists in general, favor a strict test of a hypothesis, so that its confirmation suggests acceptability, but if not confirmed, the hypothesis need not be abandoned since sights can be lowered! There is always some reluctance to abandon a hypothesis or model. Most of us are brutally objective only when reviewing the work of others.

Carnap (1950) recognized that universal laws cannot be firmly established through induction. In a search for a noninductive foundation for inductive logic, Carnap came to accept "probability" as a reasonable degree of faith and even argued at one time that the judgment as to the degree to which a hypothesis is supported by the evidence is analytic and a priori. Certainly, there is no absolute proof since regardless of how many times a hypothesis is confirmed, there is always the possibility that the next test following a finite series will be inconsistent with the hypothesis.

Since confirming consequences is a necessary but not a sufficient condition for verification, Popper (1959) argued the emphasis should be on attempting to disprove a hypothesis: the principle of falsifiability should replace that of verifiability. Popper believed the falsifiability principle got round the problem of induction. But critics point out that it is an *inductive step* to assume that a theory that has passed a variety of falsification tests is a better guide to the future than one that has not been so tested or one that has been tested but found wanting. And if we take this inductive step, then how can it be justified? The problem of induction remains.

Hypothesis testing as a process of checking predicted empirical consequences against the "facts" came to be viewed as highly simplistic. Some limitations are associated with the limitations of the "correspondence theory of truth" already described, but there are others. An obvious limitation is that the falsification of a hypothesis may simply falsify the specific application. A second limitation was suggested by Pierre Duhem (1954), a physicist, who in 1906 argued that theories are not abandoned only when observational evidence is in conflict. He claimed that observations are theory-loaded, so it may be the observations and not the theory that is at fault. Scientific hypotheses may as a consequence not be conclusively established or *conclusively refuted by observation.* Duhem pointed out that a physicist can never subject an isolated hypothesis to experimental test but can only test a group of hypotheses. When experimental results disagree with predictions, the physicist learns only that at least one of the hypotheses in the group is unacceptable. But the experiment does not indicate which of the hypotheses must be rejected.

It is true that a test does not just test the hypothesis itself but a whole set of hypotheses. Every test of a hypothesis must take account of other hypotheses in respect of

1. the initial conditions governing the conduct of the experiment (including the validity of the correspondence rules or operational definitions); and

2. auxiliary assumptions to the effect that nothing else interfered.

Thus if

$$H = \text{hypothesis}$$
$$IC = \text{initial conditions}$$
$$AA = \text{auxiliary assumptions}$$
$$P = \text{the predicted consequences}$$

we argue

If $(H, IC, AA)$, then $P$

*or*

If (not-$H$, and $IC$ and $AA$ are accepted as unproblematic), then probably not-$P$.

Because we test hypotheses in conjunction with initial conditions and auxiliary assumptions, we can never be absolutely sure we have confirmed *or refuted* the hypothesis itself. In fact, when refutation occurs, it is not unusual for investigators to maintain the hypothesis by supplementary ad hoc assumptions. Also, in behavioral science, where many initial conditions and auxiliary assumptions may not be checkable, it may well happen that a consequence is not confirmed yet the hypothesis is true. In line with this Nagel comments on Popper's falsification rules as follows:

> The difficulty in defining the potential falsifiers for theories of this sort derives from several sources, but I will limit myself to mentioning just one. These theories are not single statements, but systems of assumptions, whose component statements contain terms, such as "atom" or "light ray," which for the most part do not designate anything identifiable either by direct observation or even by laboratory instruments. Accordingly, if such theories are to be tested experimentally they must be supplemented by a distinctive set of further statements—variously called "coordinating definitions," "correspondence rules," and "bridge laws" in order to establish connections between the theoretical entities postulated by such a theory and certain matters than can in fact be observed. . . . The introduction of new bridge laws or the elimination of old ones may shift the status of an accepted basic statement from that of being a falsifier to that of being compatible with the theory, or vice versa. (1979, p. 75)

Of course, if a consequence is only probable (which is typically the case), it cannot be falsified by just one nonconfirmation. There is a need to establish the actual relative frequency of the consequence and check against what would be predicted.

Positivists hold a view of reality as something fixed regardless of the language used to describe that reality. This reality is that revealed by sensory experience. But in testing some hypothesis we may simply see what the theory directs us to see. Thus if theory teaches us to look for unconscious motives in dreams, that is what is found. That such theory can be self-validating has been the constant criticism of much of psychoanalytic psychology. Even in mainstream psychology, there is the danger of operationally defining consequences in a way supportive of the hypothesis by making the consequences conceptually indistinct from the antecedent. Thus I may argue that "the higher the consumer's attitude toward the brand, the more likely is the intention to buy" while at the same time defining "intention to buy" in a way that is conceptually embraced by the definition of a highly favorable attitude. When research in marketing commits this error the only thing established is a link between the meaning of terms, not the discovery of behavioral relationships. But more generally the basic explanatory system directs observation into finding a solution in line with the researcher's basic theoretical orientation. In any case, if theory always affects our interpretation of the facts, this casts doubts on the supposed independence of observation from theory. Nonetheless, interpretation of the facts cannot be entirely dictated by theory since interpretation must operate within confines limited by the material of reality, even though we may acknowledge that there are no completely uninterpreted "givens" that can serve as the foundation of knowledge.

The claim that the interpretation of facts will *always* depend on theories held is disputed by Hacking (1983). He does not agree that *all* scientific observations are interpretations in the light of theories held. While agreeing that interpretation is always involved, he argues nonetheless that the early development of optics depended solely on noticing surprising phenomena that preceded any formulation of theory.

There are several problems with self-reports when used to check some hypothesis. There is first the problem of establishing whether the hypothesis itself is a genuine one or simply a conceptual truth. There are indeed statements put forward for testing where the consequent is simply a conceptual extension of the antecedent, like the example quoted earlier. There is also the problem of replies simply reflecting the respondent's desire to be consistent. Thus salespeople who say they are committed to their companies' future are also likely to say that they are customer-oriented not because the one causes the other but because the respondents wish to maintain a consistency in their replies. Many hypotheses in marketing, concerned with likely behavior under different circumstances, are tested by asking respondents from the target group their likely behavior in the different circumstnaces. In their replies the respondents may confirm the predicted behavior, but such confirmation may simply reflect the fact that the hypothesis is considered the most rational or right way to behave in the circumstances. In other words, respondents are acknowledging they understand what would be the rational or right way to act but not necessarily confirming what actually happens.

## FALSIFYING MODELS BUT NOT THEORIES?

We have talked of hypothesis testing as if the hypothesis was an isolated hypothesis unrelated to any theory. More typically, we test some model or group of hypotheses. Lying behind a model are a set of theoretical presuppositions, whether formally set out or not. This is so in spite of the fact that a constant complaint of research in marketing is that it is not theory-driven in that it is ad hoc and not formally linked to any theory. Where theories are explicit, models or hypotheses are the implications of the theories and hence they, not the theory directly, are what are tested. Only a model of a theory (even if it consists of just one hypothesis) can be tested but, since there are many possible models of a theory, falsifying the single model of the theory does not falsify the theory absolutely. To refute the theory absolutely, we would have to show that all models of the theory are false. This is similar to the earlier argument that falsifying a hypothesis may simply falsify the particular application. It is also in line with the claim that we cannot be absolutely sure we have disproved a scientific hypothesis.

## ELIMINATING RIVAL HYPOTHESES

We are never able to eliminate *all* rival hypotheses and several of the hypotheses we do consider may be consistent with the evidence. Other criteria—harmonizes with the facts better, is more illuminating or promising, is less complex, and so on—then become important. A common criterion is the simplicity of the hypothesis. But there can be simplicity in the description of a theory yet considerable complexity in the background discourse needed to understand it. The criterion of simplicity is cited not to condemn complexity but to suggest to the researcher the need to justify complexity. Thus we have a need in social science to justify explanations couched in complex jargon when such explanations are so easily translated into a reason-giving format.

Another popular criterion is coherence with what was already known. Blanshard (1939) argued for a coherence theory of truth on the ground that an ideal system of knowledge is one in which the constituent members are necessarily connected one to another. However, as we have argued, coherence cannot be a sufficient condition for truth. Yet if a hypothesis does not cohere or, at least, is not congruent with existing knowledge, then confirmation of predicted consequences is less convincing. There is a great deal of evidence for extrasensory perception, but it may still be rejected on the grounds that it "just does not make sense." On the other hand, there is not much validating evidence for psychotherapy, but it may be accepted because its explanations form a self-consistent, unified whole.

Research in marketing seldom attempts to eliminate rival hypotheses. The object of testing is not to demonstrate the truth of explanations but to decide whether to accept or not to accept the hypothesis on the basis of standard testing conventions suggested by statistical theory, which is discussed later.

## EXPERIMENTATION

Experimentation has traditionally been regarded as the major way to test hypotheses. In fact, for many people the scientific method is equated with experimentation. This is because experimentation is controlled observation, defined by Nagel as follows: "More generally, an inquiry is a controlled one only if, by instituting some kind of eliminative procedure, the differential effects of a factor that is assumed to be relevant to the occurrence of a given phenomenon can be ascertained" (1979, p. 18).

In experiments the independent variable is manipulated directly whereas the dependent variable is that which is affected by the manipulation of the independent variable. But this simple cause (independent variable) and effect (dependent variable) relationship is complicated in practice. In experimenting with people there is no guarantee that all factors will remain constant except the independent and dependent variables. Those factors held constant are the "parameters," and defining these parameters defines the state of the system within which the independent variables are manipulated. The use of experiments is limited by this need to separate the independent and dependent variables and ensure other parameters are fixed (Harré, 1983).

Not all experimentation is conducted to test hypotheses. There are "heuristic" experiments designed to generate ideas and to open up new lines of inquiry. There is "boundary" research designed to establish the domain within which some theory or model is applicable. Finally, there are "simulation" experiments using the model to find out what would happen if this or that was done. Computer simulation is most common. Numbers or symbols represent the variables of the model and these are manipulated by the simulation program. The focus is not necessarily, however, on prediction but on "sensitivity analysis," whereby various changes in the values of variables are tried to see what happens and so deepen understanding of how things work.

Hacking (1983) claims that although much profound experimental work is guided entirely by theory, it is also true that many hypotheses just emerge from conducting experiments.

Experimentation is common in marketing to ensure that some behavioral response $R$ is purely due to the treatment $S$ and is not contaminated by other contemporaneous events, changes in the group itself, bias from being observed, or bias from being measured. The most common approach is to set up control and experimental groups that are matched in all relevant respects. Whether matching is done by choosing at random members of the control and experimental groups or in some other way, the fact remains that no experimenter can guarantee that members of each group are identical in all relevant respects. The net effect of the treatment on the experimental group is

$$(E_2 - E_1) - (G_2 - G_1)$$

where $E$ is an experimental group ($E_1$ and $E_2$ being the states before and after the experiment) and $G$ is the control group ($G_1$ before, $G_2$ after).

There are many possibilities in experimental designs:

1. Single group designs such as *AB*, *ABA*, *ABABA*, where *A* = untreated group and *B* = treated group.
2. Multiple experimental and control groups.
3. Factorial designs that permit the analysis of the simultaneous effects of two or more treatments by providing a group for each possible combination.
4. Other designs such as the Latin square.

There is no guarantee, however, that an experiment can isolate the true cause. There are always rival hypotheses since an experiment cannot guarantee distinguishing cause from mere coexistence. Furthermore, even random assignments to control and experimental groups to establish homogeneous groups can be dysfunctional in that we do not know the individual characteristics of those influenced by the stimulus (e.g., a new drug) and those who were not. It is for this and other reasons that Harré and Secord claim many experimental findings are banal, producing just descriptive information in quantitative form.

Brown and Gaulden (1982) claim the marketing literature displays a conspicuous absence of attempts at replicating a study. They point out that replication takes the form of having additional tests made at the same time under the same circumstances *or* on additional test units *or* having tests that are temporarily separated with perhaps some modification of the assumptions. But replication is misleading if it suggests we can replicate an experiment in every detail. We cannot and these differences in detail may be (in our ignorance) highly significant. Although replication should not be ignored, the mere accumulation of similar tests confirming a hypothesis does not add much, since the additional tests may simply overtest one facet of the hypothesis. One is reminded of something in one of Moliere's plays:

*Hypothesis:* This man has a fever.

*Deduction:* If he has a fever, he will have a red face.

*Confirmation:* He does have a red face.

*Conclusion:* Therefore, he has a fever.

However often this sequence occurred it would add little to our confidence in the hypothesis. But at least journal articles should contain enough information to make replication possible. This is not always so, which means there is no guarantee at all with regard to the results obtained. No respectable journal should permit this—but it happens.

Laboratory experiments frequently are criticized for their lack of external validity, or the ability to generalize from the results to the real world, because

1. the causal conditions triggered in an experiment may never be active in a pure form in the real world;
2. we cannot guarantee that the conditions giving rise to the events of interest are present or will occur in the real world; and
3. contamination/noise may grossly distort or even neutralize the predicted effect.

But many experiments are not undertaken in hopes of generalizing the particular results. A major aim frequently is to manipulate variables to gauge the effect in controlled conditions on behavior and other variables. As Calder, Phillips, and Tybout (1982) say, the experiment might simply be designed to test a theory and its power in controlled conditions; the question of its utility or applicability to the real world is a separate issue. However, this subject of external validity has given rise to many articles and viewpoints (see Calder, Phillips, and Tybout, 1982, 1983; Lynch, 1982, 1983; McGrath and Brinberg, 1983).

Hacking (1983), a realist, argues that experimentation provides the strongest evidence for scientific realism. This is because unobserved entities can be manipulated in an experiment. As unobserved entities (e.g., the self-image) are manipulated in order to experiment on something else, success in prediction leads to a belief in the reality of the entity itself. Thus if an experiment is designed to change behavior by manipulating "attitudes" and such manipulations did lead to a predicted change in behavior, we would have more faith in the construct of "attitude." But, as Hacking says, we may find that many long-accepted theoretical entities cannot be manipulated to change behavior and may be discarded. Finally, Hacking argues that the ability to explain in itself carries little warrant of truth but that when we know a lot about the behavior of $X$, we no longer feel the need for explanations. This may be true, though usually knowing a lot about the behavior of $X$ does mean being able to explain that behavior whereas not being able to explain that behavior would, in fact, inhibit interventions to change behavior.

In physics, experimentation is crucial and Newton himself was a master experimenter, as his seminal work on optics demonstrates. Yet the importance of experimentation in the social sciences is a matter of controversy. Laboratory research finds difficulty in replicating the motivations and behavior that would apply if the treatments were stimuli occurring in everyday living. This in turn has given rise to the claim that experimentation has so far produced very little useful knowledge for marketers. Others argue that experimentation is not designed to produce immediate practical findings but to find relationships that would not be manifested in the complex environment of social living.

## MATHEMATICS AND MEASUREMENT

Scientific method is associated with quantification if for no other reason than that mathematics is regarded as the language of science. As Davies (1983) says, mathematics allows the physicist to describe situations that are completely beyond the power of human beings to even imagine: without mathematics, physics would never have progressed beyond mechanics. However, it could be claimed that neither logical positivism nor logical empiricism requires the use of mathematics or statistics for scientific activity. This is not surprising since many of today's statistical techniques are twentieth-century inventions associated with names like R. A. Fisher, Karl Pearson, Francis Edgeworth, and Udny Yule; moreover, Kuhn (1977) points out that "thoroughgoing mathematization" in science only came about around 1840. The logical positivists were concerned with using the symbolic logic of Russell and Whitehead's *Principia Mathematica* (1910–1913) in the analysis of science. And formal logic is mathematics. George Boole in the last century showed that deductive reasoning was no different in kind from mathematical reasoning, so that Boolean algebra embraces Aristotle's system of logic.

When we speak of mathematical psychology we refer to the application of mathematical rules to data and hypotheses to deduce their implications or the use of existing models in mathematics to model behavior or market processes. Such models in mathematics like the Markov chain are synthetic models, existing quite apart from any application. There is always the possibility of a correspondence between the behavior of a specific mathematical system and the behavior of buyers and competitors. Where this is so, the mathematical system can be used as a model representing marketing phenomena.

The use of mathematics brings with it the need for measurement, which, in turn, involves getting agreement on some physical invariant as the unit for measuring so the characteristics of things can be expressed in numbers.

Measurement should be viewed purely pragmatically, neither as desirable nor undesirable but as useful or not useful in some application. Those who inveigh against measurement do not seem to eschew words like "few" and "many," which imply numbers. Yet it must be admitted that an obsession with measurement does result in a tendency to elevate method over substance. What good is a series of equations containing many unquantified or unquantifiable variables? It can in fact be misleading if it suggests measurement is possible.

The functions of measurement are to

1. test hypotheses by facilitating comparison between the actual and predicted results;
2. bring out the implications of the data through mathematical manipulation of the data;
3. express in some equation the maximum amount of information about the pattern of data collected *or* the pattern of results to be expected; and
4. discriminate categories.

Note that numbers have no properties except relational properties with each other. Mathematics does not conjure knowledge out of nothing but brings out the implications of data. Mathematics is simply a manufactured system of rules for combining symbols or numbers. Where assumptions are unrealistic, conclusions may be rigorously deduced but nonetheless may be irrelevant to real marketing problems.

Measurement makes possible subtle discriminations and more precise descriptions while facilitating comparisons. Most important, measurement may make it possible to recognize hidden qualitative differences since the gap between a quality and its possible measurement may simply represent our ignorance of how the two can be related. As Nagel (1979) words it, "Instead of ignoring or denying the existence of qualitative distinctions, techniques of measurement both presuppose qualitative differences as well as make it possible to recognize more subtle qualitative distinctions" (p. 18). And he continues, "that scale merely orders qualities in an unambiguous manner" (p. 19).

Why is mathematics often so readily applicable to real-world phenomena? Presumably because the abstract mathematical structures that have been invented have been inspired by mental models of the world. It also appears that the structures that occur in one field of experience occur in others.

In spite of what has been said about the virtues of quantification and measurement, there is a danger in marketing of regarding only the quantitative as of value, leading to an obsession with measurement and a craving to express everything in mathematical form to indicate qualifications as a card-carrying quantifier. This can direct attention away from substantive issues. Thus the attention given to attitude measurement between the wars diverted attention from the more substantive issue of affecting attitude change. But the obsession is understandable. If we were to rank the sciences in terms of the degree to which the disciplines use mathematics, we would find physics ranked higher than economics with economics ranked higher than psychology and sociology. For some physicists, "all that is not physics is stamp collecting." Yet we might remember the advice of the economist Alfred Marshall. As Buchholz (1989) comments:

> Although trained as a mathematician, Marshall feared that economists would calculate themselves into irrelevancy. Ricardo forever remained a hero to Marshall, because Ricardo thought like a mathematician without resorting to obscure symbols and secret

formulae. Marshall translated Ricardo and Mill into calculus, but never let his economic arguments rest solely on mathematical proofs. In a charming letter, Marshall put forth his system: (1) Use mathematics as a shorthand language, rather than as an engine of inquiry. (2) Keep to them till you have done. (3) Translate into English. (4) Then illustrate by examples that are important in real life. (5) Burn the mathematics. (6) If you can't succeed in 4, burn 3. This last I did often.

But then we have the advice of Lord Kelvin: "I often say that when you can measure what you are speaking about, and express it in numbers, you know something about it; but when you cannot measure it, when you cannot express it in numbers, your knowledge is of a meager and unsatisfactory kind" (Mackay, 1977).

An obsession with quantifying can narrow the range of problems considered; this is "the primacy of technique over problems." *The principal condition for progress in marketing is to improve its conceptual base.* Quantification is premature if the mathematical superstructure lacks an adequate conceptual base, since no amount of mathematical manipulation can make up for the poverty of an underlying conceptual structure. Kuhn (1977) claims that a large amount of qualitative work is usually a prerequisite to fruitful quantification in the physical sciences. Where measures are taken without such work, Kuhn argues, numbers provide no insights. Without a theory of what to expect, figures seldom make much sense.

*Measurement Models.*    There are a number of measurement models which are identified by their mathematical characteristics. They are important since the different models allow different mathematical and statistical manipulations to be carried out.

1. *Nominal scale.* The nominal scale is a simple scale that uses numbers to identify individuals or classes. Any data that are in categories can be assigned numbers, which then are counted and the categories are placed in frequency distributions. However, there must be agreement on the categories. We can easily apply the nominal scale in assigning people to category (1) male and category (2) female, but it is more difficult to put people into social classes without agreed-upon operational definitions of each and every class.

2. *Ordinal scale.* The ordinal scale is one in which numbers are used to order from "most" to "least." Thus items are ranked in order of magnitude with respect to some criterion; for example, marketers may ask respondents to arrange brands in order of preference. In an ordinal scale not only are numbers assigned to different items but every number has a reserved place in the number series. A typical ordinal scale would be the ranking of items from the smallest to the largest. There are several different ordering systems, all possessing essentially the same mathematical properties. The ordinal scale permits only the calculation of correlations on the ranked data and the calculation of medians; it does not allow addition, subtraction, multiplication, or division.

3. *Interval scale.* This scale justifies the term "measuring" rather than merely "scaling" since numbers here are used to reflect distances between items. Thus an interval between 100 and 120 is the same as that between 180 and 200. Though psychologists claim that the IQ scale is an interval scale so that a difference of 10 points at one end of the scale is the same as 10 points elsewhere along the scale, the starting point is arbitrary (in that a score of zero IQ does not mean absolutely no intelligence), so it makes no sense to say that an IQ of 200 is twice an IQ of 100. We can add and subtract intervals and calculate means but cannot carry out multiplication or division.

4. *Ratio scale.* For there to be a ratio scale it must be conceivable to have a zero amount of the quality because unless the measuring instrument has a zero point, like a ruler

does, it is not possible to say how many times bigger or smaller one thing is than another. Thus we can say one person is twice as old as another but it does not make much sense mathematically to say someone has twice the intelligence or twice the favorable attitude. The ratio scale is true measurement as there is a true zero point (as with a ruler) so multiplication and division can be carried out.

5. *Multidimensional scaling.* The interval and ratio scales assume that whatever is being measured can be measured on a single, unidimensional underlying continuum. But there are some attributes that are clearly multidimensional, even though we may treat them as unidimensional. Thus IQ is really a multidimensional construct consisting of such abilities as comprehension, memory, and reasoning ability, and it may be more meaningful to spell out each of those dimensions of intelligence and show the score on each for the purposes we have in mind. It is the same with attitude measurement. Researchers may just treat it as the dimension of "liking" and measure it in terms of how the respondent evaluates some item, person, or thing. On the other hand, it could be regarded as a multidimensional construct consisting (as one view claims) of a "cognitive" dimension, an "affective" dimension, and a "conative" dimension. With multidimensional scaling, instead of assigning a single number (scale value) to represent a point along a single dimension, as many numbers are assigned as there are independent dimensions in the relevant multidimensional space. Each number corresponds to a scale value point on one of the axes (dimensions) of the space.

Most statistical measurement in marketing assumes data are measured on a ratio scale or at least on an interval scale regardless of the true position. This is a classic case of conventionalism in marketing research, where "mathematical niceties" are ignored so that the most powerful methods can be applied to the data. We get away with this since no one is quite sure what the consequences are of violating the rules of measurement. In marketing we all too often assume a ratio (cardinal) scale when only a "greater," "smaller," or "equal" is applicable (e.g., between attitude measures). No one complains because everyone does it! Similarly, researchers favor continuous variables with linear relationship to support regression analysis, although qualitative categories may be more justified, particularly for categorical perceptions of qualities of taste and smell (Kagan, 1989).

*Statistics in Research.* Statistics has probably been more instrumental in unifying the methods of research and the interpretation of research findings than all the formulations on the philosophy of science. In fact statistics has substituted for philosophy of science and in the process substituted much conventionalism for thought and judgment. This is because statistical techniques offer a conventional way of bringing about closure in research, without which there would appear to be no end to disputes like that over the degree of support for a hypothesis. But such closure has often been purchased at a price of abandoning the elimination of rival explanations.

A good deal of research in marketing is concerned with establishing empirical generalizations that relate observables to observables (e.g., heavy users of detergents to ages of housewives), not with theoretical behavioral hypotheses relating hypothetical constructs to observables. But establishing empirical generalizations still raises problems in that finding exceptions to such generalization does not falsify the generalizations. But, by convention, we decide to count a statistical statement as provisionally falsified if the frequency it attributes to some item, event, or property (e.g., using discount coupons) in the target population is sufficiently different from that found to occur in a sample to make it highly improbable. But all this assumes our sample is a representative one.

We speak of random sampling as a way of obtaining a representative sample. If the sample is picked at random, it assumes every item has an equal opportunity of being selected. In games of chance we ensure randomization by shuffling cards or shaking up the box of lottery tickets. We may at times use a table of random numbers, although such tables have on occasion had to be modified on the ground that a truly random sample will have no recognizable patterns. But in marketing we seem to assume that selecting respondents at random ensures a representative sample or we use quota sampling and assume it will behave like a random sample if certain precautions are taken. Random sampling, covering all probability sampling, whether stratified, cluster, sequential, or inferential statistics, is based on the axiom that a random sample drawn from a fixed population will on average provide a sample that is representative of all the characteristics of the population. The size of the sample depends on the precision required and the homogeneity of the population with respect to the characteristics (attributes, properties) of interest.

The logic of probability theory is not inductive but deductive since its axioms logically imply its theorems. Thus the theoretical sampling distribution is a matter of deduction since it follows from the conditions laid down in the theory. The real problem in sampling lies in ensuring that actual conditions match the theoretical conditions being assumed. For diverse constituents within a target market population, true random sampling is almost impossible in practice, and nonavailability can lead to sampling error not accommodated in significance testing.

The *parent* population of the observed sample is *key* to statistical inference. If that population does not have stability with respect to the attributes of interest but is changing on the dimensions of interest (e.g., preferences), the resulting sample distributions will also not be stable. If we are not to go beyond the evidence, we would limit the findings to a specific population (Who), a specific time (When), and a specific place (Where). When it comes to beliefs and wants, it is naive to assume any long-term stability of consumer populations. There is no real counterpart in consumer markets to the static population of colored balls in an urn on which theoretical distributions are based. The theoretical frequency distribution is a deductive algebraic specification, an ideal type, a sort of hypothetical construct that may or may not coincide with the actual frequency distributions. Whether a binomial, Poisson, or normal distribution can be used to interpret some actual distribution has to be empirically established and not just assumed. Researchers are taught this but often ignore it if conditions *seem* right.

*Significance testing* is the statistical approach to hypothesis testing. But such hypothesis testing is simply a screening convention to decide whether to proceed or not to proceed. We ask oursleves how likely it is that sampling errors would lead to such a difference or a greater difference than that which actually occurred between the sample figure and what we would expect on theoretical grounds. On this basis, we decide whether the difference is statistically significant, that is, something greater than can be attributed to chance alone. More specifically, we set up a statistical hypothesis (the "null hypothesis") to the effect that "no change" has recurrred from known conditions. On the assumption that this null hypothesis is true, the probabiblity that the sample results obtained could arise by chance is calculated. If this probability is less than the chosen significance level, the result is said to be statistically significant and the hypothesis is rejected. If the probability turns out to be greater than the chosen significance level, then rejection of the hypothesis would entail a greater risk than is acceptable. When acceptance of the hypothesis follows, there is no suggestion that this means the hypothesis is true. Significance testing does not prove anything. If we reject a hypothesis or model as false when it is actually true, the statistician speaks of a Type I error having been made. On the other hand, if we accept a hypothesis as true when it is actually false, the statistician speaks of a Type II error having been made. Statistical testing must choose between avoiding one or the other type of error. (There can, of course, be differences that are statistically significant but are so small as to be of no practical importance to marketing; as the pragmatist would say, "a difference is a difference only if it makes a difference.")

At present we accept or reject a hypothesis on the basis of significance testing. However, in the case of a theoretical hypothesis, we should reject or reserve judgment when rival explanatory hypotheses have not been eliminated, since significance testing merely takes account of findings being the result of chance. It is not testing to eliminate major rival hypotheses. Writers do, of course, typically formulate the hypotheses in explanatory terms. This explanation then gets carried forward in the literature as if that particular explanation had been substantially corroborated by the research, which can be misleading.

Both significance testing and sampling theory are predicated on the assumption that the parent population has a true mean. This (as we have argued) is so only if the population attributes of interest have stability. The pragmatist who says that "statistics work" is suggesting that such stability is the norm. But this cannot be assumed. Anyone who has worked in manufacturing and seen how useful is the application of statistical quality control will inevitably be disappointed in applying statistical theory to populations of consumers. Marketing research in practice is the "land of dirty data" where sanity is saved by not checking for stability and trying to reconcile results. We just talk about bias as if deviation from theory were an aberration of that particular study. But it is not the science of statistics that creates false expectations: the expectations come from wishful thinking about the power of an idealized system to mirror reality and the belief that consumers in mass are essentially analogous to colored balls in a lottery urn.

Statistics is also concerned with generating hypotheses about relationships— hypotheses that are otherwise hidden as mathematics brings out relationships that cannot be discerned without such help. Of particular interest is *multivariate analysis* (MVA), which is the analysis of data that can be presented in a matrix of $N$ rows and $M$ columns. The $N$ rows refer to the groups (e.g., social classes); the $M$ columns are the variables that relate to the groups (e.g., attitudes). The purpose of MVA is twofold: data reduction and the analysis of dependence to indicate whether the variance of some variable (like attitude) can be "explained" by covariance with other variables.

*Multiple regression* is one form of dependence analysis where a single dependent variable $Y$ or several dependent variables $Y_1, Y_2, \ldots, Y_N$ are related to a number of independent variables $X_1, X_2, \ldots, X_N$. As in the case of linear regression and correlation, the aim is to identify the regression weights to get the line of best fit and calculate the (multiple) correlation coefficients. The *analysis of variance* (ANOVA) is also a form of dependence analysis where measures on a single dependent variable $Y$ are collected under a variety of experimental conditions. If we aim to predict from regression, there is an assumption in regression that a *true* line exists so that deviations about regression lines are treated as random errors. But unless we can be sure we are dealing only with random errors about a "true" line or curve, no individual measure has any more right than another to claim to be the "true" value. As one eminent scientist critic, Lancelot Hogben (1956), comments, the theory of regression uses the same formal algebra as the Gaussian theory of error but derives no sanction from it.

There are other techniques like discriminant analysis, principal components analysis, and factor analysis that also come under MVA and additional techniques for dealing with nonlinear categorical variables. Although these are beyond what can be discussed here, it can be said that none is free from controversy among philosophers of mathematics.

*Bayesian Inference.*   One statistical approach to choosing among rival hypotheses is through the use of subjective probabilities combined with Bayesian inference. Bayesian statistics or Bayesian inference starts with each person setting subjective (a priori) probabilities and updating them in the light of new information using Bayes's theorem. When viewed as a branch of probability theory, Bayes's theorem is a simple rule for computing the probability of each of a set of $N$ mutually exclusive and exhaustive events (see the appendix to this chapter). As Putnam (1981) says, the Bayesian school sees the "problem of inductive logic as the problem of defining a confirmation function, that is, a probability function which will determine the mathematical probability of each one of the hypotheses relative to the observational evidence or, in another terminology, the 'degree of support' the evidence lends to each of the alternative hypotheses." Miller (1987), in a thorough review of the approach as applied to choosing among rival hypotheses, argues that although it is helpful in choosing from simplistic hypotheses, it cannot resolve complex problems:

> Bayesian reasoning does guide us in choosing among hypotheses about the mix of red and blue marbles in an urn, on the basis of samples drawn from the urn—if we know that the marbles are uniform and thoroughly mixed after each drawing. . . . However, when we choose among hypotheses in important scientific controversies, we usually lack such prior knowledge of causal structures, or it is irrelevant to the choice. As a consequence, such Bayesian inference to the preferred alternative has not resolved, even temporarily, a single fundamental scientific dispute. (p. 269)

We can conclude the brief incursion into statistics by saying that all models operate within boundary restraints and break down at some point. Models based on statistical theory are no exception, though practitioners act as if they believe otherwise because they believe it is the best approach available. This is the argument of the conventionalist and not the argument of the positivist or the logical empiricist.

## PREDICTION

Traditional philosophy of science has given prominence to prediction in

1. comparing the predictions of a theory, model, or hypothesis against what actually occurs;
2. judging the adequacy of a model, theory, or hypothesis by its predictive power;
3. evaluating and ranking theories and models on the basis of the accuracy, scope, and power of their predictions; and
4. screening out as nonscientific theories that were not, at least in principle, capable of being tested by prediction.

Successful prediction is far from being conclusive evidence. Thus Trevor-Roper points out that both the horoscope of the German Republic dated September 9, 1918, and the horoscope of the Führer drawn up on January 30, 1933, "unanimously predicted the outbreak of war in 1939, the victories till 1941 and then the series of defeats culminating in the worst disasters in the early months of 1945. . . . After peace there would be a difficult time for Germany for 3 years but from April 1948 she would rise to greatness again" (1947, p. 98). For the realist, there is an asymmetry between explanation and prediction except in closed systems like the experimental laboratory. The realist argues that in the real world expected conjunctions are unlikely to occur because of the presence of intervening factors and countervailing causes. In real life (open systems) several generative structures are likely to be at work to produce the effect and we do not know ex ante which will be at work. All this makes the realist more concerned to understand causal structures through retroduction than testing hypotheses through checking predictions. For the instrumentalist, however, theories are simply instruments for prediction and nothing more. This is consistent with the logical positivist view that the aim of science is prediction.

Predictions are warranted if underlying assumptions are warranted, even though predictions are inevitably uncertain and approximate. Decisions not yet made, based perhaps on beliefs not yet formed, will affect the success of all marketing plans. For Popper a necessary part of predicting, say, a radical invention is to say what it is—but to say what it is means to have already invented it. Yet all prediction of social behavior like buying is helped (MacIntyre, 1981) by

1. statistical regularities that are unlikely to change (e.g., more people catch colds in winter, past weather patterns);
2. social conventions (e.g., with respect to household buying); and
3. "causal" regularities (e.g., level of education, type of magazines read).

Popper (1961) claims science is interested in "hypothetical prediction," which predicts what will happen only under certain specified conditions. Such hypothetical prediction he contrasts with "categorical prediction," which simply declares what as a matter of fact is going to happen in the future. Popper regards categorical prediction as little more than prophecy. Most scientists (Kyburg, 1983) argue *if* initial conditions are such and such *and* such and such events do not interfere, *then* the outcome (within certain limits of error) will be such and such (the prediction).

Milton Friedman (1953), the economist, claims a theory's predictions are its vindication and validation; its assumptions are unimportant even if seemingly unsound or untrue. Friedman argues that the ultimate goal of a positive science is a "theory" that yields valid and meaningful predictions about phenomena not yet observed; a theory's assumptions should not enter into the assessment of its value—in fact, focusing on the truth of assumptions gets in the way of its predictive capacity in that efficient prediction depends on simplifying reality. Friedman's view relegates explanation to rationalizations of successful predictions. Von Wright (1983) points out that no law is involved when we talk about predicting action from intention (e.g., intention to buy), so that there is no covering law to be confirmed or refuted. He argues (as Winch would) that only a conceptual connection is involved between intention and action. Predictability is simply the criterion for assessing conformity to a rule; we predict not so much the action as that people will not change their mind and other things will not interfere with their intentions.

## Conclusion

We have briefly reviewed traditional research methodology. Like all human procedures, it is far from perfect for the purpose of establishing a firm basis in knowledge. It is certainly not some fixed universal method but more a "mixed bag" of strategies, rules, tricks, and tactics upon which the researcher draws (Agnew and Pyke, 1969). In spite of wanting to be free of mere conventionalism, instrumentalism, and pragmatism, researchers seeking closure to their work find these philosophies permeate their methodology. As statistics more and more directs research methodology and interpretation of findings, there seems less concern with establishing explanatory hypotheses by ruling out rival hypotheses, though researchers from other disciplines may put forward rival hypotheses. Thus the social psychologist explains why obtaining a small favor from a buyer facilitates making larger demands later on, on the ground that people like to be consistent; the cognitive psychologist sees it as a matter of people examining their past action and coming to believe that their past approval signifies their general support of such requests from that source. Similarly, impression management research has developed as an alternative to theories such as cognitive dissonance and causal attribution theory.

What critics might claim is that problems more and more are being simplified and redefined to fit statistical methodology. Yet this methodology is frequently a conventionalist escape route that has not always served science well because of its relatively trivial amounts of explained variance, lack of comparability across studies, little predictive validity, and so on. The result is a confused field where findings are compromised by competing findings and rival hypotheses. The same is true in all branches of social science. The hidden agenda of all these studies is perhaps that suggested by Boland (1982) as applying to the field of economics—that the accumulation of studies represents an accumulation of evidence that will, for all practical purposes, solve the problem of induction. But this assumes a collective stability of beliefs and wants with static theories to be tested and confirmed over and over again.

The positivists and the logical empiricists cannot be blamed here since much that occurs in research does not meet with their approval. But even if we followed the traditional scientific method, we are still left with the problem of justifying hypotheses, inductive inferences, and explanations while we are coming to realize that all scientific inquiry has a hermeneutic (interpretive) dimension.

What we need in marketing is more honesty about our ignorance on fundamental issues and the recognitition that as long as experts can defend their mutually contradictory positions with equal logic, we in marketing can pick and choose among them, while being tolerant of other rationally defensible procedures. Hermeneutic social science is concerned with understanding human actions by making them intelligible through uncovering their meaning. This goal is a legitimate academic one. With regard to its methods, the interpretive methodology can be rationally defended. In the first place, many interpretations involve such low-level categorizations (perhaps keeping to the words of the respondents) that little controversy is generated. The problem arises when highly abstract hypothetical constructs (like the concept of "displaced meaning") enter into interpretation. Such abstractions do not always translate easily as input into managerial decision-making. Yet high-level constructs are needed in the interests of parsimony of explanation (since they embrace a wide variety of local interpretations) and because we need hypothetical constructs that are rich in sense meaning to produce a rich vein of hypotheses. If some researchers believe such interpretations are better tested by the hypotheticodeductive method rather than trying to seek better explanations, they are at liberty to do so, though they will need to think in terms of eliminating rival hypotheses, which the hermeneutic approach implicitly seeks to do. There are also those who seek collective, external causal influences or, like the realist, causal structures to explain the process by which meaning, intentions, and so on, come about. This also is a legitimate activity that can give a causal account of behavior or at least indicate the factors that entered into a decision.

# APPENDIX: BAYESIAN INFERENCE*

A prediction results from some hypothesis, and the validity of that prediction is related to the probability with which the hypothesis is true. New information can revise probabilities by the use of Bayes's theorem, which is simply conditional probability and extensions of that concept.

Essential to an understanding of Bayes's theorem in its broader aspects is the idea of total probability. Suppose we have two mutually exclusive and exhaustive events, $A$ and not-$A$ ($\overline{A}$). For example, $P(A)$ could be the probability of a machine being loaded properly, while $P(\overline{A})$ could be the probability of its not being loaded properly. Since the events are exhaustive and mutually exclusive,

$$P(A) + P(\overline{A}) = 1$$

If $P(B)$ represents the probability of getting a good product from the machine, then $P(B|A)$ is the probability of getting a good product given that the machine is properly loaded, and $P(B|\overline{A})$ is the probability of getting a good product given that the machine is not properly loaded.

TABLE 12.1. Calculating Probabilities

| Type of Probability | Symbol | Formula | |
|---|---|---|---|
| | | Statistical Independence | Statistical Dependence |
| Joint | $P(AB)$ | $P(A) \times P(B)$ | $P(B) \times P(A|B)$ or $P(A) \times P(B|A)$ |
| Conditional | $P(B|A)$ | $P(B)$ | $P(AB)|P(A)$ |
| | | Mutually exclusive | Not mutually exclusive |
| Alternative | $P(A \text{ or } B)$ | $P(A) + P(B)$ | $P(A) + P(B) - P(AB)$ |

Let us assume the following values:

$$P(A) = 0.7 \qquad P(B|A) = 0.9$$
$$P(\overline{A}) = 0.3 \qquad P(B|\overline{A}) = 0.1$$

Then the joint probability of both getting a good product and loading the machine properly is

$$P(A) \times P(B|A) = 0.7 \times 0.9 = 0.63$$

*From John O'Shaughnessy (1972). *Inquiry and Decision*. London: Allen and Unwin.

and the joint probability of both getting a good product and not loading the machine properly is

$$P(\overline{A}) \times P(B|\overline{A}) = 0.3 \times 0.1 = 0.03$$

The total probability of getting a good product, by the rule for alternative probability (mutually exclusive events), is

$$P(A) \times P(B|A) + P(\overline{A}) \times P(B|\overline{A}) = 0.63 + 0.03$$
$$= 0.66$$

If we now receive information that the machine has produced a good product, we can revise the probability of the machine being properly loaded.

$P(A|B)$ is the probability of the machine being properly loaded given the new information that it has produced a good product.

The conditional probability formula states that

$$P(A|B) = \frac{P(AB)}{P(B)}$$

But

$$P(AB) = P(B) \times P(A|B) = P(A) \times P(B|A)$$

and

$$P(B) = \text{total probability of getting a good product}$$
$$= P(A) \times P(B|A) + P(\overline{A}) \times P(B|\overline{A})$$

so that

$$P(A|B) = \frac{P(AB)}{P(B)} = \frac{P(A) \times P(B|A)}{P(B)} =$$
$$\frac{P(A) \times P(B|A)}{P(A) \times P(B|A) + P(\overline{A}) \times P(B|\overline{A})} = \frac{0.63}{0.66} = 0.95$$

The revised probability 0.95 now replaces 0.7, which was the initial probability for the machine being loaded properly.

We can use the same procedure to reconsider our choice of some hypothesis in the light of new information. Suppose we have four mutually exclusive and exhaustive hypotheses, $A$, $B$, $C$, $D$, and that hypothesis $A$ has been the one favored to date. In fact, probabilities are as follows:

$$P(A) = 0.4$$
$$P(B) = 0.3$$
$$P(C) = 0.2$$
$$P(D) = 0.1$$

In the light of the new data, $Z$, the conditional probabilities of $Z$ relative to each of the hypotheses are

$$P(Z|A) = 0.1$$
$$P(Z|B) = 0.5$$
$$P(Z|C) = 0.2$$
$$P(Z|D) = 0.2$$

The following would be the four revised probabilities:

1. The revised probability of hypothesis $A$ given the new information $Z$ is

$$P(A|Z) = \frac{(0.4)(0.1)}{(0.4)(0.1) + (0.5)(0.3) + (0.2)(0.2) + (0.1)(0.2)}$$
$$= \frac{0.04}{0.25} = 0.16$$

2. The revised probability of hypothesis $B$ given the new information $Z$ is

$$P(B|Z) = \frac{(0.5)(0.3)}{0.25} = \frac{0.15}{0.25} = 0.6$$

3. The revised probability of hypothesis $C$ given the new information $Z$ is

$$P(C|Z) = \frac{(0.2)(0.2)}{0.25} = \frac{0.04}{0.25} = 0.16$$

4. The revised probability of hypothesis $D$ given the new information $Z$ is

$$P(D|Z) = \frac{(0.1)(0.2)}{0.25} = \frac{0.02}{0.25} = 0.08$$

Although hypothesis $A$ was the one initially selected as being the most probable, $B$ would now be selected.

The foregoing process is known as Bayesian inference. The probabilities with which we start are progressively revised as we receive new information.

A problem lies in determining the basic given probabilities. Essentially these are estimates based on experience or derived through some form of analogy with similar hypotheses and types of outcomes. Such "guess-estimating" may be difficult to accept, but the initial probabilities matter less as new evidence emerges to revise them.

## References

Ackoff, Russell L. (1968). *Scientific Method.* New York: Wiley.

Agnew, Neil McK., and Sandra W. Pyke (1969). *The Science Game.* Englewood Cliffs, NJ: Prentice-Hall.

Ajzen, Icek, and Martin Fishbein (1980). *Understanding Attitudes and Predicting Social Behavior.* Englewood Cliffs, NJ: Prentice-Hall.

Bagozzi, Richard P. (1984). "A Prospectus for Theory Construction in Marketing." *Journal of Marketing* 48 (Winter), pp. 11–29.

Bartos, Rena (1982). *The Moving Target.* New York: Free Press.

Barrow, John D. (1988). *The World Within the World.* Oxford: Clarendon Press.

Belch, George E., and Michael A. Belch (1990). *Introduction to Advertising and Promotion Management.* Homewood, IL: Richard D. Irwin.

Blanshard, Brand (1939). *The Nature of Thought.* London: George Allen and Unwin.

Blattberg, R., and J. Golanty (1978). "TRACKER: An Early Test Market Forecasting and Diagnostic Model for New Product Planning." *Journal of Marketing Research* 15 (May), pp. 192–202.

Boland, Lawrence A. (1982). *The Foundations of Economic Method.* London: George Allen and Unwin.

Bridgman, P. W. (1927). *The Logic of Modern Physics.* New York: Macmillan.

Brown, S. W., and C. F. Gaulden (1982). "Replication and Theory Development." In *Theoretical Developments in Marketing,* edited by C. W. Lamb and P. M. Dunne. Chicago: American Marketing Association, pp. 240–43.

Buchholz, Todd (1989). *New Ideas from Dead Economists.* New York: New American Library.

Calder, B. J., L. W. Phillips, and A. M. Tybout (1982). "The Concept of External Validity," *Journal of Consumer Research* 9 (December), pp. 240–44.

Calder, B. J., L. W. Phillips, and A. M. Tybout (1983). "Beyond External Validity." *Journal of Consumer Research* 10 (June), pp. 112–14.

Campbell, H. R. (1920). *Physics, the Elements.* Cambridge: Cambridge University Press.

Carnap, R. (1950). *Logical Foundations of Probability.* Chicago: University of Chicago Press.

Churchill, G. A. (1979). "A Paradigm for Developing Better Measures of Marketing Constructs." *Journal of Marketing Research* 16 (February), pp. 64–73.

Churchman, W. (1966). *Prediction and Optimal Decision.* Englewood Cliffs, NJ: Prentice-Hall, p. 78.

Coombs, Clyde H. (1966). "Theory and Methods of Social Measurement." In *Research Methods in the Behavioral Sciences,* edited by Daniel Katz. New York: Holt, Rinehart and Winston.

Copeland, M. T. (1923). "Relation of Consumers' Buying Habits to Marketing Methods." *Harvard Business Review* 1 (April), pp. 282–89.

Curry, David J., and Peter C. Reisz (1988). "Prices and Price/Quality Relationships: A Longitudinal Analysis." *Journal of Marketing* 52 (January), pp. 36–51.

Davies, Paul (1983). *God and the New Physics.* New York: Simon and Schuster.

Dennett, Daniel C. (1986). *Brainstorms: Philosophical Essays on Mind and Psychology.* Cambridge, MA: The MIT Press.

Dickson, P. R., and J. L. Ginter (1987). "Market Segmentation, Product Differentiation and Marketing Strategy." *Journal of Marketing* 51 (April), pp. 1–10.

Duhem, Pierre (1954). *The Aim and Structure of Physical Theory,* translated by P. Weimer. Princeton, NJ: Princeton University Press.

Drucker, Peter (1964). *Managing for Results.* New York: Harper and Row.

Enis, B. M., and K. J. Roering (1980). "Product Classification Taxonomies: Synthesis and Consumer Implications." In *Theoretical Developments in Marketing,* edited by C. W. Lamb and P. M. Dunne. Chicago: American Marketing Association.

Foxall, Gordon (1990). *Consumer Psychology in a Behavioral Perspective.* London: Routledge.

Friedman, Milton (1953). "The Methodology of Positive Economics." In *Essays in Positive Economics.* Chicago: University of Chicago Press.

Gellner, Ernest (1968). *Words and Things.* Harmondsworth: Pelican Books.

Gellner, Ernest (1971). "Concepts and Society." In *Rationality,* edited by Bryan R. Wilson. New York: Harper Torchbooks.

Gibbon, Guy (1989). *Explanation in Archaeology.* Oxford: Basil Blackwell.
Greenwald, A. G., A. R. Pratkanis, M. R. Leippe, and M. H. Baumgardner (1986). "Under What Conditions Does Theory Obstruct Research Progress?" *Psychological Review* 93, pp. 216–29.
Hacking, Ian (1983). *Representing and Intervening.* Cambridge: Cambridge University Press.
Handy, R., and E. C. Harwood (1973). *A Current Appraisal of the Behavioral Sciences.* Great Barrington, MA: Behavioral Research Council.
Hanson, N. R. (1958). *Patterns of Discovery.* Cambridge: Cambridge University Press.
Harré, Rom (1983). *Great Scientific Experiments.* Oxford: Oxford University Press.
Hayakawa, S. I. (1950). *Symbol, States and Personality.* New York: Harcourt, Brace and World.
Hayek, F. A. (1952). "The Counter-Revolution of Science." Glencoe, IL: Free Press.
Hogben, Lancelot (1956). *Statistical Theory.* New York: W. W. Norton.
Holbrook, Morris B., and John A. Howard (1977). "Frequently Purchased Nondurable Goods and Services." In *Selected Aspects of Consumer Behavior,* edited by Robert Ferber. Washington, DC: National Science Foundation.
Humphrey, H. (1983). *Consciousness Regained.* Oxford: Oxford University Press.
Jacobson, Robert, and David A. Aaker (1987). "The Strategic Role of Product Quality." *Journal of Marketing* 51 (October), pp. 31–44.
Jacoby, Jacob, and Robert W. Chestnut (1978). *Brand Loyalty: Measurement and Management.* New York: Wiley.
Kagan, Jerome (1989). *Unstable Ideas; Temperament, Cognition and Self.* Cambridge, MA: Harvard University Press.
Kneale, W. (1949). *Probability and Induction.* Oxford: Clarendon Press.
Krugman, Herbert E. (1965). "The Impact of Television Advertising: Learning Without Involvement." *Public Opinion Quarterly* 29 (Fall), pp. 349–56.
Kuhn, Thomas S. (1970). *The Structure of Scientific Revolutions,* 2nd ed. Chicago: University of Chicago Press.
Kuhn, Thomas S. (1977). *The Essential Tension.* Chicago: University of Chicago Press.
Kyburg, Henry E. (1983). *Epistemology and Inference.* Minneapolis: University of Minnesota Press.
Laurent, G., and J. Kapferer (1985). "Measuring Consumer Involvement Profiles." *Journal of Marketing Research.* 22 (Feb.) pp. 41–53.
Lichtenstein, Donald R., and Scott Burton (1989). "The Relationship of Behavior Perceived and Objective Price-Quality." *Journal of Marketing Research* 26 (November), pp. 429–43.
Lockhart, Charles (1979). *Bargaining in International Conflicts.* New York: Columbia University Press.
Lynch, J. G. (1982). "On the External Validity of Experiments in Consumer Research." *Journal of Consumer Research* 9 (December), pp. 225–39.
Lynch, J. G. (1983). "The Role of External Validity in Theoretical Research." *Journal of Consumer Research* 10 (June), pp. 109–11.
MacCorquodale, Kenneth, and Paul E. Meehl (1948). "Hypothetical Constructs and Intervening Variables." *Psychological Review* 55, pp. 95–107.
MacIntyre, Alasdair (1981). *After Virtue: A Study in Moral Theory.* Notre Dame, IN: University of Notre Dame Press.
Mackay, A. L. (1973). *The Harvest of a Quiet Eye.* London: The Institute of Physics.
McGrath, J. E., and D. Brinberg (1983). "External Validity and the Research Process: A Comment on the Calder/Lynch Dialogue." *Journal of Consumer Research* 10 (June), pp. 115–24.
Miller, R. W. (1987). *Fact and Method.* Princeton, NJ: Princeton University Press, Chapter 6.
Mintzberg, Henry (1973). *The Nature of Managerial Work.* New York: Harper and Row.
Mintzberg, Henry (1978). "Patterns in Strategy Formation." *Management Science* (May), pp. 934–48.
Montgomery, D. B., and G. L. Urban (1969). *Management Science in Marketing.* Englewood Cliffs, NJ: Prentice-Hall.

Morris, Charles (1964). *Signification and Significance*. Cambridge MA: The MIT Press.

Mowen, J. C. (1979). "Retroduction and the Research Process in Consumer Behavior." In *Conceptual and Theoretical Developments in Marketing*, edited by O. C. Ferrell, S. W. Brown, and C. W. Lamb. Chicago: American Marketing Association.

Murphy, P. E., and B. M. Enis (1986). "Classifying Products Strategically." *Journal of Marketing* 50 (July), pp. 24–42.

Nagel, Ernest (1961). *The Structure of Science*. New York: Harcourt, Brace and World.

Nagel, Ernest (1979). *Teleology Revisited*. New York: Columbia University Press.

Narasimhan, Chakravarthi, and Subrata K. Sen (1983). "New Product Models for Test Market Data." *Journal of Marketing* 47 (Winter), pp. 11–24.

Northrop, F.S.C. (1959). *The Logic of the Sciences and the Humanities*. New York: Meridian Books.

Osgood, C. S., G. J. Suci, and P. H. Tannenbaum (1957). *The Measurement of Meaning*. Urbana: University of Illinois Press.

Peter, J. Paul, and Jerry C. Olson (1987). *Consumer Behavior: Marketing Strategy Perspectives*. Homewood, IL: Richard D. Irwin.

Popper, K. R. (1959). *The Logic of Scientific Discovery*. London: Hutchinson.

Popper, K. R. (1961). *The Poverty of Historicism*. London: Routledge and Kegan Paul.

Pringle, Lewis G., Dale R. Wilson, and Edward I. Brody (1982). "NEWS: A Decision-Oriented Model for New Product Analysis and Forecasting." *Marketing Science* 1 (Winter), pp. 1–29.

Putnam, Hilary (1981). *Reason, Truth and History*. Cambridge: Cambridge University Press.

Quine, W. V. (1987). *Quiddities*. Cambridge, MA: Belknap Press.

Rao, Akshay R., and Kent B. Monroe (1989). "The Effect of Price, Brand Name, and Store Name on Buyers' Perception of Product Quality: An Integrative Review." *Journal of Marketing Research* 26 (August), pp. 351–57.

Rosch, E. (1973). "Natural Categories." *Cognitive Psychology* 4, pp. 328–50.

Silk, A. J., and G. L. Urban (1978). "Pre-test Market Evaluation of New Packaged Goods: A Model and Measurement Methodology." *Journal of Marketing Research* 15 (May). pp. 171–191.

Thomas, David (1979). *Naturalism and Social Science*. Cambridge: Cambridge University Press.

Trevor-Roper, H. R. (1947). *The Last Days of Hitler*. New York: Macmillan.

Von Mises, L. (1949). "Human Action: A Treatise on Economics." New Haven, CT: Yale University Press.

Von Wright, G. H. (1983). *Practical Reason*. Oxford: Basil Blackwell.

Webster, F. E., and Y. Wind (1972). "A General Model for Understanding Organizational Buying Behavior." *Journal of Marketing* 36 (April), pp. 12–19.

Wilson, R. D., and E. I. Brody (1984). "An Empirical Comparison of Awareness Forecasting of New Product Introduction/Comment/Reply." *Marketing Science* 3, pp. 179–208.

Winch, P. G. (1958). *The Idea of a Social Science*. Boston: Routledge and Kegan Paul.

Zaltman, G., and T. V. Bonoma (1979). "The Lack of Heresy in Marketing." In *Conceptual and Theoretical Developments in Marketing*, edited by O. C. Ferrell, S. W. Brown, and C. W. Lamb. Chicago: American Marketing Association, pp. 474–84.

Zeithaml, Valerie A. (1988). "Consumer Perceptions of Price, Quality and Value: A Means–End Model and Synthesis of Evidence." *Journal of Marketing* 52 (July), pp. 2–22.

# 13

## Choosing Explanatory Theory: Recent Controversies in the Philosophy of Science

> A new scientific truth does not triumph by convincing its opponents
> . . . but rather because its opponents eventually die, and a new gen-
> eration grows up that is familiar with it.
>
> Max Planck (1858–1947)

### The Received View and Its Critics

In previous chapters we discussed the various systems of psychology and sociology, their explanatory modes, and their philosophical underpinnings. At every stage we found controversy, with debate being vigorous and sharp on many issues. But polarization was greatest over aims and methods in the study of human behavior. Is the goal understanding or prediction and control, or is it to be explanation broadly interpreted to embrace both understanding and, say, the realist's position? Are the methods associated with the natural sciences to be abandoned in favor of some hermeneutic approach or are both simply alternative windows on a problem rather than some good–bad dichotomy? This book favors the goal of explanation—which is tied to understanding and a help in prediction—combined with methodological pluralism, in which different methodologies suit different kinds of questions as none is suited to all questions equally. Thus to reject certain methodologies is to reject certain kinds of questions. There are, of course, social scientists who think otherwise because of their commitment to the traditional scientific method. But the scientific method sketched in Chapter 12 is no algorithm for producing truth. There is wisdom and reason in the method; nonetheless, it is a technology whose rules need to be blended with creativity and combined and allied with skill. Being a good researcher does not come from reading books on scientific method, although this may help.

Vienna Circle positivism focused on the criteria by which claims to scientific knowledge are accepted. The purpose was to distinguish genuine science from certain kinds of metaphysics linked at the time to fascism. The truth claims of the mature sciences became the dominant theme in the philosophy of science. The belief that scientific hypotheses were either true or untrue tended to push commentators "to oscillate between dogmatism and skepticism." Although it was acknowledged that the scientific method as described by philosophers was more normative than descriptive of what happens in science, it was nonetheless accepted that the method reflected what "any genuine science must be like" (Ravetz, 1990). This is not surprising since, as Harman (1986) says, it is hard to come up with normative principles except by considering how people actually do reason, yet any description of actual reasoning must involve a certain amount of idealization, which is always normative to some extent.

The hermeneutic alternative accepted the general thesis that the "scientific method" had not been produced in an observational vacuum and, though largely normative, was fairly descriptive of best practice in the natural sciences. Thus theories in physics, for example, were viewed as being verified/modified/rejected on the basis of objective facts resulting in cumulative scientific progress as more experiments are undertaken and more facts about the world come to light. But, as suggested in Chapter 12, things are not that simple and explanations are not easily reconciled by testing. Thus the two greatest achievements of physics in the twentieth century—the general theory of relativity and quantum mechanics—are actually in conflict. Nor can natural scientists rise above philosophical positions such as idealism versus realism. Thus Stephen Hawking (1988), a theoretical physicist whose research is concerned with solving the conflict between quantum mechanics and the general theory of relativity, cannot escape taking philosophical positions. From his writings he generally appears to be a realist, but occasionally he writes like an instrumentalist.

In recent years there has been considerable criticism of traditional views about the nature of the scientific enterprise. While it will take time for this criticism to be digested to separate what should be absorbed from what should be rejected, the criticism has highlighted the hermeneutical (interpretive) dimension in all science and shifted attention from "proving" theories to the general role of rationality in science and scientific progress. This chapter reviews recent philosophical controversies over the scientific enterprise: its methods, its goals, its criteria of progress. It also offers some guidance for the "backing of the right horses," or research traditions in the behavioral sciences.

Ever since Thomas Kuhn's *The Structure of Scientific Revolutions* appeared in 1962, traditional philosophy of science has been under attack with regard to both the historical accuracy of its descriptions of how science progresses and the problems it addresses. As is almost inevitable, those criticizing traditional viewpoints tend to suggest there was some unanimity of doctrine. Both Nagel (1979) and Brodbeck (1982) have decried this tendency. Traditional philosophy of science was not monolithic. As Nagel says, much criticism centers on the particular views of Carnap, who, like other members of the Vienna Circle, was a scientist and not a philosopher by training.

What Suppe (1977) calls the received view (RV) is criticized for the following:

1. A narrow focus on methods and the products of science.
2. Making a sharp distinction between observational statements and theoretical statements.
3. Accepting empiricism as the foundation for scientific endeavors.
4. Viewing the progress of science as cumulative.
5. Drawing a sharp distinction between scientific beliefs and beliefs in general.
6. Separating hypothesis generation from methods of justification.

Each of these attacks is reviewed briefly before turning to the views of the more influential critics and other more recent views about the scientific enterprise.

## Narrow Focus

The received view is regarded as focusing primarily on just two questions. What methods should be adopted by science to test and evaluate hypotheses? How should theories be structured? The followers of the RV thus are regarded as too method-centered: "they fix themselves to methods that give prestige and are assumed to be safe and they even go so far as to let the methods decide which problems they will deal with" (Radnitzky, 1970). This is also a criticism that can be made of academic research in marketing. A common criticism is that the professional journals in marketing are more interested in articles based on the latest quantitative technique than in the usefulness of the findings—that trivial findings using the latest tools are preferred to the testing of creative hypotheses yielding useful findings when there is nothing new about the techniques used. This may or may not be so, but it is certainly true that many in research search for technique applications rather than seeking out problems and issues to work on. It is because this is so that so much of what is taught in marketing comes from business itself or from researchers outside of marketing altogether like Michael Porter.

It is not surprising that the RV focuses on developing procedures for hypothesis testing since the philosophical problem was perceived as justifying claims to knowledge. The first major difficulty with all traditional methods of hypothesis testing was discussed in 1906 by the French physicist Pierre Duhem (1954). Duhem pointed out that a physicist can never subject an isolated hypothesis but only a group of hypotheses to experimental test. When the experimental results are in disagreement with the predictions, all the physicist learns is that at least one of the hypotheses in the group is unacceptable, but the experiment does not say which it is. As a consequence we can always rescue a hypothesis by making ad hoc assumptions to reconcile the evidence with the hypothesis.

We cannot verify or certify an explanatory hypothesis as true since, as Popper points out, the elimination of a finite number of rival hypotheses cannot reduce the infinity of the surviving rivals. On the other hand, we cannot be sure we have falsified a scientific hypothesis since, as Duhem showed, the falsification takes place within the presence of several other hypotheses that are inevitably tested at the same time. Laws, theories, models, hypotheses do not have experimentally isolatable, testable consequences. To predict their consequences, all kinds of auxiliary hypotheses are assumed (Harré, 1983). Even if this were not so, how can we be sure that a theory, law, or hypothesis that is false today when applied to some situation will be false in the future or when applied elsewhere?

It might seem easier to establish the probability of the theory, model, or scientific hypothesis being true. But a probability estimate is a ratio and no such ratio can be given when the denominator is infinite. Resort can be made to logical or subjective probabilities but no one has so far developed a reliable method of measuring logical probabilities, and subjective probabilities are of dubious value.

The RV is justificationist, seeking to identify knowledge with empirical proof. However, since every proof and method of proof can be questioned, there is resort in practice to conventionalism, instrumentalism, or pragmatism. Early criticism of justificationism is apparent in the later Popper. His *critical fallibilism* acknowledges there is no objective way of knowing when we have reached the truth, although Popper avoids complete skepticism by arguing that there are criteria allowing us to detect error.

The failure to discover a scientific method that would prove a theory, model, or set of hypotheses has shifted interest toward comparing rival theories or a series of theories in some research tradition. How knowledge grows or develops has attracted more attention as a reaction to the failures of verifiability, confirmation, falsification, or Bayesian inference to provide an adequate foundation for firm knowledge.

In recent years philosophers have abandoned the goal of a strong justificationist program of absolutely proving or disproving. The nonjustificationist abandons justificationism in favor of *rational criticism,* holding that all beliefs should be open to criticism all the time. There is a need in marketing for much more rational criticism beyond that supplied by statistics, which is typically used at present as a stick to beat stray mongrel dogs into orthodox conventionalist kennels.

## Sharp Distinction Between Theory and Observation

What awakened interest in the role of rationality in science is not just the recognition that testing involves testing several hypotheses, but the recognition that testing is not a matter of just checking models, hypotheses, and so on, against neutral, objective, and unproblematic "facts." In the RV, theories are said to be checked against the facts, with the facts regarded as neutral and independent of theory. Given this is so, the correspondence theory of truth is dominant. What is given in sense experience is viewed as concrete fact about reality. The RV assumes the existence of uninterpreted facts. Against this claim it is argued that theoretical concepts set up expectations that guide sensory receptors to some sensations more than to others so that interpretations are in some important sense theory-loaded. Thus different theoretical frameworks, embodying different concepts, direct attention to one type of explanation rather than another and give rise to differences in operational measures and to different interpretations of the same facts.

Quine (1953), a mathematical logician, showed there was no clear distinction between analytic and synthetic statements for reasons that undermine the view of synthetic statements "matching" some part of reality. Quine (1968) argues that what science is prepared to assert as true forms part of a seamless "web of belief." Particular observations lie on the outside of the web; explanatory laws are part of the center. When anomalies or contradictory findings occur, scientists attempt reconciliation in a way that does not disturb the core of the science. But when revolutions do occur, basic concepts like "space" and "energy" are redefined so that concepts like space that appeared analytic turn out to be revisable. Everything in the whole web of belief can be revised and no statement is necessarily true or analytic unless we wish to treat it as such.

Quine (1968) argues that our judgments about the nature of things are always embedded in some theory. Although we can substitute one theory for an entirely different one, we cannot detach ourselves from theory entirely and see the world without preconceptions of it. Quine shows that the same stimuli can with equal coherence be captured by incompatible conceptions. This means we cannot think of the concepts of our language as simply mirroring facts about the world and we cannot settle disputes among theories by pointing to "neutral" facts. Thus for Quine, what is true is what is true relative to some theory and what is true relative to some theory can always be revised. As a result, no "reality" is conceivable except through some conceptual scheme we have adopted. Quine is an empiricist and denies any position of relativism as commonly interpreted.

Scientific facts are interpreted so that what is typically believed to be factual is actually inferred. This means that two scientists (one an eighteenth-century biologist and one living today) with different conceptual frameworks will interpret reality (say, a slide with bacteria on it) in different ways. On this view, science is always mediated by theoretical frameworks so no sharp distinction can be drawn between theory and observation: observation is theory impregnated.

The claim that there are no facts at all independent of theory represents a relativist position but only in the sense that "facts" are relative to the theory proposed, as follows:

1. Facts are entirely conceptual, arising from concepts tied to theory: the classification involved in perception presupposes concepts. Because facts are theory-loaded, science is fact-correcting in that a new theory can and often does deny the facts assumed in the theories it displaces (e.g., the denial of facts like phlogiston being given off by burning). Thus we are able to classify an activity as shopping, bidding, picking, and so on, only because we understand the concepts of shopping, bidding, picking. As we have seen, different explanatory systems in psychology and sociology develop different concepts, which give rise to different interpretations of behavior.

2. There are no invariant facts on which science can build to form an independent foundation for knowledge. What rules of correspondence (operational measures) are accepted depends on their cohering with the theoretical constructs. Correspondence rules or operational definitions always remain hypotheses about the relationship of phenomena to theoretical constructs. Thus any attitude measure is tied to the theoretical construct of attitude and if different researchers hold different conceptualizations of attitutde, their measures will reflect this.

3. Experiencing is always experiencing in terms of conceptual structures already absorbed. Thus consumers in the United States who are watching television will interpret and experience the event differently from someone elsewhere who has never previously seen television. What critics here are arguing is that we need a pluralistic approach to testing that embraces an *interpretative* theory that provides the so-called facts and an *explanatory* theory that seeks to explain the facts. Those who adopt this view argue that we cannot just regard the facts as unproblematic and so refute the hypothesis if in conflict with the facts. The problem for the scientist lies in reconciling *inconsistencies* between the explanatory theory and the interpretive theory that provides the so-called facts.

The preceding views have not gone unchallenged. While accepting that observation is theory-loaded and theoretical concepts do direct what is seen, traditionalists argue that it does not follow from this that scientific observation is biased toward hypotheses confirmation as alleged. This is true. However, it misses the thrust of the argument, which is that theory directs attention toward a certain solution or type of explanation rather than considering rival explanations based on other frameworks. In other words, each of the systems of psychology and sociology will seek solutions that cohere with the basic explanatory system.

Weimer (1979) sees a movement in the philosophy of science from a belief in proof (or justificationism) to nonjustificationism. He suggests the following stages, beginning with three *justificationist* stages:

1. Proof/certainty is thought to be attainable.
2. Only probable truth is thought to be attainable.
3. Facts are seen to be theory contaminated.  ·

followed by four *nonjustificationist* stages:

4. Recognition that theories or models of theories are not evaluated in isolation against neutral facts but rather in a maze of competing hypotheses. So there is difficulty in getting others to agree over what has been falsified.

5. Science is seen nonetheless to progress in the absence of refutation.

6. Science is seen not to need any confirmation theory to make progress.

7. Growth of knowledge or theory growth replaces the idea of instant assessment or testing as the most crucial concern. (As we shall see, while there is still this interest in theory development and the growth of knowledge, there are additional concerns).

## Acceptance of Empiricism

Positivists take experience (perceptions plus the judgments emanating from these perceptions) as the foundation for all theoretical knowledge. However, theory always goes beyond sense experience since in expounding a theory the scientist goes beyond what can be observed. There is thus only an indirect connection in practice between observations and the abstract hypothetical constructs embedded in the theoretical background of any model. But if the positivist's sharp distinction between theory and observation is rejected, the claim that the only firm knowledge is that grounded in observation is seriously undermined. The constructs or terms used in theories are idealizations of the entities to which they apply. If there is a need for correspondence rules to link theory to observation, there is a need of a theory to identify the facts!

If theories cannot be proved and all theoretical entities cannot be defined in observational terms, then the claim that scientific theories necessarily capture reality becomes dubious. If we accept that there is no guarantee that truth can be reached by a continuous application of the scientific method, it is not surprising that this leads some philosophers like Quine to reject realism as a practical strategy. But Suppe (1977) claims most philosophers are still committed to realism in their analysis of the status of theories and theoretical terms. Realism is preferred as a working hypothesis to any brand of instrumentalism since realism urges the scientist to seek ever-fuller explanations, whereas instrumentalism is content with prediction. Many philosophers, too, accept the limitations of empiricism; nonetheless, they believe that too much is being inferred from these limitations in that the logical weaknesses in the RV are equated with there being nothing in science that has a firm foundation, which seemingly ignores the scientific achievements of the modern world.

## Science as Cumulative

The RV argues that science is cumulative, that is, the latest accepted theories embrace and enlarge on what went before. Apparent "breaks" (discontinuities) in this progression are viewed as temporary puzzles for scientists to resolve and reconcile with the view of cumulative progress. If scientific knowledge is accumulative and true, then this implies that new theories must cohere with older theories and subsume them. New theories will not conflict with older theories but simply update them, though there might be debates among inductivists, hypotheticodeductivists, and Bayesians about how this updating should be pursued. The idea of science being cumulative should be distinguished from the idea of science as progressing since science can progress in the sense of being able to do more things without science showing *cumulative* progress. This view of science as cumulative is now under attack with discontinuities and alternative "paradigm" approaches being emphasized. If we look at Chapters 7 and 8, which discuss the systems of psychology and sociology on which marketing academics draw, we no doubt will find some continuity and cumulative progress within each research tradition but each tradition defines itself by contrasting its assumptions and methods with earlier traditions and prides itself on rejecting the explanations of actions offered by rival approaches.

## Scientific Beliefs

Some philosophers question whether the grounds for accepting scientific statements are all that different from those found outside science. Nor is it all that obvious that "hard evidence" will shift beliefs when such beliefs are basic to the accepted orthodoxy. Thus the hard evidence of Garcia and Koelling (1966) undermined behaviorist learning theory (see Chapter 7), but the findings were dismissed by one prominent learning theorist as "no more likely than birdshit in a cuckoo clock" (quoted by Frank, 1988, p. 149).

There is the assumption that the scientist wears two hats. When wearing the hat of the scientist, he or she adopts rigorous methods and a tough, uncompromising logic. On the other hand, in everyday life the same scientist wears another hat whereby evidence is not scrutinized, thinking is sloppy, and emotional appeals can be crucial. It is true that scientists do adopt certain methods that act as precautions against committing certain common errors, but their training is likely to invade other spheres of life as well. Much of the logic associated with a training in scientific method can find analogous expression in the professional buyer's decision-making and that of other professionals. The principles of practical reasoning (and doing research is a practical technological activity) are the same whether exercised in research or in day-to-day living (see Harman, 1986). This does not mean that the scientifically trained mind has no advantage but that the advantage carries over into problem solving generally: mental training does indeed provide an edge in coping with life.

## Hypothesis Generation and Justification

The RV showed little interest in the process by which hypotheses are generated. Little or no attention was paid to the context of discovery. This was regarded as the domain of psychology. But for many philosophers a sharp distinction between discovery and justification is misleading since the two are interwoven in that theoretical orientation influences both what is discovered and how models are tested. Thus the theoretical discussion in Chapter 9 on emotion has many implications for marketing that can be set out as hypotheses. For example, it suggests that the weighting of attributes is more likely to be changed by emotional appeals based on getting the consumer to see things from a different perspective rather than by logical argument.

## Recent Influential Views on Science and the Scientific Enterprise

### Sir Karl R. Popper

Popper's philosophy of science, introduced previously, embraces Popper's early ideas. Although he later abandoned some of these views, he has remained anti-inductivist, anti-conventionalist, and anti-instrumentalist in his writings. He has also become one of the major figures in the growth of knowledge approach. Popper rejects induction when interpreted to mean that science proceeds from pure observation to general laws: universal statements cannot be inferred from singular statements, and there is no way laws or theories can be "read out of the data." To Popper, all observation in science is guided by hypotheses, so that telling a scientist to just observe is absurd without guidance on what to observe. Popper opposes instrumentalism (the view that laws, theories, or models are merely instruments for prediction and control) because he believes that instrumentalism, if generally adopted, would be fatal to scientific advance since in denying the truth or falsity of theories it abandons attempts to falsify them. Conventionalism, too, is rejected by Popper because it does not stimulate the advancement of science and would rest content with substituting correlational data for explanation.

Lakatos (1968) distinguishes three distinct stages in Popper's thinking:

$Popper_0$, the dogmatic falsificationist;

$Popper_1$, the methodological falsificationist; and

$Popper_2$, the sophisticated methodological falsificationist.

## $POPPER_0$ THE DOGMATIC FALSIFICATIONIST

Initially, Popper claimed that although science could not prove any scientific hypothesis conclusively, it could disprove conclusively. Scientific laws are *falsifiable* but not verifiable: a universal law can be shown to be false but never proved to be absolutely true. Popper argued that this falsifiability separates the genuine scientific hypothesis from the counterfeit since a genuine scientific hypothesis must run a well-specified risk of refutation. Positivists tended to interpret this falsifiability criterion as an alternative version of the verifiability principle (see Chapter 11), but Popper was never interested in developing any criterion of meaning; he sought only to develop a method of distinguishing science from its impostors. Popper rejected the Vienna Circle principle of verifiability on several grounds but notably because it would not exclude from genuine science subjects like astrology that were either superstition or dogma.

For Popper, scientific knowledge is not proven assertion but warranted assertion since science advances not by proof but by bold conjecture and attempted falsification. Bold conjecture commits the scientist to definite expectations as to what a hypothesis rules out if true and what evidence would refute it. Popper also argues that the better (potentially more fruitful) hypotheses, more often than not, are the more improbable ones; it does not follow from this, however, that he is proposing (as many have claimed) an improbability criterion for the choice of scientific hypotheses. Popper acknowledges that such "better" hypotheses may have already been refuted.

If a hypothesis stands up to attempts to falsify or refute it, it is *corroborated*. Popper speaks of the degree of corroboration but not as a measure of the probability of the hypothesis being true. The degree of corroboration is a sort of status report on the model, law, or theory at some particular point in time. It is an evaluation of the past performance of the theory, law, or model with respect to the way it solves problems; its degree of testability; the severity of tests it has undergone; and the way it has stood up to these tests. A highly corroborated hypothesis, law, model, or theory will have high information content and explanatory power. But Popper argues that all this does not increase the probability of a theory, law, and so on, being true since this would imply that the problem of induction had been solved. Ayer (1982) finds it odd to argue that high corroboration does not make a hypothesis more credible (probable). As Ayer says, would not the whole process of testing be futile if it did not help justify our beliefs?

Popper rejects the concept of "confirming" a hypothesis since there is nearly always evidence that favors some hypothesis while the concept itself has overtones of having established truth. Popper claims falsification stresses negative instances or counterexamples in contrast to the inductivist who, he claims, stresses positive instances from which nondemonstrative inferences are drawn. But whether in marketing or elsewhere hypotheses, theories, or models are not necessarily overturned by a single falsified prediction. The hypothesis, for example, may be only probable, so falsification in a strict sense is not possible except by agreement to accept statistical conventions. Even then there are problems, given the difficulty of obtaining a truly representative sample; moreover, falsification is always complicated by the presence of initial conditions and auxiliary hypotheses. This means that anomalous results can always be explained away without surrendering a theory, hypothesis, or the model's general assertions. In any case a "good" model or theory is unlikely to be abandoned unless a better one comes along, just as the consumer will continue with a deficient product to meet a need until a better product comes along. Theories are not necessarily overturned by a single falsified prediction, and scientific hypotheses, often interlocked in models, are not typically tested in isolation. Finally, although falsificationism should be a tool in research, criticism of hypotheses cannot be confined to just applying the falsification test.

## POPPER₁, THE METHODOLOGICAL FALSIFICATIONIST

Popper$_1$ accepts as problematic that the refuting "facts" can be queried, since there is always room for dispute over the interpretation of the refuting facts. In other words, the observational statements used to falsify a scientific hypothesis cannot be empirically conclusive. Test results may be vitiated through auxiliary assumptions being unfounded, and judgment is involved in deciding what outcomes or predictions are to count as disproof. But falsification is, in principle, still possible. Popper argues that even probability hypotheses are, in principle, refutable since they make assertions about the relative frequencies of some class of events. In such a case Popper would follow the statistical practice of rejecting a hypothesis if the recorded frequency differed from the predicted frequency by more than a certain amount. Though Popper insists on testing rival hypotheses, this move to statistical testing represents a move to the conventionalism of significance testing as a way to bring about closure.

## POPPER₂, THE SOPHISTICATED METHODOLOGICAL FALSIFICATIONIST

Popper$_2$ (1972) gives more prominence to recognizing that the refuting facts are not known independently of theory—that such facts are not just given but stem from theory. When a hypothesis, model, or theory turns out to be incompatible with certain alleged facts, a decision has to be made as to whether to refute the (theoretically determined) facts or whether to refute the theory, model, or hypothesis. Scientists may treat the facts as unproblematic or immunize the hypothesis from refutation by assuming ad hoc hypotheses. Theories, hypotheses, or models, too, may seemingly be falsified when they simply apply to a different or more limited domain or field of application than that in which they were tested. On this basis, all theories remain guesses, conjectures, or hypotheses since there is no way of absolutely establishing truth. Popper$_2$ thus accepts fallibilism.

*Fallibilism* is the doctrine that nothing about the world can be known for certain since such certainty presupposes we have solved the problem of induction. All our factual knowledge is probable only in that we cannot prove the contrary to be absolutely impossible. In any case there is no certainty that any law will extend indefinitely into the future. If theories cannot be conclusively proved or conclusively disproved, then fallibilism in explanation must be accepted. Whereas traditional philosophy of science focuses on the structure and testing of theories, models, or hypotheses, Popper$_2$ sees the central problem to be one of showing how science progresses by, for example, backing the right horses in choosing among rival theories. Although Popper acknowledges that there are no criteria for demonstrating the attainment of truth, he believes the rules (criteria) followed by scientists can identify error. The aim of science is thus to find errors and correct them. Hence his fallibilism does not lead to radical skepticism. [Radical skepticism is the thesis that we never have the slightest reason to believe anything. Radical skepticism is not the same as the commonsense view that nothing can be known for certain, which acknowledges that practical certainty is possible even if absolute certainty is not. Radical skepticism, except as a debating ploy of the devil's advocate, is typically rejected on the ground that it cannot be coherently stated without presupposing its own falsity. (See Harman, 1973.)]

Popper argues that the inductivist sees scientific progress as consisting of evolutionary improvements in a theory while he views scientific progress as resulting from replacing current theories with better ones.

How does Popper suggest we choose from among rival theories? How do we choose between theories spun off by the different explanatory systems in psychology and sociology? While falsification is still best for testing *within* theories to improve them, the evaluation of competing theories (*between* theory choosing) involves a wider range of criteria since the competing theories may survive all feasible types of testing. Popper$_2$ argues that the competing theories must be assessed *together rather than each in isolation,* applying all types of criticism but particularly the search for inconsistencies. Popper's position is thus labeled one of *critical* fallibilism.

According to Popper, one theory, model, or hypothesis may be considered more *logically promising* than another

1. if that theory has more empirical content. The empirical content of a theory is defined negatively in terms of the consequences or outcomes that are ruled out by the theory. A theory with high empirical content has a high class of potential falsifiers. The more the theory rules out, that is, the more the observable state of affairs the hypothesis forbids, the more its empirical content. The greater a theory's empirical content, the greater the testability of the theory and the more improbable it is, and so the more informative it is if it withstands testing. Science seeks (or should seek) improbable theories which are capable of surviving critical tests;

2. if at least some of the "excess" empirical content of the theory over its rivals predicts novel consequences that are corroborated in the sense of surviving various forms of critical evaluations.

Although Popper acknowledges that we can never *justify* a theory by claiming to know that it is true, he argues that we are able to support a *preference* for one theory over another in the sense of marshaling better reasons for choosing it. What counts is a theory's relative boldness or empirical content and its ability to survive criticism. Popper argues that scientists should choose the theories that have higher *verisimilitude.* Popper defines verisimilitude as truthlikeness. Verisimilitude combines the notions of truth and empirical content in that the verisimilitude of a theory is its truth content minus its falsity content.

Popper believes the goal of science is truth and *science can show progress toward such a goal.* Popper claims science gets better approximations to truth ("greater *verisimilitude*") through the following process:

$$p_1 \rightarrow TT \rightarrow EE \rightarrow P_2$$

where $p_1$ = the problem from which we start
$TT$ = the tentative theory, which is the imaginative conjectural solution that we first reach
$EE$ = error elimination, which consists of a severe *critical* examination of our conjectural solution
$P_2$ = the problem situation as it emerges from the first attempt to solve $P_1$, and this leads to still further attempts to get nearer the truth

$T_2$, the later theory for dealing with the problem, is nearer to the truth or more similar to the truth than the original theory $T_1$, "if and only if more true statements follow from $T_2$ but not more false statements, or at least equally as many true statements but fewer false statements." Popper acknowledges that the degree of verisimilitude is not measurable. Just as all theories are conjectural, so also are all appraisals of theories, including the comparisons of theories from the point of view of their verisimilitude. For Popper science should always be "revolutionary" to help progress toward discovering the truth. Science should proceed by bold imaginative conjectures (hypotheses) if the growth of knowledge is to be accelerated. There should be a proliferation of theories set out for evaluation; science should be an "open society" for ideas and should not be wedded at any time to just the one theory. Popper$_2$ rejects the building block (cumulative science) view of science but instead advocates bold conjectures away from existing orthodoxy.

## Criticism of Popper

Popper has been criticized for his views on *within*-theory testing and *between*-theory choosing. Ernest Nagel (1979), an early critic of Popper, while agreeing that science is an honest search for evidence to *eliminate rival hypotheses,* rejects Popper's particular conception of the role of falsification in theory development as an oversimplification that is "close to being a caricature of scientfic procedure." He views the substance of Popper's later ideas on science, even when understood to be prescriptive, as not "any less dubious than when they are taken to be descriptive" (pp. 76–77). Popper was inspired by Einstein, whose theory of general relativity appeared to be a bold conjecture with Einstein inviting scientists to falsify his claim. But what Nagel and others found simplistic about falsificationism was that it failed to show how knowledge could advance through applying tests designed to falsify hypotheses. As Ravetz (1990) says, if the hypothesis is falsified, we gain only the knowledge that some particular hypothesis is false. On the other hand, if the test does not falsify, we learn only that the hypothesis has not yet been proved false: "as a principle of method such an approach is bankrupt." Ravetz also points out that the theory of evolution seems structurally incapable of falsification but is accepted simply on the ground that it appears the only conceivable rational explanation of "how the rich and subtle order of nature has come to be."

Putnam (1981), a critic of traditional philosophy of science, does not regard Popper's scheme for *within*-theory testing to be significantly different from the more traditional approach. Both views proceed by arguing theories/hypotheses/models imply predictions which, if falsified, falsify the theory. On the more traditional view, if sufficient predictions are true, the theory is "confirmed"; Popper simply substitutes the word "corroborated." Putnam argues that scientific activity cannot in general be thought of as a matter of testing theories or models. This is in line with Harré and Secord (1973), who point out that much scientific research does not involve the sequence hypothesis $\rightarrow$ prediction $\rightarrow$ test but is simply exploratory, with the scientist having no clear idea of what is likely to occur but simply aiming to find out.

A more general criticism is of Popper's claim to avoid inductivist thinking. It has been frequently pointed out that Popper does not avoid the problem of induction with his concept of deductivism since it is in fact an inductive step to assume that some theory which has passed a variety of tests will be a better guide to the future than one that has not been so tested.

It was in a footnote to the 1959 edition of *The Logic of Scientific Discovery* that Popper went along with the view expressed earlier that observations and observation statements were always interpretations of the facts observed and that these interpretations are made in light of the theories held by the scientists. Hacking (1983) disputes that this is always so and offers support for the more traditional view. Hacking argues that not all experimentation is dominated by theory and that much research precedes the development of the relevant theory. Hacking claims that some profound experimental work is generated entirely by theory, but some great theories spring from pretheoretical experimentation. Hacking's claim would seem to revolve around the term "theory." Although much experimentation is not directed by any articulated, formally developed theory, it is not carried out uninformed by any ideas at all. Ideas lend direction to research and such ideas are embryo models or theories.

Popper's concept of verisimilitude has been criticized as potentially stultifying science. Thus Robinson writes:

> If scientists were to take Popper's conception of verisimilitude and progress seriously it would have the effect of stultifying growth and progress because what he calls "verisimilitude" and "progress" could be increased or even maximized by a policy of incurious repetition of safe experiments. (1971, p. 195)

In the process $p_1 \rightarrow TT \rightarrow EE \rightarrow p_2$ Popper emphasizes the role of criticism in error elimination. But such criticism focuses on the search for contradiction and so the question arises as to whether such a process could ever account for the growth of science. Feyerabend (1977) argues that neither proof nor the absence of contradictions (consistency) seems to be necessary for the acceptance of a theory: good reasons for accepting a theory cover more than the need for consistency.

Stove (1982), while acknowledging the "fallibilist" position that a scientific theory is never certain, claims Popper goes beyond this in asserting that a scientific theory is never even probable in relation to the evidence for it. On these grounds, he accuses Popper of being an irrationalist. A person may be called irrational if prone to indulge in invalid reasoning, but an irrationalist is someone who explicitly repudiates the generally recognized norms of valid reasoning. This is a strange charge to make against Popper. Stove says Popper's irrationalism stems from Hume's skepticism about induction. Hume argued induction was logically invalid and cannot be justified as a way to truth. Positivists accepted this but sought to get around Hume's argument by constructing a nondeductive logic, a theory of logical probability, inductive logic, and so on. Popper (1968) denies any of these are solutions. Stove claims the traumatic event for Popper was the overthrow of Newtonian physics and he was determined after that to repel any claims to truth on behalf of any scientific theory. Stove points out that Hume never actually used the term "inductive argument" but used expressions such as "inference from experiences" which capture the concept of induction. In any case the idea that induction is not a route to true knowledge when allied to the claim that there is no other route, according to Stove, leads Popper to his irrationalist position.

Stove argues that there is no point in searching for a way of turning induction into a logically valid argument ("invalidity that cannot be cured, had better be endured"). The fact that we cannot validate an inductive argument does not mean that premises about observed events are never enough to believe the conclusion. Stove is an *inductive probabilist* in contrast to Hume, Popper, Kuhn, Lakatos, and Feyerabend, who, as *deductivists,* claim an argument is *reasonable* only if it is valid, that is, *P* is a reason to believe *Q* only if *Q* is deducible from *P*. Inductive arguments are unreasonable to these philosophers because their invalidity cannot be cured by additional premises supplied either by a priori knowledge or by experience. Stove argues the acceptance of deductivism by Popper leads to a rejection of terms like "confirm" and "verify" as nondeductive, logical expressions.

## Thomas S. Kuhn

Philosophers of science typically focus on the questions of how science justifies (tests) its claims and how science structures its theories. When history is quoted it is mainly to illustrate a method or to show the chronology of scientific progress and not to provide any historical analysis of how scientific discoveries are made and how scientific progress comes about. Kuhn (1962, 1970), a historian of science, views the historical development of any science as influencing both the content and methods of that science. Kuhn moves away from the focus on theory/model testing and theory building to what he terms scientific "paradigms." A scientific paradigm is the overall conceptualization of the field involving values, concepts, theories, models, and applications. Understanding a paradigm does not come about from memorizing laws or theories or models but by mastering applications: being able to solve a certain class of problem and being able to recognize in different situations further applications.

While antipositivists in social science attacked methodological monism, they accepted the picture of natural science as traditionally described. Kuhn, however, argues that the traditional picture is distorted in several ways (Hacking, 1983):

1. There is no sharp distinction between observation and theory since theory influences what is observed.

2. A live science does not have a tight deductive structure.

3. Living scientific concepts are not particularly precise.

4. There is no methodological unity, even within the natural sciences, in that there are many very distinct methods whose use depends on the nature of the inquiry. (If natural science itself follows no one particular method, it becomes more difficult and more dubious to speak of the need for unity of method among all the sciences.)

5. The context of justifying scientific claims cannot be separated from the context in which the discovery itself is made.

6. There are no transcendent rules for justifying the claims of science. There are many explanatory theories that can be shown to be consistent with any particular body of data, so that the notion of accepting the best supported theory is a dubious one, particularly given the fact that there is no logic establishing relative degrees of confirmation. Kuhn focuses on tradition and the collective judgment of scientists working within that tradition as creating science or at least influencing what is acceptable. This view contrasts with any philosophy of science that stresses objective transcendent rules in scientific method. Kuhn's claim that scientific knowledge is what some community of scholars states it to be is essentially a conventionalist position. On this basis,

scientific knowledge is simply *assertoric knowledge,* namely, that which is acceptable to the discipline and not known to be false. A good deal of marketing is assertoric knowledge as characterized by the conventional wisdom in the field.

7. Science is not cumulative in the sense that later theories improve on earlier ones to ensure continuity in the growth of scientific knowledge. Kuhn points to the discontinuities, that is, the absence of a single, unbroken, theoretical thread connecting earlier with later theories. He claims that there are revolutions in science that result in a complete break or discontinuity with what has gone before. On this view, destruction and re-creation is a better description of the history of science than the idea of science being cumulative. If we look to the various explanatory systems in psychology (Chapter 7) and sociology (Chapter 8), we do not get the impression of a single unbroken theoretical thread running from earlier to later theories. Instead there are discontinuities and conflicts. However, Kuhn was discussing the mature, natural sciences, not the behavioral sciences, although much of what he says seems highly applicable.

Kuhn's historical approach views any science as passing through a cycle:

1. The preparadigm stage of the science.
2. Emergence of a paradigm following a breakthrough by the great scientists in the field.
3. A period of "normal" science.
4. A crisis stage leading to a questioning of the current paradigm in favor of a new one.
5. A sudden, abrupt transition to a new paradigm.
6. The return to a period of normal science acting within the new paradigm.

### PREPARADIGM STAGE

Before a field of study can be termed a mature science, Kuhn claims the field must have an accepted paradigm. It is within such a paradigm that "normal" science occurs. Kuhn (1962) saw any mature science as dominated and shaped by its paradigm.

Kuhn's initial (1962) conceptualization of a paradigm was criticized for its vagueness. Masterman (1970), for example, claimed that Kuhn used the term in at least twenty-one different ways. Kuhn (1970, 1974) later defined the term in two related senses:

1. *As a disciplinary matrix:* The paradigm is "disciplinary" because it is the common possession of some scientific community and a "matrix" because every paradigm embodies sets of orderly elements like
   • symbolic generalizations or expressions;
   • beliefs and values sought like predictive accuracy, simplicity, consistency;
   • models; and
   • *exemplars,* which are the shared set of crucial, striking, successful examples of problem-solving applications.

2. *As exemplars:* While exemplars are part of the disciplinary matrix, they are also paradigmatic of the field and as such *represent, in the most fundamental sense, the word paradigm. Exemplars represent the paradigm-as-achievement* and so serve as models for future generations of scientists. They are the concrete successes attributable to the disciplinary matrix's power. Through familiarity with the field's exemplars the scientist absorbs the rules to be followed for extending the application of the disciplinary matrix.

The concept of a disciplinary matrix comes closer to defining a social science than does the view of a science as being composed of theories along the lines suggested by Campbell (see Chapter 12).

Every scientific community at every level of science down to highly specialized areas will have its exemplars. With these exemplars acting as a guide, scientists are told what facts to look for and what they should see in the facts. Such a view ties together theory and observation. We can either say that there are no facts independent of the paradigms used to apprehend them or, at least, that two people confronting the same facts through different conceptual lenses (tied to different paradigms) will interpret the facts differently.

Traditional philosophy of science viewed the practice of science as being directed by absorbed theory linked to reality by models and rules of correspondence (operational measures). But according to Kuhn, scientists learn scientific concepts and methods through exemplars, not through being indoctrinated with any theory. Just as a child may recognize a swan without possessing any explicit criterion for distinguishing a swan, a student working on exemplars comes to understand the concepts and methods of the discipline without being taught such things as correspondence rules. (Kuhn suggests the formalization and learning of correspondence rules may be dysfunctional in representing a premature closure of class boundaries.)

Kuhn shifts the focus from theories and models to the concept of a paradigm. Unlike the understanding of a theory, understanding a paradigm signifies the ability to apply a certain set of concepts and techniques. In the language of cognitive psychology, it is procedural knowledge rather than declarative knowledge. This concept of a paradigm thus embodies within it a *performance conceptualization* of *scientific knowledge* that lends support to those who believe in exposing students to a whole range of successful applications rather than just teaching "theory." With respect to marketing, it suggests that mastering marketing is less a matter of learning "principles" than of being exposed to many detailed case studies of successful marketing that can act as exemplars so that the student sees the possibility of similar applications. It also means learning to handle and apply the concepts of marketing.

Every science will have its disciplinary matrix and exemplars. Every mature specialized area within a science will have its own exemplars. But, contrary to popular interpretations, Kuhn does not claim that the possession of a paradigm is what distinguishes science from nonscience. If the development of a paradigm does not distinguish science from nonscience, some writers have argued that it is the possession of a *shared* paradigm (i.e., the adoption of a common disciplinary matrix and set of exemplars by the scientific community) that is a necessary condition for a discipline to be a science. Some social scientists even attribute the poor state of social science to the absence of a shared paradigm (Friedrichs, 1970). However, Kuhn makes no such claim, though he does believe that a shared paradigm is what distinguishes a *mature* science.

EMERGENCE OF A PARADIGM

It is the emergence of shared exemplars that is key to the emergence of the rest of the disciplinary matrix. In working with exemplars the scientist acquires practical understanding of the scientific terms used without formal operational definitions and comes to see in the data how the principles implicit in the disciplinary matrix underlie very different phenomena and applications. However, in carrying out experiments student scientists are not testing hypotheses but simply gaining insight and understanding of the science via the exemplars. The rules for doing research stem from the exemplars; there is no one scientific method.

Kuhn argues that there is no neutral observation language: observations are paradigm-dependent. Rival paradigms may collect very different data and solve different problems. Paradigms constitute the conceptual lens or "worldviews" for interpreting findings. Working with the exemplars a scientist learns to interpret such and such as a "fact" of a certain sort. Exemplars also provide implicit criteria as to what solutions are acceptable. The existence of a disciplinary matrix within a scientific community or some specialized area of a science explains the ease of communication and wide agreement obtained. Hence, according to Kuhn, choosing between theories within an accepted paradigm is very different from choosing between paradigms because

1. choosing *between theories* within the same paradigm means using criteria that are dependent on the same paradigm; and

2. choosing *between paradigms,* however, cannot draw on any objective criteria since criteria are always paradigm-dependent.

Thus if we were to regard the various systems of psychology as various paradigms, we would choose between models or explanations within behaviorism on the basis of behaviorist criteria, whereas choosing between behaviorist models and those in cognitive psychology is made "impossible" because of an absence of a common criterion for evaluation.

## NORMAL SCIENCE

Once a paradigm has developed, there is a period of what Kuhn calls "normal" science, which is essentially solving the puzzles or questions posed by the paradigm. A "puzzle" is a problem that is believed or known to have an answer and is therefore regarded as solvable. Normal science is not concerned with testing basic paradigms or fundamental premises but is concerned with checking the individual scientist's conjectures in the light of a paradigm. If a conjecture proves wrong, it is a setback not for the basic paradigm but for the individual scientist.

This seems essentially what occurs in marketing and the social sciences. Whether the social scientist is an economist, behaviorist, cognitive psychologist, or whatever, he or she works within a paradigm, not to test it but to check out implications. Many of us are familiar with situations on doctoral defenses where some "outsider" questions fundamental presuppositions only to be told that what has been done is in line with orthodoxy in economics or some other discipline.

Normal science is trying neither to falsify nor to confirm the underlying paradigm. During this period of normal science the exemplars constitute the models to be emulated in finding solutions to the puzzles. At this stage, research is concerned with explicating what is suggested by the current paradigm. In this research, outcomes can usually be predicted; it is the way to achieve the outcome that is often in doubt. In fact, the main purpose of the research is "to add to the scope and precision with which the paradigm can be applied."

Exemplars substitute for correspondence rules but are less restrictive since the rules underlying the exemplars are never codified. Where two scientific communities use the same terms but follow different exemplars, the terms possess different meanings. As the exemplars determine meaning, they also determine what is to be observed and how results are to be interpreted. Hence there is no sharp distinction between reports of observation and theoretical statements. According to Kuhn, the sharp distinction between theory and observation ignores the role that theoretical concepts play in determining what is observed.

Normal science best fits the view of science as a cumulative enterprise. But to Kuhn, the aim of normal science is not truth but puzzle-solving as there is no theory-independent way to say what is "really out there."

The paradigm serves to evaluate research in the period of normal science and the exemplars set precedents for future actions and judgments. Commitment to the paradigm is achieved by dogmatic training in the disciplinary matrix through the absorption of the exemplars. (Every doctoral student in marketing will recognize such training in the seminars given over to reading and criticizing key journal articles and the requests for analogous research proposals.)

On Kuhn's view, progress via falsification becomes less clear. The existence of data in conflict with theory is not seen as falsification of the paradigm, but as puzzles to be solved and reconciled within the existing paradigm. The whole point of normal science is to fit nature into the various conceptual schemata provided by the scientist's training.

## CRISIS

In a period of normal science, scientists tend to confine themselves to problems that are solvable within the paradigm adopted. Failure tends to be attributed to the scientist's deficiencies rather than to some defect of the paradigm. However, in time, normal science inevitably gives rise to an accumulation of "anomalies" which ultimately lead to its demise. The general recognition among the scientific community of a large number of anomalies or puzzles that cannot be solved within the current paradigm evokes a *crisis*.

Kuhn argues that the accumulation of anomalies cannot be equated with an accumulation of falsifying tests since tests at variance with what is predicted can be attributed to many factors. It is the *collection of anomalies* that is worrying since the odd anomaly can often be ignored, shelved, or accommodated by modification of the contents of the disciplinary matrix. Falsification of the odd individual claim will, at best, demonstrate only that the theory is not suitable for the application or that other things went wrong; the theory may still apply to the next application. In fact, Kuhn claims that no physicist takes the risk of falsification by stipulating in advance the sufficient and necessary conditions defining the domain of a theory.

Kuhn shows that once a scientist is committed to practicing science in a certain way, it is difficult to switch to different conceptual lenses in viewing old problems. Kuhn claims that a scientific revolution is required before a new paradigm is adopted: Such revolutions result from the crisis triggered by an accumulation of more and more problems, or anomalies, which the existing paradigm is unable to solve. However, the old paradigm is overthrown only when a new and more promising paradigm comes along. Thus Newton's laws of motion were not rejected before a better theory came along, even though the laws gave rise to many anomalies. The same could be said of much else in Newton if judged by modern-day science. Mach showed in fact how Newton's idea of "force" was confused, his concept of "mass" incomprehensible, and his "absolute space" just nonscientific. The decision to reject an existing paradigm occurs simultaneously with the decision to switch to another one. This view conflicts with the claim that theories are discarded once falsified since in the absence of an alternative paradigm, scientists persist with the old one. This is typically what occurs in marketing, as reflected in the expression "it's not much good but it's the best we've got."

## ADOPTION OF A NEW PARADIGM

A different paradigm involves a different conceptual viewpoint. Since all perceptual identification, description, and categorization rests on some conceptual basis, a change in paradigms influences how things are described and categorized. Thus in the field of mental illness, the diagnostic categories developed by psychiatrists are seen to be ill-suited and at variance to those being currently developed by research biologists.

The adoption of any new paradigm may promise to deal with the accumulated anomalies suggested by the old paradigm and offer promising new directions for future research, but the choice between paradigms cannot be settled unequivocally by logic and experimental evidence alone. The data themselves cannot determine which paradigm to choose because different paradigms will disagree about what problems test the paradigms and different paradigms will interpret the data differently.

Although Kuhn seems to view the social sciences as preparadigmatic because of the failure to agree on any one single paradigm, this can be misleading. In the first place, different explanatory systems in psychology and sociology do not all tackle the same problems or at least provide different windows onto the same problem. Second, because the necessary and sufficient conditions for the application of the term "paradigm" have not been specified, it is not clear that any science has just one paradigm. If the different explanatory systems in psychology and sociology constitute different paradigms, the criticisms that advocates of each system make of rival systems typically reflect their own paradigm's premises.

Kuhn claims that changes in paradigms effect changes in the meaning of terms, so that competing paradigms speak different languages. Kuhn speaks of competing paradigms being *incommensurable* in that there is no common measure for judging their relative merits so that there is no incontrovertible basis for making a rational choice between them.

In arguing paradigms are incommensurable, Kuhn does not claim they cannot be compared but initially did argue that such comparisons cannot be carried out using neutral criteria as rival paradigms involve different standards for judging success. As outsiders we can compare paradigms in terms of their "goodness" for certain purposes (e.g., their seeming simplicity and depth), but those promoting rival paradigms would not agree with the criteria or how the criteria should be interpreted and applied to their own paradigm. Those holding competing paradigms will not be able to agree on a common body of observations to act as a neutral basis for evaluating their respective merits. When different paradigms address different problems, this complicates still further the problem of finding a common measure for relative success. Advocates for different paradigms will differ as to what problems to count as problems, their relative importance, and what criteria to use in judging an acceptable solution to a problem. Given the fact that no theory within some paradigm provides a perfect fit with the facts even when the facts are paradigm-dependent, refutation becomes more problematic.

In choosing between paradigms and deciding what is and what is not to be regarded as scientific knowledge, *Kuhn claims that the scientific community's judgment is the final court of appeal.* Kuhn agrees that rational debate has a role to play but claims such debate docs not settle or terminate a crisis. With the conceptual changes accompanying a change in paradigms, change is in the nature of a Gestalt switch, that is, a completely different way of viewing the phenomena of interest. Kuhn compares the Gestalt switch to a conversion, so that to understand it we must turn to the techniques of persuasion, since the case for the new paradigm cannot be proven. Thus the Copernican system was adopted not because it fitted the observation data better but because it was more elegant and simpler than its rival. (Alexander [1987] argues that, at least in sociology, the universal technique of persuasion has been to caricature the old paradigm!)

Kuhn is not criticizing science for failing to develop criteria for objectively choosing between rival paradigms. He is simply rejecting the mythology that such criteria exist. What does exist is the trained judgment of the scientific community. The new paradigm that captures the allegiance of the scientific community becomes the new reality for them. Kuhn is not asserting that collective wisdom substitutes for rational debate and objective standards but that the very concepts and standards of rationality are themselves simply a communal product.

Kuhn claims that paradigm shifts are *progressive* in spite of the absence of objective criteria for ensuring that the new paradigm is going to be better. He argues that if a scientific community overthrows one paradigm in favor of another, this in itself guarantees that the change is progressive, that is, guarantees the growth of scientific knowledge. Thus the new paradigm would preserve a large part of the explanatory capacity of the old paradigm while promising much more. Kuhn was later (1970, 1977) to argue (in answer to charges of substituting sociology for scientific methods) that choice between paradigms is very much influenced by the commitment of scientists to certain values. Thus scientists value predictive accuracy; qualities like consistency and coherence of a theory with what is already known; the suggestiveness of a theory in terms of likely findings; theory simplicity; and wide scope of application.

If the history of science involves crisis and revolutions leading to the adoption of new paradigms, then science, although perhaps progressive, cannot be said to be cumulative. The RV of science saw the move from theory 1 to theory 2 as ideally requiring that theory 2 subsume theory 1: eliminating the errors of theory 1 while extending the depth and range of explanation and prediction. With such continuity, progress was regarded as both cumulative and measurable. On Kuhn's view it may not be possible to compare theory 1 and theory 2 because the two theories may be incommensurable on three criteria:

1. Topic incommensurability. The two theories, or paradigms, will not deal with exactly the same set of problems. Although the two theories may overlap to some extent, theory 2 is unlikely to possess the whole of the predictive and explanatory power of theory 1. Thus the various systems of psychology and sociology do not tackle all the same problems so that if any system were exclusively dominant, certain questions would be ignored.

2. Meaning incommensurability. The two theories or paradigms may use the same terms for theoretical entities that are radically different in meaning. Thus the term "motive" in behaviorism has a different meaning from its use in cognitive psychology.

3. Conceptual incommensurability. The two theories or paradigms will represent different ways of viewing the same phenomena. These different viewpoints defy any attempt at developing a set of commonly agreed measures for judging their relative merits, so there remains no noncontroversial basis for choosing rationally between them. On the basis of this argument, there would be no commonly agreed basis for judging between the viewpoint that all consumer behavior results from past conditioning and the view of human beings as free agents acting in accordance with wants and beliefs.

The Kuhnian view does not guarantee that science is progressing to a more accurate picture of the world. A paradigm shift simply means that we view the world differently without any assurance that the shift gives a truer picture of the world. If observations are theory-loaded and different paradigms provide different representations of the world, Hacking (1983) argues that this implies idealism. Hacking claims that Kuhn's work reveals his antirealism, but this can be questioned. What Kuhn doubts is whether progress in problem solving can be equated with progress toward truth in the sense of representing reality better.

## Kuhn versus Popper

Both Kuhn and Popper are concerned with the process or the mechanisms that bring about growth in scientific knowledge. Both agree that there can be no absolute proof or disproof of a theory. However, Popper sees the growth of science as a matter of error elimination. Kuhn, like Lakatos (discussed next), believes such an explanation to be inadequate since scientific progress occurs in the absence of tests like that for falsification. Kuhn claims that the puzzle-solving activity of normal science brings with it anomalies that lead to a crisis that precipitates a scientific revolution. Finally, whereas for Popper science should be always revolutionary ("revolution in permanence"), Kuhn claims that scientific change is either *consolidatory* (normal science) or *revolutionary*.

## Criticism of Kuhn

The first edition of Kuhn's *The Structure of Scientific Revolutions* in 1962 gave rise to a torrent of criticism. Toulmin (1972), who holds to an evolutionary model of scientific development, takes Kuhn to task for exaggerating the depth of conceptual change actually occurring in paradigm shifts: there are, he argues, no radical discontinuities so rival paradigms never really amount to entirely different worldviews. Toulmin is more concerned with how the conceptual inventory of science changes and increases. Toulmin believes that

1. the crucial intellectual choices in any science involve changes in its most basic concepts; and
2. the rationality of any science revolves around its procedures for the discovery, development, and changes in basic concepts.

The basic question according to Toulmin in much of science is not whether concepts are true or valid but whether conceptual innovations improve the scientist's explanatory power more than rival concepts. Often conceptual innovations improve understanding while introducing impairments to understanding. Thus the concept of "attitude" might be seen as improving understanding of the job to be done by advertising but in the process has diverted attention from the concept of motive and motivational appeals.

Kuhn's sharp distinction between revolutionary and normal science is criticized. For example, the idea of scientists making incremental advances or choosing between completely different approaches makes it hard to understand how scientific advance can be guaranteed. But there is little agreement among the critics. Popper rejects the idea of the prevalence of normal science; Quine (1970) grants the prevalence of incremental shifts in theories over the idea of constant, bold, new conjectures. Toulmin (1970), on the other hand, argues that intellectual discontinuities on the theoretical level of science conceal underlying continuities at a deeper methodological level. Kuhn (1970) in fact diluted his central distinction between "consolidatory" changes in science (normal science), which take place within the boundaries of a paradigm, and "revolutionary" change, which involves a complete change in paradigm. He now views change in science as occurring in an unending sequence of smaller revolutions. Such microrevolutions open up the possibility of a gradual paradigm shift that need not be preceded by a crisis. Also, in small areas of specialization (Kuhn's basic scientific community) adherence to some basic paradigm may be short-lived.

Although Kuhn refined his definition of paradigm, criticism still persists. Bernstein (1976) argues that Kuhn's updated definition still does not help us distinguish ideological from truly scientific paradigms. Also, it is not clear to what extent the exemplars, as described by Kuhn, can be used *on their own* to model solutions to new puzzles.

Normal science is viewed as giving rise to puzzles and anomalies resulting from trying to solve the puzzles. But in marketing and the social sciences, both the puzzles and the anomalies seem to arise more from changes in the environment or in beliefs than from conducting what might be termed normal science. Thus the revived interest in demonstrating advertising's effectiveness is tightly tied to the increasing proportion of the promotional budget being diverted to sales promotion and the growing belief among many marketing managers that the returns from advertising are highly speculative.

Perhaps the major criticism aimed at Kuhn concerns the incommensurability of rival paradigms. For many, Kuhn's view undermines the rationality of science, suggesting some form of relativism. Kuhn denies this relativism characterizes his position. He insists that incommensurability means simply that adherents to different exemplars have a different view of the world. Such differences cannot be resolved through debate. Some doubt this (Musgrave, 1980). Kuhn himself denies he is suggesting that choice between different paradigms is an irrational act. He is simply asserting that there is no choice process that is logically compelling. Although choice is based on a mixture of objective and subjective factors (as in buying), he denies relativism or the view that there are no theory-independent standards. There are generally held values; for example, a theory should solve the "puzzles" presented by nature. But such values used alone cannot fully determine choice.

Suppe (1977) equates the Kuhnian concept of a paradigm with the claim that scientists operate within some *Weltanschauung,* or worldview. Consistent with this is the belief

1. that scientists classify and analyze observations in a way that is at least partially determined by the worldview; and

2. that some or all of the statements in a theory contribute to the meaning of the terms in a theory and some changes in a theory will result in changes in the meaning of terms. It follows from this that rival theories, models, and so forth, on occasion can be incommensurable.

While agreeing that the meaning of terms may be theory-dependent, Suppe argues there is little support for the view that incompatible theories are noncomparable because they are incommensurable. It must first be demonstrated that the two theories cannot be formulated in terms of a common vocabulary. Also, while agreeing that scientists do have a Weltanschauung, Suppe argues that, even within some specific scientific community, scientists are unlikely to have the exact same Weltanschauung, which is, in any case, less determining of scientific activity and theorizing than Kuhn suggests. This may be so in the behavioral sciences where scientific activity and theorizing may in fact converge even though basic presuppositions about the nature of man can differ. In any case, as Chapter 9 on emotion shows, it may still be possible to bring together different viewpoints into some overall framework.

Kuhn does not deny the possibility of comparability but denies the possibility of the acceptance of a common vocabulary by which to compare. Thus we may be able to translate the rival paradigms in psychology into a common vocabulary—the vocabulary of "wants, beliefs, and actions"—but it is doubtful if such translation would be accepted by advocates of the various systems. They would likely argue that such translation does not express the full range and richness of their particular explanatory system. With respect to the claim that even within the same scientific community paradigms will differ, it can be taken for granted that there will be differences, but whether such differences significantly affect methods and theorizing can be answered (if at all) only by empirical inquiry.

Suppe argues that the Weltanschauung approach of Kuhn is no longer regarded as a promising basis for studying the philosophy of science. There is a return to the role of rationality in the growth of scientific knowledge. Although philosophers are more interested in the role and nature of reasoning in science, this interest is surely inseparable from examination of the basic suppositions of different paradigms. At least this must be so in the behavioral sciences.

The doctrine of incommensurability has been further criticized. Rescher (1984) points out that although there may be semantic and other forms of incommensurability between scientific theories, this does not mean that pragmatic commensurability is not possible. Barbour (1980) even denies that the rival theories will be incommensurable. He agrees that all data are theory-loaded yet argues that rival theorists will find a common core of overlap in observational terms. Even with a Gestalt switch, there are lines in the picture that remain unchanged. Hacking (1983) claims that the basic problem raised by meaning incommensurability is concerned with how theoretical entities get their meaning, since operational definitions are only part of the answer.

Kuhn claims that the rules for choosing *between* theories within a paradigm are implicit in the paradigm itself, whereas there are no rules for choosing between the rival paradigms themselves. MacIntyre (1980) points out that if reason operates only within a tradition or paradigm, it becomes difficult to see how reason is used at all to move from one paradigm to another. Kuhn denies that a scientific theory can embody a true representation of reality since there is no paradigm-independent way to establish that this is so. MacIntyre will not have this, pointing out that science has decisively shown to be false many claims made about the existence of certain entities (e.g., the ether). MacIntyre also argues that the Gestalt switch as described by Kuhn assumes every area of rationality is invaded by the disagreement over paradigms. He argues it is not the case that everything is put to question simultaneously. What is achieved in a transition to a new paradigm, he argues, is not just a new way of understanding nature but a new way of understanding the old paradigm's way of understanding nature. And it is only from the standpoint of the new paradigm that the inadequacy of the old can be characterized and the new regarded as more adequate. Somewhat in line with MacIntyre's criticism, Davidson (1984) argues that the very concept of totally different frameworks or sets of beliefs is in itself unintelligible. More generally, some argue that the fact that disagreement takes place at all implies some commonality of standards for evaluation. Others argue that incommensurable theories are often just an illusion emanating from competition among rival systems.

Much of what Kuhn has to say has great intuitive appeal and seemed to many social scientists very descriptive of their own experience in their own particular discipline and also descriptive of the many frustrations that occur in trying to reconcile different explanatory systems. It would be a pity if criticism of Kuhn should blind us to the insight he provides and the illuminating discussion that his work has stimulated. What perhaps worried many critics was not just the suggestion of an absence of universal standards for judging claims to knowledge but the idea that the practice of science does not occur in an open society where reason prevails. After all, in normal science, science proceeds by puzzle solving within some imposed framework that could be cited to justify arbitrarily imposed conformity. On the other hand, the concept of the relativity of paradigms might be used to substitute "anything goes" for current orthodoxy (Ravetz, 1990).

## Imre Lakatos

Lakatos (1971), though impressed by Kuhn's work, was critical of what he viewed (wrongly, according to Kuhn) as the cultural relativism implicit in Kuhn's work. Lakatos set out to update Popper in the light of Kuhn's work, minus any suggestion that scientific rationality rested on "mob psychology." Lakatos aims to demonstrate that rejection of the utopian goal of certain knowledge (justificationism) or highly probably knowledge (probabilism) need not mean either mob psychology or conventionalism. Lakatos claims that critics of Popper assume him to be promoting some dogmatic or naive falsificationist principle where there could be "instant rationality" in theory choice; in reality, however, he moved on to the position described earlier as sophisticated methodological falsificationism. Lakatos aims to build on this. His own methodological falsificationism aims both to set down prescriptions by which science proceeds and to provide the rationale of how a science might evolve.

Lakatos sought a view of the scientific enterprise that recognizes that the testing of theories could be neither immediate nor decisive while at the same time acknowledging that scientists are justifiably unwilling to abandon past theoretical commitments when presented with some anomaly. Like Popper, Lakatos seeks to defend reason against its enemies. And like Popper, he seeks a method for assessing scientific progress.

Lakatos rejects the correspondence theory of truth for an understanding of the process by which knowledge grows. But if a scientific theory can be neither absolutely proved true nor absolutely disproved by the "facts," how do we account for the certainty that scientific knowledge has *grown?* And scientific knowledge has grown in that more is known today than in previous times. This cannot be through some process of falsification: just surviving testing will not do. Given theories are tested in conjunction with initial conditions and auxiliary hypotheses, they can neither be absolutely proved nor refuted; moreover, there is no metric for measuring degrees of corroboration for any individual theory. Lakatos suggests we need to study the events that seem to be tied to the growth of knowledge and seek in them the underlying rationality. Like Popper, Lakatos seeks a method *for assessing scientific progress* rather than a method for solving scientific problems; that is, he seeks to identify genuine scientific activity by identifying real instances of growth in science.

Lakatos borrows from Popper the idea of an interrelated series of theories that are progressive in terms of growth. Lakatos argues that the study of scientific progress must focus not on an isolated theory but on some "scientific *research programme*" (SRP), which is the set, series, or system of theories representing successive revisions and (it is hoped) progressive advances in knowledge. While an SRP is evolving, Kuhn's normal science holds; when some SRP is in the process of being discarded, however, the science undergoes a revolution. But the rejection of an SRP comes about only during the process of adopting a new theory or SRP that promises to be better. To Lakatos, the rejection of a theory can come about only *by* the process of adopting a better theory. Hence evaluation focuses not on the individual theory but on a whole series of theories within a particular scientific domain. To Lakatos, the history of science is the history of the life cycles of SRPs. He views the sequence of developing theories as possessing the continuity of

Kuhn's normal science. Such a sequence might prosper for centuries before its decline, and even then a revival is possible.

Boland (1982) views an SRP in social science as represented by a sequence of models with each being accepted following conventionalist criteria. He argues that economists see each new model as part of a chain that will (mistakenly) ultimately lead to inductive proof. This sort of thinking occurs also in marketing. Implicit in many discussions on marketing research is the belief that it will all come together in the end to form such a system of evidence that only the complete skeptic would reject on the grounds of there being no measure to actually assess the weight of evidence. But this assumes (among other things) that we all continue to operate within the same paradigm and that progress is essentially linear and cumulative.

Every SRP consists of the following:

1. A "hard core," which (like Kuhn's paradigm) is regarded as irrefutable by adherents. Thus the hard core of behaviorism would include a belief in conditioning as the source of all learned behavior while part of the hard core of cognitive psychology would be the concept of mental representation and mental information processing.

2. A protective belt of additional hypotheses that can be questioned. Testable theories are derived from the hard core plus the protective belt to test whether some hypothesis of the protective belt is admissible.

The difficulty in applying the falsification rule leads Lakatos to argue that SRPs should be treated leniently, even claiming that it is often rewarding to persist with a particular SRP in the face of seeming falsifying evidence. Lakatos recognizes that tests in the protective belt are often undertaken to support rather than refute hypotheses and falsification does not lead to theory rejection unless some more plausible theory can be found. Lakatos, like Kuhn, thus sees falsificationism as having a less significant role than Popper suggests.

Kuhn's normal science takes place during the life of a particular SRP while science undergoes a revolution when there is a change from one SRP to another. To Lakatos, normal science is rational if it results in successive improvements of the SRP defined in terms of a progressive *problem shift*. Lakatos distinguishes between progressive and degenerating problem shifts. Problem shifts are *theoretically progressive* if each successive formulation of the theory contains some "excess empirical content" over its predecessor (i.e., it predicts some novel, hitherto unexpected fact); they are *empirically progressive* if some of this excess empirical content is corroborated in the sense that later theories in the series do actually discover new facts. *To be progressive an SRP must be both theoretically and empirically progressive.* If both are not present but, for example, many ad hoc adjustments are needed to accommodate new facts, the SRP is *degenerating*. An SRP may slip from being progressive to degenerating *and vice versa. Science is distinguished by displaying a progressive SRP.* A progressive SRP will consist of a sequence of theories $T_1$, $T_2$, $T_3$, . . ., whereby each successive theory is as consistent with the known facts as its predecessor but predicts novel facts not predicted by the predecessor and some of these predictions are corroborated. A successful SRP's series of theories or problem shifts is consistently theoretically progressive and intermittently empirically progressive. When the theory with the higher corroborated content supersedes the older theory, the older theory is "falsified"—in line with what Lakatos calls sophisticated methodological falsification. Good SRPs are progressive and bad SRPs are degenerating.

A particular SRP is defined by its negative and positive heuristics, which offer guidance as to what to pursue and what to avoid. A negative heuristic relates to the hard core in stating which assumptions are not to be challenged; the positive heuristic determines the ranking of problems to be addressed that constitute at any one time the protective belt.

According to Lakatos, it is not always rational to abandon every SRP that is degenerating (content-decreasing) in its problem shifts. This is because an SRP that is degenerating may reverse itself. Also, because the hard core of any SRP cannot be proved true, this suggests there should be a proliferation of rival SRPs. If we look at the different explanatory systems of psychology and sociology as different SRPs, they appear as a proliferation of rival SRPs. But doubts about the truth or validity of the older approaches do not fully account for the new SRPs coming along. There is also dissatisfaction with their utility for the new problems being addressed.

For Lakatos there is both normal and revolutionary science. In normal science hypotheses are tested and theories evaluated within the framework of the SRP. On the other hand, in revolutionary science theories are more broadly tested and conflicts among SRPs occur. Where there are conflicts among rival SRPs, choosing from among them cannot rest on any correspondence theory of truth or falsificationist criteria. Lakatos claims that the SRP adopted will both explain the success of its rival and possess additional heuristic power. A change in SRPs or paradigms means the elimination of the hard core and its program for constructing protective belts. Lakatos claims that rival SRPs arc logically commensurate and can be compared with each other.

Kuhn views the SRP hard core as similar to his concept of the paradigm; the protective belt reflects his normal science; and the degenerating phase is equated with his concept of a crisis. But the positive heuristics associated with an SRP are not as restrictive as Kuhn's disciplinary matrix, so more theoretical and methodological pluralism is possible. Lakatos places great emphasis on the rationality of changes in SRPs to avoid any suggestion that such changes are in some way irrational.

Leong (1985) uses Lakatos to reconcile, within marketing, the logical empiricists and their opponents. Leong equates marketing's hard core with some of the basic assumptions or axioms commonly accepted. But this is hardly what Lakatos had in mind in defining the hard core of a science. Moreover, the protective belt disputes Leong discusses are actually conflicts over SRPs or paradigms such as that between behaviorism and cognitive psychology.

## Criticism of Lakatos

The SRP approach identifies ex post facto which SRPs are progressive. In other words, the method tells us an SRP is progressive only after the fact. Is such a method helpful when it comes to choosing which SRP to back in the future? This problem becomes even more acute when a particular SRP still must demonstrate a record of achievement. As Hacking says:

> Lakatos provides no forward-looking assessments of present competing scientific theories. He can at best look back and say why, on his criteria, this research programme was progressive, why another was not. As for the future, there are few pointers to be dervied from his "methodology." (1983, p. 121)

Suppe (1977) makes the following additional criticism:

1. No guidance is offered on the nature of rational positive and negative heuristics. (Lakatos is not interested in developing a methodology of this sort.)

2. Lakatos is wrong in viewing "immature" sciences as having no SRP but only a "mere patched up pattern of trial and error." There is rationality to theorizing even in immature sciences like the social sciences. (The same goes for Kuhn's paradigms.)

3. The Lakatos demand for continuity in any series of theories is based on either adding auxiliary hypotheses or reinterpreting the terms of the theory. Other reasonable ways of modifying theories are hence ruled out.

4. Lakatos overemphasizes theory development by testing and modifying theories in response. Theoretical developments more often rely on "thought experiments," and work on solving domain problems (where the theory applies) plays an important role in the development of a theory.

5. Lakatos neglects the important role of concept development in theory development. Concepts play a key role in determining what theoretical approaches are appropriate in solving some problems. We might add here that marketing also neglects the key role played by concepts in buying. Concepts are prior to attitudes in buying and represent a more fundamental focus.

6. Lakatos merely exposes only one reasoning pattern—and that only partially—in the growth of scientific knowledge. In certain circumstances this pattern characterizes good reasoning in science, but often "science does, and ought to, employ other incompatible patterns of proceeding rationally."

The last point relates to the exclusive focus by Lakatos on the hypotheticodeductive method of reasoning by which scientists make conjectures that are then tested as solutions to problems within the protective belt. Feyerabend (discussed next) argues that the Lakatos analysis applies only to the kind of knowledge produced by this one particular style of reasoning. Hacking (1983) is sympathetic, acknowledging that further styles of reasoning may produce a new kind of knowledge.

There can be no closure on what constitutes rational criteria. Take the problem of accepting a hypothesis. What would warrant a scientist accepting a hypothesis given that the evidence in favor is never conclusive? Over and above what has already been said, there are those who look at the seriousness of the consequences that would arise if a mistake were made in accepting the hypothesis as true. The more serious the consequences, the more hesitant the scientist will be about acceptance. This ties acceptance to personal values. Levi (1985) adds another criterion. He argues that in deciding which hypothesis to accept, scientists are concerned not only to avoid error but to increase their stock of information. The degree to which a hypothesis is informative is not related to its improbability or verisimilitude (Popper) but in part on the questions being addressed, so that a hypothesis selected will enhance the system of evidence relevant to the questions asked.

We might conclude this section on Lakatos by asking why we should ever be obliged to choose just one paradigm or SRP in marketing when each may simply be a different window onto a problem or at least may not deal with exactly the same set of problems.

## Paul Feyerabend

Paul Feyerabend is the most controversial figure in philosophy of science. Once a disciple of Popper, Feyerabend (1981) now argues that all theories have formal flaws so that if Popper's criteria were applied resolutely to current scientific theories, the result would be to eliminate science without replacing it with anything comparable. Similarly, he regards Kuhn's normal science as dysfunctional and argues for uninterrupted revolution in science. On the other hand, Feyerabend accepts Kuhn's view on the incommensurability of successive paradigms. Feyerabend agrees with Lakatos that it is the evolution of a theory over long periods of time and not its shape at a particular moment that is important in appraising it. On the other hand, he rejects the idea that theories lacking excess empirical content over their predecessors should be eliminated. He claims that Lakatos does not offer a methodology for determining when to accept and when to retain an SRP. Feyerabend's major arguments, however, revolve around the following claims:

1. There are no rules of scientific method setting out how science must proceed.
2. Observations and theoretical terms are paradigm-dependent.
3. Different paradigms are incommensurable.
4. There should be methodological and theoretical pluralism.
5. Theories should be tenaciously held on to even when the evidence might suggest otherwise.

Each of these is discussed in turn.

NO RULES

As Putnam (1981) says, there are virtually no philosophers of science today who believe in a purely formal scientific method. However, no philosopher has been so condemning as Feyerabend (1977) in claiming there are no absolute rules to be followed in scientific method while arguing that all attempts to discover such rules are doomed to failure. For Feyerabend argues that there are no absolute canons of rationality or privileged "good" reasons and that the history of science shows the absence of any norms or rules of scientific method that have been valid for all time. Feyerabend denies there is a specific logic to science and rejects the desirability or even the feasibility of science adhering to any fixed set of rational principles on the ground that the world is too complex for any rigid adherence to rules set up in advance without regard to changing conditions and unique circumstances.

We find echoes of this claim by Feyerabend in those who attack the idea of any fixed principles to be followed in strategic planning. Like rules in every sphere of life, the more rules there are, the greater the definiteness; the fewer rules, the greater the flexibility. Both increased definiteness and increased flexibility are desirable on occasion—the problem lies in achieving the right balance. But there will always be rules: "Without rules of the game, clubs are trumps." However, if we view doing research as a technology (see Chapter 1), we are likely to acknowledge that the rules are essentially maxims, that is, rules with exceptions.

Science, according to Feyerabend, cannot be made to follow any fixed rules of procedure without injury to scientific progress. He claims that the freedom of thought and action of *rational* people is considerably restricted by the supposition that certain infallible rules are available for deciding whether to accept or reject a paradigm or theory. Feyerabend shows that every principle of the so-called scientific method was violated to good effect by some great scientist (e.g., Galileo).

Contrary to his critics, Feyerabend is not saying people should not try to be rational but simply that scientific rationality cannot be equated and confined to the so-called canons of rationality of scientific method.

To Feyerabend (1977) the best methodology of science is nonmethodology: "There is only one principle that can be defended under all circumstances and in all stages of human development. It is the 'principle that anything goes.'" Although an early follower of Popper, Feyerabend ridicules the falsification principle on the ground that not a single theory agrees with all the known so-called facts in its domain.

## PARADIGM DEPENDENCE

Feyerabend accepts the view of Kuhn and others that observations and theoretical terms are paradigm-dependent. This means there is no neutral observation language, so it becomes debatable whether it is meaningful to talk of new theories having to be consistent with well-established ones as implied by the coherence theory of truth. On the other hand, the hypotheticodeductive method of testing a hypothesis, with its implicit acceptance of the correspondence theory of truth, rests on the unfounded assumption that observation is unproblematic. There is also no meaning invariance of concepts between theories. The necessary and sufficient conditions for the use of a scientific term do not remain constant: any change in theory 1 to theory 2 alters somewhat the meaning attached to the names of terms/concepts common to the two theories. Hence if scientists were to insist on the meaning-invariance rule as applying to some series of theories, scientific advance would be stymied.

## PLURALISM

While accepting that normal science does occur, Feyerabend argues that such conformity to one paradigm should be opposed in every way as it reflects a shift to ideological conformity that undermines the growth of science. Feyerabend's slogan is the pursuit of uninterrupted scientific revolutions by encouraging a proliferation of rival theories. In line with this Toulmin (1972) argues that in the resolution of disagreements in science, objectivity in the sense of impartiality should not have been equated with objectivity in the sense of timeless truths.

Popper argued for "revolutions in permanence"—science advancing through bold conjecture. Feyerabend goes further. If facts are theory-dependent, the more theories there are, the greater quantity of facts, and the more facts, the greater the increase in the empirical content of scientific knowledge. Hence Feyerabend claims that a proliferation of theories is the best way to scientific advance. This is his "principle of proliferation."

Feyerabend's advocacy of pluralism in methods, theories, and paradigms follows from his rejection of any one set of rules or methods for doing science and evaluating competing theories. He argues against the coercion implicit in demanding conformity to a single paradigm at the risk of being branded irrational. For Feyerabend, there is no good reason to equate being rational to toeing some particular methodological line: it is results that count.

Feyerabend is not abandoning rationality but rejecting the idea that current orthodoxy says it all. He is not even advocating the abandonment of rules or methods that have proved useful but the recognition that such rules can never be the last word.

## INCOMMENSURABILITY

Feyerabend agrees with Kuhn that if different paradigms change the meanings of scientific terms and different paradigms call for different standards of judgment, paradigms will be incommensurable. (Feyerabend has since relaxed this claim.)

## TENACITY

There are always problems with new theories and paradigms. But, Feyerabend argues, this does not mean scientists should adhere to one established paradigm. New theories inevitably contain contradictions and their relationship to facts is likely to be unclear so ambiguities abound. Feyerabend, as a consequence, advocates his "principle of tenacity"—holding on to theories, ideas, even when the evidence seems to be in conflict. We find here an echo of Lakatos.

For Feyerabend, objective evidence is never decisive when it comes to the adoption of a new theory or paradigm. Since no single interesting theory ever agrees with all the known facts in its domain, observational evidence is not decisive. Feyerabend argues that scientists compare ideas with other ideas and that we should seek to improve rather than discard views that have failed vis-à-vis rival theories.

What is always necessary for the adoption of a new theory or paradigm is persuasion. If we see the force of persuasion in prompting buying, why not in buying ideas when the evidence is indeterminate? If only cold evidence and hard calculation enter into science, we have difficulty making sense of criteria such as "elegance," "beauty," and "simplicity," which can often "swing a sale." This leads Peter and Olson (1983) to look at science as a special case of marketing! Thus McCloskey (1983) demonstrates the role of persuasion in the adoption of economic ideas. Similarly, Gellner (1985) shows how Freud's ideas were accepted in the absence of hard evidence, and Alexander (1987) shows how theories in sociology achieve great popularity even if scientifically dubious. Many scientists would agree that where choices are not clear-cut, persuasion will have a hand in bringing about a consensus and that persuasion will not always be based on just hard evidence and displays of rational acuity. On the other hand, they might also argue that, if deceived, there will always be a rebellious intellect to stop manipulated beliefs from becoming unchallengeable.

The "strong program" in the sociology of knowledge (Bloor, 1983) also places emphasis on rhetoric in the adoption of theories. It claims that all standards encountered in a social setting reflect the social interest of those installing the standards. Common observation of the world does not make people agree on what constitutes a true account of that world since it is not just experience but cultural/social/group factors that determine what will be believed. On this basis, theory choice is not entirely objective but reflects the particular scientific group's interest in maintaining and/or increasing the importance of its intellectual capital as reflected in its methods and techniques. They take the received view to task for reconstructing the history of science to coincide with some normative, rational model that is at variance with what actually goes on.

The Bloor position is essentially relativist if it claims that rationality is always culturally/context-dependent and there were no independent standards that can operate everywhere. Roth (1987) points out that much of the criticism this group levels against Popper, Lakatos, and Laudan (see pp. 351–55) could also be used to undermine their own case since it suggests their own claims are culturally/socially determined. Although this is so, it would be wrong to assume that factors other than rationality play no part in theory preference. People will not believe black is white just because of self-interest or loyalty, yet these factors can make themselves felt in choices whether in the choice of a product or in the choice of theories. As Toulmin (1990) points out, if we wish to understand what convinced Newton about the truth of his scientific beliefs, we would do well to "remove all limits on the factors that may be accepted as relevant." Thus the fact that Newton's theories about the heavens seem to mirror the Anglican church hierarchy may have supplied Newton with additional reasons for adopting them.

## Criticism of Feyerabend

Feyerabend (1977) dedicates his book to his friend the late Imre Lakatos, and one gathers from the preface that he deliberately set out to be provocative. In this he has succeeded.

His subsequent attacks on science as the secularization of theology have made him even more unpopular in many circles. The only occasion I ever remember Ernest Nagel getting angry was in a discussion on Feyerabend's views, which he regarded as "mad."

Suppe (1977) claims that Feyerabend, by assuming that all so-called facts and all theoretical terms are paradigm-dependent, either makes testing a circular argument or rules out empirical testing altogether. Under such circumstances it becomes difficult to know what would be involved in carrying out Feyerabend's tenets of tenacity and theory proliferation. Similarly, it becomes impossible to compare rival theories in any meaningful sense. In fact, it is not clear we would be able to identify when two or more theories are competing since this presupposes we can compare them as having shared objectives and a common set of problems. But whether he has been misinterpreted or has simply retreated from his initial position, Feyerabend (1987) now denies that he ever implied that theories could not be compared and seems to regard "incommensurability" as a rare event. Thus much depends on what we mean by "incommensurability." Does it mean we cannot measure the relative "goodness" of paradigms on a set of common scales? If perfect measurement is being demanded, then "incommensurability" is a fact of life. On the other hand, such incommensurability need not prohibit meaningful comparisons, and this is what is now being asserted.

Nagel denies that all observation terms involve theory and are therefore unavoidably "theory laden." He claims, in fact, that

> most if not all the terms employed in describing the observations that are made with the intent of testing a given theory usually have established meanings that are not assigned to those terms by the very same theory. . . .
>
> It is simply not true that every theory has its own observation terms, none of which is also an observation term belonging to any other theory. (1979, p. 93)

In support of Nagel's argument, there are relatively few theoretical terms that are employed throughout in social science or in marketing that stray far from the core meanings of the words as employed by educated people.

Hacking (1983) similarly argues that it is false to assume that observational reports *always* embody theoretical assumptions unless Feyerabend subsumes under the word "theory" every assumption being made. If this is, in fact, Feyerabend's definition of theory, then the assertion that every observational report is theory-loaded may be true but trivial. Hacking agrees that we see things because we have a theory that points in that direction, but it is also possible on occasion to notice things because there is no theory to give direction! Finally, Nagel makes the point that even though the weight of evidence for some given statement may not be measurable, it is often possible to objectively evaluate the evidence to judge whether it is adequate: "Even when individuals make their assessments independently of one another, they concur in their evaluations more frequently than is compatible with the supposition that evaluations are wholly subjective and idiosyncratic" (1979, p. 91). Nagel claims that the principles of scientific method were never meant to be applied without qualification or without reference to the contexts in which the principles are to be used. He sees no rigid or exhaustive set of rules as being traditionally advocated since "all methodological rules are candidates for adoption, and that only experience in applying a rule can provide the needed evidence for deciding whether or not the rule contributes to the success of inquiry" (pp. 87–88).

Feyerabend takes an extreme position and follows his own maxim on the need to dramatize if existing orthodoxy is to be undermined. But Feyerabend has a point if he is arguing that there can be no closure on rationality since new considerations and additional rational reasons develop along with experience. Just as buying is a learning experience so that buyers can change their mind during the process of buying, so scientists change their mind about what constitutes rationality in the circumstances as more familiarity with the data and the domain develops. But this is what Nagel, too, would uphold even if it took Feyerabend's exaggeration to make us recognize it more clearly. But carried to extreme the principle "anything goes" would free scientific discourse from any constraints whatever. This would suggest we abandon any attempt at objectivity in science on the ground of its being an impossible goal. Although, as Ravetz (1990) says, objectivity cannot be guaranteed by the methods of science, it can and does emerge from the integrity of individual scientists and the open debate over scientific findings.

## Popper, Kuhn, Lakatos, and Feyerabend

Stove (1982) accuses Popper, Kuhn, Lakatos, and Feyerabend of being irrationalists, on the ground that they deny there has been knowledge accumulation. Stove is puzzled by their assertion that scientific knowledge is not *cumulative* and by the belief shared by other philosophers like Quine that we are unable to justify as incorrigible any belief including our confidence in the methods used to justify scientific knowledge. Stove claims that Popper, Kuhn, Lakatos, and Feyerabend disguise their basic irrationalism by using clever rhetorical strategies to confuse the reader. These strategies, as described by Stove, are discussed in turn.

The first strategy is *inconsistency,* for example:

> Both Popper and Lakatos claim that the aim of science is to discover *true* laws and theories but then argue that the attainment of truth is impossible.

(*Comment:* We may posit truth as a normative ideal and at the same time not be inconsistent in arguing that that ideal cannot be attained with complete certainty.)

Another example:

> Popper recommends attempting to falsify a hypothesis while at the same time claims the falsity of any proposition is assured.

(*Comment:* Just as we know a model or an analogy will ultimately break down at some stage or in some application, we may reasonably sure any type of hypothesis will be shown to be false in some way. However, this does not mean the model, analogy, or hypothesis has not been revealing in the range, situations, and applications where falsification was resisted.)

And two more examples:

> Popper and Lakatos speak of the growth of knowledge yet deny the accumulation of knowledge.

> Kuhn speaks of normal science solving problems suggesting knowledge accumulates through successive paradigms. Yet, Kuhn rejects the cumulative view of the history of science.

(*Comment:* This claim by Stove is basic to his charge of irrationality. But Popper, Kuhn, Lakatos, and Feyerabend are denying the simple, linear continuity in scientific discovery, *not* that there has been no progress in science or accumulation of knowledge.)

The second strategy is *neutralizing* success words or failure words *by the use of quotation mark* and other devices, for example:

"progress"      "rational"      "confirmed"
"knowledge"     "discovery"     "explain"
"refuted"       "falsified"

A third strategy is *sabotaging logical expressions.* This can also be done by the use of quotation marks to cast doubt on the relationship specified, for example:

"entails"   "verifies"
"proves"    "confirms"

Stove is accusing Popper of inconsistency in arguing that only falsifiable propositions are scientific yet saying none is falsifiable. "Sabotaging blurs the distinction between *P* falsifying *Q* and its being regarded as doing so!"

(*Comment:* It is possible to falsify a proposition by some observation statement as a matter of *practical* certainty yet acknowledge there is no *absolute* certainty that the proposition is false.)

The fourth strategy is *upholding the thesis of the theory-ladenness of all observation statements.* Stove argues that to claim "observation statement *O* depends on theory *T*" is a ghost-logical statement that needs to be explained.

(*Comment:* As we have seen, other philosophers have had no particular problem in understanding "observation statement *O* depends on theory *T*.")

## Nicholas Rescher

Rescher (1984), an antirealist, argues that scientific progress correlates not with better approximations to the truth but with warranted confidence. Although scientific theories are dramatically better than they were centuries ago, this in itself is not proof these theories have become closer to the truth. This means that the criteria of progress should be pragmatic, not cognitive, so that prediction and control should be the criteria of progress. Success in practical problem solving and cognitive and physical mastery over nature reflects progress.

In returning to a purely *pragmatic criterion* for measuring scientific progress, Rescher rejects alternative criteria such as the following:

1. Better approximations to the truth. Rescher argues that we cannot claim better approximations to the truth but only that later theories provide us with more warrant for our claims.

2. Knowledge accumulation. Rescher rejects the criterion of knowledge accumulation for measuring scientific progress in the sense of an ever-growing set of answered questions on the ground that as science develops and abandons certain theoretical perspectives and entities, we see not only gains but also losses in "question resolution." Rescher, like Popper, Kuhn, Lakatos, and Feyerabend, rejects the idea of science as cumulative, with later theories simply augmenting or expanding on earlier theories. He even rejects the idea that science is necessarily self-correcting, as untenable hypotheses are not necessarily replaced with anything better. Like Toulmin, Rescher accepts that conceptual innovation leads to major revisions of how things happen in the world. Such conceptual innovations may amount more to a revolution in thinking than a mere supplementation of knowledge. For Rescher, science generally develops by substitution (replacement) of theories, not by any cumulative process.

3. Question enlargment. This is the claim that scientific progress allows us to pose additional questions. Rescher argues, however, that progress sometimes involves abandoning old questions and some of the old answers. Thus it is not yet clear in marketing whether asking questions about mental processing will result in meaningful answers that will be of pragmatic interest to marketing managers.

4. Increase in the volume of resolved questions. This criterion is complicated by the problem of measurement, the question of adequacy of the answers, and the importance of the questions.

5. Decrease in the volume of unanswered questions. The adequacy of answers remains a problem, as does the measurement of the stock of unanswered questions.

6. Decrease in relative proportion of answered questions. Problems of measurement and the adequacy of answers remain while the increase in question-resolving capability might be offset by expanding problem horizons.

Rescher's discussion of the criteria for assessing scientific progress is interesting in that marketing as a discipline does need to periodically take stock of its achievements. However, it is doubtful whether a purely instrumentalist's approach emphasizing prediction and control would provide adequate criteria. Such criteria would also raise the intractable problems mentioned by Rescher to discredit other criteria, namely, assessing the importance of the events predicted and the behavior controlled and determining the significance of different degrees of precision and accuracy in prediction.

## Larry Laudan

Laudan (1977) agrees with Kuhn that science has not progressed cumulatively. Theory transitions are, he claims, generally noncumulative in the sense that neither the conceptual nor the empirical content of earlier theories is completely preserved when the old theories are supplanted by newer theories. This is why it can be misleading to view the development of the social sciences as a movement from erroneous to true ideas. Newer theories seem more often to provide additional windows onto a problem or to deal with different problems altogether rather than substitute truth for past error. Old ideas in marketing do not die but hibernate, to be awakened in a more favorable climate to assume the mantle of newness.

Laudan agrees with both Kuhn and Lakatos in arguing that the more general/global theories, as reflected in Kuhn's concept of a paradigm and Lakatos's research program, are the primary tool for understanding and appraising scientific theories. They provide the dos and don'ts for doing the day-to-day research and, by sanctioning certain assumptions in advance, free scientists from having to justify all their assumptions. Thus in the social sciences researchers adopt the presuppositions of their explanatory system.

Laudan disagrees with both Kuhn and Lakatos, however, in how they account for the evolution of paradigms/research tradition. Laudan claims that Kuhn

1. fails to see the role of conceptual problems;

2. treats a scientific paradigm as something implicit yet at the same time something rigid. Laudan argues the assumptions of many paradigms were made explicit and do, in fact, change over time; and

3. believes that two scientists utilizing the same exemplars are, ipso facto, committed to the same paradigm, though this need not be so. Laudan seems here to be rejecting Kuhn's claim that the exemplars represent in the most fundamental sense the paradigm itself as they represent the paradigm-as-achievement.

Laudan says Lakatos improves on Kuhn in recognizing the coexistence of several research programs and in arguing that the progress of competing research programs can be objectively compared (i.e., *they are not incommensurable*). However, Laudan argues that Lakatos

1. has a conception of progress that is exclusively empirical, ignoring the importance of concepts (Academic marketing also makes this mistake.);

2. views later theories in the series as entailing their predecessor when successor theories may eliminate and not just add to the assumptions of predecessor theories;

3. does not provide a method of measuring progress via a measured comparison of empirical content of every member of the series which constitute the research program; and

4. has a view of a rigid research program and assumes the accumulation of anomalies to have a bearing on the appraisal of a research program.

Laudan, a rationalist and antirealist, argues that the goal of science is not to find ever truer theories but to find solutions to problems. Any theory should be evaluated on the basis of its adequacy in solving significant problems and *not* on whether it is true, corroborated, well-confirmed, or otherwise *justifiable* within the framework of some contemporary epistemology (i.e., the current ideas about what we know and how we know it). Assessing truthfulness is beyond science's ability: science cannot demonstrate either true or highly probable theories.

Laudan also rejects truth as a goal on the ground that if we cannot determine whether a proposed goal has been achieved, we cannot embark on a rationally grounded set of actions to achieve or promote the goal. But why can we not press toward a goal without knowing when we have achieved it, just as the Christian can embark on a rationally grounded set of actions to promote the goal of individual saintliness without knowing if attainment is at hand? Laudan would claim that the religious analogy is false, since "no one has been able even to say what it would mean to be 'closer to the truth,' let alone to offer criteria for determining how we could assess such proximity." (The RV also typically regards science as a problem-solving activity but identifies increasing success in problem solving and prediction with having achieved better approximations to the truth.)

Like Toulmin, Laudan sees problems as having both an empirical and conceptual dimension. Any *empirical* problem falling within the domain of the scientific theory may

1. not as yet be adequately solved by the scientific theory. Such a problem is classified as *unsolved;*

2. have been adequately solved by the theory. Such a problem is classified as *solved* in the sense that scientists no longer regard it as an unanswered question (though what counts as an adequate solution today may not be so regarded tomorrow);

3. be anomalous in that although it falls within the scientific theory's domain of problems, the theory has not solved the problem though some rival scientific theory has. Such problems are classified as *anomalous.*

Laudan claims, however, that debates over theories often relate to *conceptual issues* rather than questions of empirical support. *Conceptual* problems with theories can be *internal* (e.g., inconsistencies occurring when one part of the theory entails the negation of another part; vagueness of concepts) or *external* (e.g., in conflict in some way with another theory that is taken to be well grounded). Note that the RV did *not* ignore conceptual problems but simply did not take success in solving them as a mark of goal achievement. This was because the solving of conceptual problems was regarded as instrumental to formulating better theories.

Laudan argues that solved problems count in favor of a theory, whereas anomalous problems constitute evidence against a theory. *On this basis we should choose the theory that comes closest to solving the largest number of important problems (after weighting for relative importance) while generating the smallest number of significant anomalous and conceptual problems.* Thus Laudan does not go along with Rescher in believing that the measurement problem allied to assessing the relative importance of the questions and the adequacy of the answers makes the approach impractical. Laudan offers some guidance on the weighting problem. High weighting should be given if

1. the problem was formerly anomalous;
2. the problem is core to the discipline; and
3. the solution to the problem allows many other problems to be solved similarly.

Laudan claims that the aim of science is to maximize the scope of solved problems while minimizing the scope of anomalous and conceptual problems. The hallmark of scientific progress is thus

1. the transformation of anomalous and unsolved problems into solved ones; and
2. the solution of conceptual problems.

Laudan takes the position that although we would choose the general theory or research program with the highest problem-solving adequacy, it is always rational to pursue any research program/tradition that is currently exhibiting a higher rate of progress than its rivals even if it has at that time a lower problem-solving record. This is a middle ground between Kuhn arguing it is never rational to choose an alternative to the dominant paradigm and Feyerabend and Lakatos, who claim that the pursuit of any research tradition can always be rational.

Hacking (1983) doubts that we can compare the problem-solving capacities of rival theories. Laudan's problem-solving approach for selecting progressive research traditions offers no assurance that different scientists would not reach very different answers since Laudan's criterion does not measure up to an operational metric for ranking research programs. More critically, Rescher (1984) rejects entirely the use of the concept of problem-solving capacity as a measure of progress on the ground that what is considered interesting and hence important would be very theory-dependent.

More recently, Laudan (1984) has sought to identify the role of cognitive (as opposed to moral) values in the practice of science and the relationship of such cognitive values to the methods and theories of science. For Laudan, cognitive values in science embrace *ends* in terms of the knowledge being sought and *simplicity, elegance, scope, precision, power,* and *reliability* in theories.

According to Laudan, the received view explains how consensus among scientists comes about as resulting from the adherence of scientists to some sort of hierarchial model whereby shared values lead to agreement on methods and agreement on methods leads to agreement about factual claims. Table 13.1 shows the various levels of disagreement that might arise among scientists and the way such disagreements were assumed to be resolved, ultimately through the superordinate goal of shared values. Laudan disputes the validity of Table 13.1 on the ground that even the acceptance of a common set of cognitive values would not be sufficient to bring about the coherence of methodological

TABLE 13.1.  Received View of Consensus Process

| Level of Disagreement | Method of Resolution |
|---|---|
| 1.  Over factual issues | Methodological resolution (balance of evidence since agreement over how evidence weighted) |
| 2.  Methodological | Axiological (appeal to shared values) |
| 3.  Axiological | None (assumes scientists hold shared values) |

rules and factual choices with cognitive values. This is because cognitive values typically underdetermine (i.e., do not fully determine) methodological rules while methodological rules underdetermine factual choice. (By analogy, this argument can apply to buying in that an individual's values underdetermine product and brand choice.) Hence there is room for differences. In fact, it is possible for scientists to agree at just one or two of the levels and disagree on the other levels or level. Laudan agrees with Kuhn in claiming there are clashes between rival paradigms and that the evaluative criteria available for choosing between rival paradigms are not always equal to the job. He also agrees with Feyerabend that many successful scientists repeatedly violate the canons of scientific inquiry. Laudan, however, claims Kuhn offers no adequate account of the transition from crisis to normal science, and Feyerabend denies there are any standards or norms for scientists to agree on. Kuhn in fact just focuses on disagreement through incommensurability and consensus maintenance through normal science.

Laudan says we must distinguish between the rules or criteria that would be needed to choose unambiguously among rival theories and the less demanding criteria needed just to determine a preference. Such criteria may underdetermine choice in an absolute sense but may, nonetheless, unambiguously dictate a preference from among the rival theories under consideration. (This argument also applies to the consumer in that consumers tend to collect only enough information to determine a preference but not to become absolute experts on the product class.)

Laudan presents his reticulated model of scientific rationality (see Figure 13.1) as a replacement for the hierarchical model (see Table 13.1). Figure 13.1 shows a triadic network of justification with methods, theories, and values (aims) in mutual support and interdependence. In brief, Laudan argues as follows:

1. Methods or methodological rules are relevant as a tool for assessing the reliability of cognitive values (aims). For example, aims may be too utopian (impossible to attain) or too ambiguous or may be out of line with practices endorsed. Thus while aims justify methods, methods affect what aims (values) we consider feasible and viable as opposed to desirable.

2. Similarly, methods, while used to "justify" choices of theories, are at the same time constrained by theory. If we regard cognitive values, methodological rules, and theories as components of a paradigm or worldview, Laudan insists Kuhn is wrong in believing they form a coherent whole since the individual components are individually negotiable and individually replaceable. Change can occur on one level (one component) at a time (i.e., piecemeal change) leading to a paradigm change, or paradigm change may come from competition between rival paradigms, because
   • theories of paradigm 1 seem better than theories of paradigm 2 in adhering more to

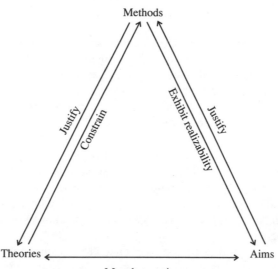

FIGURE 13.1. Laudan's Reticulated Model of Scientific Rationality. [*Source*: Larry Laudan, *Science and Values: An Essay on the Aims of Science and Their Role in Scientific Debate* (Berkeley: University of California Press, 1984). Reprinted by permission of the Regents of the University of California.]

methodological rules subscribed to by supporters of paradigm 2. (Kuhn denies this is possible.);

- methods of paradigm 1 may cohere more with the cognitive goals of former supporters of paradigm 2;
- the cognitive goals or aims of paradigm 1 may appear more realizable than the aims of paradigm 2. Laudan doubts the frequency of Gestalt-like shifts at all levels concurrently but argues for the piecemeal character of most forms of scientific change brought about by rational considerations. (Kuhn denies we can judge theories on their ability to solve the same problems, for problems, values, and methods are all defined by the paradigms.)

Laudan's focus on justification in terms of coherence among values (aims), theories, and methods fits his rationalist, antirealist position, but Figure 13.1 makes some sense psychologically.

Hunt (1990) in a recent paper attacks the Laudan position on many fronts. In particular he rejects the defintion of truth as something "unequivocally the case." He goes along with Harré in seeing this as an example of the "philosopher's fallacy," whereby some perfectly good term is subject to such "high redefinition" that the term "can no longer be applied to anything." He sees truth as being exhibited not by establishing that something is known with absolute certainty but by showing that over some significant period of time a theory "has demonstrated its ability to explain phenomena, predict phenomena, or be useful in solving pragmatic problems." He argues too that the "counting and weighting" procedure recommended by Laudan is unworkable and also "utopian" on the very criterion employed by Laudan to dismiss truth as the aim of science.

## Richard Miller

Miller (1987), a realist, returns to looking at rival theories or models rather than rival paradigms or SRPs. He claims that the mistake being made by both positivists and logical empiricists lies in viewing "confirmation" of theories, models, and hypotheses as a "lonely encounter of hypothesis with the evidence" rather than viewing confirmation as the process of comparing rival explanations to select that which seems to offer the best *causal* explanation. (This charge certainly applies to marketing research aided and abetted by significance testing.) Miller accepts that reasons for action are causes—"an elementary variety of cause, not a special case satisfying a more general definition." Although Miller assumes there will be debate over interpretation and evaluative criteria, he argues that comparing causal explanations does not lead to endless evaluations since the set of rival candidates drawn up by the scientists in the field is typically small. But for Miller, selected explanations are always tentative and subject to revision in light of further scientific developments.

Miller is implicitly assuming that we do not need to measure the relative evidence for rival theories on a ratio or interval scale to choose between them but simply need to order them on the basis of the evidence. This in turn assumes that the consideration of evidence is not entirely idiosyncratic when we adhere to a causal framework. This is probably so. Miller should be taken seriously in his claim that the set of likely hypotheses is typically small. If this is so, it eliminates the major excuse for not seeking to eliminate rival hypotheses.

## Conclusion

Scientific activity is a technology and, like every other technology, will be governed by rationally based rules that have evolved from experience. But what constitutes the most rational set of rules today may be improved upon tomorrow. This is not saying that rationality is relative to the time in which we live but that what we regard as most rational today will change as our experience widens and our intellect develops. What this chapter reviews is essentially a number of suggestions for going about the selection of rival explanatory theories, models, hypotheses, and paradigms. Which advice to select is not unlike choosing from among rival proverbs. At the abstract level, "Too many cooks always spoil the broth" and "Many hands always make light work" are contraries in that both cannot be true, though both can be false. But we recognize that both can apply on different occasions and that it is the situation that suggests relevance. Philosophy of science has not yet identified any set of methods that adequately explains the successful practice of science. At present we cannot justify methodological monism. Given this is so when allied to the richness of human behavior, the case for methodological pluralism is more defensible.

To return, though, to the matter of explanation. Is one type of explanation (e.g., the causal) always more fundamental than the others? If we accept methodological pluralism, we will accept the idea of pluralism in explanation. Kurtz (1965) views the various explanatory modes as merely different facets of a problem and uses the term "coductionism," where each type of explanation makes its contribution to understanding at different levels and perspectives.

At present the type of explanation sought might be dictated simply by methodological commitments or might rest on a belief that only one type of explanation can be considered truly scientific. This can even occur in history. Thus Gordon Wood (1964) points out how, in the first half of the twentieth century, historians focused on economic and social causes in explaining the American Revolution and disparaged the role of beliefs. From the end of the World War II to the time of his writing, the focus, he argues, was on the beliefs and principles at the time of the Revolution with efforts made to discredit the social and economic approach of an earlier generation. Wood argues that the earlier historians explicitly rejected the "causal" importance of ideas because they had absorbed the "diffused thinking of Marx and Freud and the assumptions of behaviorist psychology," whereby the reasons people give for their actions are viewed as rationalizations to mask the material self-interest that actually determines social behavior. Dogma and fashion have also played a role in marketing explanations.

Referring to a story told by Benjamin Franklin, Forrest Wood (1990) tells the story of the Susquehanna Indians listening to a missionary talking about the Garden of Eden. They were happy to accept the story of Adam and Eve but the missionary dismissed as a falsehood the Indians' own tale about a woman coming down from the sky to help them find beans, maize, and tobacco. So it is with methodological monism. If there is just one true religion, there is the inclination to regard the rest as no better than superstition.

# References

Alexander, Jeffrey C. (1987). *Twenty Lectures: Sociological Theory Since World War II.* New York: Columbia University Press.

Ayer, A. J. (1982). *Philosophy in the Twentieth Century.* London: Weidenfeld and Nicolson.

Barbour, Ian (1980). "Paradigms in Science and Religion." In *Paradigms and Revolutions,* edited by Gary Gutting. Notre Dame, IN: University of Notre Dame Press.

Bernstein, Richard J. (1976). *The Restructuring of Social and Political Theory.* Philadelphia: University of Pennsylvania Press.

Bloor, David (1983). *Wittgenstein: A Social Theory of Knowledge.* New York: Columbia University Press.

Boland, Lawrence A. (1982). *The Foundations of Economic Method.* London: George Allen and Unwin.

Brodbeck, May (1982). "Recent Developments in the Philosophy of Science." In *Marketing Theory: Philosophy of Science Perspectives,* edited by Ronald F. Bush and Shelby O. Hunt. Chicago: American Marketing Association, pp. 1–6.

Davidson, Donald (1984). *Inquiries into Truth and Interpretation.* New York: Oxford University Press.

Duhem, P. (1954). *The Aim and Structure of Physical Theory.* Princeton, NJ: Princeton University Press.

Feyerabend, Paul K. (1977). *Against Method.* London: New Left Books.

Feyerabend, Paul K. (1981). "How to Defend Society Against Science." In *Scientific Revolutions,* edited by Ian Hacking. Oxford: Oxford University Press.

Feyerabend, Paul K. (1987). "Putnam on Incommensurability." *British Journal of Philosophy of Science* 38, pp. 75–81.

Frank, Robert H. (1988). *Passions Within Reasons.* New York: W. W. Norton.

Friedrichs, Robert W. (1970). *A Sociology of Sociology.* New York: Free Press.

Garcia, John, and Robert Koelling (1966). "Relation of Cue to Consequences in Avoidance Learning." *Psychonomic Science* 4, pp. 123–24.

Gellner, Ernest (1985). *The Psychoanalytic Movement.* London: Paladin Books.

Hacking, Ian (1983). *Representing and Intervening.* Cambridge: Cambridge University Press.

Harman, Gilbert (1973). *Thought*. Princeton, NJ: Princeton University Press.

Harman, Gilbert (1986). *Change in View*. Cambridge, MA: The MIT Press.

Harré, Rom (1983). *Great Scientific Experiments*. Oxford: Oxford University Press.

Harré, Rom, and P. F. Secord (1973). *The Explanation of Social Behavior*. Totowa, NJ: Littlefield, Adams.

Hawking, Stephen W. (1988). *A Brief History of Time: From the Big Bang to Black Holes*. New York: Bantam Books.

Hunt, Shelby (1990). "Truth in Marketing Theory and Research." *Journal of Marketing* 54 (July), pp. 1–15.

Kuhn, Thomas S. (1962). *The Structure of Scientific Revolutions*. Chicago: University of Chicago Press; 2nd ed. 1970.

Kuhn, Thomas S. (1973). *The Essential Tension*. Chicago: University of Chicago Press.

Kuhn, Thomas S. (1974). "Second Thoughts on Paradigms." In *The Structure of Scientific Theories*, edited by F. Suppe. Urbana: University of Illinois Press.

Kuhn, Thomas S. (1977). *The Essential Tension: Selected Studies in Scientific Tradition and Change*. Chicago: University of Chicago Press.

Kurtz, Paul (1965). *Decision and the Condition of Man*. New York: Dell.

Lakatos, Imre (1968). "Criticism and the Methodology of Scientific Research Programmes." *Proceedings of the Aristotelian Society* 69, pp. 149–86.

Lakatos, Imre (1971). "History of Science and Its Rational Reconstructions." In *PSA 1970: In Memory of Rudolf Carnap. Boston Studies in the Philosophy of Science*, Vol. III. Dordrecht, Holland: D. Reidel, pp. 91–139.

Laudan, Larry (1977). *Progress and Its Problems*. Berkeley: University of California Press.

Laudan, Larry (1984). *Science and Values*. Berkeley: University of California Press.

Leong, Siew Meng (1985). "Metatheory and Metamethodology in Marketing: A Lakatosian Reconstruction." *Journal of Marketing* 49 (Fall), pp. 23–40.

Levi, Isaac (1985). *Decisions and Revisions*. Cambridge: Cambridge University Press.

MacIntyre, Alasdair (1980). "Epistemological Crises, Dramatic Narrative and Philosophy of Science." In *Paradigms and Revolutions*, edited by Gary Gutting. Notre Dame, IN: University of Notre Dame Press.

Masterman, M. (1970). "The Nature of a Paradigm." In *Criticism and the Growth of Knowledge*, edited by Imre Lakatos and Alan Musgrave. Cambridge: Cambridge University Press.

McCloskey, Donald N. (1983). "The Rhetoric of Economics." *Journal of Economic Literature* 21 (June), pp. 481–517.

Miller, R. W. (1987). *Fact and Method*. Princeton, NJ: Princeton University Press.

Musgrave, Alan (1980). "Kuhn's Second Thoughts." In *Paradigms and Revolutions*, edited by Gary Gutting. Notre Dame, IN: University of Notre Dame Press.

Nagel, Ernest (1961). *The Structure of Science*. New York: Harcourt, Brace and World.

Nagel, Ernest (1979). *Teleology Revisited*. New York: Columbia University Press.

Northrop, F.S.C. (1959). *The Logic of the Sciences and the Humanities*. New York: Meridian Books.

Peter, J. Paul, and Jerry C. Olson (1983). "Is Science Marketing?" *Journal of Marketing* 47 (Fall), pp. 111–25.

Popper, K. R. (1959). *The Logic of Scientific Discovery*. London: Hutchinson.

Popper, K. R. (1963). *Conjectures and Refutations*. London: Routledge and Kegan Paul.

Popper, K. R. (1968). "Theories, Experience, and Probabilistic Intuitions." In *The Problem of Inductive Logic*, edited by Imre Lakatos. Amsterdam: North-Holland.

Popper, K. R. (1972). *Objective Knowledge*. Oxford: Clarendon Press.

Putnam, Hilary (1981). *Reason, Truth and History*. Cambridge: Cambridge University Press.

Quine, W.V.O. (1953). *From a Logical Point of View*. Cambridge, MA: Harvard University Press.

Quine, W.V.O. (1968). "Ontological Relativity." *Journal of Philosophy* 65, pp. 185–212.

Quine, W.V.O. (1970). *The Philosophy of Logic*. Englewood Cliffs, NJ: Prentice-Hall.

Radnitzky, G. (1970). *Contemporary Schools of Metascience,* Vols. I and II. New York: Humanities Press.

Ravetz, J. R. (1990). *The Merger of Knowledge with Power: Essays in Critical Science.* London: Mansell.

Rescher, Nicholas (1984). *The Limits of Science.* Berkeley: University of California Press.

Robinson, G. S. (1971). "Popper's Verisimilitude." *Analysis* (Oxford) 31, p. 1995.

Roth, Paul A. (1987). "Meaning and Method in the Social Sciences." Ithaca, NY: Cornell University Press.

Stove, David (1982). *Popper and After: Four Modern Irrationalists.* New York: Pergamon Press.

Suppe, F. (1977). "Editor's Introduction." In *The Structure of Scientific Theories,* edited by F. Suppe. Urbana: University of Illinois Press.

Toulmin, Stephen (1970). "Does the Distinction Between Normal and Revolutionary Science Hold Water?" In *Criticism and the Growth of Knowledge,* edited by Imre Lakatos and Alan Musgrave. Cambridge: Cambridge University Press.

Toulmin, Stephen (1972). *Human Understanding,* Vol. 1. Princeton, NJ: Princeton University Press.

Toulmin, Stephen (1990). *Cosmopolis: The Hidden Agenda of Modernity.* New York: Free Press.

Weimer, Walter B. (1979). *Notes on the Methodology of Scientific Research.* Hillsdale, NJ: Lawrence Erlbaum Associates.

Wood, Forrest G. (1990). *The Arrogance of Faith.* New York: Alfred Knopf.

Wood, Gordon S. (1964). "Rhetoric and Reality in the American Revolution." *William and Mary Quarterly* 23 (January), pp. 671–95.

# Discussion Questions

## Chapter 1

1. Teaching marketing management or any other practical activity involves teaching rules, principles, rules of thumb, and so on. Given the student understands the rules, why do we still talk about the need to develop skill in application?
2. If management is rule-following, where does creativity come in?
3. Why might it be argued that there are no experts in marketing but only experts in markets?
4. "All techniques employed in behavioral research presuppose some explanatory theory or model whether acknowledged or not." Discuss.
5. "Rules (even the recipes in cooking) when applied without any understanding of their scientific (explanatory) basis will lead to conservatism in the practice of the technology and puzzlement when things go wrong." Why is this so? Is it always so?
6. Why do you think that Lindblom and Cohen might be right in saying that the behavioral sciences can produce only a small portion of the stock of propositions commonly employed in any type of social problem solving?
7. Why do some writers argue that no acceptable definition of science will arise until agreement is reached on what constitutes scientific rationality? Why is the debate considered so important?

## Chapter 2

1. The chapter refers to the absence of any universal laws in the behavioral sciences. Is this true if behavior includes involuntary behavior? Does this absence in any way relate to the problem of specifying the conditions under which a universal law would be universal?
2. Why is the concept of selection-explanation important to both management and behavioral scientists?
3. "There is a difference between having grounds for expecting $y$ to occur and explaining why it did or will occur." What sort of grounds might lead to expectations that would not be explanatory in any scientific sense?
4. Do you see any relationship between Mach's views and the D-N model?
5. Miller rejects (hard) determinism on the ground that it has never been seen to operate yet is prepared to explain by reference to causal mechanisms even if such mechanisms are relatively unobservable. Is he being consistent?
6. Why do some social scientists distinguish between scientific explanations of behavior and understanding it?
7. Why are marketing practitioners so interested in marketing generalizations given the comment in the chapter? Would it help if such generalizations had a theoretical base?

8. Is the Webster–Wind model of organizational buying just a refinement of the claim that people's actions are a product of their heredity and environment?
9. In saying that the reason-giving explanation is a causal explanation but not an explanation by causation, is Collin making a meaningful distinction?
10. Consider each basis of segmentation against the claim that we need to know both beliefs and wants to predict action. Can we predict relevant wants and beliefs from the habitual buying of brand $X$ by consumer $Y$? If attitudes just reflect evaluative beliefs, why do we so commonly use attitudes to predict buying action?
11. What is omitted from the practical syllogism of practical reasoning (p. 24) that makes it too simplistic a model of decision-making?
12. What distinguishes the recommendation of Kurtz about the need for coductionism and Kuhn's assertion that the adequacy of explanation depends on the scientist's paradigm?

## Chapter 3

1. If reasons can be regarded as "causes," can the Humean criteria (p. 30) still apply?
2. Do Elster's four groups of regularity models (p. 31) cover all the management science models?
3. Are Miller and Nagel defining determinism in the same way?
4. Hard determinism, hard voluntarism, compatibilism—is adherence to any one of them just a reflection of faith rather than evidence?
5. Are the examples cited by Bagozzi (p. 29) examples of causal mechanisms? Is Bagozzi consistent in his view of cause?
6. What sort of causal relationship is being assumed in talking about the relationship between causal laws and counterfactual and subjunctive conditional statements?
7. Why is defining cause as the necessary and sufficient conditions of an event inadequate?
8. No scientific law states all the necessary and sufficient conditions for an event to occur. Why must this be so?
9. Are transition theories really process laws?
10. Do you agree with Mohr about the interaction problem being the biggest stumbling block to developing causal models?
11. Can any conclusions be drawn from the following?
    a. Those who purchased brand $X$ were much more familiar with the advertisements for that brand than rival brands.
    b. It has been shown that there is a high correlation between company growth and expenditure on new product development.
12. In any closed-loop control system, the actual performance is compared with standard and the deviation is calculated. It is argued that remedial action should be taken if the deviation is outside acceptable limits. What is the problem with this advice?

## Chapter 4

1. Do Popper's views and criticism of historicism apply to the PLC?
2. If we were to accept that any retail pattern development emanates from the decisions of individuals in retail management taking account of the likely behavior of their present or future customers, how might you explain the wheel pattern?
3. How might you defend the PLC as an ideal type?
4. Why do you think Michael Porter spoke of evolutionary stages in his book *Competitive Strategy* and ignored the concept of the PLC?
5. It is frequently claimed that the same cause will produce the same effect. Can this be reconciled with the concept of multiple causal structures or is there a contradiction here?

6. Every strategy or policy will have functional or dysfunctional effects both at the time of its adoption and when it is implemented. Illustrate.

7. In a reciprocal causal structure we select as the cause that which is the more actionable. Illustrate.

8. Distinguish a process from a movement. Can we be certain that awareness/comprehension–evaluation is a process?

9. Why is the word-of-mouth communication process downplayed in the text?

10. What distinguishes a development law from a process law?

11. Is Dretske talking about identifying a causal process?

12. How can we be sure that the cognitive and affective constitute distinct steps in mental processing? Why the different breakdowns of mental steps in the hierarchy models (see Figure 4.2)?

13. Do hierarchy of effects models warrant being described as delineating the persuasive process?

14. If attitude measures come from summing up a relevant set of evaluative beliefs, why cannot attitudes be equated with evaluative beliefs?

15. If "affect" embraces emotions, feelings, mood, and temperament, how could affect be equated with attitude?

16. Why does the text claim that attitude toward the ad is not caused by the factors listed by MacKenzie and Lutz, which are more likely to be properties of attitude?

17. In the elaboration likelihood model, if we accept the distinction between central route and peripheral routes, is not the argument of Petty and Cacioppo simply a truism?

18. What does Foxall mean in claiming that improved prediction from attitude measures have arisen through demanding "situational correspondence between the circumstances under which attitudes and behavioral measurements occur"?

19. Howard consumer decision model
   a. Do any problems arise in taking Howard's definition of a product category as a group of brands that consumers view as close substitutes for each other? Any problems with his definition of brand image? Is it consistent with his saying that, under LPS, retail store atmosphere becomes part of the consumer's image of the brand? Any problems with Howard's definition of intention to buy?
   b. Can objectives/motives as Howard defines them determine the importance weights attached to brand benefits?
   c. Why does Howard claim that consumers in EPS are likely to respond to major price changes only?

20. What do you see as the problems in accepting and using the Rossiter–Percy matrix (Table 4.3)?

21. Relate the Weitz model to the Dretske claims. What value do you see in the model?

22. What do you see as the uses of the genetic explanation in marketing? What do you see as the problems likely to be encountered in seeking such explanations?

# Chapter 5

1. Making replacement sales, choosing on the basis of liking, and picking a brand at random or on whim seem to be processes that involve no deliberation on uncertainties associated with true decision-making. Do these choice categories come under the Kagan (p. 89) notion of non–fully conscious actions?

2. Collin (p. 89) shows the conceptual connection between reasons and corresponding buying actions. What function do promotion and distribution play here?

3. Prediction of buying action rests not on any scientific laws but on exploiting the principle of rationality given knowledge of belief and want normalities. Discuss.

4. Do the comments made on goals (p. 91) have any bearing on conjoint analysis? Does conjoint analysis rule out Sen's partial ordering (p. 97)?

5. Where does the criticism of subjective probabilities leave decision calculus with respect to estimating sales response to advertising expenditure and to sales effort?
6. Can buying options be incommensurable?
7. Do you agree that practical reasons are impartial rather than self-centered (See the Darwall argument)?
8. Elster sees social norms as typically leading to action not justified on the basis of self-interest and therefore as a source of nonrational motives and is seriously puzzled about how to account for social norms influencing behavior. What do you think?
9. Why is intentional action necessarily rule-following in some sense?
10. Is the distinction between purposeful and purposive action just semantic?
11. What are the implications of methodological individualism for studying organizational buying?

## Chapter 6

1. How are functionalism and methodological holism related?
2. What is
   a. the purpose of promoting brand image?
   b. the function of brand image in promotion?
   c. the role of brand image in promotion?
3. If attitudes serve the four functions suggested by Katz (p. 111) and attitudes are always a mediating variable between the input of information and buying, then Katz's four functions must identify the four motivations in buying. Discuss.
4. Apply Miller's view of the functional explanation (as describing a cause of causes) to the Katz view.
5. Why do different use functions suggest different markets for a product? Should not design functions, use functions, and service functions coincide? Why might they not do so?
6. Relate the idea of manifest functions to planning. Do these functions explain the existence of the phenomena of planning? Are there typically dysfunctional consequences?
7. Make a case for viewing functional analysis in cognitive psychology as causal analysis.

## Chapter 7

1. If behaviorism seeks a causal mode of explanation, show the causal mode represented by (a) the contiguity model, (b) operant conditioning, (c) Hull's drive reduction theory, (d) Tolman's relational behaviorism, and (e) Tolman's purposive behaviorism.
2. Does Pavlovian/classical conditioning (the contiguity model) explain human actions?
3. Why do those advocating operant conditioning see advertising as concerned with retaining customers and downplay its role in attracting new customers, converting from rivals, and increasing the level of sales to the individual?
4. It was said long ago that a good metaphor in psychology (e.g., the brain is a computer) is bursting with suggestions and hints to be taken up and as such is a research project waiting to be started. If and when the metaphor runs out of suggestions it will be abandoned by all but the diehards. What are the implications of the metaphor of the brain as a computer?
5. Could we reduce Freud's three structural systems of the mind to views about wants and beliefs?
6. In the Freudian system we work back from goals to desires and likely triggers in the environment. Using an example from consumer behavior, illustrate what might be considered an unconscious desire.
7. "Early damage to self-esteem can result in an everlasting desire for admiration, avoidance of criticism, and the urge to power and positions of dominance." Can conditioning explain this?

8. On page 130, Gellner's reasons for the market success of the Freudian system are discussed. Can you think of some management theory to which the explanation could equally apply?
9. How are mental representations, or information-processing steps, identified in cognitive psychology?
10. "Human actions cannot be interpreted in terms of laws because they occur within certain cultural and institutional constraints so that behavior is always being formed anew as circumstances change." Discuss.
11. Contrast the view of consumer decision-making in the multiattribute model with the idea that buyers simply have felt expectations as to how buying brand $X$ rather than brand $Y$ will be personally experienced.
12. Is intersubjective understanding required to understand the consumer?
13. "People's verbalizations of their actions can be read as a text." What do you see as the limitations of this view?
14. Existential phenomenology
    a. rejects any compelling external causes of action.
    b. claims that people are not a bundle of unrelated wants and habits so that the fundamental choices people make are a key to understanding their behavior.
    c. searches for the interpretation of the "text."
    d. searches for global themes without rising to abstractions. Comment.
15. In ethogeny we let consumers talk "off the top of their heads" before, during, and after buying, using no questionnaires or formal interview questions. What is the advantage of such an approach over questionnaires and focus groups?

# Chapter 8

1. Structural functionalism
   a. Why did Parsons (unlike Fishbein) take for granted the motivation to conform to social norms?
   b. Show how a fund-raising campaign might appeal to the symbolic rewards of love, respect, and prestige.
   c. How would operant conditioning explain infants identifying with external things and such interpretations being generalized to analogous objects later in life?
   d. Can a housewife be affected by role conflict, role strain, and role anomie in buying?
   e. What example in Chapter 7 might illustrate the concept of equilibrium in a dyad being upset by expectations not being realized?
   f. Is the influence of social norms diminishing or is it just with respect to societal norms?
2. Conflict theory
   a. Is the root metaphor of functionalism human physiology, as alleged by Rex?
   b. Is conflict inevitable in bringing about fundamental change in marketing strategy?
3. Exchange theory
   a. Does the Blau view have implications for the prediction of behavior from the compensatory model?
   b. Does customer orientation as a universal philosophy in marketing ignore the relative power of the firm vis-à-vis the customer?
   c. Think of an example in buying where two brands with identical attributes and attribute levels may not be equally preferred because consumers believe one brand carries more risk regarding attributes.
   d. Considering the factors on pages 156–57, is Heath suggesting a move toward satisficing behavior?
   e. Why is exchange theory as so far developed inadequate for explaining all buyer behavior?

4. Mead saw "social adjustment" as the key social motivation. How does this concept differ from (a) social conformity and (b) social adaptation?
5. Is the Blumer concept of (symbolic) meaning as defined on page 159 interchangeable with the Krugman concept of involvement?
6. Goffman's interest lies in the art and practice of deception. What would Goffman hope to gain through understanding how deception or impression management is carried out?
7. Take the three sets of expectations mentioned by Goffman (p. 160) and apply them to a mother buying clothes for her young son. Which is likely to be strongest?
8. What sort of evidence would you accept for claiming consumers have (a) a self-concept, (b) self-esteem, and (c) an ideal self-image?
9. Schutz advocates the need to explore the concepts people use to describe and structure their environment. Schutz argues such exploration rests on intersubjective understanding. Do you think that exploring the concepts used by some subculture or subgroup would be facilitated by the services of an "insider"?
10. Ethnomethodologists claim that "all interactions are highly indexical yet such indexicality is lost when social science attempts generalization." Discuss.
11. What is the weakness of the metaphor of action as a text?
12. Geertz would have us view culture as a system of meaningful symbols which the anthropologist is to identify. Is this a useful approach for studying buying within a market?
13. Relate Geertz's concept of symbolic models of the mind being used to interpret and guide actions to the cognitive psychologist's view of beliefs tending to be part of some system of beliefs.
14. Distinguish between hermeneutic understanding and empathy.
15. Does Gadamer's concept of the fusing of horizons relate to Parson's claim that interpretation rests on having standards for comparison purposes?

# Chapter 9

1. If emotions emanate from past paradigm scenarios that form our values to determine the salience of considerations, attributes, and things, what does this imply about human nature if we accept the self-interest, calculative, model of man offered by the economist?
2. If Etzioni is right (p. 186), then does it follow that the multiattribute model will predict brand choices any better than a respondent's ranking of the rival brands being considered on overall preference?
3. Emotional responses signal what we value. Does this imply that emotional responses signal specifically what we want?
4. If the target audience is known to place a high value on a thin self-image, which is tied to self-esteem, how might you induce them to eat more bread if you omit the possibility of advertising a low-calorie bread?
5. Do appeals to self-esteem really exploit the self-assessment emotions of pride, envy, shame, guilt, and integrity?
6. Carroll's claim suggests that we do not so much identify with the fictional characters in a television ad (though we may do so) than assimilate the situation, coming to see the situation both from the point of view of the characters in the commercial and from the outside as well. Comment on this in considering "slice of life advertising."
7. Pleasure is contingent on change. How can this be reconciled with the pleasure we derive from hedonic ads such as those showing a beautiful woman on a beach?
8. "Advertising may activate emotion but the problem is still to channel that emotion in the direction of the brand advertised." Discuss.
9. Assuming that attitudinal reasons for wishing $X$ to occur or not to occur are strong but epistemic emotions may be weak, why do we focus on strengthening epistemic reasons if we wish to intensify an emotional state (p. 202)?

## Chapter 10

1. "A person's motivational capacities are made up not merely of a set of needs, wants, or desires but include the capacity of imagination, sensitivity, and so on."
   "The consumer is best viewed by the marketer as a bundle of wants which act as a filter determining what products he or she will buy."
   Contrast these two statements. What are the implications of the first statement for marketing?
2. Can you classify habit, picking, intrinsic preference, and extrinsic preference under the compensatory and noncompensatory rules?
3. "Few, if any, company offerings meet in full what is sought so how can we speak of satisfying the consumer? On the other hand, just meeting the 'core need' may not be satisfying at all." Comment.
4. Is impulse buying intentional buying?
5. Can changing attitudes be equated with changing beliefs assuming one way of measuring attitudes is by the multiattribute model?
6. Why can it be said that consumers are generally open to persuasion right to the point of sale?
7. Explain why habit, picking, and intrinsic preference are likely to favor the brand leader in a market that consists of largely undifferentiated offerings.
8. Are integrative criteria rational?
9. Does providing a consumer with what she or he wants always lead to customer satisfaction with the purchase?
10. Do you think the choice criteria (including intrinsic) discussed in the text could be applied to choosing a spouse?

## Chapter 11

1. Is rationalism versus empiricism simply a matter of emphasis with respect to establishing knowledge?
2. The text claims that few marketing academics are likely to adhere completely to methodological monism. Why?
3. Does behaviorism adhere to physicalism and aim purely at descriptive regularities?
4. Why did the logical positivists eschew all talk of causal explanation given that some causes are surely observable?
5. Are "nominalism" and the avoidance of nonobservable entities related?
6. Would Tolman's purposive behaviorism violate the logical positivist tenet of avoiding teleological explanation?
7. Why is logical positivism against starting off with theory?
8. What would be your objection to a thorough, universal application of operationalism to all marketing theory?
9. "The ontological question regarding 'attitudes' depends on our epistemological position." Discuss.
10. What are the various reasons Quine has for rejecting the concept of analytic statements? Do you agree?
11. "The degree of confirmability provided by supportive evidence has proved too difficult to measure." Why do you think this is so?
12. Putnam defines relativism as claiming there are no standards of truth or rationality that transcend particular cultural or linguistic communities. Can this be reconciled with Goodman's constructivism? Does the denial of some aboriginal reality lead to an "anything goes" relativism?
13. Why has the dispute between realism and idealism not been settled? Is the belief in realism an act of faith?

14. Bhaskar sees some causal sequence such as the following: social facts and happenings → organism (psychology/physiology) → reasons → action. Could we work back from action alone to the rest of the causal antecedents?
15. It has been claimed that a focus on verification gives rise to methodological rather than conceptual innovation. Why?
16. Is there a rigid distinction between testing and interpreting?
17. What are the various interpretations of action being rule-following?
18. What is the difference between changing concepts and changing (a) perceptions and (b) attitudes?

## Chapter 12

1. Why would the logical positivist accept justificationism as a reasonable demand given their tenets?
2. Is retroduction/abduction related to realism?
3. A letter to *Business Week* (March 18, 1991) about dissatisfaction with market research ended with the following: "Meanwhile, the professional publications in the field are full of articles on statistical models instead of addressing the real problem: the limitations of the question-and-answer survey and the need to find alternative means of studying markets." What do you consider the limitations of the question-and-answer survey?
4. "The researcher's image of the domain is basic." Relate this to the assertion that the most basic job of persuasion is to change the target audience's perspective.
5. Why does rational choice theory entail a particular danger of confusing internal checks of any models it embraces with the empirical confirmation of the models?
6. "The hypothetical constructs embodied in a theory are richer than their operational measures. It is this surplus meaning that helps drive research." Discuss.
7. State what you believe to be
   a. the sense meaning of "market potential."
   b. an operational definition/referential meaning of "market potential."
   c. the likely response meaning of market potential by market managers.
8. "Getting a target audience to accept a certain analytic definition can lay the basis for a change in behavior." Discuss.
9. "When operational definitions/measures differ among studies, we cannot get consistency of findings." Discuss.
10. Relate Humphrey's comments on the two descriptions of the House of Commons in session to the debate over relativism.
11. "Marketing thinking and analysis are empty without some model to drive them. Discuss.
12. Does an uncritical stance and passive absorption of a television ad always mean noninvolvement with the product?
13. What do you think Handy and Harwood have in mind in their criticism of game theory and utility theory?

## Chapter 13

1. What are the dysfunctional consequences for marketing arising from
   a. an exclusive focus on techniques justifying claims to knowledge?
   b. a view of theory and observational support as independent?
   c. a belief that all firm knowledge is based on sense experience/observation?
   d. an acceptance of marketing knowledge as necessitating cumulative progress?
   e. the separation of hypothesis generation from justification?

2. Has Popper provided an operational criterion for choosing between theories or explanatory systems?
3. Can some of the criticisms made of evolutionary models apply to Kuhn's cycle in science?
4. Does it matter much that the various systems of psychology are incommensurable providing they are nonetheless comparable?
5. Is the information-processing approach as a scientific research program showing a progressive problem shift?
6. Is Feyerabend right about the importance of persuasion in science?
7. Use Laudan's reticulated model of scientific rationality as a basis for describing the relationships that exist between beliefs, wants/goals, and buying actions.
8. How does Miller come to grips with Weber's claim that in explaining human behavior there should be adequacy at the level of cause and adequacy at the level of meaning?
9. "Every way of seeing is also a way of not seeing." Relate this statement to the debate over relativism.
10. "In ridding ourselves of the search for truth we have merely shifted the concept of truth, not its abolition."
   "Any strategy of persuasion must court a belief in truth and come up with a standard of truth by which its own conclusions will follow."
   Discuss these two statements.
11. "In the social sciences those who still wait for a Newton are not just waiting for a train that won't arrive—they're in the wrong station altogether." Discuss.

# NAME INDEX

# SUBJECT INDEX